Modern East Asia

Modern East Asia
A Brief History

Conrad Schirokauer
Senior Scholar, Columbia University
Professor Emeritus, City University of New York

Donald N. Clark
Professor of History, Trinity University

Houghton Mifflin Company   Boston   New York

Library of Congress Control Number: 2006937039

ISBN-13: 978-0-618-92070-9

4 5 6 7 8 9—DOC—11 10 09 08

Contents

List of Primary Source Document Boxes

Preface

Our decision to expand an earlier brief history of modern China and Japan to include all of East Asia is based on our belief in the intellectual value of regional approaches and the growing importance of East Asia as a major part of our world. We hope to introduce students to the region in a way that will help them make comparisons and go on to explore in greater depth some of the topics and areas we discuss.

Following our initial decision, we had to decide on the geographic and temporal parameters of our project. The vast land mass of Eurasia does not consist of clearly demarcated zones any more than time comes neatly packaged into periods. Our choices in this respect, as in others, result from our understanding of current scholarship as well as the experiences and approaches that we have found useful in our own teaching.

To the best of our knowledge, everyone considers China, Japan, and Korea as belonging to East Asia, and we give these countries primary emphasis in our book. We also discuss Vietnam, although in somewhat less detail. Vietnam is often treated as belonging to Southeast Asia, and we acknowledge its position as being roughly on the boundary of the two regions. Vietnam exemplifies how East and Southeast Asia are not entirely exclusive of each other. However, we put it in a special category and exclude the rest of Southeast Asia for two basic reasons.

First, Vietnam shares the commonalities we discuss in Chapter 1, and its differences from the rest of East Asia are probably no greater than those of, say, Japan. In none of the four countries under consideration are the commonalities the whole or "essential" story, but at the same time, in none can they be ignored. And they are by no means confined to the past, as is clear from the continuing persistence of official Marxism in Vietnam, China, and North Korea.

The second reason for including Vietnam is that its history has always been intertwined with that of China and, in the twentieth century, with that of Japan, and it shares with Korea the experiences of colonialism, division, and the devastation of war fought under American auspices. If one of the reasons for studying East Asian history is to provide a framework for reflection, then surely Vietnam—and by that we mean Vietnam as a nation and not just as a war—belongs in our book. We are sure that including Vietnam is the right thing to do and worry only lest we have not done it well enough.

In an age that is often called "post-modern" and even "post-post-modern," "modern" remains an elusive term with shifting meanings. What was modern in one period tends to be regarded as old-fashioned in the next, and today, in some contexts, the word *modern* is itself out of date. To compound the problem, historians studying East Asia disagree on when and how to use the term. Thus some would begin "modern" China around the year 1000 whereas others might argue that China is not completely modern even today. Much of the diversity of views depends on definition. In our case, we use the word *modern* broadly and sparingly. Its function in our title is to signal that we are not tracing the history of East Asia back to its beginnings but are covering the general period from 1600 to the present, with the focus on the period when the people of the region could no longer ignore the multifaceted power of Western, and now global, civilization. We also discuss prior developments, including events that set the stage for "modernization" in East Asia as well as features that parallel "modern" developments in the West, such as industrialization and state building. We leave open the question of how many different ways there were and are to be "modern." We hope our readers will develop their own nuanced understanding of both "East Asia" and "modern."

History is woven of many strands, and so we include economic and political history and also give much attention to social structure, thought, and the arts. The challenge facing us as it does instructors who use our book is to fashion a balance between these areas of human activity and to grapple with the impossible task of confronting all the dying and suffering that runs like a red thread through the history we recount in this book while at the same time giving full measure to human achievement. We believe that it is important to provide a general map of the historical and cultural terrain so that the student can find his or her bearings and learn enough to consider further explorations in many areas, with some idea of the rewards to be gained for the effort. This book is not a catalog of cultures, but it is meant to be an introduction to the main narrative and the present state of our understanding of East Asian history.

The themes of change and continuity pervade our writing. In looking at the "modern" period in this region we have not begun with a blank slate, and like many writers before us we have faced the duty of weighing the change within the continuity, the continuity within the change. Such a determination requires, in the final analysis, as much art as science, and no assessment is ever final. This is so not only because of the continual discovery of new evidence and new techniques (for example, in the dating of materials) but also because scholars' intellectual frameworks and analytic concepts change, and we all learn to ask new questions. Even if that were not the case, history would still have to be rewritten at intervals, inasmuch as the ultimate significance of any individual historical episode depends in the final analysis on the whole story: As long as history itself is unfinished, so is its writing.

Acknowledgments

Our book is a joint effort, but the reader is entitled to know who wrote what. Donald Clark wrote everything on Korea. We divided the work on Vietnam, with Clark contributing the discourse in Chapter 14 and the discussion through the

Vietnam War in Chapter 18. The Afterword is a joint effort. The rest of the book was written by Schirokauer.

We have benefited from and been challenged by an efflorescence of scholarship that has enriched our field even as it has made it impossible to read everything. This has made the role of those who have guided us all the more important. It would take a volume in itself to name everyone who has contributed by offering suggestions, criticism, and encouragement, or who has helped by suggesting references, supplying a date or a translation of a term, or to acknowledge individually teachers, students, and colleagues who have influenced our thinking about broader issues of history, the East Asian region itself, teaching, and writing.

We do need to acknowledge our continuing indebtedness to those who contributed to our earlier books, but we will not repeat their names here. However, some directly involved in the first edition of this book should be named. Foremost among them is Barbara Brooks, who has been a valued advisor from start to finish: She helped get us started, provided invaluable guidance (especially on the treatment of Japan and on colonial Vietnam), and gave our manuscript a final critical reading before sending it off to the publisher. It is our loss that unforeseen circumstances kept her from being a co-author as originally planned. Donald Clark also wishes to thank Conrad Schirokauer for his invitation to participate in an expanded volume on modern East Asia that includes Korea and Vietnam, and Conrad Schirokauer wants to thank Don Clark for making it possible to include Korea and Vietnam. Both of us thank Nicole Cohen for help on the boxes.

The brief history of this book is no longer all that brief! It is deeply indebted to numerous people associated with its first edition as well as those who contributed to its predecessors, going back to William A. Pullin who inspired and nurtured the original book. The leading anchors for the first edition of *Modern East Asia* were Drake Bush and Clark Baxter. Without them, it would not have seen the light of day. Clark also organized and supervised the preparation of the present edition, which benefited enormously from the exceptionally thorough and thoughtful editing of Jessica Kim. This book is unusual in that late in the game there was a change in publisher. It is fortunate that we landed in the stable of Houghton Mifflin, publisher of the leading text by Fairbank/Reischauer during our formative years. For their dedication to this project we thank Nancy Blaine, Vastavikta Sharma, Samantha Ross, and everyone else at Houghton Mifflin who worked on the book.

The reports of reviewers of both editions helped us rethink and reformulate certain issues and saved us from embarrassing errors. For the present edition we received five reviews without indication of authorship but subsequently learned the identities of four of these scholars: James Anderson (The University of North Carolina, Greensboro), Ling Arenson (DePaul University), Nortrud Niehuss (The University of Texas at San Antonio), and Brian Platt (George Mason University). We wish to thank all five for their careful critiques. We appreciate their help and hope they will not be disappointed that we did not always adopt their suggestions. No matter how much care we have all taken, inevitably, some errors will remain, and we may even have produced some new ones. In all cases, the responsibility is ours.

We also thank our students for providing the basic stimulus for this book. Schirokauer owes a special debt to the delightful young scholars with whom he has been coteaching East Asian courses during the past few years: Letty Chen, Nicole Cohen, Naomi Fukumori, Jimin Kim, Yasu Makimura, Suzanne O'Brien, Kerry Ross, Katherine Rupp, and Jaret Weisfogel. Also deserving special mention are the staff of the East Asian Library at Columbia for their help with books; Robert Scott, head of Columbia's Electronic Text Service, Butler Library, and master electronic scanner; and Rongxiang Zhang and Yangming Chu, for vital assistance in obtaining permissions from China.

Finally, the completion of a demanding project such as this would have been impossible without the understanding and support of our families.

Note on Names and Romanization

In East Asia surnames precede given names, and that is the order we follow in this book except for men who are commonly known by their given names (for example, Tokugawa Ieyasu and Ngo Dinh Diem). Similarly, we have transcribed them according to the standard system of romanization as indicated below, except where common usage indicates otherwise, as with Confucius, Syngman Rhee, Kim Daejung, Sun Yat-sen, Chiang Kai-shek, and all Chinese Taiwanese names. Except for Edo (modern Tokyo), contemporary geographical names have been used for the sake of easy identification even though this results in some anachronisms.

For Korean words and names we have used the McCune-Reischauer system. Japanese terms are rendered in accordance with the standard Hepburn system, except that macrons have been omitted for Kyoto, Osaka, and Tokyo. For Vietnamese, this book, like others intended for a general readership, omits diacritical marks and follows the Roman alphabet even when doing so conflates two separate Vietnamese letters.

Chinese is rendered in the Pinyin transcription; conversion tables into and from the older Wade-Giles system and provided on the book's website, at college .hmco.com/info/schirokauer. This system prevailed in the West prior to 1979, remains in use in Taiwan, and is still occasionally used in Western publications.

Note on the Figures in the Part and Chapter Openers

Origami, the art of paper folding, and kirigami, the art of paper cutting (seen in the bamboos on the cover of Part II), like paper itself, originated in China but became popular throughout East Asia. The figures used in this book were folded and cut by Lore Schirokauer. After studying these arts in Kyoto, she created and diagrammed her own designs and exhibited her work. Throughout the making of this book, she has demonstrated the strength of a tiger, the faith that raises pagodas, the resilience of bamboo, and the elegance of a crane.

About the Authors

Conrad Schirokauer Conrad Schirokauer currently serves as Senior Scholar and Adjunct Professor at Columbia University as well as Professor Emeritus at the City University of New York. In addition to *A Brief History of Chinese and Japanese Civilizations* (and its separate volumes on China and Japan), he has published articles on Song intellectual history, served as co-editor (with Robert Hymes) of *Ordering the World: Approaches to State and Society in Sung Dynasty China*, and served as translator of *China's Examination Hell*, by Miyazaki Ichisada.

Donald N. Clark Donald N. Clark is Professor of History and co-director of the East Asian Studies program at Trinity University in San Antonio, Texas. He earned his Ph.D. in East Asian history at Harvard University and is a leader in the field of Korean studies. His publications include *Christianity in Modern Korea* (1986), *Culture and Customs of Korea* (2000), and *Living Dangerously in Korea: The Western Experience, 1900–1950* (2003). He has co-authored books on the history of Seoul, on Korean politics, and on U.S.–Korean relations. His shorter works include many articles, reviews, and chapters, including one on Sino-Korean tributary relations in the *Cambridge History of China*.

Modern East Asia

Part One

Early Modern/Late Traditional

Part I considers the last period when East Asian history flowed at its own pace, influenced, but not deflected, by outside forces. Scholars who emphasize this period's continuity with the past tend to label these centuries as "late traditional" or "late imperial." Others prefer "early modern" because of similarities with "early modern" European history, the period's considerable continuity with its future, and developments that prepared the way for future developments. However assessed, clearly it was during the last traditional dynasties that the stage was set for later developments.

We begin by setting the stage ourselves. Whether we want to emphasize the immensity of change or are more impressed by the persistence of old patterns, we need a basis for comparison. We would also do well to bear in mind that even by the sixteenth century, East Asia had a very old history and a strong sense of history. For better or worse, its statesmen and theorists could draw on traditions that had stood the test of time.

Many of these traditions were shared. For this reason, and to spare the reader repeated discussions of rice paddies or Confucianism, we begin by considering commonalities before turning to individual countries and to the first encounters between East Asia and modern Europe.

Foundations, Traditions, Commonalities

1

During their formative years, Korea, Japan, and Vietnam adopted salient aspects of Chinese civilization and, over long centuries of adaptation and digestion, developed them to suit conditions and proclivities very different from those of China. Each maintained and developed its own patterns and systems while looking to Chinese antiquity as the font of civilization much as Europeans and Americans long revered classic Greece and Rome—except that China could not be relegated to a distant past: it persisted as a living source of inspiration and challenge. It still does so today, except that now China, literally "the central kingdom," no longer occupies the center of the cultural and geopolitical world of anyone but itself.

Geographical Parameters

In East Asia, complex political organization, cities, and other components of civilization appeared first in China, which was separated by formidable oceans, mountains, deserts, and steppes from the other early civilizations of Eurasia. During China's formative years, its neighbors either were largely illiterate tribal peoples or had cultures that derived writing and other aspects of higher civilization from China.

Unlike Korea and Japan, which by 1600 had attained their present territorial extent, China had not yet reached its present size. However, as in later times, the overwhelming majority of the Chinese population lived in the area south of the Great Wall, where soil and climate were suitable for the intense agriculture characteristic of East Asian civilization. Within this area, known as China Proper or Inner China, the basic division was between north and south, with the dividing line roughly along the thirty-third parallel, following the Qinling Mountains and the Huai River.

The outstanding feature of the north is the Yellow River, which flows from the highlands of the west through the alluvial lowlands of the Great Plain to the sea near the Shandong Peninsula. In its slow progress toward the sea, the river carries an enormous load of fine-grained, yellowish-brown silt (loess), which gives the river its color and name. It also accounts for the river's reputation as "China's sorrow," because the steady silting process has raised the bed so high that dikes are necessary to confine it to its channel. In many places the riverbed rises higher than the surrounding countryside, and a break in the dikes can have devastating effects. It may take several years of flood and famine before the river digs itself a new bed. Such a catastrophe occurred from 1851 to 1855. By the end of the devastation, the mouth of the river had shifted from the south side of the Shandong Peninsula to its present location on the north side.

The north is a region of temperate climate, cold winters, and warm summers, but rainfall is scarce. This is particularly true in the arid west; even in the wetter areas the annual rainfall is extremely variable. Although the area is subject to drought, it benefits from thick layers of fertile loess that retains moisture, and is easy to work. The north is suitable for millet, sorghum (*gaoliang*), and, in the moister areas, wheat and beans, notably soybeans.

Different conditions prevail to the south, where rain is abundant and the climate is subtropical, but minerals and nutrients have been drained out of the soil. The dominant river is the Yangzi, which is about 3,200 miles long, roughly 500 miles longer than the Yellow River. In 1600 it was still clean and sparkling. Unlike the Yellow River, the Yangzi is navigable for 1,500 miles, all the way to Sichuan. However, large modern vessels have to stop 630 miles upriver at Wuhan. Once the necessary technology was developed and land laboriously drained, a process that took centuries, the Yangzi Basin and the adjoining region proved ideal for rice culture.

Farther to the south, the West River flows through a mountainous landscape, emerging in the rich delta that forms the hinterland of Canton (Guangzhou) and Hong Kong. In the interior are the mountains and jungle of Guangxi and Yunnan, home to many ethnic minorities who have gradually been pushed into the hills by Chinese settlers.

Here China ends. South of this rugged, but not impenetrable, region lie Vietnam and the densely populated Red River Basin, cradle of Vietnamese civilization and location of Hanoi. Like the Yellow River, dikes restrain the Red River to prevent it from flooding. In Vietnam, as in Yunnan and Guangxi, the mountains have long provided refuge for minorities; the seas also offer people in Vietnam opportunities for fishing and trade. This is true of coastal China as well, but there the great Chinese land mass predominates. Champa, an Indianized Southeast Asian maritime state, prevailed in central Vietnam until the Vietnamese annexed it in the fifteenth century. Historically, Vietnam stood at the frontier between two highly sophisticated and very different civilizations, but throughout their history the Vietnamese have defined themselves in Chinese, rather than Indian, terms. Sometimes, as when an early Vietnamese ruler claimed to be Emperor of the South paralleling the Chinese Emperor of the North, the Vietnamese even have defined themselves as equals.

Vietnam's second major river delta, the Mekong in the south, was incorporated in modern times to form the present long and narrow shaped state, which stretches just over a thousand miles from northwest to southeast. Even with the additional land, Vietnam remains predominantly a country of mountains, with only about one quarter of the land suitable for agriculture. In this respect it resembles Korea and Japan, where the ratio is even less: about one fifth in both cases.

In Korea and Japan, as in Vietnam, the ocean provides a rich source of nourishment as well as trade, but in all three rice is king. In Korea, 600 miles long and 125–200 miles wide, rice is grown most plentifully in the river valleys and relatively wide coastal plains of the west and south. In Japan just three noteworthy plains exist, all on Honshu, the main island, and each ending in a bay. At 500 square miles, the Kinai Plain at the head of Osaka Bay is the smallest in size but the earliest in historical importance. The 600-square-mile Nobi plain at the head of Ise Bay is the home of Japan's most sacred shrine. The Kanto Plain at the head of Tokyo Bay measures around 5,000 square miles.

In modern times, Korea's border has been defined by two rivers: the Yalu, flowing westward, and the Tumen, flowing eastward from the slopes of Mount Paektu, the Koreans' sacred peak in the Ever White Mountains. Southward from the Ever White Mountains runs the backbone of Korea, the T'aebaek Mountains, which extend the length of the peninsula and divide it into a sharply defined coastal area on the east and a series of broad valleys to the west. Korea's best farmland is in the southwest; its richest mineral resources, forests, and water-power potential are in the north.

In both Korea and Japan mountains have challenged the soldier and merchant, but they prevented neither the achievement of Korean political unity in the seventh century, nor the emergence of central authority in Japan at about the same time. Mountains, however, are not just impediments—throughout East Asia, they have provided congenial settings for the sacred, a home to spirits, and a source of legends, as well as inspiration for poets and painters. China's Mount Tai, Korea's Mount Paektu, and Japan's Mount Fuji come to mind as the best known. The majestic mountain that towers over the natural and human landscape in Fan Guan's painting remains unidentified, but that enables it all the better to evoke a general sense of mountain grandeur (Figure 1.1).

Unlike the island state of Japan, Korea occupies a peninsula firmly anchored on the East Asian mainland where the Yalu River and massive mountains separate it from Manchuria, home to the founders of China's last dynasty. The mountains provided an even more effective barrier to Chinese immigration than did the mountainous jungles and seas to China's south. In modern times, the population flow has been from Korea into Manchuria.

Korea and Vietnam were close enough to China to experience Chinese aggression early on: during the second century B.C.E., China's Han dynasty established colonies in the Red River Delta and in Korea, where the largest occupied a site across the river from P'yŏngyang, the present capital of North Korea. Thanks to geography and military resistance, however, the Chinese never dominated, even in the north where their power was concentrated, and eventually had to withdraw entirely. This occurred much earlier in Korea than in Vietnam. In the seventh century, the Korean state of Koguryŏ successfully fought off a mighty Tang invasion and, except for a period of Mongol dominance, the Koreans retained their autonomy, despite further invasions from the north in subsequent years.

Vietnam freed itself from Chinese sovereignty in the tenth century, but underwent a final period of Chinese domination from 1407 to 1427. In both states,

FIGURE 1.1 *Travelers Among Mountains and Streams,* Fan Guan (Fan K'uan, d. ca. 1023). Employing the classic Chinese perspective, the picture surface divides into three planes, one near, one distant, and a middle plane of water or mist. Hanging scroll, ink and light color on silk, 129.6 × 74.9 cm.

NATIONAL PALACE MUSEUM, TAIPEI, TAIWAN, REPUBLIC OF CHINA.

admiration for Chinese civilization went hand in hand with a determination to avoid Chinese political domination. By 1600, both states had long participated in China's tributary system, sending envoys acknowledging Chinese hegemony and bearing "tribute," but receiving handsome gifts befitting the generosity of a superior toward an inferior. Frequently such embassies became occasions for engaging in trade. Korea and Vietnam thus valued the Chinese connection even as they avoided Chinese interference. In general, Korea's and Vietnam's experiences with foreigners, even when painful and destructive, helped each people develop a strong sense of self-reliance and identity.

In contrast to Korea and Vietnam, Japan has never been threatened by China. At its closest point, the island of Kyushu is about 120 miles from the continent, across the Korean Straits. It had never been successfully invaded prior to the twentieth century, and only the thirteenth-century Mongols had made the attempt. Historically, the Japanese have been free from military or political interference from abroad, and their leaders have been determined to keep it that way.

Rice

In early times, people farming the dry fields of the north lived primarily on millet. By the seventeenth century the modern pattern was established, with wheat and millet predominating in the north while rice reigned in the south. Although it remained a special treat in northern areas, the majority of East Asians lived on rice. The main advantage of growing rice is that it yields more nutrition per land unit than any other crop. Other advantages have been summarized by Francesca Bray:

> It is highly adaptable, can be grown under almost any conditions, does not necessarily require fertilizers (although it does respond well to their use) and will produce as many as three crops a year if there is sufficient water, without exhausting the fertility of the paddy field. The techniques of rice cultivation are such that farmers themselves have been able to select for desirable traits through the centuries, and so a very wide range of cultivates has been developed.[1]

These varieties include drought-resistant strains, early ripening varieties, and rice suited for different tastes and/or purposes, such as brewing. The reason for its low fertilizer requirements is that flooding of the paddy brings in nutrients. A high yield-to-seed ratio and ease of transport are other advantages.

Although dry rice is grown on steep fields in the hills, rice is mostly, and most productively, grown in wet paddy fields. Rice can feed many people, but, traditionally, it also requires many people working long hours to prepare the paddy fields, plant and transplant the seedlings, weed, harvest, thresh, and husk. It is no accident that throughout the world the most densely populated agrarian areas are those that grow rice.

Irrigating the fields is an intricate process involving the allocation of water, which demands careful local coordination, whether provided by lineages (descent groups) as in China or provided by villages as elsewhere in East Asia. Historically, it also affected political geography. Except in China, the political centers of East Asian states were close to the rice-based economic centers. In China, the political center generally remained in the north, with the Grand Canal, actually a series of canals and rivers, linking it to the rich south. Thus in China, transportation requirements as well as agricultural demands contributed to the transformation of the landscape. Throughout the region dikes were built, swamps drained, and hills and mountains terraced.

Material Culture

In the seventeenth century, as through most of history, life in East Asia was at least as safe and comfortable as in Europe, and technology at least as advanced. As we read this book, it is appropriate to bear in mind that paper, a Chinese invention, was just one of East Asia's gifts to the world. Others include three that are often cited as transforming Europe: the gunpowder that destroyed its castles and brought down its knights; the printing that revolutionized the circulation of ideas; and the compass that enabled the Portuguese and their successors to find their way to China and Japan. Even our vocabulary reflects the excellence of Chinese textiles and ceramics: *silk* derives from the Chinese word for that most prized of fabrics, while the source of *china* is obvious.

Just as a variety of ingenious and complex looms were invented in East Asia to facilitate the weaving of cotton and silk, much East Asian thought and creativity went into the construction of pumps and other devices to raise water, ships protected by watertight compartments and steered by axial rudders, steel bits for drilling salt wells, and steel chains for hanging suspension bridges over steep ravines. A complete list would go on and on, ranging from the Korean submarine and plated warship to the Japanese folding fan.

The delicious variety of East Asian cuisines need hardly be mentioned except that good food contributed greatly to the pleasures of life. Perhaps people ate better than they were housed, but the Japanese gave the world its first modular houses, and North Chinese and Koreans battled winter cold by devising flues— the Chinese used them to heat beds made of clay, and the Koreans ran them under their floors. In contrast, houses in the tropical climate of Vietnam were built to avoid the heat. Walls were made of palm leaf matting, and palm fronds formed the roof. In all four lands, items of superb workmanship decorated the lives of those who could afford them and traditions of fine arts developed from calligraphy and landscape painting to furniture and garden design, with many more in between. In these and many other areas—particularly theater, tea, lacquer, and jade—a connoisseurship developed that, as elsewhere, set apart insiders and outsiders, rich and poor, elite and vulgar, reflecting the complexity of the societies.

Of course, the most delicious food, luxurious clothes, fine houses, and art collections are lost on those who are ill. People in East Asia were as apt to become ill as people elsewhere on the globe. However, as S. A. M. Adshead has suggested,[2] thanks to the work of the urban nightsoil collector, Chinese rivers were spared the sewage polluting the rivers of London, Rome, and Paris, and the resulting spread of disease. The Japanese addiction to the bath certainly made for good personal hygiene. Throughout the region, bamboo supplied a natural source for pipes used for plumbing and in salt wells. It seems likely that people in East Asia were no less healthy than their European counterparts.

Those who became ill had as good a chance for recovery in East Asia as in the West. During his stay in Vietnam, the Jesuit missionary Alexander de Rhodes (1591–1660) found the medicine there by no means inferior to that practiced in Europe, where, at the time, bleeding was the standard treatment. The doctors who treated him practiced a form of medicine originating in China. By his time, there was a rich medical tradition with treatments based both on practical experience and theory. This, in turn, was based on more general concepts of the structure and dynamics of nature.

Theories of the Natural Order

The Chinese and other East Asians thought of nature in dynamic rather than static terms. As illustrated by Fan Guan's paintings (Figures 1.1 and 1.2), humans did not dominate but were a part of the world.

Basic to East Asian medicine is the concept of qi, in this context translated as "life breath" but with the potential for broader meaning and thought of as "forming everything" (see page 15). In the dynamic universe everything is structured and animated by *yin* and *yang*, paired complementary opposites whose interaction keeps the world going. *Yin* is associated with the feminine, the passive, the negative, the weak; *yang* with the opposite qualities and forces: the masculine, the active, the positive, the strong. *Yin* is cold and winter; *yang* hot and summer. *Yin* is response, *yang* stimulus. Neither can do without the other, nor does either ever appear alone. As illustrated by South Korea's flag, there is a bit of each in the other (Figure 1.3). The resulting configurations can become complicated, as when a woman (*yin*) has a problem with her liver (*yang*) in the evening (*yin*) of the first day (*yang*) in a winter (*yin*) month.

The two terms appear in many contexts, from the popular to the technical, from the

FIGURE 1.2   Detail from *Travelers Among Mountains and Streams*. Fan Guan reduces the travelers to their proper dimensions while a road invites us to enter and contemplate nature's grandeur.

National Palace Museum, Taipei, Taiwan, Republic of China.

concrete to the abstract. For instance, the Chinese word for "landscape" is conceived in terms of water (*yin*) and mountains (*yang*); diagnosing *yin* and *yang* is fundamental to the geomancer examining a site to determine its suitability for a house or grave.

FIGURE 1.3   The famous circle that represents the interaction of *yin* and *yang* forms the heart of South Korea's flag.

Another important concept is the Five Phases: wood, fire, earth, metal, and water. Because this idea recalls the four elements of Greek philosophy, it has been translated as the "Five Elements." This translation is misleading, for it implies inertia and passivity rather than the dynamic self-movement inherent in the original conception, and it obscures the point that the processes of nature occur in a particular sequence.

The East Asian view of the world is formed by a sensitivity to change as the fundamental constant in life. *The Classic of Changes,*[*] an ancient and still popular divination manual, is based on this idea. The book gives 64 readings, each corresponding to a different *hexagram,* or configuration of solid lines (*yang*) and broken lines (*yin*), and indicative of various, constantly shifting situations requiring different responses. Four *trigrams* (which form the upper and lower halves of the hexagrams) appear on the flag of the modern Republic of Korea (Figure 1.3).

Language and Writing

Nothing is more fundamental to a culture than language, and speaking precedes writing in the life of a people as it does in that of an individual. In East Asia, as in Europe, many people used strong local dialects, and spoke mutually unintelligible languages. Even within modern China, speakers of the local languages of Shanghai, Canton, and Xiamen are incomprehensible to each other as well as to people from elsewhere in China. However, these languages are at least members of the Sino-Tibetan linguistic family. Some linguists propose that Vietnamese is also Sino-Tibetan. It resembles Chinese in distinguishing words by tones, indicating the function of a word by its placement in a sentence, and in using modifiers to express mood, tense, and so on, yet it is often characterized as an Austro-Asiatic language related to Khmer and Mon, spoken in Cambodia and Burma, respectively. Other scholars argue that Vietnamese does not fit into any larger grouping

---

[*]Now Romanized *Yi Jing,* the title is *I Ching* in the Wade-Gile system of transcribing Chinese. In English this book is also known as *Book of Changes.*

BOX 1.1 CHINESE WRITING

The characters, or symbols, developed in China may be divided into four broad categories. The earliest were **pictographs** of objects increasingly abstracted over time. We may no longer recognize 馬 as a horse, but 木 still resembles a tree. Among things that cannot be seen are a few that can nonetheless be visualized and rendered as simple **ideographs**, such as 一, 二, 三, (one, two, three), or 上 (up) and 下 (down). More interesting are the complex ideographs formed by association: 林, two trees for a forest, or 好, woman and child to represent good. Another way to increase the written vocabulary was to use an already existing character to represent one or more words with the same sound. Examples of such phonetic borrowings, or **phonograms**, are 不, a flying bird, used to write the homonym "no," and 而, beard, for "and" or "but." However, this could become extremely confusing, as 馬, for example, could stand not only for horse but also for agate, weights, leeches/locusts, panel/board, to abuse or scold, an interrogative particle, or mother/old woman, all pronounced alike. To deal with this, a signifier (or radical) was added to form a **compound character**. A tree was placed next to a horse, 榪, to signal a word pronounced like horse but having something to do with wood, hence wooden panel. A jade or gem was added for agate, 瑪; a stone for weights, 碼; and insect for leeches, 螞; etc. The majority of characters are of this kind. Unfortunately, with changes in pronunciation the phonetic is not necessarily an accurate guide to present-day pronunciation. One further change that needs to be noted is that in The People's Republic many characters were further simplified so that 馬 became 马. The Japanese also adopted some simplified characters but stayed closer to the traditional forms.

but is unique. Korean and Japanese belong to yet another group. As Altaic languages, they differ from Chinese in cadence and sound, as well as in their complex grammatical structures completely alien to Chinese.

Vietnamese, Koreans, and Japanese had no script to render their diverse languages prior to the introduction of Chinese writing. Throughout East Asia the first books were written in Chinese, and until modern time, full literacy continued to be defined in terms of command of Chinese texts. Familiarity with the classical language of China was seen as a prime criterion for high status, and literacy was considered the basis of civilization. Although the majority of Chinese symbols include a phonetic component, they are primarily units of meaning rather than sound. Thus people who spoke mutually unintelligible tongues could and did read the same canonical texts considered valid everywhere and for all ages.

In China, the vernacular and the formal classical language remained separate until the twentieth century, though they did influence each other. Beyond China, even people literate in Chinese had a desire to write their own languages but found it very difficult to use Chinese symbols for this purpose. It would probably be more difficult to use Chinese characters to write Korean or Japanese, with their wealth of word-endings and particles, than it would be to write English in this manner. One way of rendering native words lacking a Chinese equivalent was to use Chinese characters for their sounds as well as for meaning. But this made for endless difficulties and confusion, and eventually Japan, Korea, and Vietnam turned to phonetic scripts.

The first of these was developed in Heian Japan (794–1185). It was a hybrid system, retaining Chinese characters for nouns, the stems of verbs, and adjectives, but rendering grammatical markers as well as indicators of mood, voice, tense, and the like phonetically in *kana,* or more accurately, *hiragana,* since a second form called *katakana* is employed primarily for foreign words and for emphasis. As a result, a page of Japanese looks like Chinese characters afloat in a sea of squiggles. In the fifteenth century Korea devised an alphabet known as *han'gŭl* (Figure 3.2) while Vietnam continued to use *nom,* a complex system based on Chinese characters, into the twentieth century. Then it turned to the phonetic *quoc-ngu* system of transcribing Vietnamese into Latin script, devised by seventeenth-century Jesuits, most notably Alexander de Rhodes.

Even after the development of indigenous scripts, Chinese remained the language of government and of formal prose throughout East Asia. Members of the elite, who prided themselves on their command of the language and the Chinese literary and intellectual tradition, continued to write poetry in Chinese. On the other hand, the most valued poetry tended to be in the vernacular. In Japan this was also the case for prose. There, the most prized diaries and novels were composed by women, who were not supposed to use Chinese. The *Tale of Genji,* written by a court woman a thousand years ago, is an outstanding example. Centered on the life and loves of its "shining prince," it occupies a very special place in Japanese culture. Not only has it inspired poets and painters, but, to quote its most recent English translator, "It is not just a book, but a cultural phenomenon. It has been turned into movies, plays, dance, modern novels, Kabuki, comic books (manga), musical theaters, and operas."[3]

Confucianism

The term *Confucianism* has been used by students of thought to identify a set of texts and ideas, while social scientists employ it to refer to a way of life. This might well have pleased Confucius (c. 549–449 B.C.E.) and later thinkers committed to a tradition much concerned with the practical consequences of ideas. However, they believed that their Way had been realized only in remote antiquity when, under the aegis of the sages, peace and harmony had prevailed throughout the world. We will therefore consider Confucianism as a teaching while keeping in mind that, like other faiths, it also influenced and was influenced by how people lived.

By 1600 the teachings of Confucius had been around for two millennia and undergone considerable evolution and change. The most influential version by the time we encounter it, known generally in the West as Neo-Confucianism, was developed in Song Dynasty China in the eleventh and twelfth centuries.

An earlier core text, *The Analects,* was accepted as conveying the authentic words and conversations of Confucius. It is now regarded as consisting of layers dating from between 479 and 249 B.C.E. It formed one of *The Four Books,* selected by Zhu Xi (1130–1200) to constitute the basic curriculum of classical learning and of the civil service examination system in China, Vietnam, and Korea. In Japan, *The Four Books* were equally revered. In all four lands they were internalized by youngsters who memorized the texts before they were capable of understanding their meaning.

The second of *The Four Books* bears the name of Mencius (387–303 B.C.E.), who is famous for maintaining that human beings are basically good, although their potential for goodness will turn sour if not properly nourished and cultivated. Mencius also advocated benevolent rule, with the threat that failure would cost the ruler "The Mandate of Heaven." In the common view, such loss of divine sanction would be preceded by abnormalities such as eclipses, earthquakes, floods and droughts, as well as famine and revolts. If these warnings went unheeded, the mandate would be lost. This became the standard Confucian explanation for dynastic change.

Both of the remaining books, *The Great Learning* and *The Doctrine of the Mean,* were chapters of *The Record of Rites* selected for special emphasis by Zhu Xi. Actually "rites" only captures a part of the meaning of *li,* a term also featured in *The Analects.* To be sure, it denotes sacred rites, but it further includes all ceremonies, proper behavior, and good manners. The *li,* if performed in good faith, with everyone keeping to his or her proper role, were thought to produce universal harmony so that there would be no need for physical sanctions, no necessity for laws or punishments. The model for society was the patriarchal family headed by a virtuous and wise father. For mainstream Confucians, family values came first, both in terms of human development and in terms of value: according to *The Analects,* a son should not turn in a father for stealing a sheep. Confucians stressed the claims of filiality, the wholehearted obedience a child owes his or her parents in return for their love and concern. The parent/child relationship served as a model for the rest of the classic "Five Relationships": ruler/subject, husband/wife, elder brother/younger brother, and (senior) friend/(junior) friend. Beyond that, however, the devout Confucian should have a feeling of obligation to everyone. Zhang Zai (1020–1077), one of Zhu Xi's predecessors, took it even further:

> Everyone is my father and Earth is my mother, and even such a small creature as I find an intimate place in their midst. Therefore that which fills the universe I regard as my body and that which directs the universe I regard as my nature. All people are my brothers and sisters, and all things are my companions.[4]

Foremost among the Confucian moral values was *Ren* 仁. Written by combining the graphs for *person* and *two*, it is the ground for the other virtues, the condition for being fully human in dealing with others. Translated variously as humanness, humaneness, or benevolence, it permeates all human relations—in the State, as in the family. According to Mencius, we are all endowed with a sense of compassion that needs to be cultivated to produce *Ren*. Our native sense of shame is the germ of dutifulness, our sense of modesty the germ of courtesy, our inborn sense of right and wrong the germ of wisdom.

According to Confucianism, every individual can become a sage by recovering his original nature or finding his lost mind. Self-cultivation was a major theme in Confucian thought and practice, given psychological and philosophical depth by *The Doctrine of the Mean* as well as by Song thinkers. *The Great Learning* stressed the link between self-cultivation and government, viewing the perfection of the individual as prerequisite for the perfection of society. Good government required good officials. The implied meritocratic ideal, though rarely achieved, inspired the government examination system of China, Korea, and Vietnam, which went to great lengths to prevent cheating, and theoretically selected men according to the breadth and depth of their Confucian learning.

Neo-Confucians accepted the discourse of *yin* and *yang* and the five phases, as well as *qi*, but coupled the latter with *li* (written differently from the *li* above), usually translated "principle" or "pattern." Because Chinese does not distinguish between singular and plural, the word can be understood as a network of principles, with each *li* a part of the entire system. For Zhu Xi, the *li* constituted the underlying pattern of moral and physical reality. Nothing could exist if there were no *li* for it. But *li* also required *qi*, which here can be thought of as a kind of material energy that occupies space. In its refined form it is a rarefied ether, but condensed it becomes the most solid metal or rock. Zhu Xi envisioned the world as a sphere in constant rotation, so that the heaviest *qi* is held at the center by the centripetal force of the motion. The *qi* becomes progressively lighter and thinner as we move away from the center. This explains why the air at high altitude is thinner than at sea level.

Human beings, too, are composed of *li* and *qi*. The *li* assures the fundamental goodness of people, but the *qi* accounts for human imperfection. Neo-Confucianism had a moral seriousness that found expression in a variety of ways. It made especially heavy demands on women. A girl was taught to obey her father. After marriage to the husband who had been selected for her, she had to obey him as well as his mother, who usually ran the household. If she were widowed, she was not supposed to remarry and was expected to listen to her eldest son. She was required always to be modest and to help everyone in the family live up to moral principles. A woman's sphere of action was within the home, while men managed the external world.

Confucians concerned themselves with institutions, policies, and statecraft. Some may have shown an interest in law, but as Confucians they distinguished themselves from the Legalists, advocates of punitive law, who were discredited after the harsh regime of the Qin (221–206 B.C.E.). On the other hand, since self and society, inner and outer, were seen as intimately linked, some Confucians concentrated on self-perfection. In doing so they could well adopt Daoist or Buddhist techniques, but unlike the followers of these two teachings, the Confucians understood the self as a social self and sought sagehood within, not beyond, society. Unlike Legalism, Daoism and Buddhism continued to flourish on their own, even while influencing Neo-Confucianism.

Daoism

Daoism and Buddhism are exceedingly complex; they include texts of philosophy and of popular religious practices. Furthermore, the two main Daoist classics, *The Dao De Jing* (or *De Dao Jing*, also known by the name of its purported author, Lao Zi) and the *Zhuang Zi*, were widely read and savored as literary masterpieces by people not necessarily Daoists. This is ironic, since both texts share a suspicion of language: the former begins by saying that the permanent Way cannot be spoken of, and maintains that those who know do not speak and those who speak do not know. Daoists are immune to the charge of self-contradiction, because they do not believe in logic. To grasp the Way in its entirety one has to transcend language and logic and see things not from our limited human perspective but from the total perspective of the Way (*Dao*) itself. By doing so, a person is released from social conventions and is able to regain oneness with nature.

Both texts use language poetically. *The Dao De Jing* is itself a poem—allusive and elusive. The *Zhuang Zi* delights in flights of fantasy, paradox, and evocative anecdotes, as when it relates that Zhuang Zi once woke from a nap not knowing whether he was Zhuang Zi dreaming he was a butterfly or a butterfly dreaming he was Zhuang Zi. In China and beyond, Daoism was an inspiration for literature and art, fostering the appreciation of nature and spontaneity. According to an old cliché, a Confucian in office easily turned into a Daoist when he returned home, cast off his official robes and cares, relaxed, tried out some poetry with friends over a cup of wine, and perhaps even dreamed.

The relationship between the Daoism of the literary elite and that of the religious sects was highly tenuous despite the common acceptance of Lao Zi as their founder. Another link was the references of classical texts to breathing exercises, designed to foster longevity and enable practitioners to attain a kind of immortality. In developing such ideas, Daoists contributed to the advancement of chemistry/alchemy, undifferentiated in China as in medieval Europe. They took an interest in *yin* and *yang* and other concepts concerning the operation of the physical world. Daoism was also engaged with everyday life, and Daoist priests performed numerous rites for the well-being of their patrons. Reminiscent of the Chinese State, Daoism developed a rich hierarchic pantheon headed by the August Jade Emperor and welcoming local deities in China and Vietnam. Although Daoist influences can be found in Korea and Japan, Daoism did not send out missionaries and its presence there was limited. In contrast, Buddhism, introduced to the rest of East Asia mainly from China, took deep root in all four lands.

Buddhism

Gautama Siddhartha (c. 563–483 B.C.E.), the founder of Buddhism, was roughly contemporary with Confucius. (Gautama refers to his clan and Siddhartha was the name he received at birth. He is also known as Sakyamuni, sage of the Sakya tribe. After he attained enlightenment he was called the *Buddha* or the *Tathagata*.) By the time Buddhism reached East Asia from India, the original teachings, directed at satisfying the spiritual quest of a small group, had broadened into a universal faith with wide appeal. It took further centuries for this religion to take root in China, but it came to pervade the culture of Tang China (617–907), from which it spread to Korea and Japan. In Vietnam, although monks also brought South Asian Buddhism to Vietnam by sea, the East Asian Buddhism that originated in China predominated. Throughout East Asia, it became "indigenized" into the domestic religious landscapes.

At the core of the Buddha's teachings are the *Four Noble Truths*. The first of these is that life is suffering. Pain and unhappiness are unavoidable. Death is not the answer. Like other Indians, Buddhists believed that living beings are subject to reincarnation. According to the law of karma, for every action there is a moral reaction. A life of good deeds leads to reincarnation at a higher level; a life of evil deeds leads in the opposite direction. However, the ultimate goal is not rebirth as an emperor or a billionaire: it is to achieve *Nirvana* and thus never be born again.

The second Truth explains the first: the cause of human suffering is craving or desire. This leads to the third Truth: that to stop the suffering, desire must be stopped. The cause of suffering must be completely understood and dissolved. The Fourth Truth proclaims the eightfold path as the way to accomplish this: right views, right intention, right speech, right action, right livelihood, right effort, right mindfulness, and right concentration. Most sects understood the religious life as practiced by monks and nuns to entail vegetarianism, celibacy, and abstinence from alcohol, as well as positive religious practices and meditation.

As Buddhism evolved and spread, the Buddha was transformed from a teacher of superlative wisdom, but a man nonetheless, into a god whom people could worship and to whom they could pray. The image of the Buddha appeared, art and iconography developed, as did ceremonies accompanied by musical chants and the burning of incense.

Many problems of doctrinal interpretation were left unanswered by the Buddha, for he was a religious teacher concerned with showing the way to salvation, not a philosopher interested in metaphysics for its own sake. As in other traditions, later commentators worked out the implications of the founder's teaching. The ultimate result was a vast literature and a rich variety of schools and sects, with a major distinction between the Theravada sects, which still predominate in Southeast Asia, and the Mahayana schools, which were most influential in East Asia.

Buddhism appealed to people in East Asia because it addressed itself to human suffering with a directness unmatched in the native traditions. It also provided a well-developed body of doctrine, art, magic and medicine, music and ritual, even heavens and hells, and a rich pantheon of deities. The historic Buddha was joined by other Buddhas: Bhaisajyaguru, the Buddha of Medicine; Amida, the Buddha who presides over the Western Paradise; and Maitreya, the Buddha of the Future whose coming would usher in a new and perfect age. Because of his messianic appeal, Maitreya was often associated with rebel movements.

One sect influential throughout East Asia was the School of Meditation, known as Zen in Japan. Even more popular were schools that offered less arduous or exclusive paths to salvation such as faith in Amida or the efficacy of the *Lotus Sutra*, a sermon attributed to the historic Buddha that became the most venerated Buddhist scripture in East Asia. Shinran (1173–1262), founder of Japan's True Pure Land sect, still the largest in that country, was convinced that salvation depended on faith in Amida, accessible to laity even more than to clergy, so he left the monastery for worldly life and married a nun.

Most beloved among Mahayana objects of worship were the bodhisattvas, beings who postponed their own salvation in order to help other living beings. Foremost among them was Avalokitesvara, the embodiment of mercy. In India and China, Avalokitesvara originally appeared as a male, but over the centuries this bodhisattva gradually came to be considered a woman (Figures 1.4 and 1.5).

By 1600, Confucianism generally overshadowed Buddhism intellectually and politically. It is also fair to say that except in Vietnam and in some Japanese Zen temples, Buddhism's power to inspire artistic creativity had declined as well. But, before and after 1600, temples continued to be built and maintained, and patronage was not lacking. There were, to be sure, those who bent the rules: a local Chinese gazetteer complained about local monks taking "vegetarian wives," and the church's enemies delighted in spreading scurrilous tales, but men and women continued to enter the religious life, and Buddhism remained a living faith. The sects retained their independence even as Buddhism also contributed to religious syncretism.

Syncretism

None of the East Asian religions commands exclusivity on the part of its worshippers. There has been an underlying tendency on all levels of society to compartmentalize or combine Confucianism, Buddhism, and Daoism (Figure 1.6). As a matter of course people performed their Confucian duty by offering ritual homage to tablets representing their ancestors, but this did not keep them from offering incense to a Buddha, praying to a local goddess for progeny, or calling on

FIGURE 1.4 Buddhist sculpture of Avalokitesvara, the bodhisattva embodiment of mercy, depicted with multiple hands and arms to better aid the multitudes.

FIGURE 1.5 *Detail of Figure 1.4.* Avalokitesvara is a favorite subject of Buddhist sculpture, including this statue, regarded as the most beautiful in Vietnam.

a medium to supplement the efforts of a doctor. The human world was pervaded by the supernatural. Some deities were specialized. A fisherman would no more appeal to the smallpox deity for a bountiful catch than we would consider purchasing marine insurance at our local ice cream parlor.

Buddhism and Daoism were amenable to local deities whose presence often predated their own arrival in a community and whose goodwill was seen as essential by the local people. Every body of water had its dragon, each hollow its spirits; ancient heroes might live on as gods, while special trees or rocks were charged with numinous energy. Such deities and cults were local, with great

FIGURE 1.6 *Patriarchs of the Three Creeds.* Attributed to Josetsu. The artist shows the three great teachers—Sakyamuni in the center, with Confucius to his right and Lao Zi to his left—in harmonious agreement, yet renders each figure in its own style. In the abbreviated brushwork beloved by Zen artists, every stroke, every line, counts. Hanging scroll, ink on paper, 98.3 × 21.8 cm. RYOSOKUIN MONASTERY, KYOTO.

variation within as well as among the four East Asian lands. In Japan the spirits were loosely subsumed under Shinto, a religion centered on deities (*kami*) so well established that it was regarded as a purely native religion. (Today scholars see it as an amalgam of imported and local gods and practices.) Here, too, they did not form a unified, ordered pantheon. At the pinnacle of State and society, sovereigns gained legitimacy by claiming that the Confucian Mandate of Heaven had been bestowed on them, but beyond China they also drew on native myths, values, and traditions. By the time we begin our account, the male political elite throughout East Asia was reading the same books and professing similar values, but this hardly implies uniformity in public or private.

This chapter has stressed commonalities, but we must not lose sight of major differences even in basic institutions. That includes the family. The patriarchal family, supported by Confucianism, was the norm, and the perpetuation of the family was important everywhere, but inheritance practices differed radically. In Japan a single heir inherited by far the largest portion of an estate, but in China, after providing for dowries for unwed daughters, it was divided equally among all surviving sons. These inheritance practices not only affected the quality of life of those concerned but had a major impact on the size and economic viability of land-holdings and on the degree of social mobility.

Women were subordinate throughout East Asia, but only in China—and more in some regions than in others—did mothers wrap their daughters' feet in tight bandages, bending the four toes of each foot into the sole and bringing sole and heel as close together as possible, to form tiny feet. Thought to enhance a girl's attractiveness, tiny feet also deterred her from straying into mischief and demonstrated to the world that her family could dispense with her labors in the field.

More broadly, the need to define and delimit our generalizations applies to such very general traits as deference to authority, stress on ritual form, and respect for scholarship and scholars (including students, scholars in the making). It is not merely that one can cite major counterexamples and that similar traits may appear in very different forms. Traits also varied according to place and changed over time. Furthermore, regarded broadly, many such traits hardly seem unique to East Asia. Perhaps they strike us now because we no longer practice or value them.

Notes

1. Francesca Bray, *The Rice Economies: Technology and Development in Asian Societies* (Berkeley, CA: Univ. of California Press, 1994), pp. 25–26.

2. S. A. M. Adshead, *Material Culture in Europe and China, 1400–1800* (New York, NY: St. Martin's Press, 1997), p. 161.

3. Murasaki Shikibu, *The Tale of Genji*, trans. by Royall Tyler (New York, NY: Penguin Putnam, 2001), p. xii.

4. *A Source Book in Chinese Philosophy*, trans. by Wing-tsit Chan (Princeton, NJ: Princeton Univ. Press, 1963), p. 147 (converted to *pinyin*).

Qing China

c. 1600	1644				1911

Rise of Manchu Power

QING DYNASTY

Late Qing

Later Jin (1616–1636)

Kangxi (166–1722)

Qianlong (1736–1795)

Opium War (1839–1842)

In this chapter we will consider the Qing Dynasty (1644–1911) until approximately 1800. This was a century and a half of major achievements: the state reached its greatest geographical extent (Figure 2.1); the economy and the population grew; scholars and artists were productive; popular culture flourished. In terms of cultural and political sophistication and the dynamics of economic development, China was comparable to the most advanced societies on Earth, including those of Europe, whose "great divergence"[1] into sustained industrial growth was still to come. But by 1800 the Qing had seen its best days, even if no one could yet imagine that it was to be China's last dynasty.

The establishment of the new dynasty was a momentous event, but it did not represent a radical break with the past. Social and cultural transformations tend to be more gradual than political change, and given the limitations of seventeenth-century communication and transportation technology, the new rulers could not have refashioned China even if they had wanted to. In recognition of the considerable continuity between the Qing and its Ming predecessor (1368–1644), scholars interested in the long view frequently include both under the rubric "late imperial" China.

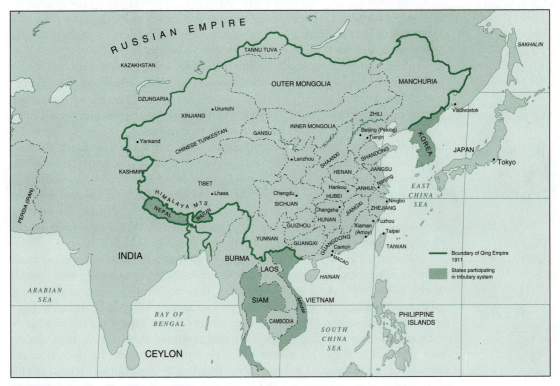

FIGURE 2.1 The Qing Empire, 1775.

Society and the State

As in most agrarian societies, elites dominated local life in late imperial China. They formed an interface between society and government, represented on its lowest level by a magistrate who, from his county seat, had authority over a population that even in Ming times averaged over 50,000. Because his staff was small, his tour of duty limited to three years, and the "law of avoidance" prohibiting officials from serving in their native locality assured that he was a stranger, he needed to work with members of the local gentry with whom he shared a world view grounded in common education, common values, and, when the system worked smoothly, common objectives. The gentry took the lead in the construction of public works such as bridges and waterworks, in social welfare measures, in temple building, and in defense. Such activities complemented rather than challenged the State. However, the local elite could also balk at or even sabotage tax collection, and they could resist other efforts at revenue extraction or policies that went against their interests.

Ideally, members of the elite derived their status from learning, their power from eligibility for office and access to officials, and their wealth from land-owning. The most solidly established were *literati*, officials and landlords all in one, whose learning, power, and wealth each reinforced the other. Wealth allowed a family to dispense with the labors of a son in the fields and pay for his education. Education was both a source of local prestige and a prerequisite for taking the civil service examinations that led to government office, which, in turn, provided opportunities for the acquisition and retention of wealth.

However, these three attributes did not always overlap: there were able scholars who were poor as well as men of wealth who lacked the education and polish to be welcome in polite society, let alone pass examinations. Elite families frequently engaged in commerce, even though the classic Confucian view considered merchants nonproductive and relegated them to the bottom of a four-place hierarchy headed by scholars (*shi*), followed by farmers, with artisans in third place. Because status was not hereditary, elite families could and did fall to commoner status, while merchants and others could raise themselves by educating their sons. Economically, movement up or down was furthered by the ready transferability of land and other forms of wealth. Generational fragmentation of wealth resulted from the practice of dividing estates among male heirs after providing dowries for unmarried daughters, rather than passing on the family property intact to a single heir.

Although eligibility for office remained important, the local elite perpetuated themselves by forming marriage ties with similar families to build powerful networks. Still more basic than marriage ties was membership in common descent groups, consisting of families with the same surname who traced themselves back to a common ancestor. Especially in the wealthy Lower Yangzi and the southeast, such groups formed lineages that controlled property, most notably land to support ancestral halls and graveyards where ceremonial sacrifices for lineage ancestors were performed. Lineages also frequently maintained schools. The compilation of genealogies, which identified those entitled to lineage membership and fostered a sense of identity, further promoted lineage cohesion. Solidarity was also protected and sustained by formal lineage rules enforced by punishments including expulsion for the most serious infractions.

In practice, as in theory, the basic social unit was the family, but the ideal joint family with "five generations under one roof," including the nuclear families of brothers, required a degree of wealth seldom enjoyed by commoners. The senior male normally headed the family, although a widowed matriarch could be the major force. Age prevailed over youth, yet men generally outranked women. The "interior" world of the household was regarded as the women's sphere, while men dealt with the external world. Marriages were arranged by and for families, with the bride becoming a member of her groom's family and subject to supervision and discipline by her mother-in-law. Giving birth to a child, preferably a boy, raised her standing in the family, and in the end, "the lonely disaffected young bride became the pillar of the joint family as a mother-in-law" and "the girl who shrieked her childhood away in agony as her foot bones were crushed grew up to insist on binding her daughter's feet."[2] Women as well as men accepted prevailing norms. Dorothy Ko has pointed to the common saying "a plain face is given by heaven, but poorly bound feet are a sign of laziness" as evidence "that a pair of nicely shaped small feet represented the triumph of individual willpower and effort."[3]

We should note here the variety of lifestyles in a land as vast as China. There were regional differences: small feet were more common in the south than in the north though they were a mark of status and prosperity in both regions. Poor and lower-class women had hard lives but normal feet. There were differences between urban and rural, rich and poor. A criminal, say a salt smuggler, might well enjoy high standing within his community though despised by the official elite. Within China proper, in the south and southwest there were many ethnic minorities with their own ways, and beyond the Great Wall non-Chinese traditions prevailed.

Local societies moved to their own rhythms; nevertheless, the localities were part of a larger whole. G. William Skinner has proposed the existence of a pattern of market towns, 45,000 by the middle of the nineteenth century, "each the nucleus of an autonomous economic system . . . structured spatially according to the principle of centrality and temporally by the periodicity of the market days."[4] Although this theory may be overly schematic, it helps explain how local structures survived dynastic upheaval. Additionally, markets as forums for theatrical performances, along with itinerant peddlers and practitioners of medical and religious arts, provided for a considerable degree of cultural integration. Political integration was supplied by the State.

Supreme over State and society was the emperor, who claimed to have received Heaven's Mandate. Ming and Qing emperors, like their predecessors, performed all the sacred rites demanded of the "Son of Heaven," who linked the human and natural orders. Although constrained by custom and tradition, the emperor's power was absolute in theory. Under harsh emperors, officials who refused to toady to their superiors and criticized the ruler did so at the risk of torture and death. An official who became famous for his uprightness, concern for the common people, frugality, and great courage was Hai Rui (1513–1587). Hai Rui suffered imprisonment and torture after submitting a memorial to the emperor criticizing His Majesty's vanity and erratic conduct, while holding him responsible for the injustice, corruption, military weakness, heavy taxation, and the impoverishment of the people that prevailed during his reign. The emperor was an autocrat, but his reach was limited by his need to work through a vast bureaucracy. To succeed in the long run, he had to avoid alienating the officialdom or provoking the people into rebellion.

Like all governments, that of China provided security, collected taxes, maintained large-scale projects such as the dikes along the Yellow River, and administrated a judicial system. Beyond that, in keeping with Confucian imperatives, the government joined the local elite in activities meant to assure the physical and moral welfare of its subjects. A populace panicked by the threat of starvation or spurred by "immoral" heterodox ideas to resist the status quo posed a threat equally to the gentry and the State.

A key institution, dating back to the Sui (581–617) and continued by the Qing, was the civil service examination system that linked State and society, as well as political and intellectual life. With the exception of a small minority of men whose family backgrounds included criminals, brothel keepers, or other undesirables, the examinations were open to all. There were documented cases of men from truly humble backgrounds winning the coveted highest degree, but the need for years of intensive study favored candidates from elite families who could afford to dispense with the labor of their sons and to educate them. Great pains were taken to avoid dishonesty, since the credibility of the government was at stake.

To pass the examination required a thorough command of Confucian classics and literature. Attempts to test for an ability to apply this knowledge to current problems were only sporadically successful. The tendency was to reward formal competence in composing essays along the lines of the models readily available at the local bookstore. Nevertheless, the examination system retained enormous prestige and produced China's most impressive statesmen. Dominating education, it fostered a gentlemen elite bound by a shared conceptual framework of references and ideals.

The Fall of the Ming

By the seventeenth century there were numerous signs that, after well over two centuries, the Ming was in trouble. In the 1590s the dynasty could still conduct campaigns in Mongolia and send large armies to fight the Japanese invaders of Korea (see Chapter 3). These military operations, as well as later military efforts in Manchuria, put enormous financial burdens on a government undermined by corruption, divisiveness, and incompetence in the highest places. The resulting financial crisis was a symptom of profound malaise.

The traditional Chinese analysis of dynastic decline holds that internal decay precedes external disaster. The Ming fits this formula. During its last half century it clearly lacked the vitality to renew a decaying political apparatus. The balance between the central government and the local elite was upset when the dynasty made too many concessions to the gentry. Too much was given away, too many fields were removed from the tax rolls. Large landowners were able to find tax shelters through manipulation, leaving only peasant freeholders to pay taxes. Local resentment against the gentry grew, while lack of funds forced the dynasty to neglect public works. Grain stored for emergencies was sold off. Even the postal system was shut down. Finally, the regime failed to pay even its most strategically placed troops. Desperate men formed outlaw gangs that gradually coalesced into full-fledged rebel organizations. One of these, led by Li Zicheng (c. 1600–1645), a former postal attendant, seized Beijing, and the last Ming emperor committed suicide. Li, however, was unable to found a new dynasty, for he had failed to take the necessary ideological and administrative steps to gain the backing of the scholar-official elite.

The Founding of the Qing

A major theme in Chinese history is the interaction between the Chinese and their nomadic and semi-nomadic neighbors whose way of life made them formidable horsemen and fierce warriors. When united under effective leadership, the Chinese, with their superior economic resources and larger population, normally had the upper hand, but they could never fully control their mobile adversaries. To deal with these troublesome neighbors, Chinese governments worked out various strategies ranging from diplomacy of accommodation and alliance to attempts at outright military suppression. One military alternative was the kind of static defense that prompted the Ming to engage in bursts of wall-building during the 1470s, 1540s, and 1570s, turning the Great Wall into the impressive structure it is today. In the northeast, the Ming relied on the Willow Palisades, a barrier formed by lines of willows and a deep trench fortified by military checkpoints.

Beyond the Willow Palisades lay Manchuria, home of the Jurchen, who spoke a language related to Korean but not to Chinese. Although the Jurchen traced themselves back to the Jin Dynasty (1115–1234) that had once dominated north China, they had long been divided into tribes. In the north they subsisted by hunting and fishing, but in the south, where they were in contact with Chinese speakers, they farmed, raised livestock, and took pleasure and pride in their horsemanship and hunting skills. The ethnic origins of the inhabitants of the agricultural lands of Liaodong and southern Manchuria were diverse. They were not necessarily descended from Chinese settlers, but they spoke Chinese and overall were Chinese culturally. There was also a major Mongolian presence in Manchuria, and Mongol influence on the Jurchen was strong.

To bring the various peoples of Manchuria into a state and create a regional power took Nurgaci (1559–1626), a clan and tribal chief, more than 25 years as he fought, negotiated, and married his way to leadership and power. To facilitate state building he ordered the creation of a script, based on Mongolian, to write the Jurchen language. Originally favored by the Ming, Nurgaci continued to send tribute to Beijing until 1609. But he was powerful enough to defy the Chinese dynasty when he wished, and in 1616 declared himself emperor of the Later Jin. However, it was his successor, Hong Taiji (r. 1626–1643), who created a new ethnic identity called "Manchu," and envisioned a broader empire. In 1636, while remaining "divine khan" to his tribal subjects, Hong Taiji signaled his ambition to rule China by founding the new "Qing" (pure) dynasty. Nothing in the Chinese tradition stipulated that the imperial house had to be ethnically Chinese.

From the beginning, the new dynasty drew support from an alliance with Mongols and Chinese speakers, mostly from Manchuria. This was reflected in the organization of its armies into "banners," each with its own colors. By the time of the conquest, there were eight Manchu banners (278 companies), eight Mongol (120 companies), and eight "Chinese" (165 companies). Membership in the banners was hereditary. After the conquest, they were stationed in garrisons strategically located throughout the empire. There the bannermen lived apart from the local population under a general who reported directly to Beijing.

After Li Zicheng overthrew the Ming, the key to the military situation was in the hands of the Ming general Wu Sangui (1612–1678), whose army guarded Shanhaiguan, the strategic pass between the mountains and the sea that formed the eastern terminus of the Great Wall. When Wu threw his lot in with the Manchus, Li Zicheng's fate was sealed.

After the Manchus entered the capital, Beijing, in June 1644, the Qing ruler announced he had come to punish the rebels, buried the deceased Ming emperor and empress with full honors, and claimed to be the legitimate successor of the old dynasty. To consolidate and expand their control, the new rulers needed the support and participation of Chinese officials and the tacit assent of the Chinese populace. Even before they gained the capital, the dynasty sought to draw on the talents of Chinese scholars and reassure the Chinese elite by holding its first examinations. Also prior to the conquest they formed a political system that balanced an Assembly of Princes and High Officials composed almost exclusively of Manchus, with such traditional Chinese institutions as The Six Ministries (personnel, revenue, rites, war, justice, and public works) and the Censorate, charged with reporting on the conduct of the civil service with the right and duty to criticize the emperor.

Despite such reassuring measures, the subjugation of the rest of China, especially the south, involved long and bloody warfare including a terrible ten-day massacre in Yangzhou that left the city's gutters filled with corpses. After the capture of Nanjing, which Ming loyalists had made their capital, the Qing emperor forced all men to shave the forward portion of their heads and braid their hair in back into a long queue (pigtail). The Manchus were not the first to force their hairstyle on their subjects; the Ming had done the same in Vietnam.

After the fall of Nanjing, the Qing still faced prolonged resistance. For approximately 40 years, warfare, banditry, and peasant uprisings, along with periods of starvation and epidemics, took a heavy toll. From 1646 to 1658 much of the southeast coast was controlled by Zheng Chenggong (1624–1662), the son of a Chinese pirate adventurer and a Japanese mother, widely known as Coxinga. From 1661 to 1669, in order to deprive Zheng of support and supplies, a 17-mile strip along the coast, extending from Zhejiang to the Vietnamese border, was completely cleared of people. Barriers, guard posts, and watch towers were erected to prevent anyone from entering. Originally based in Xiamen (Amoy), Zheng moved to Taiwan (Formosa), from which he expelled the Dutch in 1662. His son held out against the Manchus, who finally subdued the island in 1683 and placed it under the administration of Fujian Province. By then the southwest, too, was pacified, but only after the War of the Three Feudatories (1673–1681), one of whom was Wu Sangui, who had created a practically autonomous state for himself in Yunnan and Guizhou.

In their new empire, the Manchus, who comprised only about two percent of the population, and their Mongol associates formed a conquest elite who were conscious of their non-Chinese heritage, forbidden to intermarry with the Chinese, and distinguished from them in dress, family rituals, diet, and lifestyle. For example, Manchu women were not allowed bound feet. Shamanistic practices brought from their homeland were continued at court. An inner circle of this elite dominated the inner court and exercised profound influence on government throughout the life of the dynasty.

While claiming to be heirs of the Ming and recipients of Heaven's Mandate, Qing emperors (Table 2.1), as Manchus, concurrently asserted the claim to rule

TABLE 2.1 THE QING EMPERORS

Beginning with the Ming period emperors used a single era name (*nianhao*, literally "year designation") throughout their reigns. Normally the era name remained in use until the end of the lunar year in which the emperor died. Consequently, the emperors are often referred to by their era names rather than by their formal posthumous names used in the imperial ancestral temple (their temple names) or by their personal names, although these are also employed in the scholarly literature. Qing emperors followed the Ming practice of using a single era name.

Era Name	Temple Name	Personal Name	Era Dates
Shunzhi	Shizu	Fulin	1644–1661
Kangxi	Shengzu	Xuanye	1662–1722
Yongzheng	Shizong	Yinzhen	1723–1735
Qianlong	Gaozong	Hongli	1736–1795
Jiaqing	Renzong	Yongyan	1796–1820
Daoguang	Xuanzong	Minning	1821–1850
Xianfeng	Wenzong	Yizhu	1851–1861
Tongzhi	Muzong	Zaichun	1862–1874
Guangxu	Dezong	Zaitian	1875–1908
Xuanzong	[none]	Puyi	1909–1911

as khans, thus appropriating the title long revered by Mongols and other people of the steppe. In the Western regions, as in the inner court, non-Chinese traditions made for non-Chinese identities. The Manchus also drew on Buddhist traditions to make their rule acceptable to people beyond the Great Wall. Non-Chinese ritual observances solemnly enacted by the rulers legitimized their rule. Potent symbolism was a major component of Qing authority and power.

China proper was divided into eighteen provinces further subdivided into circuits, prefectures, and counties, but Inner Asian affairs were handled by the Court of Colonial Affairs using the peoples' own languages and appealing to their own political traditions. The emperors themselves regularly studied Mongolian, Manchu, and Chinese. Although the trend was toward increasing bureaucratization, Inner Asians saw themselves as subjects of a universal empire. But China was the Center.

Early Qing Thinkers and Painters

While many literati accepted service under the new dynasty, the most original work came from the brushes of men who refused to serve the Qing. Among those who found tranquility in a Buddhist monastery during these turbulent times was Hongren (1610–1663; Figure 2.2), who "represented the world in a dematerialized cleansed vision . . . revealing his personal peace through the liberating form of geometric abstraction."[5]

Although Hongren had his followers, other painters who lived through the change of dynasties were too individualistic to attract followers or perpetuate styles. One such was Zhu Da, also called Bada Shanren (c. 1626–1705), whose behavior was distinctly odd: he sang and laughed frequently but refused to speak. His painting was equally unusual: surging landscapes, huge lotuses, and birds and fish with the eyes of a Zen patriarch. His handscroll "Fish and Rocks" (Figure 2.3) begins with a section (not shown here) done with a dry brush, and the brushwork becomes wetter as the painting proceeds. Although there are references to the Ming dynasty and himself in the poems and in the painting, the work remains enigmatic. Zhu Da had to wait several centuries for his fame, but he exemplifies the self-expression favored by the aesthetic theory of his time, which regarded representation as crude and unworthy of gentlemen amateurs even if the distinction between amateur and professional was one more of theory than practice.

Like Zhu Da in the world of painting, Wang Fuzhi (1619–1704) had no followers in his own time, but late in the dynasty came to be admired as a philosopher who gave primacy to *qi*, and as a student of history who emphasized that institutions and policies of one age or culture were not necessarily applicable to another. Another Ming loyalist with trenchant political views that had to wait centuries for a hearing was Huang Zongxi (1610–1695), who complained that in antiquity the people had been the master, and the prince the tenant, but that now the situation is reversed. The prince lords it over the people and exploits them. "Thus he who does the greatest harm in the world is none other than the prince."[6]

Among the policies advocated by Huang was the restoration of the pre-Ming strong chief ministership, the introduction of tax and land reforms, increasing the authority of local officials, and the strengthening of education, including the creation of independent schools.

Huang's most influential work was a great compendium of Ming thought, still widely used. The writings and teachings of Huang's contemporary, Gu Yanwu (1613–1682), made a deep impression on mainstream Qing scholarship. Objecting to the abstract speculations of Song and Ming philosophers, Gu insisted on what he considered real and practical learning, based on scholarship in the original sources rather than relying on later commentaries. He himself wrote important studies on historical geography and inscriptions but is most famous for his work in historical phonetics. His essays, collected under the title *Records of Daily Knowledge (Rizhilu)*, discuss government, the examination system, and economics as well as the classics and history, showing a range and critical spirit representative of the best of seventeenth-century thought. He was influential in founding Qing philological scholarship and what came to be known as "evidential learning." Subsequent Qing scholars contributed greatly to this textual scholarship.

Not all painters of the early Qing were eccentric or even persistently loyal to the Ming. Outstanding among the more orthodox painters were four artists all named Wang, among whom Wang Hui (1632–1717) was considered the most gifted. One of his paintings is a rendition of Fan Guan's *Travelers* (Figure 1.1). His *Summer Mountains, Misty Rain* (Figure 2.4) is representative in that Wang here follows the style and composition of the masters of the Song and Yuan in "an almost magical composite" to create a painting very much his own. Wang himself formulated his agenda and expressed his aspiration: "I must use the

FIGURE 2.2 Hongren's masterpiece, *The Coming of Autumn,* displays a marvelous sense of structural depth. Hanging scroll, ink on paper, 122.4 cm high.
HONOLULU ACADEMY OF ARTS, GIFT OF WILHELMINA TENNEY MEMORIAL COLLECTION, 1995 (NO. 2045.1).

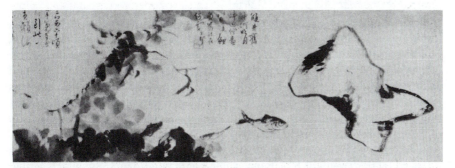

FIGURE 2.3 *Fish and Rocks,* Zhu Da (Bada Shanren 1624–c.1705), Qing dynasty. Note the water plants and lotuses on the left and the strange rock that invites speculation. Section of handscroll, ink on paper, 29.2 × 157.5 cm.
© THE CLEVELAND MUSEUM OF ART, 2002. JOHN L. SEVERANCE FUND, 1953.247.

FIGURE 2.4   *Fishermen Returning Home,* third and last panel of *Summer Mountains, Misty Rain* (1668), Wang Hui (1632–1717). In this handscroll, as frequently in others, the landscape dominates, forcing the viewer to search carefully for the two boats carrying the fishermen. Handscroll, ink on paper, 17 in. × 19 in.

brush and ink of the Yuan to move the peaks and valleys of the Song and infuse them with the breath-resonance of the Tang. I will then have a great synthesis."[7]

In 1691 Wang Hui received an imperial command to supervise the painting of a series of scrolls commemorating Kangxi's southern tour. He was only one of many painters and other talented men to enjoy the patronage of Kangxi and in turn enhance the aura of the throne and the glory of its occupant.

The Reign of Kangxi

The dominant force at the beginning of the dynasty was Dorgon (1612–1650), the fourteenth son of Nurgaci, acting as regent for the dynasty's first emperor, Shunzhi (1638–1661, r. 1644–1661). When Kangxi (b. 1654) inherited the throne in 1662 another regency was formed, but Kangxi himself took control in 1668 and ruled until his death in 1722. As already noted, the Manchu conquest of China was completed during the early years of his reign. This was accomplished in campaigns fought largely by Chinese troops under Chinese generals. After the incorporation of Taiwan, he turned his attention to China's borders in the north and west. In the Amur River region his army destroyed a Russian Cossack base. This success was followed by the Treaty of Nerchinsk, signed with Russia in 1689, which settled frontier problems between the two great empires and regularized relations between them. It also removed the threat of a possible alliance between the Russians and a confederation of Western Mongols. Against the latter, Kangxi personally led his troops from 1696 to 1697 and won a great victory. Around the middle of the seventeenth century, Western Mongols had intervened in the political and religious struggles taking place in Tibet and had remained as conquerors. In 1720 Kangxi's armies entered Tibet and installed a pro-Chinese Dalai Lama (the spiritual and secular ruler of Tibet). This was the first, but not the last, Qing intervention in Tibet.

Kangxi's martial exploits reflected his identification with his forebears and his desire to preserve a Manchu way of life, which he saw as essential for maintaining Manchu supremacy. Another expression of this feeling was his zest for great hunts.

To help preserve Manchu distinctiveness, one of the first acts of Kangxi's reign was the closing of Manchuria to Chinese immigration. Kangxi was very much the Manchu, but he was by no means anti-Chinese. Kangxi maintained a strict balance between Manchus and Chinese in the top central administrative posts. In the provinces, a Chinese governor usually was counterbalanced by a governor-general, who was a Manchu, a Mongol, or a Chinese bannerman mostly presiding over two provinces. Banner garrisons continued to be the main source of security. The emperor also used Chinese bondservants, who managed the imperial household and the emperor's personal treasury. Furthermore, they performed confidential tasks such as sending secret reports on provincial conditions.

Kangxi was a vigorous man. He rose well before dawn each day to go through a great stack of memorials before receiving officials, beginning at 5 A.M. (later changed to 7 A.M. to accommodate officials not living near the palace). His personal tours of inspection in the south are famous. To show his benevolence, he reduced taxes and forced Manchu aristocrats to desist from seizing Chinese lands. He was also a man of wide intellectual interests, including Western learning. He won the affection of many Chinese literati by holding a special examination in 1679. He not only patronized artists but sponsored the compilation of the official Ming history, a great phrase dictionary, a giant encyclopedia, and an exhaustive dictionary of Chinese characters. He gave special support to the philosophy of Zhu Xi.

Kangxi was one of the most successful emperors in all of Chinese history, but he was unable to provide for a smooth succession. Although he had 56 children, only one son was by an empress. He was designated heir apparent, but disappointed his father, who complained that he was "dissolute, tyrannical, brutal, debauched."[8] He also showed signs of mental instability, and in the end Kangxi placed him in confinement, but failed to appoint a successor. The claim that 14 years later he named his fourth son on his deathbed appears to be a later fabrication. During these years, various sons, suspicious of one another and each backed by his own political faction, conspired and maneuvered for the succession. The upshot was that after Kangxi's death, the throne was seized in a military coup by the fourth son, who became Emperor Yongzheng (r. 1723–1735).

Yongzheng

Yongzheng censored the record of his accession and suppressed other writings deemed inimical to his regime or hostile to the Manchus. Like his father, he used military force to preserve the dynasty's position in Mongolia. When Tibet was torn by civil war from 1717 to 1728, he intervened militarily, leaving a Qing resident backed by a military garrison to pursue the dynasty's interests. After the dynasty ended in the twentieth century, this provided a basis for Chinese claims of sovereignty over Tibet.

Yongzheng was a tough, hard-working ruler bent on effective government. During the early Qing, the emperor had been assisted by the Grand Secretariat, a six-man board composed of three Manchu and three Chinese, but under Kangxi the Grand Secretariat lost its influence. In a move toward greater efficiency and control, Yongzheng created a five-man Grand Council whose members linked the inner court with the outer bureaucracy, headed by the chiefs of the six ministries. By expanding the number of officials entitled to submit secret memorials and sending them confidential replies, he operated his own channel of communication apart from the general bureaucracy.

The emperor saw the need for administrative and fiscal reform and restructured the financing of local government in order to free magistrates from dependence on private and informal funding. Active in tax reform, he simplified the system of tax registers by combining the land and personal service taxes. This and other measures, along with strong imperial oversight, led to increased government efficiency. In the long run, though, effective reform below the county level proved unattainable.

Yongzheng's reign was despotic, efficient, and vigorous. By the simple device of sealing the name of the heir-apparent in a box kept in the throne room, he was able to assure that on his death there would be no struggle over the succession. Thus he prepared the way for what was to be the dynasty's most splendid reign, that of Qianlong.

Qianlong

During Qianlong's reign (1736–1795), the Qing achieved its greatest prosperity. By 1760 the size of the empire had doubled, and expansion into Central Asia had reached its greatest extent (see map, Figure 2.1). This was the result of Qing diplomatic skill in practicing "divide and rule" policies, its ability to work with local leaders and manipulate inner Asian symbols of authority, and the sheer power of its armies. The Qing also took advantage of the disunity and declining strength of the Inner Asian peoples. The weakening of these peoples has been subject to various interpretations. According to Morris Rossabi, the most plausible explanations include the diminishing importance of the international caravan trade in an age of developing maritime commerce, a trend toward the development of sedentary societies marked by urbanization, and Russian expansion that reduced the area to which tribes could flee in retreat, thereby reducing their mobility.[9]

Under Qianlong, Chinese Turkestan was incorporated and renamed Xinjiang. To the West, Ili was conquered and garrisoned. This brought into the empire Muslim leaders, including followers of the activist Naqshbandiyya order, difficult to convince of the legitimacy of Qing rule. The Qing also dominated Outer Mongolia after inflicting a final defeat on the Western Mongols. Its policy there was to preserve Mongol institutions, but it allowed Chinese merchants to enter and exploit the people, thus reinforcing the anti-Chinese animosities of the animal-herding Mongols. It is no accident that after the Qing fell in the twentieth century, the Mongols promptly declared their independence. Throughout this period there were continued Mongol interventions in Tibet and a reciprocal spread of Tibetan Lamaism in Mongolia. Qianlong again sent armies into Tibet and firmly established the Dalai Lama as ruler, with a Qing resident and garrison to preserve Qing suzerainty. Other than that, no further attempt was made to integrate Tibet into the empire after the manner of Xinjiang. To foster the loyalty of Mongols and Tibetans, Qianlong drew on the Buddhist tradition. Six tangkas (Tibetan religious paintings) survive portraying the emperor as Manjusri, boddhistava of compassion and wisdom. Tibetan records often refer to him by that name.

Further afield, military campaigns against Vietnam, Burma, and over the Himalayas into Nepal forced local rulers to accept Qing hegemony and render tribute. Qianlong's imperialism involved millions of square miles and brought into the empire non-Chinese peoples, such as Uighurs, Kazakhs, Kirghiz, and Mongols, who were at least potentially hostile. It was also a very expensive enterprise. The dynasty enjoyed unprecedented prosperity and managed to accumulate a healthy financial reserve in the mid-1780s, but even its resources had their limits. Qianlong delighted in the glory and wealth. He built a sumptuous summer residence, partly of Western design, and undertook grand tours of the empire. In his policy toward the literati, he combined Kangxi's generous patronage of scholarship with Yongzheng's suspicion of anti-Manchu writings. The greatest project he sponsored was the *Complete Library of Four Treasuries (Siku quanshu)*, employing 15,000 copyists working 12 years to produce 3,462 complete works in 36,000 volumes. This "final affirmation of the unity of knowledge and power in Chinese history"[10] preserved many books but also merged with a campaign to ferret out and suppress writings offensive to Manchu sensibilities.

Some 80 percent of Qianlong's officials were Chinese, but the emperor was much concerned that Manchus did not become Chinese. To this effect he ordered compilation of Manchu genealogies and histories, promoted the study and the use of the Manchu language by Manchus, and insisted on all that set Manchus apart from Chinese down to the details of feminine adornment. Three earrings in each ear were mandatory for Manchu ladies, and woe to her who made do with just one in the Chinese manner. Qianlong's measures standardized Manchu lore and practices; they reaffirmed Manchu identity but rendered the tradition inflexible.

Eighteenth-Century Governance

The eighteenth century was generally a time of prosperity, when institutions functioned as smoothly as they ever had. A system of state and local granaries ensured adequate and affordable food supplies. In the rich Lower Yangzi region, the local elite constructed and operated community granaries, but elsewhere government assumed a more active role in providing these sources of emergency food.

In the eighteenth century it also performed formidable feats of information gathering and coordination over the breadth of the land.

The State's concern with encouraging popular morality was expressed in the promotion of village lectures based on edifying imperial pronouncements and its compilation of an officially sanctioned pantheon of local gods and spirits, and included others as long as they were not considered subversive. It also fostered schools. As in the case of community granaries, in the more advanced areas education was left to local initiative, but in outlying provinces officials played a more active role. Thus, a dedicated eighteenth-century governor of Yunnan established 650 schools for the instruction of the numerous minorities of the province.

When the system operated effectively, as in the eighteenth century, State and society formed a continuum without a fixed boundary. Though local gentry might resist tax collection and examination candidates might resent the bitter competition that left little hope for success, essentially officials and elite shared a broad spectrum of values and ideas pushing them to cooperate rather than compete. As one study puts it:

> Because the state understood the art of ruling to include shaping people's moral behavior, it was inclined to be meddlesome, authoritarian, and censorious. But at the same time, because only people who freely choose to do the right thing can be said to have high moral standards, the state accepted and even promoted initiatives among its subjects that it saw as likely to make people take their moral and social agency seriously.[11]

Eighteenth-Century Literati Culture

Following the lead of Gu Yanwu, but without his breadth, Qing scholars engaged in "evidential research," rejected philosophical speculation, and relied on careful textual study to reveal the meaning of the classics:

> If only they [those who seek the Way] correct primary and derived characters, discern their pronunciation, read the explanations and glosses, and master the commentaries and notes, the meaning and principles will appear on their own, and the Way within them.[12]

Scholars of evidential learning made important, even iconoclastic, discoveries concerning the questionable historicity of parts of such canonical texts as *The Classic of Changes, The Classic of History*, and *The Records of Rites*. However, the concentration on philology (historical linguistics) easily led to the view that textual studies alone were truly "solid" (in the sense that they avoided abstract speculation) and "practical."

Yan Yuan (1635–1704), on the other hand, condemned both quiet meditation and book learning as standing in the way of true self-cultivation, which should lead to the capability of changing the world. He studied military science and medicine, but his chief disciple Li Gong (1659–1733) expounded his teachings in the form of commentaries on the classics.

A major eighteenth-century thinker was Dai Zhen (1723–1777), who made important contributions to linguistics, astronomy, mathematics, and geography as well as philosophy. Like most of the creative seventeenth-century thinkers, he rejected the metaphysical existence of *li*, which he considered simply the pattern of things. He also disputed Zhu Xi's dualistic theory of human nature, insisting that it contradicted the teachings of Mencius, that human nature is one whole and all good, and that moral perfection consists in fulfilling one's natural inclinations.

Dai Zhen shared his age's faith in philology, but this was not true of his contemporary Zhang Xuecheng (1738–1801), who strongly disliked philological studies and sought meaning in the study and writing of history. Zhang is perhaps most famous for his thesis that "the six classics are all history," by which he meant that they are not "empty" theoretical discussions but that they document antiquity and illustrate the Dao. A scholar must not stop at the facts but get at the meaning. Zhang once compared a work of history to a living organism: its facts are like bones, the writing is like the skin, and its meaning corresponds to the organism's vital spirit.

Along with history and philosophy, another subject of perennial concern to Chinese scholars was the function and evaluation of literature. The poet Yuan Mei (1716–1797) held that the purpose of poetry is to express emotion and that it must give pleasure; he rejected the didactic view, held by Zhang Xuecheng, that it must convey moral instruction. Yuan's poetry and prose reflect the life of a talented, refined eighteenth-century hedonist, unconventional within the bounds of good taste, and marginally aware of the exotic West. One of his prize possessions was a large Western mirror much admired by his female pupils. Among Yuan's less conventional works are a cookbook and a collection of ghost stories. His interest in the latter was shared by his friend, the painter Le Ping (1735–1799), the youngest and last of the Eight Eccentrics of Yangzhou, a man who claimed actually to have seen the apparitions he painted.

In the eighteenth century, painters of various schools were at work: professionals working in the meticulous and mannered "northern" style, eclectics drawing on diverse traditions and models, and individualists striving, sometimes excessively, for originality. An unusually interesting and prolific artist was the painter Gao Qipei (1660–1734). Even in the Song dynasty and earlier, artists had experimented with unconventional materials instead of using a brush, but none had gone as far as Gao in using his fingernail (Figure 2.5).

Qing painters and scholars generally perceived themselves as latecomers in a long and revered tradition. As such, they faced a dilemma similar to that of painters, poets, and composers of our own time who no longer feel they can contribute to the traditional lines of development in their arts—that is, to be another Rembrandt, Beethoven, and so forth. What had been valid for one age could not serve another.

Thus some literati artists cultivated the notion that the epitome of art was non-art—that is, the deliberate cultivation of innocent awkwardness. Unusual behavior was tolerated, and it became quite acceptable to sell one's paintings. Both Gao and Le did so without jeopardizing their "amateur" status. Meanwhile, openly professional artists, who did not claim literati status, sold their work to ordinary, unsophisticated folk who appreciated bright colors and verisimilitude. Colored

FIGURE 2.5 *Tiger Seen from Above* (c. 1700), Gao Qipei (1660–1734). At the upper right, Gao Qipei wrote the following text: "Life with the fingers from the man from outside the Shanhai gate." Beneath it are several red seals. Artists often stamped their seals on their paintings, and collectors frequently added theirs as well. They even wrote poems in the empty spaces. Emperor Qianlong particularly liked to do so. Ink and colors on paper, 105.3 × 51.5 cm.

RIJKSMUSEUM, AMSTERDAM AK-RK-1991-10.

woodblock prints also appealed to a wide audience, as did antiques of varying authenticity and quality (Figure 2.6).

Fiction

Many of the dynasty's best writers and thinkers were men who had failed in the examination route to success, an experience that perhaps helped them to view society with a measure of critical and even satiric detachment. The examinations themselves were a favorite target. Pu Songling (1640–1715) wrote this account of the seven transformations of a candidate in the provincial examination:

> When he first enters the examination compound and walks along, panting under his heavy load of luggage, he is just like a beggar. Next, while undergoing the personal body search and being scolded by the clerks and shouted at by the soldiers, he is just like a prisoner. When he finally enters his cell and, along with the other candidates, stretches his neck to peer out, he is just like the larva of a bee. When the examination is finished at last and he leaves, his mind in a haze and his legs tottering, he is just like a sick bird that has been released from a cage. While he is wondering when the results will be announced and waiting to learn whether he passed or failed, so nervous that he is startled even by the rustling of the trees and the grass and is unable to sit or stand still, his restlessness is like that of a monkey on a leash. When at last the results are announced and he has definitely failed, he loses his vitality like one dead, rolls over on his side, and lies without moving, like a poisoned fly. Then, when he pulls himself together and stands up, he is provoked by every sight and sound, gradually flings away everything within his reach, and complains of the illiteracy of the examiners. When he

calms down at last, he finds everything in the room broken. At this time he is like a pigeon smashing its own precious eggs. These are the seven transformations of a candidate.[13]

This examination was held in a labyrinthine compound, with the candidates housed in individual cells where they had to spend the night. It was an eerie place sealed off from the rest of the world, for during an examination session the great gates remained firmly shut: if a man died during the examination, his body was wrapped in straw matting and thrown over the wall. Thus it was a perfect setting for numerous tales of ghosts, usually the spirits of jilted maidens come to wreak vengeance on the men who had done them wrong.

As David Rolston points out, "neither landscape painting nor traditional Chinese fiction is structured around the use of the convention of fixed perspective or viewpoint so important in western painting or fiction."[14] *The Scholars* (*Rulinwaishi*), a novel by Wu Jingzi (1701–1754), is a good case in point. Characterized by Shang Wei as "a literati novel driven by conflicting impulses toward irony and the Confucian moral imagination,"[15] it satirizes the examination system, catches in its net an assortment of human follies, and unveils the intricacies of social life in vignettes of the pompous and the ignorant, the unworldly scholar and those who

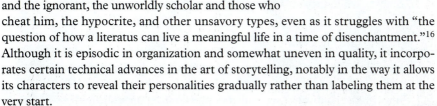

FIGURE 2.6 *Antique Dealer in Beijing, Late Qing.* John Thomson, *Illustrations of China and Its People: A Series of Two Hundred Photographs, with Letterpress Descriptive of the Places and People Represented* (London: S. Low, Marston, Low, and Searle, 1873–1874. Reprinted in 1900.) Vol.4, Plate 28.
This vendor works on a street given to "curiosity shops," catering to collectors hoping to discover a treasure, and to travelers looking for a souvenir from the capital. When they see something they like they will have to match bargaining wits with the proprietor. The Manchu hairstyle clearly visible here was abandoned as soon as the dynasty collapsed.

cheat him, the hypocrite, and other unsavory types, even as it struggles with "the question of how a literatus can live a meaningful life in a time of disenchantment."[16] Although it is episodic in organization and somewhat uneven in quality, it incorporates certain technical advances in the art of storytelling, notably in the way it allows its characters to reveal their personalities gradually rather than labeling them at the very start.

China's most beloved and exhaustively studied novel is *The Dream of the Red Chamber* (*Honglou Meng*), also translated as *The Story of the Stone* [Box 2.1]. Like *The Scholars*, it offers priceless insights into Qing society, this time from the vantage point of a large, eminent family in decline. With rich detail and a cast of hundreds, it reveals how such a family was organized, how it functioned, the relationships between the generations and the sexes, the lives of women, the status of servants; and it does all this with fine psychological characterizations based on the personal experience of the author, Cao Zhan (d. 1763). But it is far more than a novel of manners. Conscious of its own fictionality, it prompts the reader to contemplate the distinction between the real and the unreal and to ponder the nature of desire. C. T. Hsia has written that "it embodies the supreme tragic expression in Chinese literature," and that "the ultimate tragic conflict lies in a tug of war between the opposing claims of compassion and detachment."[17]

BOX 2.1   HUMOROUS EPISODE FROM DREAM OF THE RED CHAMBER

The gap between the life of privileged gentry and the life of ordinary folk is revealed when Grannie Liu, distantly related to the wealthy Jia family, comes for a visit hoping for financial assistance. She is astounded at the wealth her distant relatives enjoy and has an amusing encounter with a Western mirror. In the following episode her hosts have fun at her expense by giving her a pair of heavy ivory chopsticks inlaid with gold, but Grannie Liu is invariably good humored.

"What's this you have given me?" said Grannie Liu, "A pair of tongs? They are heavier than one of our iron shovels. I shall never be able to manage with these."

The others all laughed.

A woman-servant now entered carrying one of the luncheon boxes. . . . There were two dishes inside. . . . The second a bowl of pigeon's eggs (deliberately chosen for their mirth provoking possibilities) was taken out by Xi-feng and set down in front of Grannie Liu.

. . . Even your hens here are special," remarked Grannie Liu. "I must see if I can get one of these under me belt."

"They cost a silver tael a piece," said Xi-feng as Grannie Liu continued to praise the diminutive "hen's" eggs. "You should eat them quickly, while they're still hot. They won't be so nice when they're cold."

Grannie Liu obediently held out her chopsticks and tried to take hold of one, but the egg eluded her. After chasing it several times around the inside of the bowel, she did at last succeed in getting a grip on it. But as she craned forward with open mouth to reach it, it slipped through the chopsticks and rolled on the floor. At once she laid down the chopsticks and would have gone down on hands and knees to pick it up, but before she could do so one of the servants had retrieved it and carried it off for disposal.

"That's a tael of silver gone," Grannie Liu said regretfully, "and we didn't even hear it clink."

Cao Xueqin, *The Story of the Stone*, Vol. 2, trans. by David Hawkes (Middlesex, England & New York, NY: Penguin Books, 1977), pp. 287–289.

Despite the literary excellence of *The Dream*, neither it nor other novels ever gained Confucian legitimacy as high literature. In Japan the novel was an honored part of literary culture, but in China reading a novel was a surreptitious pleasure indulged in by students when their teacher was not looking—or vice versa.

A Buoyant Economy

During the initial 40 cataclysmic years following the founding of the Qing, warfare, destruction, dislocation, and cold weather combined to bring widespread hardship, famine, disease, and population decline. However, then both the economy and the population revived and went on to reach new heights (Figure 2.7). By the end of the eighteenth century, the Chinese population was around 300 million, about double what it had been around 1600. More people lived in China than even in Europe. The century saw an increase in life expectancy and an all-around improvement in the standard of living.

In agriculture, increased production and commercialization went hand in hand. Yields improved with the geographical spread of crops, such as specialized strains of rice suitable to local conditions, and of improved irrigation techniques

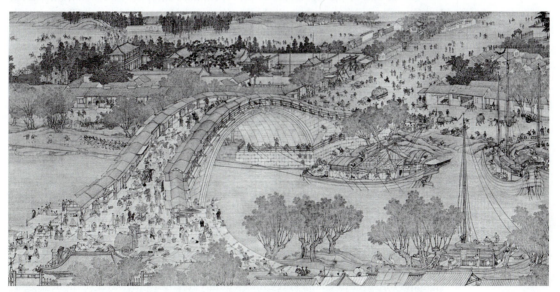

FIGURE 2.7 *Rainbow Bridge.* Detail of a 1736 rendition and embellishment by five of Emperor Qianlong's court painters of an eleventh-century handscroll that takes the viewer on a journey in the imagined past that often reflects the actual present. Here two boats, masts taken down, are being pulled under a bridge lined with shops that are filled with shoppers. The countryside was served by periodic markets while cities and towns acted as permanent hubs of commercial activity, wholesale and retail, large and small. Handscrolls are intended to be held one end in each hand and unrolled gradually, permitting the viewer to travel through the scenes depicted in the painting.

National Palace Museum, Taipei, Taiwan, Republic of China.

and better fertilizers, such as soybean cakes. Production was also significantly increased by the introduction of new plants from the Americas: sweet potatoes, peanuts, tobacco, and corn. These could be grown on land previously left uncultivated because it was unsuitable for traditional Chinese crops.

A rising population spurred demand. The economy became more complex with the expansion of markets for commercial crops such as tea, sugar, cotton, hemp, tobacco, and for other products of agricultural activity, most importantly mulberry trees for feeding silkworms. Rice was grown commercially to feed cities and towns and for sale to farmers who had converted rice paddies to more profitable cash crops.

The developments in agriculture had their counterparts in manufacturing. The products of China's kilns were world famous; Chinese ceramics were copied in Europe and Japan. Brewing, papermaking, mining, and metal working industries thrived. China led the world in silk and cotton textile production. The demand for raw cotton exceeded what could be grown in China, so it was imported from India via Thailand. Until the 1770s, Chinese shipping predominated in coastal trade and in foreign shipping, as Chinese junk owners took advantage of the winds associated with the monsoons and engaged in business dealings with a thriving overseas Chinese community.

By the end of the eighteenth century, Chinese shipping no longer dominated, but China's maritime trade with the West continued to contribute to Chinese well-being. Throughout the century, the balance of overseas trade had been in China's favor, as it had been ever since the sixteenth century, when China became the world's "sink" for silver, which flowed in from Japan and the Spanish colonies of Mexico and Peru to pay for Chinese textiles and ceramics. To quote William Atwell, writing of the 1570s:

> Within a short time Chinese silks were being worn in the streets of Kyoto and Lima. Chinese cottons were being sold in Filipino and Mexican markets, and Chinese porcelain was being used in fashioning homes from Sakai to London.[18]

The major distribution center in the intercontinental trade connecting Europe and China was Manila in the Philippines (held by Spain since 1565), which attracted a community of Chinese traders.

While this trade was disrupted by the troubles of the seventeenth century, silver imports resumed after trade restrictions were lifted in 1683. The silver flow declined in the 1720s and again at mid-century, but it rose again after 1760. The demand for silver in China and China's ability to absorb the silver without triggering inflation attest to the productivity of the Chinese economy and to the absence of a market for European products in China.

Eighteenth-century China, like all large countries at this time, was primarily agricultural, but Beijing remained the world's largest city until London surpassed it around 1800. Increased trade fostered growth of market towns linked by empire-wide merchant groups and serviced by a sophisticated banking system. As William Rowe has concluded, "the uniquely efficient water-transport system and marketing mechanism of preindustrial China allowed it to overcome the barriers of long distance and low technology, and to develop a national market by mid-Qing, even though in Europe and elsewhere such a development may have been conditional upon the advent of steam-powered transportation."[19]

Despite the spread of a "national market," generalization about China's local social and economic foundations remains difficult and potentially misleading because conditions varied greatly from area to area then as they do today. Economic growth and transformation were most evident along the coast and along the major river arteries, with the Yangzi and Pearl River Delta areas profiting most from the new prosperity.

The population continued to increase even though Chinese families took various measures to limit the number of children. People married young but practiced sexual abstinence in the early years of marriage when living with their parents. Infanticide, especially female infanticide, as well as neglect, also reduced the number of offspring. Still the population grew. With more people there was mounting pressure on land. As an official put it in a memorial to Yongzheng, "while the population increases daily, the land does not."[20] Under Yongzheng the government actively pursued a policy of land reclamation, while under Qianlong market forces encouraged the maximum spread of agriculture up into the hills, with terraces all the way to the summits, and out into the hinterlands. In 1793 Hong Liangji (1748–1809) became the first official to warn against excessive population growth.

These developments changed the balance between the human and the natural environment. Deforestation, which began long before this period, became more acute. "The earth was loose; when the big rains came, water rushed down from the highlands and mud and silt spread out below. Fertile areas near the mountains were repeatedly covered with sand and were abandoned."[21] Another result of a long-term trend toward deforestation was the shortage of wood that in the sixteenth century had prompted salt extractors to shift from boiling to less effective solar evaporation. In the sixteenth and seventeenth centuries, highland and lowland communities frequently fought over woodlands to the point that the State had to intervene. As more accessible forests were cut down, the primary sources of timber were increasingly distant from the center; Guizhou in the southwest and the Yalu region in the northeast became the major suppliers.

The environmental history of China and East Asia is complex, because there were major differences within as well as between regions, and much remains to be learned. However, a start has been made, revealing the frequently complex interrelations among technology, commerce, climate, government policies, and social practices. Indications are that major parts of China were heading into environmental crisis by the late eighteenth century as forests disappeared, soil eroded, and silted rivers flooded, rendering human life more dire and condemning to extinction animals deprived of habitat. However, the worst was still to come. As Kenneth Pomeranz has shown, China, environmentally as well as economically, did not yet compare unfavorably to Europe, which was able to avoid intensified land use by exploiting the ecological "windfall" provided by the New World.[22]

Dynastic Decline

The mounting expenses of military campaigns far beyond the bounds of China proper strained the resources of even the prosperous Qianlong regime, while simultaneous laxity and corruption rendered government less effective and more expensive. The worst offender was Heshen (1750–1799), a handsome and clever Manchu bannerman who enjoyed the aging emperor's complete trust for 23 years. He controlled the Ministry of Personnel and Ministry of Revenue, held many offices concurrently (20 at one time), built a network of corruption, and amassed an enormous fortune. Although bitterly detested, he could not be removed, for he never lost Qianlong's confidence and affection. An attack on Heshen implied an attack on His Majesty's own judgment and suggested the presence of factionalism. Perhaps Qianlong was especially sensitive to any signs of factionalism since his father, Emperor Yongzheng, had written a strong critique on this subject. Like his political authority, the moral and intellectual authorities of the emperor were beyond question. Qianlong abdicated after his sixtieth year as emperor in order not to rule longer than his illustrious grandfather, but he continued to dominate the government until his death in 1799. Only then was Heshen removed from power.

FIGURE 2.8 *A Cheating Shirt*. Before entering the examination compound where they were to spend three days and two nights, candidates underwent a thorough body search. Absolutely forbidden to bring anything with writing on it, the wearer of this undershirt clearly hoped to beat the system.

As always, the common people bore the burden of extravagance and corruption. As a result, many of them joined in the White Lotus Rebellion (1796–1804). At its height it affected Sichuan, Hubei, Henan, Gansu, and Shaanxi. The rebellion drew its following by promising the coming of Maitreya (the Buddha of the future), a restoration of the Ming, and the rescue of the people from all suffering. It gained momentum as it attracted the destitute and displaced, and proved the wide popular appeal of its cause. The ineffectiveness of the dynasty's response assisted the movement: government generals used the occasion to line their own pockets, and bannermen, largely untrained and long accustomed to peace, proved their total incompetence. Not until after Heshen's fall did the government make real headway: A new, capable commander was appointed, disaffected areas were slowly taken back from the rebels, and militia bands organized by the local elite proved effective in putting down insurgency.

The civil service was not expanded to keep pace with the growth of the population and economy or to accommodate the growing number of thwarted candidates, many of them superbly qualified. Already in the Song there had been men who spent a lifetime taking examinations—when the emperor asked one such candidate his age, he replied, "fifty years ago twenty-three." The aged candidate became a stock figure in literature. The government even relaxed standards for men over 70 so that, past retirement age, they could at least enjoy the satisfaction of receiving a degree. In an effort to weed out candidates, new examinations were introduced. Thus, in 1788 the reexamination of provincial and metropolitan graduates was introduced. That brought the total minimum number of examinations required for the final degree to eight, not counting a final placement examination. By this time the criteria for judging papers had become exceedingly formalistic. Candidates spent years practicing highly complex, artificial "eight-legged essays," required in the examinations, and bookshops did a thriving business selling model answers. In the meantime, the old battle of wits between examiners and cheaters remained a draw (see the "cheating shirt," Figure 2.8). The unsatisfactory state of the examination system, and the tendency of the government to tinker and elaborate rather than reform and innovate, suggests a dangerous hardening of the institutional arteries just as China's place in the world was about to change.

Notes

1. The term is taken from Kenneth Pomeranz, *The Great Divergence: China, Europe, and the Making of the Modern World Economy* (Princeton, NJ: Princeton Univ. Press, 2000).

2. Susan Mann, "The Education of Daughters in the Mid-Ch'ing Period," in Benjamin A. Elman and Alexander Woodside, eds., *Education and Society in Late Imperial China, 1600–1900* (Berkeley, CA: Univ. of California Press, 1994), p. 21.

3. Dorothy Ko, *Teachers of the Inner Chambers: Women and Culture in Seventeenth-Century China* (Stanford, CA: Stanford Univ. Press, 1994), p. 171.

4. G. William Skinner, "Chinese Peasants and the Closed Community: An Open and Shut Case," in *Comparative Studies in Society and History* 13 (1971), p. 272.

5. James Cahill, *The Compelling Image: Nature and Style in Seventeenth-Century Chinese Painting* (Cambridge, MA: Harvard Univ. Press, 1982), p. 183.

6. W. Theodore de Bary, trans., *Waiting for the Dawn: A Plan for the Prince. Huang Tsung-hsi's Ming-i Tai-fang lu* (New York, NY: Columbia Univ. Press, 1993), p. 92.

7. Chin-sung Chang, "Mountains and Rivers, Pure and Splendid: Wang Hui (1632–1717) and the Making of Landscape Panoramas in Early Qing China," Ph.D. dissertation, Yale University, New Haven, CT, 2004, p. 118 and p. 126 with the quotation as translated by Wen Fong in Wen Fong et al., *Images of the Mind: Selections from the Edward L. Elliott Family and John B. Elliot Collections of Chinese Calligraphy and Painting at the Art Museum, Princeton University* (Princeton, NJ: The Art Museum, Princeton University 1984), p. 184.

8. Jonathan D. Spence, *Emperor of China: Self-Portrait of Kang-hsi* (New York, NY: Alfred E. Knopf, 1974), p. 128.

9. Morris Rossabi, *China and Inner Asia—From 1638 to the Present Day* (New York, NY: Pica Press, 1975), pp. 139–40. Rossabi does not think

Buddhism was a major factor, although it may have contributed to the decline (pp. 140–41).

10. R. Kent Guy, *The Emperor's Four Treasures: Scholars and the Rise of the State in the Late Ch'ien-lung Era* (Cambridge, MA: Harvard Univ. Press, 1987), p. 37.

11. R. Bin Wong, Theodore Huters, and Pauline Yu, "Introduction: Shifting Paradigms of Political and Social Order," in Huters, Wong, and Yu, *Culture & State in Chinese History: Conventions, Accommodations, and Critiques* (Stanford, CA: Stanford Univ. Press, 1997), pp. 4–5.

12. Wang Mingsheng (1725–1798) as translated in Benjamin A. Elman, "Social Roles of Literati in Early to Mid-Ch'ing," in Willard J. Peterson, ed., *The Cambridge History of China, Vol. 9, Part 1: The Ch'ing Empire to 1800* (Cambridge, MA: Cambridge Univ. Press, 2002), p. 395.

13. Quoted in Ichisada Miyazaki, *China's Examination Hell*, trans. by Conrad Schirokauer (New Haven, CT: Yale University Press, 1981), pp. 57–58.

14. David L. Rolston, *How to Read the Chinese Novel* (Princeton, NJ: Princeton Univ. Press, 1990), p. 14.

15. Shang Wei, *Rulin Waishi and Cultural Transformation in Late Imperial China* (Cambridge, MA: Harvard Univ. Press, 2003), p. 279.

16. Ibid, p. 285.

17. C. T. Hsia, *The Classical Chinese Novel* (New York, NY: Columbia Univ. Press, 1968), pp. 246 and 264.

18. William Atwell in Frederick W. Mote and D. Twitchett, eds., *The Cambridge History of China*, Vol. 7 (Cambridge, England: Cambridge Univ. Press, 1988), p. 587.

19. William T. Rowe, *Hankow: Commerce and Society in a Chinese City, 1796–1889* (Stanford, CA: Stanford Univ. Press, 1984), p. 62.

20. Han Liangfu as quoted in Robert B. Marks, *Tigers, Rice, Silk, and Silt: Environment and Economy in Late Imperial South China* (Cambridge, England: Cambridge Univ. Press, 1998), p. 291.

21. Quoted from the Gazetteer for Chengde (Hunan) in Peter C. Perdue, *Exhausting the Earth: State and Peasant in Hunan, 1500–1850* (Cambridge, MA: Harvard Univ. Press, 1987), p. 88.

22. See note 1. Another major factor in Europe's "great divergence" was the proximity of coal to the center of textile production, whereas in China they were far apart.

3

Chosŏn Korea

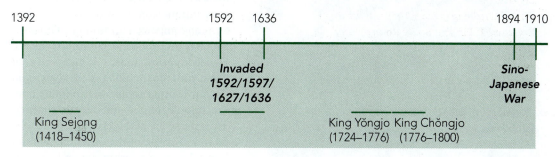

CHOSŎN DYNASTY

1392   1592   1636   1894 1910

**Invaded
1592/1597/
1627/1636**

**Sino-
Japanese
War**

King Sejong
(1418–1450)

King Yŏngjo   King Chŏngjo
(1724–1776)   (1776–1800)

Korea's Chosŏn dynasty (1392–1910), established in the same century as China's Ming, became the longest-lasting regime ever to rule in East Asia. As noted in Chapter 1, by 1392 Korea already had a long tradition of political independence and cultural borrowing. Though partially colonized once, during the Han dynasty, the Koreans successfully repelled attempts by China's Sui and Tang dynasties to reassert control in the seventh century. After unification under the Kingdom of Silla in 668 C.E., the Koreans maintained an autonomous state that covered most of the peninsula. However, they also respected Chinese civilization, emulated many of its cultural patterns, and pursued a policy of loyal submission to the emperor on the Chinese throne.

In the centuries prior to the Chosŏn dynasty, the Korean people consolidated their unique combination of local traditions and imported institutions. The institutional and cultural continuity of the Chosŏn period makes it necessary to begin with the founding of the dynasty in the fourteenth century and continue until the middle of the nineteenth century. Thus the scope of this chapter exceeds the temporal scope of the other chapters in Part I, beginning earlier and ending later.

Korea under the Chosŏn dynasty continued developing its own language and literature, art, social structure, economy, and many unique forms of daily life such as food, work patterns, and folk religion. On top of this cultural base, Korea studied Chinese models and adapted Chinese patterns for its higher culture, including government institutions, Confucian philosophy, the Chinese written language, Chinese patterns in art and architecture, and refinements such as the Chinese lunar calendar, Chinese herbal medicine, and Ming clothing styles. These two streams of tradition—the local and the imported—are sometimes referred to as the "Small Tradition" and the "Great Tradition," and they exist in all nations in the Chinese cultural sphere. Korean culture offers many examples of the conflict, coexistence, and even blending of the two streams, as Figure 3.1 illustrates.

FIGURE 3.1 *Sansindo (Mountain Spirit with Tiger),* 18th-century Korean painting. Themes from Daoism (the mountain hermitage), classical Chinese symbolism (the pine symbolizing endurance), the tiger (a Korean reference), and the mountain spirit (a figure from Korean shamanism) blend in one of the most common representations in all of Korean art. Unidentified artist, Chosŏn Dynasty, 18th century. Inks and colors on paper.

GEORGE AND MARY ROCKWELL COLLECTION, COURTESY OF HERBERT F. JOHNSON MUSEUM OF ART, CORNELL UNIVERSITY (99.067.001).

The Chosŏn Dynasty: Foundations

At its beginning, the Chosŏn dynasty replaced the state of Koryŏ, a medieval kingdom that had been subjected to Mongol domination and had suffered serious internal corruption. In its later years, the Koryŏ Kingdom's problems included excessive concentrations of power and property in a few aristocratic families, some of which had ties to the Mongols, and too much influence in the hands of the Buddhist establishment. The aristocratic families paid no taxes on their vast estates, called *nongjang*, and their tendency to own slaves reduced the number of taxpayers.

In the fourteenth century, a rising faction of Confucian-educated officials in the Koryŏ capital began calling for reform. Their rise coincided with the rise of the Ming and the fall of the Mongols in China, a change that robbed pro-Mongol elements in Korea of their most important external prop. In 1392 the Koryŏ reform faction overthrew the Koryŏ ruling house and established the new state of Chosŏn. The founder, King T'aejo (1335–1408), moved the royal capital to Hanyang, modern Seoul, to symbolize a new beginning. He built a new Chinese-style royal palace to symbolize his position as a king (*wang*) within the universe ruled by his superior, the Emperor of China.

Continuing Korea's long practice of submission to the Middle Kingdom, King T'aejo sent tribute envoys to the Ming emperor. He swore that Korea had cut all its ties to the Mongols and that it would not make alliances or have relations with any of China's enemies in the future. The emperor eventually rewarded the Korean monarch with "investiture" (that is, recognition, which was essential to the king's status), valuable gifts, a tacit promise of military support in case of foreign attack, and permission for a certain amount of tributary trade. By the early fifteenth century Sino-Korean relations were on firm footing.

As part of its effort to institutionalize Confucian ethics in the new regime, the government of Chosŏn adopted the Ming criminal code and a council structure for decision making in the royal court. To keep the kings mindful of Confucian values, they were tutored from boyhood and subjected to Chinese-style "royal lectures" (*kyŏngyŏn*). To enforce Confucian virtue in the officialdom, the government set up a censorate to review and criticize the actions of officials, and an inspectorate to uncover corruption and report evildoers to the authorities in the capital.

In their capital, the kings of Chosŏn were assisted by officials organized by rank in six Chinese-style ministries (Personnel, Revenue, Rites, Military, Justice, and Public Works), palace officials including secretaries, advisors, inspectors, censors, tutors, and a coterie of palace staff that included eunuchs, ladies-in-waiting, guards, servants, and government-owned slaves.

The officialdom was organized into two branches, civil and military, with the civil branch exceeding the military in prestige. As in China, the civil service was Chosŏn's most prestigious profession, and families invested much in preparing their sons for the qualifying examinations necessary for obtaining a bureaucratic appointment. Preparation involved the moral lessons of the Confucian classics, development of a refined style in classical Chinese, which was the written language for all Korean documents, and success in preliminary examinations at the local and provincial levels. Candidates who passed the mid-level literary examinations won the coveted *saengwŏn* or *chinsa* degrees and were eligible to take the capital examinations, known as the *munkwa*, which enabled them to display mastery of the high traditions of history, philosophy, and ethics. Only the most talented and disciplined candidates passed the entire series of examinations and emerged ready to govern. As in China, the Chosŏn examination system was a meritocracy, at least in theory. However, access to the examinations was much more limited than in China: the archives reveal that most of the exam passers at the *munkwa* level were members of Chosŏn's leading families. Thus it appears that Korea's landed aristocracy found ways to protect itself despite the reform impetus of the early Chosŏn period.

The Enlightened Reign of King Sejong (r. 1418–1450)

The early Chosŏn kings promoted Neo-Confucianism as their regime's official ideology. This reflected the Chosŏn founders' distaste for the inflated influence of Buddhism on the Koryŏ court. Though the Chosŏn Kingdom's Confucian reforms did not succeed in every respect, they did succeed in giving the kingdom a moral basis for all judgments. Chosŏn Neo-Confucianism stressed the "encouragement of learning," and there was no better example of the scholar-king than King Sejong (r. 1418–1450), the fourth and most celebrated of Chosŏn's 27 monarchs. Sejong sponsored important new studies in history, literature, astronomy, and philosophy by scholars working in a palace institute known as the "Hall of Worthies" (*Chiphyŏnjŏn*).

They are best remembered for their invention of the alphabet now known as *han'gŭl* ("Korean writing"), an alphabet that has consonants and vowels arranged into clusters representing the sounds of word syllables in spoken Korean (Figure 3.2). This enabled Koreans to put their language into writing accurately and phonetically, as we do with Western alphabets. Over time, Koreans learned to combine the two written styles, using Chinese symbols for words with Chinese roots and *han'gŭl* syllables for words of Korean origin and for Korean grammatical elements in sentences. This system resembles the mixture of *kana* and Chinese characters used in Japan.

King Sejong enjoyed convening his retinue of scholars and challenging them to explore new avenues of learning. One, Chŏng Inji, wrote an exhaustive history of the entire Koryŏ dynasty (the *Koryŏ-sa*). Others invented a clock, a rain gauge, new ways of calculating mathematics, and various musical instruments. One significant innovation was a font of movable copper type that could be rearranged to print different texts. This copper font was used to print eight different works between 1403 and 1484, including King Sejong's proclamation of the *han'gŭl* alphabet, in a work entitled *The Correct Sounds for the Instruction of the People* (*Hunminjŏng'ŭm*).

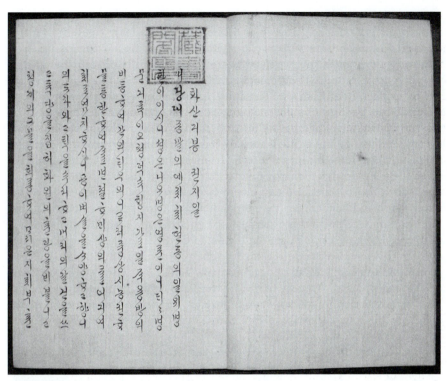

FIGURE 3.2 Handwritten *han'gŭl* script in the 13-volume *Strange Encounters on Mount Hwa* (18th century). Page 1, volume 1.

Chosŏn Society

The elite class of Koreans during the Chosŏn period were called *yangban* ("of the two branches"), a term that referred to membership in the civil or military branches of the government. *Yangban* officials and their family members enjoyed public esteem by virtue of their learning, presumed moral fitness, and willingness to shoulder the heavy responsibilities of public service. They also enjoyed material privileges based mainly on land ownership, because official salaries were paid in the form of land grants at the beginning of the dynasty, and there was a tradition of investing income in additional land increments. Certain *yangban* families were associated with certain places. These had clan seats in rural counties where they maintained primary households, often in imposing mansions that overlooked valleys where tenant farmers and slaves worked their land and provided them with income. The ideal *yangban* displayed an attitude of noblesse oblige toward common people in his jurisdiction, sometimes supplying emergency charity. But mainly the *yangban* sought to perpetuate the privileges of their families and class by educating sons to pass the examinations, rise in the officialdom, and win more wealth and power for the clan. Even when the local *yangban* landlords were not actually in office, their social access to the nearby magistrates and governors made them extensions of the power structure. Thus it was rare for any commoner, even if he were a wealthy farmer who amassed enough money to educate his sons, to win acceptance in this self-perpetuating ruling elite.

In addition to officials who passed the examinations, Korea's *yangban* class included "merit subjects," individuals who had been rewarded by the king for loyal service during times of crisis. Chosŏn's founder, King T'aejo, for example, rewarded several groups of merit subjects for helping him overthrow the previous king and consolidate his own control. His merit subjects were close associates whom he appointed to high positions without making them pass the examinations. Their rewards included permanent tax-free grants of government land and slaves that could be inherited by their children, making them instantly wealthy. Their fast track to power was often resented by "ordinary" *yangban,* giving rise to an undercurrent of conflict between them and their descendants throughout the dynasty. There existed a third door into the *yangban* class for talented young people who could win the favor or protection ("shade" *ŭm,* Chinese *yin*) of a high official, and who could thereby receive a recommendation for direct appointment. The recommendation system was supposed to provide a way to promote the deserving, but it, too, was a problem because high officials were known to accept favors in return for their "shade."

The scholar-official-landlord *yangban* class occupied the top rank of Korean society, the rank of people who labored with their minds. Commoners labored with their hands, doing the society's productive work. They paid a share of what they produced to the government in the form of taxes, and many paid a share to their *yangban* landlords and other patrons. Commoners also did the labor service on public works and facilities that was required of every taxpayer for a set number of days each year. Additionally, they supplied sons to the military as draftees when there was trouble. In theory, Chosŏn Korea had a four-tiered class structure along Chinese lines, with the *yangban* at the top, producers (farmers) second, specialists (artisans) third, and the "lowborn" (slaves and people who did distasteful work such as butchers) at the bottom. The Neo-Confucian ethos of the Chosŏn period made fine distinctions between people and their occupations, but in practice the greatest gulf was between the *yangban* and everyone else, whether they were peasant landowners, sharecroppers, merchants, or slaves. Slavery was significantly more common than in China, where it was limited and largely took the form of household slavery.

Male privilege was also basic to Chosŏn society. The leading families maintained genealogies that carefully documented the history, patriarchy, and relationships of males in the lineage, as well as the fathers-in-law of the lineage's daughters. Because male succession was so important to the continued prosperity of the family, *yangban* men often had secondary wives and concubines to help produce sons. Sons of concubines, however, were not fully entitled members of the male line. Though most were educated and many were treated like their "legitimate" brothers, when it came time to perform ancestral rituals, get married, or engage in anything that represented the lineage, the sons of concubines suffered direct discrimination. In their careers, they were barred from taking the civil service examinations and achieving high office. Instead they had to settle for jobs as clerks and low-level bureaucrats in the *chung'in* class, positions for which they qualified through specialized examinations called *chapkwa*. Their marriages were arranged with partners who were from secondary lineages, making for continued discrimination that lasted for generations.

Korean patterns of patriarchy, reinforced by the teachings of Confucius, made it necessary for women to defer to the men in their families. *Yangban* women were kept secluded, protected from prying eyes and outsiders. Their parents arranged their marriages, and the custom was to keep them from meeting their grooms until the actual wedding ceremony, after which they were transferred to their husbands' houses as new members of their in-laws' families. They had no rights to property and little say in decisions about how or where they would live. *Yangban* women were supposed to be models of morality and chastity, and their loyalty to their husbands lasted even into widowhood, since it was unacceptable for a widow to marry a second time.

The Problem of Legitimacy

King Sejong died in 1450 and his son, King Munjong, reigned only two years before his own death. King Munjong's young son was next in line, and he ascended the throne only to die in exile after a palace coup staged by his uncle, Prince Suyang, who became King Sejo, ruling from 1455 to 1468. Sejo's usurpation of the throne was widely regarded as a crime, and to consolidate his power he had to fend off condemnation by many of Chosŏn's most respected elders and reward his supporters with merit subject titles and lavish grants of land and slaves. This created an instant faction and began a rivalry between the lineages of the two brothers, Kings Munjong and Sejo. King Sejo punished many of his critics, but the controversy raged for several generations.

Sejo usurped the throne of Chosŏn at a time when the legitimacy of the dynasty itself was still in question. Its founder, King T'aejo, had been guilty of usurpation in 1392, and for more than a decade thereafter the imperial court in China had regarded him with suspicion. The first Ming Emperor never granted him investiture, and it was not until 1403 that the Yongle Emperor finally recognized Chosŏn by investing the third king of the dynasty. The question of the regime's legitimacy was so sensitive a subject that King Sejong had made it a major theme of one of his reign's greatest literary works, *Songs of the Dragons Flying to Heaven* (*Yongbi ŏch'ŏn'ga*), which compared his ancestors to the greatest of China's imperial ancestors. Much of King Sejong's emphasis on history—in particular his commissioning of the *Koryŏ-sa*—had been aimed at providing justification for his grandfather's usurpation of the Koryŏ throne in 1392. Now, scarcely more than 60 years later, the legitimacy of the ruling house was again in doubt because of King Sejo's coup.

The collective power of the *yangban* class as they argued over this problem is evidence of the weak position of the monarchy in Korea as compared to that of the emperor in China. The Korean king had to win and maintain support from several quarters, beginning with the Chinese emperor but including factions of the *yangban* aristocracy and his own Korean officials, whose help he needed in order to govern. King Sejo tried to bolster the authority of the throne at the expense of the *yangban* by packing his court with newly named merit subjects, making it harder for *yangban* to accumulate land through inheritance, and subjecting the *yangban* to taxation. These were unpopular moves that further alienated the country's landed elite and generated animosities that fueled factional infighting for many years.

Intellectual Flowering in the Sixteenth Century

During the sixteenth century, Korea produced several significant Neo-Confucian philosophers. One of these was Yi Hwang (better known by his literary name of T'oegye, 1501–1570), Korea's foremost proponent of the ideas of the Chinese neo-Confucian philosopher Zhu Xi, and a scholar who occupies an analogous position to Zhu Xi in the history of Korean thought. T'oegye is best known for his *Ten Diagrams on Sage Learning,* which explicates "the essential framework of, and linkage among, Neo-Confucian metaphysics, psychological theory, moral conduct, and spiritual discipline."[1] T'oegye, like Zhu Xi before him, stressed disciplined study of the textual tradition to apprehend principle (*i*, Chinese *li*) and thus to know how to live a principled life. He is also famous for his part in the "Four-Seven Debate," which pertains to the origins of and relation between the "four beginnings"—humanity, righteousness, propriety, and wisdom—which Mencius had taught were inherent in all people, and on the other hand, the "seven feelings" (desire, hate, love, fear, grief, anger, and joy). T'oegye separated the "beginnings" and "feelings" at their source, arguing that the former take precedence over the latter (which derive from material essence or force, *ki*).[2]

T'oegye's younger contemporary Yi I (better known as Yulgok, 1536–1584), argued a different view, which placed primary emphasis not on "principle" but on "material force," or "matter" (*ki*, Chinese *qi*). The differences between T'oegye and Yulgok reflected a highly refined version of the ancient philosophical debate in East Asia that appears in many forms, including the complementary halves of the symbol for *yin* and *yang*. They were struggling for a better understanding of what it means to be human and spiritual at the same time. Their scholarship and refined moral tone made them famous as Korean exemplars of Confucian learning. Still today they are important national figures, and their works are widely read.

The second half of the sixteenth century saw the foundation of numerous local academies, or *sŏwŏn*, that were typically headed by a famous *yangban*-class teacher who taught his protégés his own theories on philosophical problems like the Four-Seven debate. The first of these was T'oegye's own *sŏwŏn* near the town of Andong, a center for scholars who were interested in his theories about the primacy of principle. The government recognized T'oegye's *sŏwŏn* by granting it a royal charter that, among other privileges, exempted it from tax. Before long, other *sŏwŏn* were springing up around the country. The founder or leading scholar of each *sŏwŏn* was regarded with reverence by his disciples. His theories on philosophy and politics became the *sŏwŏn* scholars' central ideas, to be defended in debates with scholars from rival academies. Chosŏn-era *sŏwŏn*, like their counterparts in Ming China, became headquarters for political cliques as ambitious young scholars competed to put their teachers' versions of Neo-Confucian theory into practice by getting themselves appointed to office. The rivalries drew on philosophical differences like the ones that had occupied T'oegye and Yulgok; however, the personal loyalties and regional political conflicts that complicated the debates and turned them into petty, even violent, feuds would have displeased the two great scholars.

The Imjin War and the Manchu Invasions

The worst crisis faced by the Kingdom of Chosŏn occurred in the 1590s when Japan invaded the peninsula as part of a war to establish hegemony over Korea and China. The invasion was launched in 1592 (the year with the name *Imjin* in the Korean calendar) by Toyotomi Hideyoshi, after he had completed the unification of Japan. The invasion used experienced samurai veterans from the war for unification. In the first assault, an estimated 160,000 Japanese troops, many of them carrying firearms, landed near Pusan on the southeast coast and fought their way through southern Korea as far as Seoul. Though the Korean royal army resisted, the kingdom was caught unprepared for the invasion. King Sŏnjo (r. 1567–1608) was forced to abandon his capital and flee to the Manchurian border, where he appealed to the Ming for military assistance. Chinese armies intervened and stopped the Japanese advance at P'yŏngyang.

Korea, meanwhile, had become a battlefield. The failure of Korean army defenses forced civilians to bear the brunt of the fighting. *Yangban* landlords, common farmers, and even Buddhist monks rallied villagers into informal militia units and fought heroic rear-guard actions. These "righteous troops" (*ŭibyŏng*) occupied large portions of the invading army and inflicted significant damage, even though they were usually defeated by the better-armed Japanese.

To keep their troops supplied and reinforced, the Japanese had to cross the straits separating the islands from the Korean peninsula (Figure 3.3). On the south coast of Korea, a *yangban* official named Yi Sunsin took advantage of Japanese vulnerability on the sea and distinguished himself with a naval campaign that sank many Japanese ships and disrupted the invaders' supply lines. To enable his boats to fend off arrows and fire bombs so that they could attack at close range, he covered their decks with canopies made of copper, giving rise to the name "turtle ships" (*kŏbuksŏn*). Using oarsmen below decks, he maneuvered his turtle boats around the islands and narrow waterways of the south coast, drawing the Japanese into traps where he was able to outmaneuver and destroy them. His success in these battles earned him a reputation for great daring and military skill, and he died a hero in the last engagement of the war off Hansan Island in 1598.

FIGURE 3.3 Korea during the Chosŏn dynasty.

FROM JOHN FAIRBANK, EDWIN REISCHAUER, AND ALBERT CRAIG, *EAST ASIA: TRADITION AND TRANSFORMATION*, FIRST EDITION. COPYRIGHT © 1973 BY HOUGHTON MIFFLIN COMPANY. USED WITH PERMISSION.

Japan's invasion of the mainland stalled with the Battle of P'yŏngyang, and it was not until 1597 that Hideyoshi sent a second wave. This too was a failure, and Japan called off the war when Hideyoshi died in 1598. Korea, meanwhile, suffered greatly. Many Koreans died in the fighting or were captured or kidnapped and taken to Japan. There was much vandalism and looting. Many of Korea's remaining Buddhist temples were ransacked and burned, their precious gold-leafed images and paintings being stolen not only by the Japanese enemy but also by the "friendly" Chinese. In Seoul, when the king and the royal court fled the city just before it fell to the invading Japanese, Korean citizens, reacting to being abandoned by their ruler, attacked the central palace and set it ablaze, after which it lay in ruins until the 1860s.

The war in Korea coincided with the rise of the Manchus under their powerful new chief Nurgaci, whose sons went on to destroy the Ming and establish the Qing dynasty in China. Part of the Manchu strategy required forcing the Koreans to break their ties with the Ming and alter their allegiance. For a short time the Koreans managed a balancing act between their commitment as a Ming tributary state and the need to placate the Manchus. However, when the Koreans briefly tried to side with the Ming in the 1620s, the Manchus invaded. In 1627 they extorted a promise that Korea would behave like a loyal younger brother to the Manchu ruler. However, in 1636 when the Koreans refused to receive a Manchu envoy and gave signs of going back on their promise, the Manchus invaded again. In their second invasion, they penetrated all the way to Seoul and forced King Injo to surrender. Chosŏn had to break relations with the Ming, send troops to help the Manchus conquer the Ming, accept the newly founded Qing Empire as its suzerain, offer tribute, and give the Manchus two of the king's eldest sons as hostages.

Although the Manchus wreaked less havoc in Korea than the Japanese a generation earlier, the humiliation of being forced to submit to people whom the Koreans had always regarded as barbarians was a severe blow to the morale of the Korean monarchy and ruling class. They were never comfortable with the Manchus as their overlords, and although they carried on correct tributary relations until the 1890s, internally they continued to mourn for the Ming as their legitimate "older brother." To symbolize this they engaged in quiet forms of protest such as numbering the dates on their internal documents according to the defunct Ming calendar and wearing clothing and hairstyles from the Ming period.

Struggles within the Yangban Class

Military defeats at the hands of the Japanese and Manchus caused the government of Chosŏn to reorganize its military defenses. The Office of Border Defense grew in importance and actually emerged as a key decision-making body. Much attention was paid to conscription and training, and a new system of garrisons was put in place. Though the army evolved into a force devoted mainly to suppressing internal rebellion, the effort to raise an effective defense represented a positive response to the bitter experiences of the early 1600s.

The invasions of Korea happened just as its government was embroiled in a major power struggle among political factions. Before the Japanese invasion there were "Easterners" (Tong'in) and "Westerners" (Sŏ'in), so named for the location of their residences in the capital city. No sooner had the "Easterners" achieved ascendancy and purged the "Westerners" than they proceeded to divide into "Northern" (Pugin) and "Southern" (Namin) subfactions over the question of a successor to King Sŏnjo, who died without an heir in 1608. The Northerners won and put King Kwanghae on the throne, only to see him overthrown in 1623 by the Westerners, who had been biding their time. The Westerners then spent most of the seventeenth century feuding with the Southerner subfaction, but when they won decisively in 1694, they too proceeded to split into subfactions: the "Old Doctrine" (Noron) and the "New Doctrine" (Soron). The infighting was about power, but the factions took positions based on ethical interpretations. For example, one debate between the Southerners and Westerners concerned the length of time a king's mother should spend mourning the death of her son. Another concerned whether the son of a royal concubine could be named crown prince. In the competitive atmosphere of Chosŏn politics, people drew little distinction between a person's political beliefs and his moral virtue. Dissent was dangerous, and criticizing a person's politics was very close to attacking his moral virtue. When political disagreements were defined in moral terms there was little incentive for compromise. Instead, the process created winners and losers, with the winners trying to purge the losers and prevent them from ever returning to office. When a group lost power it retired to the countryside, often to a *sŏwŏn*, where it brooded and plotted revenge.

Korea in the Eighteenth Century

The factional feuding that plagued the Chosŏn's middle years and the resulting weakness and confusion generally defines the period for scholars. However, the same period saw considerable intellectual vitality. The feuding cooled during the eighteenth century under two particularly able Chosŏn kings, Yŏngjo (r. 1724–1776) and his grandson Chŏngjo (r. 1776–1800). After 50 turbulent years during which the kingdom of Chosŏn seemed to reach its nadir, King Yŏngjo reinvigorated the government by asserting himself as a model Confucian sage-ruler. He mastered the classics and was recognized as a scholar. He used court ceremonies and the rituals of Confucian culture to uplift public life. He inspired people by putting his policy of *tangp'yŏng* ("pacifying the factions") into effect, quieting the rivalries among the four main factions—the Old Doctrine, New Doctrine, Northerners, and Southerners. He ordered proportional appointments to the bureaucracy designed to prevent any one group from acquiring dominance.

King Yŏngjo also effected economic reforms, including a halving of the military cloth tax on commoners and the institution of a land tax. The years of disruption had created a serious social problem in the form of homeless people. One of the causes had been the crushing burden of taxation on free commoner landlords. King Yŏngjo's reform was a partially successful attempt to spread the burden more equally. *Yangban* landlords, however, continued to find ways to pay less than their fair share.

As a strong ruler, King Yŏngjo might have gone down in history as a great king, but his reign was tainted by one shocking and controversial act. In 1762, the king put his own son, Crown Prince Sado, to death after a chain of events that showed the prince to be deranged and possibly plotting to kill Yŏngjo himself. The killing of his only son was technically within King Yŏngjo's rights as monarch, particularly since the prince was guilty of several murders, but not everyone in the royal court accepted the deed. They split into critics and defenders of the prince's execution, forming new factional combinations that launched a new era of political infighting.

When Yŏngjo passed from the scene in 1776, he was succeeded by the dead prince's son, who became King Chŏngjo. King Chŏngjo complicated the issue by honoring the spirit of his dead father, making obvious his criticism of King Yŏngjo. The royal family itself was torn by these developments, and once again the dynasty suffered a legitimacy crisis.

The Cultural Environment of Late Chosŏn

While these political events were occurring in the eighteenth century, Korea experienced a renaissance in fields ranging from literature to art to philosophy. While continuing to follow Chinese models, Koreans also refined their own creations. A good example is the work of the painters Kim Hongdo (b. 1745) and Shin Yunbok (b. 1758). Kim Hongdo's paintings show children in school and at play and ordinary working people in everyday situations, some of them humorous. Shin Yunbok's favorite themes were social and romantic, and often featured *kisaeng* courtesans keeping company with male patrons in *yangban* costumes (Figure 3.4). Kim Hongdo was the more formal of the two, and he produced classical landscapes, plums, orchids, and lotus flowers in addition to more whimsical themes such as the tiger in Figure 3.5. Koreans appreciate both artists for their honoring of their native culture. Their genre paintings are today some of the most descriptive documents of Korean life in the 1700s.

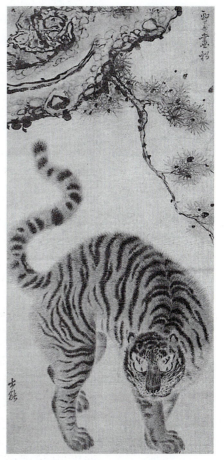

FIGURE 3.5 *Tiger and Pine Tree*, Kim Hongdo (1745–1806?). Chosŏn dynasty, late 18th century. Ink and light colors on silk, 90.4 × 43.8 cm.

Ho-Am Art Museum, Seoul, Korea.

FIGURE 3.4 *Sunyu* (Party on a Boat), Shin Yunbok (18th century). Kansong Art Gallery.

Kansong Gallery, Seoul, Korea

FIGURE 3.6   Cyclindrical water-dropper with design of bamboo and prunus (plums). Water-droppers were used when mixing ink in the inkstones. An indispensable item on a Korean and East Asian scholar's desk, water-droppers formed an artistic genre of their own. Unidentified artist, porcelain, underglaze in blue, diameter 9 cm. Korean, Chosŏn dynasty, 18th century.

GIFT OF COLONEL JOHN R. FOX, COURTESY OF HERBERT F. JOHNSON MUSEUM OF ART, CORNELL UNIVERSITY (65.219).

On the more formal side, Kings Yŏngjo and Chŏngjo sponsored court artists who were commissioned to produce inspirational works that encouraged reason, respect, and an aesthetic appreciation of tradition and discipline. The kings themselves led austere lives, and the artists in their painting academy, called the Tohwawŏn, were expected to do likewise. Their works include screens depicting the orderly rituals of court life, portraits of worthy officials, and depictions of virtuous and unselfish acts.

Ceramics and ink painting flourished. Bamboo, which bends but does not break, and the plum, which alone blooms in the dead of winter, were East Asian symbols of the upright and stalwart gentleman who maintains his principles even under the most dire circumstances. Thus they are fitting decorations for the accouterments found on a scholar's desk (Figure 3.6).

The era also brought advances in literature written in *han'gŭl* script. This followed many years during which King Sejong's alphabet was little used. Korean writers, who were mainly *yangban* schooled in the Chinese classics, had actually scorned the alphabet as too simple and too limiting, and they had continued to write in the much more difficult Chinese characters. It took many years and a great deal of money to learn to write Chinese well. Few people who were not *yangban*-class men could afford this kind of education. Accordingly, the few who could write Chinese were able to use literacy and their writing ability as a social barrier, protecting their privileged position while denying basic communication skills to the less fortunate.

In the eighteenth century, however, the educated women who belonged to the royal family, along with other cultured women of the *yangban* class, began to write their own literature. They wrote not in Chinese but in the Korean *han'gŭl* alphabet. Their works were diaries, memoirs, and stories about palace life, expressive of the emotions and conflicts of daily life.[3] Certain commoners also learned *han'gŭl* well enough to write stories and novels. These works survive as commentaries on life in the *yangban*-dominated Chosŏn Kingdom. By the turn of the nineteenth century, *han'gŭl* had become a tool for non-*yangban* to communicate and even organize rebellions against their rulers.

The *yangban* class, however, had its own reformers. The Chinese Neo-Confucian philosopher Zhu Xi had taught that truth could be found through a better understanding of reality—"the investigation of things," as he called it. By the eighteenth century, certain *yangban* groups had become highly critical of their own class and its grip on Korean wealth and institutions. In the seventeenth century, the *yangban* scholar Yu Hyŏngwŏn conducted extensive studies on Korean society, beginning with the agricultural system, and concluded that thorough reform was called for in the system of official appointments, national defense, and the land system. His great treatise, *Pan'gye Surok*, is a catalog of Chosŏn's institutions and their workings, and it inspired later scholars to seek their own reforms. Analysts and reformers in this school of thought came to be known as the Silhak ("Practical Learning School").[4] Taking the agricultural system as the basic enterprise of the Korean people, they concentrated their attention on the farming class of commoners who actually worked the land. The conditions in which they worked, verging on serfdom in many cases, was of great concern to the Silhak scholars. They began to think in terms of justice and security for workers, generating ideas that threatened the privileges of the landholding *yangban* class. Since criticism of the social and economic system amounted to an attack on the *yangban*, the Silhak scholars were seen as subversive.

One variant of the Silhak School was a group of Korean scholars who had traveled to China and were thus aware of different methods for ordinary tasks. Since the road to China led northward, they were known as the "Northern School" (Pukhak). Pukhak scholars pointed out that the Chinese themselves were

BOX 3.1 KISAENG ENTERTAINERS AND SIJO POETRY

Figure 3.4 shows one of Shin Yunbok's famous genre paintings featuring *kisaeng,* or female entertainers. In a culture where women were forbidden to keep company with males who were not their relatives, "public women" were on the social margins. Like the geisha in Japan, kisaeng broke the mold, and they ranged in type from palace staff to common prostitutes. In refined society, *kisaeng* were hired to entertain men in elegant surroundings, where they sang, played instruments, made jokes, told stories, and generally kept the mood light and convivial.

Many *kisaeng* were famous for their mastery of the arts. Among these were a number of notable poets whose short-form *sijo* poems are an important part of Korean literature. *Sijo* poems consist of three lines, 14–16 syllables long. They are sung, usually very slowly, with pauses at the end. They are not as rigid in form as the Japanese *haiku,* but they do have a prescribed structure. In general, the first line states a problem, question, or riddle. The second elaborates or contradicts it, and the third resolves it.

(continued)

BOX 3.1 KISAENG ENTERTAINERS AND SIJO POETRY (CONTINUED)

One of Korea's most famous *sijo* was by a *kisaeng* named Hwang Jini (c. 1506–1544), generally regarded as Korea's greatest female poet.

> I will break in two the long strong back
> of this long midwinter night,
> Roll it up and put it away
> under the springtime coverlet.
> And the night that my loved one comes back again
> I will unroll it to lengthen the time.

The slow cadence of *sijo* was well-suited to wistful love poetry. There are many more examples, such as this one by the *kisaeng* Hongnang (late sixteenth century):

> I chose a wild willow branch
> and plucked it to send to you.
> I want you to plant it
> by the window where you sleep.
> When new leaves open in the night rains,
> think it is I that have come to you.

Most *kisaeng* poets were male, mainly because there were more men in the educated class. But the *sijo* of the *kisaeng* are a particularly romantic rendition of literary life in the Chosŏn period.

Richard Rutt, *The Bamboo Grove* (Berkeley: University of California Press, 1971), p. 61.

adaptable and not afraid of change when circumstances called for it. They attacked the unproductive *yangban* class and the kingdom's social system. Using Zhu Xi's teaching about the "investigation of things," they sought better understandings of reality. They were open-minded enough to experiment with Catholicism, which had acquired a foothold in Beijing through the Jesuit presence that began in 1583. This window to the West suggested new ways of understanding many things, including astronomy, mathematics, health, and social ethics. It even led a small circle of Silhak scholars to found a secret branch of the Catholic religion in Korea, in 1784.

The Crisis of the Nineteenth Century

Conflict between reform-minded officials and established *yangban* interests in the royal court is one major theme of Korean politics in the nineteenth century. The Silhak scholars suffered retribution for their departures from established orthodoxy. Especially the Catholic community was viewed with suspicion because of its loyalty to a foreign faith as well as its associations with outlying political factions in the Chosŏn political system. Bloody anti-Catholic purges took place in 1801, 1811, 1849, and 1866, and thousands of believers lost their lives.

Throughout the Chosŏn dynasty, Korean society experienced shifts in its social structure. In the seventeenth and eighteenth century, for example, many slaves won their freedom either by buying it or by leaving their owners and becoming wanderers and commoners. Another, opposite, trend was the difficulty experienced by *yangban* families in keeping their high social status when they were unable to produce sons who could find their way into government office. By 1800 there were many nominal *yangban* who had little means and had lost most of their property and prestige. In the meantime, the barriers that had prevented the sons of *yangban* men and concubines from attaining office had broken down. Significant numbers of concubines' sons had been permitted to take jobs as government specialists (for example, clerks, accountants, legal specialists) under the permissive rules of King Chŏngjo's administration. These specialists sparked the growth of a new class of "middle persons" (*chung'in*), who were fundamentally interested in social reform because of their own social positions. Many of Korea's earliest Catholics were from the *chung'in* class, attracted by the religious idea that all are equal before the throne of God. Other marginal but educated categories of people on the margins of the *yangban* aristocracy, like the *chung'in*, were eager to adapt to new opportunities that came with the dying of the dynasty. These included the military, which had slipped in status but was poised for reorganization into modern-style units with modern-style weapons.[5]

The impetus to change was fueled in the early nineteenth century by the growing autonomy of large landlords in the provinces. In the southwestern Chŏlla provinces and in the northwest near the Chinese border, the power of local *yangban* came to exceed the power of the central government, and they sent growing numbers of sons to pass the examinations and take more prominent places in the central bureaucracy. Change was also on the minds of ordinary workers such as farmers and miners, who raised the standard of revolt several times during the early nineteenth century. While the royal court continued to be preoccupied with factional politics and the struggles between the royal line and powerful families, such as the ones who supplied queens for the successive kings, the country as a whole experienced a ripening for reform generated by many different constituencies. This pressure for change was significant by the mid-nineteenth century and coincided with the arrival of Western military and cultural forces in China and Japan that served as catalysts for change in Korea's neighbors. The Koreans themselves tried for a time to resist being influenced by these outside developments. Their failure to do so and the subsequent rapid intervention of foreign influence created the conditions for Chosŏn's decline in the late 1800s.

Notes

1. Peter H. Lee and W. Theodore de Bary, eds. Sources *of Korean Tradition,* vol. 1 (New York, NY: Columbia Univ. Press, 1997), p. 350.

2. For the thought of Yi Hwang (T'oegye) see Michael C. Kalton, *To Become a Sage* (New York, NY: Columbia Univ. Press, 1988).

3. Of these, the most famous is the Hanjungnok, by Lady Hyegyŏng. See JaHyun Kim Haboush, *The Memoirs of Lady Hyegyŏng: the Autobiographical Writings of a Crown Princess of Eighteenth-Century Korea* (Berkeley, CA: Univ. of California Press, 1996).

4. James B. Palais, *Confucian Statecraft and Korean Institutions: Yu Hyŏngwŏn and the Late Chosŏn Dynasty* (Seattle, WA: Univ. of Washington Press, 1996), especially pp. 6–14.

5. The social status and historical role of people in between the yangban aristocracy and the commoner population of Korea at the end of the dynasty is the subject of Kyung Moon Hwang's *Beyond Birth: Social Status in the Emergence of Modern Korea* (Cambridge, MA: Harvard Univ. Press, 2005).

Tokugawa Japan: Background, Establishment, and Middle Years

4

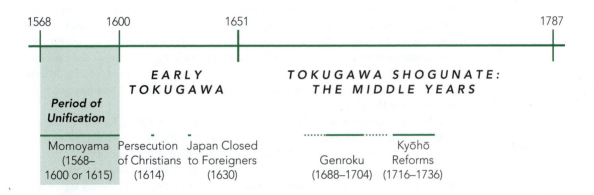

| 1568 | 1600 | 1651 | 1787 |

EARLY TOKUGAWA

TOKUGAWA SHOGUNATE: THE MIDDLE YEARS

Period of Unification

Momoyama (1568–1600 or 1615)

Persecution of Christians (1614)

Japan Closed to Foreigners (1630)

Genroku (1688–1704)

Kyōhō Reforms (1716–1736)

During its formative years Japan had drawn deeply on Chinese models, often mediated through Korea. However, by the time the Tokugawa Shogunate was founded in 1600, Japan had been blending the imported and the native for over a millennium, developing its own ways and institutions. Under the Tokugawa, Japan experienced peace, economic growth, a vibrant urban culture, and an intense intellectual life. This chapter considers its origins in the period of unification, as well as its early and middle years. By the time the stresses inherent in the system began to tear it apart, it had developed foundations for a very different future.

Unification (1573–1600)

Although Chinese influence still ran deep in Japan, from around the middle of the ninth century, the trajectory of political and social change diverged from that of the continent. Japan, alone in East Asia, experienced the rise to dominance of a warrior class. Known as *bushi* or samurai, the warriors belonged to a hierarchy bonded by ties of vassalage culminating in a hereditary leader, the shogun. While the shogun's power was basically military, his legitimacy came from the emperor, who traced his descent to the Sun Goddess and retained an aura of sanctity. The emperor held court in Kyoto (his capital since 794), attended by an aristocracy who continued to set standards of refined culture long after the court had lost political and economic power. Meanwhile, the shogun administered his affairs through the *bakufu*, a term originally designating a military field-headquarters but later used for the shogun's government.

The first *bakufu* was the Kamakura Shogunate (1185–1333), located in the city of that name in Eastern Japan. It was succeeded by the Ashikaga Shogunate (1336–1573), which ruled from Kyoto and ended in a century of warfare (1467–1573) during which feudal lords (*daimyo*) used their vassal samurai as they strove to preserve or enlarge their domains (*han*), turning them into small states centered around castle-towns. The trend was for the samurai to become concentrated in these castle-towns, supported by stipends from their *daimyo*, rather than continuing to live on the land. Thus, the fragmentation of Japan into virtually independent domains was accompanied by increased centralization within the individual domains.

The restoration of central authority entailed curbing and controlling the *daimyo* but not eliminating them. The result was not a unitary state in the Chinese model but a third dynasty of shoguns presiding over a hybrid system. This came about through a cumulative process, directed by three leaders who each built on the work of his predecessors.

The first was Oda Nobunaga (1534–1582), known for his ruthlessness in destroying enemies, including militant Buddhists, and for his use of firearms, first introduced by shipwrecked Portuguese in 1543. By the time he was assassinated by one of his own generals, he controlled about a third of Japan.

Toyotomi Hideyoshi (1536–1598), the invader of Korea (see Chapter 3), was born a peasant but rose to become one of Nobunaga's generals. After defeating his rivals for the succession, he continued to amass power, inducing *daimyo* to acknowledge his supremacy by arms, marriage politics, and diplomacy. Unable to subdue the strongest *daimyo*, Tokugawa Ieyasu, he gave his sister to Ieyasu in marriage and assigned him substantial holdings in the East (Kanto), thus assuring that Ieyasu was both content and at a distance. Hideyoshi also relocated his own vassals, placing the most trusted in strategic positions and discouraging those thought to harbor territorial ambitions by providing them with hostile neighbors. To demonstrate their loyalty, vassals were sometimes required to leave wives and children with Hideyoshi as virtual hostages. By 1590 all *daimyo* had sworn oaths of loyalty to him and he was, in effect, overlord of all Japan.

Hideyoshi was intent on suppressing the ambitious *daimyo*, but he did not want to eliminate them. On the contrary, his policies strengthened the *daimyo* locally vis-à-vis their warriors and farmers, even as he took steps to assure their subordination. When a *daimyo* was relocated, he took many of his vassals with him into his new domain where they had no hereditary links to the land, accelerating the tendency for samurai to be concentrated in castle-towns.

In his "sword hunt" of 1588, Hideyoshi ordered all peasants who had not already done so to surrender their weapons. The metal was used to build a great statue of the Buddha. This was followed in 1591 by class-separation edicts prohibiting fighting men from becoming peasants or townsmen, forbidding peasants from leaving their fields and becoming merchants or artisans, and preventing the latter from becoming farmers. Hideyoshi, who rose from the peasantry to the greatest heights, sought to ensure that henceforth everyone would remain within his hereditary social status. Although in theory applicable everywhere, in practice confiscation of swords and implementation of the class-separation edicts was up to the local *daimyo*, who determined the degree and pace of compliance based on their assessment of local conditions. However, the long-term trend was toward compliance.

Another far-reaching measure was the land survey (1582–1598) conducted to assess cultivated land in terms of average annual productivity, measured in *koku* of rice (4.96 bushels). Again, individual domains varied in the degree of implementation, but the holdings of each *daimyo* were now calculated in terms of the assessed value of his domain rather than acreage. From this time on, a *daimyo*, by definition, held land assessed at a minimum of 10,000 *koku*. Wealthy *daimyo* held much more than that. Some had several hundred thousand *koku*, and there were a few with over a million. Hideyoshi personally held two million, not including those of his wealthiest, most trustworthy vassals. Tokugawa Ieyasu held 2,555,000.

Hideyoshi's vision of the world, and his own place in it, extended well beyond Japan. He took an active interest in overseas trade and suppressed the pirates and freebooters who had long plagued the Chinese and Korean coasts. One of his two great castles was at Osaka (Figure 4.1), which soon eclipsed nearby Sakai as a trading center, and remains today the largest city in western Japan. But Hideyoshi looked abroad for more than trade—he thought in terms of empire. In the 1590s, he demanded the submission of the Philippines by its Spanish governor, although he never enforced this demand. He also planned to conquer China and divide it among his vassals. After China would come India and the rest of the world as he

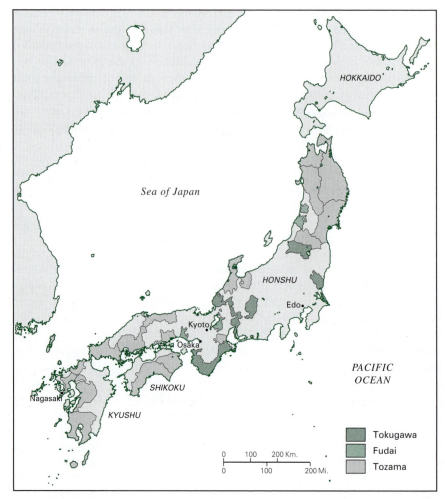

FIGURE 4.1 Japan c. 1664.

knew it. His invasion of the continent can partially be seen as an attempt to satisfy the perpetual land hunger of his vassals or, at least, to find employment for restive samurai. It would also convince everyone of Hideyoshi's power. Another factor was his personality, but Jurgis Elisonas has suggested that "not so much megalomania as ignorance moved the entire enterprise."[1]

Whatever Hideyoshi's motivation, the outcome was a disaster. Similarly, his hopes to found a dynasty came to naught. He left his five-year-old son and heir in the care of regents who had their own ambitions. The winner in the ensuing struggle for supremacy was Ieyasu (1542–1616). He became shogun in 1603, though this merely confirmed the hegemony he had established at the decisive battle of Sekigahara in 1600, a victory marking the effective beginning of the Tokugawa Shogunate.

Consolidation of the Tokugawa Order (1600–1651)

Ieyasu, drawing on the heritage of Hideyoshi, devised the structure of the Tokugawa political system that gave Japan three and a half centuries of peace. His two immediate successors, Hidetada (1616–1623) and Iemitsu (1623–1651), completed it. By the middle of the seventeenth century, the system was in full operation.

Ieyasu rose to supremacy as the leader of a group of *daimyo*, each backed by his own vassals and supported by an independent power base. Appointment by the emperor as shogun gave Ieyasu legitimacy. The *daimyo*, however, were by no means all deeply committed to the Tokugawa. Hideyoshi's recent failure to establish a dynasty had demonstrated the folly of relying solely on the loyalty of such men, especially when passing on the succession to a minor. Ieyasu himself assured the smooth transfer of power to his son by resigning from the office of shogun in 1605, after holding it for only two years. But he continued in actual control until his death.

All the *daimyo* were the shogun's vassals, bound to him by solemn oath. When a *daimyo*'s heir succeeded to his domain, the new *daimyo* had to sign his pledge of vassalage to the shogun in blood. Still, some vassals were more reliable than others, and the Tokugawa classified them into three groups. Least trusted and potentially the most dangerous were the "outside," or allied, *daimyo (tozama)*, who were too powerful to be considered Tokugawa subordinates. Some had supported Ieyasu at the battle of Sekigahara, but others came over to the Tokugawa only after the outcome of that battle left them no other choice. More trustworthy were the "house" *daimyo (fudai)*, most of whom had been family vassals raised to *daimyo* status by the Tokugawa, and who thus were indebted to the *bakufu* for their status and domains. The third group, the "collateral" *daimyo (shimpan)*, belonged to Tokugawa branch families ordinarily out of the line of succession but eligible to supply a shogun if there was no heir from the main line. The Tokugawa also had its direct retainers on its own lands. Some of these held fiefs of less than the 10,000 *koku* required for *daimyo* status, and many received stipends directly from the *bakufu*.

When Ieyasu was transferred to the Kanto region by Hideyoshi, he chose the centrally located village of Edo (modern Tokyo) as his headquarters, although it consisted of only one hundred houses at the time. Edo remained the Tokugawa capital, and the shogunate also maintained castles at Osaka and Shizuoka (then called Sumpu), as well as the Nijō Castle in Kyoto, residence of a *bakufu* official responsible for governing the city and representing the shogun at the imperial court. To secure itself militarily, the Tokugawa placed its house *daimyo* strategically to dominate the Kanto, central Japan, and the Kyoto-Osaka area, while relegating the outside *daimyo* to outlying areas. To keep the *daimyo* weak, they were limited to one castle each and needed *bakufu* permission before they could repair this castle. They were allowed only a fixed number of men-at-arms and forbidden to build large ships. To prevent alliances that might threaten the *bakufu*, the *daimyo* had to obtain its consent for their marriage plans.

During the first half of the seventeenth century the shogunate further increased its strength at *daimyo* expense. In this period, there were 281 cases in which *daimyo* were strengthened or weakened by transfers from one fief to another. Another 213 domains were confiscated outright. This could happen when a lord proved incompetent or a domain was torn by a succession dispute. More often, confiscation resulted from failure to produce an heir. Deathbed adoptions were not recognized. By such means the Tokugawa more than tripled their holdings to 6.8 million *koku*, about a fourth of Japan. The distribution of their holdings also favored the Tokugawa economically, as they included many important cities such as Osaka, Kyoto, and Nagoya. In the mid-Tokugawa period, collateral *daimyo* held land worth 2.6 million *koku*; house *daimyo*, 6.7 million; and outside *daimyo*, 9.8 million. Religious institutions held around 600,000 *koku*, and the emperor and his court could draw on land worth only 187,000 *koku*.

To ensure the *daimyo* obeyed *bakufu* orders, the shogun had his own inspectors. He also kept the *daimyo* under surveillance by requiring them to spend alternate years in residence at Edo. When they returned to their domains, they had to leave their wives and children behind. This system of alternate attendance (*sankin kōtai*) forced the *daimyo* to spend large sums traveling back and forth with their retinues and to maintain suitably elaborate residences in Edo. They were also called on to support public projects such as waterworks or repair of the shogun's castle at Edo, but such exactions were not as burdensome as the constant expense of alternate attendance. These requirements turned Edo into the capital of Japan, as well as of the *bakufu*.

The shogun's dual role as feudal overlord and the emperor's deputy made him responsible for the conduct of foreign affairs. The early *bakufu* also reserved the right to issue paper money. It even issued regulations for the dress of the *daimyo*, and in 1635 it declared, "all matters are to be carried out in accordance with the laws of Edo,"[2] though that sounds like wishful thinking. The *bakufu* usually interfered only when a *daimyo* proved incompetent or when an issue involved more than one domain. Meanwhile, the emperor remained in Kyoto under the surveillance of the shogun's representatives.

Bakufu–Han Relations

Whatever even an assertive shogun might wish, the *daimyo* remained largely free to manage affairs in their own *han*. The tendency of *daimyo* and their samurai to identify with their own domain, at times even generating *han* chauvinism, was strongest among the outside *daimyo*. Of course, the others also focused on managing their *han*. Thus, they had a stake in maintaining and enlarging the decentralized aspect of the larger political system. Under the fourth shogun, Ietsuna (1651–1680), the centralizing policy of the *bakufu* was reversed. There was a drastic decline in the number of *daimyo* transferred and *han* confiscated. Deathbed adoptions were recognized as legitimate. The shogunate even began permitting *han* to issue their own paper money. A proliferation of local currencies ensued. To protect their own money, some *han* in the eighteenth century prohibited the use of outside currencies—including the *bakufu*'s money.

The vigorous but eccentric fifth shogun, Tsunayoshi (1680–1709), presided over a reassertion of *bakufu* power, which earned him the enmity of the *daimyo* and lasting ignominy and ridicule. He was an easy target, for he was extreme in his Buddhist devotion to the preservation of animal life, especially with his solicitude for dogs, which was sometimes even at the cost of human life. This earned him the epithet "dog shogun." Nevertheless, his period saw a great flourishing of culture as well as a resurgence of centralizing activity. But this neither led to a permanent shift in the power balance nor initiated a long-term trend toward greater *bakufu* control. If it had, this shogun's historical image would have been different.

Until the end of the Tokugawa, the pendulum continued to swing between the *bakufu* and the *han*. In his analysis of the history and dynamics of this process, Harold Bolitho has shown that periods of *bakufu* assertiveness tended to occur under vigorous shoguns working with trusted advisors drawn from among the shogunate's low-ranking retainers. Unencumbered by fief or vassals, totally dependent on the shogun, they became his men, free from potential conflicts of interest. Under such regimes, the high-ranking Senior Councilors, always selected from among the house *daimyo*, were treated with an outward show of respect while they were actually bypassed and disregarded. These *fudai* and the new advisors often feuded.

When the shogun was a minor or an incompetent, control over the *bakufu* reverted to the Senior Councilors, descendants of the Tokugawa's most favored and highly trusted vassals. The service of these vassals had formed the core of Ieyasu's strength, and his house relied on their descendants for continued loyal service. While these men were conscious of their heritage and special obligations toward the shogunate, they also had responsibilities and opportunities as *daimyo*. The tensions between shogunate and *han* were mirrored in their own persons as they faced the often conflicting demands of *bakufu* and *han*. The usual pattern was for them to act more as *daimyo* than as *bakufu* officials. Such Senior Councilors were not prepared to sacrifice *han* privileges. Cases existed of even *han* held by incumbent Senior Councilors refusing to export grain badly needed to combat famine elsewhere. The balance of power between the *bakufu* and the *han* never resolved completely in favor of one or the other. This probably proved beneficial in the long run since it allowed for considerable divergence in Japan while still maintaining a centeral power.

The more than 250 *han* varied widely in size, natural resources, and local conditions. All the lands held by a *daimyo* were not necessarily contiguous; some domains were more easily organized than others. Nevertheless, operating on a smaller scale than the *bakufu*, the *daimyo* were more successful in controlling their retainers. The trend for the samurai to be concentrated in the *han* capitals, divorced from the land, continued to be strong. By the last decade of the seventeenth century, over 80 percent of the *daimyo* were paying stipends to their samurai. By the end of the eighteenth century, 90 percent of samurai were entirely dependent on these stipends. Only 10 percent still retained local roots in the country.

Economic and Social Change

The Tokugawa peace made economic growth possible. There was a rise in demand to meet the needs of the samurai and the growing expenses of the *daimyo*. The system of alternate attendance stimulated the commercialization of agriculture. Consequently, agricultural productivity increased substantially, especially in the seventeenth century. Cultivated acreage doubled thanks to vigorous irrigation and land reclamation. Technological improvements, the practice of multiple cropping, better seed strains, and improved fertilizers helped, as did the dissemination of knowledge through agricultural handbooks and manuals. The spread of market networks was accompanied by regional specialization in cash crops such as cotton, mulberry trees for the rearing of silk worms, indigo, tobacco, and sugar cane, but grain (especially rice and millet) continued to be grown in all parts of Japan.

The population rose from about 18 million at the beginning of the Tokugawa to around 30 million by the middle of the period. Afterward, there were fluctuations in population, but there was no major long-term increase during the rest of Tokugawa; in 1872 the population was only 33.1 million. Although famine and disease took their toll, mortality rates were comparatively low. The average life span was very likely longer than in premodern Europe, since Japan was free from war and less susceptible to epidemics. Late marriage, the custom of having only one son marry and inherit, as well as abortion and infanticide kept population growth under control. Family planning was widespread. Even when times were good, life was by no means easy for Japanese peasants who remained at the mercy of the elements. Many were poor, but for most of the period, the standard of living rose.

With samurai now largely removed from the land, outside authority over villages, though affirmed by decree (Box 4.1), diminished in practice as many villages were left virtually free to collect themselves the taxes due to their overlord. Regardless of the role of outside authority, within the village neither the benefits of agricultural growth nor the burdens of taxation were shared equally: there were wide gradations in wealth, status, and power backed by the State. Since tax reassessments were infrequent, wealthy peasants who were able to open new lands and otherwise increase their yields found their incomes rising.

Traditionally, the main house of an extended family had claims on the services of the lesser households, along with some obligations to look after the poorer members. Furthermore, the heads of the main houses formed the traditional village leadership. With more money in circulation, wealthy villagers turned increasingly to hired laborers or tenant farmers to work their land. They also put their money to work in rural commerce, money lending, and such rural industries as processing vegetable oils, brewing sake, producing soy sauce, and making paper. Since the wealthy villagers did not necessarily belong to the old main houses, tensions ensued.

These tensions were aggravated by economic disparities, as poorer villagers and the landless did not share in the prosperity of the countryside and suffered when contractual relationships replaced those based on family. Most often they endured in silence, but at times they gave vent to their resentment in uprisings. Peasant unrest increased in the late Tokugawa. In contrast to early Tokugawa rural uprisings, often

BOX 4.1 THE MUTUAL RESPONSIBILITY SYSTEM

Although Chinese in origin, the idea of holding a group of people responsible for one another also appealed to political authorities in Japan. The *goningumi*, literally "five-man groups," established in the countryside as well as urban centers, normally consisted of five propertied households, although they could be expanded to as many as a dozen. Members were to assist one another by coming to each other's aid and protection, helping prevent and fight fires, build roads, bridges, irrigation works, and maintain peaceful relations between community members. The head of each *goningumi* was responsible for seeing that its members were law-abiding citizens and that they paid their taxes on time. If one person in the group was caught transgressing the law, the entire group was punished.

The degree to which the system was implemented varied as did the balance between local autonomy and centralized power. It could be considered the lowest rung of a chain of command reaching all the way to the shogun, but in practice, especially in the villages, made for considerable self-governance.

The *daimyo* of Echizen, a *han* located on the west coast of Honshu, issued the following order in 1632. The six injunctions reflect the importance of having a dependable, stable, and peaceful population of peasant farmer producers who performed their appropriate role in life and in the Tokugawa class system by tilling the land and responsibly paying their taxes.

The Group of Five (*Goningumi*)

1. If there is anyone in the group of five who is given to malfeasance, that fact must be reported without concealing anything.
2. If there is anyone in the group of five who fails to pay his annual taxes or perform the services required, other members of the group must quickly rectify the situation.
3. If there is anyone in the group of five who runs away, those who are remaining must quickly search for and return him [to the original domicile]. If the return of the runaway cannot be secured, the group of five will be rendered culpable.
4. No one in the group of five may ask to work outside the domain, or to work in a mine elsewhere. Even if he wishes to work within the

(*continued*)

BOX 4.1 THE MUTUAL RESPONSIBILITY SYSTEM (CONTINUED)

domain at places such as Maruoka, Oné . . . he must secure permission from the authorities ahead of time.

5. If there is anyone in the group of five who is exceptionally strong, that fact must be reported.

6. Members of the group of five must not permit anyone who absconds, or any stranger who is not beyond suspicion regardless of being man or woman, to lodge in his house. Nor can they provide lodging for any single person. However, if the stranger is an express messenger, lodging may be provided after his letter box is examined.

If there is anyone who violates any of the provisions above, that fact must be reported to the office of the village head (shôya) without delay. The village head must report the same to the *tedai* (minor magistrate's) office immediately. If there is any violation of the above rules, we [as members of the group of five] shall be deemed to be culpable, and at that time we shall bear no grudges.

In witness whereof, we have jointly affixed our seals for the group of five.

Translated in David J. Lu. Japan: A Documentary History: The Dawn of History to the Late Tokugawa Period. (New York: East Gate, 1997).

led by village headmen, those of the later period were frequently directed against those wealthy and powerful villagers. However, neither the uprisings nor the changes in agricultural technology seriously threatened the basic stability of the village. Violence was a form of protest, not a means toward revolution. Changes in agriculture increased yield but did not alter the basic pattern of rice farming, with its need for intensive labor and community cooperation. The experience of calculating work in terms of money and time was to prove a legacy useful in the future.

Internal peace and economic vigor were conducive to expansion of the Japanese presence in the far north, homeland of the non-Japanese Ainu people who, by the end of the eighteenth century, accounted for only about half the population of Hokkaido. The Japanese presence then accelerated, partly out of concern over Russian expansion. In the early nineteenth century, they pursued a policy of turning the Ainu into Japanese in eastern Hokkaido, forcing them to abandon their bear festival, to cut their hair in the Japanese manner, and to give up tattooing and ear-piercing. Many died of disease. Others labored in fisheries that sent their products south to Japan. The decline in Ainu numbers and identity proved to be a long-term trend.

Economic expansion also left a dubious ecological legacy. In the seventeenth century, both the *bakufu* and the domains promoted land clearance. Old-growth forests were cut. By the end of the century, producers and consumers were faced with a lumber shortage. In the eighteenth century there was a countervailing move to save natural resources and to reforest cleared areas. However, government policies were inconsistent, because agriculture brought in more tax revenue than did forestry. Conrad Totman concludes, "How best to balance the need for both woodland and arable was a dilemma that early modern Japan never resolved."[3]

Much of the lumber went to the cities, homes of officials and merchants, who became rich as the economy flourished and the political authorities found their services indispensable. Merchants supplied an economic link between the cities and the rural hinterlands as well as between localities and the capital. They handled the transport, warehousing, and sale of rice and other commodities. Frequently, they were licensed to operate *han* monopolies and organize commodity production. Important merchants acted as financial and forwarding agents for the *daimyo*, handling shipments to Osaka for exchange or to Edo for the *daimyo*'s consumption. They supplied banking services, dealing in the manifold *han* currencies, transferring funds, and issuing loans to political authorities and hard-pressed samurai. They were the backbone of widespread and diverse commercial networks. The position of individual commercial establishments could be precarious—in extreme cases, a wealthy merchant with heavy loans out to the powerful might suffer confiscation so that the loans could go unpaid, as happened to a great Osaka merchant in 1705. However, these cases were exceptions. Government measures forcing creditors to settle for less than full repayment, or accept cancellation, simply had the effect of raising the cost of new loans, because the authorities never found a way to eliminate the need for such borrowing.

With the *bakufu*, *daimyo*, and samurai dependent on them, the merchants prospered; in the second half of the eighteenth century there were over 200 mercantile establishments valued at over 200,000 gold *ryŏ*, a monetary unit worth roughly a *koku* of rice. Such merchants were fully the economic equals of *daimyo*. Some of the great modern commercial and financial empires go back to the early Tokugawa, including the house of Mitsui, founded in 1620 (figure 4.2).

By the beginning of the eighteenth century, Edo had a population of about a million, a little over half of them townspeople (*chŏnin*). Osaka, too, developed as a prosperous commercial and shipping center, and Kyoto remained a major city. The capitals of the *han* also became trade centers, with merchants and artisans playing an active role in shaping the character of each city. The most prominent merchants, as City Elders, Ward Representatives, and the like, had a role in administration.

As in the villages, there were also great differences in status and wealth among the town dwellers; for every great merchant there were many more humble shopkeepers, peddlers, artisans, laborers, and servants. At the bottom of society, constituting under 2 percent of the population at the end of the Tokugawa period, were *hinin* ("non-people"), mostly beggars, and *eta*, or outcasts (today called *burakumin*

FIGURE 4.2   Mitsui Kimono Shop, Edo (Nihoinbashi). *Scenic Mementos.* Mitsui grew from humble beginnings into a major enterprise including not only the kimono shop illustrated here (the forerunner of today's Mitsukoshi Department Store) but also a lucrative money exchange business that became a modern bank. The illustration on the left shows deliveries being made. That on the right depicts the entrance to the store and a typical street scene. Perhaps the kimonos worn by the elegant ladies were bought at Mitsui. The company crest is prominently displayed and "Mitsui" (Three Wells) is written in large characters on the pillars.
NATIONAL DIET LIBRARY, TOKYO, JAPAN.

because *eta* is considered pejorative), who mostly engaged in butchering and tanning, tasks considered unclean. The *bakufu* placed one powerful outcast house in charge over all outcasts in its own domains in return for supplying leather goods and men to serve as prison guards and executioners. As Eiko Ikegami has pointed out, "The identical action of killing, whether human beings or animals, was, however, interpreted variously as either a source of pollution and exclusion (in the case of the outcasts) or a source of honor and power (in the case of the samurai)."[4]

Classes and Values

To create an enduring order, Ieyasu followed Hideyoshi in drawing a clear line between samurai and commoners. Occasionally, destitute *rōnin* (masterless samurai) dropped out of their class, or through marriage an alliance was formed between a wealthy merchant family and that of an impoverished samurai.

Assigned to various duties, the samurai staffed the increasingly bureaucratized administrative machinery of the domains and the *bakufu*. Most were now occupied more with civil than with military affairs. The most visible sign of the samurai's privilege was his sole right to wear swords, symbols of his status even after they had ceased to be his major tools. While he was expected to acquire some proficiency in at least one of the martial arts, this became "a matter of formal gymnastics and disciplined choreography."[5] Nevertheless, the ethos of the samurai remained that of a loyal military vassal imbued with a strong and prickly sense of personal honor and a proclivity to violence, which the *bakufu* needed to tame as well as exploit.

Success in civil office depended on study. Although Ieyasu patronized the Confucian scholar Hayashi Razan (1583–1657), whose family continued to supply the heads of the *bakufu*'s Confucian Academy, it was not until the end of the century that Confucianism came to prevail. The ideal was for the samurai to combine the virtues of a Confucian scholar and those of a traditional warrior. An early proponent of the fusion of Confucian and warrior values was Yamaga Sokŏ (1622–1695). A student of Hayashi Razan and of the martial arts, he is considered a founding father of the modern way of the warrior (*bushidŏ*). One of his followers became the leader of the famed 47 *rŏnin*, who sought vengeance for the wrong done to their dead lord. In 1703 their carefully nurtured plans were rewarded with success, as they stormed into the Kyoto mansion of the offending *daimyo* and killed him. They were immediately considered heroes, and have remained popular examples of ideal loyalty. Their act was full of warrior courage and devotion, but it was also illegal. The shogunate debated what should be done, finally finding a solution that upheld the substance of civil law while preserving the warriors' honor: they ordered the *rŏnin* to commit ritual suicide. Playwrights lost no time in adapting the story for the stage. *Chūshingura* (*Treasury of Royal Retainers*) was popular with commoners and samurai alike, and has remained a Japanese favorite; in the twentieth century both the cinema and the television versions enjoyed great success.

In Tokugawa times, samurai and commoner could agree on plenty. The official Confucian morality was promoted in periodic lectures and spread by the many schools founded during the Tokugawa period. As a result by 1800, 40 to 50 percent of Japanese males were literate to some degree. Fewer girls went to school, but as in China, special texts were published for their benefit. It is estimated that 10 percent of girls were in school by the end of the Tokugawa in 1868.

Hierarchical principles of organization operated throughout the society, as did a tendency to rank people in grades. Like samurai, even the inhabitants of the urban pleasure quarters were carefully ranked. The great merchant houses resembled feudal fiefs not only in their wealth but also in their expectation of lifelong loyal service from their employees, who, in turn, were entitled to be treated with paternalistic solicitude. A similar relationship survives in Japanese industry to this day.

Although merchant and samurai held many values in common, it was a mark of samurai pride to regard financial considerations with contempt. Fukuzawa Yukichi (1853–1901) tells in his autobiography how his father took his children out of school when, to his horror, their teacher began to teach them arithmetic, a subject fit only for merchants and their offspring. But business had its defenders, including the Kaitoku Academy in Osaka, which taught the importance of trade and of those who engaged in it. A strain of Buddhism that considered all occupations as valid forms of devotion further legitimated the merchants' calling. Shingaku ("Heart Learning"), a religion founded by the Kyoto merchant and philosopher

Ishida Baigan (1685–1744), combined elements of Shinto, Confucianism, and Buddhism to create an ethic for the artisan and merchant stressing honesty, frugality, and devotion to one's trade. Diversity in classes and lifestyles made for similar diversity in the visual, literary, and performing arts as well as in thought.

The Aesthetic Culture of the Aristocracy

The aristocracy inherited a rich cultural tradition. The subtle arts of the tea ceremony and flower arranging continued, and the *Nŏ* drama, which had flourished during the Muromachi period (1336–1573), continued to have its devotees, including the shogun Tsunayoshi, who himself performed in *Nŏ* plays. In architecture, the classic aesthetic of restraint was exemplified by the imperial villa at Katsura, outside Kyoto, but it coexisted with a love for the ornate, displayed at Nikko, the mausoleum north of Tokyo where Ieyasu's remains are interred. Here brightly painted and gilded decorations luxuriate in chaotic flamboyance, saved from empty vulgarity by their setting in a magnificent forest, creating in Alexander Soper's words, "a serene depth of shadow into which their tumult sinks without an echo."[6]

In Kyoto, aristocratic aesthetics enjoyed a surge of vitality in a movement led by Hon'ami Kŏetsu (1558–1637), who established a community of artists and craftsmen on a site granted to him by Ieyasu in recognition of his prominence as a member of that city's Nichiren Buddhist community. Nichiren was a thirteenth-century religious leader whose adopted name combines the words for sun (*ni*) and lotus (*ren*) to express his faith in Japan, Land of the Rising Sun. Kŏetsu was trained in his family's hereditary art of sword repair and connoisseurship, but his far-reaching talents found masterly expression in tea bowls, lacquer inlay work, cast metal vessels, painting, and above all, calligraphy. Frequently he worked in collaboration with other artists, as with the bold and free calligraphy he contributed to the handscroll *Thousand Cranes*, painted by Tawaraya Sŏtatsu, a highly gifted younger contemporary (Figure 4.3). The result is a decorative elegance that does honor to an aristocratic tradition going back to the Heian period (794–1185).

The third great Kyoto artist was Ogata Kŏrin (1658–1716), represented here by a pair of iris screens, which Elise Grilli has compared to Mozart's variations on a musical theme, the artist "first stating his motif, then adding variations, shifts, repetitions, pauses, leaps, intervals, changes of tempo, accents, chords, rise and fall, with changes of mood from major to minor."[7] Kŏrin's color orchestration and his superb eye for the decorative are visible even in a monochrome reproduction (Figure 4.4).

Genroku Urban Culture

Urban culture reached a high point during the Genroku Era, technically the era name for the 16 years from 1688 to 1704, but more broadly used for the cultural life of the 50-year period beginning in the last quarter of the seventeenth century, when some of Japan's most creative artists were at work. These include

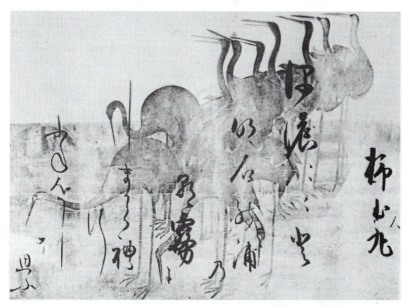

FIGURE 4.3 *Thousand Cranes.* Section of a hand-scroll. Painting by Tawaraya Sōtatsu, calligraphy by Hon'ami Kōetsu. Gold and silver underpainting on paper, 341 × 1460 cm.
PHOTOGRAPH COURTESY OF KYOTO NATIONAL MUSEUM.

the playwright, Chikamatsu (1653–1724); the short story writer, Saikaku (1642–1693); Moronobu (1618–1694), generally credited with developing the Japanese print; and Bashō (1644–1694), master of the haiku.

Most large cities have "pleasure districts," parts of town devoted to bohemian life, erotic activities, entertainment, and gambling. Tokugawa cities were no exception. But rarely, if ever, have such quarters produced a first-rate aesthetic as they did in seventeenth-century Yoshiwara, the home of Edo's "floating world." Here, and in similar quarters in the other large towns, there was a world that savored

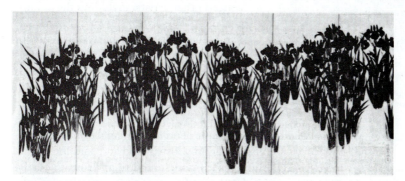

FIGURE 4.4 *Irises*, from a scene of *The Tale of Ise*, Ogata Kōrin. One of a pair of six-fold screens. Color on gold foil over paper, 151.2 × 360.7 cm.
NEZU INSTITUTE OF FINE ARTS, TOKYO, JAPAN.

sophisticated stylishness in dress, coiffure, perfume, gesture, and life itself. The tone was set by the worldly flair of the man-about-town and the elegance of the spirited courtesans who presided over this world and who looked down with disdain on the country boor.

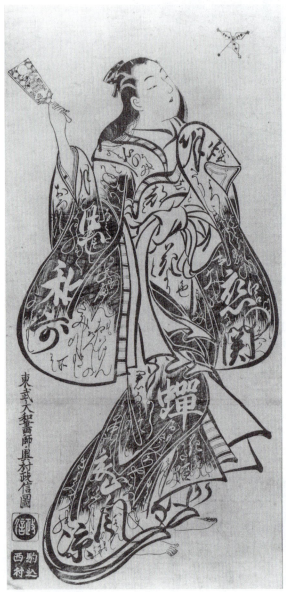

FIGURE 4.5 *Courtesan Striking a Shuttlecock with a Battledore,* Okumura Masanobu (1710s). Poetic verses written in calligraphic script decorate the courtesan's kimono. Woodblock print, ink on paper, 65.2 × 32.2 cm.

ALLEN MEMORIAL ART MUSEUM, OBERLIN COLLEGE, OHIO. MARY A. AINSWORTH BEQUEST (1950.202).

The Print

Courtesans and actors were favorite subjects of the *ukiyo-e* ("pictures of the floating world") paintings and illustrations for books such as the *Yoshiwara Pillow* (1660), a combination sex manual and "courtesan critique." Later, *ukiyo-e* woodcut prints were produced by taking portraits of courtesans, theater scenes, nature subjects, or scenes from urban life and carving into wood blocks. These were then inked and printed on paper. The process was highly experimental until Hishikawa Moronobu consolidated the early efforts.

At the beginning the prints were in black and white, but soon color was added, first by hand, then by developing techniques for printing red and green, and by the eighteenth century three- or four-color prints were produced. A versatile master and major contributor to the development of the print was Okumura Masanobu (c. 1686–1764), who produced the eighteenth-century beauty seen in Figure 4.5 dressed in a characteristically sumptuous kimono, gracefully at play.

Masanobu, a master of various styles, influenced other artists, including the creator of the hand-colored print shown in Figure 4.6. Depicting the interior of a theater, the composition experiments with the receding perspective of European painting.

Masanobu was a publisher as well as an artist, although usually these functions were carried out by different people. Numerous people had a hand in creating a print. The publisher not only distributed and sold the prints, but also commissioned them from the artist with more or less explicit instructions on subject and style. The artist drew the picture and designed the print, but then turned it over to the engraver and the printer. The craftsmanship

FIGURE 4.6 *Perspective View of Kyogen Play Stage.* Okumura Masanobu (c. 1745). The actors on stage had to compete for attention with refreshment hawkers and private conversations, and some of the affluent spectators in the balcony seem as interested in the goings-on in the pit as they are in the performance of the actors. Prints such as these, like the inexpensive seats in the pits, were within the means of ordinary urbanites and made prized mementos for travelers. Everyone loved *kabuki.*
BURSTEIN COLLECTION/CORBIS FROM BETTMANN/CORBIS.

of these men helped determine the quality of a print, but the artist contributed the essential vision.

Theater and Literature

An unceasing source of inspiration for the print artist was the *kabuki* theater, whose celebrated actors enjoyed as much acclaim and attracted as avid a following as did the most elegant of Yoshiwara courtesans. *Kabuki* originated in the dances and skits performed in Kyoto early in the seventeenth century by a troupe of female performers. But this women's *kabuki* lasted only until 1629, when it was banned by the *bakufu* to put an end to the outbursts of violence that erupted as rivals competed for the favors of these ladies. For the next two decades young men's *kabuki* flourished, until it ran into similar difficulties and was prohibited in 1652. Afterward all actors were mature men. Even then *kabuki* continued to be under restrictions, tolerated but licensed and controlled, because like other indecorous pleasures, it could not be suppressed.

Kabuki's spectacular scenery, gorgeous costumes, and scenes of violent passion enchanted audiences. It was very much an actor's art, dominated by dynasties of actors who felt quite free to take liberties with the texts of plays. The audience greeted the virtuoso performances of the stars with shouts of approval. Particularly esteemed was the artistry of the men who played the female roles.

These masters devoted their lives to achieving stylizations of posture, gesture, and voice conveying the quintessence of femininity, always operating in that "slender margin between the real and unreal"[8] that Chikamatsu, sometimes called Japan's Shakespeare, defined as the true province of art.

Chikamatsu wrote for the *kabuki* stage but preferred the puppet theater (*bunraku*), where his lines were not at the mercy of the actors. In *bunraku*, large wooden puppets, each manipulated by a three-man team, enacted a story told by a group of chanters, accompanied by three-stringed samisen, an instrument that looks like a square banjo. This theater became so popular that live actors came to imitate the movements of the puppets. Even after *kabuki* carried the day in Edo, *bunraku* continued to flourish in Osaka. The puppets, like the masks employed in *Nō*, assured that the action on stage would not be a mere mirror of ordinary life but would be more stylized and symbolic. It also made possible scenes of violence and fantastic occurrences on stage, which are impossible for live actors but pose no problems to figures that do not bleed and are not bound by the usual limits of human physiology. Chikamatsu frequently used spectacular elements in his plays on historical subjects, such as *The Battle of Coxinga*, his most famous work in this genre.

Chikamatsu also wrote more subtle domestic plays. These center on conflicts between moral obligation (*giri*) and human emotion (*ninjō*). Feeling usually wins out over duty, but at a heavy price. One play, for example, tells of the tragic love of a shopkeeper and a lovely courtesan whom he cannot ransom from her house for lack of funds. Frequently the poetic high points of these plays are the lovers' flight to death. Often the women exhibit greater strength of character than the men, but both are turned into romantic heroes through the purity and intensity of their emotions. Art imitates life, but life also imitates art: the plays produced such a rash of love suicides that the *bakufu* finally banned all plays with the words "love suicide" in the title.

Ihara Saikaku loved to write about love in his stories and books. Sometimes he wrote about samurai, but his best work deals with recognizable city types: the miser and money-grubber, the playboy who squanders his patrimony, the young beauty mismatched to an elderly husband, men and women in love with love. Exuberant and witty, he mixed humor and sex, and wrote with a robust directness. He was also a prolific composer of *haikai* linked verse, a light verse that grew out of *renga*, in which one poet starts off, leaving it up to friends to continue. Enlivened by infusions of everyday speech and humor, *haikai* turned its back on aristocratic refinement, as seen in this famous pair of links in a sixteenth-century anthology:

> Bitter, bitter it was
> And yet somehow funny.
> Even when
> My father lay dying
> I went on farting.[9]

Vulgar as it is, the second verse does contrast sharply with the first, as is required in this poetic form. The popularity of *haikai* is attested by several seventeenth-century anthologies, one containing verses by over 650 contributors.

Classical poems (*tanka*) and *renga* often began with 17 syllables arranged in three lines five/seven/five, which, when standing alone, form a haiku. The greatest haiku master was Matsuo Bashō, who was born a samurai but gave up his rank to live the life of a commoner, earning his living as a master poet with pupils from all strata of society.

Not every 17-syllable poem is a true haiku, for the real measure of a haiku lies not in its formal structure or surface meaning but in its resonance; not in what it says but in what it leaves unsaid. It presents the reader with a series of images, which when connected in the imagination, yield a wealth of associations, visions, and emotions. Consider, for example, Bashō's best-known haiku:

> An old pond
> Frog jumps in
> Sound of water.

The inner spring of the poem is the juxtaposition of two contrasting natural elements, a juxtaposition that (like the frog in the water) sets off waves in the reader's mind. The old pond supplies the setting, but implies a condition of ancient stillness that contrasts with the sudden action, and results in a delightful image. It raises the question, "How does one explain the relationship between the pond that has been there for centuries and a tiny splash that disappears in a moment?" This question was posed by Professor Makoto Ueda, who responded, "Different people will give different answers, though they will all experience the same sort of 'loneliness' when they try to give an explanation. It seems that Bashō was more concerned with the loneliness than with the answer."[10] Some of his finest poems were composed on his travels and are contained in his *The Narrow Road of Oku*. One reads:

> At Yoshino
> I'll show you cherry blossoms
> Cypress umbrella.[11]

He wrote the poem on his umbrella, and there is a gentle whimsy in Bashō's idea of sharing the beauty of the cherry blossoms with his umbrella. The word translated "umbrella" can also mean "hat." Figure 4.7 is a portrait of Bashō dressed for travel, with this haiku inscribed on it.

This painting is an example of the genre known as *haiga* in which a haiku and a painting (*ga*) are integrated. It is by Yokoi Kinkoku (1761–1832) in the general manner of Yosa Buson (1716–1783), the most eminent artist in the literati mode. Like Chinese gentleman painters, the creators of

FIGURE 4.7 *Portrait of the poet Bashō*, Yokoi Kinkoku (1761–1832). Bashō, the greatest haiku master, composed some of his finest poems on his travels and appears here ready for his next trip with his traveling hat. Ink and color on paper, hanging scroll, 21.6 × 18.4 cm.

Japanese "literati painting" (*bunjinga,* Chinese *wenrenhua*) also cultivated calligraphy and poetry as means of self-expression. They looked to China for inspiration but did not limit themselves to Chinese subjects in their art.

Intellectual Currents: Confucianism

Tokugawa Confucians were deeply influenced by developments in China, but their writings also reflected the vast differences between the two countries. In Japan, there was no civil service examination system to reward mastery of Confucian texts. Most Confucian scholars came from lower samurai or commoner ranks and made their living as teachers or doctors. One attraction of Confucianism to such men was its advocacy of government by the meritorious rather than the well-born. At the same time, even the sinophiles among them took pride in Japan. Some argued that Japan came closer to Confucian ideals than Qing China, while others played an ingenious "game of one-upmanship."[12]

The beginnings of Tokugawa Confucianism are usually traced back to Fujiwara Seika (1561–1619), an aristocrat who did not find it beneath his dignity to write a letter for a Kyoto merchant sending a trade mission to Vietnam. He drew up a ship's oath that began: "Commerce is the business of selling and buying in order to bring profit to both parties." He defined profit as "the outcome of righteousness," and admonished merchants not to be greedy.[13]

In Japan, as in China and Korea, Confucian teachings found a home in academies. Edo's premier Confucian academy was founded by Hayashi Razan (1583–1657) under *bakufu* patronage, but Edo did not dominate Tokugawa thought. The fragmentation of political authority made for intellectual diversity.

An outstanding early exponent of Song Confucianism was Yamazaki Ansai (1618–1682), a stern and forceful teacher who stressed "devotion within, righteousness without," and was so dedicated to Zhu Xi that he said he would follow the master even into error. When asked the hypothetical question, 'What should be done were Confucius and Mencius to lead a Chinese invasion of Japan?' he answered that he would capture the two sages and put them at the service of his own land. Deeply versed in Shinto, Ansai attempted to fuse Confucian ethics with Shinto religion. Most Confucians justified the shogunate by incorporating it into the hierarchy of loyalty, but Ansai's contemporary Muro Kyūso (1658–1734) argued that the Tokugawa ruled by virtue of a heavenly mandate.

Muro Kyūso found it necessary to defend the thought of Zhu Xi against increasingly vigorous challenges from other schools. In Japan as in China the followers of Wang Yangming challenged the teachings of Zhu XI. The man considered the founder of Wang Yangming school in Japan, Nakae Tōjū (1608–1648), had died before Kyuso was born but not so his influence. Like the Chinese philosopher, he stressed the inner light and insisted on the importance of action. His lofty and unselfish character attracted the admiration of his contemporaries and of later activist intellectuals. His best-known disciple, Kumazawa Banzan (1619–1691), ran into political trouble, not because of his philosophic ideas, but for such policy recommendations as relaxing the *daimyo*'s attendance requirements to save expenses. His deep concern for the well-being of the peasantry went hand in hand with lack of sympathy for the merchant class, as reflected in his advocacy of a return to a barter economy using rice in place of money.

Like Yamazaki Ansai and Kumazawa Banzan, Kaibara Ekken (1630–1714) found much of value in Shinto, but his philosophy of nature was based on *qi* (see Chapter 1). The writings of this remarkable man range from botany to ethics, from farming to philology, and include precepts for daily life and a primer for women. They express his breadth of mind, commitment to the welfare of society, and faith in the unity and value of knowledge.

In Japan, as in China, there were men who denied the authority of Song thinkers and insisted on going back to the foundation texts. This was the stance of Yamaga Soko, the formulator of *bushidō*, and of Itō Jinsai (1627–1705), who drew inspiration from the *Analects:*

> The *Analects* is like the boundless universe which men live in without comprehending its full magnitude. Enduring and immutable throughout the ages, in every part of the world it serves as an infallible guide. Is it not, indeed, great![14]

Jinsai rejected the distinction between *li* and *qi* and stressed self-cultivation with an emphasis on *Ren* (humaneness).

Another opponent of Song philosophy was Ogyū Sorai (1666–1728), who insisted on going back earlier than the *Analects* all the way to the classics. He has been described by Kate Nakai as effecting an intellectual "sea-change." Rejecting the unity of the inner human realm and the outer world of heaven and earth, "Sorai challenged the notion that through the practice of *li* (rites and propriety) the individual realized an innate capacity for alignment with a natural order."[15] A complex, many-sided thinker and prolific writer, Sorai emphasized rites and institutions and wrote on many topics including philosophy, politics, literature, linguistics, music, military science, and economics.

A younger contemporary of Sorai, Goi Ranju (1697–1726), head of the Kaitokudo Academy, did not believe that the ancients had exhausted all knowledge, and even envisioned intellectual progress. A member of the next generation who studied at the academy was Tominaga Nakamoto (1715–1746), a skeptic who argued that all historical texts were unreliable. In the work of these and others were the roots for ideas which exceeded the confines of the Tokugawa order and, indeed, the normal bounds of Confucian thought. Of course, Confucian thought, too, could take men's minds in unanticipated directions.

Historiography and Nativism

A perennial field of Confucian scholarship was the study of history. Hayashi Razan began work on a history of Japan that was completed by his son and accepted as the official history of the shogunate. Another major contributor to scholarship was the statesman and scholar Arai Hakuseki (1657–1725), noted for his careful attention to evidence and willingness to reexamine traditional beliefs.

A different emphasis appeared in *The Great History of Japan* (*Dainihonshi*), sponsored by Mito, a Tokugawa collateral house, and begun in the seventeenth century under the Lord of Mito, Tokugawa Mitsukuni (1628–1700). It was not completed until the twentieth century. Mitsukuni, a grandson of Ieyasu, enlisted the services of Zhu Shunshui (1600–1682), who, faithful to the Ming Dynasty, left his homeland rather than serve China's new masters and was admired by the Japanese for his loyalty as well as scholarship. The resulting history was highly moralistic and exalted the Japanese imperial house. Since the shogun derived his legitimacy from the emperor, there was nothing inherently anti-*bakufu* in this, but its focus on the emperor rather than on the shogun was potentially subversive. Indeed, it later became an emperor-centered source for nationalistic sentiments, and eventually supplied intellectual ammunition for the anti-*bakufu* movement to "restore the emperor," which culminated in the Meiji Restoration of 1868.

Interest in Japan's past often went hand in hand with a new appreciation of native traditions. Ansai had advocated both Confucianism and Shinto, but Kada Azumamaro (1669–1736) urged a return to a Shinto purified of Confucian elements. Rejection of Confucianism and celebration of the native tradition became a defining theme in the nativist thought of the *kokugtaku* ("National Learning") scholars.

Frequently this was linked to a championship of Japanese literature and aesthetics. Thus Tokugawa Mitsukuni commissioned the Shingon priest Keichū (1640–1701), a great philologist, to write a commentary on the Manyoshu, the oldest anthology of Japanese poetry. Motoori Norinaga (1730–1801), a gifted philologist, enjoyed wide influence as a teacher, political adviser, and champion of a supposedly pure Shinto found in antiquity and as yet uncorrupted by Buddhist and Confucian influences. Admitting that there was much that was immoral in the *Tale of Genji*, he wrote the following:

> Genji's conduct is like the lotus flower that grows in muddy water yet blooms with a beauty and fragrance unlike any other in the world. Nothing is said about the water's filth; the monogatari [that is, the *Tale*] concentrates instead on Genji's deep compassion and his awareness of what it means to be moved by things and holds him up as the model of a good man.[16]

Motoori's views on *Genji* remain influential, but his life's work was the study of the *Kojiki,* one of the first histories of Japan that contains accounts of the *kami* (gods/spirits—the *shin* in Shinto). Motoori thought it wrong to try to understand these stories rationally and arrogant not to recognize the limitations of the human intellect. Indeed, the irrationality of the old legends was a sign of their truth, for "who would fabricate such shallow sounding, incredible things?"[17] Supreme among the *kami* was the Sun Goddess, and though she spread her favor everywhere, foremost among the countries of the world was the land of her birth.

Motoori left a dual heritage, academic philology and ideological nativism. Of those who drew on the latter aspect of his thought, the most influential was Hirata Atsutane (1776–1843), whose narrow Japanism proved attractive to many nineteenth- and twentieth-century ultranationalists.

Dutch Learning

As the Dutch were the only Westerners allowed access to Japan (see Chapter 5), it is from them that the Japanese got their information about the West. Their annual audience with the shogun allowed the Japanese to satisfy their curiosity about the exotic:

> He [the shogun, mistaken for the emperor by the Dutch chronicle] order'd us to take off our Cappa, or Cloak, being our Garment of Ceremony, then to stand upright, that he might have a full view of us; again to walk, to stand still, to compliment each other, to dance, to jump, to play the drunkard, to speak broken Japanese, to read Dutch, to paint, to sing, to put our cloaks on and off . . . I join'd to my dance a lovesong in High German. In this manner, and with innumerable such other apish tricks, we must suffer ourselves to contribute to the Emperor's and Court's diversion.[18]

This is from an embassy report of 1691 or 1692. "The Red-haired Barbarians," as the Dutch were commonly known, continued to be the objects of wild rumor. But they also drew the attention of serious scholars after 1720, when the *bakufu* permitted the import of books on all subjects except Christianity. These scholars wrestled with the difficulties of the Dutch language, laboriously made translations, compiled the first dictionaries, and wrote treatises on geography, astronomy, medicine, and other Western subjects. Shiba Kōkan (1738–1818), the first in Japan to produce copper engravings, was fascinated by the ability of Western art to portray objects as they appear to the eye. Arai Hakuseki had earlier recognized the practical value of Western studies, and Shiba valued this as well. For spiritual nourishment such men continued to turn to their own heritage, thus foreshadowing the nineteenth-century formula "Eastern ethics-Western science." Because of *bakufu* policy, they knew little about Western political, philosophical, or religious thought.

By the end of the eighteenth century, there were also scholars of "Dutch Learning" who, alarmed by Western expansionism, discussed political, military, and economic matters at considerable personal risk. Hayashi Shihei (1738–1793) was arrested for defying a *bakufu* prohibition by publishing a book dealing with political issues: he advocated defense preparations against the threat he saw impending from abroad. Honda Toshiaki (1744–1821) looked north and advocated settling Ezo (Hokkaido). He envisioned turning Japan into the England of the East complete with a mercantile empire, but escaped persecution by not publishing his ideas.

Implicit in the views of the scholars of Dutch Learning was dissatisfaction with the Tokugawa seclusion policy, which stood in the way of their learning more about Western civilization and prevented them from traveling overseas. Meanwhile, by stressing the royal line, Mito Confucians and National Learning scholars also helped weaken the *bakufu* ideologically. And even orthodox Confucianism did not really require a shogun or a *bakufu*. Thus, by 1800 there were fissures in the Tokugawa's intellectual, as well as in its political and economic, foundations.

Eighteenth-Century Art and Literature

Genroku was the classic age of popular theater, prints, and haiku, but artists and writers continued to create works in these genres that are often considered to mark another highpoint in cultural history. Notable among the *ukiyo-e* artists was Tōshūsai Sharaku, famous for the psychologically penetrating and bitterly satirical prints of actors he turned out during a ten-month outburst of creativity in 1794. More in keeping with the spirit of the time was Suzuki Harunobu (1724–1770), who excelled in the subtle use of color and the freshness of his young beauties.

Controversial and uneven was the prolific Kitagawa Utamaro (1754–1806), who achieved great popularity with his prints of the ladies of the "floating world" (Figure 4.8).

With the end of the eighteenth century, there was a falling off in the quality of the figure print, but as if in compensation, the landscape print flourished. A master of this art was the "old man mad with painting," Katsushika Hokusai (1760–1849), an eclectic genius. One of his depictions of Mt. Fuji can be seen in Figure 4.9. Less versatile, but at his best producing works imbued with a delicate lyricism, was Andō Hiroshige (1797–1858), who lived to see Commodore Perry arrive in Japan in 1853 (see Chapter 7).

Literature also flourished and equally defies summation. As indicated by Haruo Shirane, it was marked "by a complex fusion of Japanese and Chinese cultures, and by a mixture of popular and elite culture."[19]

Kobayashi Issa (1763–1827) was perhaps the best loved of the later haiku poets. He achieved a wide identification with nature and showed sympathy for even the humblest of animals and insects.

FIGURE 4.8   *A Flirt,* from the series *Ten Studies in Female Physiognomy,* Kitagawa Utamaro. Woodblock print, ink, color, and mica on paper, 37.8 × 25.1 cm. MR. AND MRS. JOHN D. ROCKEFELLER, 3RD COLLECTION OF ASIAN ART 1979.219. ASIA SOCIETY, NEW YORK: PHOTOGRAPH BY LYNTON GARDINER.

> Lean frog,
> don't give up the fight!
> Issa is here![20]

FIGURE 4.9 "Fuji at Torigoe" from *Fugaku Hyokkei*, Hokusai. The instrument shown here is an orrery, a mechanical model of the solar system.

Reform and Its Limits

The underlying discrepancy between official theory and socioeconomic reality was brought home to the *bakufu* in a series of financial crises, some aggravated by poor harvests due to natural causes. Major famines during 1732 to 1733 and again after 1783 brought death and starvation as well as rural uprisings and urban riots highlighting the government's ineptness.

Repeatedly, revenue failed to keep up with government needs. Retrenchment was one standard response. Often, as in the Kyōhō Reforms (1716–1736), a spending cut was seen as morally desirable as well as fiscally necessary. Calls for reduction in government spending were accompanied by admonitions for samurai to revive warrior morality and detailed laws to limit merchant expenditure. More effective was the granting of merchant monopolies in exchange for an annual fee. To make it easier to fill high offices with capable men of low inherited rank, the practice of granting such men permanent high hereditary rank was abandoned in favor of raising their rank and stipends only during their tenure of office.

Among the sources of additional needed revenue were special payments imposed on the *daimyo*, programs of land reclamation, and campaigns to squeeze more taxes out of the peasantry. But in the long run these yielded diminishing returns. The same can be said of the *bakufu*'s attempts to set prices of essential commodities. Some initially successful measures backfired, as when monetary deflation quelled a destructive inflation only to bring on a deflation so severe that it provoked urban riots in 1733.

Later in the century, the *bakufu* made some additions to its reform repertoire as when, under the leadership of Tanuma Okitsugu (1719–1788), it encouraged foreign trade, tried to develop mines, created new monopolies, imposed new merchant licenses, and showed interest in developing Hokkaido. Tanuma, however, was resented for favoring the *bakufu* vis-à-vis the *han*, and his enemies emphasized his corruption. In 1787, food shortages caused by crop failures the previous year led to uprisings throughout Japan and violent rioting in Edo. Tanuma died in disgrace. Whether the *bakufu* was capable of leading the country in new directions remained a question for the future.

Notes

1. Jurgis Elisonas, "The Inseparable Trinity: Japan's Relation with China and Korea," in John W. Hall, ed., *The Cambridge History of Japan,* vol. 4, *Early Modern Japan* (New York, NY: Cambridge Univ. Press, 1991), p. 271.

2. Harold Bolitho, *Treasures Among Men: The Fudai Daimyo in Tokugawa Japan* (New Haven, CT: Yale Univ. Press, 1974), p. 17.

3. Conrad Totman, *Early Modern Japan* (Berkeley, CA: Univ. of California Press, 1993), p. 229.

4. Eiko Ikegami, *The Taming of the Samurai: Honorific Individualism and the Making of Modern Japan* (Cambridge, MA: Harvard Univ. Press, 1995), p. 116.

5. Ronald P. Dore, *Education in Tokugawa Japan* (Berkeley, CA: Univ. of California Press, 1965), p. 151.

6. Robert Treat Paine and Alexander Soper, *The Art and Architecture of Japan* (Baltimore, MD: Penguin Books, 1955), p. 274.

7. Elise Grilli, *The Art of the Japanese Screen* (Tokyo, Japan and New York, NY: John Weatherhill, 1970), pp. 111–12.

8. Attributed to Chikamatsu by his friend Hozumi Ikan. Hozumi's account of Chikamatsu's views has been translated by Donald Keene as "Chikamatsu on the Art of The Puppet Stage," in Donald Keene, ed., *Anthology of Japanese Literature* (New York, NY: Grove Press, 1955), p. 389.

9. Ryusaku Tsunoda, W. Theodore de Bary, and Donald Keene, comps., *Sources of Japanese Tradition* (New York, NY: Columbia Univ. Press, 1958), p. 454.

10. Makoto Ueda, *Matsuo Bashō* (New York, NY: Twayne, 1970), p. 53.

11. Calvin French, *The Poet-Painters: Buson and His Followers,* exhibition catalog (Ann Arbor, MI: Univ. of Michigan Museum of Art, 1974), p. 132.

12. See Kate Wildman Nakai, "The Naturalization of Confucianism in Tokugawa Japan: The

Problem of Sinocentrism," *Harvard Journal of Asiatic Studies,* 40 (1980), pp. 157–99.

13. Ryusaku Tsunoda et al., *Sources of Japanese Tradition* (New York, NY: Columbia Univ. Press, 1958), p. 349.

14. Ibid., p. 419.

15. Ibid., p. 524.

16. Kate Wildman Nakai, "Chinese Ritual and Japanese Identity in Tokugawa Confucianism," in Benjamin A. Elman, John B. Duncan, and Herman Ooms, eds., *Rethinking Confucianism: Past and Present in China, Japan, Korea, and Vietnam* (Los Angeles, CA: UCLA Asian Pacific Monograph Series, Univ. of California, 2002), p. 272.

17. Haruo Shirane, ed., *Early Modern Japanese Literature: An Anthology, 1600–1900,* trans. Thomas Harper (New York, NY: Columbia Univ. Press, 2002), pp. 624–25.

18. E. Kaempfer, quoted in Donald Keene, *The Japanese Discovery of Europe* (Stanford, CA: Stanford Univ. Press, 1969), p. 4.

19. Shirane, *Early Modern Japanese Literature,* p. 19.

20. Harold G. Henderson, *An Introduction to Haiku,* (New York, NY: Doubleday, 1958), p. 133.

5

East Asia and Modern Europe: First Encounters

Key Dates

The story of the early contacts between post-Renaissance Europe and East Asia can be conceived as an overture setting the tone, introducing basic themes, and establishing the harmonics of the history to come. Between 1405 and 1433 China's Ming dynasty had sent maritime expeditions that reached as far as the East Coast of Africa but were abandoned as costly displays of imperial splendor. That left the initiative for world exploration to the Europeans motivated by prospects of economic gain and religious zeal. The general failure of the early intermediaries to build frameworks of mutual understanding made it all the harder to do so later when East Asia had to deal with a Europe transformed by the French and Industrial Revolutions.

The Portuguese in East Asia

The pioneers of European global expansion were the Portuguese, who reached India in 1498, China in 1514, and Japan in 1543. Having wrested control of the seas from their Arab economic, religious, and political rivals, they established their Asian headquarters in 1510 at Goa, a small island off the coast of West India. In 1511 they captured Malacca, a vital center for the lucrative spice trade located on the straits separating the Malay Peninsula from Sumatra (Figure 5.1). The desire to break the spice-trade monopoly of the Arab and Venetian middlemen supplied the

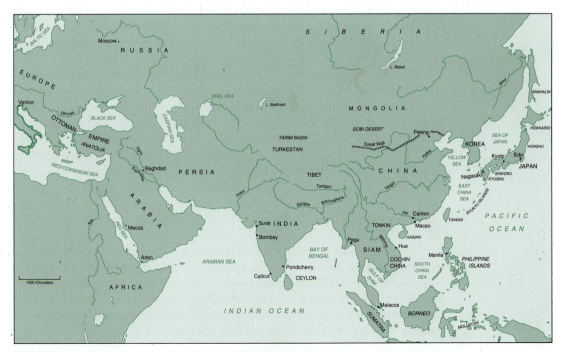

FIGURE 5.1 Eastern Europe and Asia in the 16th and 17th centuries.

economic motive for the Portuguese. Spices were highly valuable relative to their bulk and weight. Easily transported and fetching a high price, they formed an attractive cargo. And there was an assured market for them in Europe, where they added flavor to an otherwise dull diet and made meat palatable in an age when animals were slaughtered in the fall for want of sufficient fodder to sustain them through the winter. They were also used in medicine and religious ceremonies.

Prospects for trade were hampered, however, by the absence of any European commodities that could be marketed in Asia. Lacking access to silver, the Portuguese initially financed themselves by a mixture of trade and piracy, taking advantage of their superior ships, weaponry, and seamanship. They derived income from transporting goods from one Asian country to another: Southeast Asian spices to China, Chinese silk to Japan, and Japanese silver to China. They used their profits from this trade to purchase spices and other products for European markets. But before this trade could prosper, they had to secure entry into China and Japan. This posed problems quite different from those they had encountered in seizing a small island off the coast of politically divided India or in driving the Arabs from Malacca.

In China the Portuguese got off to a bad start. Not waiting for official permission to trade, they engaged in illegal commerce and even built a fort on Lintin Island, located at the mouth of the river that connects Canton to the sea. Their unruly behavior did not endear them to the Ming authorities, and served to confirm that these "ocean devils" were a new kind of barbarian. The outrageous behavior of the Portuguese traders was further embellished by the Chinese imagination. When the Portuguese bought kidnapped Chinese children as slaves, the Chinese concluded that their purpose was to eat them. The Chinese long continued in the firm belief that they were dealing with barbarous child-eaters. More than just a popular rumor held by the ignorant, this belief found its way into the official history of the Ming dynasty.

The first Portuguese envoy to China failed to obtain commercial concessions and later ended his life in a Cantonese prison. It was an inauspicious beginning. But the Portuguese would not leave, and their superiority on the seas made it impossible for the Chinese to drive them out. In 1557 an arrangement was reached permitting the Portuguese to establish themselves in Macao in exchange for an annual payment. There the Portuguese were in control, although legally the territory remained under Chinese jurisdiction until Macao was ceded to Portugal in 1887.

The Jesuits in Japan

Trade and booty were not the only objectives of the Europeans who ventured into Asian waters. Missionary work was also important: mid-sixteenth-century Goa boasted some 80 churches and convents. From the beginning, the missionary impulse provided a strong incentive as well as religious sanction for European expansion. It was the missionary, rather than the trader, who served as prime intermediary between the civilizations of East Asia and the West from the sixteenth century until the twentieth century.

Among the early missionaries, the great pioneers were the Jesuits, members of the Society of Jesus. Founded in 1540, this tightly disciplined religious order formed the vanguard of the Catholic Counter-Reformation. They were the "cavalry of the church," prepared to battle the Protestant heretics in Europe and the heathen in the world beyond. Along with its stress on martial discipline and intensive religious training, the Society was noted for its insistence on intellectual vigor and depth of learning. The latter included secular as well as sacred studies, and the ideal Jesuit was as learned as he was disciplined and devout.

Thanks to the Jesuits, Europeans were no longer dependant on accounts such as that of Marco Polo (1254–1324) to learn about East Asia. Jesuit accounts of Chinese society and thought were to influence such major thinkers as Leibniz (1646–1716) and Voltaire (1604–1778).

In 1549, less than 10 years after the founding of the Jesuit order, St. Francis Xavier (1506–1552), one of the original members of the Society, landed on Kyushu. This was just six years after the Japanese had first encountered Europeans in the form of shipwrecked Portuguese who had landed on the island of Tanegashima. Xavier was well received and soon established relations with important men in Kyushu. First impressions on both sides were favorable. The Japanese were impressed by the strong character and dignified bearing of the European priests. The Jesuit combination of martial pride, stern self-discipline, and religious piety fitted well with the ethos of sixteenth-century Japan. Even the Christian religion was not completely strange.

Initially Christianity, brought to Japan from Goa, seemed like just another type of Buddhism. It was similar in some of its ceremonies, and it was difficult for the early priests to convey the subtleties of theology. For example, explaining the difference between God and the cosmic Buddha, or distinguishing Paradise from the Buddhist Pure Land was complicated. At last the Jesuit fathers concluded that the devil, in all of his malicious cleverness, had deliberately fashioned Buddhism to resemble the true faith so as to confound and confuse the people.

The initial meeting of the Jesuits and the Japanese was facilitated by similarities in their feudal backgrounds. In Japan, the Europeans found a society that resembled their own far more than did any other outside Europe. "The people," wrote Alessandro Valignano (1539–1606), "are all white, courteous and highly civilized, so much so that they surpass all the other known races of the world."[1] Only the Chinese were to receive similar praise—and, indeed, to be regarded as "white." Donald Lach has summarized the qualities the Jesuits found to admire in the Japanese: "their courtesy, dignity, endurance, frugality, equanimity, industriousness, sagaciousness, cleanliness, simplicity, discipline, and rationality."[2] The Jesuits, however, were also appalled by some Japanese characteristics besides the obvious paganism, including the prevalence of sodomy among the military aristocracy and the monks. They criticized the Japanese propensity for suicide and also found fault with the "disloyalty of vassal to master, their dissimulation, ambiguity, and lack of openness in their dealings, their bellicose nature, their inhuman treatment of enemies and unwanted children, their failure to respect the rule of law, and finally their unwillingness to give up the system of concubinage."[3]

Nevertheless, the similarities between Japanese culture and their own gave the Jesuits high hopes for the success of their mission.

In their everyday behavior the Jesuits tried to win acceptance by adapting themselves to local manners and customs, as long as these did not run counter to their own creed. "Thus," Valignano observed, "we who come hither from Europe find ourselves as veritable children who have to learn to eat, sit, converse, dress, act politely, and so on . . . ."[4] They learned how to squat Japanese style, learned to employ the Japanese language with its various levels of politeness, and mastered the art of tea—the Jesuit dwelling was usually equipped with a tea room so that their guests could be properly entertained. C. R. Boxer has pointed out that the Christian monks came from a land with rather different standards of personal cleanliness: "Physical dirt and religious poverty tended to be closely associated in Catholic Europe where lice were regarded as the inseparable companions of monks and soldiers."[5] But in Japan the devoted monks even learned to wash, a major concession to Japanese sensibilities. Still there were limits: Valignano could not bring himself to endorse the Japanese custom of taking a hot bath every day. That would really be going too far in his eyes.

The Jesuit fathers' strategy of working from the top down required them to pay careful attention to the niceties of etiquette. They hoped to transform Japan into a Christian land by first converting the rulers and then allowing the faith to seep down to the populace at large. The purpose of their labors was not to Europeanize Japan or China, but to save souls. They realized that the enthusiastic support of the ruling authority would be an invaluable asset, while without at least a ruler's tacit approval they could do nothing.

This approach met with considerable success in Kyushu, where they converted important local lords, who ordered their people to adopt the foreign faith. Although there were numerous genuine conversions, some lords simply saw the light of commerce and adopted a Christian stance in hopes of attracting Portuguese trade to their ports. At least once, when the great Portuguese ship did not appear, the local *daimyo* promptly turned his back on the new faith. The Jesuits themselves became involved in this trade and in politics. For seven years they even held the overlordship of Nagasaki, granted to them by a Christian lord.

Xavier and the monks who came after him realized that real progress for their mission depended on the will of the central government as well as that of local Kyushu lords. Xavier's initial trip to Kyoto came at an unpropitious time—the city was in disorder. But Nobunaga (1532–1584), the first of Japan's three great unifiers after a century of division, soon became a friend of the Jesuits. He was attracted by their character and his interest in hearing about foreign lands, and perhaps he was also happy to talk with someone not part of the hierarchical order that he himself headed. This personal predilection coincided nicely with reasons of state. It was consistent with his hostility toward the Buddhist orders and with his desire to keep the trading ships coming in. Hideyoshi (1536–1598), Nobunaga's successor, was at first similarly well disposed toward the foreign religion. He liked dressing up in Portuguese clothes, complete with rosary, and once said that the only thing that kept him from converting was the Christian insistence on monogamy.

The political and economic success of the Jesuits helped the spread of Christianity. However, power, or the semblance of power, always entails risks. There was a danger that the ruler might perceive the activities of the monks not as assets bolstering his own position but as liabilities. A portent of future disaster came in 1587 when Hideyoshi issued an order expelling the monks. Eager to encourage trade and not really feeling seriously threatened, he did not enforce the decree, but it foreshadowed the persecutions that were to begin in earnest 27 years later.

Meanwhile, there was a surge of popularity for things Western, for instance, "Southern Barbarian Screens," showing the giant black ships of the foreigners and the foreigners themselves (Figure 5.2). Other scenes, based on paintings from Europe, depicted various barbarian topics: the battle of Lepanto, an Italian court, European cities, maps of the world, not to mention religious subjects. While some artists painted European subjects Japanese style, others experimented with Western perspective and techniques of shading to produce three-dimensional effects. Nor were Western motifs limited to painting. Western symbols were widely used in decoration: a cross on a bowl, a few words of Latin on a saddle, and so forth.

FIGURE 5.2   Detail from a "Southern Barbarian" (Namban) screen. 17th century. Pair of six-panel folding screens. By the time this screen was painted, the trade with the "southern barbarians" was limited to the Dutch, but interest in the giant ships and their exotic passengers did not abate. Ink and gold on paper.

The Impact of Other Europeans

Despite the order of 1587, Western influences continued to enter Japan. The situation was further complicated when the Portuguese were followed by other Europeans. Foremost were the Dutch, who established themselves in what is today Indonesia, which was then a source of excellent spices. However, the Spanish, whose conquest of the Philippines (named after Philip II) was completed in 1571, preceded the Dutch in Japan. To the Japanese, Manila presented a new source of profitable trade, but the colonization of the Philippines also alerted them to the imperialist ambitions of the Europeans and revealed connections between Christian evangelism and colonialism. In contrast, when Dutch and English Protestants arrived in the early 1600s, there were finally Europeans in Japan who broke the link between trade and missionary activity, and they did their best to fan Japanese suspicions of their Catholic rivals. Now, as later, the "West" did not represent a single interest nor did it speak with a single voice.

The Spanish empire differed from that of Portugal in kind as it did in scale. Whereas the Portuguese maintained themselves by the proceeds from the inter-Asia trade, the Spanish commanded the precious metals of the New World, including the silver to pay for Chinese silks, which reached China through Manila. In its heyday, this silver financed Ming and Qing prosperity (see Chapter 2). However, the immediate effect on Japan of the Spaniards' arrival was to complicate the situation for the Jesuits. The Spanish were as committed to the missionary enterprise as the Portuguese, but they patronized Franciscan monks rather than Jesuits. The first Franciscan arrived in Japan from Manila in 1587. Much less well informed about conditions in Japan than the Jesuits, the Franciscans were less discreet. They rejected the Jesuit strategy of working from the top down, and instead of associating with the elite, worked among the poor and forgotten, the sick and miserable, those at the very bottom of society. The Jesuits did not disguise their contempt for the ignorance and poverty of the Franciscans, the "crazy friars" (*fraile idiotas*) as they called them, and these sentiments were heartily reciprocated by the friars, who scoffed at Jesuit pretensions.

The "Closing" of Japan

It was an omen of things to come when, in 1597, Hideyoshi crucified six Franciscan missionaries and 18 of their Japanese converts after the navigator of a Spanish ship driven ashore in Japan reportedly boasted about the power and ambitions of his king. Like Nobunaga and Hideyoshi, Tokugawa Ieyasu, the last of Japan's three unifiers, was at first friendly to the Christians but later turned against them. In 1606 Christianity was declared illegal, and in 1614 he undertook a serious campaign to expel the missionaries.

By 1614 there were over 300,000 converts in Japan. The destruction of Christianity was long and painful. Tortures, such as hanging a man upside down with his head in a pit filled with excrement, were used to induce people to renounce their faith. Before it was all over, there were more than 3,000 recognized as martyrs by the Vatican, of whom fewer than 70 were Europeans. Others died without achieving martyrdom. From 1637 to 1638 there was a rebellion in Shimabara, near Nagasaki, against a lord who combined merciless taxation with cruel suppression of Christianity. Fought under banners on which Christian slogans were written in Portuguese, and led by *rōnin*, it was a Christian version of the rural uprisings characteristic of the century of warfare before Nobunaga. In its suppression, some 37,000 Christians lost their lives.

Persuasion as well as violence was employed in the campaign against Christianity. Opponents of Christian dogma argued that the idea of a personal creator was absurd and asked why, if God were both omnipotent and good, he should have tempted Adam and Eve and devised eternal punishment in Hell for non-Christians even though they led exemplary lives. According to Christian teaching, even the sage emperors Yao and Shun would end in Hell. The First Commandment was attacked as leading to disobedience of parents and lord; a loyal retainer should accompany his lord even into Hell.

Such arguments suggest that the Japanese saw Christianity as potentially subversive of the political order and basic social structure, because it challenged accepted values and beliefs and demanded a radical reappraisal of long-revered traditions. Its association with European expansionism posed a threat from abroad, and, as exemplified by the Shimabara Rebellion, it also harbored the seeds of radical disruption at home. Thus, the motivation for the government's suppression of Christianity was secular. The government was not worried over the state of its subjects' souls, but it was determined to wipe out a dangerous doctrine.

New restrictions followed. The Spaniards were expelled in 1624, one year after the English had left voluntarily. In 1630, the government forbade Japanese from going (or returning from) overseas and from building ships capable of long voyages. The Portuguese were expelled after the Shimabara Rebellion on the grounds of complicity with that uprising. When they sent an embassy in 1640, its members were executed. The only Europeans left were the Dutch (Figure 5.3), who as we saw in Chapter 4, were willing to do just about anything for trade. They kept other Europeans from trying their luck in Japan until the English and Russians challenged Dutch naval supremacy in the late eighteenth and early nineteenth centuries. In 1641, the Dutch were moved to a tiny artificial island of Deshima in Nagasaki Harbor, where they were virtually confined as in a prison. The annual Dutch vessel to Deshima was all that remained of Japan's contact with Europe, but it sufficed to spark the "Dutch Learning" discussed in Chapter 4.

Japan's "closing" was far from complete. Trade and diplomatic contacts with Korea and the Ryukyu Islands continued to provide Japan a window to the rest of the world. Japan refused to participate in the Qing tribute system, but this did not prevent an annual average of 26 Chinese ships from coming to Nagasaki or Chinese traders settling there.

FIGURE 5.3 *A Dutch Dinner Party.* Prints such as this satisfied the public's curiosity about the strange customs of the Westerners—and may or may not have been accurate portrayals. Color print, 22 × 33 cm.

RIJKSMUSEUM VOOR VOLKENKUNDE NATIONAL MUSEUM OF ETHNOLOGY, LEIDEN, THE NETHERLANDS (5824-6).

The Jesuits in Vietnam

As elsewhere, the first Europeans to arrive in Vietnam were Portuguese adventurers and traders. In 1525 they established a trading center at Hoi An, which attracted a community of Japanese and Chinese merchants and developed into a thriving international port. Although the Portuguese first brought Dominicans to Vietnam, the most lasting impact was made by Father Alexander de Rhodes, the Jesuit who developed a phonetic script for Vietnamese (see Chapter 1). Born into a Portuguese family in Avignon, then under papal rule, he was well connected in Paris and Rome.

The Jesuit activities in China, Japan, and Vietnam were closely linked. Rhodes was originally bound for Japan. When staying in Japan was no longer possible, he was transferred to Vietnam after spending a year in Macao. The account of his travels provides a good reminder of the hazards of the voyage from Europe to and within East Asia, and of the dedication and courage demanded of these hardy travelers, who were sustained by faith in their sacred mission and obeyed the will of a God who would not abandon them. Rhodes attributed narrow escapes at sea to the magical efficacy of his most treasured possession, a hair of the Virgin.

By the time Rhodes arrived in Vietnam in 1624, a church had already existed in Danang for nine years, founded by a Jesuit trained in Macao. Like his confreres in Japan, Rhodes was enthusiastic about the people and impressed with the steadfast faith of the converted. His account also includes details which might otherwise have gone unrecorded, such as what happened to a woman caught in adultery:

> The punishment inflicted on her is to lead her into a field; she is laid on the ground completely bound; an elephant is commanded to throw her into the air with his trunk, to catch her on his tusks, and finally trample her underfoot.[6]

Control over Vietnam at this time was divided between the Trinh lords in the north and the Nguyen in what is now central Vietnam but then constituted Vietnam's south (see Chapter 6). Although the Jesuits sought to work from the top down, and did convert a Nguyen princess, government policy under both the Nguyen and the Trinh vacillated from tolerance—often motivated by desire for trade and military technology—to suppression, lax at times but at others escalating to outright persecution, as when two Vietnamese catechists were executed in 1645.

Most of the time Rhodes himself had to work clandestinely, traveling and meeting the faithful at night. Several times he was expelled, but managed to smuggle himself back. Among those converted by Rhodes were Japanese merchants residing in Hoi An, many of their Vietnamese wives, and their headman (governor). By 1640 there were a reported 39,000 converts in central Vietnam and 82,000 in the north.

In 1658, the French, disregarding Portuguese objections that Vietnam lay within the sphere the Vatican had assigned to them for missionary work, sponsored the Société de Mission Etrangère. Two years later this body sent out its first French priest, who opened a seminary in Ayutthaya (Thailand) as part of an ongoing effort to foster development of a native clergy. In 1664, the French showed their interest in developing trade with the area by founding the Compagnie des Indes de l'Indochine, chartered to foster French commerce. Thus, the French strengthened their early presence and laid foundations for what was to become French Indochina.

The Jesuits in China

Xavier had hoped to begin the work in China himself, considering this not only a great project in itself but also a major step in the Christianization of Japan, providing an answer to the question he was constantly asked there: "If yours is the true faith why have not the Chinese, from whom comes all wisdom, heard of it?"[7] Xavier died before he could reach his goal, and three further Jesuit attempts to enter China also failed. Then Valignano established a special training center in Macao so that missionaries could study the Chinese language and culture in preparation for work in China. As elsewhere, it was Jesuit policy in China to concentrate on gaining the support and, if possible, the conversion of the upper classes. To this end, they once more accommodated themselves as best as possible to native sensibilities and traditions.

Again, the strong character and attractive personalities of the first missionaries were of great importance in gaining them entry. The outstanding pioneer was Matteo Ricci (1551–1610). A student of law, mathematics, and science, he also knew a good deal about cartography and practical mechanics. Once in the East, he was able to master the Chinese language and the classics. Slowly Ricci made himself known in Chinese officialdom, impressing scholars and officials with his knowledge and his prodigious memory. At last in 1601, after 18 strenuous years, Ricci was received in an imperial audience and won permission for himself and his colleagues to reside in the capital. (By this time they had discarded the Buddhist robes worn by Jesuits in Japan and had adopted the gowns of Confucian scholars as more acceptable to the Chinese.) In Beijing, Ricci converted a number of prominent men. By the time Ricci died in 1610, the mission was well established in the capital and accepted by the government. Ricci's body was laid to rest in a plot donated by the emperor.

During the period when the Japanese were persecuting Christians with increasing ferocity, the Jesuits in China labored fruitfully, building on the foundations laid by Ricci. They were particularly successful in demonstrating the superior accuracy of European astronomical predictions. Thereby they succeeded in displacing their Muslim and Chinese competitors, and established themselves in the Bureau of Astronomy, an important and prestigious office. Jesuit gains in this area were solidified by the work of Adam Schall von Bell (1591–1666), a German Jesuit who was a trained astronomer and served as chief government astronomer in Beijing. Schall von Bell also assisted in casting cannon for the Ming, although it did not save the dynasty.

The Jesuits made some notable converts among the literati, particularly during the troubled years of the declining Ming. Most notable was Xu Guangqi (Paul Hsu, 1562–1633), who translated Euclid's *Elements* and other works on mathematics, hydraulics, astronomy, and geography, making him the first Chinese translator of European books. With the help of such men, Western science and geography were made available to China, but European influence remained limited. When Li Zhi (1527–1602), one of the most forceful and independent Late Ming thinkers, met Ricci, he was impressed with the Jesuit's personality but saw no merit in his proselytizing mission. The triumph of the Manchus did not seriously disrupt Jesuit activity. Schall von Bell was retained by the new dynasty as their astronomer. He was followed by the Belgian Jesuit, Ferdinand Verbiest (1633–1688), the last of the trio of great and learned missionary fathers. Verbiest, like Schall von Bell, cast cannon and in other ways won the favor of Kangxi. A good account of Jesuit activities at court comes from the emperor's own brush:

> With Verbiest I had examined each stage of the forging of cannons, and made him build a water fountain that operated in conjunction with an organ, and erect a windmill in the court; with the new group . . . I worked on clocks and mechanics. Pereira taught me to play the tune "Puyanzhou" on the harpsichord and the structure of the eight-notescale, Pedrini

taught my sons musical theory, and Gheradini painted portraits at the Court. I also learned to calculate the weight and volume of spheres, cubes, and cones. . . .[8]

The emperor accepted the Jesuits' science with alacrity and took their quinine for the sake of his health. He also discussed religion with them, but here they were less successful: "I had asked Verbiest why God had not forgiven his son without making him die, but though he had tried hard to answer I had not understood him."[9] In China, as in Japan, the fathers found it most difficult to explain the central tenets of their faith to people with very different ideas about the nature of the universe and of the divine.

The high point for early Catholicism in China came in the middle years of Kangxi's reign, but by 1700 there were no more than 300,000 Christians in China, roughly the same number as in much smaller Japan a century earlier. In both cases the missionaries were there on sufferance, dependent on the good will of the authorities. And in China, as earlier in Japan, divisions between the Europeans themselves strongly contributed to their undoing.

The Rites Controversy

The controversy that brought an end to the missionary activity in China centered on the Jesuit policy of accommodation, which was opposed by rival orders, particularly and vigorously by the Dominicans. It revolved around the question of the proper attitude a Christian should adopt toward Confucian doctrines and practices. A similar dispute also undermined the Jesuits in Vietnam but not in Japan, where Catholic fathers of all orders agreed in their condemnation of Buddhism and Shinto and in their absolute refusal to allow their converts to have anything to do with such heathen religions.

In China, however, the basic strategy used by Ricci and followed by his successors was to accept the teachings of Confucius, "the prince of philosophers." They argued that they had come not to destroy Confucius, but to make his teachings complete, capping his doctrines with the truths of revealed religion. Like Chinese thinkers intent on using Confucius in new ways, the Jesuits also discarded and condemned previous interpretations and commentaries on the classics. They attacked Neo-Confucianism and developed new theories of their own. In their enthusiasm for the classics, the Jesuits turned Confucius into a religious teacher. Some members of the order went as far as to trace the origin of the Chinese people to the eldest son of Noah. The most extreme even claimed to find Christian prophecies in the *Classic of Changes*. Meanwhile, the Dominicans held that the ancient Chinese were atheists, and argued against the Jesuit portrayal of Confucius as a deist. The resulting literature greatly influenced Western understanding of Chinese philosophy. At its best, the debate was a serious effort by Europeans to understand Chinese thought in what they believed to be universally valid terms.

The status of Confucius and the acceptability of the classics were major issues for missionaries operating in a society dominated by the Confucian examination system. Even more troublesome, however, was the related problem posed by Confucian observances. Were the ceremonies in veneration of Confucius, held in the temples of Confucius throughout the land, acts of religious devotion and therefore anathema to a Christian? Or were they social and political, secular expressions of respect for China's greatest teacher? Even more important was the status of the rites performed by every family in front of the tablets representing its ancestors. Was this worshiping of the departed spirits and thus the most iniquitous idolatry? Or did these acts of commemoration for one's forebears merely convey a deep sense of filial piety? Were the two kinds of ceremonials civic and moral in nature, or were they religious, and therefore sacrilegious? Consistent with their stand on Confucianism, the Jesuits claimed the ceremonies were nonreligious and therefore permissible. The Dominicans disagreed.

The issue was fiercely debated because much was at stake. Theology aside, it is easy to see the practical reasons for the Jesuit standpoint. To exclude Christians from performing the ceremonies for Confucius would be to exclude them from participation in Chinese political life. Worse still, to prohibit the ritual veneration of ancestors would not only deprive Chinese Christians of their sense of family but also make them appear as unfilial, immoral monsters in the eyes of their non-Christian fellows. If Christianity rejected the classics and advocated this kind of nonconformist behavior, it would be turned into a religion subversive of the Chinese State and society. Persecuted and condemned, Christianity would be unable to reach many souls, who would thus be deprived of their chance for salvation.

However, the Dominicans could muster strong counterarguments. Why should a church that condemned Protestant Christianity condone Confucian Christianity? The issue was not the acceptability of Christianity to the Chinese, but whether the salvation of souls would be fatally jeopardized by tolerating false Confucian doctrines. In their eyes, nothing could be allowed to interfere with the Christian's sacred duty to maintain the purity of the faith.

The Decline of Christianity in China

The question 'When does Christianity cease to be Christianity?' was to reappear in the nineteenth century and is not all that different from the question, 'When does Marxism cease to be Marxism?' which agitated some thinkers in the twentieth century. Such questions are never easy to resolve, and perhaps only true believers need to grapple with them. However, the church had a source of authority that could rule on what was acceptable—the papacy. The process of reaching a decision was complicated and involved. Eventually, though, the outcome went against the Jesuits. In 1704 the pope condemned Chinese rituals, and in 1742 a decree was issued that settled all points against the Jesuits. This remained the position of the Catholic Church until 1939. Grand and powerful emperors like Kangxi, however, resented Rome's claim of authority over their subjects, and they saw no reason to abide by the papal judgment. They naturally favored the Jesuit point of view. In the end, the pope would send only those missionaries the emperor of China would not accept.

Some missionaries remained in China after the break, including the Jesuit Giuseppe Castiglione, who served as court painter for half a century, from 1715 to 1766. Among other things, he designed a miniature Versailles for the Summer Palace, destroyed in the nineteenth century. Michael Sullivan has described his fusion of artistic traditions as a "synthetic style in which with taste and skill and the utmost discretion, Western perspective and shading, with even an occasional hint of chiaroscuro, were blended to give an added touch of realism to painting otherwise entirely Chinese in manner."[10] Figure 5.4 shows a painting in the European manner done at the Chinese court. Just as Louis XV of France sometimes amused himself by having his courtiers and their ladies assume Chinese dress, the Qing emperor Qianlong enjoyed exotic Western costume on occasion. Meanwhile Western perspective appeared in color prints intended for a broad popular market.

Regardless of the Rites Controversy, the Christians also had opponents in China motivated by the usual combination of self-interest and conviction. There was no Chinese counterpart to the town of Nagasaki or to the Dutch on Deshima island. Instead, Canton and the surrounding area, the part of China most exposed to the Europeans, already at this time took a negative view of the foreigners. Christianity was proscribed in 1724. Some churches were seized, and other acts of persecution occurred, but the suppression of Christianity was not as thorough as it had been in Japan. This was probably because there was no Chinese equivalent to the Shimabara Rebellion—at least not yet. Not until the nineteenth century did the potential of Christianity as an ideology for peasant rebellion become evident in China. By the end of the eighteenth century, the number of Chinese converts had been reduced to about half what it had been at the beginning of the century. Western contact did influence some areas of intellectual life, such as astronomy and cartography, but remained that peripheral to the mainstream of Chinese intellectual life. There was

FIGURE 5.4 A lady's portrait in Western-style costume (inspired by Daiyu). Anonymous, mid-18th century.

Collection of the Palace Museum, Beijing, China.

no revolution in thought or art. Those of the Qing elite who came in touch with things Western rarely progressed much beyond the appreciation of European exotica, such as clocks and other mechanical devices. Ricci himself lived on as the patron saint of clockmakers. The influence was much stronger in the other direction, for the Jesuit reports on China were well received in Europe and helped create the image of an ideal China, which the philosophers of the European Enlightenment cherished.

A major difference between the course of events in China and Japan was that in China trade considerations did not influence government decisions concerning missionary policies.

Trade with the West and the Canton System

After 1683, the Qing recognized that flourishing maritime trade with Southeast Asia was of great economic importance to coastal communities and posed no security problems for the empire, and thus the Qing left its management to local authorities. Though Kangxi instituted some restrictions on foreigners trading in the Chinese market, it was Qianlong who restricted them to Canton, where a special area was set aside for the warehouses (called "factories") of the foreign traders, who were allowed to reside there but not to bring their wives and settle down (Figure 5.5).

FIGURE 5.5 The Canton waterfront, c. 1760. Artist unknown. One of four panels creating a panorama of the waterfront. Notice the flags of Western nations in front of their respective warehouses. Gouache on silk, 47.7 × 73.7 cm.

PHOTOGRAPH COURTESY PEABODY ESSEX MUSEUM, SALEM, MASSACHUSETTS.

There were other restrictions under this Canton System, which lasted from 1760 to 1842. In all transactions, foreign traders were required to deal with a group of Chinese merchants who had been granted a monopoly on foreign trade. These merchants belonged to the Cohong, an association of firms (*hong*) established for that purpose. The Cohong could be composed of a maximum of 13 *hong*, although in practice there were only seven or eight *hong*, supervised by an imperial official who usually squeezed a good deal of personal profit out of his position. Each foreign ship was placed under the responsibility of a particular *hong*, which handled commercial matters, ensured that duties were paid, and guaranteed that the foreigners conducted themselves properly.

Under this system, the foreigners were not granted direct access to Chinese officials, nor were there any provisions for government-to-government relations. On the British side, the prime agent was the East India Company, which was under government charter. It enjoyed a monopoly of trade between England and China, and it governed much of India—an arrangement not challenged until the nineteenth century, when the idea and forces of free trade triumphed.

The Qing taxed foreign maritime trade more heavily than that of Chinese ships, but both were administered separately from the tributary system of conducting foreign relations. Consequently, when Macartney, in 1793—and later Lord Amherst in 1816—came to China to try to expand trade and open European-style diplomatic relations, he faced a well-established dynastic practice that the Qing court saw no reason to change. The system continued to operate until China faced a Europe that could no longer be contained.

Korea has not figured in our account because it was only marginally involved. Koreans first learned of Christianity through a Chinese book written by Matteo Ricci. This aroused keen interest among a small group of Korean scholars, who subsequently persuaded the son of the tribute envoy to Beijing to accompany the mission and learn more. Converted in Beijing, he returned with books, crucifixes, and images, and in 1784 organized a lay congregation. Ten years later they obtained the services of a Chinese priest, but he was put to death in 1801 by the government, intent on wiping out what it considered a dangerous heresy. Thus, Korea's initial encounter with Christianity was a story of enthusiasm and suppression.

Along with enthusiastic participation in the trade opportunities offered by the Chinese tributary system, Koreans continued to trade with Japan regardless of political changes there. Like China and Japan, Korea used silver as an ultimate standard of value and to store wealth. However, it did not participate directly in world trade, nor did a Korean port serve as an international transshipment site as Manila and Hoi An did. Therefore, Korea was affected only indirectly by the world silver flow.

Notes

1. Quoted in C. R. Boxer, *The Christian Century in Japan* (Berkeley, CA: Univ. of California Press, 1951), p. 74.

2. Donald F. Lach, *Asia in the Making of Europe*, vol. 1, *The Century of Discovery* (Chicago, IL: Univ. of Chicago Press, 1965), p. 728.

3. Ibid.

4. Quoted in Boxer, *The Christian Century in Japan,* p. 214.

5. Boxer, *The Christian Century.*

6. *Rhodes of Viet Nam: The Travels and Missions of Father Alexander de Rhodes in China and Other Kingdoms of the Orient,* trans. by Solange Hertz (Westminster, MD: The Newman Press, 1966), p. 61.

7. A. H. Rowbotham, *Missionary and Mandarin* (Berkeley, CA: Univ. of California Press, 1942), p. 46.

8. Quoted in Jonathan Spence, *Emperor of China* (New York, NY: Alfred A. Knopf, 1974), pp. 72–73.

9. Ibid., p. 84.

10. Michael Sullivan, *The Meeting of Eastern and Western Art* (New York, NY: New York Graphic Society, 1973), pp. 60–67.

Part Two

The Nineteenth Century

In the nineteenth century the whole world came to feel the might of Europe, where intellectual, political, and economic forces at work since the Renaissance were producing unprecedented wealth and power. This process was accelerated in the late eighteenth century by the Industrial and French Revolutions, gaining momentum with the emergence of new technologies, new appetites, new ideas, new values, and new problems setting off tremors that were to reverberate throughout the globe. It was a tumultuous period of intense economic competition, stringent national rivalries, bitter class conflicts, and sharp clashes between old and new values and ideas. Yet few Europeans questioned the superiority—moral, intellectual, economic, or political—of their civilization or, indeed, of their century.

A major development was the nation-state, which won unprecedented and enthusiastic acceptance as the "natural" and uniquely legitimate political entity worthy of being the primary object of political loyalty even though what constitutes a "nation" remained ill defined. The nation-states were able to mobilize human and natural resources to an unprecedented degree, as demonstrated in World War I, which ended Europe's global predominance while destroying Czarist Russia and Austro-Hungary, Europe's last old-style multinational empires.

Nineteenth-century nationalism prompted European patriots to revolt against foreign rule, and it also glorified commercial, military, and cultural expansion abroad. Reflecting the accelerating pace of change in East Asia as in Europe, we devote two chapters to the first two-thirds of the century (with the terminal dates adjusted to the history of the individual countries) and two chapters to the last third of the century, when the emergence of a unified Germany changed the map of Europe, and the intensified competition for new colonies known as "the new imperialism" changed the map of the world. Although in terms of European and even global history, the century came to a close with World War I, the pivotal event in East Asia occurred 20 years earlier when the Sino-Japanese War radically affected Korea, China, and Japan.

The West was never uniform, nor its course of events smooth. It helps place East Asian turbulence in perspective if we keep in mind that the forces of nationalism and republicanism erupted in revolutions on the European continent in 1830 and 1848, that in 1839 English Chartists took to the streets demanding political reforms, that warfare played a crucial role in the creation of Italian and German national states (completed by 1870), that Americans slaughtered each other in civil war, and that bitter fighting and strife marked the transition from Napoleon III, through the Paris Commune, to the establishment of the conflicted Third Republic in France (1870). The violence of the nineteenth century is matched only by that of its successor.

Vietnam and China: Internal Crises and Western Intrusion

In both China and Vietnam internal crisis preceded Western intrusion. In 1800 the Chinese were busy suppressing the White Lotus Rebellion, while in Vietnam the Tay Son Uprising (1771–1802) was in its final phase. Both upheavals were fueled by the widespread discontent of impoverished peasants alienated by government corruption and ineptitude while drawn by the vision of a better world sanctioned by the divine. Both revealed deep fissures in government and society. Both failed. In China the Qing continued while a new dynasty, the Nguyen, rose in Vietnam. Each had to grapple with major internal problems even as it faced new external threats. Neither was adequately prepared for confronting the expanding and aggressive Western powers or for grasping and handling the enormity of the civilizational challenge facing them.

I. Vietnam

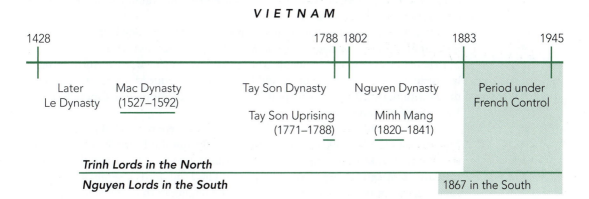

VIETNAM

| 1428 | | | 1788 | 1802 | | 1883 | 1945 |

Later
Le Dynasty

Mac Dynasty
(1527–1592)

Tay Son Dynasty

Tay Son Uprising
(1771–1788)

Nguyen Dynasty

Minh Mang
(1820–1841)

Period under
French Control

Trinh Lords in the North

Nguyen Lords in the South

1867 in the South

*Historical Background: The Later Le Dynasty
(1428–1788)*

The Tay Son Uprising (1771–1802)

*The Nguyen as Rulers of All Vietnam
(1802–1867)*

Scholarship and Literature

The Loss of Independence

Historical Background: The Later Le Dynasty (1428–1788)

The Le dynasty was founded in 1428 by Le Loi (1385–1430), who put an end to 13 years of Ming rule. In his youth, Le Loi had passed the civil service examinations under the brief Ho dynasty (1400–1407), and after founding the new dynasty, continued a policy of looking to China for institutional models. The later Le reached its greatest success in the fifteenth century, particularly under Emperor Le Thanh Tong (1460–1497), who reformed and strengthened the Chinese-style six ministries (Rites, War, Justice, Interior, Public Works, and Finance) and the bureaucracy, thereby weakening the landed aristocracy. He promulgated a new legal code that combined Confucian and Vietnamese traditions, including those giving women greater rights. While the code stipulated that all land belonged to the emperor, it followed the policy of Le Loi in setting limits, based on status, rank, profession, and age on the amount anyone could actually hold. Neo-Confucianism was firmly established as the state orthodoxy, and the emperor effectively patronized scholarship.

Forceful abroad as well as at home, in 1471 Le Thanh Tong invaded and vanquished his country's ancient rival, Champa, the Indianized state established in central Vietnam by the Cham, a people who speak a Malay Polynesian (Austronesian) language. He annexed some of the old kingdom, and reduced the rest to a protectorate with the existing internal political structures continuing to function under Viet supervision and control.

In the sixteenth century the dynasty suffered a severe reversal of fortunes. The Mac dynasty (1527–1592) gained control briefly, but the Le were able to regain the throne, thanks to the support of Trinh military leaders. However, the Le permanently remained dependent on the Trinh. The Trinh lords resembled Japanese shoguns, except that a dynasty of rival lords belonging to the Nguyen family controlled what is now central Vietnam. For the remainder of the dynasty, a Le Emperor in Hanoi, controlled by the Trinh, was recognized in Beijing as a tributary and accepted as legitimate sovereign in Vietnam, but in reality Vietnam was divided in two. Trinh rulers prevailed in the traditional Vietnamese heartland centered on the Red River Basin but were unable to prevent the Nguyen from ruling the lands south of the eighteenth parallel from their capital in Hue (Figure 6.5).

Meanwhile in the Deep South, the Lower Mekong Region constituted a "Water Frontier" with the "frequent movement of peoples and exchanges of commodities and cultural practices among Viets, Siamese, Mon-Khmer, and Malays with Chinese settlers, sojourners, and junk traders forming a common thread weaving them all together."[1] Fueled by trade in rice, tin, rubber, and various commodities, Bangkok and Saigon developed into major economic centers.

Confined by mountains and the sea, neither the Trinh nor the Nguyen could expand east or west. The north under the Trinh, known as Tonkin, was also hemmed in by the Chinese to the north and the Nguyen to their south. The Nguyen state, however, faced only weaker obstacles to its south, and Vietnamese expansion had always been to the south. During their ascendancy, the Nguyen continued this process, pushing south at the expense of the Chams (today a small minority in Vietnam) and in the Deep South displacing the Khmers, the inhabitants of Cambodia. Frequently, Vietnamese from the north were encouraged to farm southern lands, as were Chinese, including 3,000 Ming loyalists who fled from the Qing and were settled by the Nguyen into the northeast Mekong Delta, incorporating and transforming what had been Cambodian lands.

Expansion at the expense of Cambodia remained a recurrent theme. Champa was fully incorporated in 1692. Beginning in 1658, Vietnamese troops frequently intervened in Cambodian succession disputes as rival princes sought either Vietnamese or Siamese support. In 1674, Vietnamese forces entered Saigon (then Cambodian) before going all the way to seize Phnom Penh. Other incursions took place in 1699, 1747, 1753–1755, and 1771–1772, leading to cession of territory in what a Nguyen general described as "the policy of slowly eating silkworms."[2]

Six provinces of present Vietnam were obtained in this manner by 1750. While the south was being incorporated into a Vietnamese state, influence also worked in the other direction, creating "a new way of being Vietnamese."[3] People living in the Nguyen territory were deeply influenced by the customs and beliefs of the local Cham and those of other cultures. Accustomed to a world filled with numerous spirits and supernatural beings, newcomers readily paid their respects to resident deities. For example, the polyandrous Cham goddess, Po Nagar, acquired a Vietnamese name but retained her naturalism and sexuality. In the 1880s, she was honored with many titles by a pious ruler, and today the polyandrous deity, properly draped, is venerated by Vietnamese as intensively as by Chams (Figure 6.1). Southerners were more mobile than the inhabitants of the long-settled north. They differed in cuisine, dress, poetry, and lifestyle. In keeping with Southeast Asian traditions, the Nguyen kings were attributed aspects of divinity. They did adopt Chinese institutions, but not until the eighteenth century, and then only slowly. For instance, after Chinese-style civil service examinations were instituted in 1740, they were suspended for 26 years. Southeast Asian ways were particularly strong in the military, with special attention paid to the use of elephants, abundant in the south,

FIGURE 6.1   Temple of Po Nagar in Nha Trang. The figure of the dancing Siva that graces the temple originated in India, as did much of the old Cham culture.
PHOTOGRAPH © LORE SCHIROKAUER.

rare in the north. Elephants were used effectively in warfare, and they were even employed as a means of administering capital punishment: women guilty of adultery were some of the numerous criminals who suffered death by elephant (see Chapter 5).

We should also bear in mind that the Nguyen territory ranged from older lands in central Vietnam to parts of the Mekong Delta further south, and from the ocean to the mountains. Local cultures retained their diversity. For example, inlanders remained ignorant of "The Great Fish of the Southern Seas" venerated in annual ceremonies along a section of the coast. This whale cult was limited to the former Cham area: in the north the whale remained a mere fish. Both the east-west and the north-south divisions were significant.

The Tay Son Uprising (1771–1802)

In the eighteenth century, people under both the Trinh and Nguyen suffered from misgovernment, political divisiveness, excessive taxation, corruption, and the privatization of communal land. Exacerbating conditions in the north were natural disasters resulting in famine and disease. The south was better off, but also had problems including the economic dislocations associated with a failed attempt by the government to impose a zinc currency in place of traditional copper.

The harsh conditions in the north fueled numerous rebellions, but the most significant one began in the central-southern mountains around the village of Tay Son, from which it derived its name. Led by three brothers and fortified by signs of supernatural support (some fabricated), it attracted both people living in the hills and disaffected peasants in the lowlands. It also found support among many small merchants, four wealthy merchants—two of them Chinese—and even a Cham princess.

During these turbulent years of almost uninterrupted fighting, the Tay Son gave top priority to military matters, with emphasis on army recruitment, weapons procurement, and the like. They also encouraged commerce and fostered education. Displaced people were returned to their villages, where communal land was restored. We cannot tell what might have been accomplished given stability and more time, but corruption remained a problem, as did failure to develop an original ideology or a compelling program.

The rebellion put an end to the Trinh. In 1789 the Qing intervened with 200,000 troops on behalf of the Le emperor, but the expedition turned into a disaster for the Chinese and marked the end of any hopes for a Le restoration. In the south, the Nguyen were thoroughly defeated, and seemed on the verge of extinction.

However, Nguyen An, a prince who had been driven to seek shelter in Siam, was eventually able to draw on the profitable water frontier trade and defeat the Tay Son, for he proved to be "an opponent who lost battle after battle but always came back, an opponent with an eye to the long-term campaign rather than the single confrontation, for whom success came not from armed combat but was the result of organization, training, the marshalling of resources, preparation, planning, and waiting, waiting, waiting . . . ."[4] By utilizing men from many lands, he achieved naval supremacy and was able to transport armies by sea, while in Saigon he gained the backing of Chinese and other commercial interests. Among his foreign supporters were a small number of French mercenaries and two ships paid for by funds raised by Pigneau de Behaine, a French cleric long active in central Vietnam, who earlier had taken Nguyen An's son to Paris in pursuit of an ambitious plan to gain French government support.

The spread of Catholicism had enjoyed French patronage ever since the pope founded the Société de Mission Etrangère at the urging of Father Alexander de Rhodes, but the French government had other priorities. When he failed to gain official support, Pigneau de Behaine acted on his own. Nguyen's cause had already made considerable progress by the time the French contingent joined in, but this was a harbinger of future French military involvement.

The Nguyen as Rulers of All Vietnam (1802–1867)

After his victory, Nguyen An proclaimed himself Emperor Gia Long (r. 1802–1820) and ruled a unified empire with its capital at Hue. The emperor's name, combining the first syllable of Gia Dinh, the largest city in the south, and the second syllable of Thang Long, the original name for Hanoi, signified the unification of north and south. Vietnam now assumed its present form, which has been compared to a pole carrying a basket at each end, representing the fertile and wealthy Red River and Mekong Deltas, in the north and in the south, respectively. To sustain this entity required a sturdy pole and a strong back. Whereas earlier "the south" referred to everything below Tonkin, we now and hereafter need to differentiate between the narrow central region including Hue, and the south, dominated by Saigon and the Mekong Delta. Another image, reflecting less happy times, describes Vietnam as "a slightly bent half-moon country shaped like a starved sea horse trapped inside the sky."[5]

In assuming the imperial title, Gia Long was claiming the legacy of the Le and the Confucian legitimization that supported it. At the same time, he was keenly aware of his Nguyen heritage, and claimed to have restored Nguyen rule, thanks to the cumulative spirit-influence of a long line of rulers. This self-image had nothing to do with a Confucian Mandate of Heaven, but appealed to people of the south in familiar terms.

Gia Long was succeeded by Minh Mang (1820–1841), an equally vigorous emperor who did all he could to model his regime on that of China. He transformed Hue into a typical Chinese capital complete with forbidden city, six ministries, and Censorate. The Vietnamese legal code copied that of the Qing. The examination system, complete with the eight-legged essay, flourished. The emperor's tomb is approached by a Chinese-style spirit-way with statues of military men, civil officials, and animals standing guard. Along with the other structures, it serves as a reminder of the continued power of the Chinese imperial tradition to serve as a compelling model (Figures 6.2 and 6.3). At the same time, included within the walls of the forbidden city and departing from the Chinese model were temples to predynastic ancestors, placed there "to enshrine the Restoration myth,"[6] first promoted by Gia Long. Minh Mang sponsored many Chinese institutions, not all of them suitable for a smaller country. He brought northerners into the government, while continuing to sponsor Buddhism and native cults. The central political elite, based near the capital, was able to manipulate the examination system so that by the 1860s only three southerners had won the top degree.

This suggests inadequate integration of the south. However, the Nguyen had ambitions in Cambodia, where they remained deeply involved. For seven years, from 1834 to 1841, they even reduced Cambodia to a Vietnamese province administered in a Sino-Vietnamese manner. However, they had bitten off more than they could chew, even with Chinese-style teeth. The Cambodians revolted, throwing

FIGURE 6.2   Tomb of Minh Mang (1820–1843): Gate. The tomb for the emperor and his empress is reached through the Hien Due Gate, one of a number of gates and other structures displaying the wealth and power of the Nguyen dynasty as well as its Chinese orientation—for a gate such as this would not be out of place in an imperial Chinese tomb.
PHOTOGRAPH © LORE SCHIROKAUER.

FIGURE 6.3   Tomb of Minh Mang: Spirit-Way. Statues of officials and animals line the "spirit-ways" of imperial Chinese tombs. Minh Mang's array is relatively modest, but imperial nonetheless.
PHOTOGRAPH © LORE SCHIROKAUER.

off Vietnamese rule, only to be dominated by Siam from 1841 to 1845. The Cambodian kings, pressured on both sides, then tried to assert some independence by declaring vassalage to both Bangkok and Hue, until the French took control in 1863.

Scholarship and Literature

As in China and Korea, Vietnam was theoretically an examination-based meritocracy based on "epistemological self-righteousness"[7] and fortified by an array of old texts and current scholarship such as the *Survey of the Institutions of Successive Courts* by Phan Huy Chu (1782–1840) covering geography, the military, civil institutions, and classical literature among other topics.

Poetry remained the heart of Vietnamese literature, and best reflected the tensions of the age. The greatest poet of the century was Nguyen Du (1765–1820). He was not related to the royal house—Nguyen is a common name, even shared by the brothers who led the Tay Son Uprising. Nguyen Du belonged to a northern scholar-official family who supported the Le dynasty to the end. During the Uprising, he avoided office, but then reluctantly served the new Nguyen dynasty. His experiences of humiliation, political debasement, and of suffering wrongs are echoed in *The Tale of Kieu,* a long narrative poem written in *nom.* Based on a Chinese novel and cast in powerful, evocative verse, it relates the sufferings of *Kieu,* who in order to rescue her father from debtor's prison, agrees to a marriage for money. She is sold into a brothel, from which she is eventually rescued, only to fall again. But throughout, she remains pure at heart, and in the end overcomes adversity. The beauty of the poem's language as well as empathy for *Kieu* were to stir the hearts of many Vietnamese, including men who, like Nguyen Du, felt forced to prostitute their political beliefs and serve an illegitimate master (see pp. 275 and 460 including Figure 18.4).

Northern elites had a reputation for puritanism, but a very different ethos flourished elsewhere, and women tended to see things differently than did men. There are many stories but few facts concerning the life of Ho Xuan Huong, born around 1775–1780 and deceased by the 1820s. The poem in Figure 6.4 may be autobiographical, but we cannot be sure. Writing in the native *nom* script, Ho is known for her skillful use of double meanings, frequently sexual. Beloved for its free spirit, her poetry remains widely popular. To quote a modern appreciation:

Ho Xuan Huong's poems are so effortless in construction, so simple and spontaneous, that they rank as the most charming in Vietnamese. . . . Her daring has won her a reputation as an early feminist. She preaches free love, equality of the sexes, and the cause of unmarried mothers; she derides social conventions, ignorant scholars and high officials and impious monks.[8]

BOX 6.1 "ON SHARING A HUSBAND"

On Sharing a Husband

Screw the fate that makes you share a man.
One cuddles under cotton blankets, the other's cold.
Every now and then, well maybe or maybe not.
Once or twice a month, oh, it's like nothing.
You try to stick to it like a fly on rice
but the rice is rotten. You slave like the maid,
 but without pay. If I had known how it would go
I think I would have lived alone.[9]

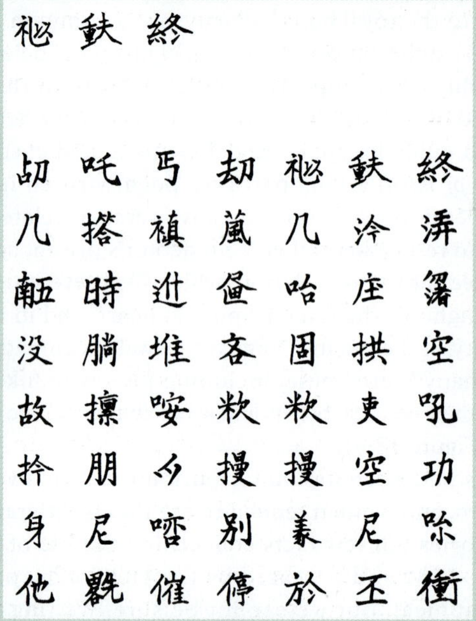

FIGURE 6.4 "On Sharing a Husband" by Ho Xuan Huong, written in the native *nom* script.

Spring Essence: The Poetry of Ho Xuan, Ed. and Trans. John Balaban (Port Townsend, WA: Copper Canyon Press), p. 24.

The Loss of Independence

Situated at the border between the Southeast Asian cultural sphere and that of China, the new Vietnam was a diverse place in just about every respect. Keeping it together required a great effort—political, cultural, economic, and military—that proved beyond the capacity of the dynasty. Maintaining a regime based in Hue, in Vietnam's narrow middle, required the support of at least one of the rich and populous lands to the north or south, but the government failed to win strong backing in either region. Threatened by internal rebellion and confronting French commercial and territorial ambitions, the dynasty "almost inevitably maneuvered themselves into a deadly crossfire—hostile subjects challenging them on the one hand and French imperialists encroaching on the other."[10]

As already noted, French expansionists included missionaries as well as naval officers and commercial types. Earlier, although Christianity was outlawed by both Trinh and Nguyen, missionaries had been tolerated, especially by the Nguyen, who were eager for trade. Gia Long combined uneasy tolerance for the missionaries with suspicion of French commercial and political intentions. Minh Mang, aware of missionary and local Catholic support for internal rebellion and foreign intervention, issued increasingly severe decrees, beginning with the proscription of Christianity in 1825, by which time there were already an estimated 300,000 converts. Proscription turned into repression. In 1832, he had a missionary strangled to death for being involved in a rebellion.

Relations deteriorated further under Emperor Thieu Tri (1841–1847), whose efforts at settling disputes over missionaries were undermined by the French bombardment of Danang in 1847. The fourth Emperor, Tu Duc (1847–1883), faced internal rebellion and, in 1858, a French-Spanish invasion. Several years of fighting were concluded with the Treaty of Saigon (1862), under which the Vietnamese agreed to lift restrictions on religion and trade, to give France a major voice in the conduct of foreign policy, and to cede Saigon along with three neighboring provinces. To these the French added another three in 1867 to form a colony they called Cochin China (Fr. Cochinchine). (The origin of this name is in dispute. According to one popular theory, "Cochin" was derived from an old Chinese term for the Red River Delta, and "China" added to distinguish it from Cochin in India.)

Under the French Third Republic (1870–1914), French politicians sought to compensate for the loss of territory and national pride in the Franco-Prussian War of 1870–1871 by imperial conquest overseas, but the real initiative for further expansion into Vietnam was taken by Frenchmen already there. First, in 1873, a French merchant-adventurer seized part of Hanoi. To restore order and Vietnamese control, the Vietnamese government permitted a French force into the area. However, the French commander, Francis Garnier (1839–1873), who had been sent by the Governor of Cochin China, Admiral Jules-Marie Dupré (1813–1881), actually supported his countrymen in Hanoi. Garnier's gunboats went marauding down the northern rivers and streams between Hanoi and the sea until he was killed in battle. This episode led to serious debates in Paris and the forced resignation of Dupré. French encroachment continued, but at a slower pace. Under the Treaty of 1874 the French withdrew, but the Red River was opened to foreign trade, and Vietnam

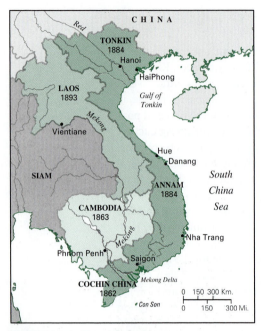

FIGURE 6.5   French Indochina.

recognized Cochin China as a French colony, subsequently promising to follow France in its foreign policy.

The south was now permanently lost, and the north was precarious, as local armed forces (usually led by the elite), Chinese fleeing the suppression of the Taiping Rebellion, armed Vietnamese Catholic units, rebellious mountain tribes, Chinese and Vietnamese bandits organized as the "Black Flags" under a Chinese secret society leader, as well as Qing border troops and French consular troops, all pursued their own agendas. Meanwhile, the French were determined not to allow any other power to dominate the north. When they seized Hanoi in 1882, the Nguyen court responded by seeking help from both the Qing and the Black Flags. The Qing sent troops, but after losing the Sino-French War (see Chapter 9), they were eliminated as a factor in Vietnam, leaving the French supreme, but loyalist Vietnamese bitterly resentful.

According to a treaty signed in 1883, Tonkin in the north and Annam (an old Chinese designation adopted by the French) in central Vietnam, like Cambodia, became French "protectorates." In 1887 the addition of Laos completed the formation of French Indochina. "Protectorate" is an official euphemism, since power over all Vietnam was in the hands of a French governor-general in Hanoi. However, while Cochin China was governed according to French law administered by Frenchmen and Frenchified Vietnamese, the "protectorates" were under dual jurisdiction, with French citizens responsible to French authority, but the old Vietnamese bureaucracy still in place, their officials surviving "as traumatized, moldering tokens of the classical past."[11]

II. China

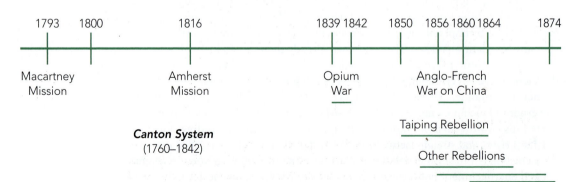

Nineteenth-century China was beset by internal and external difficulties, each contributing to the severity of the other. Opium, for example, came from abroad, but its spread in China was made possible by official corruption, and the appeal of the drug to bannermen (see p. 125) exacerbated the situation. The Qing now faced long-term problems that would have taxed the ingenuity and energy of even an honest and effective government. Foremost were the problems created by population pressures, for the population continued to increase in the nineteenth century as it had in the eighteenth. By 1850 the number of inhabitants in China had risen to 430 million from 300 million at the beginning of the century, without any comparable increase in productivity or resources. As the pressures of the struggle for survival strained old humanistic values to the breaking point, it left little room for honesty, let alone charity. Life became brutish and hard. As always, the poor suffered most, and they were legion, for the uneven distribution of land left many people landless, destitute, and despairing. The situation was made worse by government neglect of public works.

Emperor Jiaqing (1796–1820) tried to remedy the government's financial problems by cutting costs and selling official posts and titles, but was unable to solve the underlying fiscal and economic problems, reform the bureaucracy, or help the people, who ultimately supplied the funds. Emperor Daoguang (1820–1850) continued his father's policy of frugality but could not stem the decay. Internal pressures were building, but external crisis preceded internal eruption.

The Opium War (1839–1841) and Its Causes

Before turning to the opium crisis that triggered the war, we need to consider the long-range factors that made it a turning point in China's foreign relations. Underlying the tensions between China and the West was the incompatibility of the Chinese and Western views of themselves and the world. Both were supremely self-confident and proud of their own civilizations. Both were narrowly culture-bound. Thus, when the Macartney mission arrived in Beijing in 1793 hoping to broaden the terms of trade and to initiate treaty relations, the Chinese labeled presents sent to Emperor Qianlong from England's George III as "tribute." Qianlong responded to the English monarch by praising his "respectful spirit of submission" and in the gracious but condescending language appropriate for addressing a barbarian king residing in the outer reaches of the world, turned down all his requests. He saw no merit in the British request for representation in Beijing nor did he favor increased trade: "As your Ambassador can see for himself, we possess all things. I set no value on objects strange or ingenious, and have no use for your country's manufactures."[12]

The sources are inconsistent on whether Lord Macartney performed the ceremonial kowtow expected of inferiors and performed by emperors themselves toward Heaven, but he was confident that the Chinese would perceive "that superiority which Englishmen, wherever they go, cannot conceal."[13] The English sent another mission to China in 1816, headed by Lord Amherst, but he was not granted an audience at court.

The British motive for coming to China remained primarily economic. In contrast to China's self-sufficiency and Emperor Qianlong's disdain for foreign products, there was a Chinese product in great demand in Britain: tea. First imported in tiny quantities in the late seventeenth century, tea was initially taken up as an exotic beverage with medicinal properties, then popularized as a benign alternative to gin, and finally was considered a necessity of English life. The East India Company, which enjoyed a monopoly of trade with China until 1834, was required by Act of Parliament to keep a year's supply in stock at all times. Tea imports reached 15 million pounds in 1785, and double that amount in the decade preceding the Opium War. Not only did the East India Company depend on the income from tea trade, the British government also had a direct stake in tea, since about one-tenth of its entire revenue came from a tax on Chinese tea. Not until the 1820s did the Company begin experimenting with tea growing in India, and it was many years before Indian tea would provide an alternative to the tea of China. The importance of Chinese tea extended even to American history: it was Chinese tea that was dumped from East India Company ships in the famous Boston Tea Party (1773).

The British problem was how to pay for this tea. There was no market for British woolens in China, and the "singsong" trade in clocks, music boxes, and curios was insufficient to strike a balance of trade. Until the last third of the eighteenth century, the sale of British imports covered 10 percent or less of the cost of exports, with the rest paid for in cash and precious metals. Unable to find anything European that the Chinese wanted in sufficient quantity, the English turned toward India and the "country trade" between India and China, conducted under East India Company license by the private firms of British subjects. Money obtained in Canton by the "country traders" was put on deposit there for the Company against bills of exchange on London. In this way, England, India, and China were connected by a trade-and-payments triangle.

Until 1823 the largest commodity imported to China from India was cotton, but this never reached the volume necessary to balance the trade. That was accomplished by opium. Opium had long been used for medicinal purposes, but the smoking, or more accurately, the inhaling of opium fumes through a pipe, began in the seventeenth century. The spread of the practice was sufficient to provoke an imperial edict of prohibition in 1729, but this and subsequent efforts to suppress the drug were unsuccessful, and opium consumption continued to increase. Distributed partly through older salt-smuggling networks, and protected by the connivance of corrupt officials, it spread steadily and proved particularly attractive to soldiers and government underlings. The drug was debilitating and habit forming (Figure 6.6). Withdrawal was excruciatingly painful. Over time the addict developed a tolerance for opium and needed more of the drug to achieve a "high." Thus, to pay for tea, the Chinese were sold a poison. Since the opium was brought to China by private "country traders," the East India Company disclaimed responsibility for the illegal traffic in China. At the same time, however, it profited from the sale of opium in India. However, within India, where the British, as the paramount power, felt a certain sense of responsibility, consumption of opium for nonmedicinal purposes was strictly prohibited.

The Chinese market for opium developed at such a pace that the balance of trade was reversed. During the 1820s and 1830s silver seems to have left China in large quantities to pay for opium imports. This caused an increase in the number of copper coins needed to buy a specific amount of silver, thereby destabilizing the Qing monetary system. What began as a public health problem now became a fiscal problem as well.

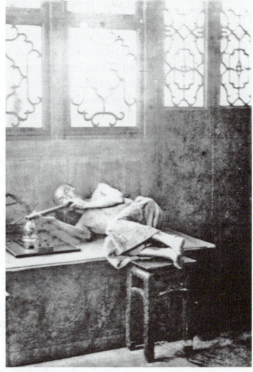

FIGURE 6.6 *Opium Smoking in a Restaurant.* Those who could afford to do so indulged in high-quality opium prepared for them by servants at home. The less affluent had to prepare their own. But the least fortunate were left to smoke opium ash or refuse on rudimentary benches in shoddy surroundings in dismal opium dens. John Thomson, *Illustrations of China and Its People: A Series of Two Hundred Photographs, with Letterpress Descriptive of the Places and People Represented.* London: S. Low, Marston, Low, and Searle, 1873–1874. Reprinted in 1900.
© MANSELL/TIME & LIFE PICTURE COLLECTION/GETTY IMAGES.

In 1834, the Company's monopoly of the China trade was abolished by the British government. This opened the gates of trade still wider on the British side, resulting in an increased flow of opium to China, and an increased flow of silver out of China.

Abolition of the Company's trade monopoly was a victory for English advocates of free trade, who were as antagonistic to restraints on trade abroad as at home. The immediate effect in China was to put an end to the system of channeling official Company communications through the Cohong which, however, continued to handle commerce with the country traders. Instead of the Select Committee of the East India Company, an official of the crown now represented the British government. To initiate the new relations, Britain sent Lord Napier as First Superintendent of Trade with instructions to establish direct contact with the Qing viceroy, to protect British rights, and to assert jurisdiction over Englishmen in Canton. To accomplish these aims, he was ordered to use a moderate and conciliatory approach. Napier, however, was more ambitious than diplomatic and immediately took an adamant stand on the issue of direct communication with the viceroy. He violated Chinese regulations by not waiting in Macao for permission to proceed to Canton and by sending a letter rather than petitioning through the *hong* merchants. With neither side willing to back down, the impasse developed into a showdown. All Chinese employees were withdrawn from the British community, food was cut off, and trade was stopped. Napier finally withdrew to Macao, where he died. This all took place in 1834. Unfortunately, in the ensuing lull, no progress was made toward finding a new modus vivendi between the two sides.

For a brief moment the Chinese considered legalizing opium, but in 1836 the emperor decided on suppression. In doing so, he sided with the Spring Purification Circle of reform-minded literati officials, who were seeking influence in government decision making. Thus an "Inner Opium War," to use James Polachek's formulation, developed parallel to and intertwined with the external conflict.[14]

Opium dealers and addicts were prosecuted with great vigor, and imprisonments and executions were widespread, with the result that the wholesale price of opium dropped precipitously. This program was well under way when the vigorous and determined reformer Lin Zexu (1785–1850) arrived in Canton in March 1839. As imperial commissioner, he was charged with stamping out the drug trade once and for all.

Lin conducted a highly successful campaign against Chinese dealers and consumers. He also severely punished corrupt officials who had connived in the trade. To deal with the foreign source of the opium, he appealed to Queen Victoria: "Suppose there were people from another country who carried opium for sale to England and seduced your people into buying and smoking it; certainly your honorable ruler would deeply hate it and be bitterly aroused."[15] He also admonished the foreign merchants, and he backed moral suasion with force. He demanded that the foreigners surrender all their opium and sign a pledge to refrain from importing the drug in the future at the risk of confiscation and death. To effect compliance, he used the same weapons of isolating the foreign traders employed successfully in 1834 against Napier. Elliot, the British Superintendent of Trade, took a fateful step in response when he ordered the British merchants to turn their opium over to him for delivery to the Chinese authorities. By this act he relieved the merchants of large amounts of opium they had been unable to sell because of the efficacy of the Chinese prohibitions, and he made the British government responsible for eventual compensation. No wonder that the merchants enthusiastically dumped their opium: 21,306 chests were delivered to Lin Zexu. It took twenty-three days to destroy it all.

In England, firms interested in the China trade exerted great pressure on the government for prompt and vigorous military action. Lin, meanwhile, pleased with his victory, continued to press Elliot on the issue of the pledges but was unsuccessful. The Superintendent of Trade argued that it was against British law to compel the merchants to sign the pledges which would make them subject to

Chinese jurisdiction, and that the imposition of the death penalty without the benefits of English judicial procedure was also contrary to British law. What was at stake here was the issue of British jurisdiction over British subjects, a source of Anglo-Chinese friction since 1784, when the British had refused to submit to Chinese justice. The issue came to the fore again in the summer of 1839, when a group of English sailors killed a Chinese villager in the Canton hinterland. Refusing to turn the men over to Lin Zexu, Elliot tried them himself and found them guilty, but when they were returned to England the men were freed, because the home court ruled that Elliot had exceeded his authority.

The first clash of the war took place in November 1839, when the Chinese tried to protect one of the only two ships whose captains had signed the pledge so that they could receive official Qing permission to trade, despite Elliot's stand. When a British ship fired a shot across the bow of the offending vessel, the Chinese intervened with 21 war junks. However, they were no match for the foreign ships. In December, trade with the British was stopped, and on January 31, 1840, a formal declaration of war was announced by the governor-general of India acting in the name of the home government.

In June 1840, the British force, consisting of 16 warships, 4 armed steamers, 27 transports, 1 troop ship, and 4,000 Irish, Scottish, and Indian soldiers, arrived in China. First the British blockaded Canton, and then they moved north. Lin and his associates remained confident of victory, holding that the British, like their maritime pirate predecessors, depended on the spoils of war to finance their military operations, and thus had grossly overextended themselves.

The British were fired on at Xiamen (Amoy) while trying to deliver a letter from Prime Minister Palmerston under a white flag of truce, a symbol the Chinese did not understand—just one example of mutual cultural misunderstanding. They then seized Chusan Island, south of the Yangzi estuary, and Dinghai, the chief city there. The main body of the fleet sailed another 800 miles north to Beihe, near Tianjin, where Palmerston's letter was accepted. By this time the emperor had lost confidence in Lin Zexu, whose tough policy had led to the military retaliation.

Lin was dismissed, disgraced, and exiled to Ili in Central Asia. His place was taken by the Manchu prince Qishan (d. 1854), who in September 1840, by flattery and accommodation, got the British to return to Canton for further negotiations. When these came to naught, the British resumed military operations, with the result that in January 1841 Qishan was forced to sign a convention that provided for the cession of Hong Kong, payment of an indemnity to Britain, equality of diplomatic relations, and the reopening of Canton. Both Qishan for the Qing and Elliot for the British thought they had done very well, but neither government accepted their work. The Chinese emperor was indignant at how much had been conceded, while Palmerston fumed that Elliot had demanded too little. The reactions of the Chinese and British governments showed all too clearly how far apart they still were. Caught in the middle were the negotiators. Like Lin Zexu earlier, now Qishan came to feel the imperial displeasure: his property was confiscated and he was sent to exile on the Amur. Elliot too was dismissed; his next position was as consul-general in Texas.

In the renewed fighting, the British besieged Canton in February 1841, but the siege was lifted on payment of a ransom of 6 million Spanish silver dollars. However, before their departure, the British experienced the growing hostility of the local population. They were attacked by a body of troops organized by the local gentry. Although militarily ineffective, the attack was an indication of popular sentiment, and its results were embellished by Chinese hard-liners to support their advocacy of continued intransigence toward the British. In August, Elliot was relieved by Pottinger, and the last phase of the war began when the British moved north, occupying Xiamen in August and Dinghai in October. Reinforcements were sent from India, increasing the naval force and bringing troop strength up to 10,000. With this force, Pottinger continued the campaign, advancing up the Yangzi until his guns threatened Nanjing. There on August 29, 1842, the treaty was signed that ended the war. It was a dictated peace imposed by the Western victor on the vanquished Chinese.

The Treaty of Nanjing and the Treaty System

The Treaty of Nanjing (together with the supplementary Treaty of the Bogue, October 1843) set the pattern for treaties China later signed with the United States and France in 1844, established the blueprint for China's relations with the West for the next century, and supplied the model for similar treaties imposed on Japan. The Canton System and the Cohong monopoly (see Chapter 5) were abolished. Five ports—Canton, Xiamen, Fuzhou, Ningbo, and Shanghai—were opened to British trade and residence. Britain received the right to appoint consuls to these cities.

The treaty also stipulated that henceforth official communications were to be on a basis of equality. The Qing was forced to pay an indemnity of 21 million Spanish silver dollars. Of this, 12 million was for war expenses, in keeping with the European practice of forcing the loser to pay the costs of a war. Another 6 million was paid as reparations for opium handed over to Commissioner Lin, while the remaining 3 million went to settle the debts owed by the *hong* merchants to British merchants.

An important provision of the treaty established a moderate Chinese tariff of 4 to 13 percent on imports, with an average rate of 5 percent. The Chinese, whose statutory customs had been even lower, did not realize that by agreeing to this provision they were relinquishing the freedom to set their own tariffs. On the British side there was the conviction that, as Adam Smith had taught, the removal of constraints on trade would benefit all by allowing everyone to concentrate on what he did best.

The British, having acquired an empire in India, with all the burdens of government that it entailed, did not seek to create another in China. Trade, not territory, was their aim. However, they did demand and obtain a Chinese base for their trade and their navy. Hong Kong Island, at that time the site of a tiny fishing village, was ceded to them in perpetuity. Well located and with an excellent harbor, it developed into a major international port.

The issue of legal jurisdiction over British subjects was settled by the Treaty of the Bogue, which provided for extraterritoriality—that is, the right of British subjects to be tried according to British law in British consular courts. Having only recently reformed their own legal system, the British were convinced of its superiority. There were precedents in Chinese history for allowing "barbarians" to manage their own affairs, but in the context of modern international relations, extraterritoriality amounted to a limitation on Chinese sovereignty.

The Treaty of the Bogue also provided for most-favored-nation treatment. This obliged China to grant Britain any rights China conceded in the future to any other power. Its effect was to prevent China from playing the powers against each other. It meant that once a nation had obtained a concession, it was automatically enjoyed by all the other states granted most-favored status. In the 1844 treaties, the United States and France gained this status. In the American treaty, China agreed to allow for the maintenance of churches in the treaty ports and to treaty revision in 12 years, while the French won the right to propagate Catholicism.

The status of the opium trade was left unsettled in the original treaties. An agreement to outlaw smuggling did not slow down the growth of the traffic, which was legalized under the next round of treaty settlements (1858–1860), and opium even functioned as a kind of money. From the annual 30,000 chests prior to the Opium War, the trade expanded to reach a high of 87,000 chests in 1879. It then declined as Chinese production of opium increased. British opium imports were down to about 50,000 chests when, in 1906, the Qing took strong measures against the drug. British imports finally came to a stop in 1917, but opium smoking remained a serious social problem until the early 1950s.

For China, the treaties solved and settled nothing. A particularly ominous development was the permission granted foreign gunboats to anchor at the treaty ports, for when additional ports were opened, it gave foreign powers the right to navigate China's inland waterways. Today, with the benefit of hindsight, it is apparent that the cumulative effect of the treaties was to reduce China to a status of inequality unacceptable to any modern nation.

Although it is now universally regarded as a milestone, the treaty settlement did not seem so to the Qing authorities who, as John Fletcher has shown, had made many of the same concessions as recently as 1835 in reaching a settlement with the tiny Central Asian state of Kokand. This treaty involved an indemnity, a tariff settlement, the abolition of a merchant monopoly, and a special position exceeding that of most-favored-nation status, and seen by the Qing as simply a case of "impartial benevolence."[16] From the vantage point of Beijing, Hong Kong seemed as remote as Kokand.

Foreign policy remained deeply imbedded in political conflicts revealing deep lines of division in the body politic. When the Manchu-led centralizers, who advocated peace, came into power, they purged their opposition so thoroughly that Chinese scholar-officials of various intellectual persuasions found common ground in pressing for open discussion in official channels, administrative decentralization, and a policy of determined resistance against the foreigners. Few men had any inkling of the dimensions of the challenge facing the empire. Even Wei

Yuan (1794–1857), author of the influential *Illustrated Treatise on the Sea Kingdoms* (first version, 1844), limited himself to incorporating new information into old categories and persisted in underestimating the British threat.

Under the circumstances, the best that experts could suggest was for China to acquire "barbarian" arms and to employ the old diplomacy of playing one "barbarian" against another. Less-well-informed officials suggested that future military operations take advantage of the supposed physical peculiarities of the "barbarians," for example, their stiff waists and straight legs, which made them dependent on horses and ships, or their poor night vision.

Internal Crisis

The encroachments of the foreign powers was ominous, but the internal crisis was even more dangerous. Government leadership remained totally inadequate. Earlier, Emperor Daoguang's partial success in reforming the official salt monopoly system had not compensated for his failure to reinvigorate the Grand Canal or Yellow River managements. The Grain Transport Administration was "in effect a free-wheeling taxation agency that preyed upon officialdom and populace alike."[17] By 1849, the Grand Canal was impassable. Afterward, tax grain had to be shipped by sea. The abandonment of the canal cost thousands their jobs. Emperor Daoguang did not even live to see the Yellow River disaster of 1852. Since 1194, the greater river had flowed into the sea south of the Shandong Peninsula, but now it shifted to the north, spreading flood and devastation over a wide area.

The next emperor, Xianfeng (1851–1861), was 19 when he inherited the throne and proved equally incapable of dealing with an increasingly menacing situation. Even while rebellion threatened the dynasty, a major scandal involving bribery and cheating shook the examination system.

Famine, poverty, and corruption gave rise to banditry and armed uprisings, as had so often happened in the past. The most formidable threat to the dynasty came from the Taiping revolutionaries. To aggravate the crisis, the dynasty also had to contend with rebellions elsewhere. In the border regions of Anhui, Jiangsu, Henan, and Shandong, there was the Nian Rebellion (1853–1868) led by secret societies, probably related to the White Lotus Society. There was also a Muslim rebellion in Yunnan (1855–1873) and the Dongan Rebellion in the Northwest (1862–1875). Yet it was the Taiping who came closest to destroying the Qing, in a civil war that, in terms of bloodshed and devastation, was the costliest in human history. It is estimated that more than 20 million people lost their lives.

The Taiping Rebellion (1850–1864)

The founder of the Taiping movement was a village school teacher named Hong Xiuquan (1814–1864). He belonged to the Hakka, ethnically a Han subgroup, which many centuries earlier had migrated from the north to the southeast, where they remained a distinct ethnic group. Originally, Hong hoped for a conventional civil service career, and four times went to Canton to participate in the civil service examination, only to fail each time. In 1837, shocked by his third failure, he became seriously ill and for 40 days was subject to fits of delirium during which he experienced visions. These visions he later interpreted with the aid of a Christian tract he picked up in Canton, where Protestant missionaries had started to bring their faith to China. He also received some instruction from an American Southern Baptist missionary. On the basis of his limited knowledge of the Bible and Christianity, he proceeded to work out his own form of Sinicized Christianity.

Central to Hong's faith was his conviction that in his visions he had seen God, who had bestowed on him the divine mission to save humankind and exterminate demons. He also believed that he had met Jesus, and that Christ was his own elder brother. This recasting of Christianity into a familistic mode appealed to Hong's Chinese audience but dismayed Western Christian missionaries, who were further appalled by Hong's claims that he was a source of new revelation. The emphasis in Taiping Christianity was on the Old Testament—on the Ten Commandments, not the Sermon on the Mount. Hong's militant zeal in obeying the first commandment by destroying "idols," including Confucian ancestral tablets, soon cost him his position as a village teacher. He became an itinerant preacher among the Hakka communities in Guangxi, gaining converts and disciples among the downtrodden and dispossessed, whom he recruited into the Association of God Worshippers. To the poor and miserable, he held out a vision of the Heavenly Kingdom of Great Peace (*Taiping tianguo*), an egalitarian, God-ordained utopia.

In keeping with both Christianity and native traditions, the Taiping stressed a strict, even puritanical, morality. Opium, tobacco, gambling, alcohol, prostitution, sexual misconduct, and foot binding were all strictly prohibited. Women were made equal to men in theory and to a remarkable extent in practice. Consonant with both Christian egalitarianism and native Chinese utopian ideas was a strong strain of economic egalitarianism, a kind of simple communism. Property was to be shared in common, and in 1850 the members of the Association were asked to turn over their funds to a communal treasury that would provide for everyone's needs.

The Taiping land program was based on a system of land classification according to nine grades found in *The Rites of Zhou*, which long had been a source of Chinese radical thought. The idea was that everyone would receive an equal amount of land, measured in terms of productivity of the soil. Any production in excess of what was needed by the assignees was to be contributed to common granaries and treasuries. The system did not recognize private property (Box 6.2).

The basic political structure was a unit of 25 families consisting of five groups of five families each. The leaders of these, and larger units, were to combine civil and military duties and look after the spiritual welfare of their people by conducting Sunday religious services. The Taiping developed their own hymns, primers, and literature, which served as the subject matter for a new examination system open to women as well as men. Similarly, there were female as well as male military units. Marriages took place in church and were monogamous.

BOX 6.2 SPECIFICS OF THE TAIPING LAND SYSTEM (1853)

After decreeing that the land is to be divided equally and laying down how this is to be accomplished, this official pronouncement continues:

> Everywhere in the empire mulberry trees shall be planted beneath the walls. All women shall raise silkworms, spin cloth, and sew dresses. Every family in the empire shall have five hens and two sows without exception. At the harvest the platoon chief shall supervise the section-chief in storing away the amount of new grain needed for the twenty-five families and surrender the rest to the public storehouse. The same applies to wheat, beans, nettle-hemp, cloth, silk, chickens, dogs and so on; it applies to money also. For under Heaven all belongs to the family of the Heavenly Father, Supreme Lord, and August God. In the empire none shall have any private property, and everything belongs to God, so that God may dispose of it. In the great family of the Heavenly Father every place is equal and everyone has plenty. This is the edicts of the Heavenly Father, Supreme Lord and August God, who especially commanded the Taiping True Lord to save the world.

Quoted and translated in Wolfgang Bauer, *China and the Search of Happiness: Recurrent Themes in Four Thousand Years of Chinese Cultural History*, translated from the German by Michael Shaw (New York: The Seabury Press, 1976), p. 288.

What stood in the way of realizing this utopia were the "demons," mostly Manchus. By July 1850 the Association had attracted 10,000 adherents, primarily in the remote and neglected province of Guangxi. In defiance of the Qing, they now cut off their queues, the long braids of hair hanging down from the back of the head, which had been forced upon the Chinese by the Manchus as a sign of subjugation. Since they also refused to shave the forepart of their heads, the government called them the "long-haired rebels." Millenarian religious beliefs, utopian egalitarianism, moral righteousness, and hatred of the Manchus proved a potent combination when fused into a program of organized armed resistance. In November 1850 there were clashes with government troops, and on January 11, 1851, Hong's thirty-seventh birthday, his followers proclaimed him "Heavenly King," thus formally defying the Qing.

At this stage, the Taiping enjoyed strong leadership. One of the outstanding secondary leaders was Yang Xiuqing, originally a charcoal burner, who was a talented organizer and strategist. Starting from their base in Guangxi, the Taiping forces made rapid military progress. One of their favorite tactics in attacking cities was to use their contingent of coal miners to dig tunnels that undermined the defending walls. The incompetence of the government forces also helped. As the Taiping armies advanced, they picked up strength. It has been estimated that their number reached over one million by the time they took Nanjing in 1853.

After such a quick advance, with their ranks swollen by new adherents only partially versed in Taiping tenets, it was time to call a halt and consolidate. They had formally proclaimed the Heavenly Kingdom of Great Peace in 1851. Now, with their capital at Nanjing, they attempted to turn it into a solid regime. To continue military operations, two expeditions were sent out. A small force was dispatched north and came within 20 miles of Tianjin before suffering reverses and defeat. Large forces went west and enjoyed considerable success until 1856, but they too were eventually defeated.

Taiping treatment of Westerners was cordial but clumsy. They lost much good will by employing condescending language and expressions of superiority not unlike those used by Beijing. After the British failed to obtain Taiping recognition of their treaty rights, they decided on a policy of neutrality, and the other powers soon followed suit. This remained the policy of the foreign powers through the 1850s.

A turning point for the Taiping regime came in 1856 in the form of a leadership crisis they could ill afford. Yang Xiuqing had increased his power to the point of reducing Hong to a mere figurehead. Yang, too, went into trances, and claimed to be acting on God's orders, but he was unable to convince the other leaders. When he over-reached, they turned on him. Yang, along with his family and thousands of followers, was killed, but no strong successor appeared to take his place. By the time Hong's cousin Hong Rengan (1822–1864) came into prominence in 1859, it was too late to restructure the regime. Hong Rengan was the most Westernized of the Taiping leaders, but had neither the time nor the power to build the centralized and modern state he had in mind. His leadership lasted only until 1861. Hong Xiuquan, meanwhile, was immersed in his religious mission, occupied with writing elaborate commentary on the Bible, and lost to the world around him.

Failure of the leadership was one source of Taiping weakness. Inadequate implementation of stated policies was another. Practice did not conform to theory. For example, Hong Xiuquan, as well as other Taiping leaders, kept numerous concubines despite the Taiping call for monogamy. Moreover, there were many missed opportunities: the failure to strike before the dynasty could regroup; the failure to cooperate with secret societies and other opponents of the regime who did not share the Taiping faith; the failure to cultivate good relations with the foreign powers.

To make matters worse, Taiping revolutionary ideas repelled all those Chinese who identified with the basic Confucian way of life and understood that the Taiping program was not merely anti-Manchu but anti-Confucian, and thus subversive to the traditional social order. Consequently, the Taiping failed to recruit gentry support, and worse, they antagonized this key element of Chinese society. To the literati, rule by "civilized" Manchus was preferable to rule by "barbarized" Chinese.

Zeng Guofan and the Defeat of the Taipings

What ultimately prolonged the Qing dynasty's life was a new kind of military force organized by Zeng Guofan (1811–1872), a dedicated Confucian and a product of the examination system. Unlike the old armies organized under the Qing banner system, Zeng's army was a strictly regional force from Hunan, staffed by officers of shared regional and ideological background personally selected by him. They, in turn, recruited soldiers from their own home areas or from members of their own clans. A paternalistic attitude of officers toward their men, a generous pay scale honestly administered, careful moral indoctrination, and common regional ties combined to produce a well-disciplined force high in morale. Qing statesmen were aware that strong regional armies such as Zeng's threatened the balance of power between the central government and the regions, and were ultimately dangerous to the authority of the dynasty. Nonetheless, the traditional armies of the regime had proved hopelessly inadequate, and the Manchu rulers had no choice but to trust Zeng. Although organized in Hunan, where it began its operations, the army also fought the Taiping in other provinces. It was not always victorious: twice Zeng suffered such serious defeats that he attempted suicide. However, in the long run this well-led and highly motivated army, honestly administered and true to its purpose, proved superior to the Taiping forces.

The dynasty also benefited from the services of two other remarkable leaders: Zuo Zongtang (1812–1885) and especially Li Hongzhang (1823–1901), whose Anhui Army became the strongest anti-Taiping force. After the treaties of 1860, the Western powers sided with the government that had made such extensive concessions to them, and Western arms were of great assistance, particularly to the Anhui Army. An American adventurer was succeeded by a British officer as leader of 4,000 or 5,000 Chinese in the "Ever Victorious Army." Meanwhile, French officers commanded the "Ever Triumphant Army," composed of Chinese and Filipino mercenaries. Customs revenues helped loyalists purchase foreign arms and steamers and establish arsenals.

After a series of victories, the loyalist armies laid siege to Nanjing. When the situation became desperate, Hong Xiuquan relied on divine intervention, ordering the starving people to eat manna. According to a Taiping general, "The Sovereign himself, in the open spaces of his palace, collected all sorts of weeds, which he made into a lump and sent out of the palace, demanding that everyone do likewise."[18] The same source attributes Hong's subsequent fatal illness to his eating of these weed concoctions. Shortly after Hong's death, on July 19, 1864, the city fell to an army commanded by Zeng Guofan's brother. As had happened often in this bitter war, the fall of Nanjing was followed by a bloodbath. Hong's son managed to flee, but was discovered in Guangxi and executed. The Taiping, once so close to victory, were completely eradicated. Similarly, the loyalist forces succeeded in quelling the Nian, Muslim, and other rebels.

The Taiping's example was to inspire future revolutionaries, while conservatives continued to admire Zeng Guofan. That others were restless and defiant is suggested by the famous life-size self-portrait of Ren Xiong (1820–1857), who served in a military headquarters but did not rest easily with his choice (Figure 6.7). Painted in Shanghai, which was beginning to assume its role as a major meeting place between China and the West, this original, unsettling work of art mirrors the stress of its time and foreshadows future conflict and distress.

China and the World from the Treaty of Nanjing to the End of the Taiping Rebillion

As we have seen, the Treaty of Nanjing established a pattern, but satisfied neither side. Frustrated in attempts at local negotiation, the British demanded direct representation in Beijing. They also pressed for treaty revision, because the opening of the new ports had not led to the anticipated increase in trade. Behind the demands for freer trade was the persistent belief that only artificial restrictions prevented the development of a giant market in China for British textiles and other products.

One cause of friction between the English and the Chinese was the repeated postponement of Canton's opening because of the strong antiforeign feeling of its people. The continuation of the opium trade did not help matters, nor did the development of a new commerce in Chinese laborers. These men were often procured against their will, crowded into dismal "coolie" vessels, and transported as contract laborers to work the plantations of Cuba and Peru. The boom set off by the discovery of gold in California in 1848 also brought Chinese immigrants to the United States, but they came as free laborers, their passage organized by Chinese merchants. By 1852 there were 25,000 Chinese in the American West, and by 1887 there were twice that number in California alone.

There were some efforts at cooperation during these years, as the foreign powers sided with the dynasty rather

FIGURE 6.7 Ren Xiong. In a self-portrait unlike any ever painted before, Ren depicts himself with a military haircut and expresses both belligerence and anxiety. Hanging scroll, ink and color on paper. 177.5 × 78.8 cm.
COLLECTION OF THE PALACE MUSEUM, BEIJING, CHINA.

than the Taipings. With Chinese consent, the British set about suppressing piracy. More important was the establishment of the Foreign Inspectorate of Customs in Shanghai, in 1854, after the Qing officials had been ejected by rebels. The Inspectorate became responsible for the collection of tariffs and the prevention of smuggling. By the new treaties of 1858, its authority was extended to all treaty ports. It remained an important source of support for the dynasty during and after the Taiping Rebellion.

Nevertheless, there was more discord than harmony, and in 1856 war broke out once more. The immediate cause of war was the Arrow Affair. The Arrow was a Chinese-owned but Hong Kong-registered vessel which, although flying the British flag, was boarded by Chinese officials, who seized 12 Chinese men whom they charged with piracy. When the viceroy returned the men but refused to apologize and guarantee that it would not happen again, the British responded by seizing Canton. There was a lull in the fighting while the British were occupied fighting a war in India set off by the Mutiny of 1857. When the war in China was resumed in December 1857, the English were joined by the French.

As in the first war, the Europeans moved north, and in Tianjin the British and French negotiated the Treaties of Tianjin, providing for permanent residency of diplomats in Beijing, the opening of ten new ports, unrestricted foreign travel throughout China, reduction of inland transit dues, an indemnity, and freedom of movement for all Christian missionaries. However, hostilities resumed after the British envoy discovered that the Qing planned to exchange ratifications of these treaties in Shanghai rather than Beijing, thus avoiding the appearance of full diplomatic relations between equals. Although the Chinese defeated the British at Taku, where the river leading to Tianjin enters the sea, overall victory went to the allies who entered Beijing, where Elgin, the British commander, vented his anger by burning down the imperial summer palace consisting of around 200 buildings northwest of Beijing. In October, the Conventions of Beijing were signed to supplement the Treaties of Tianjin, which now also took effect. In addition to the usual indemnity, China was forced to open 11 new ports, to grant rights to travel in the interior, and to allow foreign envoys to reside in Beijing. In 1860 the French also surreptitiously inserted into the Chinese text a provision granting missionaries the right to buy land and erect buildings in all parts of China.

The peace agreements were secured through the mediation of the Russian ambassador to Beijing, who used the opportunity to advance his country's interests. Russia now gained most-favored-nation status. Although it received only minor concessions in Central Asia, Russia made massive gains in the Northeast where, in 1860, it was ceded the entire area north of the Amur and east of the Ussuri River. That year also saw the founding of Vladivostok ("Ruler of the East," in Russian). The gains Russia made at this time remain a source of friction between Russian and China. They also turned Russia into a major player in the politics of Northeast Asia, ultimately bringing it into conflict with Japan.

Notes

1. Nola Cook and Li Tana, eds., *Water Frontier: Commerce and the Chinese in the Lower Mekong Region, 1750–1880* (London, U.K. and New York, NY: Rowan & Littlefield Publishers, 2004), p. 3.

2. Quoted in Alexander B. Woodside, *Vietnam and the Chinese Model: A Comparative Study of Vietnamese and Chinese Government in the First Half of the Nineteenth Century* (Cambridge, MA: Harvard Univ. Press, 1988), p. 247.

3. Li Tana, *Nguyen Cochinchina* (Ithaca, NY: Southeast Asia Program, Cornell University, 1998), Chapter 5.

4. K. W. Taylor, "Surface Orientations in Vietnam: Beyond Histories of Nation and Region," in *The Journal of Asian Studies 57*, No. 4 (Nov. 1998), p. 965.

5. Lan Cao, *Monkey Bridge* (New York, NY: Penguin Putnam, 1997), p. 150.

6. Nola Cooke, "The Myth of the Restoration: Dang-trong Influences in the Spiritual Life of the Early Nguyen Dynasty (1802–47)," in Anthony Reid, ed., *The Last Stand of Asian Autonomies* (New York, NY: St. Martin's Press, 1997), p. 277.

7. See Alexander Woodside, *Lost Modernities: China, Vietnam, Korea, and the Hazards of World History* (Cambridge, MA: Harvard Univ. Press, 2006), p. 41.

8. Maurice M. Durand and Nguyen Tran Huan, *An Introduction to Vietnamese Literature,* trans. by D. M. Hawke (New York, NY: Columbia Univ. Press, 1985), p. 99.

9. John Balaban, ed. and trans., *Spring Essence: The Poetry of Ho Xuan Huong* (Port Townsend, WA: Copper Canyon Press, 2000), p. 35.

10. David G. Marr, *Vietnamese Anticolonialism 1885–1925* (Berkeley, CA: Univ. of California Press, 1971), p. 26.

11. Alexander B. Woodside, *Community and Revolution in Modern Vietnam* (Boston, MA: Houghton Mifflin, 1976), p. 3.

12. Franz Schurmann and Orville Schell, *The China Reader: Imperial China* (New York, NY: Vintage Books, 1967), pp. 105–13, which reproduces Harley F. MacNair, *Modern Chinese History, Selected Readings* (Shanghai, China: Commercial Press Ltd., 1923), pp. 2–9.

13. John K. Fairbank, *Trade and Diplomacy on the China Coast: The Opening of the Treaty Ports, 1842–1854* (Cambridge, MA: Harvard Univ. Press, 1953), p. 59, which quotes H. B. Morse, *The Chronicles of the East India Company Trading to China, 1635–1834,* 5 vols. (Oxford, England, 1926, 1929), 2: pp. 247–52.

14. James M. Polachek, *The Inner Opium War* (Cambridge, MA: Harvard Univ. Press, 1992).

15. Ssu-yü Teng and John K. Fairbank, *China's Response to the West: A Documentary Survey, 1839–1923* (Cambridge, MA: Harvard Univ. Press, 1954), p. 26.

16. John Fletcher, *The Cambridge History of China,* vol. 10, ed. John K. Fairbank (Cambridge, England: Cambridge Univ. Press, 1978), pp. 375–85.

17. Philip Kuhn, *Origins of the Modern Chinese State* (Stanford, CA: Stanford Univ. Press, 2002), p. 56.

18. Quoted in Jonathan D. Spence, *God's Chinese Son: The Taiping Heavenly Kingdom of Hong Xiuquan* (New York, NY: W. W. Norton, 1996), p. 325.

Japan from Tokugawa to Meiji: *1787–1873*

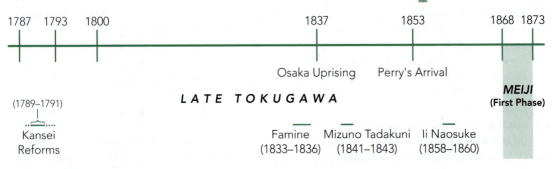

| 1787 | 1793 | 1800 | | 1837 | 1853 | 1868 | 1873 |

Osaka Uprising   Perry's Arrival

LATE TOKUGAWA

MEIJI
(First Phase)

(1789–1791)

Kansei
Reforms

Famine   Mizuno Tadakuni   Ii Naosuke
(1833–1836)   (1841–1843)   (1858–1860)

Internal crisis and Western intrusion are the main themes of this chapter, as of the last. Although prior to the 1830s there were some good years, the Tokugawa system was showing major symptoms of stress well before challenges from abroad put the old order to a final test. However, the dynamism of the forces subverting Tokugawa state and society ultimately helped Japan develop into a modern country.

Economy and Society: Pressures and Strains

Nature rescued the land from the famine of the 1780s but could not resolve the country's deeper economic problems or rescue the *bakufu* and the *daimyo* from fiscal difficulties that ultimately threatened the whole system.

When *daimyo*, burdened with biyearly attendance in Edo and the expense of maintaining headquarters in Edo as well as at home, found themselves in financial difficulty, they frequently reduced samurai stipends. This hurt even the small minority of high-ranking men with large stipends, but worst off were low-ranking samurai who had to convert a substantial portion of their rice stipend into cash, and who were constantly at the mercy of a fluctuating market that they did not understand and would not study.

Some samurai married daughters of wealthy merchants, but many lived in increasingly desperate circumstances. They pawned their swords, worked at humble crafts such as umbrella making and sandal weaving, and tried to hide their misery from the world. A samurai was taught that his mouth should display a toothpick even when he had not eaten. The samurai were not dissatisfied with the premises of a social system that placed them at the top, but they were enraged by the discrepancy between the theoretical elevation of their status and the reality of their poverty. Not only was their poverty demeaning, but the spectacle of merchant wealth hurt their pride. It seemed the height of injustice that society should reward the selfish money-makers and condemn to indigence the warrior whose life was one of service. They harbored deep resentment against incompetence and corruption in high places, and called on governments to employ more capable men from the lower samurai ranks.

City merchants and rural entrepreneurs flourished, but the increasing scope of the market had diverse effects on ordinary folk. In the Kanto there were villages left with untilled fields as people fled rural poverty in the hope of a better life in industry or commerce, but the market often proved a hard taskmaster. Charismatic religious teachers and cults offered consolation for misfortunes and hope for a better future. One such cult, Fujiko, was centered on pilgrimage to Mount Fuji and worship of Maitreya, associated in Japan as elsewhere with millenarianism (see Chapter 1).

When, as during a famine, things became unbearable, people resorted to violence. The best estimate claims 465 rural disputes, 445 peasant uprisings, and 101 urban riots between 1830 and 1844. A great impression was made by the 1837 uprising led by Ōshio Heihachiro (1793–1837), a low-ranking *bakufu* official and follower of Wang Yangming's philosophy of action. Although poorly planned and quickly suppressed, the uprising expressed a general sense of malaise and of the disintegration of authority. This was the case also in the countryside, where in earlier conflicts, villagers had united behind their headmen, but now the gap between the rich and poor had reached the point where interests diverged too widely for the village to speak with a single voice. Meanwhile, political leaders and thinkers sought to deal with the situation as best they could.

The Bakufu: 1787–1841

The Kansei Reforms (1789–1791) were an attempt to resolve the *bakufu*'s fiscal problems. They were led by Matsudaira Sadanobu (1787–1793), an earnest Confucian who served a young shogun and owed his position as head of the *bakufu* to the support he received from an inner circle of *daimyo*. Matsudaira encouraged a return to simpler times. He launched a campaign against corruption and made an effort to improve public services in Edo. His fiscal and economic program relied on edicts mandating lower prices for rice, restrictions on merchant guilds, cancellation of some samurai loans, and rent control. Matsudaira also sought to freeze foreign policy, reducing contact with the Dutch and proposing to leave Hokkaido undeveloped as a buffer against foreign intervention.

To improve administration, he sought to advance "men of ability," yet he tried to control what they thought by promoting education and by making the Neo-Confucianism of Zhu Xi the official doctrine. He proscribed heterodoxy from the official *bakufu* school, but this had little effect elsewhere. There was also a hardening of censorship. All told, these measures "institutionalized and hardened tradition . . . and left a regime less flexible and more concerned with preserving a tradition that had now been defined."[1]

It did not take long for the *bakufu*'s systemic fiscal ills to reappear. By 1800 its annual budget showed a small deficit, the beginning of a trend. Forced loans and 19 currency devaluations between 1819 and 1837 brought only temporary relief. The political authorities remained dependent on the market and on the merchants who understood and manipulated the market. The government could not simply borrow, because there was no system of deficit financing. When famine struck again, beginning in 1833 and reaching a crescendo in 1836, the *bakufu*'s response was once again inadequate.

The Bakufu: Mizuno Tadakuni's Reforms

In 1841 the *bakufu* embarked on a new round of reforms under Mizuno Tadakuni (1793–1851), a house *daimyo* (*fudai*) who rose to *bakufu* leadership. His measures included recoinage, forced loans, dismissal of officials to reduce costs, and sumptuary laws intended to preserve morals and save money. Censorship became stricter. An effort (by no means the first) was made to force peasants to return to their lands. This was in keeping with the Confucian view of the primacy of agriculture as well as with the Tokugawa policy of strict class separation—but it solved few if any problems.

A program to create a solid area of *bakufu* control around Edo and Osaka called for the creation of a *bakufu*-controlled zone of 25 square miles around Edo and 12 square miles around Osaka by moving certain *daimyo* and direct retainers out of these areas. This could have rationalized administration and strengthened the shogunate, but the plan proved too ambitious and could not be implemented. In the hope of fighting inflation, merchant monopolies were broken up and an attempt was made to bar the *daimyo* from engaging in commercial monopolies. Despite the retrenchment policy, an expensive and ostentatious formal procession to the Tokugawa mausoleum at Nikko was organized in an effort to reassert the *bakufu*'s preeminence. However, the *daimyo* were not easily bridled, and the reform lasted only two years.

The Domains

Reflecting Japan's geographical and political diversity, there were major local differences in the economy and in society. Fortunately, a number of local studies are currently helping correct overemphasis on the center, which was less important at the time. Thus, in his study of the herring fisheries in Hokkaido, which supplied fertilizer to the rest of Japan, David L. Howell found "a vibrant proto-industrial complex of commodity production for distant markets, dominated by merchant capitalists who used their ties to the local feudal authorities to good advantage."[2] A number of other domains pursued market-oriented policies, and commercial networks developed that linked communities in ways beyond the control of individual political authorities.

Change varied geographically and was complex socially. Nonetheless, the problems faced by the *daimyo* were similar to those confronting the *bakufu*, prompting attempts at local reform programs. In some cases, *han* government machinery was restructured, with stipends and other costs being cut. Some domains even rewarded the expert assistance of outstanding members of the merchant community by promoting them to samurai status. Agriculture was encouraged and commercial policies were changed. In the *han* as in the *bakufu,* the reforms ended in various ways, "some whimpering their way into oblivion, others culminating in an explosion in which the reformers were dismissed . . . and sometimes thrown into prison as well. . . . Whatever the end, they were ignored until their resurrection as models for fresh reforms in the 1850s and 1860s."[3]

A major domain in which the reforms did take hold was Satsuma in Kyushu (Figure 7.1). Subsequently, Chōshū in southwest Honshu enjoyed similar success. In important ways these were atypical domains. They were both large, outside *han* (*tozama*), which had accepted Tokugawa supremacy only when they had no alternative. Both had had their domains transferred and reduced in size, which consequently kept alive an anti-Tokugawa tradition and left them with an above-average ratio of samurai to land. In Satsuma, this led to the formation of a class of samurai who worked the land (*goshi*) and maintained a tight control of the countryside,

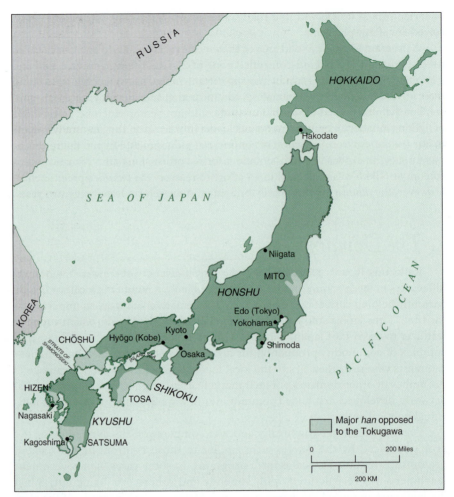

FIGURE 7.1   Map showing Satsuma in Kyushu and Chōshū in southwest Honshu, 1850s–1860s.

which experienced not a single peasant uprising throughout the Tokugawa period. Satsuma economic backwardness became an asset to the domain because it worked against the erosion of samurai values found in economically more advanced and urbane regions. Both Chōshū and Satsuma had special family ties with the court in Kyoto, the most likely focus for any anti-*bakufu* movement.

In both *han*, finances were put in order and a budget surplus was built up, although by different means. In Chōshū, rigorous cost-cutting was initiated, major improvements were made in *han* financial administration, and the land tax was reformed. Most monopolies were abolished, since they were unprofitable for the government and unpopular among the people. Only the profitable shipping and warehouse monopolies at Shimonoseki were continued. Otherwise, commodity transactions were turned over to merchants for a fee. Satsuma, in contrast, derived much of its income from its monopolies, especially the monopoly on sugar from the Ryukyu Islands, a Satsuma dependency that continued sending tribute to China in order to foster trade. Thus the Ryukyus served as a source of Chinese goods for Satsuma. The sugar monopoly was strictly enforced: private sale of sugar was a crime punishable by death. The sugar was brought to market in Osaka in the *han*'s own ships, and at every stage, from production to sale, everything was done to maximize profit for the Satsuma treasury.

These programs required vigorous leadership because they naturally ran up against the opposition of merchants and others who benefited from doing things the old way. Both Chōshū and Satsuma were fortunate in having reform-minded *daimyo* who raised to power young samurai of middle or low rank, men who tended to be much more innovative and energetic than conservative samurai of high rank. However, particularly in Chōshū, such differences in background and outlook among the samurai class led to bitter antagonisms and political turbulence.

The fact that reform was more successful in Chōshū and Satsuma than in the *bakufu* suggests that it was easier to implement reform in a well-organized, remote domain than in the central region where the economic development was most advanced and political pressures and responsibilities were far greater. Reform attempts in other *han* varied in success, but Chōshū and Satsuma are particularly important, since these two large and wealthy domains were to play a crucial role in the eventual overthrow of the Tokugawa.

Intellectual Currents

Economic, social, and political changes were accompanied by intellectual restiveness. Perceptions and ideas advanced by Shinto Revivalists of the School of National Learning, the Mito school with its emphasis on the centrality of the emperor, followers of Dutch Learning, and advocates of social restructuring ate away at the intellectual foundations of Tokugawa rule (see Chapter 4).

The roles of emperor and shogun continued to be subjects of discussion. In Mito, noted for its work on history, scholars emphasized that the emperor ruled by virtue of his unique descent and that the shogun's legitimacy came from the mandate he derived from the emperor. Aizawa Seishisai (1782–1863), a leading Mito thinker, combined Confucian values and *bushidō* with Shinto mythology in discussing Japan's unique polity (*kokutai*). In 1825 he wanted the emperor to create in Japan the kind of unity that he saw as the basis for the strength of Western states and attributed to (iniquitous) Christianity. As Bob Wakabayashi has indicated, in 1825 Aizawa's "argument for using the emperor's religious authority to bolster *bakufu* political supremacy was sensible and compelling."[4] However, 30 years later the emperor and shogun had grown so far apart that this would have been inconceivable. Nevertheless, Aizawa's glorification of the emperor was to outlast the very idea of a *bakufu*.

As a collateral domain, Mito was close to the center of power, but it was not alone in supporting new and potentially subversive ideas. From the very different world of Osaka came the bold ideas of Yamagata Bantō (1748–1821), a great financier who recommended making written Japanese more accessible by using only the phonetic *kana* script and eliminating all Chinese characters. An even more unorthodox thinker was Kaihō Seiryō (1748–1821), who spent his life traveling Japan free from the encumbrances of status or family, and saw all relations, including that between lord and samurai, in economic terms: the samurai sells his service to the lord in exchange for a stipend. For Kaihō Seiryō, this was merely accommodating to *li* (principle). Here a key Neo-Confucian concept is employed to structure a new theory of social conduct. The old bottles were capable of holding remarkably new wine—domestic or foreign.

Most students of Dutch Learning took a more positive attitude. Interest in practical Western sciences such as astronomy, medicine, and mathematics continued to grow. The *bakufu* itself, in 1811, set up a bureau to translate Dutch books even while it maintained its closed-door policies toward the West. However, Takano Chōei (1804–1850) and Watanabe Kazan (1795–1841), persecuted for disagreeing with the *bakufu*'s seclusion policy, eventually committed suicide.

Outstanding among the students of Western science was the Confucian scholar Sakuma Shōzan (1811–1864), who conducted experiments in chemistry and glass making, and later became an expert in the casting of guns. He was a serious thinker about the principles as well as the products of Western technology. There was ample room in his thought for Western learning, which he saw as part of the ultimate unity of *li* as taught by Zhu Xi, supplementing, not supplanting, his own tradition. His formula, "Eastern ethics and Western science," conveying the primacy of Japanese values as well as the compatibility of Western science, became an influential slogan after the Meiji Restoration. However, Sakuma did not live to see the day, for he was murdered by an antiforeign extremist from Chōshū in 1864.

Like Kaiho among others, Sakuma found room for new ideas within the old traditions, but beyond that, his intellectual strategy was essentially one of compartmentalization. The basic framework was left intact, with native and foreign traditions assigned different functions. Each had its distinct role isolated from the other. Most students of Dutch painting would have agreed, for they valued Western techniques more for their practical results than for any aesthetic merit. Yet, like all generalizations, this demands qualification. Hokusai, who lived until 1849, once contrasted the use of shading for decorative purposes in Chinese and Japanese art with its employment to create an effect of three-dimensionality in the West. He concluded, "One must understand both methods: there must be life and death in everything one paints."[5]

The Opening of Japan

As we have seen, the opening of China was a result of the Opium War, but in Japan, the *bakufu* knew that it could not prevail militarily and was determined to avoid war when confronted with an armed mission led by Commodore Matthew C. Perry of the United States Navy in 1853 (Figure 7.2). The treaties that followed that momentous event ended the Tokugawa policy of seclusion. This undermined the authority of the *bakufu,* and more importantly, the entire Tokugawa system.

Before 1853 there were a number of Western attempts to induce the Japanese to broaden their foreign policy, but these efforts were sporadic because they were

FIGURE 7.2 *Commodore Matthew C. Perry* (1794–1858) of the United States Navy. Artist unknown. In 1853–1854, Perry successfully led an armed mission to force isolationist Japan's agreement to open trade and diplomatic relations with the United States. Woodcut, nineteenth century, 26 × 24.5 cm.

PHOTOGRAPH COURTESY PEABODY ESSEX MUSEUM, SALEM, MASSACHUSETTS.

not supported by substantial economic and political interests like those at work in China. Regarded as poor and remote, Japan was considered a low priority by the great powers. The first approaches came from Japan's nearest Eurasian neighbor, the Russian Empire, and took place in the north, in the Kurile, Sakhalin, and Hokkaido islands. In 1778 and again in 1792, the Russians requested trade relations in Hokkaido, and in 1804 a similar request was made in Nagasaki. All were refused. British ships seeking trade or ship's stores were also turned away. British whaling ships sometimes requested supplies, but in 1825 the *bakufu* ordered that all foreign ships should be driven from Japanese waters. In 1837 a private American-British attempt to open relations with Japan fared no better. In 1842 the shogunate finally relaxed the edicts of 1825 and ordered that foreign ships accidentally arriving in Japan were to be provided with water, food, and fuel before being sent on their way.

China's defeat in the Opium War and the opening of new ports increased the number of Western vessels in East Asia, and hence the pressure on Japan. This changing situation could not be ignored. The lessons of Chinese weakness and Western strength were not lost on Japanese observers. Information concerning Western science, industry, and military capabilities continued to be provided by scholars of Dutch Learning and by the Dutch at Nagasaki. Information also came from China: Wei Yuan's *Illustrated Treatise on the Sea Kingdoms* was widely read after it appeared in a Japanese edition in 1847. Furthermore, the Japanese were making progress in mastering Western technology. By the 1840s, Mito, Hizen, and Satsuma were casting guns using Western methods. In 1850, Hizen possessed the first reverberatory furnace needed to produce iron suitable for making modern cannons. As already noted, a few courageous students of the West had suggested abandoning the policy of seclusion well before the arrival of Perry. The Dutch, too, had warned the *bakufu* of the designs of the stronger Western nations.

In 1846 an American mission to Japan ended in failure, but with the acquisition of California in 1848, the interest of the United States increased, because

Nagasaki, 500 miles from Shanghai, was a convenient fueling stop for ships bound from San Francisco to that port. Thus the United States, rather than Britain or Russia whose interests remained marginal, took the lead and sent Commodore Perry with four ships. Perry and his fleet reached Japan in July 1853, forced the Japanese to accept a letter from the American president to the emperor, and announced that he would return for an answer the following spring.

No match militarily for the American fleet, the *bakufu* realized that it would have to accede at least in part to American demands. In preparation for that unpopular move, it took the unprecedented step of soliciting the opinions of even the outside *daimyo*. This turned out to be a serious miscalculation. Instead of hoped-for support, the *bakufu* received divided and unhelpful advice, while undermining its exclusive right to determine foreign policy in the future.

When Perry returned in February 1854 with eight ships, an initial treaty was signed that provided for the opening of Shimoda and Hakodate to ships seeking provisions, assured that the shipwrecked would receive good treatment, and permitted the United States to send a consul to Japan. Similar treaties with Britain and France followed in 1855, and the Dutch and Russians negotiated broader agreements in 1857. The task of negotiating a commercial treaty was left to the first American consul, Townsend Harris, who arrived in Japan in 1856 and gradually succeeded in persuading the shogunate to make concessions (Figure 7.3). The resulting treaty was signed in 1858, and another round of treaties with the Dutch, Russians, British, and French followed.

FIGURE 7.3 *Harris's Procession on the Way to Edo.* Artist unknown. Townsend Harris, first American consul to Japan, traveled to Edo (Tokyo) in 1856 to negotiate a commercial treaty with Japan—a treaty that contained terms unfavorable to Japan. Watercolor, 53.5 × 38.8 cm. PHOTOGRAPH COURTESY PEABODY ESSEX MUSEUM, SALEM, MASSACHUSETTS.

At the end of this process, Japan's international situation was essentially that of China under the unequal treaty system. First there was the matter of opening ports. This began with Shimoda on the Izu Peninsula and Hakodate in Hokkaido; it was extended to Nagasaki and Kanagawa (for which Yokohama was substituted); dates were set for the opening of Niigata, Hyogo (modern Kobe), and admission of foreign residents, but not trade, into Osaka and Edo. As in China, the treaties gave extraterritoriality rights to foreigners. Japan lost its tariff autonomy and was limited to relatively low import duties. Most-favored-nation treatment obliged Japan to extend to all such states any concession it granted to another state.

Domestic Politics

For the *bakufu*, forced to accede to the foreign demands without enjoying support at home, these were difficult years. Each concession to the powers provided additional ammunition to its domestic enemies. Compounding its difficulties, the *bakufu* was itself divided by factionalism and policy differences. An attempt was made after Perry's arrival to broaden the shogunate's base by drawing on the advice of non-house *daimyo*. The Lord of Mito, Tokugawa Nariaki (1800–1860), a persistent advocate of resistance to the West, was placed in charge of national defense. These measures, however, failed to strengthen the *bakufu*—too many men were pulling in opposite directions.

When the shogun died without an heir in 1858, a bitter dispute took place over the rival claims of two candidates for the succession. One was still a boy, but had the strongest claim by descent. He also had the backing of most house *daimyo*, including Ii Naosuke, greatest of the *fudai*. The other candidate was Tokugawa Yoshinobu (then known as Hitotsubashi Keiki), the capable son of the Lord of Mito.

The immediate issue in the succession dispute concerned control over the *bakufu*, for Keiki's accession was seen as a threat to the continued control over the shogunate by the *fudai*. At the same time, foreign policy was involved, because the *bakufu* officials were inclined to make concessions to the foreigners, as they had little other choice. The great lords, however, demanded a vigorous defense policy against the intruders from the West. Furthermore, the Lord of Mito and some of his peers envisioned their own *han* as playing important roles in building up military strength. Thus, his advocacy of a strong foreign policy was consistent with his desire to strengthen his own domain at the expense of the center. Meanwhile, the split in the *bakufu* increased the political importance of the imperial court. Nariaki even appealed to Kyoto for support of his son's candidacy. Further increasing the court's importance was the shogun's attempt to obtain imperial approval for the treaty negotiated with Harris, which he failed to get.

The crisis of 1858 was temporarily resolved when Ii Naosuke took charge of the *bakufu* as Grand Councilor (*tairo*), a high post usually left vacant, and one that had previously been held by several members of the Ii family. The effective power of this position depended on the authority of the incumbent, and the strong-minded

Ii Naosuke used it to dominate the shogunate. He proceeded to sign the treaty with the United States without prior imperial approval, vigorously reasserted *bakufu* power, purged his enemies, forced into retirement or house arrest the *daimyo* who had opposed him, including the Lord of Mito, and punished some of the court nobles and Mito loyalists. For a moment the *bakufu* was revitalized. But only for a moment: in March 1860 Ii was assassinated by a group of samurai, mostly from Mito. They were advocates of *Sonnō*—"Revere the Emperor"—and *Jōi*—"Expel the Barbarians."

Sonnō Jōi

As we observed earlier, Mito was the home of an emperor-centered school of historiography and political thought, and its lord was one of the most fervent advocates of a strong military policy to "expel the barbarians." It is therefore not surprising that Mito thought influenced the passionate and brilliant young man who became the main spokesman and hero of the Sonnō Jōi movement. This was Yoshida Shōin (1830–1859), the son of a low-ranking Chōshū samurai. Yoshida was influenced by *bushidō* in the tradition of Yamaga Sokō, by books on military science, and by Confucianism. From Sakuma Shōzan he learned about the West. Then he became acquainted with Mito ideas on a study trip to northern Japan, which, since it was unauthorized, cost him his samurai rank. Apprehensive of the West and convinced of the importance of knowing one's enemy, he tried to stow away on one of Commodore Perry's ships, but was caught and placed under house arrest in Chōshū. After his release, he started a school there and attracted disciples, including Kido Kōin (or Takamasa, 1834–1877), one of the three leading statesmen of the Meiji Restoration, and the future leaders Itō Hirobumi and Yamagata Aritomo. Yoshida condemned the *bakufu* for its handling of the foreign problem. He charged that its failure to expel the barbarians reflected incompetence, dereliction of duty, and a lack of proper reverence for the throne. Like many men of lower samurai origins, he resented a system that rewarded birth more than ability or talent, and blamed the *bakufu*'s inability to reject the foreigners on this system. He believed that pure and selfless officials were necessary to redress the situation, because they would act out of true loyalty rather than mindless obedience. Thus, Yoshida's teaching combined elements of moral revival at home, opposition to foreigners, and championship of the throne.

Initially, Yoshida favored the appointment of new men to the *bakufu*, but after the signing of the treaty with the United States in 1858, he concluded that the *bakufu* must be overthrown. Both personal fulfillment and national salvation required an act of unselfish self-sacrifice by a national hero. In 1858 Yoshida, seeking to achieve both aims, plotted the assassination of the emissary sent by the shogun to the imperial court in order to persuade the emperor to accept the commercial treaty with the United States. But word leaked out. Yoshida was arrested and sent to Edo, where he was beheaded the following year.

Mixed Responses to the West

In this turbulent era, Japanese reactions to the West varied widely. Some Japanese, like the Confucian Shinoya Tōin (1810–1867), had an absolute hatred for everything Western. He even belittled the script in which the foreigners wrote, describing it as:

> confused and irregular, wriggling like snakes or larvae of mosquitoes. The straight ones are like dog's teeth, the round ones are like worms. The crooked ones are like the forelegs of a mantis, the stretched ones are like slime lines left by snails. They resemble dried bones or decaying skulls, rotten bellies of dead snakes or parched vipers.[6]

It is not surprising that a culture which prized calligraphy should find the strictly utilitarian Western script aesthetically unappetizing, but Shinoya's invective goes beyond mere distaste. Every word betrays, indeed is meant to express, horror and disgust at the beasts that had now come among them.

However, there were others who were determined to learn from the West, even if only to use that knowledge to defeat the foreigner. Their slogan was *kaikoku jōi:* "open the country to drive out the barbarians." In 1857 the *bakufu* opened the "Institute for the Investigation of Barbarian Books" near Edo Castle. Both *bakufu* and *han* sent men on study trips abroad; in the latter case this was often done illegally. The process of adopting Western technology, begun even before Perry's arrival, was accelerated. An indication of the people's receptivity to the new knowledge is provided by the popularity of the writings of Fukuzawa Yukichi (1835–1901), who went abroad twice in the early 1860s and published seven books prior to the Restoration; beginning with the first volume of *Conditions in the West* (*Seiyō jijō*), which appeared in 1866 and promptly sold 150,000 copies. Another 100,000 copies were sold in pirated editions. These works, written in a style easy enough for Fukuzawa's housemaid to read, were filled with detailed descriptions of Western institutions and life: hospitals, schools, tax systems, museums, climate, clothes, cutlery, beds, and chamberpots. Fukuzawa went on to become a leading Meiji intellectual, but the turbulent years just prior to the Restoration were dangerous for men of his outlook.

Unlike Yoshida Shōin, some people hoped for a reconciliation of the court and the *bakufu,* and there were some who still hoped the *bakufu* could transform itself and take the lead in creating a more modern state. These issues, at work during the 1860s, were finally buried in the Restoration.

Last Years of the Shogunate: 1860–1867

After the assassination of Ii Naosuke in 1860, the *bakufu* leadership tried compromise. An effort was made to effect a "union of the court and military" that was substantiated by the shogun's marriage to the emperor's sister. In return for affirming the emperor's primacy, the *bakufu* obtained assent for its foreign policy. It also sought to win *daimyo* support by relaxing the requirements for attendance at Edo. However, this policy ran into the opposition of Kyoto loyalists, activists of the *Sonnō Jōi* persuasion, samurai, and voluntary *rōnin* who had escaped the bonds of feudal discipline by requesting to leave their lords' service. Psychologically this was not difficult, as their loyalty to their lords had become bureaucratized and they now felt the claims of a higher loyalty to the throne. Men of extremist dedication, ready to sacrifice their lives for the cause, terrorized the streets of Kyoto in the early 1860s and made the capital unsafe for moderates, who risked losing their heads and having them displayed as a warning to others.

This also happened to statues: their location in a temple did not save the statues of Ashikaga shoguns from decapitation at the hands of some followers of Hirata Atsutane who, unable to reach prominent living targets, exercised vengeance on the Ashikaga for wronging the emperor in the fourteenth century. Mito, too, was unsafe for moderates. Women as well as men were moved to protest (see Box 7.1).

BOX 7.1 A FEMALE POET SPEAKS OUT

Descended from a well-off peasant family in central Japan, Matsuo Taseko (1811–1894) became a poet, local activist, and scholar in the tradition of Hirata Atsutane. She traveled to Kyoto in 1862 as a 51-year-old to support the anti-*bakufu* activists aiming to restore the Japanese emperor to power and expel the Western barbarians. She especially resented the interference of Westerners in Japan's trade, and the weakness of the *bakufu* in dealing with them. Matsuo also saw the *bakufu* as backward in its embrace of Chinese teachings and its inability to change with the times.

> In the eastern provinces
> where the birds sing,
> in place of the emperor
> who once had taken charge
> of the great affairs of government
> for the realm
> in his palace far away
> above the clouds,
> the despicable charlatans
> who run the administration
> have abandoned the way
> of the foundation for the sun
> and learned even from
> superficial Chinese teachings

(continued)

BOX 7.1 A FEMALE POET SPEAKS OUT (CONTINUED)

Matsuo dreamed of a day when the emperor, released from *bakufu* control, would be free to exercise his power. Here she reflects the perspective of non-elite actors in the events leading up to the Meiji Restoration. In other poems Matsuo expresses her feelings of constraint as a woman, and vents frustration at her inability to do more.

> Even though I am not worthy to be counted
> among the mighty warriors
> who go out to serve
> on that way
> graced with
> the departed souls
> of the imperial ancestors
> I shout bravely
> to enflame
> true Japanese hearts.
>
> How awful
> to have the ardent heart
> of a manly man
> and the useless body of a weak woman

Source: Anne Walters, *The Weak Body of a Useless Woman: Matsuo Taseko and the Meiji Restoration* (Chicago: University of Chicago Press, 1998), pp. 107, 229, 231.

For ordinary people this was a time when their frustrations came to a head, a time of messianic visions and religious fervor, of amulets falling from the sky, and of people finding temporary escape from misery by dancing wildly in the streets, shouting "*ee ja nai ka*" ("ain't it great," or "what the hell"), barging into the houses of the rich and powerful demanding food and drink, forcing them to join the dance, and wreaking general havoc. Beginning in the cities of central Japan and spreading along the Tōkaido, these riots showed that the Tokugawa order was falling apart. George M. Wilson says of the Meji Restoration that "a pervasive urge to remedy distress at home was just as compelling to most participants as the patriotic intent to elevate Japan in the international area."[7]

Westerners, too, were blamed for the distress, for the opening of the ports was followed by a marked rise in the price of rice, causing great hardship and reinforcing nativistic hatred of foreigners. Fervent samurai assassinated several foreigners in 1859. In 1861, Townsend Harris's Dutch interpreter was murdered, and the British legation in Edo was attacked. In 1862, a British merchant lost his life at the hands of Satsuma samurai. When the British were unable to obtain satisfaction from the *bakufu*, they took matters into their own hands. In August 1863 they bombarded Kagoshima, the Satsuma capital, in order to force punishment of the guilty and payment of an indemnity.

A similar incident involving Chōshū took place in the summer of 1863. By that time extremists had won control of the imperial court, and with Chōshū backing, had forced the shogun to accept June 25, 1863, as the date for the expulsion of the barbarians. The *bakufu*, caught between intransigent foreigners and the insistent court, interpreted the agreement to mean that negotiations for the closing of the ports would begin on that day, but Chōshū loyalists interpreted it more literally. When Chōshū guns began firing on foreign ships in the Straits of Shimonoseki, the foreign ships fired back. First, American warships came to shell the fortifications, and then French ships landed parties that destroyed the fort and ammunition. Nevertheless, Chōshū persisted in firing on foreign vessels, until in September 1864 a combined French, Dutch, and American fleet demolished the forts and forced Chōshū to come to terms. These losses, plus a defeat inflicted on Chōshū adherents by a Satsuma-Aizu force in Kyoto in August 1864, stimulated Chōshū to overhaul its military forces. It had already undertaken the purchase of arms and ships. Now peasant militia were organized, and mixed rifle units were formed, staffed by commoners and samurai, a radical departure from Tokugawa practice and from the basic principles of Tokugawa society. One of these units was commanded by Itō Hirobumi, recently returned from study in England.

Satsuma's response to defeat, although not as radical as Chōshū's, was similar in its appreciation of the superiority of Western weapons. With British help, the domain began acquiring Western ships, forming the nucleus of what was to become the Imperial Japanese Navy. The British supported Satsuma partly because they were disillusioned with the *bakufu* and partly because the French were supporting the shogunate with arms, hoping to lay the foundations for future influence in a reconstituted shogunate. By now, many *bakufu* officials appreciated the need for institutional change as well as modernization. During the closing years of the Tokugawa, the issue was no longer one of preserving the old system but of who would take the lead in building the new one. In Chōshū and Satsuma, too, there was now less talk about "expelling the barbarians" and more about "enriching the country and strengthening the army," at least among the leaders.

The politics of these years were especially full of complications and intrigues, and as long as Chōshū and Satsuma remained on opposite sides, the situation remained fluid. Traditionally unfriendly to each other, competing for power in Kyoto, and differing in their policy recommendations, they were nevertheless unified in their opposition to a restoration of Tokugawa power. There were two wars against Chōshū. In the first, from 1864 to 1865, a large *bakufu* force with men from many domains defeated Chōshū. This in turn set off a civil war in Chōshū from which the revolutionaries, with their mixed rifle regiments, emerged victors. This led to a second *bakufu* war against Chōshū, but before this second war began, in 1866, Chōshū and Satsuma made a secret alliance. When the war did come, Satsuma and some other powerful *han* remained on the sidelines. Although outnumbered, the Chōshū forces, better trained, better armed, and high in morale, defeated the *bakufu*.

After this defeat by a single *han*, the *bakufu*, under Tokugawa Yoshinobu (who inherited the position of shogun in 1866), tried to save what it could. There were attempts to work out a *daimyo* coalition, and calls for imperial restoration. In November the shogun accepted a proposal that he resign in favor of a council of *daimyo* under the emperor. According to this arrangement, he was to retain his lands and, as the most powerful lord in Japan, serve as prime minister. However, this was unacceptable to the *sonnō* advocates in Satsuma and Chōshū and to the restorationists at court, including the court noble Iwakura Tonomi (1825–1883), a master politician. On January 3, 1868, forces from Satsuma and other *han* seized the palace and proclaimed the restoration. The shogunate was destroyed. Tokugawa lands were confiscated, and the shogun himself was reduced to the status of an ordinary *daimyo*. A short civil war ensued. There was fighting in Edo and in northern Honshu, but no real contest. Last to surrender was the *bakufu* navy, which finally did so in May 1869.

Formation of a New Government: The Meiji Restoration

The men who overthrew the Tokugawa in January 1868 did not subscribe to any clear and well-defined program. There was general agreement on the abolition of the shogunate and "restoration" of the emperor, but this meant no more than that the emperor should once again be at the center of the political system, functioning as the source of legitimacy and providing a sense of continuity. It definitely did not mean that actual power should be given to the sixteen-year-old Meiji Emperor (1852–1912; r. 1867–1912),[*] nor did it necessarily imply the destruction of feudalism, for there were those who envisioned the Restoration in terms of a new feudal system headed by the emperor. On the other hand, Japanese scholars had long been aware that the Chinese system provided a bureaucratic alternative to feudalism. This, very likely, eased the shift to bureaucratic centralization.

The new leaders did not always see eye to eye, but they did share certain qualities: they were all of similar age (35–43) and rank, and came from the victorious *han* or the court aristocracy, although the *han* coalition was soon broadened to include men from Tosa and Hizen. The three most eminent leaders in the early years of the Restoration were Ōkubo Toshimichi (1830–1878), Kido Kōin (1833–1877), and Saigō Takamori (1827–1877). Both Ōkubo and Kido had risen

---

[*]His name was Mutsuhito but, as in the case of the Qing emperors in China, it is customary to refer to him and his successors by the designation given to their reign periods.

to leadership in their own domains (Satsuma and Chōshū), through their influence in that domain's bureaucratic establishment and among it's loyalist activists. Of the two, Ōkubo was the stronger personality—disciplined, formal, and somewhat intimidating; completely dedicated to the nation, cautious, and practical. Kido was livelier but more volatile, less self-confident but more concerned than Ōkubo with strengthening the popular base of the government. Nonetheless, he was equally devoted to building a strong state.

Ōkubo's was the single strongest voice in government during 1873 to 1878. One of his initial tasks was to retain the cooperation of Saigō, the military leader of the Satsuma forces who had joined with Chōshū to overthrow the Tokugawa. Saigō was a man of imposing physique and great physical strength. He was known for his outstanding courage, and possessed many of the traditional warrior virtues, such as generosity and contempt for money. More conservative than the others, he was devoted to Satsuma and its samurai, but worked with the others at least until 1873. They were united in their conviction that the country must be strengthened to resist the West.

For the sake of national self-preservation, the leaders were prepared to enact vast changes, but it took time to plan and carry these out, and indeed, to consolidate their own power in a land where, as Kido complained, "we are surrounded on four sides by little *bakufu*."[8] To insure that the emperor would not become a focus of opposition to reform, Ōkubo argued that he should be moved to Edo, renamed Tokyo (Eastern Capital) in September 1868. This took place the following year when the emperor moved into the shogun's former castle, which in 1871, after much debate, was renamed the "imperial palace."

The Charter Oath

Even before the move, in April 1868, while the emperor was still in Kyoto, a Charter Oath was issued in his name to provide a general, if vague, statement of purpose for the new regime. It consisted of five articles:

1. An assembly widely convoked shall be established and all matters of state shall be decided by public discussion.

2. All classes high and low shall unite in vigorously promoting the economy and welfare of the nation.

3. All civil and military officials and the common people as well shall be allowed to fulfill their aspirations, so that there may be no discontent among them.

4. Base customs of former times shall be abandoned and all actions shall conform to the principles of international justice.

5. Knowledge shall be sought throughout the world and thus shall be strengthened the foundation of the imperial polity.[9]

Although the government was reorganized to provide for an assembly in keeping with the first article, power remained with the original leadership, and the attempt to implement this provision was soon abandoned. In contrast, the end of seclusion, the acceptance of international law, and the openness to foreign ideas conveyed by the last two articles did take place. Symbolic of this shift was the audience granted representatives of the foreign powers by the emperor in Kyoto just a month before the Charter Oath was issued. The document itself was drafted by two men familiar with Western thought; it was then revised by Kido. The ramifications of the Charter Oath were far from clear, but the last article, to seek for knowledge "throughout the world," was taken very seriously. Furthermore, with its call for an assembly and its strong internationalism, the entire document illustrates the gulf between Japanese and Chinese leaders at this time. No Chinese government would have issued such a document in an attempt to gain political strength.

Dismantling the Old Order

While the machinery of the central government underwent various reorganizations, the prime need was for the government to extend and consolidate its authority and ability to collect taxes. Since the continued existence of the feudal domains was a major obstacle to this, the government leaders undertook the delicate but essential task of abolishing the *han*. In March 1869, Kido and Ōkubo were able to use their influence to induce the *daimyo* of Chōshū and Satsuma to return their domains to the emperor. The lords of Tosa and Hizen joined them in this act. Many others followed suit, anxious to be in the good graces of the new government and expecting to be appointed governors of their former domains, which they were. The real blow came in 1871 when, in the name of national unity, the domains were completely abolished and the whole country was reorganized into prefectures. This was made palatable to the *daimyo* by generous financial arrangements. They were allowed to retain a tenth of the former domain revenue as personal income while the government assumed responsibility for *han* debts and financial obligations. The *daimyo* were also assured continued high social standing and prestige. Finally, in 1884, they were elevated to the peerage.

As a result of background and experience, the new leadership was keenly sensitive to the importance of military power. Initially, the new government was entirely dependent on forces from the supporting domains, but this was unacceptable for a government truly national in scope. Accordingly, the leaders set about forming a new army freed from local ties. Rejecting the views of Saigō, who envisioned a samurai army that would ensure the warrior class a useful and, he hoped, brilliant role in Japan's future, the leaders decided in 1872 to build their army on the basis of commoner conscription. In January 1873, the new measure, largely the work of Yamagata Aritomo (1838–1922), "father of the Japanese Army," became law.

The Restoration had a profound effect on the samurai. The new army, by eliminating distinctions between commoners and samurai, cut right to the heart of the status system. Anyone could become a warrior now. Other marks of samurai distinctiveness were eliminated or eroded. In 1870 commoners were allowed to acquire surnames and were released from previous occupational and residential restrictions. In 1871 the wearing of swords by samurai became optional; five years later it was prohibited entirely.

The samurai's position was further undermined by the abolition of the *han*, which left them without any political or social function. Furthermore, continued payment of their stipends at the customary rate was too expensive for the central government. Accordingly, they were forced to accept pensions. However, because the samurai were numerous, the government could not afford to treat them as generously as it did the *daimyo*. At first, samurai stipends were reduced on a sliding scale from half to a tenth of what they had been, then they were given the right to commute these into 20-year bonds (in 1873), and finally they were forced to accept the bonds (in 1876).

Reduction and commutation of samurai stipends was just one measure taken to establish the new government on a sound financial basis. In addition to monetary and banking reform, a tax system was created (1873). The fiscal measures were largely the work of Ōkuma Shigenobu (1838–1922), a man from Hizen who was to remain prominent in Meiji politics, and Itō Hirobumi (1841–1909) of Chōshū. The main source of government revenue was, as before, agriculture. However, in place of the old percentage of the crop payable by the village to the *daimyo*, the government now collected the tax in money according to the assessed value of the land. It was payable by the owner, and for this purpose ownership rights had to be clearly established. This was not done in favor of the absentee feudal interests long divorced from the land, nor did ownership pass equitably to all peasants. Instead, certificates were issued to the cultivators and wealthy villagers who had paid the tax during Tokugawa times. In this way, tenancy was perpetuated. Since poor peasants, often unable to meet their taxes, were forced to mortgage their land, the rate of tenancy increased, rising from about 25 percent before the new system to about 40 percent 20 years later.

Disaffection and Opposition

The creation of a modern political, military, and fiscal system benefited the state but left many people bitterly disappointed. Peasants who had been led to expect a better life felt they had been duped when their burdens remained as heavy as ever, while they additionally were saddled with military conscription, compulsory education, and high taxes. Such grievances along with resentment at the removal of the restrictions on outcasts (*burakumin*, see p. 75–76) motivated a series of peasant insurrections from 1866 to 1876. In 1873 alone, 37 disturbances occurred, including one in Fukuoka that involved three million people and the destruction of 4,590 buildings.

The new order favored commerce, but many of the large merchant houses that had developed symbiotic relationships with the *bakufu* or *daimyo* suffered during these years, and some even went bankrupt.

More serious for the regime was samurai discontent. The new government was itself led by former samurai, and for many men the new order meant a release from old restrictions and the opening of new opportunities. Since the samurai were the educated class with administrative experience, it was they who supplied the personnel for local and national government, provided officers for the army, furnished teachers for the schools, and produced colonists for Hokkaido. Casting aside tradition, some entered the world of business and finance. Yet many did not make a successful transition; men who resented the erosion of their stipends and privileges, were unable or unwilling to take advantage of the new vocations opened to them, or to use their payments to establish themselves in new endeavors. Among the leaders, as well as the supporters, of the Meiji government were men who firmly believed that its purpose was literally the restoration of the old, not the creation of the new. A split between conservatives and modernizers developed early in the Restoration and culminated in 1873.

The Crisis of 1873

The crisis of 1873 centered on the issue of going to war with Korea in order to force it to open its doors to Japan. Those who advocated war, such as Saigō and Itagaki Taisuke (1836–1919) from Tosa, did so for nationalist motives, and because they viewed war as a method to provide employment for the samurai, an opportunity to give them a greater role in the new society, and a means to preserve their military heritage. Saigō, a military leader with great charisma and devotion to the way of the warrior, asked to be sent to Korea as ambassador so that he could get himself killed and provide a cause for going to war.

A decision for war was made in the summer of 1873, in the absence of Ōkubo, Kido, and other important leaders who were abroad in America and Europe. They were on a diplomatic and study mission headed by Iwakura Tomomi, the noble who had played a leading role at court in bringing about the Meiji Restoration. The purposes of the Iwakura mission were to convey the Meiji Emperor's respects to the heads of state of the treaty powers and build good will, to discuss subjects for later treaty revision, and to provide its distinguished members with an opportunity to observe and study the West first hand. It took 631 days, including seven months in the United States, four in England, and seven in continental Europe. The Japanese leaders did not just have audiences with heads of state and observe parliaments and courts; they took an interest in everything.

> They toured cotton mills, iron foundries, shipyards, newspaper plants, breweries, prisons, banks, stock exchanges, cathedrals, telegraph offices, military fortifications, lunatic asylums, libraries and art galleries. . . . [They] visited zoos; attended the theater and opera; and took in endless concerts, ballets, and an occasional masked ball, circus performance, and fox hunt.[10]

They returned home in September 1873 with a new appreciation of the importance and complexity of modernization and a new realization of the magnitude of the task facing Japan in its quest for equality. They were convinced of the urgent priority for domestic change.

When the mission returned, Ōkubo led the opposition to the Korean venture on the grounds that Japan could not yet afford such an undertaking. Ōkubo, Kido, and Iwakura prevailed, with the support of many officials and the court. In October it was decided to abandon the Korean expedition and to concentrate on internal development. The decision split the government. Bitterly disappointed, the war advocates, including Saigō and Itagaki, resigned. They provided leadership for those who were disaffected by the new government and its policies, an opposition that later proved troublesome to those in power, although samurai uprisings in 1874 and 1876 never became too threatening. Furthermore, the government was left in the hands of a group of men unified by a commitment to modernization. Most prominent among them were Ōkubo, Itō, Ōkuma, and Iwakura.

By 1873 the Meiji government had survived the difficult period of initial consolidation. It had established the institutional foundations for the new state, had found a means of defense and national security, and with the resolution of the 1873 crisis, had charted the basic course of development at home and peace abroad that was to dominate Japanese policies during the next 20 years.

The Meaning of the Restoration

Like other major historical events, the Meiji Restoration meant and continued to mean different things to different people. Most visible was increased openness to the West in all matters. Already in the early 1870s, the gentleman of fashion sported a foreign umbrella and watch and, as recommended by Fukuzawa Yukichi, strengthened his body by eating beef. Faddish Westernism was satirized in one of the bestsellers of the day, *Aguranabe* (*Sitting around the Stew Pan,* 1871) by Kanagaki Robun (1829–1903). Ōkubo ate bread, drank dark tea for breakfast, and wore Western clothes even at home. In 1872, Western dress was made mandatory at court and other official functions. The Gregorian calendar was adopted the same year. After the Tokyo fire of 1872, the city's main avenue, the Ginza, was rebuilt under the supervision of an English architect. It boasted brick buildings, colonnades, and gas lamps (Figure 7.4).

The inhabitants of Tokyo could take pleasure and pride in the Ginza, but the glitter of the capital was not shared by the countryside. Already in 1874 the widening contrast between the prosperous modern capital and the hinterland prompted Fukuzawa Yukichi to warn:

> The purpose [of the government] seems to be to use the fruits of rural labor to make flowers for Tokyo. Steel bridges glisten in the capital, and horse-drawn carriages run on the streets, but in the country the wooden bridges are so rotten one cannot cross them. The cherry blossoms bloom in Kyōbashi [in Tokyo] but weeds grow in the country fields. Billows of smoke such as rise from city stoves do not rise from the farmer's furnace. . . . We must cease making Tokyo richer and concentrate on rural districts.[11]

Unfortunately for those at the bottom of society, this was not to be.

Ideologically, the main thrust was to use the old to justify the new, a process that produced a new vision of the past as well as of the future. Invoking the name of the emperor, a symbol of continuity with the old, the Meiji leaders were able to

FIGURE 7.4 The Ginza, 1873. The Ginza's facade and lamp posts represent the Meiji Restoration's most visible feature—an increased openness to the West in matters small and large.

PHOTOGRAPH © TSISEI CORPORATION, JAPAN. USED BY PERMISSION.

innovate even as they assured the survival, in new forms, of old values and ideas. Along these lines, there was an effort to turn Japan into a Shinto state. In 1868, Shinto was proclaimed the basis for the government and a Department of Shinto was established with precedence over the other departments. There was a drive to purify Shinto from Buddhist influences that had seeped into Shinto and to make Shinto the only religion of Japan. This drive, however, ran into opposition from Buddhists, and conflicted with Western pressures for the legalization of Christianity. In 1872 the Department of Shinto was abolished, and in 1873 the ban on Christianity was lifted. Settlement of the legal status of Shinto had to wait until 1882 (see Chapter 8).

The Restoration was revolutionary because it destroyed the old system and created a centralized state. It eliminated the old class lines and legally opened all careers to all men. In all areas of human activity it paved the way for the profound changes that, during the next century, were to transform the very countryside of Japan. But if it was a revolution, it was a revolution from above, an "aristocratic revolution," to borrow a term from Thomas C. Smith.[12] Though popular unrest helped undermine the Tokugawa, the Restoration was not the product of a mass movement nor of a radical social ideology. It did not radically change the structure of village life or the mode of agricultural production. It eliminated the samurai elite as a legally defined, privileged class, but led by men who were themselves samurai, did so in terms the samurai could understand.

The legacy of the Restoration was complex and perhaps is still incomplete, since it provided a base for both the successes and the failures that were to come.

Notes

1. Marius B. Jansen, ed. *The Cambridge History of Japan,* vol. 5: *The Nineteenth Century* (Cambridge, England: Cambridge Univ. Press, 1989), p. 60.

2. David L. Howell, *Capitalism from Within: Economy, Society and the State in a Japanese*

Fishery (Berkeley, CA: Univ. of California Press, 1995), p. 91.

3. Harold Bolitho in Howell, *Capitalism from Within,* p. 159.

4. Bob Tadashi Wakabayashi, *Anti-Foreignism and Western Learning in Early Modern Japan: The*

New Theses of 1825 (Cambridge, MA: Harvard Univ. Press, 1986), p. 134.

5. Michiaki Kawakita, *Modern Currents in Japanese Art, Heibonsha Survey of Japanese Art,* vol. 24, trans. by Charles S. Terry (New York, NY and Tokyo, Japan: Weatherhill/Heibonsha, 1974), p. 29.

6. Marius B. Jansen, ed., *Changing Japanese Attitudes Toward Modernization* (Princeton, NJ: Princeton Univ. Press, 1969), pp. 57–58, which quotes van Gulik, "Kakkaron: A Japanese Echo of the Opium War," *Monumenta Serica* 4 (1939): 542–43.

7. George M. Wilson, *Patriots and Redeemers in Japan: Motives in the Meiji Restoration* (Chicago, IL: Univ. of Chicago Press, 1992), p. 2. For *ee ja nai ka,* see p. 98.

8. Albert Craig and Donald Shively, eds., *Personality in Japanese History* (Berkeley, CA and Los Angeles, CA: Univ. of California Press, 1970), p. 297.

9. Ishii Ryosuke, *Japanese Legislation in the Meiji Era,* trans. by William J. Chai (Tokyo, Japan: Pan-Pacific Press, 1958), p. 145.

10. John Hunter Boyle, *Modern Japan: The American Nexus* (Fort Worth, TX: Harcourt Brace Jovanovich, 1993), p. 92.

11. Quoted by Mikiso Hane, *Peasants, Rebels, and Outcastes: The Underside of Modern Japan* (New York, NY: Pantheon Books, 1982), p. 33.

12. See Thomas C. Smith, "Japan's Aristocratic Revolution," *Yale Review* 50 (Spring 1961), pp. 370–83. Also see Marius B. Jansen, "The Meiji State: 1868–1912," in James B. Crowley, ed., *Modern East Asia: Essays in Interpretation* (New York, NY: Harcourt Brace Jovanovich, 1970), pp. 95–121, which cites Smith on p. 103.

8

The Emergence of Modern Japan: 1874–1894

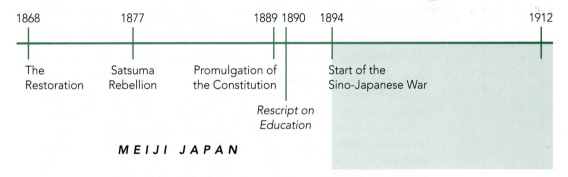

1868	1877	1889	1890	1894	1912
The Restoration	Satsuma Rebellion	Promulgation of the Constitution		Start of the Sino-Japanese War	

Rescript on Education

MEIJI JAPAN

Political Developments

Formation of Parties

The Emperor and the Constitution

Western Influences on Values and Ideas

"Civilization and Enlightenment"

Social Darwinism

The Arts

Conservatism and Nationalism

Education

Modernizing the Economy

The Zaibatsu

The Military

After the Meiji leaders consolidated their new regime, their top priority was to transform Japan into a modern nation accepted as an equal by all the powers of the world. During the next 20 years, a new political framework was devised, the foundations for a modern economy were laid, and profound change occurred in institutions as well as in values and ideas. Just as tradition had different meanings for different people, throughout the nineteenth and twentieth centuries there were diverse (and changing) versions of modernity. Rather than attempting a substantive definition of the modern, we use the term in a purely temporal sense, to mean "up to date." During the nineteenth and twentieth centuries, the West largely defined modernity by virtue of its great power.

Change was neither smooth nor simple. In the intricate interweaving of old and new, some old customs went the way of the samurai's sword and topknot, but others were retained or transformed for new uses. Early Meiji saw the appearance of the patently new as well as the emergence of new versions of the past. As John Dower, summarizing a body of recent scholarship, has written:

> Thus they [recent scholars] called attention to the careful and adroit manner by which elites and molders of popular opinion, in Japan as elsewhere, routinely create modern myths under the rubric of "tradition" or cultural uniqueness—whether these be myths involving the emperor, or an idealized hierarchical "family system," or a code of "obedience and filial piety," or a harmonious "traditional employment system," or a simple and egalitarian rural community, or a pure "national essence" rooted in the past before the corruption of foreign influences from China and the West.[1]

As we have seen, myths centered on a "national essence" could draw on Tokugawa nativist thought, but they became modern myths participating in Japan's process of becoming modern. That process continued, but Japan's victory over China in 1895 marked the conclusion of the crucial initial phase of modernization, for by then it had achieved many of its initial objectives: a centralized government, a modernizing economy, and sufficient military strength to warrant international respect.

Political Developments

Acting in the name of the emperor, a small inner circle dominated the government during the 1870s and 1880s, but not without opposition. To mollify those disappointed by the abandonment of the Korean expedition so earnestly sought by Saigō and his friends, Japan sent a military force to Taiwan in 1874, ostensibly to punish aborigines who had killed some shipwrecked Okinawans. This expedition was a smaller and safer undertaking than a military confrontation with Korea. It was successful, resulting in China paying an indemnity and recognizing Japanese sovereignty over the Ryukyu Islands. Thus, the expedition ended the ties that the Ryukyus had maintained with China even while they were Satsuma vassals.

The success of the expedition, however, did not alleviate the situation of disoriented and embittered samurai who felt betrayed by the Meiji leaders. Such men resorted to arms in an uprising in Hizen in 1874, Western Kyushu in 1876, and most seriously, in Satsuma in 1877. Saigō Takamori led the Satsuma Rebellion, after he had withdrawn from the government in 1873 following the decision against the Korean expedition. The rebel force rose as high as 42,000. Its suppression strained the military resources of the Restoration government, but after half a year the rebellion was crushed.

The Satsuma Rebellion was the last stand of the samurai. When the military situation became hopeless, Saigō committed ritual suicide. His was a martyr's death for a lost cause. Saigō died under official condemnation as a traitor, but the force of his personality, the depth of his sincerity, and the magnanimity of his spirit were widely admired. To quote Ivan Morris:

> There are times in the history of many countries when growing internal discord and fear of dangers from outside create a special need for some unifying symbol in the form of national hero who will give the people sense of pride and cohesion and help them confront their difficulties.[2]

The Meiji government soon rehabilitated Saigō for exemplifying the "nobility of failure." Along with conservatives, representatives of the most diverse political persuasions praised the magnanimity of his spirit and transformed Saigō into a legendary hero; celebrating him in poems and songs (including an army marching song), portraying his saga on stage and in an extensive literature, depicting him in portraits and prints, and even identifying him with the planet Mars.

Protest against the government continued, on occasion, to take a violent turn. Less than half a year after Saigo Takamori's death, some of his sympathizers assassinated Ōkubo Toshimichi, also from Satsuma, who had worked so hard to create the new Japanese state. There were other assassination attempts, both successful and not. More important in the long run, however, was the formation of nonviolent political opposition. This opposition objected to various aspects of government policy, but more importantly it protested against the monopoly on power held by the few men from Chōshū and Satsuma. Basing their position on the first article of the 1868 Charter Oath, opposition leaders demanded the creation of an elected legislature early in 1874. Prominent among them was Itagaki Taisuke, the Tosa leader who, along with Saigō, had left the government over the Korean issue.

In Tosa and subsequently elsewhere, antigovernment organizations voiced the discontent of local interests, demanding political rights, local self-government, and formation of a national assembly. The advocates of a constitution and the leaders of this movement for popular rights drew upon Western political theories. Constitutionalism itself was an idea with wide currency and a long pedigree in the West, where it was associated with ideas concerning the supremacy of law, a "social contract," and human rights highlighted in eighteenth-century political thought. In the West, constitutions limited the powers exercised by heads of state by providing for representative institutions to share in governing, however, a strong argument advanced in Japan was that representative institutions would create greater unity between the people and the emperor. In this view, a constitution was not needed to limit the emperor's powers, but rather to control his advisors. The men in power were not averse to some kind of constitution as a necessary and even desirable component of modernization. Indeed, Kido, as a participant in the Iwakura mission to Europe, became persuaded of the need for a constitution.

By 1878, Kido, Ōkubo, and Saigō were all dead. Of the older men, only Iwakura remained important, and three younger men who had already contributed significantly to the Meiji state now assumed leadership: Itō Hirobumi and Yamagata Aritomo, both from Chōshū, and Ōkuma Shigenobu from Hizen. Yamagata was the creator of the new army, while Itō took the lead in political modernization, and Ōkuma served as Finance Minister. They agreed that Japan should have a constitution, but could agree neither on the structure of the constitution nor on a schedule for devising and implementing it. Tensions between Itō and Ōkuma culminated in 1881 when the latter wrote a memorandum advocating the adoption of an English-style political system. His proposals that the majority party in parliament form the government, that the cabinet be responsible to parliament, and that the first elections be held in 1883 clashed with the conservative and gradualist views of his colleagues. First his proposals were rejected; then, when Ōkuma joined in public criticism of the government over its sale of a certain government project in Hokkaido, the emperor consented to having Ōkuma ousted from the government. At the same time, the government announced that the emperor would grant a constitution to take effect in 1890.

Formation of Parties

In response, Itagaki and his associates formed the Jiyutō (Liberal party), and Ōkuma followed by organizing the Kaishintō (Progressive party). Both parties advocated constitutional government with meaningful powers exercised by a parliament, but they differed somewhat in ideology and especially in composition. The Jiyutō, linked to Tosa, drew much of its support from rural areas, where peasants and landlords were unhappy that their taxes were as high as they had been under the Tokugawa, and resented bearing a heavier tax burden than that required of commerce and industry. The Jiyutō proclaimed itself "devoted to the expansion of liberty, protection of rights, promotion of happiness, and reform of society."[3] Ōkuma's party (linked to Hizen) was, in contrast, more urban and more moderate, advocating English-style liberalism and setting forth more specific proposals. It had the backing of merchants and industrialists. Although both opposed the government and advocated representative government, the two parties fought each other energetically. At the same time, the parties were troubled by internal factionalism; party splits were based on master-follower and patron-client relations rather than on differences in programs.

Restrictive laws, including those controlling political criticism, further hampered the organized oppostion. One source of such criticism was the press. Japan's first newspaper appeared in 1871. Early papers had a small but elite readership and focused on politics, but restrictive press laws enacted in 1875 and revised in 1877 gave the Home Minister power to suppress publications and fine or imprison critics. The 1880 Public Meeting Law placed all political meetings under police supervision. Included among those prohibited from attending such meetings were teachers and students. Nor were political associations allowed to recruit members or to combine or correspond with similar bodies. Finally, the 1887 Peace Preservation Law increased the Home Minister's powers of censorship and gave the police authority to expel people from a given area: 570 were shortly removed from Tokyo.

The Liberal party was hurt by differences among its leaders, but was damaged even more by antagonism within its membership, including conflicts between tenants and landlords. It proved impossible to contain within one party both radicals who supported, and even led, peasant riots and the substantial landowners who were the objects of these attacks. In 1884 the party was dissolved. At the end of the same year, Ōkuma and his followers left the Progressive party, although others stayed to keep it in existence. Criticism of the government continued, but this initial attempt to organize political parties turned out to have been premature.

While suppressing its critics, the government was also taking steps to increase its effectiveness. A system of centralized local administration was established that put an end to the Tokugawa tradition of local self-government. Villages and towns were now headed by officials appointed by the Home Ministry in Tokyo, which also controlled the police. In the late seventies (1878–1880), local assemblies were created as sounding boards of public opinion, but their rights were limited to debate and their membership restricted to men of means. The details of bureaucratic procedure were worked out and a civil service system fashioned. A new code of criminal law was enacted, and work was begun on civil and commercial codes.

For the parties and the government alike, the promulgation of a constitution was seen as an essential component in fashioning a modern state uniting the people into a nation, as exemplified by the advanced countries of the West. However, the West offered a range of ways to accomplish this with varying degrees of popular participation and power. To prepare for drawing up a constitution, Itō spent a year and a half in Europe during 1882–1883, mostly studying German theories and practices because they were similar to the kind of constitution he and the other oligarchs wanted. After his return, a number of steps were taken in preparation for the constitution: a new peerage was created in 1884 composed of the old court nobility, former *daimyo,* and some members of the oligarchy; in 1885 a European-style cabinet was created with Itō as premier; and in 1888 the Privy Council was organized as the highest government advisory board.

The Emperor and the Constitution

In the last chapter we noted the abandonment of the original effort to turn Japan into a Shinto state and the subsequent granting of religious tolerance, but this did not settle how such tolerance should coexist with belief in the divine descent of the emperor and the legends that supported this belief. The matter was settled in 1882 with the division of Shinto into Shrine Shinto and Sect Shinto. Most Shinto shrines, including the most prominent, such as Ise and Izumo (sacred to the Sun Goddess and her brother, respectively), came under Shrine Shinto. Thus, they were transformed into State institutions operating on a higher plane than the merely "religious" bodies of Buddhism (in its various forms), Christianity (legalized in 1873), and ordinary Shinto shrines subsumed under Sect Shinto. This formula permitted the government to identify itself with the Shinto tradition from which it derived the mystique of the emperor, who was the source of its own authority, while concurrently meeting the demands for religious tolerance voiced by Japanese reformers and Western nations.

In the name of the "restoration" of the emperor, strands of nativist thought and notions of modern monarchy were combined to form an image of the emperor—promoted by careful manipulation of the emperor himself and spread by word and picture. In his person, he represented both old and new: he was a divine being embodying a timeless spirit, but this was a modern divinity, resplendent in his flashy, new, world-class uniform (Figure 8.1).

In 1889, after work on the constitution was completed, it was promulgated as a "gift" from the emperor to his people. The Meiji constitution remained in force until 1945. The emperor, "sacred and inviolable" father of the family state, was supreme. He was the locus and source of sovereignty: the land and people belonged to him. He had the power to declare war, conclude treaties, and command the army. He also had the right to open, recess, and dissolve the legislature, the power to veto its decisions, and the right to issue his own ordinances. The ministers were responsible not to the legislature, but to the emperor. The legislature, called the Diet (derived from *dieta*, Late Latin for public assembly), consisted of two houses, the House of Peers and the House of Representatives. The latter was elected by a constituency of tax-paying property owners amounting to about 450,000 men, or 1.1 percent of the total population. The most consequential power of the Diet was the power of the purse, but following the example of the Prussian constitution, the Meiji constitution provided for automatic renewal of the previous year's budget whenever the Diet failed to pass a new budget.

FIGURE 8.1 *Portrait of the Meiji Emperor*, Takahashi Yuichi. Emperor Meiji—the reign name of the emperor of Japan from 1867 to 1912 (his given name was Mutsuhito)—ascended the throne when he was 15. He is depicted here in a modern medium, dressed in a manner appropriate to an emperor appearing on the world stage during the "long nineteenth century" that ended in 1914. Oil, 1880.
COLLECTION IMPERIAL HOUSEHOLD, TOKYO, JAPAN.

Only the emperor could take the initiative to revise the constitution. The emperor was the final authority, but he was also above politics; the actual exercise of imperial authority was divided between the Privy Council, the cabinet, the Diet, and the general staff. The constitution failed to provide for coordination between these bodies, but this was done by the men who already had been governing in the emperor's name. Gradually, the practice developed of deciding on the selection of prime minister and other major questions by consulting the *genrō*—elder states-men and leaders of the Meiji Restoration, such as Itō and Yamagata, who talked things out in private. Obviously, this could work only as long as there were *genrō* to consult.

The oligarchs who framed the constitution viewed the government, like the emperor in whose name it functioned, as above the divisive and unedifying world of party politics. But the parties turned out to be stronger than the oligarchs had expected. In the first election of 1890, the reconstituted Liberal party (Jiyutō) won 130 seats, the Progressives (Kaishintō), led once again by Ōkuma, won 47, while only 79 members favoring the government were elected. As a result of this grow-ing party strength, there was a stiff parliamentary battle over the budget in the first session of the Diet, which was resolved only after the premier, Yamagata, resorted to bribery and force. When the budget failed to pass the following year, the Diet was dissolved. During the subsequent elections (1892), the government used the police to discourage the opposition, but failed to obtain a more tractable Diet. Imperial intervention in 1893 worked only temporarily. Another election was held in 1894, but the majority remained opposed to the government, and the Diet was dissolved after only a month and a half.

Japan's war with China over Korea (1894–1895), marking the end of a period of history and therefore of this part of our book, broke the political deadlock and provided temporary unity in the body politic. During the war, the government enjoyed enthusiastic support at home. By that time, Japan was quite different from what it had been 20 years earlier, when the oligarchs rejected intervention in Korea. The political developments were just one dimension of the transformation of Japan.

Western Influences on Values and Ideas

Enthusiasm for aspects of Western science and technology went back, as we have seen, to Tokugawa proponents of Dutch Learning, and from the very start of Meiji, Western styles were in fashion, especially styles of dress. Representative of Japanese attitudes, the Meiji Emperor himself wore Western clothes and dressed his hair in the Western manner, as in his portrait by Takahashi Yuichi (1828–1894), shown in Figure 8.1. In fact, both subject and artist were influenced by Western styles. Takahashi was very conscious of his precursors, and he revered Shiba Kōkan. Like Shiba and his own teacher, the prominent Western-style painter Kawakami Tōgai (1827–1881), Takahashi placed great value on realism. Most of his works, unlike the emperor's portrait, were still-life studies of familiar objects, and his most famous work is a realistic painting of a salmon. A major difference between Kawakami Tōgai and Takahashi is that whereas the former saw Western art as no more than a necessary component of Western learning to be mastered for technical reasons, Takahashi also valued it as art.

Similarly, men turned to the West in other fields for practical reasons and because they were attracted by the intrinsic nature of Western achievements. Prominent among such men were the intellectuals who, in 1873, formed the Meirokusha, a prestigious society devoted to all aspects of Western knowledge. These same men led what was known as the movement for "civilization and enlightenment" (*bummei kaika*). A leading theorist of this movement was Fukuzawa Yukichi, whose books on the West were mentioned earlier.

"Civilization and Enlightenment"

In eighteenth-century Europe, the intellectual movement known as the Enlightenment sought to put all traditional ideas and institutions to the test of reason. Impressed by the achievements of science as exemplified in the work of Sir Isaac Newton (1642–1727), such philosophers as Voltaire (1694–1778) and Diderot (1713–1784) believed that reason could produce similar progress in solving human problems, and that the main obstacles to truth and happiness were irrationality and superstition. Their greatest monument was the encyclopedia compiled by Diderot and his associates, a summation of the accomplishments of reason in all fields of human knowledge.

Japanese intellectuals like Fukuzawa Yukichi were strongly influenced by the European Enlightenment, particularly the emphasis on reason as an instrument for achieving progress. Their faith in progress was also confirmed by influential Western historians such as H.T. Buckle (1821–1862) and Francois Guizot (1787–1874). Firm belief in progress remained widespread during the nineteenth century, even after faith in reason had faded.

A corollary to this new concept of historical progress, in Japan as in the West, was a negative reevaluation of Chinese civilization, now regarded as unchanging, and therefore decadent. No longer did the Japanese look up to China as the land of classical civilization; on the contrary, China was now a negative model, and as China's troubles continued, the Japanese tended to regard it with condescension as well as concern. Now the source of "enlightenment" was in the West.

One of Fukuzawa's prime goals in advancing the cause of "civilization and enlightenment" was to stimulate the development of an independent and responsible citizenry in Japan. "It would not be far from wrong," he complained, "to say that Japan has a government but no people."[4] Tracing the lack of individual independence back to the traditional family, Fukuzawa advocated fundamental changes in that basic social institution. Ridiculing the ancient paragons of filial piety, he urged limitations on parental demands and authority. While he viewed the role of women in terms of family and home, Fukuzawa also, on occasion, recommended greater equality between the sexes, championed monogamy, argued that women should be educated and allowed to hold property, and compared the Japanese woman to a dwarfed ornamental tree: artificially stunted.

According to Fukuzawa, history was made by the people, not by a few great leaders, and he thought it wrong to place too much faith in government or to give the political authorities too much power. His view of the role of government resembled the concept of the minimal state held by early European liberals. Consistent with these ideas, he did not enter government himself, but disseminated his views in books and through a newspaper he founded. He also established what became Keiō University, a distinguished private university in Tokyo whose graduates were important in business and industry.

In Fukuzawa's mind, the independence of the people and the independence of the country were linked; indeed, the former was a prerequisite for the latter. This view was widely held among the proponents of "enlightenment." For instance, the translator of the best-seller *Self-Help* by Samuel Smiles, whose Japanese version was published in Tokyo in 1871, explained that Western nations were strong because they possessed the spirit of liberty. John Stuart Mill's *On Liberty* appeared in Japanese translation the same year, and Rousseau's *The Social Contract* was published in installments from 1882 to 1884. Fukuzawa, with his faith in progress, believed that the ultimate universal movement of history is in the direction of democracy, and that individual liberty makes for national strength.

Fukuzawa's liberalism of the early 1870s was based on the Western Enlightenment concept of natural law, the belief that human affairs should be governed by inherent concepts of justice like the physical world is governed by laws of nature. This belief resembled the Neo-Confucian concept of *li* ("principle") in linking the natural and human orders, except that the European doctrine, unlike the Chinese, included the affirmation of innate human rights. It postulated an affirmative body of law stating the inherent rights of people in society, in whose name societies could overthrow unjust governments and establish new ones. It was to natural law that the American colonists appealed when they declared their independence in 1776, and this was also the case when the French revolutionaries promulgated their Declaration of the Rights of Man in 1789.

Social Darwinism

After the "civilization and enlightenment" of the 1870s, discourse became multi-faceted, but the concept of natural law was soon displaced by a more recent Western import: Social Darwinism. There were various versions of this doctrine, most notably those developed by the enormously influential Herbert Spencer (1820–1903), but all were based on the theory of evolution by natural selection presented in Darwin's famous *On the Origin of Species* (1859). Darwin held that over time the various forms of life adapt to changing natural conditions and that those that adapt best are most likely to survive. This theory was summarized by the catch phrase "survival of the fittest." Social Darwinism was the application of these doctrines to the human realm. Applied to the success or failure of individuals within society, it justified brutal competition. Similarly, applied to the rise and fall of nations, it focused on military as well as civil competition. In both cases, "the fittest" were those who came out on top and thereby contributed to human progress.

Social Darwinism, purporting to have a scientific basis, offered a persuasive explanation of the present, while holding out hope for a different future. It explained why Japan had been unable to resist the Western powers, but held out the promise that a nation did not have to accept permanent inferiority. Thus, it justified Japanese efforts to develop national strength by mastering the learning and techniques of the West. Unlike natural law with its moral rules, it turned strength itself into a moral criterion, and justified not only resisting foreign aggression but also engaging in aggressive expansionism of one's own.

In the mid-1870s, Fukuzawa first became skeptical of natural law, and then abandoned it. He lost confidence in international law and formed a new view of international relations as an arena where nations struggle for survival. In 1876 Fukuzawa remarked, "a few cannons are worth more than a hundred volumes of international law."[5] By 1882 he was willing to accept even autocracy if it meant strengthening the nation. Furthermore, he favored imperialist expansion both to assure Japan's safety and to bring the benefits of "civilization" to neighboring countries such as Korea. Therefore, he welcomed the war when it came in 1894.

Fukuzawa found words of praise for some aspects of the Japanese tradition, including the samurai value of loyal service, but continued to look primarily to the West for his models and ideas. However, he avoided the extremes of Westernization. In early Meiji some thinkers allowed their enthusiasm to get the better of their judgment, and there were all kinds of extreme proposals for radical Westernization, including one to abolish the national language and another to intermarry with Europeans. However, not all supporters of Westernization were genuine enthusiasts. Many desired to impress Westerners in order to be accepted as equals and to speed treaty revision. This was the motive behind a variety of movements, ranging from a drive to reform public morals to the revision of the legal code. It also accounts for one of the symbols of the era, the Rokumeikan, a hall completed in 1883 to accommodate mixed foreign and Japanese social gatherings. Designed by an English architect in the elaborate manner of the European Renaissance, it provided the setting for dinners, card parties, and fancy dress balls.

The Arts

In the arts, Western influence was both audible and visible. It affected music taught in the schools and that performed in military bands. In literature, the 1870s and 1880s have been defined as "the age of translation,"[6] during which Japanese versions of European novels were published and read with great enthusiasm, to be joined in the mid-1880s by the first modern Japanese novels, worthy forerunners of great achievements to come. In painting, we have already noted the work of Takahashi, but the impact of the West was visible also in more traditional genres. Kobayashi Kiyochika (1847–1915) has been called the last of the major *ukiyo-e*

FIGURE 8.2 *Train at Night,* Kobayashi Kiyochika. This was the great age of the railway, a force as well as symbol of technological and economic transformation. With his unique techniques of light and shadow, the artist sets his train rushing through the night against a calm, seemingly eternal Japanese landscape. Woodcut.

artists. He introduced Western light and shading into *ukiyo-e,* using the principles of Western perspective, but retaining a traditional Japanese sense of color (Figure 8.2).

Western styles of painting were advanced by foreign artists who taught in Japan and by Japanese who studied abroad, particularly in France, bringing back new styles and ways of looking at the world. Kuroda Seiki (1866–1924) studied in France from 1884 to 1893, and it was there that he painted *Morning Toilet* (Figure 8.3), which caused a stir when exhibited in Tokyo in 1894 and unleashed a storm of controversy when shown in more conservative Kyoto the following year. Japan and East Asia had no tradition of painting the nude. There were protests that Kuroda's painting was pornography, not art. But Kuroda won the battle, and went on to become one of Japan's most influential Western-style painters.

The initial enthusiasm for Western art led to the neglect of, and even disdain for, traditional art. This shocked the American Ernest Fenollosa (1853–1908) when he came to Japan in 1878 to teach at Tokyo University. Fenollosa did what he could to make the new generation of Westernized Japanese aware of the greatness of their artistic heritage. He himself was an admirer of the last of the masters of the China-influenced Kano school, Kano Hōgai (1828–1898), and together with the younger Okakura Tenshin (1862–1913), sparked a revived interest in traditional styles. Meanwhile, Japanese art fascinated such Western artists as Gaugin, Van Gogh, and Whistler.

FIGURE 8.3 *Morning Toilet,* Kuroda Seiki. Kuroda learned an academic style under the French painter Louis-Joseph-Raphael Collin, but also acquired an Impressionist vision that incorporated bright outdoor light. Oil, 1893, 178.5 × 98 cm. NATIONAL RESEARCH INSTITUTE OF CULTURAL PROPERTIES, TOKYO, JAPAN.

Conservatism and Nationalism

The reaction against the enthusiasm of the early Meiji Westernizers was not limited to the arts. Starting in the late-1980s, there was a tide of conservative thought. Many were attracted by the old formula, "Eastern ethics; Western technology," a concept earlier advanced by Sakuma Shōzan.

Some feared that acceptance of a foreign culture was a step toward national decline, and sought ways to be both modern and Japanese by adopting universalist aspects of Western culture while retaining valuable aspects of their past. The educated and sensitive were especially troubled by the tensions inherent in a program of modernization under traditionalist auspices. Western scientific rationalism could, by questioning the founding myth, undermine the throne itself. In 1892 a Tokyo University professor was forced to resign after he wrote that Shinto was a "survival of a primitive form of worship."[7] That was sacrilege. Similarly, Western individualism, fostered by the policy of modernization, clashed with the old family values that, Fukuzawa notwithstanding, continued strong and remained in official favor.

Drawing on German thought, new conservative voices affirmed Japanese uniqueness along with their belief in national progress, arguing that change should come about gradually, growing organically out of past traditions with emphasis not on the individual but on the state. There was talk about a national "essence," though little agreement on how it should be defined. Akira Iriye has drawn attention to the weakness in Japan of the liberal elements that Western nationalism inherited from its origins, when it "had been part of the democratic revolution in which national identity was sought less in a country's ethnic and historical uniqueness than in the belief that it embodied certain universal values such as freedom and human rights." Such a nationalism "could often be transformed into internationalism because a nation could envision a world order that embodied some of the universalistic principles that it exemplified itself."[8] Japanese particularism often took a benign form, but sometimes it led to cultural exceptionalism and political chauvinism, even if Japanese nationalists were hardly unique in celebrating (and exaggerating) the uniqueness of their nation. Such views could easily lead to a sense of special national mission.

Some Japanese intellectuals, notably Okakura, soon went on to define a wider world role for Japan by emphasizing Japan's Asian roots. Thus, in a book bearing the revealing title, *The Ideals of the East* (1902), Okakura presented the nation's mission in terms of preserving an "Asian" cultural essence. Japan's cultural place in the world remained a key issue throughout modern times, but more notably, its political mission did so as well.

Education

Japanese intellectual and political leaders were quick to realize the importance of education in fashioning a new Japan capable of competing with the West. In this, as in other areas, they showed great interest in the practices and institutions of European countries and of the United States. One member of the Iwakura mission paid special attention to education, and wrote 15 volumes on the subject after his return from abroad.

At the beginning of the Meiji period, Japan sent many students overseas to obtain the advanced training it could not provide at home. One-eighth of the Ministry of Education's first budget (1873) was designated for this purpose, and 250 students were sent to the United States and Europe on government scholarships that year. Furthermore, many foreign instructors from the same countries were brought to Japan to teach in various specialized schools. However, these were temporary expedients until Japan's own modern educational system was in operation. By the late 1880s, the number of foreign instructors was down, and only 50 to 80 students were being sent abroad by the government annually. A landmark in the history of higher education was the establishment of Tokyo University in 1877, with four faculties: physical science, law, literature, and medicine.

Considerable progress was made in building a complete educational system to replace the uncoordinated network of outdated academies as well as *han*, temple, and family schools. Yet actual accomplishments fell short of the ambitious plan drawn up in 1872 calling for 8 universities, 256 middle schools (equivalent to American high and junior high schools), and 53,760 elementary schools. Thirty years later, in 1902, there were only 2 universities, 222 middle schools, and 27,076 elementary schools. Similarly, the government had to retreat from its 1872 ordinance making four years of education compulsory for all children. Among the difficulties this program encountered were money problems (elementary education was locally financed), teacher shortages, and the reluctance of rural parents to send their children to school. However, by the time four years of compulsory education were reintroduced in 1900, the great majority of children who were supposed to be in school were in actual attendance, and in 1907 the government was able to increase the period to six years. By that time the teachers were predominantly graduates of Japanese Normal Schools (teacher training institutes), the first of which was established in Tokyo in 1872 with the assistance of Marion M. Scott, an American educator.

When the Ministry of Education was first established in 1871, the French system of highly centralized administration was adopted. Although local schools were locally financed, the ministry prescribed textbooks, supervised teacher training, and controlled the curriculum of schools throughout the country. Government educational policy therefore was decisive in determining what was taught.

There was wide agreement among political leaders that an essential function of the educational system was to provide the people with the skills necessary for modernization. They realized that factories and businesses, as well as armies and navies, require a certain level of literacy and command of simple arithmetic among the rank and file, and higher education for managers and officers. Beyond that, the leaders recognized that schools foster values and used them to help mold the Japanese people into a nation. On the question of specific moral content, however, there were intense disagreements reflecting different visions of Japan's future. In the 1870s, when enthusiasm for the West ran high, even elementary readers and moral texts were frequently translated from English and French for use in Japanese schools. However, there were also critics who insisted that schools should preserve traditional Confucian/Japanese values. Another influential position opposed both Western liberal values and traditionalist ideals being taught in schools. Instead, it wanted schools to indoctrinate the populace with modern nationalist values. An influential proponent of this last position was Mori Arinori (1847–1889), Minister of Education from 1885 until, ironically, a nationalist fanatic assassinated him in 1889.

Although Mori had a strong hand in shaping the educational system, the most important Meiji pronouncement on the subject was drafted under the influence of Motoda Eifu (1818–1891), the Emperor's lecturer on Chinese books who provided Confucian guidance and advice. This was the *Rescript on Education,* issued in 1890. For half a century it remained the basic statement of the purpose of education, memorized by generations of schoolchildren. It begins by attributing "the glory of the fundamental character of Our Empire" to the Imperial Ancestors who "deeply and firmly implanted virtue," calls on His Majesty's subjects to observe the usual Confucian virtues beginning with filiality toward their parents, and enjoins them to "pursue learning and cultivate arts" for the sake of intellectual and moral development, and "to advance public good and promote common interests." Furthermore, "should emergency arise, offer yourselves courageously to the State, and thus guard and maintain the prosperity of Our Imperial Throne coeval with heaven and earth."[9] In this document, Confucianism is identified with the throne (no mention is made of its foreign origins), and a premium is placed on patriotic service to the state and the throne. These values were further drummed into schoolchildren with compulsory ethics classes. Education prepared Japan for the future in the name of the past.

Modernizing the Economy

In the 20 years that followed consolidation of the Meiji regime, Japan laid the foundations for a modern industrial economy. The nation was still primarily agrarian, but Western experience had shown that capital accumulated through the sale of surplus agricultural production and labor obtained through the migration of surplus rural population to the cities were necessary conditions for industrial development. Both conditions existed in Meiji Japan.

Japanese agriculture had become more efficient with the introduction of new seed strains, new fertilizers, and new methods of cultivation. New land for farming was being opened, especially in Hokkaido. New applications of science to agriculture were being tried at experimental labs and agricultural colleges. Consequently, during the 14 years preceding the Sino-Japanese War, rice yields increased by 30 percent, and other crops showed comparable gains. Agriculture was further stimulated by the development of a substantial export market for silk and tea, and a growing domestic demand for cotton. Thus, trade also helped generate capital needed for investment in manufacturing.

Increased agricultural production did not result in major changes for the grower. Village government and the organization of village labor remained largely the same. Rents remained high: it was not unusual for a peasant's rent to equal half his rice crop. Profits resulting from the commercialization of agriculture went to the landlord, who handled the sale, rather than to the tenant. Even the creation of factory jobs did little to relieve population pressure on the land. Much of the factory labor was performed by peasant girls sent to the city to supplement farm incomes until they were married. Housed in company dormitories and strictly supervised, they were an inexpensive work force (see Box 8.1). Conditions were often appalling as owners squeezed as many women as possible into rooms where they froze in the winter and boiled in the summer. The food was terrible. "Toilets were not kept clean, and with a hundred girls using the same bathwater it became grimy."[10] No wonder dormitories resembled prisons and were enclosed in high fences topped by bamboo spears or bared wire. When times were bad and factory operations slowed down, the women were laid off and returned to their villages. The system was advantageous to the landlord and the industrialist at the expense of those who tilled the fields and reeled the thread.

In Western countries, the industrial revolution was largely carried out by private enterprise. In Japan, however, where it was government policy to modernize and catch up with the West, the government took the initiative. The Meiji regime invested heavily in the economic infrastructure—those basic public services that must be in place before an industrial economy can grow: education, transportation, communication, and so forth. As previously mentioned, students were sent abroad at public expense to study Western technologies and techniques, and foreigners brought to Japan to teach in their areas of expertise. A major effort went into railroads. The first line was completed in 1872, running between Tokyo and Yokohama (see Figure 8.4). By the mid-1890s, 2,000 miles of track existed, much of it privately owned because government initiative was followed by private investment once the feasibility, and especially the profitability, of railroads had been established. Transportation within cities began to improve as Kyoto, in 1895, became the first Japanese city to have trolleys.

BOX 8.1 "THE PRISON LAMENT"

The songs of the workers reveal the conditions under which young factory women labored as well as their resentment at how they were treated.

The Prison Lament
Factory work is prison work
All it lacks are iron chains.
More than a caged bird, more than a prison,
Dormitory life is hateful.
Like a horse or a cow,
The reeler is fenced in.
Like the money in my employment contract,
I remained sealed away.
If a male worker makes eyes at you,
You end up loosing your shirt.
How I wish the dormitory could be washed away,
The factory burned down.
And the gatekeeper die of cholera!
At six in the morning I wear a devil's face,
At six in the evening, a smiling face.
I want wings to escape from here,
To fly as far as those distant shores.
Neither silk reeling maids nor clops
Are promoted or kept for long.

Translated from Yamamoto Shigemi, *AA namudi tōge* (*Ah The Nomugi Pass!*) (Tokyo: Kadokawa, 1977), pp. 388–89 in E. Patricia Tsurumi, *Factory Girls: Women in the Thread Mills of Meiji Japan* (Princeton: Princeton University Press, 1990), p. 198–99.

This sequence of state initiative followed by private development also occurred in manufacturing. The government took the lead in establishing and operating cement works, plants manufacturing tiles, textile mills (silk and cotton), shipyards, mines, and munitions works. The government felt these industries were essential, but private interests were unwilling to risk their capital in untried ventures with little prospect of profits in the near term. Thus, the government had to start such ventures and finance the initial period of operations.

FIGURE 8.4 Yokohama Print, an example of a genre popular in early Meiji juxtaposing such recent inventions as the paddlewheel steamer and the train with traditional boats, dress, and Mt. Fuji clearly visible from downtown Tokyo as well as Yokohama. Sometimes discrepancies between the traditional and modern led to awkwardness. A story that may be apocryphal but is worth telling nonetheless has it that passengers on the first train from Tokyo to Yokohama discovered on arrival that their shoes were still in Tokyo where they had carefully removed them before entering their carriages.

The Zaibatsu

The expenditure of capital required for this effort, the payment due to samurai on their bonds, the costs of the Satsuma Rebellion, and an adverse balance of trade combined to create a government financial crisis. Rising inflation damaged the government's purchasing power and hurt the samurai, whose income depended on the interest paid on their bonds. These problems culminated in 1880. The government's response was mainly to cut back on expenditures, leading to a deflation that is seen as preparing the way for a period of economic growth sustained to the end of World War I.

As part of its economic move, the government decided, late in 1880, to sell at public auction all its enterprises with the exception of the munitions plants. Most of the buyers were men who were friendly with government leaders and who recognized the long-term advantages of buying the factories, which were selling at bargain prices. These enterprises did not become profitable immediately, but when they did, this small group of well-connected firms enjoyed a controlling position in the modern sector of the economy. These were the *zaibatsu*, huge financial and industrial combines.

The *zaibatsu* were usually organized by new entrepreneurs, for most of the old Tokugawa merchant houses were too set in their ways to make a successful transition into the new world of Meiji. The outstanding exception to this generalization was the house of Mitsui, originally established in Edo as a textile house, and later enriched by its banking activities (see Chapter 4). When it became apparent that government initiatives were creating new economic opportunities in commerce and industry, Mitsui brought new men into the firm to take advantage of these opportunities. The new leadership was vigorous and capable, establishing first a bank and then a trading company. These institutions became important factors in Japan's foreign commerce; they also engaged in domestic transactions, profiting handsomely from handling army supply contracts during the Satsuma Rebellion. In 1881 Mitsui bought government coal mines, which ultimately contributed greatly to its wealth and power. By that time, the traditional drapery business had been relegated to the sidelines and delegated to a subordinate house.

The Mitsubishi *zaibatsu* stands in contrast to Mitsui. Iwasaki Yataro (1834–1885), a former Tosa samurai who was bold and ruthless in the wars of commerce, founded this new *zaibatsu*. Iwasaki developed a strong shipping business by obtaining government contracts, government subsidies, and for a time, even government guarantee of its dividend payments. At one point the government lent the company ships, a loan that eventually became a gift. Mitsubishi also benefited greatly from doing government business during the Taiwan expedition of 1874 and again during the Satsuma Rebellion. The firm grew strong enough to displace some of its foreign competitors, and around its shipping business it developed banking and insurance facilities. It even entered foreign trade. Mitsubishi also went into mining, and its acquisition of the government-established Nagasaki shipyard assured its future as the leader in shipbuilding and heavy industry, although Iwasaki did not live long enough to see the shipyard turn a profit. Iwasaki ruled the combine like a personal domain, but he also recruited an able managerial staff composed largely of graduates from Fukuzawa's Keiō University.

For Iwasaki, personal ambition and patriotism were fused. As he conceived it, his mission was to compete with the great foreign shipping companies, and he was convinced that whatever benefited his company was also good for the nation. Not everyone, however, agreed with this assessment. For a time Iwasaki had to face the competition of a rival company, one of whose organizers was Shibusawa Eiichi (1840–1931), one of the great Meiji entrepreneurs and bankers, founder of the Tokyo Chamber of Commerce and Bankers' Association, a believer in joint-stock companies, in competition, and in business independence from government. Iwasaki won this battle, but Shibusawa remained enormously influential, not only because of his economic power but also because of his energetic advocacy of higher business standards and the view that business could contribute to public good by remaining independent of government.

The success of such men as Iwasaki and Shibusawa should not obscure the fact that new ventures continued to entail risk. Not all new ventures were successful. For example, the attempt to introduce sheep-raising into Japan was a failure. Initial attempts at organizing insurance companies were similarly ill-conceived, since they used rates and tables appropriate for European rather than Japanese conditions. But insurance companies were finally established, and altogether successes outnumbered failures.

One reason for the success of the *zaibatsu* and other new companies was their ability to attract capable and dedicated executives. Formerly, many capable members of the samurai class had refused to enter the business world because concern with moneymaking was considered abhorrent. However, this obstacle was largely overcome after the Restoration, not merely because these were now ex-samurai families, but because commercial and industrial development was required for the good of the state. Those who helped build a strong bank, trading company, or manufacturing industry were seen as rendering a service to the emperor and to Japan. Indeed, the government's initial sponsorship of many enterprises lent them prestige of government service. Business became more socially acceptable as men of samurai origins created many companies.

The association of business with government also influenced business ideology in Japan. From the beginning, the ethos of modern Japan business focused on its contributions to the Japanese nation, not on the notions of economic liberalism that prevailed in the West. The company did not exist only, or even primarily, to make a profit for its shareholders. Likewise, provisions were made in the internal organization of the business to encourage group solidarity and mutual responsibility, to give participants in the venture a strong sense of company loyalty, and to keep workers in their place. The association of business and government also helped justify the government's influence on business, and helped account for continued acceptance of policies that kept consumption low even as national income rose.

Similarly, in the 1890s an argument appeared that Japanese factories were "exceptional sites of warm-hearted social relations,"[11] a contention that grew more insistent in the early twentieth century as movements for legislation concerning factory conditions, working hours, child labor, and so on gained momentum.

The *zaibatsu* remained important economically and politically in the twentieth century, but in discussing them and other modern firms, it should not be supposed that large-scale trading, mining, and manufacturing represented the whole of Japanese business. On the contrary, many small-scale establishments continued to function well past the early Meiji era. But the new firms did represent major growth and change in economic activity, and signaled a change in Japanese perceptions of Japan's role in international affairs. This was reflected in economic terms by efforts to preserve economic independence—for example, by protecting home markets, conserving foreign exchange, and avoiding dependence on foreign capital to ensure Japanese ownership of railways and other large-scale enterprises. It was reflected also in Japanese foreign policy and especially in the modernization and deployment of the Japanese military.

The Military

Japanese military forces engaged in three major operations in the 20 years following the Restoration: the Taiwan expedition of 1874, the Satsuma Rebellion of 1877, and the Sino-Japanese War of 1894–1895. The first two operations were fought primarily for domestic purposes, as the new Meiji government sought to consolidate its power. The Sino-Japanese War, on the other hand, was an outward-looking venture from the start, a test of strength with China on the Korean Peninsula. An even more striking difference was the quality of Japanese military organization, armament, and tactical skill in 1874 and 1877 versus 1894.

The Taiwan expedition of 1874 was far from brilliant. The landing was poorly executed, hygiene was so defective that disease took a great toll, and equipment had to be abandoned because it was unsuitable for use in a tropical climate. Similarly, the force that suppressed the Satsuma Rebellion did so because of its superiority in numbers and equipment rather than its military excellence.

To improve the quality of the army, Yamagata directed a major reorganization in 1878. He established a general staff along German lines, and Germany became the overall model for the army, which had previously been influenced by France. By strengthening the reserves, the military potential was greatly increased. During the 10 or 15 years before the Sino-Japanese War, generous military appropriations enabled the army to acquire modern equipment, mostly manufactured in Japanese arsenals and plants, while the creation of a Staff College and improved training methods further strengthened and modernized the army. Like Yamagata, most of the leading generals were from Chōshū.

Naval modernization was similar to that of the army, except that England was the model and continued to be a source from which larger vessels were purchased. In 1894 the navy possessed 28 modern ships with a total displacement of 57,000 tons, and 24 torpedo boats. Most important, Japan had the facilities to maintain, repair, and arm its fleet. From the start, most of the naval leadership came from Satsuma.

The military is a good example of the way various facets of modernization intertwined and supported each other, for the armed forces both benefited from and contributed to the process. Not only did they stimulate new industries, ranging from armaments to tin cans, but the army was also the first time rural conscripts were exposed to a wider and more modern world. Indeed, when conscription was first introduced, many men from backward districts were quite bewildered by the accouterments of modern life. There are reports that some bowed in reverence to the stove in their barracks, taking it for some kind of god. For many men, the army provided the first introduction to shoes. Before the spread of education, some men learned to read and write in the army. All were exposed to the new values of nationalism and loyalty to the emperor. Most also learned to smoke (cigarettes were first reported in 1877) and to drink native alcoholic beverages including excellent Japanese beer, first brewed in the 1870s, and had their first experience with the modern city. Soldiers enjoyed a better diet, receiving more meat than the average Japanese. But discipline was very harsh, and draft-dodging was rampant. Nevertheless, the majority did serve.

Life was changing for the majority of Japanese, but compared to later, it was changing very slowly. Styles changed, such as glass replacing paper inside the house or the use of Western umbrellas outside, but as Susan B. Hanley has shown, the essential consumption patterns and basic components of the material culture of the Japanese people remained traditional and stable.[12]

Notes

1. John W. Downer, "Sizing Up (and Breaking Down) Japan," in Helen Hardacre, ed., *The Postwar Development of Japanese Studies in the United States* (Leiden, Netherlands: Brill, 1998), p. 14.

2. Ivan Morris, *The Nobility of Failure: Tragic Heroes in the History of Japan* (New York, NY: Holt, Rinehart and Winston, 1975), p. 272.

3. First article of the party platform as quoted by Kyu Hyun Kim, "Political Ideologies of the Early Meiji Parties," in Hardacre, *Postwar Development*, p. 400.

4. Quoted in Carmen Blacker, *The Japanese Enlightenment: A Study of Fukuzawa Yukichi* (London, U.K.: Cambridge Univ. Press, 1964), p. 111.

5. Ibid., p. 128.

6. Donald Keene, *Dawn to the West: Japanese Literature of the Modern Era: Fiction* (New York, NY: Holt, Rinehart and Winston, 1984), Chapter 3, "The Age of Translation."

7. Quoted in Kenneth Pyle, *The New Generation in Meiji Japan: Problems in Cultural Identity, 1885–95* (Stanford, CA: Stanford Univ. Press, 1969), p. 124.

8. Akira Iriye in Marius Jansen, *The Cambridge History of Japan,* vol. 5, p. 754.

9. "Rescript on Education," in John Lu, *Sources of Japanese History* (New York, NY: McGraw-Hill, 1974), vol. 2, pp. 70–71.

10. E. Patricia Tsurumi, *Factory Girls: Women in the Thread Mills of Meiji Japan* (Princeton, NJ: Princeton Univ. Press, 1990), p. 133. People wash and rinse before soaking in a Japanese bath.

11. Andrew Gordon, "The Invention of Japanese-Style Labor Management," in Stephen Vlastos, ed., *Mirror of Modernity: Invented Traditions of Modern Japan* (Berkeley, CA: Univ. of California Press, 1998), p. 19.

12. Susan B. Hanley, "The Material Culture: Stability in Transition," in Marius Jansen and Gilbert Rozman, eds., *Japan in Transition: From Tokugawa to Meiji* (Princeton, NJ: Princeton Univ. Press, 1986), pp. 467–69 and passim.

China and Korea: 1870—1894

While the Meiji government brought about major changes in Japan, governments on the continent were less successful in preparing their people for a new world. As we have seen, Vietnam lost its independence in 1883 (see Chapter 6) despite the Qing war with France (1884—1885). Attempts at dynastic renewal and "self-strengthening" in China and Korea, while not negligible, in the end failed to solve problems of dynastic decay. Meanwhile, the histories of the three Northeast Asian powers increasingly intertwined, ending with China and Japan at war over Korea.

I. China

1861   1872   1884   1894

THE SELF-STRENGTHENING MOVEMENT

(Phase 1)   (Phase 2)   (Phase 3)

Sino-French War   Sino-Japanese War
(1884–1885)   (1894–1895)

The Post-Taiping Revival

Self-Strengthening and the Empress Dowager

Education

Economic Self-Strengthening

The Traditional Economic Sector

Missionary Efforts and Christian Influences

Self-Strengthening—The Theory

Old and New Wine in Old Bottles

The Post-Taiping Revival

Confucian pragmatism was nothing new. Willingness to adopt new means to strengthen and reform the state had animated a long line of Confucian scholars from the Song onward, and as it became clear during the early years of the nineteenth century that the Qing was in serious trouble, some scholars turned against philology to focus on policy studies. The *Anthology of Qing Statecraft Writing (Huangchao jingshi wenbian)*, published in 1827, is a case in point. It is a collection of essays on social, political, and economic matters written by Qing officials and published by He Changlin (1785–1841), with the actual work done by Wei Yuan (see Chapter 6). Concern for reform and willingness to take a hard, critical look at financial and political institutions characterized the writings of leading intellectuals, and Wei Yuan began to merge these concerns with an interest in the West

During the 1860s the government was receptive to reformist advice. With a minor on the throne, the Dowager Empress Cixi (1835–1908) (Figure 9.1) became the dominant figure at court and continued as such until her death. The intelligent, educated daughter of a minor Manchu official, she entered the palace as a low-ranking concubine, and had the good fortune to bear the emperor his only son. After that emperor's death, she became co-regent for her son, the Tongzhi emperor, whom she dominated. It was also rumored that she encouraged him in the debaucheries that weakened his constitution and sent him to the grave in 1875 at the age of 19. She then manipulated the succession in order to place on the throne her four-year-old nephew, the Guangxu emperor (r. 1875–1908), and continued in power even after he ostensibly assumed the imperial duties in 1889.

During the Tongzhi period (1862–1874), Zeng Guofan, Li Hongzhang, and other leaders in the victory over the Taiping sought to cope with the dislocations wrought by warfare and to revive the dynasty by launching a program of Confucian reform. Expenses and taxes were cut in the ravaged south, relief projects were instituted, public works projects were initiated, land was reclaimed, water was controlled, and granaries were established. As always, agriculture had priority.

An aspect of the revival dear to its Confucian sponsors was a strengthening of scholarship by reprinting old texts, founding new academies, opening libraries, and the like. Examination system reform was similarly a high priority, as was the elimination of bureaucratic corruption. Questions dealing with practical issues of statecraft were introduced, and attempts were made to limit the sale of degrees and offices. By such measures the reformers sought to raise the level of honesty.

However, the reforms did not penetrate to the crucial lower level of the bureaucracy—many county magistrates continued to gain office through purchase—and nothing effective was done to curb the rapacity of the solidly entrenched and notoriously corrupt sub-bureaucracy of clerks and underlings. Furthermore, with the leadership for reform coming primarily from provincial governors, the dynasty was

FIGURE 9.1   The Empress Dowager Cixi (1835–1908) seated on the Imperial Throne. Scholars, too, grew long fingernails to show the world that they worked with their minds, not their hands.

powerless to reverse the trend toward regionalism. The disruption of old bonds with the central government removed many of the political constraints on local wealth and power, and set in motion a restructuring of local society that ultimately proved dangerous for both the State and the social order.

Self-Strengthening and the Empress Dowager

The aim of the Self-Strengthening Movement was to fortify the Qing through selective borrowing from the West (Figure 9.2). In the words of Feng Guifen (1809–1874), the first to see the West as a source for solving the problems it had

FIGURE 9.2 China during the Self-Strengthening Period.

created, "we should adopt the instruments of the barbarians but not adopt the ways of the barbarians. We should use them so that we can repel them." The full formulation of the underlying theory did not take place until later (see p. 191), but from the beginning it entailed reorganization based on the superiority of foreigners in military and other practical areas, along with a commitment to the preservation of the existing social, political, and intellectual order.

Self-strengthening began in the Tongzhi period with a focus on military modernization and international relations, and was expanded in its middle phase (1872–1885) to encompass transportation (shipping and railways), communications (telegraph), and mining. Finally, after China's defeat by France in 1885, it was further broadened to include light industry.

During the first phase, Li Hongzhang created gun factories in Shanghai (1862) and Suzhou (1864), established an arsenal in Shanghai with Zeng Guofan (1865), and founded another in Nanjing (Nanking) in 1867. In 1870, Li also expanded machinery works first built in Tianjin in 1867. Another leader founded a shipyard in Fuzhou using machinery from France, with shipbuilding and a navigation schools attached, one teaching French, the other English.

With the emperor a minor, foreign policy was largely under the direction of Prince Gong, who expressed the regime's order of priorities thus:

> The situation today may be compared (to the diseases of a human body). Both the Taiping and the Nian bandits are gaining victories and constitute an organic disease. Russia, with her territory adjoining ours, aiming to nibble away our territory like a silk worm, may be considered a threat at our bosom. As to England, her purpose is to trade, but she acts violently, without any regard for human decency. If she is not kept within limits, we shall not be able to stand on our feet. Hence she may be compared to an affliction of our limbs. Therefore we should suppress the Taipings and the Nian bandits first, get the Russians under control next, and attend to the British last.[1]

It was apparent to Prince Gong that new approaches to foreign policy were required to meet these objectives. In 1861, to deal with foreign powers and related matters, he sponsored the establishment of the Zongli Yamen (Office of General Management), as a subcommittee of the Grand Council, to supervise a number of offices (Figure 9.3). Since its influence depended on that of its presiding officer and his associates, it was most influential during the 1860s, when Prince Gong was at the height of his authority. An important innovation introduced by the Zongli Yamen was appeal to international law, using Henry Wheaton's *Elements of International Law,* a standard text translated by the American missionary W. A. P. Martin.

Prince Gong, recognizing that Chinese officials would be at a disadvantage in dealing with foreigners unless they had a better understanding of foreign languages and learning, was instrumental in having the Zongli Yamen establish a school for foreign languages and other nontraditional subjects in 1862. The language staff was foreign, and included Martin, who became the school's president in 1869. By

FIGURE 9.3   Three members of the Zongli Yamen and states-
men of the Tongzhi period. Left to right: Shen Guifen, President
of the Ministry of War; Dong Xun, President of the Ministry of
Finance; Mao Changxi, President of the Ministry of Works. John
Thomson, *Illustrations of China and Its People: A Series of Two
Hundred Photographs, with Letterpress Descriptive of the Places and
People Represented.* London: S. Low, Marston, Low, and Searle,
1873–1874. Reprinted in 1900.
PHOTOGRAPH © HULTON-DEUTSCH COLLECTION/CORBIS (HU038080).

that time, astronomy and mathematics had also been introduced, despite the
objections of the distinguished Mongol scholar, General Secretary Woren
(d. 1871), who memorialized: "From ancient down to modern times your slave
has never heard of anyone who could use mathematics to raise the nation from a
state of decline or to strengthen it in time of weakness."[2] Woren was not alone in
his objections to this extension of "barbarian" influence.

Nevertheless, similar schools were established at Shanghai, Canton, and
Fuzhou. Foreigners were relied on to run both the military and educational establishments. In this way, the foundations of self-strengthening and modernization
were laid, but the emphasis remained heavily on the military. This was true even of
Feng Guifen, the advocate of learning from the barbarians, who had the audacity

to propose that examination degrees be presented to men demonstrating accomplishment in Western mechanical skills.

During the 1860s, an important area of Chinese cooperation with foreign powers was the Maritime Customs Service. Its first director, Horatio Nelson Lay, had acquired a fleet of eight gunboats for the Chinese in England. Although these were paid for by the Chinese, Lay arranged that the captain of the fleet should receive all orders through and at Lay's own discretion. This was unacceptable to the Qing, and there were protests. China's first effort to acquire a modern navy ended with disbandment of the little fleet, and Lay was pensioned off. Matters improved, however, when Robert Hart succeeded Lay in 1863. Hart's attitude was the opposite of Lay's. He insisted that the customs was a Chinese service, that Chinese officials were to be treated as "brother officers," and he gave the Qing government well-intentioned and frequently helpful advice on modernization, while building the service into an important source of support for the dynasty (see Box 9.1).

BOX 9.1 FROM THE JOURNALS OF ROBERT HART

Robert Hart (1835–1911) wrote about his goals and ambitions as head of the Maritime Customs Service in a journal entry dated December 24, 1863. The primary purpose of the customs service was to collect tax revenue from maritime trade with China, but it was also responsible for tasks ranging from postal administration to currency reform. Although Hart had assumed the post only one month prior, he was not a newcomer to China, having moved there from his native Belfast in 1854.

My life has been singularly successful: not yet twenty-nine, and at the head of a service which collects nearly three millions of revenue, in,—of all countries in the world!—the exclusive land of China... Now what objects have I to live for, to act for officially in China?

1. I must whip the Foreign Inspectorate into shape, getting good commissioners, good office men, and seeing that all do their work properly; the duties must be properly collected; office work must be thoroughly performed; the merchant not only must have no cause to grumble against the Customs, but must be assisted; his business must be facilitated, & in that way increased, and increase of business will in the end swell the Imperial coffers.

(continued)

BOX 9.1 FROM THE JOURNALS OF ROBERT HART (CONTINUED)

2. I must learn more about the Chinese; about the littoral provinces, about taxation, about official duties—all with an eye to being useful, and preserving myself from being "trapped."

3. I must try to induce among such Chinese as I can influence a friendlier feeling towards foreigners: right conduct: and in that way keep things straight and ensure peace.

4. I must do what I can to prevent any growth of or encouragement to antiforeign feeling on the part of the Imperialists [i.e., the Qing government], now, that the rebellion is being put down.

5. I must endeavor to ascertain what products of our Western civilization would most benefit China: and in what ways such changes could most affirmatively be introduced.

6. I must set a good example, in conduct, to all my subs.

7. I must assist those who are engaged in the noblest of all works, the preaching of the Gospel, & the teaching of Christianity, —the highest & purist morality, the most comforting religion, and the most civilizing of all influences in its purity & entirety.

Robert Hart and China's Early Modernization: His Journals, 1863–1866. Edited and with narratives by Richard J. Smith, John K. Fairbank, and Katherine F. Bruner. The Council on East Asian Studies, Harvard University. Cambridge, MA: Harvard University Press, 1991. 53–54.

this source says his title was Inspector General

Cooperation between the Qing and the powers produced the first Chinese diplomatic mission to the West, which was headed by the retiring American minister to Beijing, Anson Burlingame, on Robert Hart's recommendation. For a multi-ethnic Confucian state like the Qing to employ a trusted foreigner on such an important mission did not appear as extraordinary as it would have later, after nationalism had taken hold. Accompanied by a Manchu and a Chinese official, Burlingame left China in 1867 for a trip to Washington, several European capitals, and St. Petersburg, where he died. Carried away by his own eloquence, he told Americans that China was ready to extend "her arms toward the shining banners of Western civilization."[3] In Washington, he concluded a treaty rather favorable to China.

The most important negotiations for treaty revision were conducted in Beijing by the British. These culminated in the Alcock Convention of 1869, which included some concessions to the Chinese on duties and taxes, and stipulated that under the most-favored-nation clause, British subjects would enjoy privileges extended to other nationals only if they accepted the conditions under which those privileges had been granted. It also allowed China to open a consulate in Hong Kong. These concessions may appear minor, but the English merchant community felt threatened by them, and their opposition proved strong enough to prevent ratification of the convention.

A fatal blow to the policy of cooperation occurred in 1870 in Tianjin. A Catholic nunnery there had made the mistake of offering small payments for orphans brought to the mission. Rumors spread that the children had been kidnapped and that the sisters removed the children's hearts and eyes to make medicine. The tense situation erupted into violence. A mob took the life of the French consul and 20 other foreigners, including 10 nuns, in what came to be known as the Tianjin Massacre. The powers mobilized their gunboats. Diplomacy finally settled the issue, largely because France's defeat in the Franco-Prussian War the same year deprived France of military power and forced the French to concentrate on domestic problems.

As indicated earlier, in its middle and final phases the Self-Strengthening agenda continued to expand. However, there were also strong forces working in the opposite direction. Opinion at court was divided, and the decisions of the Empress Dowager Cixi were decisive. At first Prince Gong had provided a counterforce, but his power declined in the 1870s, and in 1884 he was removed from the government altogether.

The Empress Dowager was a strong-willed woman, and an expert at political infighting and manipulation. One of her most reliable supporters was the Manchu bannerman Ronglu (1836–1903), to whom she gave important military commands. Yet, it was an anomaly to have a woman in control of the court, and her prestige was not enhanced by rumors that she was responsible for the murder of her rivals. Corruption in high places also took its toll. The powerful eunuch Li Lianying (d. 1911) was completely loyal to his mistress, but also completely corrupt, using his influence to amass a fortune. Cixi herself accepted payments from officials and misspent funds. The most notorious case of financial abuse was her use of money intended for the navy. The Navy Department, established in 1885, became a branch of the imperial household, and China's most famous and magnificent "ship" was made of marble (Figure 9.4).

Cixi's prime political aim was to continue in power. She had no aversion, but neither did she have any commitment, to the policy of selective modernization advocated by the champions of self-strengthening, and her understanding of the West was very limited. It was to her immediate political advantage to avoid dependence on any single group of officials and to manipulate a number of strong governors-general who had gained in power while suppressing the Taiping Rebellion. These indispensable provincial administrators could no longer be controlled by the court at will, but fortunately for Beijing, they remained absolutely loyal to the dynasty. The governors-general operated their own political and financial machines and commanded substantial military forces, but they were still

FIGURE 9.4   On the shore of Kunming Lake, the Marble Pavilion has become a popular recreational site attracting ordinary Chinese visitors as well as foreign tourists—the kind of folk it was intended to exclude. Summer Palace, Beijing.
© DIMITRI KESSEL/TIME & LIFE PICTURE COLLECTION/GETTY IMAGES.

dependent on Beijing's power of appointment. Major policy decisions continued to be made in Beijing. The central government was also strengthened financially by receipts from the Maritime Customs. Thus, the West helped to preserve the dynasty even as it was undermining its foundations.

The most powerful governor-general was Li Hongzhang, from 1870 onward firmly established in Tianjin, where he commanded an army, sponsored self-strengthening efforts, and successfully avoided transfer. A protégé of Zeng Guofan, he shared his master's devotion to the dynasty, but not his Confucian probity. From his headquarters, not far from Beijing, Li dominated China's policy toward Korea, but he could not control its foreign policy elsewhere. Arguing for the priority of maritime defense, he objected to overemphasis on inner Asia and unsuccessfully opposed two military campaigns conducted there during the 1870s.

In the next decade he failed to prevent the war from 1884 to 1885 with France over Vietnam. In this war, fought on Taiwan and the Pescadores as well as in Vietnam, the Qing suffered the destruction of the Fuzhou dockyards and the loss of the fleet built there. Since the defeated dynasty was forced to relinquish all claims to Vietnam, Li was vindicated, but his opposition to going to war against

France earned him the denunciations of his enemies, who castigated him as a traitor. Li, however, survived these attacks and remained the most important patron of self-strengthening, now broadened to include light industry in hopes of better results.

Education

Crucial to every phase was the need for officers, managers, and technical personnel such as scientists and engineers. The fastest way to fill this need was to send students abroad. However, this approach experienced mixed success. The most extensive effort was made between 1872 and 1881, when 120 students were sent to the United States under the supervision of Yung Wing (Rong Hong, 1828–1912), Yale Class of 1854 and the first Chinese to graduate from an American university. The boys were between 15 and 17 years old, young enough to master new subjects, but immature and easily swayed by their foreign environment. To assure continued Confucian training, they were accompanied by a traditional Confucian mentor. Nevertheless, they soon adopted American ways, participating in American sports, dating and in some cases eventually marrying American girls, and in a few instances even converting to Christianity. Yung Wing himself married an American and ended up living in Hartford, Connecticut. The mission had been launched with the backing of Zeng Guofan and Li Hongzhang, but Li withdrew his support when the students were denied admission to West Point and were fiercely attacked by Beijing officials for neglecting their Confucian studies. The mission, poorly managed from the start, was abandoned. Among its participants were some of the first, but by no means the last, Chinese students who, during their overseas stay, became alienated from their culture.

The obvious alternative to study abroad was to supply instruction in modern subjects at home. This was the purpose of the language school established by Prince Gong, and other schools at several arsenals and the Fuzhou dockyard. By 1894 a telegraph school, a naval and military medical school, and a mining school were also in operation. The curriculum of these schools typically encompassed both the classical studies required for success in the examination system and the new subjects. Since command of traditional learning remained the key to entry into government service, the students naturally tended to concentrate on that, for otherwise their career opportunities were very limited. The most famous graduate of the Fuzhou dockyard school was Yan Fu (1853–1921), who was sent to England to continue his studies at the naval college in Greenwich, but after returning home to China was unable to pass the provincial examination, and gained fame not as an admiral, but as a writer and translator.

Some reformers wanted to broaden the content of the examinations and allow candidates credit for mastering modern subjects, but suggestions along such lines encountered formidable opposition, since they affected the Confucian core of the civilization. A minor concession was finally made in 1887. Three out of 1500 provincial examination candidates might now be granted that degree after being examined in Western along with (not in place of) traditional subjects. They would then be eligible for the highest examination (the *jinshi*) on the same terms as the other candidates.

Economic Self-Strengthening

The accomplishments of the second phase of self-strengthening included a shipping company, textile mills, the beginnings of a telegraph service, and the Kaiping Coal Mines. Li Hongzhang took the lead in sponsoring and protecting the new ventures. During the first phase, the new factories, arsenals, and the like, run by officials with the help of foreigners, had suffered from bureaucratic corruption and poor management. To avoid this, Li enacted a policy of "government supervision and merchant operation." Capital came from both the public and private sectors. Private financing was greatly desired, but capital was scarce, and other forms of investment were more lucrative and prestigious. Private investment came primarily from Chinese businessmen residing in the treaty ports and familiar with modern-style business ventures and techniques.

The records of these companies were mixed. The China Merchants Steam Navigation Company is a good example. When private capital proved insufficient to finance the company, Li Hongzhang put up the rest from public funds. To help the company, Li secured the shipping line a monopoly on the transport of tax grain and official freight bound for Tianjin. He obtained tariff concessions for the company and protected it from its domestic critics and enemies. In exchange, Li exercised a large measure of control, appointing and dismissing its managers, employing its ships to transport his troops, and using its payroll to provide sinecures for political followers. He also used its earnings to buy warships. To advance his policy in Korea, Li had the company lend money to the Korean government.

Eventually, the investors began to make money and their political sponsor benefited, but after an initial spurt, the companies stagnated. Moreover, they failed to train Chinese technical personnel, and were plagued by incompetent managers, nepotism, and corruption. Even their political sponsors exploited the companies, regarding them as sources of patronage and revenue rather than as key investments for the modernization of the country.

By the mid-1890s, there was a modern sector in the Chinese economy, but it was largely limited to the periphery of the empire, mostly in the treaty ports where an important class of middlemen developed. Known as compradors and generally Cantonese, these men played an indispensable role in the foreign firms that employed them. Using their own staffs, the sharp-witted business operators conducted transactions with Chinese merchants, monitored Chinese markets, took charge of all Chinese personnel, and generally served as the interface between the large foreign firms and China. In the process, some of them amassed great wealth. It was compradors who financed Li Hongzhang's China Merchants Company. As a group, they formed the nucleus of a modern business class.

A number of them acquired a sophisticated understanding of the West, and some Westerners took a scholarly interest in China. However, most foreign business men refused to study Chinese. Contact between Chinese and Westerners remained distant and communication limited to practical matters conducted in pidgin ("business") English, a hybrid language disdained by all.

The Traditional Economic Sector

While the new enterprises proved disappointing, developments in the traditional sector were hardly encouraging. Chinese tea merchants, despite sophisticated institutions and techniques adequate to sustain dominance of the domestic market, found it increasingly difficult to compete internationally against tea grown in India and Sri Lanka (Ceylon). The large-scale producers of these countries had an advantage over the small Chinese growers in their ability to sustain a high-quality product by investing in fertilizer, replacement bushes, and labor at the crucial picking time. Furthermore, the elaborate structure of the Chinese collection system, which worked adequately internally, was too unwieldy to organize an adequate response to international competition. After 1887, with the decline of exported tea, raw silk became China's main export. In the mid-1890s China was the world's largest exporter of silk, although by 1904 Japan, with better quality control, had supplanted her in that respect.

Beyond the treaty ports and their immediate hinterlands, the penetration of foreign imports appears to have been slow, and their impact varied. Statistics are minimal, and there is no consensus about the ways or extent to which the world economy interacted with the Chinese countryside. Thus Philip Huang's study of an area of North China where farmers had been growing cotton for a long time remains controversial as well as suggestive. According to Huang, since cotton brought a better price than grain but, being susceptible to drought, entailed larger risks, the gap between the successful rich and those pushed into poverty by failure increased. Combined with population pressure and an absence of other opportunities for employment, this set in motion an invidious process of "agricultural involution," a term first applied by the anthropologist Clifford Geertz to Java, where poor peasants worked the land for marginal and diminishing returns. According to Huang, while the men farmed, their wives and daughters supplemented family income by laboring at spinning wheel and loom, often at less than subsistence wages. Whereas spinning was practically eliminated by machine-made thread, the low prices paid to the weavers kept the price of native cloth below that of the factory-made product, which had to be shipped into the interior. "The world economy thus did not undermine the rural economic system or stimulate new departures but accelerated processes already underway. The incorporation of Chinese agriculture into the world economy telescoped and greatly accelerated change in the small peasant economy."[4]

Missionary Efforts and Christian Influences

The Western presence in nineteenth-century China was no more confined to trade and politics than it had been during the Late Ming encounter. Once again, missionaries were drawn to China, but now there were Protestants as well as Catholics. An early Protestant arrival was Robert Morrison of the London Missionary Society. He reached Canton in 1807, learned the language, produced a Chinese-English dictionary and a Chinese version of the Bible (later used by the Taipings), founded the school where Yung Wing received his early education, and set up a printing press. Other missionaries, many of them Americans, brought modern medicine and other aspects of Western secular knowledge to China.

The missionaries made a notable effort in education: by 1877 there were 347 missionary schools in China with almost 6,000 pupils. Such schools helped spread knowledge about the West as well as propagate the religion. A notable missionary-educator was W. A. P. Martin, who contributed to the self-strengthening movement and became the first president of Beijing University. The first foreign language newspaper published in China was a missionary publication, and missionaries also contributed to scholarship. Outstanding among the missionaries who became Sinologists was James Legge, a master translator who rendered the Chinese classics into sonorous Victorian prose. In this and other ways, missionaries with varying degrees of sophistication and self-awareness served as cultural intermediaries.

As indicated by the growth of their schools, the missionaries met with some success, but their strength was largely in the treaty ports, and the results were hardly commensurate with their efforts. By the end of the century, the number of Catholic missionaries in China had climbed to about 750, and there were approximately half a million Catholics in China, up from around 160,000 at the beginning of the century. The Protestants had less success. In 1890 there appear to have been only slightly over 37,000 converts served by roughly 1,300 missionaries, representing 41 different religious societies. The Tianjin Massacre of 1870 had demonstrated the potential fervor of antimissionary sentiment, and nothing happened to reduce hostilities during the next quarter of a century.

The reasons for the poor showing of Christianity are many and various. They include difficulties in translation and communication analogous to those that plagued Buddhist missionaries a millennium and a half earlier. The most important concepts of Christianity, such as sin or the Trinity, were the most difficult to translate, none more so than the most sacred idea of all, the idea of God. Agreement on how to translate "God" into Chinese was never reached; three versions, one Catholic and two Protestant, remained current. As before, differences in culture compounded the difficulties in communication.

The nineteenth-century missionary, however, also encountered problems that he did not share with his predecessors, for the Chinese associated Christianity with both the Taiping Rebellion and the unequal treaties. The former showed Christianity as subversive to the social and political order, while the latter brought the missionaries special privileges. Both were resented. Furthermore, the aura of power also attracted false converts, individuals attracted by the possibilities of a treaty port career, and opportunists out to obtain missionary protection for their own ends. Popular resentment of the missions was fired by scurrilous stories and bitter attacks (Figure 9.5). This hostility was encouraged by the elite, who saw Christianity as a superstitious religion that threatened their own status and values. It was no accident that anti-Christian riots often occurred in the provincial capitals during examination time, when they were filled with candidates committed to the status quo.

FIGURE 9.5   *The [Foreign] Devils Worshipping the Incarnation of the Pig [Jesus]*. This print employs a homonym for the transliteration of "Jesus" to depict Christ as a pig.

Here there is an interesting contrast with the situation in Japan, where 30 percent of Christian converts during the Meiji period were from samurai backgrounds. Christianity served the spiritual needs and provided a vehicle for social protest for samurai who found themselves on the losing side of the Restoration struggle. As a result, in the 1880s and 1890s a prestigious native clergy was developing in Japan, and Christianity remained more influential than the slow growth of the churches would indicate. In post-Taiping China too, Christianity continued to appeal to people dissatisfied with the status quo, and it counted among its converts some notable protesters, including Sun Yat-sen. But the elite remained hostile, and the real cutting edge of protest was to be elsewhere: too radical for the nineteenth century, Christianity turned out to be insufficiently radical for the twentieth.

In the meantime, missionaries contributed to the Western perception of China. Working in the treaty ports, dealing not with Confucian gentlemen but with men on the margin of respectable society, the missionaries frequently developed a negative view of China and its inhabitants, an image the reverse of the idealistic picture painted earlier by the Jesuits.

Self-Strengthening—The Theory

Up until the Sino-Japanese War, many of China's most energetic and forward-looking thinkers and statesmen remained committed to increased and more intensive self-strengthening as the solution to the dynasty's and China's problems. However, it was not until after it was challenged that it received its classic formulation. This came in 1898 from the brush of Zhang Zhidong (1837–1909), a governor-general and practitioner of self-strengthening. Like Sakuma Shōzan earlier in Japan, Zhang wanted to preserve traditional values while adopting Western science and technology. The idea was that Chinese learning would remain the heart of Chinese civilization, while Western learning would have a subordinate and supporting role. This was expressed in terms of the traditional Neo-Confucian dichotomy of *ti* (substance) and *yong* (function): Western means for Chinese ends. The basic pattern of Chinese civilization was to remain sacrosanct, but it was to be protected by Western techniques.

Conservative opponents of self-strengthening feared that Chinese civilization would be contaminated by borrowing from the West, since ends cannot be separated from means. In the Confucian formulation, *ti* and *yong* are aspects of a single whole. The Confucian tradition had always been concerned with means as well as ends, and generations of scholars had insisted that the Way did not consist merely of "empty" abstractions, but concerned practical realities. There was no essence apart from application. And there was a great deal more to the West than mere techniques. It was fallacious to believe that China could merely borrow techniques from the West without becoming entangled in manifestations of Western culture. If China went ahead with efforts to adopt Western techniques while preserving traditional culture, the best-case situation would be an uneasy compartmentalization. To preserve tradition in a period of modernization, the country would have to be protected from the kind of radical social reappraisal hailed in Japan by champions of "reason" like Fukuzawa Yukichi.

The contrast with Japan is instructive, for there social change was sanctioned by an appeal to nationalism as symbolized by the throne, whereas in China Confucianism was much too closely associated with the social structure to allow for a similar development. Meiji Japan demonstrated that elements of Confucianism were compatible with modernization, but that modernization involved changes reaching into the very heart of a civilization.

Old and New Wine in Old Bottles

In this difficult age, as in most, there were artists and poets who aimed at "transcending turmoil"[5] by working within the rich tradition they inherited. Their accomplishments can give much pleasure, but others more directly convey a sense of the anxieties and hopes of an age. For example, the poetry of Wang Pengyun (1848–1904), an official who served as a censor, sounds notes of uncertainty, apprehension, and regret in an age of dynastic decay.

In Reply to a Poem from Cishan, Thanking Me for the Gift of Song and Yuan Lyrics I Had Had Printed

(To the tune "The Fish Poacher")
　　Now that the lyric voice wavers in wind-blown dust
　　Who is to speak the sorrows of his heart?
　　Two years of carving, seeking from each block
　　The truest music of the string unswept,
　　Only to sigh now
　　Finding my grief in tune
　　With every beat that leaves the ivory fret!
　　I sigh for the men of old
　　Pour wine in honor of the noble dead:
　　Does any spirit rhymester
　　Understand my heartbreak?

　　The craft of letters
　　Furnishes kindling, covers jars:
　　True bell of tinkling cymbal, who can tell!

　　Du Fu,⋆ who lifelong courted the perfect phrase
　　—Did his verse help him, though it made men marvel?
　　Take what you find here,
　　See if an odd page, a forgotten tune
　　Still has the power to engage your mind.
　　My toiling over
　　I'll drink myself merry, climb the Golden Terrace,
　　Thrash out a wild song from my lute
　　And let the storms rage at will.6

　　　Late Qing writers were much given to writing sequels, new versions, and parodies of China's classic novels, often at great length. *The Dream of the Red Chamber* was a favorite (see Chapter 2). Publication of *The Dream of the Green Chamber* (about a brothel) in 1878 was preceded by *A Precious Mirror for Judging Flowers* (1849), a homosexual romance. *Quell the Bandits* (1853), characterized by David Der-wei Wang as anticipating China's modern political novel,[7] plays off *The Water Margin* (also translated as *All Men Are Brothers*), a classic novel recounting the deeds of 108 bandit heroes driven by the cruel corruption of a decadent government to take justice into their own hands. Such works, for all their flaws, looked toward the future when the old forms would no longer suffice to hold new and corrosive content.

⋆Du Fu (712–770), along with Li Bo (or Li Bai, 701–763) was one of China's most revered poets.

A literary man and political reformer hopeful of the future was Huang Zunxian (1845–1905), who spent 1877 through 1879 in Tokyo as part of the Chinese legation. A collection of his poems describing Japan was published by the Zongli Yamen in 1879. He also wrote a history of Japan, and served as a diplomat in San Francisco, Singapore, and London. Rejecting the conventional poetic genres, he sought to preserve tradition through innovation.

Among those who welcomed the winds from the West were a small group of remarkable men, some with experience abroad in official or unofficial capacities. Guo Songdao (1818–1891) was China's first minister to England and the first Chinese representative to be stationed in any Western country. Wang Tao (1828–1897) spent two years in Scotland assisting James Legge in his translations, and also visited Japan. One of the founders of modern journalism in China, he favored the adoption of Western political institutions as well as science and technology. Another remarkable man was Zheng Guangyin (1842–1921), a famous scholar-comprador, modernizer, and writer. Such men were interested in Western "substance" (not just "function"), while remaining committed to the Confucian tradition.

Important for the future were a number of younger men whose formative years fell into this period, although they did not become influential until the late 1890s. There are three names in particular to which we will return: Yan Fu, born in 1853; Kang Yuwei, born in 1858; and Sun Yat-sen, born in 1866. The discussion of their ideas must wait, however, for it was not until China was jolted by her defeat in the Sino-Japanese War that they came to the fore.

II. Korea

Key Dates

1866	Skirmishes with Americans; battle with France
1871	Clash with US Naval forces
1875	Clash with Japan
1876	Kanghwa Treaty with Japan
1882	Chinese Intervention
1885	Li Hongzhang and Itō Hirobumi agreement
1894–1895	Sino–Japanese War
1895	Treaty of Shimonoseki

The Politics of Reform

The Incursion of the Powers

Gradualists versus Advocates of "Enlightenment"

Christianity and Western Thought

The Tonghak Rebellion and the Sino-Japanese War

The Treaty of Shimonoseki (1895)

The Politics of Reform

In Korea, as in China, the period opens with a program of dynastic restoration conducted under a regency for a minor sovereign. In 1864, following the death of the childless King Chŏljong, a 12-year-old boy from a collateral line of the royal family was chosen to be king. He is known to history as King Kojong (r. 1864–1907), and his father, Yi Ha'ŭng, became regent, serving until Kojong was an adult. Yi Ha'ŭng, better known by his princely title of Taewon'gun, was determined to fight corruption and boost the power of the monarchy. To combat corruption, he punished officials guilty of robbing the treasury and made appointments based on merit and ability rather than family or factional ties. To put an end to decades of "in-law politics" that had resulted from the special position of the queens' relatives, he chose for his son a consort from the less-powerful Min clan of Yŏhŭng. To fight corruption in the bureaucracy, he punished officials who had been skimming the country's grain reserves. To diminish the power of the strongest *yangban* outside the capital, he struck at the *sŏwŏn* academies (see Chapter 4), taxing their lands and ordering them closed. And to display the importance of the king, he ordered the enormously expensive reconstruction of the Kyŏngbok Palace, the original Chosŏn dynasty palace in Seoul that had lain in ruins since the Japanese invasions of the 1590s.

The Prince Regent Taewŏn'gun's personal prestige was confirmed by his command of the brush, for he was a skilled calligrapher and ink artist whose orchids (Figure 9.6) were widely appreciated. Although he established himself as one of the strongest courtiers of the late Chosŏn dynasty, he soon discovered that he had a rival. His daughter-in-law, Queen Min, and her male relatives almost immediately assumed a stance opposing him. Not surprisingly, the Taewŏn'gun also encountered strong opposition from the *yangban* class in general, since his reforms threatened the privileges of the landed aristocracy. However, opposition also came from merchants who resented being assessed to pay for the rebuilding of the royal palace. Commoners, too, suffered from the aggregate burdens of forced labor, taxation, and inflation caused by the government's excessive minting of cash to pay the bills.

The Incursion of the Powers

It was during the Taewŏn'gun's regency that Chosŏn first experienced military pressure from the West. Though the Koreans were well aware of China's losses in the Opium War and of the unequal treaty system, for decades they had managed to fend off attempted visits by British, Americans, Germans, French, and Russians, earning for their country the nickname of "Hermit Kingdom." When approached, the Koreans refused to open relations with the foreigners, citing their special relationship with China under the terms of the tributary system. The single exception to Korea's closure to the West was the continuation of French missionary activity and the resilience of the Korean Catholic community despite waves of official persecution. By the 1860s, the heterodox ideas of Catholicism, together with its tendency to attract the discontented, once more caused such concern at court that it brought forth a final, full-scale attack on the foreign faith. When the Taewŏn'gun ordered the massive purge of 1866, there were more than 20,000 Catholic believers in Korea. By year's end, more than 8,000 converts had been killed along with 9 of the 12 French missionaries known to be residing in the country.

France responded by sending part of its Asiatic naval squadron to seek redress and "open" Korea to French commerce and missionary work. The French flotilla entered the mouth of the Han River and was fought off by a determined Korean defense. This apparent success emboldened the Korean court in its opposition to contact with the West. The Taewŏn'gun proclaimed, "The barbarians are attacking us. We must fight or surrender. Whoever advises conciliation betrays his country. Let this be a warning to our people and all future generations!" (now inscribed on a stone monument on the palace grounds).

Coincidentally in 1866, an American merchant vessel, the *General Sherman,* tried to open contact with Korea by sailing into the mouth of the Taedong River as far as P'yŏngyang. The authorities were outraged by this bold intrusion, and ordered the ship out of Korean waters. The crew disregarded this order, and made threatening gestures toward local

FIGURE 9.6 *Orchids,* Yi Ha'ŏng (1821–1898). Better known as the Taewŏn'gun (Prince Regent), Yi Háŭng was a student of the Chusa style that revolutionized Korean calligraphy. Ink on paper. 117.3 × 29.8 cm.

FROM KOREAN PAINTNG BY KEN VOS (LONDON: BAMBOO PUBLISHERS, 1992), P. 53.

officials, whereupon the *General Sherman* was attacked, set afire, and destroyed, with the loss of all hands.

In 1871 the United States government responded to the destruction of the *General Sherman* by sending a naval force to investigate, and it was hoped, to "open" Korea, as Commodore Matthew Perry had "opened" Japan in 1853 and 1854. When the American squadron approached the mouth of the Han River it was met by Korean defenders determined to repel the Westerners as they had the French in 1866. The Americans landed Marines on Kanghwa Island, however, and there was a brief but bloody battle. Though the Korean side suffered heavier casualties than the Americans, the U.S. side failed to win its objective, and was obliged to depart without a treaty or apology for the destruction of the *General Sherman*. The Koreans thus reaffirmed their seclusion policy with renewed confidence.

As the Koreans learned of the changes surrounding the Meiji Restoration in Japan, they redoubled their determination to "resist heterodoxy and uphold orthodoxy" *(chŏksa wijŏng)* in their own country. They continued the ban on Christianity, renewed their pledge to maintain the purity of Confucian civilization, and bolstered their coastal defenses. Korean thinkers such as Yi Hangno (1792–1868) recommended an all-out nationwide resistance to further foreign incursions, including any from China and Japan, which were no longer "pure." The Korean court even sent a message to the Japanese government chiding the Meiji leaders for their craven willingness to copy the Western barbarians.

Such insults were part of the inspiration for the "conquer Korea" debate *(seikan ron)* that raged within Japan in the 1870s. The Japanese made their move in 1875 when they sent a naval vessel, Perry-style, to the mouth of the Han River. When Korean shore batteries opened fire, the Japanese organized a show of force and demanded that the Koreans sign a modern-style international treaty, their first with any foreign state, on Kanghwa Island. There was considerable argument in Seoul over whether to sign the treaty, which contained language defining Korea as a sovereign state independent of China, opened additional ports to Japanese trade, permitted Japanese citizens to live and work in Korea, and allowed a Japanese ambassador to take up residence in Seoul. As a disciple of Yi Hangno pointed out, "The Japanese who come nowadays dress in Western clothes, use Western guns, and sail in Western ships—clear evidence of the Japanese being one with the Westerners."[8] Ultimately, however, Japanese military force prevailed, and the Koreans signed. One by-product was the rise in Seoul of a reform faction, or "progressive party," of younger *yangban* who recommended studying the new Meiji system and adapting elements of Japan's modernization program for Korea.

As regent, the Taewŏn'gun had campaigned to upgrade the power of his son, King Kojong, expecting him to remain steadfast in the conservative mold after he reached the age of majority. However, after the king came of age and started making decisions on his own, he displayed an unexpected independent streak by showing an interest in some of the progressive faction's ideas. Kojong also took the advice of China's Li Hongzhang to seek "self-strengthening" through controlled reform. The result was a significant policy shift that combined the traditional close relations with China, the tracking of reform in Meiji Japan, the opening of relations with Western nations, and limited toleration for Western ideas, including Christianity. In 1882, with Li Hongzhang's blessing, Chosŏn signed a treaty with the United States, its first with a Western power. The following year it received its first Western diplomat, U.S. Minister Lucius Foote. Negotiations leading up to the U.S.–Korean treaty in 1882 were difficult, and the treaty itself was written with great attention to Korean sensibilities. For example, Americans did not get the right to send missionaries to Korea. They did promise to use their "good offices" to assist Korea in relations with other states, a provision that later became an issue when Koreans accused the United States of failing in its duty to protect Korea from Japanese imperialism in the early 1900s. However, when Great Britain, France, Russia, Germany, Italy, and Belgium signed treaties with Korea in the mid-1880s, the door swung wide open to missionary work, exploration, trade, and investment. By the mid-1890s Protestant and Catholic missionaries, traders, concessionaires, speculators, teachers, mining engineers, and even a few random expatriates had taken up residence in Korea, forever ending the era of Chosŏn as "the Hermit Kingdom."

The spate of treaties with foreign powers triggered the escalation of an already existing conflict between conservative and progressive factions in the Korean court. King Kojong's dispatch of study missions to Japan and diplomatic missions to the West exacerbated the conflict and sparked a reactionary backlash. In 1881 there was an abortive attempt to replace King Kojong with a more cooperative prince. In 1882, soldiers of the old Korean army staged a mutiny to oppose the creation of Japanese-style modern military units. King Kojong was obliged to call his father back from retirement to get control of the situation, and the old regent then proceeded to dismantle the modern army units and then continued by dismantling the T'ongni Kimu Amun, Korea's newly established version of China's foreign office, the Zongli Yamen. Japan reacted by sending troops, ostensibly to collect reparations for damages to its diplomatic mission during the soldiers' mutiny. Seeing Japan's forces in Korea, China responded by sending a larger force and establishing military supremacy in Korea. Upset with the Taewŏn'gun for provoking chaos and military confrontation in Korea, the Chinese engineered his kidnapping and removal to China under virtual arrest.

This began a period of intense Chinese meddling in Korea's internal affairs. The Chinese "recommended" advisors, both Chinese and Western, to direct various aspects of Korean policy and to administer foreign affairs and the newly founded Customs Service. In a departure from tradition, the Qing government stationed a permanent representative, or "resident," in Seoul to protect Chinese interests and act as a special advisor. This was Yuan Shikai, the protégé of Li Hongzhang, who was destined eventually to become President of China after the revolution of 1911–1912. His presence in Seoul in the early 1880s encouraged a wave of Chinese merchant immigration to the Korean peninsula.

Gradualists versus Advocates of "Enlightenment"

Chinese interference in Korea thwarted some of the more radical proposals that were emanating from the progressives at court, who started calling themselves the "Enlightenment Party" (*kaehwa dang*). The gradualists were mild reformers who were interested in preserving the Korean class system, and they saw Chinese military backing as a way to stave off fundamental change. The Enlightenment Party, on the other hand, included people who had been abroad and were determined to strengthen Korea in the style of Meiji Japan rather than Li Hongzhang's China. Like their Japanese mentors, they were ready to challenge the political and social structure in fundamental ways. They proposed the abolition of classes, a sweeping revision of Korea's educational system, and liberation from Qing influence, which they saw as an obstacle to progress.

Certain members of the Enlightenment Party had studied with the great Meiji intellectual Fukuzawa Yukichi. Fukuzawa did not want his protégés to provoke a full-scale confrontation between China and Japan over Korea, and he gave only tepid support to the enlightenment faction's more militant ideas. Nevertheless, the enlightenment group staged a violent coup in December 1884 that took the lives of several gradualists. They actually seized control of the palace for several days before being routed by counterattacking Chinese troops. In the aftermath of the coup, the surviving enlightenment group members fled to Japan. The following spring, Li Hongzhang and Itō Hirobumi signed an agreement committing both China and Japan to withdraw their forces from Korea, to refrain from giving military aid to Korea, and to consult before acting in the future if intervention appeared necessary again. With the Li-Itō Convention, otherwise known as the Treaty of Tianjin, the dangerous Sino-Japanese military rivalry over Korea came to a standstill that lasted until 1894.

Christianity and Western Thought

Despite Korea's new international contacts, many Korean *yangban* remained steadfastly opposed to Western heterodoxies that competed with orthodox Neo-Confucianism, and insisted that Korea maintain its ideological purity. However, in April 1885, the same month as the Li-Itō Convention, Korea received its first Protestant missionaries. In the decade that followed, American Presbyterians and Methodists founded numerous churches in and around Seoul as well as in the ports that had been opened for trade. A clinic founded in 1885 later developed into a leading modern hospital and medical school. A Presbyterian boys' school that was founded in the same year and a Methodist girls' school founded in 1886 evolved into Yonsei and Ewha, two of contemporary Korea's greatest universities. Paejae Academy, a Methodist boys' school, produced several of Korea's most important modern leaders, including Syngman Rhee (1875–1965).

Though Western missionaries at first had difficulty recruiting converts and students, they were unhampered by the association with gunboat diplomacy and violent Taiping-style revolution that repelled and frightened many people in China. By 1900, the Korean Protestant community was growing rapidly and attracting many who were curious about modern life in the West as well as many who became authentic spiritual converts. Catholic missions also returned in the 1890s, reinvigorating Korea's earlier Christian community. The Central Cathedral in Seoul, completed in 1898, became one of the city's defining landmarks.

The disillusionment that gripped many Korean intellectuals at the end of the nineteenth century contributed greatly to the positive response that many gave to foreign ideology. Though the Chosŏn and its institutions had lasted so long that a Chosŏn-less Korea seemed inconceivable, even pedigreed *yangban* were tired of the reaction and corruption that were intertwined with the country's political culture. One young *yangban* who had an extraordinary opportunity to study abroad, first in China under American missionaries and then in the United States at Vanderbilt and Emory Universities, was Yun Ch'iho (1865–1945). As he was leaving America to return to Asia in 1893, he reflected on his homeland with criticism and concern:

> It suffocates me (literally) to think that there is a country of 80,000 square miles where millions of souls cannot think or say or act as they please; where talents have no market; ambition, no sphere; patriotism, no play; where infernal despotism breeds and nurses generations of slaves, beggars, and idiots; where men are dying in life and living in death; where moral and material putrefaction and filth are destroying thousands every year. How long will this political hell last?[9]

The Korea to which Yun Ch'iho was returning was caught in a true political whirlpool, weakened by internal factions and feckless leadership, and surrounded by larger countries that had designs on its future. Since the Li-Itō Convention of 1885, China had tightened its grip on Korea, thwarting King Kojong's feeble attempt to conduct an independent foreign policy, and supervising the country's internal affairs through pro-Chinese officials in key positions. Queen Min's male relatives had created an oligarchic faction for themselves, controlling the tax system, the civil service examination system, official appointments and promotions, and the issuing of licenses for every kind of private enterprise.

The Japanese, meanwhile, had created their own sphere of operations in Korea centering on the ports, where they dominated trade and transport. Japanese merchants busied themselves penetrating the domestic market, overwhelming Korean small businesses with better-quality textiles from Japan and daily use items such as matches. The treaty system limited the Seoul government's ability to use customs duties to protect the Korean market from Japanese sellers. Meanwhile, itinerant Japanese buyers gathered up rice and other foodstuffs in Korea and exported them to Japan, creating scarcity and high prices for Korean consumers. As the intrusion of foreign influence started affecting daily life across the country, the government's essential weakness was revealed in its inability to manage the imbalances.

The Tonghak Rebellion and the Sino-Japanese War

As Sino-Japanese rivalry over Korea simmered in the early 1890s, events within Korea began setting the stage for war. War was precipitated by a peasant outbreak in southwestern Korea called the Tonghak Rebellion, led by a visionary named Chŏn Pongjun.

Though Korea was remarkably quiet in the seventeenth and eighteenth centuries, a combination of bad harvests, high taxes, and social injustice drove many commoners to the brink of revolt in the nineteenth century. There was a serious uprising in northwestern Korea in 1811. In the 1860s, a southern Korean named Ch'oe Che'u (1824–1864) invented a millenarian religion combining Buddhist, Confucian, shamanist, and Christian ideas into a body of teachings called "Tonghak" (Eastern Learning), which he promoted as an alternative to the corrupt political and social system. Oppression by the Korean ruling class was a central grievance in his teaching, and his call for resistance led to his arrest and execution in 1864.

The "opening" of Korea in the 1870s and 1880s simply deepened the distress of peasants everywhere, but nowhere more than on the rice-growing plains of the southwestern Chŏlla provinces, where sharecroppers and small farmers were struggling to stay alive while making their rent and tax payments. They were infuriated further by the government's "selling out" to foreigners, both by the sale of Korean rice to Japan when Koreans were starving and by permitting an influx of foreigners both as merchants (the Japanese) and as purveyors of alien ideologies (Christian missionaries). Their protests grew into a movement that burst upon the national scene when more than 20,000 angry farmers demonstrated at Po'ŭn in April 1893. The Po'ŭn riot was followed by a Tonghak petition to the king in Seoul, complaining of the government's failure to address the dire conditions of the people.

The king answered the petition by accusing the Tonghaks of stirring up trouble, and the delegates reported, in effect, that the people of Chŏlla would have to redress their grievances themselves. When more abuses followed, a young teacher named Chŭn Pongjun gathered a group of peasants and took over the local magistrate's establishment, seized weapons out of his armory, raided his granary, and distributed the accumulated tax grain to the people to eat. This fracas brought government troops who proved to be no match for the armed rebels, and in a short time the Tonghaks were in control of several important counties. Until this point, the rebels had demanded fairer taxes, the sacking of the worst officials, and an end to rice exports, but now they added new demands that included land reform and an end to social discrimination, especially against the lowest classes. They justified their demands in religious terms with slogans such as "People Are Heaven!" or "People Are the Most Important Thing," a basically modern idea that government should serve the people and not the other way around.

The Tonghaks gathered momentum and beat back several attempts by government forces to stop their northward advance. When they occupied the capital

BOX 9.2   A TONGHAK PETITION

Like the Taipings, the Tonghaks combined religious fervor with outrage at the suffering of ordinary people. The following is an excerpt from the petition they submitted to the king just a year before the eruption of rebellion and war.

> Luxury and indulgence run rampant throughout the country while ordinary people everywhere suffer from deprivation. When the governors and ministers are corrupt and greedy, how can the people avoid being poor and distressed? The people constitute the nation's foundation. When that foundation is undermined, the nation will fall. Rather than helping and comforting the people, officials build themselves country residences, look after their own selfish interests and usurp high salaries and official honors. How can such behavior be justified?

Yongho Ch'oe, Peter H. Lee, and Wm. Theodore de Bary (eds.), *Sources of Korean Tradition: Volume II: From the Sixteenth to the Twentieth Centuries* (New York: Columbia University Press, 2000), p. 265.

of North Chŏlla Province and seemed headed for Seoul in May 1894, King Kojong appealed for Chinese intervention. When Li Hongzhang dispatched a contingent of 1,500 troops and notified Japan as called for in the earlier Li-Itō Convention, the Japanese responded with troops of their own. With neither power willing to back away at this point, Japanese forces made their move on July 23 and took effective control of the royal palace, putting King Kojong under their "protection." Japanese ships opened fire on Chinese naval forces in Asan Bay, on Korea's west coast, and the Sino-Japanese War began.

Most observers expected China to prevail. All parties, including the Japanese, were therefore surprised when Japan decisively defeated China on both sea and land during nine months of fighting. The Japanese crushed Li Hongzhang's army in a battle at P'yŏngyang, invaded Manchuria, and completely destroyed Qing sea power. Dalian and Port Arthur were captured by land, rendering useless the artillery pointing toward the sea and the naval bases financed at great cost by Li.

As they won the upper hand in the war, the Japanese forced the opening of several new southwestern ports to Japanese trade. In October 1894, as they saw their annual harvest being loaded onto boats for export to Japan, the people of the Chŏlla Provinces rose up in a final rage, being led into the town of Nonsan by Chŏn Pongjun. Japanese forces turned from fighting the Chinese and opened a slaughter of Korean Tonghaks that succeeded, with great violence and mass death, in crushing the Tonghak movement. It was Chŏn Pongjun's fate to be caught by Korean authorities and put to death.

The Tonghaks were no match for the Japanese. Similarly, in retrospect, the reasons for Japan's victory over China are easy to see. Japan was better equipped, better led, and more united than China. Chinese battle tactics were astonishingly inept: for example, in the Battle of Korea Bay, the admiral in charge of the Chinese fleet arranged his ships in cavalry formation, like horses, thus opening them to destruction by the Japanese admiral, who was using a disciplined modern naval formation. However, China's greatest disadvantage was its officials' disinterest in defending their stakes in Korea. Regional governors in southern China saw the war not as a national struggle, but as a project of the northern viceroy Li Hongzhang, and they withheld their forces.

The Treaty of Shimonoseki (1895)

The war ended with a peace treaty that was signed at Shimonoseki on the western tip of the Japanese main island of Honshu. In the Treaty of Shimonoseki, China renounced its traditional special role in Korea, and recognized it as a fully independent state. In addition, China ceded to Japan the island of Taiwan and the nearby Pescadores Islands, a significant increase for the Japanese empire. As if to recognize that Japan was now a world power on a par with the Western imperialist nations, China paid Japan a large indemnity, granted Japan most-favored-nation status, and opened seven additional ports to Japanese trade. The treaty also granted Japan control of the Liaodong Peninsula at the northern end of the Yellow Sea, a foothold on Manchuria that would have opened the way for Japanese development on the continent beyond Korea. However, Russia, France, and Germany reacted with diplomatic pressure to block this transfer, in what is known as the "Triple Intervention" of 1895, and China paid Japan a supplemental indemnity instead. The Sino-Japanese War thus resulted in a dramatic shift in the East Asian balance of power from China to Japan, a condition that was to continue until Japan's defeat in World War II. The world learned that China was even weaker than previously believed. Korea became a pawn in the great game of empire, with the enlightenment clique in the ascendancy and Japanese officials pulling strings in the background. To the north, Czarist Russia was consolidating its presence in Siberia and Manchuria with railroads and bases. Japan, therefore, turned from its victory against China to face a new continental rival, Czarist Russia.

Internally, too, there were changes in each of the war's participants as Japan became an empire and China was confronted with the inadequacies of self-strengthening. It also altered the course of Korean history. Japan's control over the Korean government fostered another attempt at Japanese-style reform. These were the Kabo Reforms, named for the Sino-Korean calendar year *kabo* (1894), which ended the old class system, the traditional examination system, various forms of graft, and corrupt social practices such as child marriage (see Chapter 12).

A decade after the war, the ideas behind the Tonghak Rebellion emerged again in the form of the Ch'ŏndogyo ("Religion of the Heavenly Way"). Its new leader, Son Pyŏnghŭi, was a leader of the Korean independence movement of 1919, and Ch'ŏndogyo has remained even today as a "new religion" of modern Korea, though much diminished in influence.

Notes

1. Ssu-yu Teng and John K. Fairbank, *China's Response to the West: A Documentary Survey, 1839–1923* (Cambridge, MA: Harvard Univ. Press, 1954), p. 48. Parentheses inserted by the translator.

2. W. Theodore de Bary and Richard Lufrano, eds., *Sources of Chinese Tradition*, 2nd ed. vol. 2 (New York, NY: Columbia Univ. Press, 2000), p. 238. Adapted from Ssu-yu Teng and John K. Fairbank, *China's Response to the West*, p. 76.

3. Quoted in Immanuel C. Y. Hsu, *China's Entrance into the Family of Nations: The Diplomatic Phase, 1858–1880* (Cambridge, MA: Harvard Univ. Press, 1960), p. 168.

4. Philip C. C. Huang, *The Peasant Economy and Social Change in North China* (Stanford, CA: Stanford Univ. Press, 1985), p. 137.

5. Claudia Brown and Ju-hsi Chou, *Transcending Turmoil: Painting at the Close of China's Empire 1796–1911* (Phoenix, AZ: Phoenix Art Museum, 1992).

6. Cyril Birch, ed., *Anthology of Chinese Literature*, vol. 2 (New York, NY: Grove Press, 1971), p. 294.

7. David Der-wei Wang, *Fin-de-siecle Splendor: Repressed Modernities of Late Qing Fiction, 1849–1911* (Stanford, CA: Stanford Univ. Press, 1997), p. 125.

8. Ch'oe Ikhyŏn quoted in Peter H. Lee, ed., *Sourcebook of Korean Civilization*, vol. 2 (New York, NY: Columbia Univ. Press, 1996), p. 333.

9. *Yun Ch'iho Ilgi (Yun Ch'iho's Diary)*, vol. 3 (Seoul, R.O.K.: National History Compilation Committee, 1974), p. 182.

Part Three

Continental East Asia and Imperial Japan: 1895–1945

During this half-century, interaction between the world's civilizations increased in intensity and complexity until all became involved in World War II, which brought in its wake drastically redrawn mental as well as physical landscapes in East Asia as elsewhere. Earlier, World War I had encouraged ethnic nationalism but failed to achieve a stable multinational state system. Resulting from the war, the Russian Revolution and the establishment of the Soviet Union offered a radical vision of equality and world revolution. The mostly prosperous 1920s gave substance to the claim that the war had ended in a "victory for democracy," and seemed to prove Henry Ford a better visionary than Karl Marx. However, the Great Depression in the 1930s demonstrated the precariousness of the victory that was rooted in the debacle of the war. The legitimacy of the existing order was challenged not only by Marxists longing for "the withering away of the state" after the triumph of the proletariat, but equally by Fascists and other ethno-nationalists advocating a special destiny for their "people," "nation," or "race" (whatever they might mean). Advances in international cooperation achieved in the 1920s were negated during a decade when economic crisis intensified ideological passions to an extent difficult to imagine in the present time of economic prosperity and political apathy.

World War I shattered old European verities and led to a period of cultural and intellectual ferment. Einstein, Freud, and Picasso achieved major breakthroughs prior to the war, but it was in the 1920s that their ideas became current. Now people read and argued over Joyce and Pound, delighted in or sneered at Bauhaus architecture, applauded or were puzzled by surrealism, futurism, the antics of the Dadaists, and the sounds of Schoenberg, Hindemith, and Stravinsky. Popular culture also developed, spreading through radio and film as well as through print.

As we will see, World War I had major repercussions also in East Asia. However, Japan's defeat of China in 1895 looms even larger in East Asian history, for it marked the beginning of a half-century of Japanese empire building that had a profound effect throughout and beyond the region.

10

China: Endings and Beginnings, 1895–1927

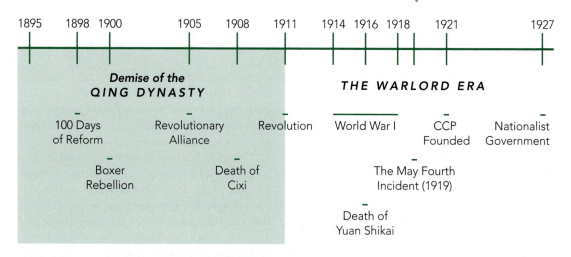

1895	1898	1900	1905	1908	1911	1914	1916	1918	1921	1927

Demise of the QING DYNASTY

THE WARLORD ERA

100 Days of Reform

Revolutionary Alliance

Revolution

World War I

CCP Founded

Nationalist Government

Boxer Rebellion

Death of Cixi

The May Fourth Incident (1919)

Death of Yuan Shikai

China's defeat by Japan ushered in a period of accelerated change as the forces of reform, reaction, and revolution interlocked in complex patterns in an international environment full of menace. After the demise of the Qing, it proved easier to do away with the old than to create the new.

I. The Last Years of the Last Dynasty

The New Reformers

The Scramble for Concessions

The Boxer Rising

Winds of Change

Stirrings of Protest and Revolution

Eleventh-Hour Reform

The Revolution of 1911

The New Reformers

The shock of defeat allowed new voices to be heard. They differed from the proponents of self-strengthening both in the scope of the changes they advocated and in their willingness to reexamine basic assumptions. At the same time, the radicals of this generation still had received a Confucian education and had a command of traditional learning.

A major influence was Yan Fu, the one-time naval student at Greenwich, who voiced the bitter resentment of many:

> We thought that of all the human race none was nobler than we. And then one day from tens and thousands of miles away came island barbarians from beyond the pale, with bird-like language and beastly features, who floated in and pounded our gates requesting entrance and, when they did not get what they asked for, they attacked our coasts and took captive our officials and even burned our palaces and alarmed our Emperor. When this happened, the only reason we did not devour their flesh and sleep on their hides was that we had not the power.[1]

Emboldened by the more open atmosphere, Yan publicized his ideas, first in a series of essays, and then in a number of extremely influential translations, notably Thomas Huxley's *Ethics and Evolution* (1898), Adam Smith's *Wealth of Nations* (1900), and John Stuart Mill's *On Liberty* (1903). Yan argued that Western learning was needed to release Chinese energies, and rejected much of Chinese tradition including even Confucius. He was especially attracted to Social Darwinism, with its dynamic view of history as evolutionary and progressive, and the hope it held out, on a supposedly modern scientific basis, for those who would struggle.

Yan Fu was no political activist, but others, notably Kang Yuwei (1858–1927) and his followers Tan Sitong (1865–1898) and Liang Qichao (1873–1929), not only spread their ideas through their writings and in study groups but also tried to implement political programs. Kang, an original thinker deeply grounded in Buddhism as well as Confucianism, elaborated a highly original theory to construct a Confucian basis for ideas that went well beyond the Confucian tradition. Drawing on an unorthodox school of classical interpretation, he argued that Confucius was not merely a transmitter of ancient teachings but a prophet whose language was full of hidden meanings. Kang's Confucius saw history as a universal progress through three stages, each with its appropriate form of government: the Age of Disorder (rule by an absolute monarch), the Age of Approaching Peace (rule by a constitutional monarch), and the Age of Great Peace (rule by the people). His Confucius was a seer and prophet for both China and the entire world. Tan Sitong went beyond Kang to argue that the monarchy should be replaced by a republic, and attacked the traditional Confucian family distinctions in the name of *ren*, the central Confucian virtue. Neo-Confucian thinkers had earlier given *ren* a cosmic dimension, but Tan drew on modern scientific concepts in identifying *ren* with ether. Kang Youwei, too, equated *ren* with ether and electricity.

In their political program, Kang and his followers sought to transform the government into a modern and modernizing constitutional monarchy along the lines of Meiji Japan. Thanks to a sympathetic governor, they were able to carry out some reforms in Hunan, but their greatest opportunity came during the "Hundred Days of Reform" (actually 103 days, June 11 to September 20), when Emperor Guangxu asserted his authority by issuing a flood of edicts aimed at reforming the examination system, remodeling the bureaucracy, and promoting modernization. It was an ambitious program, but the edicts remained more significant as expressions of intent than as indicators of accomplishment, for most were never implemented.

Moderately experienced statesmen initiated the reforms, but later accounts exaggerated the influence of Kang and his associates, as well as the initial struggle between a progressive emperor and a supposedly reactionary Empress Dowager (see Figure 9.1). However, rumors of Kang's allegedly extremist influence on the emperor helped to solidify the opposition and pave the way for Cixi, backed by General Ronglu, to stage a coup. She placed Emperor Guangxu under house arrest and turned him into a figurehead for the remaining 10 years of his life.

After the coup, Tan Sitong remained in China and suffered martyrdom. Kang Yuwei and Liang Qichao managed to flee to Japan, where they continued to write and work for renewal and reform. Kang, elaborating on his utopia, dreamed of a future when the whole world would be united in love and harmony under a single popularly elected government, which would operate hospitals, schools, and nurseries, administering a society without any divisive institutions, including even the family. Meanwhile, Liang continued to expand his intellectual horizons. Like many of his contemporaries elsewhere, he championed evolution and progress, processes that he conflated, and contrary to Darwin, saw as products of human will. But in his eyes, this will had to serve the group. Like most Chinese and Japanese thinkers, Liang was not an individualist.

The Empress Dowager's coup sent China's most advanced thinkers into exile, but it did not mean a wholesale reaction against reform. She approved moderate reforms, including military modernization, changes in education, and alterations to the monetary and fiscal systems. Although little was accomplished, this was due to the weakness of the central government and the magnitude of the problems facing the dynasty. Some of the greatest problems came from abroad.

The Scramble for Concessions

China's display of weakness in the war against Japan set in motion a scramble for special rights and privileges in which Russia, France, Britain, Germany, and Japan pursued their national interests and jockeyed for position in case China collapsed completely, as seemed quite likely at the time. The concessions extracted from China were economic and political. Loans were forced on the Qing, secured by tax revenues, such as maritime customs. Long-term leases of Chinese territory were granted, including the right to develop economic resources such as mines and railroads. Germany leased territory in Shandong; Russia leased Port Arthur in the southern Liaodong Peninsula; France held leases on land around Guangzhou Bay; and Britain obtained Weihaiwei and the New Territories, adjacent to the Kowloon area of Hong Kong. The powers frequently obtained the right to police the leased areas. Often they combined leaseholds, railroad rights, and commercial rights into a "sphere of interest," where they were the privileged foreign power, as for example, Germany was in Shandong. Finally, there were "nonalienation" pacts in which China agreed not to cede a given area to any power other than the signatory: the Yangzi Valley to Britain, the provinces bordering French Indochina to France, and Fujian to Japan. Russia received special rights in Manchuria.

Britain, as the prime trading nation in China, pursued an ambiguous policy concerned with retaining access to all of China while still obtaining its own concessions. The United States at this time was acquiring a Pacific empire. In 1898 it annexed Hawaii and, after war with Spain, the Philippines and Guam. At the urging of Britain, the United States then adopted an open-door policy enunciated in two diplomatic notes. The first of these (1899) merely demanded equality of commercial opportunity for all the powers in China, while the second (1900) also affirmed a desire to preserve the integrity of the Chinese State and Chinese territory. This was a declaration of principle, not backed by force; neither its altruism nor its effectiveness should be exaggerated.

The Boxer Rising

The Boxers, members of the *Yihequan* (Righteous and Harmonious Fists), developed in response to harsh economic conditions. Popular anxieties were also fueled by antiforeignism, stemming from alarm over the spread of railways, which cut across the land regardless of the ancestors' graves or the requirements of geomancy—railways along which stood telephone poles carrying wires from which rust-filled rainwater dripped blood-red. As a counterforce, the Boxers relied on *qigong* (ritualized exercise), spells, and amulets to endow them with supernatural powers, including invulnerability to bullets. In 1898, flood and famine in Shandong, combined with the advance of the Germans in that province, led to the first Boxer rising. It occurred there in May of that year; but it was drought in the spring and summer of 1900 that brought many new members and wide popular support.

Originally antidynastic, the Boxers changed direction when they received the support of high Qing officials prepared to use the movement against the foreign powers. Thus encouraged, the Boxers spread, venting their rage on Chinese and foreign Christians, especially Catholics. On June 13, 1900, they entered Beijing. Eight days later the court issued a declaration of war on all the treaty powers. The Boxers were officially placed under the command of imperial princes. There followed a dramatic two-month siege of the legation quarter in Beijing, where 451 guards defended 473 foreign civilians and some 3,000 Chinese Christians who had fled there for protection. The ordeal of the besieged was grim, but they were spared the worst, for the Boxers and the Chinese troops were undisciplined, poorly-organized, and uncoordinated. The city was full of looting and violence, but the legation quarter was still intact when an international relief expedition reached Beijing on August 15 and forced the court to flee the capital.

During these dangerous and dramatic events, southern governors-general ignored the court's declaration of war, claiming it was made under duress. The powers, nevertheless, demanded from the Qing court a very harsh settlement. It included a huge indemnity (450 million taels, or 67.5 million pounds sterling) to be paid from customs and salt revenues. Other provisions required the punishment of pro-Boxer officials and of certain cities, where the civil service examinations were suspended. The powers received the right to station permanent legation guards in the capital and to place troops between Beijing and the sea.

The Boxer rising also provided Russia with an excuse to occupy Manchuria, where some Russians remained until Russia's defeat by Japan in the war of 1904–1905. The Boxer rising became a source of literature. Most of it focused on one of the leading figures, Sai Jinhua (1874–1936), who was a courtesan, the concubine of a Chinese diplomat in Europe, and supposedly the mistress of the German field marshal who commanded the allied forces occupying Beijing. Depraved strumpet to some, selfless heroine to others, she fills both roles in *A Flower in a Sea of Sins* (*Niehai hua*, 1907) by Zeng Pu (1872–1935).

Winds of Change

Between 1895 and 1911, the modern sector of the Chinese economy continued to grow, but it was dominated by foreign capital. Extensive railway concessions were granted to the treaty powers, and Chinese railroads, like that linking

Beijing and Hankou, were financed by foreign capital. Foreigners also controlled much of China's mining and shipping, and were a major factor in manufacturing, both for export (tea, silk, soybeans, and so on) and for the domestic market (textiles, tobacco, and so on). Modern banking was another area of foreign domination, prompting the Qing government in 1898 to approve the creation of the Commercial Bank of China as a "government-operated merchant enterprise." Two more banks were formed in 1905 and 1907.

Except for railways and mines, foreign investments were concentrated in the treaty ports. It was also there that Chinese factories gradually developed, taking advantage of modern services and the security found in foreign concession areas. Chinese enterprises were particularly important in textile manufacturing. Most remained small (by 1912 only 750 employed more than 100 workers), but they were an important part of China's economic modernization. It was during this time that Shanghai became China's largest city.

In Shanghai and, to a lesser extent, in other treaty ports, changes in social structure occurred. During the last five years of the dynasty a bourgeoisie emerged, "a group of modern or semi-modern entrepreneurs, tradesmen, financiers, industrial leaders, unified by material interests, common political aspirations, a sense of their collective destiny, a common mentality, and specific daily habits."[2] There were also the beginnings of an urban working class, who at times expressed their resentment over terrible working conditions by going on strike. In the city, too, the old family system lost some of its economic underpinnings, and an audience developed receptive to new perspectives.

There were now 170 presses supplying 2 to 4 million readers for the "depravity novels," "chivalric/court case novels," "exposé," and "science fantasy" novels studied by David Der-wei Wang. More often than not, they took a jaundiced view of those in power, though few were as blunt as the prostitute in the "depravity novel" *Nine-tailed Turtle* who tells her customer, "The whole of officialdom is just like a big whorehouse."[3] In *The New Story of the Stone* (1908), Wu Jianren (1866–1910) brings back the main protagonist of *Dream of the Red Chamber,* and at one point has him arrested as a dissident, but also takes him to "The Civilized World," filled with technological wonders, a utopia (unlike Kang Yu-wei's) not meant to be actually attainable.

Meanwhile, a strong influence on provincial affairs was exercised by a semi-modern urban elite composed of merchants and bankers (more or less traditional), military and professional men (among them journalists) trained in modern methods, and absentee landowners—an elite whose interests and even values often differed from those of both the landed gentry and the central government. The very definition of elite status was changed forever when the examination system was abolished in 1905, putting an end to a key institution that had linked government and society, thought and action, local and central for well over 1000 years.

The government had taken this radical step in recognition of the need for more modern specialists, as well as to secure the loyalty of graduates of new schools by reassuring them in their career expectations.

Stirrings of Protest and Revolution

Some were caught off balance by the winds of change, others trimmed their sails, but there were also those who looked to the future with hope and organized attempts to induce further change. An early and notable example was the formation of the first anti-footbinding movement in 1894, which resulted in a law banning the practice in 1902. However, even in the cities the law was largely ignored. Footbinding persisted longest in rural areas, and old women with bound feet can still be seen in remote areas. Other expressions of public opinion included a flurry of criticism at what appeared to be a maneuver to depose the emperor (1900), protests at Russia's refusal to leave Manchuria (1903), a boycott against the United States protesting exclusionary immigration laws (1905), and a boycott against Japan (1908), as well as movements to regain railway rights.

Readers of the political press that emerged after 1895 were now exposed to articles and cartoons linking dissatisfaction with the government to resentment against foreign exactions (Figure 10.1).

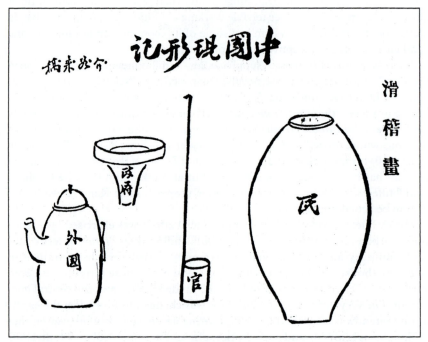

FIGURE 10.1   "A record of the situation in China." Cartoon in *Shibao,* August 26, 1907. The ladle in the center represents officials scooping from the jug of the people (on the right) and pouring their resources through a government funnel into the foreigners' teapot.

FROM *PRINT AND POLITICS: "SHIBAO" AND THE CULTURE OF REFORM IN LATE QING CHINA*, BY JOAN JUDGE (STANFORD: STANFORD UNIVERSITY PRESS, 1996), P. 184. REPRINTED COURTESY STANFORD UNIVERSITY PRESS.

Politically, the defeat of 1895 opened the door to radical reformism and, additionally, set Sun Yat-sen (1866–1925) on the path of revolution. Sun was born into a Guangdong peasant family, received a Christian education in Hawaii, and studied medicine in Hong Kong. He founded his first revolutionary organization in 1894. Throughout his life overseas, Chinese communities remained an important source of moral and financial support. Over the years he elaborated his "Three Principles of the People"—nationalism, democracy, and the people's livelihood. He called for the overthrow of the dynasty and the establishment of a republic, principles broad enough to attract the varied and loosely organized membership of Sun's Revolutionary Alliance (Tongmenghui), formed in Tokyo in 1905 by merging revolutionary groups. Afterward, his supporters included students, many from elite families.

Many looked to political revolution to solve China's ills, but some more radical voices sought social revolution as well. One such voice was that of the pioneer feminist Qin Jin, born in 1877 and executed as a revolutionary in 1907. In 1904, shortly after leaving the husband her family had selected for her, as well as a son and a daughter, she wrote the following poem:

Regrets: Lines Written en Route to Japan
> Sun and moon have no light left, earth is dark;
> our women's world is sunk so deep, who can help us?
> Jewelry sold to pay this trip across the seas,
>
> Cut off from family I leave my native land.
> Unbinding my feet I clear out a thousand years of poison,
> With heated heart arouse all women's spirits.
> Alas, this delicate kerchief here
> Is half stained with blood, and half with tears.[4]

Eleventh-Hour Reform

The abolition of the examination system was the most drastic of a series of reforms by which the Empress Dowager hoped to save the dynasty after the failure of the Boxers. Some reforms, like the drive against opium, accomplished much, but the program as a whole failed to inspire officials to change their ways. The momentum was all downhill. In *Modern Times: A Brief History of Enlightenment* (*Wenming xiaoshi*, 1905) Li Boyuan (1867–1906), a widely read author of exposé novels, depicts officials whose venality is matched only by the ignorance and arrogance of purveyors of the new Western learning. According to David Der-wei Wang, "Li Boyuan saw in this campaign for reform and modernization less a promise of new economic and political structure than an omen of collective self-delusion, incompetence, and procrastination."[5]

Frequently, measures taken to save the Qing ended up undermining it. The educational reforms are an example. By 1911 even remote provinces boasted new schools, teaching new subjects and ideas. Students also studied abroad in record numbers, especially in Japan where, by 1906, there were at least 8,000 Chinese students, many supported by their provincial governments. There, away from home, they enjoyed new personal and intellectual liberty. Even those who did not manage to complete their education drank in the heady wine of new ideas. From the writing of the highly influential Liang Qichao, many learned about the major events of world history and were introduced to Western social and political thought. The example of Japan was itself a powerful influence, as were books translated from Japanese. More books were translated into Chinese from Japanese than from any other language. Many Japanese loanwords entered the Chinese language, thus reversing the flow that had taken place over a millennium earlier.

Chinese students thus learned about Western history, law, science, and logic; became convinced of the truths of Social Darwinism; and were inspired by the visions of nationalism. As non-Chinese, the Manchus were an obvious target. The Japanese example showed that nationalism was compatible with the preservation of elements of traditional culture, but a commitment to nationalism entailed a willingness to jettison those elements of tradition that failed to contribute to national development. Toward the end of the decade, students became increasingly restive and revolutionary.

Manchu political reform included restructuring the government along modern lines and developing a constitution. After a study mission abroad (1905–1906) and subsequent deliberations, in 1908 the government announced a nine-year plan of constitutional reform, beginning with provincial assemblies in 1909. Although elected on a limited franchise, these assemblies, as well as the central legislative council convened in 1910, became centers of opposition rather than sources of popular support for the government.

Nothing was more urgent than the creation of a modern military, but here, too, the reform program backfired. The new forces proved unreliable because they were either influenced by new, subversive ideas or were loyal to their commanders rather than to the throne. The main beneficiary of military modernization turned out to be Yuan Shikai, who, after his service in Korea (see p. 203), had advanced his career by siding with Cixi in her coup and by standing firm against the Boxers. He became commander of the New Army in 1895 and, as governor-general of Zhihli from 1901 to 1907, continued to build up the army with which he retained ties even after he was dismissed from the government in 1909.

The government had some foreign policy success, especially in reasserting sovereignty over Tibet, but the government still failed to emerge as a plausible focus for nationalism. Not only was it handicapped by its non-Han ethnic origins but at this critical juncture there was confusion and disorganization after the Empress Dowager and Emperor Guangxu both died in November 1908. Since the Emperor had seemed in good health, there were rumors that his death, one day before that of the Empress Dowager, was due to poison. The rumors were never proven, but this was not a propitious way to start a new reign. The new emperor was an infant, and the regent was inept but bitterly resentful of Yuan Shikai, who was fortunate to be allowed to retire in 1909.

The Revolution of 1911

In its program of modernization, the dynasty was handicapped by its financial weakness. This became painfully apparent in its handling of the railway issue. In order to regain foreign railway concessions, a railway recovery movement was organized by provincial landed and merchant elites, who created their own railway companies. The Qing government, however, wanted to centralize, and in 1911 decided to nationalize the major railway lines. Lacking the necessary financial resources, it was able to do so only by contracting foreign loans, inevitably with strings attached. The loans and the subsequent disbanding of provincial railway companies caused a furor, particularly in Sichuan, where the local investors felt cheated by the price the government was willing to pay for their shares. Provincial interests resented the threat to provincial autonomy. Nationalists were indignant over the foreign loans that financed the transaction. This was the prelude to revolt. The insurrection that set off the revolution took place when a New Army regiment mutinied in Wuchang on October 10. It was carried out by men only loosely connected with the Revolutionary Alliance, the main revolutionary organization in the land. Its leader, Sun Yat-sen, was traveling in the United States raising money, but rushed home when he heard the news.

After the October 10 incident, province after province broke with the dynasty. The rebellion turned for help to Yuan Shikai, who had served as Grand Councilor and Foreign Minister in 1907 through 1908, but had been dismissed on January 2, 1909 after the death of his patron Cixi. Yuan was the obvious choice, for he enjoyed foreign support as well as the loyalty of China's best army, and he had prestige as a reformer. However, he was not about to sacrifice himself for a losing cause, and he was not strong enough to impose his will on all of China. The revolutionaries had in the meantime formed a government at Nanjing with Sun Yat-sen as provisional president. A compromise between Yuan and the revolutionaries was necessary for China to avoid prolonged civil war and the nightmare of direct foreign intervention. An agreement was reached. The Manchu child-emperor formally abdicated on February 2, 1912, bringing an end not only to a dynasty but also to a political system whose foundations had been laid in 221 B.C.E. China became a republic.

II. From Yuan Shikai to Chiang Kai-Shek

Yuan Shikai

The Warlord Era

Intellectual Ferment

Yuan Shikai

After the Qing abdication, Sun Yat-sen stepped aside, and Yuan accepted the presidency of a republic with a two-chambered legislature. He also agreed to move the capital to Nanjing, but once in office he evaded this provision, and Beijing remained the capital of the Republic. In the absence of well-organized political parties or deep-rooted republican sentiment among the public, there was little to restrain Yuan from rapidly developing into a dictator. To be sure, elections were held in February 1913 with about 5 percent of China's population entitled to vote.

The Guomindang (GMD or Nationalist party), the successor to the Tongmenghui, was the largest party in the new parliament. Yuan, however, was not about to share power. He bullied the elected parliament, and in March 1913, Song Jiaoren (1882–1913), architect of the constitution and leader of the parliamentary GMD, was assassinated on Yuan's orders. That summer, Yuan forced a showdown by ordering dismissal of pro-Nationalist southern military governors. When they revolted in what is sometimes known as the Second Revolution, Yuan crushed them easily. For the next two years, the other military governors remained loyal, but Yuan remained dependent on military authority.

Yuan sought to continue the late Qing program of centralization, but he had to struggle against the forces of reformist provincialism as well as revolutionary nationalism. Often the two combined, because to finance a program regarded with suspicion by provincial interests, Yuan needed funds, and in the absence of a radical social revolution, this meant obtaining foreign loans. This antagonized nationalists because the loans came with foreign strings and "advisors." The *Shibao* cartoon rang truer than ever (Figure 10.1).

In 1915, taking advantage of the great powers' preoccupation with World War I, Japan presented China with the notorious Twenty-One Demands, divided into five groups: (1) recognition of Japanese rights in Shandong; (2) extension of Japanese rights in Mongolia and Manchuria; (3) Sino-Japanese joint operation of

China's largest iron and steel company; (4) China not ceding or leasing any coastal area to any power other than Japan; and (5) provisions that would have obliged the Chinese government to employ Japanese political, financial, and military advisors, to give the Japanese partial control over the police, and to purchase Japanese arms. Yuan managed to avoid the last and most onerous group of demands, which would have reduced China to a virtual Japanese satellite. However, with the other powers preoccupied in Europe, Yuan was forced to accept Japan's seizure of Germany's holdings in Shandong, grant Japan new rights in southern Manchuria and Inner Mongolia, and acknowledge its special interest in China's largest iron and steel works, which had previously served as security for Japanese loans. The domestic result was a wave of anti-Japanese nationalist outrage, which expressed itself in protests and boycotts.

Yuan made no attempt to harness nationalist feelings for his own cause, but instead prepared for restoration of dynastic rule with himself as emperor. According to an American advisor to Yuan, China was not ready for a republic. Yuan probably was not wrong in believing that reinstating the emperorship would match the preferences and expectations of the majority of China's population, but he did nothing to tap or mobilize mass support or to mollify the resentment of the educated. He just went ahead. The new regime was proclaimed in December 1915, to begin on New Year's Day. Hostility to the new dynasty was so overwhelming that in March 1916 Yuan gave way and officially abandoned his imperial ambitions. He never regained his old prestige, and died a failure in June of that year.

The Warlord Era

After the fall of Yuan Shikai, the pattern of Chinese politics became exceedingly complex, as military men came to the fore. In 1917 there was even a two-week restoration of the Qing. In August of that year, China, under the premier and warlord Duan Qirui (1865–1936), entered World War I by declaring war on Germany. During the next year the Chinese government received loans of some 145 million yen from Japan (the Nishihara loans), ostensibly to strengthen the Chinese ally, but actually siphoned off to support Duan's military and political plans.

Although a national government ruled in Beijing, actual power lay in the hands of regional strongmen (warlords) who came to dominate civil administration in the areas under their control largely through force of arms, and who struggled with one another to enlarge or protect their holdings. They constantly made and unmade alliances with one another, while the foreign powers (especially Japan and the Soviet Union), fishing in these troubled waters, sought to play the warlords off against one another for their own benefit.

Some of the warlords, including Duan, had been generals under Yuan Shikai; others had begun their careers as bandits, and more or less continued to behave as such. One of the most notorious was the "Dog-Meat General" of

Shandong, with his entourage of White Russian guards and women. A huge brute of a man, greedy and cruel, he decorated his telegraph poles with the severed heads of secret society members. Other warlords showed a genuine interest in social welfare and education, and tried to build up their areas economically, but they lacked the vision and organization to clear a way to the future. Conditions varied widely, but for many these were years of great insecurity and suffering.

In the long run, the Treaty of Versailles (1919) ending World War I was a disaster, but the 1920s was peaceful throughout the globe. Yet China's sovereignty was more impaired than ever. Its customs and salt revenues were committed to paying foreign obligations, and tariffs were kept artificially low. China's major cities were designated as treaty ports, some—most notably Shanghai—with foreign concession areas under foreign jurisdiction. In these enclaves, foreigners led privileged lives. They also continued to enjoy extraterritoriality wherever they went. While the foreigners' economic impact should not be exaggerated, both commercial travelers and missionaries used British steamers to travel inland on waterways, policed if necessary by foreign gunboats. Foreigners were everywhere. It was politically offensive and profoundly degrading.

Economically, the modern sector expanded during the global postwar boom so that 1917 through 1923 has been called "the golden age of Chinese capitalism."[6] The influence of the world economy on China expanded, with for example, the sale of kerosene spreading into interior villages. Overall, though, these economic developments were insufficient to destabilize the economy enough to bring about a fundamental breakdown, or to create breakthrough growth. However, economic activity can never be separated from other aspects of life. We may speculate that with the State too weak to exert pressure, the examination system no longer in place to reward Confucian learning, and the old paternalistic ideology tarnished, there was increasingly little to prevent former gentry families from turning into just landlords. If so, this suggests fragmentation of the social fabric analogous to the political fragmentation produced by the warlords. Meanwhile, the shattering of the old world was most visible in the intellectual arena.

Intellectual Ferment

Revolutionary ideas had already been current among Chinese students in Tokyo during the first decade of the twentieth century, and they even had been discussed in magazines and schools at home. We have already noted the beginnings of feminism. In China, as in Japan, radicals were drawn to the teachings of anarchism—especially the idea that the State is inherently oppressive and that natural human social tendencies can create a just society. The abolition of the examinations and the collapse of the Qing opened the floodgates to new ideas, but destroyed neither the respect accorded scholars and intellectuals nor their commitment to society and their sense of their own importance.

A major landmark was the founding in 1915 of *New Youth*, the journal that came to stand at the core of the new intellectual tide. In the first issue, its founder, Chen Duxiu (1879–1942), issued an eloquent call for the rejuvenation of China, accompanied by an equally strong denunciation of tradition. Chen and the new intellectuals castigated Confucianism as responsible for all that was found wanting in the old state and society, the old class system, the old politics, and the old family system, as well as for stifling human creativity, suppressing women, and standing in the way of freedom and progress. Chen called on the youth to create a new culture based on Science and Democracy to cure "the dark maladies in Chinese politics, morality, learning, and thought."[7]

Few were convinced by Kang Youwei, who tried to cast Confucianism in a new role as the official state religion. Unsuccessful in his earlier attempt to construct a Confucian justification for modernization that would persuade scholars grounded in the classics, he now failed to make Confucianism acceptable to those whose primary loyalty was to the nation. He was not the only intellectual who began as a radical and ended as a conservative not because he had changed his ideas but because the climate of opinion had changed. Confucianism was not destroyed, but it was put on the defensive.

New Youth opposed both the traditional teachings and the language in which they were written. The journal opened its pages to Hu Shi (1891–1962), a former student of the American philosopher John Dewey, and China's leading champion of the vernacular language (*baihua*). Hu Shi argued that people should write the spoken language, not the language of the classics, and that the vernacular should be taught in the schools. He praised the literary merits of the old novels written in the vernacular, which had long been widely read but had not been considered respectable. The campaign for the vernacular was a success, although classical expressions had a way of creeping into the vernacular and newly borrowed terms stood in the way of easy comprehension. Nevertheless, the new language was both more accessible and more modern than the old. Introduced into the elementary schools in 1920, it was universally used in the schools by the end of the decade.

New Youth was also the first magazine to publish Lu Xun, pen name of Zhou Shuren (1881–1936), who became China's most acclaimed twentieth-century writer. Lu Xun had gone to Japan to study medicine, but decided to devote himself to combating China's spiritual ills rather than physical ailments. His bitter satire cut like a sharp scalpel, but a scalpel wielded by a humanist who hoped to cure, not kill. The protagonist in "A Madman's Diary" (*New Youth*, 1918) discovers the reality underneath the gloss of "virtue and morality" in the old histories: a history of man eating man. He ends with the plea, "Perhaps there are still children who have not eaten men? Save the children. . . ."[8]

Chen Duxiu and many other intellectual leaders taught at Beijing University. Their ideas found a ready following among the students at this and other universities. On May 4, 1919, some 3,000 students staged a dramatic demonstration in Beijing to protest the assignment at the Versailles Peace Conference of Germany's former possessions in Shandong to Japan, even though China, like Japan, had entered World War I on the allied side and sent labor battalions to France. The students were outraged. Their demonstrations became violent. The house of a pro-Japanese minister was burned, and another minister was beaten badly. In clashes with the police one student died. There were arrests followed by more protest, a wave of strikes, and a show of merchant and labor support for the students. In the end, the government had to retreat. Those arrested were released, and those who had ordered the arrests were forced to resign. China never signed the ill-fated Treaty of Versailles.

The May Fourth incident came to symbolize the currents of intellectual and cultural change first articulated in *New Youth,* and gave rise to the broader term "May Fourth Movement" (c. 1915 to early 1920s). After the incident, there was a new sense of urgency. What had been a trickle of protest became a tide of attacks on just about every aspect of Chinese culture in a total rejection of the past—including such basic institutions as the family. Simultaneously, the movement introduced a host of new and radical ideas. New journals appeared, and there was much excited talk, but also action, as young people spurned arranged marriage and increasingly engaged in social movements, including organization of labor unions. The May Fourth Movement had long-term revolutionary consequences, both in what it destroyed and in what it introduced. In the short term, although the current of nationalism ran deep and strong, there were intense disagreements over the future direction of Chinese culture, and a tremendous variety of ideas, theories, and styles swelled the eddies of intellectual and cultural life.

Intellectual Alternatives

Europe's self-destruction in war and the failure of liberal principles at Versailles prompted Liang Qichao to turn back to the Chinese tradition in the hope of synthesizing the best of China and the West, with Chinese elements predominating. An important debate began in 1923 between the proponents of science and those of metaphysics, involving different evaluation of Chinese and Western cultures. Among the advocates of the latter were proponents of scientism, who believed that science holds the answers to all problems and that the scientific method is the only method for arriving at truth. Their opponents argued that science is applicable only to a narrow field of study and that moral values have to be based on deeper metaphysical truths, which by their very nature are beyond the reach of scientific methodology. Since similar problems agitated the West at this time, Chinese thinkers drew on the ideas of such classic European philosophers as Immanuel Kant and also on the thought of contemporaries widely different in methodology and results. For example, some promoted the ideas of John Dewey (1859–1952), the American pragmatist who would replace "absolute truth" with truths that worked as solutions to problems; but others turned to Henri-Louis Bergson (1859–1941), the French exponent of vitalism, a doctrine centering on life as a force that cannot be explained in material terms.

Those who identified with the Chinese tradition further drew on the insights of Neo-Confucianism and Buddhism, particularly the former. One of the most noteworthy defenders of tradition was Liang Shuming (1893–1988), who put his Confucian principles into action by working on rural reconstruction. Another was Zhang Junmai (1887–1969), later the leader of a small political party opposed to both the Communists and the Nationalists. Other philosophers such as Feng Yulan (Fung Yu-lan, 1895–1990) and Xiong Shili (1885–1969) drew on Neo-Confucian thought, but the trend of the times was against them.

Among the champions of science and Western values were the scientist Ding Wenjiang (1887–1937) and the father of the vernacular language movement, Hu Shi. Hu Shi was a leading liberal who advocated a gradualist, piecemeal problem-solving approach to China's ills in the face of attacks both from the traditionalists on the right and from the radicals on the left. His message increasingly fell on deaf ears, for his approach required time, and time was precisely what China lacked. More often than not, this included time to digest the heady dose of new intellectual imports or, for that matter, to study the old traditions in depth.

Cultural Alternatives

Qi Baishi (1863–1957), probably the most beloved painter of the century, was singularly unaffected by the turmoil of the times. Qi began as a humble carpenter and did not turn to painting until his mid-20s, but his industry and longevity more than made up for a late start. It is estimated that he produced more than 10,000 paintings. Qi was a great admirer of the seventeenth-century individualist Zhu Da, but followed his own inner vision. He was not given to theorizing, but did express his attitude toward representation: "The excellence of a painting lies in its being like, yet unlike. Too much likeness flatters the vulgar taste; too much unlikeness deceives the world."[9] His works show, to quote a Chinese critic, "a loving sympathy for the little insects and crabs and flowers he draws," and have "an enlivening gaiety of manner" so that "his pictures are really all pictures of his own gentle humanism"[10] (Figure 10.2).

There were other painters and calligraphers who remained uninfluenced by the West, but many felt that the new age required a new style. Among those who tried to combine elements of the Chinese and Western traditions were the followers of a school of painters established by Gao Lun (Gao Jianfu, 1879–1951). Gao sought to combine Western shading and perspective with Chinese brushwork, and was also influenced by Japanese decorativeness. He sought to bring Chinese painting up to date by including in his works new subject matter, such as the airplanes in Figure 10.3.

In Shanghai, meanwhile, a small group of artists tried to transplant French-style bohemianism into that international city. Xu Beihong (1895–1953), for example, affected the long hair and general appearance popular in the artists' quarter of Paris. When he returned from that city in 1927, Xu also brought back a thorough mastery of the French academic style. Somewhat more advanced in his Western tastes was Liu Haisu (1896–1994), founder of the Shanghai Art School

FIGURE 10.2 *Grasshopper and Orchid Leaves,* Qi Baishi (Qi Huang). Although Qi also painted landscapes and portraits, he excelled in depicting the humble forms of life, such as rodents and insects, with a loving and gentle humor reminiscent of the haiku of Kobayashi Issa.
Ink on paper, 21.5 × 30.5 cm, signed Baishi.
Courtesy Far East Fine Arts, Inc. San Francisco.

(1920), where he introduced the use of a nude model. This was also one of the first schools to offer a full course of instruction in Western music. Liu was inspired by French postimpressionists like Matisse and Cezanne. Later, however, Liu returned to painting in a traditional manner, and Xu, too, abandoned his Western dress for a Chinese gown. Today Xu is perhaps most appreciated for his paintings of horses (Figure 10.4).

Modern Chinese literature had its origins in the novels of the late Qing. A very popular but superficial genre was "Butterfly" literature, named after poems inserted into a novel, comparing lovers to pairs of butterflies. Between 1910 and 1930, around 2,215 such novels offered a literate but unlearned public amusement and escape. Dating back to the late Qing, a steady and swelling stream of translations were made. Lin Shu (1852–1924), the most famous and prolific early translator, rendered into classical Chinese the novels of Charles Dickens, Sir Walter Scott, and others in an opus that grew to some 180 works. Thanks to the labors of Lin and other translators, soon all the major European literary traditions, as well as that of Japan, were available in translation.

The May Fourth Movement had a strong effect on literature. The intellectual revolution was accompanied by a literary revolution. This included experiments, such as those of Xu Zhimo (1896–1931), who modeled his poetry on English verse, complete with rhyme. More widespread was a tendency toward romantic

FIGURE 10.4 *Standing Horse,* Xu Beihong. 1935.

FIGURE 10.3 *Flying in the Rain,* Gao Lun (Gao Jianfu), 1932. Chinese painters, like writers and intellectuals throughout East Asia, devised different ways to combine traditionalism and modernism in style and subject matter, but lyrical landscapes with airplanes bouncing through the sky are rare anywhere. Ink and color on paper.

emotionalism, an outpouring of feelings released by the removal of Confucian restraints and encouraged by the example of European romanticism. One strain, as analyzed by Leo Ou-fan Lee, was the passive-sentimental, presided over by the hero of Goethe's *The Sorrows of Young Werther,* read in China and Japan as "a sentimental sob story." The subjectivism of these writers was similar to that of the writers of "I novels" in Japan (see Chapter 11). Another strain was dynamic and heroic. Its ideal was Prometheus, who braved Zeus's wrath and stole fire for mankind. Holding a promise of release from alienation, it was compatible with a revolutionary political stance. For Guo Moruo (1892–1978), once an admirer of Goethe, Lenin became, beyond all else, a Promethean hero. Perhaps the strongest expression of Promethean martyrdom came from Lu Xun, "I have stolen fire from other countries, intending to cook my own flesh. I think that if the taste is good, the other chewers on their part may get something out of it, and I shall not sacrifice my body in vain."[11]

Controversies and rivalries stimulated the formation of literary and intellectual societies, as like-minded men joined together to publish journals advocating their causes and denouncing the opposition. Revolutionaries were not alone in arguing that literature should have a social purpose, but as the years passed without any improvement in Chinese conditions, the attractions of revolutionary creeds increased.

Writers of revolutionary persuasion such as the Communist Mao Dun (Shen Yanbing, 1896–1981) depicted and analyzed the defects in the old society and portrayed the idealism of those who were out to change the status quo. Such themes appeared not only in the work of Communist writers like Mao Dun but also in the work of the anarchist Ba Jin (Li Feigang, 1905–2005), best known for his depiction of the disintegration of a large, eminent family in the novel appropriately entitled *Family* (1931), a part of his *Turbulent Stream* trilogy (1931–1940). Such works provide important material for students of social as well as literary history (see Box 10.1).

BOX 10.1 SHATTERED DREAMS

Many young people, especially those educated in Western studies, had to face a painful choice between self-fulfillment and obedience to the demands of their family. Ba Jin spoke for a whole generation in his account of Quexin, an excellent student who hoped to study physics and chemistry in Germany.

In his fourth year at middle school, Quexin lost his mother. His father later married again, this time to a younger woman who had been his mother's cousin. Quexin was aware of his loss, for he knew full well that nothing could replace the love of a mother. But her death left no irreparable wound in his heart; he was able to console himself with rosy dreams of his future. Moreover, he had someone who understood him—his pretty cousin Mei, "mei" for "plum blossom."

But then, one day, his dreams were shattered, cruelly and bitterly shattered. The evening he returned home carrying his diploma, the plaudits of his teachers and friends still ringing in his ears, his father called him into his room and said:

(continued)

BOX 10.1 SHATTERED DREAMS (CONTINUED)

"Now that you've graduated, I want to arrange your marriage. Your grandfather is looking forward to have a great-grandson, and I, too, would like to be able to hold a grandson in my arms. You're old enough to be married; I won't feel easy until I fulfill my obligation to find you a wife. Although I didn't accumulate much money in my years away from home as an official, still I've put by enough for us to get along on. My health isn't what it used to be; I'm thinking of spending my time at home and having you help me run the household affairs. All the more reason you'll be needing a wife. I've already arranged a match with the Li family. The thirteenth of next month is a good day. We'll announce the engagement then. You can be married within the year. . . ."

Quexin did not utter a word of protest, nor did such a thought ever occur to him. He merely nodded to indicate his compliance with his father's wishes. But after he returned to his own room, and shut the door, he threw himself down on his bed, covered his head with the quilt and wept. He wept for his broken dreams.

He was deeply in love with Mei, but now his father had chosen another girl, a girl he had never seen, and said that he must marry within the year. What's more, his hopes of continuing his studies had burst like a bubble. It was a terrible shock to Quexin. His future was finished, his beautiful dreams shattered.

He cried with disappointment and bitterness. But the door was closed and Quexin's head was beneath the bedding. No one knew. He did not fight back, he never thought of resisting. He only bemoaned his fate. But he accepted it. He complied with his father's will without a trace of resentment. But in his heart he wept for himself, wept for the girl he adored—Mei, his "plum blossom."

From *Family* by Ba Jin. Copyright © 1964 Foreign Language Press, 24 Baiwanzhuang Rd., Beijing 10037, P.R. China.

Marxism in China: The Early Years

Marxism was not unknown in China, but it had little appeal prior to the Russian Revolution. The few who were drawn to socialism were attracted more by its egalitarianism than by concepts of class warfare. The writings of Marx and Engels offered the vision of a perfect society, but their thesis that socialism could only be achieved after capitalism had run its course suggested that Marxism was inappropriate for a society only just entering "the capitalist stage of development." The success of the Russian Revolution (1917) changed all that. Faced with a similar problem in applying Marxism to Russia, Lenin amended Marxist theory to fit the needs of his own country, and thereby also made it more relevant to the Chinese. His theory that imperialism was the last stage of capitalism gave new importance to countries such as China, which were the objects of imperialist expansion and the places where capitalism was particularly vulnerable. Most significant was Lenin's concept of the Communist Party as the vanguard of revolution, for now party intellectuals could help make history even in a precapitalist state.

Furthermore, Marxism was modern, and claimed "scientifically" valid doctrines. It shared the prestige accorded by Chinese intellectuals to Western and "advanced" ideas, even as it opposed the dominant forms of economic and political organization in the West. A Western heresy to use against the West, it promised to undo China's humiliation, and persuaded its converts that "dialectic materialism" assured that Communism was the wave of the future. Thus, China could once again be in the forefront of world history. And the Russian Revolution demonstrated that it worked.

Li Dazhao (1888–1927), professor and librarian at Beijing University, was initially attracted by its promise as a vehicle for national revolution, while Chen Duxiu turned from science and democracy to Marxism as a more effective means of achieving modernization. Others were drawn to it for a mixture of reasons, high among them the promise it held for solving China's ills. By spring of 1920, when Grigorii Voitinsky arrived in China as an agent of the Communist International (Comintern), a core of Marxist intellectuals was available as potential leaders for the organization of the Chinese Communist Party (CCP) that took place the following year.

At its first gathering in July 1921, the CCP elected Chen Duxiu its Secretary General. Despite considerable misgivings, the party submitted to a Comintern policy of maximum cooperation with the Guomindang. A formal agreement was reached in 1923 that allowed CCP members into the GMD as individuals, subject to GMD party discipline. The CCP leaders found it difficult to accept the Comintern's theoretical analysis of the GMD as a multiclass party, but submitted to Comintern discipline and the logic of the situation, where the few hundred Communists were outnumbered by the thousands of GMD members and had little contact with the masses. This initial period of cooperation lasted until 1927. The CCP grew, but the GMD remained the senior partner.

The Guomindang and Sun Yat-sen (1913–1923)

After the failure of the "second revolution" of 1913, Sun Yat-sen was again forced into exile in Japan, where he tried to win Japanese support for his revolution. After the death of Yuan Shikai, Sun was able to return to China and establish a precarious foothold in Canton, where he depended on the good will of the local warlord. Denied foreign backing from Japan and elsewhere, Sun was also handicapped by the weakness of the GMD party organization, which was held together only loosely, largely through loyalty to Sun himself. The success of the Russian Revolution provided a striking contrast to the failure of Sun's revolution. Sun was also favorably disposed to the U.S.S.R. by the Soviet Union's initial renunciation of Czarist rights in China. This corresponded to a new anti-imperialist emphasis in his own thought and rhetoric, after the end of Manchu rule had not led to marked improvement in China's position in the world. Additionally, the mass nationalism of the May Fourth Movement impressed him.

Sun was therefore ready to work with the Communists, and in 1923 concluded an agreement with the Comintern that concurred with Sun's view that China was not ready for socialism, and that the immediate task ahead was the achievement of national unity and independence. Through this pact, Sun received valuable assistance and aid. Under the guidance of the Comintern agent Mikhail Borodin (originally named Grusenberg), the GMD was reorganized into a more structured and disciplined organization than ever before, while General Galen, alias Vassily Blyukher (or Blücher), performed the same service for the army. Sun made some minor ideological compromises, but overall did not depart from his previous views.

GMD and CCP Cooperation (1923–1927)

For both sides this was a marriage of convenience. At first it worked. The GMD gained guidance and support. CCP members rose to important positions in the GMD, and the party grew. A good example of a CCP leader occupying an important GMD office is Zhou Enlai's (1898–1976) service as chief of the political department of the Whampoa Military Academy under Chiang Kai-shek (1887–1975). Here the best of the GMD officer corps was trained and prepared to lead an army to reunify China and establish a national regime.

The CCP devoted itself mainly to organizing the urban labor movement, which had already won its first victory in the Hong Kong Seamen's Strike of 1922. Shanghai and Canton were particularly fertile grounds for labor organizers, since in these cities the textile and other light industries continued their pre-World War I growth, assisted by the wartime lull in foreign competition. Of some 2.7 million cotton spindles in China around 1920, 1.3 million were in Chinese-controlled factories, and 500,000 were owned by Japanese. In Chinese and foreign plants alike, wages were very low, working hours long (averaging nine and one-half hours in Shanghai, up to thirteen in the provinces), and all-around conditions remained very harsh. Under these circumstances, the CCP's work met with substantial success. It gained greatly by its leadership during and following the incident of May 30, 1925, when police of the International Settlement in Shanghai fired upon Chinese demonstrators, killing 10 and wounding more than 50. A general strike and boycott followed; in Hong Kong and Canton the movement held out for 16 months. The strike did not achieve its goals, but CCP party membership increased from around 1,000 in early 1925 to an estimated 20,000 by the summer of 1926.

Sun Yat-sen did not live to witness the May 30 incident, for he died of cancer in March 1925. He was an energetic speaker and tireless visionary, glorified as the father of the revolution, but he left no clearly designated heir and an ambiguous ideological legacy. His last major statement, "Three Principles of the People" (1924), stressed the first principle, nationalism—now directed against foreign imperialism—and provided for self-determination for China's minorities. The second principle, democracy, contained proposals for popular elections, initiative, recall, and referendum, but full democracy was to come only after a preparatory period of political tutelage. He emphasized the need for a disciplined people and believed that the Chinese people had too much freedom, not too little. The state would be a republic with five branches of government: legislative, executive, judicial (as in the West), plus an examination branch to test applicants for government posts, and a censorial branch to monitor government officials and control corruption, as under the emperors. Finally, the third principle of the people's livelihood aimed at both egalitarianism and economic development. It incorporated a proposal by the American reformer Henry George (1839–1897) to tax the unearned increment on land values in order to equalize holdings. An additional refinement was a land tax based on each landowner's assessment of the value of his land. To prevent underassessment, the state was to have the right to purchase the land at the declared value. Beyond that, Sun had a grandiose vision of "building the wealthiest, most powerful and happiest nation on earth,"[12] but his plan for Chinese industrialization was unrealistic. More realistic was a proposal for State ownership of major industries, but he remained critical of Marxist ideas of class struggle.

After Sun Yat-sen's death, Wang Jingwei (1883–1944) was well placed for succession to the GMD leadership, for he had been associated with Sun in Japan and was considered a revolutionary hero for his attempt to assassinate the Manchu Prince Regent in 1910. However, in 1926 it became apparent that he had a formidable challenger in Chiang Kai-shek. In 1923, Sun had sent Chiang to Moscow to study the Soviet military. On his return to China, Chiang became head of the Whampoa Military Academy, where he was highly successful, esteemed alike by the Soviet advisors and by the officer candidates.

While Wang Jingwei loosely presided over the GMD, the CCP steadily gained influence in the party, much to the alarm of the GMD right and of Chiang Kai-shek. In March 1926, Chiang decided to act: he declared martial law, arrested Soviet advisors, took steps to restrain the CCP influence in the GMD, and yet

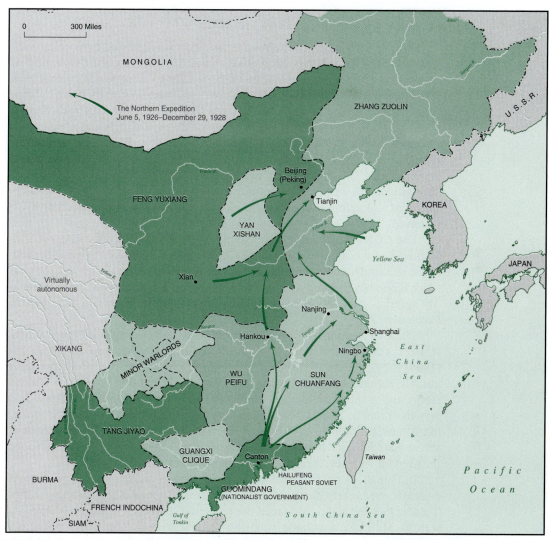

FIGURE 10.5   China and the Northern Expedition, 1926–1928.

managed to retain the cooperation of both the CCP and of its Soviet supporters, whose assistance he needed for the military unification of the country. This he began in the summer of 1926 by launching the Northern Expedition (Figure 10.5), setting out with his army from Canton. Although there was some heavy fighting against warlord armies, the force made rapid headway on its march to the Yangzi, and some warlords decided to go over to the Nationalist side. In the fall of 1926, the Nationalist victories enabled them to shift the capital from Canton to more centrally located Wuhan. There, Wang Jingwei headed a civilian government, but could not control Chiang and his army.

The Break

On its march north to the Yangzi, the army was assisted by popular support. Nowhere was this support more enthusiastic than among the Communist-led workers of Shanghai, where the General Labor Union seized control even before the arrival of the troops. Elsewhere, too, there was an increase in labor activity. This alarmed Chinese bankers and industrialists, who ready to support a national but not a social revolution, financed the increasingly anti-Communist Chiang Kai-shek. In April 1927, Chiang finally broke with the CCP completely by initiating a bloody campaign of suppression in Shanghai, which then spread to other cities. Union and party headquarters were raided, those who resisted were killed, and suspected Communists were shot on sight. CCP cells were destroyed and unions disbanded in a devastating sweep that left the urban CCP shattered.

The CCP's emphasis on city factory workers was entirely consistent with Marxist theory, but the majority of the Chinese people continued to work the land. Marx, as a student of the French Revolution, despised the peasantry as "the class which represents barbarism within civilization."[13] But Lenin, operating in a primarily agrarian land, assigned the peasantry a supporting role in the Russian Revolution.

The CCP, although it concentrated on cities, had not neglected the peasants. In 1921, China's first modern peasant movement was organized by Peng Pai (1896–1929), and by 1927 the CCP was at work in a number of provinces, most notably Hunan, where the young Mao Zedong (1893–1976) wrote a famous report urging the party to concentrate on rural revolution and predicting, "In a very short time . . . several hundred million peasants will rise like a mighty storm, like a hurricane, a force so swift and violent that no power, however great, will be able to hold it back." In another famous passage in the same report, he defended the need for violence, saying, "A revolution is not a dinner party."[14]

In Hunan, as in other rice areas, tenancy rates were high, and the poorer peasants were sorely burdened by heavy rental payments and crushing debts. Tenants had few rights and faced the recurring specter of losing their leases. It was, as Mao saw, a volatile situation fraught with revolutionary potential. However, the Chinese Communist Party and its Soviet advisors remained urban-minded.

After Chiang's coup, the CCP broke with him but continued to work with the government at Wuhan, which also broke with Chiang, but still depended for military support on armies officered largely by men of the landlord class, the prime object of peasant wrath. In this situation, Comintern directives were wavering and contradictory, reflecting not Chinese realities but rather the exigencies of Stalin's intraparty maneuvers back in Moscow. The end result was that in June the CCP was expelled from Wuhan. Borodin and other Soviet advisors were sent back to the U.S.S.R. The CCP entered a difficult period of regrouping and reorganization.

Establishment of the Nationalist Government

After Chiang Kai-shek's coup in Shanghai, he established a government in Nanjing, which remained the capital until 1937. The Northern Expedition resumed in 1928, by which time the Wuhan leaders, bowing to the inevitable, had made their peace with Chiang, as had a number of warlords whose forces now assisted the Nationalist drive north and actually outnumbered Chiang's own troops. In June 1928, after a scant two months of fighting, Beijing fell. China again had a national government, but the often only nominal incorporation of warlord armies into the government forces meant that national unification was far from complete. Warlordism remained an essential feature of Chinese politics until the very end of the Republican period in 1949.

In 1927, anti-imperialist mobs attacked British concessions in two cities, and violence in Nanjing left six foreigners dead, a number wounded, and foreign businesses and homes raided. Such incidents were officially attributed to Chiang Kai-shek's leftist rivals. The foreign powers concluded that he was the most acceptable leader, who would negotiate rather than expropriate their holdings. Chiang's victory reassured all the powers except Japan, which had plans of its own for Manchuria and Inner Mongolia. Japan had restored its holdings in Shandong to Chinese sovereignty in 1922, but now sent troops to Shandong, claiming they were needed to protect Japanese lives and property. In 1928 they clashed with Chinese soldiers. Still more ominous was the assassination that year of the warlord of Manchuria, Zhang Zuolin, by a group of Japanese army officers who acted on their own, hoping this would pave the way for seizing Manchuria. The Japanese officers did not get their way in 1928, but their act was to serve as a prelude to the Japanese militarism and expansionism that threatened China during the 1930s, even as the Nanjing government was trying to cope with warlords and revolutionaries at home in its attempt to achieve stable government.

Notes

1. Quoted in James Reeve Pusey, *China and Charles Darwin* (Cambridge, MA: Harvard Univ. Press, 1983), p. 50.

2. Marianne Bastid-Bruguiere, "Currents of Social Change," in John K. Fairbank and Kwang Ching Liu, eds., *The Cambridge History of China*, vol. 2 (Cambridge, England: Cambridge Univ. Press, 1980), pp. 558–59.

3. David Der-wei Wang, *Fin-de-siecle Splendor: Repressed Modernities of Late Qing Fiction, 1849–1911* (Stanford, CA: Stanford Univ. Press, 1997), p. 216.

4. Quoted in Jonathan D. Spence, *The Gate of Heavenly Peace: The Chinese and Their Revolution, 1895–1980* (New York, NY: Viking, 1981), p. 52.

5. David Der-wei Wang, *Fin-de-siecle*, p. 223.

6. Marie-Claire Bergère, in John K. Fairbank, ed., *The Cambridge History of China*, vol. 12 (Cambridge, England: Cambridge Univ. Press, 1983), pp. 745–51.

7. Ssu-yü Teng and John K. Fairbank, eds., *China's Response to the West: A Documentary Survey, 1839–1923* (Cambridge, MA: Harvard Univ. Press, 1954), p. 239.

8. Joseph S. M. Lau and Howard Goldblatt, *The Columbia Anthology of Modern Chinese Literature* (New York, NY: Columbia Univ. Press, 1995), p. 15.

9. See the biographical entry for Ch'i Pai-shih in Howard L. Boorman, ed., *Biographical Dictionary of Republican China,* vol. 1 (New York, NY: Columbia Univ. Press, 1967–71), pp. 302–04. Qi's statement is quoted on p. 302.

10. Michael Sullivan, *Chinese Art in the Twentieth Century* (Berkeley, CA: Univ. of California Press, 1959), p. 42.

11. Quoted in Leo Ou-fan Lee, *The Romantic Generation of Modern Chinese Writers* (Cambridge, MA: Harvard Univ. Press, 1973), p. 74.

12. Quoted in David Strand, "Calling the Chinese People to Order: Sun Yat-sen's Rhetoric of Development," in Kield Erik Brødsgaard and David Strand, eds., *Reconstructing Twentieth-Century China: State Control, Civil Society, and National Identity* (Oxford, England: Oxford Univ. Press, 1998), p. 155, citing Lu Fangshan, *Zhu Zhixin yu Zhongguo geming (Zhu Zhixin and the Chinese Revolution)* (Taibei, Taiwan: Sili dongwu daxue, 1978), p. 236.

13. Karl Marx quoted in Lucien Bianco, *Origins of the Chinese Revolution, 1915–1949,* trans. by Muriel Bell (Stanford, CA: Stanford Univ. Press, 1971), p. 74.

14. Mao Tse-tung, "Report on an Investigation of the Peasant Movement in Hunan," in *Selected Works of Mao Tse-tung*, vol. 1 (Peking, P.R.C.: Foreign Language Press, 1967), reprinted in Ranbir Vohra, *The Chinese Revolution: 1900–1950* (Boston, MA: Houghton Mifflin, 1974), pp. 115–17.

Imperial Japan:
1895—1931

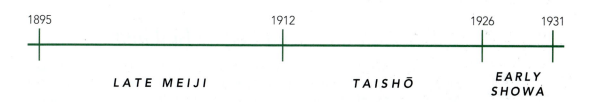

1895		1912		1926	1931
LATE MEIJI		**TAISHŌ**		**EARLY SHOWA**	

Between the founding of an empire in 1895 and the advent of militarism in 1931, Japan increasingly participated in world history and often seemed to be following the economic and political patterns pioneered by the Western powers ruling overseas empires, while pursuing liberal and democratic policies at home. Japan's tale was in many respects a success story, but later history would eventually reveal the potential for disaster. The death of the Meiji emperor in July 1912, while not as momentous as the abdication of China's last emperor earlier that year, marked a watershed and was experienced as such at the time. The passing of the emperor, who had presided over Japan's transformation for more than 40 years, signified the end of an era, a judgment with which many later scholars have concurred. We have divided this chapter accordingly. In contrast, the death of the Taishō emperor and his succession by the Showa emperor had little immediate impact on the course of events.

I. Late Meiji: 1895–1912

Foreign Policy and Empire Building

Economic and Social Developments

Politics

Literature and the Arts

Foreign Policy and Empire Building

From the very beginning, Meiji foreign policy aimed to achieve national security and equality of national status. But how were these to be defined and attained? As Louise Young put it, "In an international order where the 'strong devour the weak,' Japanese concluded they could either join with the West as a 'guest at the table' or be served up with China and Korea as part of the feast."[1] Both the army's German advisor and Yamagata, the hard-headed, realistic architect of Japan's modern army, held that Korea was the key to Japan's security, and in 1890 propounded the thesis that Japan must defend its "line of sovereignty" and secure its "line of interest," which ran through Korea. At the same time, the Japanese navy, heavily influenced by the ideas of Admiral Alfred T. Mahan (1840–1914), an American advocate of the importance of sea power, demanded Japanese naval domination of the surrounding seas. Colonies were desired both as "the ultimate status symbol", and for strategic reasons. Economic and other considerations also played a part, but an authority on the subject concluded "no colonial empire of modern times was as clearly shaped by strategic considerations."[2]

Equality was as elusive a concept as security, but minimally it required the end of extraterritoriality and the restoration of tariff autonomy. In the 1870s, work began on revision of the law codes to bring them into line with Western practices, so that the powers would no longer have reason to insist on maintaining jurisdiction over their own subjects. Even before the lengthy process of revising the codes had been completed, there was strong and vociferous public demand for an end to extraterritoriality. In 1886, this demand forced the government to back down from a compromise it had negotiated providing for mixed courts under Japanese and foreign judges. The intensity of public pressure also helped induce the British to agree in 1894, shortly before the start of the Sino-Japanese War, to give up extraterritoriality when the new legal codes came into effect (1899). Other countries followed suit. In return, foreign merchants were no longer limited to the treaty ports. These treaties also secured tariff autonomy, and in 1911 Japan regained full control over its customs duties.

By that time, Japan, under the most-favored-nation clause of the Treaty of Shimonoseki, was enjoying extraterritorial rights in China and benefiting from

China's lack of tariff autonomy. As a result, Japan's exports to China increased both absolutely and in proportion of total exports, rising from less than 10 percent before 1894 to 25 percent by World War I. A commercial treaty negotiated with China in 1896 gave Japan and other nations enjoying most-favored-nations treatment the right to establish factories in the treaty ports, spurring investment in China, but limiting China's ability to nurture its own industries.

The acquisition of Taiwan gratified the navy, but most of the public shared the army's disappointment and outrage when French, German, and Russian intervention forced Japan to give up the strategic Liaodong Peninsula. The government's response to this setback was to follow a prudent foreign policy while increasing military spending. Accordingly, Japan exercised careful restraint during the Boxer Rebellion (1900) and earned respect for the disciplined behavior of its soldiers.

Japan's chief rival in northeast Asia was Russia, which had demonstrated its intent to become a major power in the area by constructing the Trans-Siberian Railway (1891–1903). In 1896, Russia had obtained permission to run tracks across northern Manchuria directly to Vladivostok. In 1898, it obtained the lease of Port Arthur on the Liaodong Peninsula, thereby acquiring a crucial warm-water port, but further alienating the Japanese, who had just been denied the peninsula, and were concerned about holding their own in the scramble to gain concessions from China.

Russia also interfered in Korea, allying itself with conservative opponents of Japanese-backed reformers. Agreements reached in 1896, 1897, and 1898 kept the Russo-Japanese rivalry from exploding into immediate war, but Russian use of the Boxer Rebellion to entrench its interests in Manchuria intensified Japanese apprehensions.

Japan was not alone in its concern over Russian expansion. Great Britain, which had not joined in the intervention after the Sino-Japanese War, had long been alarmed over Russia's eastward expansion. In 1902 it abandoned its policy of "splendid isolation" to form an alliance with Japan. Great Britain recognized Japan's special interest in Korea, and each nation recognized the other's interests in China. Britain and Japan agreed that each would remain neutral in any war fought by the other against a single enemy in East Asia, and that each would assist the other if either were attacked by two powers at once. This meant that if Japan and Russia went to war, British forces would join Japan if France or Germany supported Russia. Japan would not have to face a European coalition alone. This alliance with the foremost world power gave Japan new prestige and confidence. However, Russia remained determined to maintain and expand its position in East Asia.

These conflicting ambitions led to the Russo-Japanese War of 1904–1905, fought both on land (mostly in Manchuria, which was actually Chinese territory) and at sea. For both belligerents the cost was heavy, but victory went to Japan. Despite some hard fighting, Russian troops were driven back on land, while in two separate naval actions the Japanese destroyed virtually the entire Russian navy. The naval war was spectacular, and much celebrated in Japan (Figure 11.1). Japan

FIGURE 11.1   *Sea Battle near Port Arthur, March 10, 1904: A Sailor from the Sazanami Jumps to the Russian Ship and Kicks Its Captain into the Sea,* Migita Toshihide (1866–1905). Woodcut print triptych, ink and color on paper, 1904.

ARTHUR M. SACKLER GALLERY OF ART, SMITHSONIAN INSTITUTION, WASHINGTON, D.C. GIFT OF GREGORY AND PATRICIA KRUGLAK (51999.1319-c).

attacked the Russian Pacific fleet at Port Arthur, just before the declaration of war. Russia's Baltic fleet then embarked on an 18,000-mile trip, sailing all the way around Africa because Britain refused passage through the Suez Canal. Its destination was Vladivostok, but the fleet was demolished by the Japanese in a decisive battle in the Tsushima Straits, between Japan and Korea. Only 4 of the 35 Russian ships reached Vladivostok.

Throughout Asia, people were deeply impressed by this first victory of a non-Western nation over a European power. In Russia, these defeats had fateful consequences. The failed Revolution of 1905 was a precursor of the successful Revolution of 1917. Though victorious, the Japanese were thoroughly exhausted. Thus both sides were happy to accept the offer from the United States to mediate and to participate at a peace conference in Portsmouth, New Hampshire.

In the resulting Portsmouth Treaty, Japan gained recognition of its supremacy in Korea, the transfer of Russian interests in Manchuria (railways and leaseholds on the Liaodong Peninsula), and cession of the southern half of Sakhalin Island (north of Hokkaido). Japan had demanded all of Sakhalin and a war indemnity, but Russia successfully resisted these demands. This aroused the anger of the Japanese public, which drunk on victory and ignorant of their country's inability to continue the war, had expected more. In Tokyo, the treaty was greeted by three days of rioting.

One immediate result of Japan's victory was economic expansion in Manchuria, where the semiofficial South Manchurian Railway Company was soon engaged in shipping, public utilities, and mining, as well as railroading. The Japanese government held half of the company's shares and appointed its officers. Although private Japanese firms also entered Manchuria, it has been calculated that in 1914, 79 percent of all Japanese investments in Manchuria were in the South Manchurian Railway. Furthermore, 69 percent of all Japanese investments in China prior to World War I were in Manchuria. Japan's economic reach stretched beyond its formal empire.

Economic and Social Developments

Both the Sino-Japanese and the Russo-Japanese wars stimulated the Japanese economy. Both wars were followed by an outburst of nationalist sentiment that gave a strong boost to heavy industry (for example, the Yawata Steel Works, established in 1897) and to armaments, including shipbuilding. After 1906, Japan produced ships comparable in size and quality to any in the world. Japanese technology continued to progress, with advances in new fields such as electrical engineering. Light industry, particularly textiles, continued to flourish and dominate the modern sector. The single most important item of export, amounting to nearly half the total, was in partly finished goods, especially silk. (Superior quality control enabled Japanese silk exports to overtake those of China.) Trade figures revealing an increasing emphasis on the import of raw materials and the export of manufactured goods are indicative of economic change, and in 1912 the industrial sector accounted for 36 percent of the GNP (gross national product). Other statistics indicate increases in labor productivity and in urbanization, widening the gulf between city and country. The government, guided by pragmatic conservative reformers, sponsored a program of rural cooperatives, which were established by an act of the Diet in 1899. Through the cooperatives, which helped with credit, marketing, and production, and through intense propaganda, the government hoped to avoid class conflict.

Not everyone in the industrial sector benefited from economic growth. Those working in the numerous small, traditional establishments experienced little change in their living conditions. Especially harsh were the working and living conditions of those who labored in the factories and shops. These were comparable to those in Western countries at a similar early stage of industrialization. During the first decade of the twentieth century, 60 percent of the work force was still female. An act promulgated in 1900 outlawed strikes, but when conditions became too bad, male workers, for whom a factory job was not an interlude prior to marriage but a lifelong occupation, rebelled, sometimes violently. Thus in 1909, three infantry companies were required to quell violence in the Ashio Copper Mines. Another labor action that made a deep impression was the 1912 Tokyo streetcar strike.

Conservative reformers, mindful of the social legislation of Bismarckian Germany, insisted early on that the government had the responsibility to ensure a balance between capital and labor, but the first factory laws were not passed until 1911. Efforts to improve the lot of women and children working in the factories also made headway only slowly. Not until 1916 did a law take effect giving them some protection, such as limiting their working day to 11 hours.

The distress of workers was of great concern to radicals. Beginning in the early 1890s, there was a small group of radicals composed of Christian socialists and anarchists. They courageously opposed the war with Russia, holding antiwar rallies in the Tokyo YMCA even after the war began. However, barred by the government from forming a political party and facing government repression, they were unable to expand their influence beyond the world of intellectuals and college students. In 1911, twelve of their leaders were convicted, on most flimsy evidence, of plotting the death of the emperor, and were executed.

Among the main beneficiaries of economic growth were the huge industrial-financial combines (*zaibatsu*), which retained close ties with government. The dominant political party during this period, the Seiyūkai (Association of Friends of Constitutional Government), also had a stake in economic development because it won regional support and built local power through projects for railway and harbor development.

Politics

During the Sino-Japanese War, the oligarchs and the party-controlled Diet were united in pursuit of common national aims. But after the war, political struggles resumed. A handful of men, enjoying the prerogatives of elder statesmen (*genrō*), advised the emperor on all major matters. They tended to see themselves as guardians of the general public good in contrast to the private interests represented by the parties, and they stressed the need for national unity in a hostile world. As participants in fashioning the new state and architects of its major institutions, they enjoyed great prestige as well as the support of their protégés and associates. The party politicians, on the other hand, resented the perpetuation of the *genrō*'s power and their propensity to limit political decision making to a few hand-picked insiders.

The politicians' main weapon against a prime minister responsible only to the emperor (see Chapter 8, p. 165–167) who defied them was that under the constitution only the Diet could authorize increases in the budget. Complicating the political situation were divisions within both the oligarchy and the party leadership. Among the former, Yamagata, a disciplined, austere military man, was committed to "transcendental government"—dedicated to emperor and nation and above political partisanship. His main *genrō* rival was Itō, the more flexible conservative who had supervised the writing of the constitution. Itō was more willing than Yamagata to compromise with the parties. Similarly, not all Diet members were adamantly opposed to collaborating with the *genrō*. Some lost their enthusiasm for opposing a government that could dissolve the Diet and thereby subject them to costly reelection campaigns. Additionally, the oligarchs could trade office for support. Accommodation had its appeal, but initially it was an uneasy accommodation; there were four dissolutions of the Diet between 1895 and 1900.

Another political factor was the influence of the military. As stipulated by the constitution, the chief of the general staff reported directly to the emperor concerning command matters, thus bypassing the Minister of War and the cabinet. In 1900, the military's power was further strengthened when Yamagata obtained imperial ordinances specifying that only officers on active duty could serve as Minister of the Army or Minister of the Navy. In effect, this gave the military veto power over any cabinet, for it could break a cabinet simply by ordering the army or navy minister to resign. Still, control over funds for army expansion remained in the hands of the lower house.

Until 1901 the oligarchs themselves served as prime minister, but after that date Yamagata's protégé Katsura Tarō (1847–1913) and Itō's protégé Saionji Kimmochi (1849–1940) alternated as prime minister for the remainder of the Meiji period. Katsura, like Yamagata, was a general from Chōshū; Saionji was a court noble with liberal views, but little inclination toward political leadership.

Katsura and Saionji were able to govern because they had the cooperation of the Seiyūkai, which Itō had founded in 1900 in order to obtain assured support in the Diet. In 1903, Itō turned the presidency of the party over to Saionji, but the real organizing force within the party was Hara Kei (1856–1921), an ex-bureaucrat who became the leading party politician of his generation. Hara greatly strengthened the party by building support within the bureaucracy during his first term as home minister (1906–1908), and also used his power to appoint energetic partymen as prefectural governors. He linked the party to the provinces and freely resorted to pork barreling to build up constituencies among the local men of means who formed the limited electorate.

The business community, including the *zaibatsu,* was interested in maintaining a political atmosphere favorable to itself, while political leaders welcomed business support. Thus Itō, when he organized the Seiyūkai, obtained the support of Shibusawa Eiichi and other prominent business leaders, although many remained aloof. The head of Mitsui was so intent on establishing his firm's independence from government that he even discontinued the practice of extending loans to Itō without collateral. However, the trend was toward closer association between the *zaibatsu* and politics, as exemplified by the relationship between Mitsubishi and Katsura after 1908. During Katsura's second ministry (1908–1911), his chief economic advisor was the head of the Mitsubishi Bank.

The relative strength of the participants in the political process changed. The *genrō* enjoyed great influence as long as they remained active, but their power was personal, not institutional. It tended to diminish with time. As the number of living participants in the Restoration decreased, the power of the oligarchs to orchestrate politics declined. As prime minister, Katsura did not always follow Yamagata's advice. Furthermore, the *genrō* lost an important source of support when a new generation of bureaucrats came to the fore. These men did not owe their positions to *genrō* patronage, because after 1885 examinations determined entrance and promotion in the bureaucracy. As servants of the emperor, bureaucrats enjoyed high prestige and considerable influence.

Political compromise eroded much of the idealism found in the early movement for people's rights, but the Seiyūkai prospered. Its strength in the Diet alarmed the opposition, which was divided and diverse. It included men opposed in principle to the Seiyūkai's compromises, as well as small and shifting groups of independents and a series of "loyalist" parties that habitually supported the cabinet. Decision making was complicated, as government policies were determined by the interaction of various power centers, none of which could rule alone. The arrangement functioned as long as funds were sufficient to finance both the military's and the Seiyūkai's highest priority projects and as long as none of the participants felt their essential interests threatened. When that ceased to be the case, it brought on the Taishō political crisis.

Literature and the Arts

The beginnings of modern Japanese literature can be traced to Tsubouchi Shōyō (1859–1935), a translator and the author of *The Essence of the Novel* (1885), in which he opposed both didacticism and writing solely for entertainment. Instead, he advocated Western realism—the view that literature should portray actual life. Futabatei Shimei (1864–1909) followed with *Drifting Cloud* (1887–1889), a psychological study of an ordinary man told in an unusually colloquial style.

Following the introduction of realism, Western romanticism came with its emphasis on expression of feelings and on naturalism, which aimed at scientific detachment as advocated by the French writer Emile Zola. Although in Europe naturalism was hostile to romanticism, this was not necessarily the case in Japan, where Shimazaki Tōson (1873–1943) won fame for his romantic poetry as well as for *The Broken Commandment* (1906), a naturalistic account of a member of the pariah class (burakumin) who tries to keep his pledge to his father never to reveal that he was born into this group (which continued to suffer discrimination and contempt even though not subject to legal restrictions).

Two Late Meiji writers, Mori Ōgai (1862–1922) and Natsume Sōseki (1867–1916), produced works of lasting literary merit. Ōgai identified with his family's samurai heritage, while Sōseki was a proud son of plebeian Edo. Their writings differed in substance and style, but both men, though deeply influenced by the West, achieved greatness by drawing on their Japanese heritage. Both spent time abroad. Ōgai was sent by the army to study medicine in Germany. After returning to Japan, he had a distinguished career as an army surgeon, rising in 1907 to the post of surgeon-general. He was both a modern intellectual profoundly influenced by his time in Europe and a samurai-style army officer, not an easy combination, but one that stimulated major achievements. Admired for the masculine, restrained style of his original works, he was also a prolific and excellent translator. Among his finest translations are his renderings of Goethe, including the full *Faust*, and of Shakespeare, which he translated from the German. He also translated modern German poetry, with the result that more modern German verse was available in Japanese translation than in English. Furthermore, he introduced German aesthetic philosophy to Japan and influenced the development of modern Japanese theater; the performance of his translation of an Ibsen play in 1908 was a major cultural event.

Ōgai's first story, "Maihime" ("The Dancing Girl," 1890), recounts the doomed romance between a Japanese student sent by his government to Germany and a German girl named Alice. It became a precursor of the many "I novels," thinly disguised autobiographical works, which became one of the standard genres of modern Japanese fiction and also owe something to the Heian tradition of literary diaries. After his initial romantic period, Ōgai began writing works of increasing psychological insight and philosophical depth. He turned more to Japanese themes, as in his novel *The Wild Goose*. Ōgai was greatly moved when his friend General Nogi (1849–1912), hero of the Russo-Japanese War, followed the Meiji Emperor into death by committing ritual suicide along with his wife. Afterwards Ōgai published painstakingly researched accounts of samurai. A particularly acclaimed late work is his *Chibu Chūsai*, an account of a late Tokugawa physician with whom Ōgai identified.

Natsume Sōseki studied in England, where a meager government stipend forced him to live in poverty, and he had virtually no friends. Later he described himself as having been "as lonely as a stray dog in a pack of wolves."[3] Both this experience of loneliness and the extensive reading he did while in England were reflected in his subsequent work. Sōseki returned from Europe to teach English literature at Tokyo Imperial University, before resigning this position to devote himself wholly to writing. He was acclaimed for his fiction, his poetry in Chinese, his haiku, and his literary criticism. He once described his mind as half-Japanese and half-Western, and his early novels reflect English influence, particularly that of George Meredith, but in his mature work the Japanese element predominates.

Sōseki's early novels, *I Am a Cat* (1905) and *Botchan* (1906), present slices of Meiji life with affectionate good humor. Additionally in 1906, in a mere week, he wrote the remarkable painterly and diary-like *The Grass Pillow*, also translated as *The Three-Cornered World*, for "an artist is a person who lives in the triangle which remains after the angle which we may call common sense has been removed from this four-cornered world."[4] Travel in that world was by railway train:

> It is an unsympathetic and heartless contraption which rumbles along, carrying hundreds of people crammed together in one box. . . . People are said to board and travel by train, but I call it being loaded and transported. Nothing shows greater contempt for the individual than the train. Modern civilization uses every possible means to develop individuality and then having done so, tries everything to stamp it out. It allots a few square yards to each person within that area. At the same time, it erects railings around him, and threatens him with all sorts of dire consequences if he should dare to take but one step beyond their compass.[5]

The main theme of Sōseki's mature works is human isolation, studied in characters given to deep introspection. Like Ōgai, Sōseki was stricken by the death of the Meiji Emperor and General Nogi's suicide, which entered into *Kokoro* (1914), a novel concerning the relationship between a young man and his mentor, called Sensei (literally, master or teacher). Sōseki links Sensei's personal tragedy and suicide to the deaths of the emperor and the general, as well as to the larger tragedy of the passing of a generation, and with it the loss of the old ethical values. Sensei perceives he has become an anachronism.

Painters, like writers, were grouped into several schools. The disciples of Okakura Tenshin, for example, continued to avoid the extremes of formalistic traditionalism and imitative modernism, while seeking a middle ground that would be both modern and Japanese. One such painter was Yokoyama Taikan (1868–1958). His screen shown in Figure 11.2 depicts the Chinese poet Tao Qian (365–427), whose blend of regret and relief at withdrawal from public life continued to strike a responsive chord.

Among the artists working in European styles was Kuroda Seiki, whose nude had so shocked Kyoto in the 1890s. Kuroda continued to paint in a Western manner, and he had many students. At the time of his death in 1924, he had come to be "the Grand Old Man of Western painting in Japan."[6] Some attempts at rendering Japanese themes in Western style produced paintings that are little more than historical curiosities, but in other cases there was a happier result. The painting by Sakaki Teitoku (1858–1925) shown in Figure 11.3 was executed in oil around 1910. While young men blow traditional bamboo flutes, two young women play violins.

Western influence on the visual arts was often direct and immediate, as it was for Umehara Ryūzaburō (1888–1986), who studied in France, met Renoir in 1909, and became his favorite pupil. The strongest influence on Japanese sculpture during this period was Rodin, who enjoyed a great vogue in Japan, especially after a major exhibition of his work in Tokyo in 1912.

Music also changed. The Meiji government early on sponsored Western military music, and in 1879 the Ministry of Education agreed to a proposal made by Izawa Shūji (1851–1917) to combine Japanese and Western music in the schools. Izawa had studied vocal physiology in the United States, and persuaded the Ministry of Education to bring Luther Whiting Mason (1828–1896) from Boston to Japan to help develop songs for use in elementary schools. The first song book (1881) consisted half of Western songs supplied with Japanese words ("Auld Lang Syne," for example, turned into a song about fireflies) and half of Japanese pieces harmonized in the Western manner.

Meiji popular music was more freely eclectic than that taught in schools. Beginning during the last decade of the nineteenth century, Japanese composers began working

FIGURE 11.2 *Tao Qian* (Chinese poet, 365–427). Detail from one of a pair of six-fold screens, *Master Five Willows,* by Yokoyama Taikan. Taikan favored tradition, but his style resonates with his own time. Color on paper, 1912, 169.4 × 361.2 cm.
Tokyo National Museum/DNPArchives.com.

FIGURE 11.3 *Concert Using Japanese and Western Instruments,* Sakaki Teitoku (1858–1925). Playing the violin while kneeling must have taken much practice—one can only hope the ensemble's music was as charming as the painting.
Oil, 1910.
Photograph © Lore Schirokauer.

with sonatas, cantatas and other Western forms, and thanks to the Tokyo School of Music, good performers were available on the piano and violin, as well as on the *koto* and other traditional instruments taught at the school. However, performers made greater progress than composers. As suggested by William P. Malm, training in Western harmonics, "created a series of mental blocks which shut out the special musical potentialities of traditional styles."[7] The rediscovery of the latter and their creative employment did not take place until after World War II.

II. The Taishō Period (1912–1926) and the Twenties

The Taishō Political Crisis: 1912–1913

Japan during World War I

Parliamentary Government: 1918–1924

Parliamentary Government: 1924–1931

Popular Culture

Fine Arts

Mingei

Literature

Intellectual Trends

The Taishō Political Crisis: 1912–1913

The Taishō period began with a political crisis whose ramifications extended well beyond the reign of the weak and mentally disturbed Taishō Emperor. The late Meiji program of satisfying both the civilian political parties and the military broke down when financial conditions forced a cutback in government spending that made it impossible to fund both the Seiyūkai's domestic program and two new divisions for the army. Although the Seiyūkai won support at the polls, Prime Minister Saionji was forced out of office in December 1912, when the army ordered the Minister of the Army to resign. While the *genrō* deliberated about a successor to Saionji, a number of politicians, journalists, and businessmen organized a movement "to protect constitutional government." The ensuing mass demonstrations were reminiscent of those protesting the Portsmouth Treaty in 1905.

Again asked to form a government, Katsura, no longer willing to compromise with the Seiyūkai, attempted to organize a party strong enough to defeat it, but failed. When the Seiyūkai threatened a vote of no confidence, Katsura tried to save the situation by obtaining an imperial order forcing the Seiyūkai to give up its planned no-confidence motion. This was a stratagem previously employed by embattled prime ministers, but this time it did not work: the Seiyūkai turned down the order. The crisis ended with Katsura's resignation. Such use of an imperial order was discredited and never tried again.

For the first time, a party majority in the Diet, backed by public opinion and a vociferous press, had overthrown a cabinet. Katsura died in 1913, but the coalition he had created held together under the leadership of Katō Takaaki (Katō Komei, 1860–1926) whose background included graduation from Tokyo Imperial University, service in Mitsubishi, and a career in the Foreign Office capped by an appointment as Foreign Minister at the age of 40. He also enjoyed a financial advantage from his marriage into the family that controlled Mitsubishi. A capable and determined man, he was personally reserved. However, this was not a handicap because there was no need for party leaders like Katō or Hara to cultivate mass support. The power of a party leader depended on his strength within his party, although this was influenced by the party's showing at the polls.

The emergence of a strong second party meant that now the Seiyūkai faced a rival for control of the lower house. The parties represented a cross section of skills and resources needed to make participation in government viable. To quote Arthur

E. Tiedemann, "Each party had associated with it the three essential ingredients for achieving political power: professional politicians to do the nitty-gritty of day-to-day party management; former bureaucrats who had the administrative talents required to form a viable alternative government acceptable to the *genrō*; and businessmen who could supply the funds and influence essential to successful election campaigns."[8]

Although the Taishō political crisis confirmed the importance of the Diet and the parties, they were not the only power center. Again there were compromises: not until Hara became prime minister in 1918 did the top government post go to a man who had made his career as a party politician. Before Hara, there were three prime ministers: Admiral Yamamoto Gombei (1913–1914), a military bureaucrat from Satsuma whose government was brought down by a scandal in naval procurement; the septuagenarian Ōkuma Shigenobu (1914–1916), who was intent on destroying the Seiyūkai but failed; and Terauchi Masatake (1916–1918), a Yamagata-backed Chōshū general who had been governor-general of Korea. It was the Ōkuma and Terauchi governments that guided Japan during World War I.

Japan during World War I

When the Western powers became immersed in war, new opportunities opened up for Japan. In August 1914, Japan declared war on Germany and within the next three months seized German holdings in Shandong and the German islands in the Pacific. In January 1915 the Ōkuma government, with Katō Takaaki as Foreign Minister, presented the Twenty-One Demands to China. Even liberal party leaders were not to be left behind in advancing the cause of Japanese nationalism. As we have seen, Japan obtained additional rights, but at the cost of stirring up strong Chinese resentment. A prominent critic of this policy was the pro-German Yamagata, who wanted Japan to be on good terms with China in order to prepare for the war he anticipated against the West.

Much larger and more costly than the military effort against Germany during World War I was Japan's attempt to prevent the extension of Bolshevik power over territory that had belonged to the Russian Empire but had become a battleground after the Revolution of 1917. Russia and Japan had been wartime allies, but in March 1918 the Bolsheviks signed a separate peace with Germany (the Treaty of Brest-Litovsk). Complicating the situation in the East was the presence of Czech troops fighting their way out of Russia and determined to continue the war against Germany.

The Japanese intervened and by mid-summer 1918 controlled the eastern Trans-Siberian Railway and Vladivostok. The United States then changed its earlier opposition to intervention, although President Wilson envisioned only a limited military operation. The Japanese, however, sent 75,000 troops, triple the number sent by the Allies (United States, Britain, France, and Canada). Faced with Russian Communist victories and the absence of a viable alternative, the United States withdrew its forces in January 1919. The other Allies soon did likewise, leaving only the Japanese, who continued their efforts in the vain hope of at least keeping the Bolsheviks from controlling eastern Siberia. Though failure was apparent by 1920, the last Japanese troops did not withdraw until 1922.

Japan could pay for such a costly undertaking largely because its economy boomed during the war, which brought an unprecedented demand for its industrial products and the withdrawal of European competition. Old industries expanded, new ones grew up, and exports surged, turning Japan from a debtor into a creditor. But while some prospered, others suffered. The sudden economic expansion produced inflation, but workers' wages, as well as the income of those in fishing and other traditional occupations, failed to keep pace. The price of rice rose until people could no longer afford this basic food. In August 1918, rice riots erupted in cities, towns, and villages all over Japan. Even as Japanese troops were setting off for Siberia, other soldiers were firing on hungry people rioting at home. The bitter irony was not lost on Japanese radicals. The immediate effect of the turbulence was to bring down the Terauchi government. When the *genrō* met to choose the next prime minister, they settled on Hara Kei.

Parliamentary Government: 1918–1924

Hara Kei had spent his career building up the Seiyūkai in preparation for the day of party rule, but by 1918 he was too set in his ways to embark on significant new policies or initiate meaningful change and remained partisan in his concerns. From then until his assassination by a demented fanatic in November 1921, he initiated only minor changes. Tending to be conciliatory at home and abroad, he achieved only an uneasy, temporary, and weak consensus. Democratic intellectuals, students, and the leaders of labor and farmer unions were disillusioned when the government turned a deaf ear to their demands for universal suffrage, and instead passed an election law that retained a tax qualification for voting and reconstructed local electoral districts to favor the Seiyūkai. Abuse of office, financial scandals, and narrow partisanship had damaged the public image of the parties for years, and the record of the first party prime minister did nothing to alter this. Liberals who had placed their hopes in parliamentary reform either became cynical or looked elsewhere, while the public at large was apathetic.

In foreign affairs, Hara's prime ministership began with the peace conference at Versailles, where Japan failed to obtain a declaration of universal racial equality but did gain acquiescence to its claims in China and the Pacific. His government then adopted a policy of cooperation with the United States, the only possible source for capital badly needed by Japanese industry facing difficult adjustments after peace brought an end to wartime prosperity. The first product of the new policy was the Washington Conference of 1921–1922, resulting in Japan's alliance with Britain being replaced by a Four Power Pact signed by France, Great Britain, Japan, and the United States. The signatories also agreed to limit construction of capital ships (ships over 10,000 tons with guns over eight inches) so as to maintain the existing balance of naval power at a ratio of three-five-five for Japan, the United States, and Britain, calculated in tonnage. In February 1922, Japan further agreed to a Nine Power Treaty, acceding to the American Open Door Policy. In October 1922, Japan agreed to withdraw from Siberia.

That October, Japan also reached an agreement with China, where nationalist sentiment had turned bitterly anti-Japanese. At Versailles, Japan had agreed, in principle, to the restoration of Chinese sovereignty in Shandong, provided that it retained economic rights there. This was now officially agreed upon. To secure and advance Japanese interests in Manchuria, Zhang Zuolin, the local warlord, was supported by the Japanese army. However, Shidehara Kijūrō followed a general policy of getting along with the United States and conciliating China during his tenure as foreign minister from 1924 to 1927 and again from 1929 to December 1931.

The purpose of this policy was to avert anti-Japanese outbursts and costly boycotts of Japanese goods, which would hinder continued Japanese economic expansion. After 1914, Japanese investments in China accelerated so that by 1931 over 80 percent of Japan's total foreign investments were in China, where they amounted to 35.1 percent of all foreign investments in that country.* Within China, by 1930, 63 percent of Japanese investments were in Manchuria, and another 25 percent in Shanghai, where Japanese engaged in trade, banking, and textile manufacturing. In 1930, Japanese owned 39.6 percent of the Chinese textile industry (calculated in number of spindles). They were also a major factor in China's iron industry, with interests in Hankou and Manchuria. China, and particularly Manchuria, were major foreign policy concerns.

Hara was succeeded by his finance minister, but this man lacked political skills and lasted only until June 1922. Signaling the continued weakness of the parties, three non-party prime ministers followed: two admirals and one bureaucrat who organized his cabinet entirely from the House of Peers but resigned when faced by a three-party coalition in control of the Diet. The leader of the strongest of these parties, the Kenseikai (Constitutional Government Association, established 1916) was Katō Kōmei, who had last served as foreign minister under Ōkuma during the war. He was now called upon to form a new government.

The most momentous event of the years between Hara and Katō was geological, not political. In September 1923, the Tokyo-Yokohama area was devastated by a severe earthquake followed by a conflagration, which came close to leveling the area. The red sky was visible all night from a distance of 100 miles. Around 100,000 people lost their lives. As so often in a disaster, the earthquake and fires brought out the best and the worst in people. While some courageously and selflessly helped their fellows, others joined in hysterical racist mobs rampaging through the city killing Koreans. The police reacted to the emergency by rounding up socialists, anarchists, and communists as a "security measure," and there were cases of police torture and killing.

---

*Great Britain accounted for 36.7 percent of foreign investment in China, but this was only 5 to 6 percent of all British overseas investments. Three other countries each accounted for over 5 percent of foreign investment in China: The U.S.S.R. for 8.4 percent, the U.S.A. for 6.1 percent, and France for 5.9 percent.

Parliamentary Government: 1924–1931

The increase in the power of the parties signified a shift in the balance of power rather than a systemic reordering of power centers. It was the power of the parties that induced Tanaka Giichi, a Chōshū general much favored by Yamagata, to accept the presidency of the Seiyūkai in 1925 when it was out of power. But the party's choice also confirmed the willingness of the parties to work within the existing parameters, and highlighted the continued prestige and influence of the army, even during the peaceful 1920s when liberalism was at its height, advocating international cooperation abroad and greater democracy and respect for civil liberties at home.

The main accomplishments of party government came while Katō was prime minister (1924–1926). Foremost among them was passage of a "universal" suffrage act, which gave the vote to all males 25 and over. This was a victory for liberals but was not followed by an attempt to rally public opinion. Instead, to still the fears of conservatives apprehensive over the possible spread of radical ideas, a Peace Preservation Law was also passed. This made it a crime to advocate change in the national political structure or to urge the abolition of private property. The Katō government never invoked the law, but it was available to later, less liberal regimes.

Katō also tried to reform the House of Peers (changing its composition and reducing its powers), but succeeded in making only minor changes. His government was more successful in introducing moderate social reforms, including the legalization of labor unions, the establishment of standards for factory conditions, the setting up of procedures for mediating labor disputes, and the provision of health insurance for workers. There was, however, no similar program to alleviate the problems of the rural poor.

Katō soon became embroiled in difficult political negotiations that included other parties and the House of Peers. When Katō died in 1926, he had not transformed Japanese politics, but he did leave a record of accomplishment that might, under different circumstances, have served as a basis for building a strong system of party rule. That this did not happen is partly the result of the problems Japan had to face during the next five years, but it also reflects the weakness of the parties. Even the increased suffrage was a mixed blessing, for the larger electorate made election campaigns costlier and politicians more open to corruption. The evident opportunism of party politicians undercut their credibility.

From 1927 to 1929 the government was led by Tanaka. In foreign policy Tanaka departed from Shidehara's conciliatory approach. In 1927, when Chiang Kai-shek resumed the military expedition to unify China, Tanaka, under political pressure at home, sent an army brigade to Shandong, where clashes with Chinese soldiers ensued. Still more ominous was the assassination, in June 1928, of Zhang Zuolin by a group of Japanese army officers who did not think him sufficiently pliant and hoped their action would pave the way for the seizure of Manchuria. This did not happen—at least not then. Instead, Manchuria was brought under the new Chinese government by Zhang's son, and Tanaka had to recognize the

Guomindang regime in Nanjing as the government of China. Tanaka's government collapsed when he incurred the displeasure of the Showa Emperor (r. 1925–1989) and court by failing to obtain from the army suitable punishment for Zhang's murderers. This episode was a harbinger of future unilateral army actions, but first, party government had one more chance.

In 1929, Hamaguchi Ōsachi became prime minister, and in 1930 his party, the Minseitō, won the election. Shidehara once again became foreign minister, and resumed his policy of reconciliation with China. He cooperated with Britain and the United States in negotiating the London Naval Treaty of 1930, which provided for a ten:ten:seven ratio for other than capital ships. The treaty was ratified only after heated debate and the forced resignation of the naval chief of staff. It generated bitterness among the military and members of patriotic societies, such as the young man who shot the prime minister in November, 1930. Hamaguchi never recovered from his wounds, but hung on in office until April 1931. From then until December 1931, the Minseitō cabinet continued under Wakatsuki Reijirō (1866–1949), who earlier had served as home minister under Katō and as prime minister from January 1926 to April 1927. He was an experienced politician, but during 1931 the government lost control over the army.

The restlessness of the military was not the government's only problem. During most of the 1920s, Japan was beset by persistent economic difficulties, including an unfavorable balance of payments, failure of job growth to match population growth, and a sharp decline in the price of rice, which helped consumers but hurt farmers (see Box 11.1). The giant *zaibatsu* profited from new technology, economies of scale, and the failure of weaker firms, but times were hard on small operators. In 1921, a dramatic dockyard strike in Kobe resulted in an eight-hour day, which was extended to other heavy industries. However, overall the union movement progressed slowly. This was also the case for unions of tenants, many of whom now worked for landlords who had moved to the city. Carol Gluck aptly summed up the situation when she characterized Japan as being in "a hiatus between a traditional agrarian paternalism that was disintegrating and a modern industrial paternalism that was still in its formative stages. The landlords were no longer offering succor to distressed tenants, and the companies were not yet acting in a paternalist role on any significant scale."[9]

To solve the balance-of-payments problem, there were calls for the government to cut expenses and retrench in order to reduce the cost of Japanese goods and improve their competitive position in international trade. This policy was followed by Hamaguchi, who also strengthened the yen by returning to the gold standard. Unfortunately, he initiated this program just as the Great Depression began, and persisted in it despite great economic dislocations and suffering. From 1925 to 1930 the real income of farmers declined by about one-third. The poorest were, as always, the hardest hit. As in earlier periods of famine, there were cases of peasants eating bark and digging for roots, or maintaining life by selling daughters into brothels.

The government's economic failure undermined the credibility of the political parties, which even in normal times had little public esteem. No mass movement arose directed against them, but there was little in their record to inspire

BOX 11.1 AGRARIAN DISCONTENT

Although urban centers flourished during the 1920s, this was a time of decline in the countryside. One of the most notable trends was a growing chasm between the way of life of the city and that of the countryside. As economic depressions caused agricultural prices to fall, and tillable land became concentrated in the hands of a select few, farmers witnessed a drop in living standards. Agrarian poverty drove some farmers to leave the countryside altogether and join the military or seek employment in factories. For farming communities throughout Japan, it was a period of dislocation and upheaval.

It was concern for such trends that prompted a farmer in central Japan named Shibuya Teisuke (1905–1989) to join the agrarian reform movement where he came under the sway of Marxism. Shibuya believed that cities were centers of capitalist forces that exploited the peasant farmers. In 1925, he helped form the Agriculturalists' Self-Rule Society. Its proclamation declared:

> The cities grow more luxurious day by day . . . while the villagers have to live on moldy salted fish and wear shopworn clothes. And even these are not readily available to propertyless farmers, who are covered with dirt like moles and are suffocated in poverty like homeless mice. To begin with, the cities are living off the sweat of the farmers. They pilfer and live on what the peasants have produced with their sweat and blood. While the cities and city dwellers prosper, becoming daily more used to luxury, the peasants who labor to support and keep them alive are on the verge of starvation and death.

Shibuya kept a diary, where he recorded his day-to-day activities as well as his private thoughts, frustrations, and ambitions. One entry on March 1, 1926, stated, "Now, the tillers of the soil, tenant farmers as well as farmowners, must unite in a single body and declare war on modern industrial commercialism and urban centered ways."

Seven months later, on October 1, 1926, he wrote:

> I went home. The house is not lit and is pitch dark. My sick father is groaning. . . . The children are crying. Oh, what misery! This is the true picture of the life of the producers of food. My body is exhausted.

(continued)

BOX 11.1 AGRARIAN DISCONTENT (CONTINUED)

My mother has taken off her work clothes soaked in sweat and does not move a muscle. The "people of culture" enjoy the glory of life while the producers of essential goods for human life—food, housing, and clothing—have to live like this. The skies of Tokyo light up the eastern horizon. You, together with the landlords, are leeches who bleed us.

Hane, Mikiso. *Peasants, Rebels, & Outcastes: the Underside of Modern Japan.* (New York: Pantheon Books, 1982). pp. 32, 36–37.

people to battle in their defense. Their enemies included those dissatisfied with their policies and politics, as well as those disgruntled with nearly every facet of 1920s liberalism, internationalism, and "modernity."

Popular Culture

This period of parliamentary government is sometimes compared to that of Germany's Weimar Republic. That applies to culture as well as politics. During the 1920s, a wave of Western influence affected lifestyles, diet, housing, and dress, particularly in Tokyo and other great cities, where there was a boom in bread consumption, Western dress became prevalent in public, and fashionable houses included at least one Western room. On the Ginza, the "modern boy" (*mobo*) and "modern girl" (*moga*) dressed and coiffured in the latest imported styles might be on their way to listen to jazz or see a movie. Although there was always an audience for films filled with melodrama and swordplay, others dealt with the problems and joys of daily life.

Western sports gained ground, including baseball, although the first professional teams did not appear until the 1930s. People began playing golf and tennis. Friends met in cafes, or a fellow could practice the latest steps with a taxi dancer at The Florida or another of Tokyo's dance halls. The old demimonde dominated by the geisha, a world fondly chronicled by Nagai Kafū (1879–1959), was declining while modern mass culture ascended.

Centered in the cities, the new popular culture was steadily diffused, as even the remotest village became accessible by train and car, and of course the radio, introduced in 1925. Mass circulation magazines, some directed at a general audience, others written especially for women or young people, catered to the unquenchable thirst of the Japanese public for reading matter.

Fine Arts

Internationalism was represented not only in politics but also in the arts. Tokyo was not far behind Paris or London in experimenting with the latest styles and techniques. Indeed, it sometimes led the other capitals, as when in 1922 Frank Lloyd Wright built the Imperial Hotel in Tokyo, a break with Japan's own version of the European Art Nouveau. The American architect, himself influenced by the Japanese tradition, was not the only stimulating visitor from abroad during the Taishō and early Showa years. Japanese scientists, for example, could converse with Einstein on his visit to their country in 1919, and music lovers enjoyed concerts by eminent foreign performers: both Kreisler and Heifetz gave concerts in Tokyo in 1923. Bach, Mozart, and Beethoven were becoming as much a part of the musical life of Japan as of any other country, foreshadowing the time when, after World War II, the Japanese pioneered in teaching young children to play the violin and also became the world's foremost manufacturers of pianos.

A grand piano dominates the four-panel screen (Figure 11.4) painted in 1926 by Nakamura Daizaburō (1898–1947), which is representative of the followers of

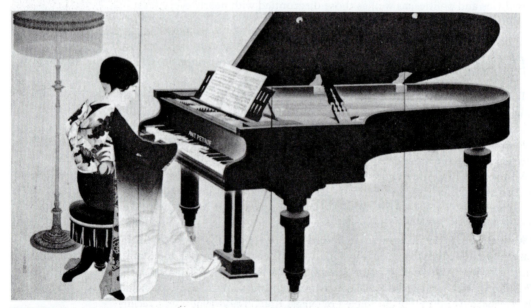

FIGURE 11.4 *At the Piano,* Nakamura Daizaburō. Not only the traditional dress of the young woman playing by the light of an electric lamp but the technique and aesthetics of the painting recall the earliest Japanese art rather than contemporary Western styles. Four-fold screen, color on silk, 1926, 164.5 × 302 cm.
KYOTO MUNICIPAL MUSEUM OF ART, JAPAN.

the Okakura school. Conversely, there were Japanese artists who, like Xu Beihong in China, depicted traditional subjects in Western style.

A major influence for modernism was the *White Birch* (*Shirakaba*) journal (1910–1923), one of whose editors was Shiga Naoya (1883–1971). In contrast to the school of naturalism and the advocates of proletarian literature, the *White Birch* group was dedicated to the exploration of the inner self and the pursuit of deeper personal understanding and self-expression, as in the "I novel" or in individualistic art. Seeking to become "children of the world," they introduced many European writers and published articles on the work and theories of such artists as Van Gogh—whose suicide for art's sake they praised as superior to that of General Nogi.

Much of the art produced during this period was imitative, but one artist who developed his own style was Umehara Ryūzaburū. A disciple of Renoir, Umehara also owes something to his childhood in Kyoto, where he became thoroughly familiar with the styles of Sōtatsu and Kōrin as still practiced in his family's silk kimono business (see Figures 4.3 and 4.4).

European pointillism, cubism, futurism, dadaism, and surrealism all had their impact on the Japanese avant-garde, here represented by a painting dated 1926 (Figure 11.5). Tōgō Seiji (1897–1978), in Europe at the time, was especially influenced by French and Italian futurism and dadaism, but here shows an inclination toward cubism.

FIGURE 11.5 *Saltimbanques*, Tōgō Seiji. The title of this cheerful, decorative picture is French for "traveling showmen," and it would take a very keen eye, not to say considerable imagination, to detect a particularly Japanese element. Oil, 1926, 114 × 71 cm.

© TOGO TAMAMI. COURTESY TOGO TAMAMI AND THE NATIONAL MUSEUM OF MODERN ART, TOKYO, JAPAN.

Mingei

Many trends converged in the "folk craft" or "folk arts" movement promoted by Yanagi Muneyoshi (or Sōetsu, 1889–1961), who spent 20 years traveling all over the country studying local pottery, textiles, lacquerware, and objects made of metal, wood, bamboo, leather, and paper. In 1926 he coined the term "mingei," the people's art or folk art. His deep belief in the creative genius of the people was in tune with Taishō democracy. His rejection of machine mass production and his devotion to the strong, honest beauty created by anonymous craftsmen working together to create objects for daily use are reminiscent of John Ruskin (1819–1900) and William Morris (1834–1896), founder of the late Victorian Arts and Crafts Movement. Yanagi, like Morris, championed the dignity of the craftsman, and linked the aesthetic beauty of folk art to the ethical qualities under which it was produced. His attempt to establish a commune for *mingei* artists failed, but he succeeded in inspiring a new appreciation for traditional woodcarving, housewares, woven and dyed cloth, and all kinds of articles made of bamboo, straw, handmade paper, wood (including furniture and traditional buildings), metal, and leather. A full list would be very long and include virtually all the products of traditional workmanship. Such works found a home in the museums, such as the Japan Folk Art Museum in Tokyo (1936), where they continue to be displayed, studied, enjoyed, and celebrated.

Yanagi's interest in folk culture was shared by Yanagida Kunio (1875–1962), Japan's foremost scholar of folklore. The massive survey he directed in the thirties laid the foundations for a whole field of studies. Beyond preserving and studying the folk craft (his preferred translation of *mingei*) of the past, he also strove to further the production of *mingei* as a living force. Foremost among his associates in the *mingei* movement were four potters: Tomimoto Kenkichi (1886–1963), the British potter Bernard Leach (1887–1979), Kawai Kanjirō (1890–1966), and Hamada Shōji (1894–1978). Others worked in textiles and other crafts. Among the woodcut artists influenced by Yanagida was Munakata Shikō (see p. 420–421).

Literature

Naturalism, symbolism, social realism, neo-perceptionsim—in literature as in the visual arts, a multitude of agendas had their proponents and special vocabulary, "pushing this or that 'ism,' this or that school and inflicting on the reader who wishes to comprehend the book's argument prior belief in this jargon." These words were written in 1930 by Kobayashi Hideo (1902–1983), Japan's foremost modern critic, who went on to say, "I don't trust the jargon. I believe that not trusting jargon is the mark of the critical spirit."[10]

Kobayashi admired Shiga Naoya, already mentioned as a member of the *White Birch* group, master of the autobiographical short story and "I novel," and of a concise, unaffected (though carefully crafted), sensitive style. Shiga was much admired and imitated, but he also had his detractors. Prominent among those who rejected the autobiographical mode were the advocates of proletarian literature exemplified by such novels as *The Cannery Boat* (1929) by Kobayashi Takiji (1903–1933), in which the workers revolt against a brutal captain. Although much of this literature was propagandistic, it did make the reader and writer more sensitive to social conditions.

A gifted writer who defies classification was Akutagawa Ryūnosuke (1892–1927), author of some 150 short stories between 1917 and 1927, many of them modern psychological reinterpretations of old tales. Because of the famous film of the same name released in 1950 by Kurosawa Akira, he is probably best known in the West for "Rashomon," which presents the story of a murder and rape as told from the viewpoint of three protagonists and a witness. In doing so, it raises questions about all our perceptions of historical truth. Akutagawa's stories are frequently eerie, but are saved from being merely macabre by the keenness of his psychological portrayals. Pessimistic, given to self-doubt, and distressed at the changing world about him, he committed suicide in 1927, citing "a vague unease."

In poetry as in art, some dedicated themselves to new experiments, while others continued working with the old forms. In the nineteenth century, Masaoka

Shiki (1867–1902), known primarily as a haiku poet, contributed toward revitalizing traditional poetry, which continued to be written and published throughout the twentieth century. Others, however, looked to the West, and some even employed the Roman alphabet (*rōmaji*). Foreign influence did not necessarily produce timeless verse; one poet proclaimed, "My sorrow wears the thin garb of one-sided love."[11] The most admired master of free verse was Hagiwara Sakutarō (1886–1942), whose collection *Howling at the Moon* (1917) caused a sensation. Moving from the canine to the feline, he published *Blue Cat* in 1923—using "blue" in the sense of the blues. *Age of Ice* (1934), his last book of new free verse, includes a poem in which he identifies with a caged tiger.

A major prose writer was Tanizaki Junichirō (1886–1965), who began with a fascination with the West, but increasingly turned to the Japanese tradition. The protagonist of *Some Prefer Nettles* (1917), unhappily married to a "stridently" modern wife, finds comfort in the arms of a Eurasian prostitute, symbolic of the West; but as the novel unfolds, he is increasingly attracted to a traditional Kyoto beauty. Tanizaki himself moved to Kyoto following the great earthquake of 1923. Some of his best work still lay in the future, including his masterpiece, *The Makioka Sisters*, written during World War II. One theme in this long, panoramic novel is the contrast between two of the sisters, one traditional in appearance and mentality, the other modern. Tanizaki's devotion to tradition also led him to translate *The Tale of Genji* into modern Japanese.

A similar trajectory from avant-garde to tradition was followed by Kawabata Yasunari (1899–1972), whose main works and fame were still to come. A very different writer also at the beginning of her career during this period was Uno Chiyu (1897–1996), whose persona and writings were more in tune with the 1920s and the post-World War I years than with the 1930s, when she published her best-known novel, *Confessions of Love* (*Iro Zange*, 1935), based on the well-known failed love suicide attempted by Tōgō Seiji (see Figure 11.5) in 1929. Uno's interview with Tōgō a month later led that same night to a famous liaison that lasted five years.

Intellectual Trends

Philosophers and political theorists, like artists and writers, were challenged by claims that modern Western ideas possessed universally valid principles, and by their need to make sense of and find value in their own tradition. On the left, there was a revival of interest in anarchism and socialism, suppressed in 1911, and Marxism enjoyed new prestige after the Russian Revolution. Some were active in the labor movement, but the labor parties formed after passage of the universal suffrage act suffered from an excess of factionalism and a lack of mass participation. This was also true of the Japanese Communist Party, which was dominated by intellectuals, some of great personal status. There was also a fledgling feminist movement, which campaigned for equality and women's rights, particularly the right to vote, because at the time women were legally minors and remained completely excluded from the political process.

Most widely read among liberal theorists were Minobe Tatsukichi (1873–1948) and Yoshino Sakuzō (1878–1933), both deeply versed in German thought. Minobe was a legal scholar who followed his teacher at Heidelberg, Georg Jellinek, in making a distinction between sovereignty, which belongs to the whole state, and the power to rule, which is supervised by the emperor. In this sense, the emperor becomes the "highest organ" of the state, limited by the other components of the state and by the constitution. The constitution, furthermore, in Japan as elsewhere (according to Minobe), allows, and indeed requires, continuing change in the direction of increasing rationality, responsible government, and popular participation. Minobe's work gained wide currency, and his book was the most frequently assigned text in courses on constitutional law. In 1932, he was appointed to the House of Peers, but his prominence was later to cost him dearly.

Yoshino did not obtain such Establishment approval, but his many articles were widely read. A Christian populist and a democrat, he was a philosophical idealist who argued for democracy as an absolute rather than on utilitarian or pragmatic grounds. He also held an idealistic view of the nation and rejected any suggestion that democracy was incompatible with the Japanese tradition: "Those who argue that democracy is not compatible with the national spirit believe in the anachronistic and erroneous notion that the Emperor and people are mutually exclusive of each other."[12] Democracy would fulfill, not diminish, the emperor's role.

After World War I, Japanese intellectuals were attracted to Hegel, Kant, and Nietzsche, the phenomenalism of Husserl, the hermeneutics of Heidegger, and the vitalism of Bergson and Eucken. Outstanding among the philosophers who digested Western philosophy and assimilated it into their own original work was Nishida Kitarō (1870–1945), strongly steeped in Buddhism and best known for his philosophy of transcendent nothingness. Other theorists used Western philosophy to differentiate an authentic Japaneseness from the West and what they perceived as the diluted or hybrid culture that they disliked and dismissed. Nishida was not alone in refraining from discussing politics, but others defined Japanism in political terms, and demanded political action.

Some ideologues, conscious of the hardships suffered by the countryside, condemned the life and values of the cities and called for a return to virtuous agrarianism. Among the most severe critics of the parties and *zaibatsu* was Kita Ikki (1883–1937), who combined advocacy of imperialistic assertiveness abroad with a call for egalitarianism at home to bring emperor and people together. Unhappy with Japan's political organization and its stance in the world, he looked not to the electorate or a mass popular movement for salvation, but placed his faith in change from above enacted by a few dedicated men. Accordingly, his ideas found a friendly reception in small societies of superpatriots and among army officers who saw themselves as continuing in the tradition of the *rōnin* who had selflessly terrorized Kyoto during the closing days of the Tokugawa. Kita also found more recent exemplars among the ex-samurai who, after Saigō's death, had formed the Genyōsha (Black Ocean Society, 1881) and the Kokuryūkai (Amur River Society, also translated Black Dragon Society, 1901). The former was dedicated to expansion in Korea; the latter concentrated on Manchuria. Both employed intimidation and assassination.

The story of the attempts made by these men to effect a "Showa Restoration" belongs in the 1930s, but Kita Ikki's most influential book was written in 1919. The rejection in the 1930s of party government and internationalism that had prevailed in the 1920s revealed that these still had shallow roots.

Notes

1. Louise Young, *Japan's Total Empire: Manchuria and the Culture of Wartime Imperialism* (Berkeley, CA: Univ. of California Press, 1998), p. 21.

2. Mark R. Peattie in Ramon H. Myers and Peattie, eds., *The Japanese Colonial Empire, 1895–1945* (Princeton, NJ: Princeton Univ. Press, 1984), p. 8. See p. 10 for colonies as "the ultimate status symbol."

3. Quoted in Sōseki Natsume, *Ten Nights of Dream–Hearing Things–The Heredity of Taste*, trans. by Aiko Ito and Graeme Wilson (Rutland, VT, and Tokyo: Charles E. Tuttle, 1974), p. 12.

4. Natsume Sōseki, *The Three-Cornered World*, trans. by Alan Turney (Chicago, IL: Henry Regnery, 1965), p. iii.

5. Ibid., p. 181.

6. Shuji Takashina and J. Thomas Rimer, with Gerald D. Bolas, *Paris in Japan: The Japanese Encounter with European Painting* (St. Louis, MO: The Washington Univ. Press, 1987), p. 105.

7. William P. Malm, "The Modern Music of Meiji Japan," in Donald H. Shively, ed., *Tradition and Modernization in Japanese Culture* (Princeton, NJ: Princeton Univ. Press, 1971), p. 300.

8. Arthur E. Tiedemann, "Big Business and Politics in Prewar Japan," in James W. Morley, ed., *Dilemmas of Growth in Prewar Japan* (Princeton, NJ: Princeton Univ. Press, 1971), pp. 278–79.

9. Carol Gluck, *Japan's Modern Myths* (Princeton, NJ: Princeton Univ. Press, 1985), p. 282.

10. Quoted in *Literature of the Lost Home: Kobayashi Hideo—Literary Criticism 1924–1939*, ed. and trans. by Paul Anderer (Stanford, CA: Stanford Univ. Press, 1995), p. 108.

11. Quoted in Donald Keene, ed., *Modern Japanese Literature: An Anthology* (New York, NY: Grove Press, 1956), p. 20.

12. Tetsuo Najita, "Some Reflections on Idealism in the Political Thought of Yoshino Sakuzo," in Bernard Silberman and H. D. Harootunian, eds., *Japan in Crisis: Essays on Taishō Democracy* (Princeton, NJ: Princeton Univ. Press, 1974), p. 40.

12

Vietnam, Korea, and Taiwan under Colonial Rule

All East Asian countries experienced imperialism to varying degrees. Macao and Hong Kong were the first lands to be taken over by European powers, but they differ in scale as well as in their maritime character from Vietnam, Korea, and Taiwan. As colonies, these three large territories became completely and—at least from the colonizers' perspective—permanently under foreign jurisdiction, ruled primarily for the benefit of the "home" countries. Though colonialism was a worldwide phenomenon, its forms and dynamics differed depending on the time, place, and parties involved. For example, when Japan acquired Taiwan, it took a lightly populated island that had been only recently and incompletely sinicized, but when it took Korea it seized a foreign civilization in its entirety, complete with its own history, language, and customs. In Indochina, the French were overlords to people who were entirely different from themselves linguistically, racially, and culturally, but in Korea, the Japanese took over a neighboring people with whom they were able to communicate readily via Chinese characters and with whose culture they already had much in common.

Nevertheless, French colonialism in Vietnam and Japanese colonialism, especially in Korea, offer several intriguing points of comparison. One obvious similarity was the use of force and intimidation in the process of taking over the colony, and the maintenance of enough military and police power to overwhelm any possible local resistance. Another was the establishment of a colonial administration that employed colonial people in the lower ranks of the bureaucracy, police, and educational systems, and provided avenues for limited advancement to colonized people who were willing to identify with the colonial regime. A third similarity was the spontaneous development of anticolonial resistance movements. The resistance grew out of a burgeoning nationalism that manifested itself in violent acts of resistance. But it also had more subtle origins. One of the most volatile was the anger felt by Vietnamese or Koreans who tried sincerely to mold themselves into authentic French or Japanese but found that no matter how hard they tried, the binary divide between colonizer and colonized always kept them in the status of second-class citizens.

I. Vietnam under the French

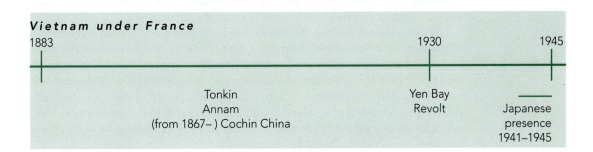

Vietnam under France

1883		1930	1945
	Tonkin Annam (from 1867–) Cochin China	Yen Bay Revolt	Japanese presence 1941–1945

Economic Policy

Social Change

Education

New Stirrings of Opposition

Ferment Intensified: The Twenties and Thirties

The Rise of Ho Chi Minh

We begin with Vietnam because it was the first of the three considered here to experience colonization. As we have seen (Chapter 6), France's annexation of the south, called Cochin China, begun in 1862 and completed in 1867, was followed by the establishment of protectorates over Annam in the center and Tonkin in the north in 1883–1884 (see Figure 6.5). In 1887, the French added the protectorates of Cambodia, under their control since the 1860s, to form the Indochinese Union, expanded in 1893 to include Laos.

A governor-general residing in Hanoi oversaw the entire Union. Cochin China was directly administered by the French colonial service, but in Annam and Tonkin the French retained the Vietnamese emperor and court at Hue as well as the old "mandarin" bureaucracy. However, after 1897 a French resident superior controlled the Tonkin mandarinate. In Annam, too, the authority of the emperor was increasingly limited. There, beginning with the rule of Governor-General Paul Doumer (1897–1902), the French assumed administrative control, including tax collection.

The French also controlled the emperor, his succession, and even his physical movements. There had been resistance from the beginning of French encroachments on the Nguyen Dynasty, but attempts by the elite to use the throne to rally opposition to the French, such as the "Save the King" Movement (*Can Vuong*) begun in 1885, were suppressed. A 1916 insurrection marked the last such attempt. Emperors were forced to comply with the French.

While a minority of the old elite resisted, in Annam and Tonkin a generation of traditional scholar-officials continued their old-fashioned devotion to the court and served in its now collaborative bureaucratic structures. Despite their direct experience of modern Western colonialism and the scientific inventions that had overwhelmed their traditional society, these men struggled to maintain the tradition of Sino-Vietnamese scholarship and participated in the examination system, which continued until 1915 in Tonkin and until 1919 in Annam, 15 years after it had been abolished in China.

Economic Policy

From the beginning of the Cochin China colony in 1862, the French authorities favored the formation of large, and preferably French, landholdings. Initially, they gave out enormous grants of land, much of it confiscated from people who had resisted or fled when France invaded. The unequal distribution of land persisted until the end of French rule, with many people left landless or nearly so. The trend in the protectorates was similar in favoring large landowners. The Nguyen had taxed indirectly through the villages and done so lightly and in kind, but the French taxed family heads directly and in cash. Many small farmers lost their land. As Ngo Vinh Long points out, "A common technique used by the French was to exploit traditional Vietnamese court law in depriving the peasants of their rights of landownership and then to apply French laws to assert the rights of ownership to the same lands."[1]

In keeping with the French policy of having its colonies supply raw materials for the factories back home, Doumer initiated a major program of building railroads, roads, harbors, ports, and bridges so that the production of the country's mines (mainly coal), farms (especially rice), and plantations (mainly rubber) would find their way to France (Figure 12.1). Under the French, work on dikes, drainage, and irrigation facilities increased agricultural production. Between 1918 and 1930, French investment, primarily in rubber, coffee, tea, and sugar plantations but also in mining and industry, increased over 600 percent, but a small group of French syndicates controlled almost all operations and profits. A handful of Frenchmen within the colonial administration and in the private sector of the colonial economy exerted near-total control. France's order of priorities was demonstrated when Cochin China exported rice abroad rather than shipping it north to alleviate rice shortages there.

France also valued the colonies as markets, and thus discouraged the formation of local industries that might compete in that market. When the Great Depression of the 1930s resulted in a decline in world trade, it merely reinforced a system in which the colonies provided secure markets "favoring the survival in France of the least modern sector and preventing economic progress in the colonies."[2]

Until the mid-1920s, the colonial regime derived as much as 70 percent of its tax income from monopolies over the production and sale of commodities such as opium, wine, and salt. The French only encouraged, but did not require, Vietnamese to purchase opium imported and sold at a profit of 400–500 percent. However, they forced villagers who had previously consumed home-brewed rice wine to buy set quotas of foreign-tasting, high-priced, alcoholic beverages. Heavy demands for *corvée* labor further added to peasant burdens. In 1908, this led to local demonstrations and riots in central Vietnam that were severely repressed by the colonial police. The French also trafficked in coolie labor, shipping large numbers of peasants from the overpopulated north to work on southern rubber plantations or in Tahiti and other French possessions in the South Pacific. At best, colonial rule brought mixed benefits to the Vietnamese people. Although not widely available, Western medicine did lengthen life expectancy and raise birth

Pont Doumer, à Hanoï.

FIGURE 12.1 *The Pont Doumer,* drawn by Georges Fraipont. Named after Governor-General Paul Doumer (1897–1902), who facilitated rapid exports to France by modernizing transportation networks throughout Indochina. The bridge, like the French colonization, did not last (see Figure 18.2).

FROM *HANOI, BIOGRAPHY OF A CITY,* BY WILLIAM S. LOGAN. COURTESY UNIVERSITY OF NEW SOUTH WALES PRESS, SYDNEY. QUOTED FROM *INDO-CHINE FRANÇAIS (SOUVENIRS)* (PARIS: VIUBERT ET NONY EDITEURS, 1905), P. 312.

rates, and there was sufficient improvement in agriculture to increase food production. However, population increases outstripped rises in living standards. Most people experienced declining living standards in the 1920s and the 1930s. There were cases of acute impoverishment in the countryside.

Life changed more rapidly in the cities than in the country, but Vietnamese villagers who had traditionally relied on a largely self-sufficient subsistence economy now entered into wider and more modern market networks and participated in the new material culture. As described by one writer depicting life in the Red River Delta region in 1938:

> In the countryside life has not changed as it has in the city. But farmers used to grow rice to eat, weave clothing to wear, use bamboo from their gardens to build their houses; now they have to take their rice and

sell it in order to purchase in turn other things they need which are brought to them from the city by merchants and peddlers. . . . The rural folk no longer find the French to be a terrifying race of people, nor do they find their artifacts to be miraculous or fantastic any longer.[3]

Some even converted to Catholicism. By the time of the French conquest about five percent of the population had been converted, and the church continued to emphasize the development of a native clergy. Although architecturally most of the churches were European transplants, the massive cathedral at Phat Diem is a local product. Built between 1875 and 1899 under the direction of a Vietnamese priest, it follows the overall plan of a Roman church, but its curling roofs, massive interior columns, and the scarlet red lacquer work on its altar are more common in Sino-Vietnamese Buddhist temples. There are also overtones of Vietnamese community houses (*dinh*). On the cathedral's roof, a great bell and a large gong stand ready to sound the message of the faith (Figure 12.2).

FIGURE 12.2   The Cathedral at Phat Diem, about 81 miles south of Hanoi and 17.5 miles from Ninh Binh, was built on marshland. An architectural hybrid, it is topped by a cross proclaiming its religious affiliation.

PHOTOGRAPH © LORE SCHIROKAUER.

Social Change

As elsewhere in East Asia, most Vietnamese continued to work the land. Increasingly, this was not their own land, as even in the north wealthy landowners increased their holdings by extending credit and foreclosing on the less fortunate. Meanwhile, ownerships of newly opened lands in Cochin China went to the wealthy and well-connected absentee landlords, to be tilled by sharecroppers at rents as high as 60 percent.

Much of this rice was exported through Saigon, which grew to supplant Hanoi as Vietnam's, and Indochina's, largest and richest city. It also became a center for rubber export, textile mills, a cement industry, and fish-sauce and other food-processing plants.

Enjoying this newly found wealth was a class of Vietnamese, French, and Chinese entrepreneurs. Although a good number of the Chinese who immigrated in the eighteenth and nineteenth centuries intermarried with the Vietnamese, many others retained their identity. This was facilitated by both the French and the Nguyen treating the Chinese as separate communities with their own leaders, schools, and clan organizations. Favored by the French, many engaged in commerce and manufacturing: the Chinese section of Saigon is still called Cholon, meaning "Big Market." Others worked as miners, longshoremen, or fishermen.

Some of the most successful Vietnamese and Chinese obtained French citizenship. At the same time, a small but growing lower bourgeoisie developed. The more well-to-do segment engaged in business or pursued professional careers in such emerging professions as engineering and medicine. Many of them were self-made, without the historic connection to the scholar-officials that had ruled Vietnam's past. Less well-off than members of this social stratum were an urban intelligentsia including teachers, journalists, students, and clerks, who were often from elite families who had a tradition of Confucian emphasis on public service and education, and who had maintained their distance from the French.

In Saigon and elsewhere, leadership for the emerging anticolonial movements and protests came overwhelmingly from members of this urban intelligentsia, but for many years, the diversity in their views stood in the way of their forming a coherent movement. Regional differences in historic background and experience under colonialism made for disagreement and disunity. Furthermore, as William Duiker has pointed out, these elites lacked a common religion to help build national bonds or provide a basis for a national consciousness.[4]

The success of Cao Dai, founded in 1926 by an official in the French service with a deep interest in spiritualism and séances, showed that many in the south were ready to embrace a new religion. Cao Dai, literally "high platform," a Daoist epithet for the highest god, got its name from Daoism, fostered Confucian morals, endorsed Buddhist belief in karma and reincarnation, modeled its organization on that of the Roman Catholic Church, and included Confucius, Jesus, and Mohammed in its pantheon (Figures 12.3 and 12.4). It was similarly synthetic in its choice of more modern exemplars, paying special reverence to Sun Yat-sen, Victor Hugo, and Nguyen Binh Khiem (1491–1587), whose poetry was marked "by a strange combination of resigned fortitude, robustness of character, and irony which explodes at times into outrage, as in 'The Hated Rats,' but most often expresses itself in patient humor." Depicting officials as rats goes back to the Chinese *Classic of Poetry,* but it did not require much effort for twentieth-century Vietnamese to find in their own world rats who gorge on taxes with "those yellow teeth whose hunger maims our flesh."[5]

Education

In Vietnam, as elsewhere, education helped mold people's values and ideas. In French Indochina, change came only slowly. This was particularly the case in the protectorates, especially in Annam, where the court was located and where, during the first 50 years of colonial rule, changes in curriculum were inhibited by voices at court insisting that education remain geared to the traditional examination system. Meanwhile, in Cochin China education was in French along with *quoc ngu,* the phonetic script devised in the seventeenth century. However, throughout Vietnam, primary education was scarce, limited to urban centers. *Lycées* (French secondary academic schools) were extremely few.

The French seem never to have quite decided between a policy of assimilation, designed to make Vietnamese French in every way, and a policy of association, "which considered that colonies and the colonized people are distinct entities with their own cultures and institutions, albeit ultimately convertible to 'civilization' and to the high status enjoyed by France and the French."[6] Albert Sarraut, governor-general from 1911 to 1913 and 1919 to 1923, pursued the latter policy, and attempted to expand education—but he was equally intent on having Vietnam contribute to France's economy (Figure 12.5). He ordered schools built in the villages—at village expense. However, his successor, Martial Merlin, reversed this policy in the 1920s, restricting secondary and post-secondary

FIGURE 12.3 The Great Temple of Cao Dai in the sacred city Tay Ninh, southwest of Ho Chi Minh City (Saigon). Here, as in other Cao Dai temples, rituals are performed four times a day.
PHOTOGRAPH © LORE SCHIROKAUER.

FIGURE 12.4 *Window of the Great Temple of Cao Dai.* The omniscient and omnipresent eye emanating sunrays is the central symbol of Cao Dai, a fitting design for the windows of the great hall of worship.
PHOTOGRAPH © LORE SCHIROKAUER.

FIGURE 12.5   His Excellency M. Albert Sarraut, governor-general of Indochina, and His Majesty Khai-Dinh, emperor of Annam (central Vietnam). Governor-general from 1911 to 1913 and again from 1919 to 1923, Sarraut attempted to expand education in village schools throughout the Indochinese Union.

From *L'Indochine Français* (Hanoi: Government General de L'Indochine, 1931).

education, shutting down traditional schools that remained in Tonkin and Annam, and ensuring that village schools would provide only three years of primary instruction in Vietnamese, taught by minimally qualified and poorly paid instructors. By 1930 only 10 percent of school-age Vietnamese children actually went to public or private schools, and the next decade saw only modest increases.

Only a small number of Vietnamese youths received education beyond the primary level. Until 1940, at any given time, approximately 500 students found places in the *lycées,* and only a dozen or so graduated from university per year—this out of a population which in 1936 amounted to 18.6 million. Those who ventured to France for higher education experienced a far freer social and intellectual atmosphere. There they were able to absorb French culture, and were exposed to the ideals of the French Revolution and leftist political philosophies, but when they returned home they had to endure demeaning employment and prejudicial treatment. Their objections to colonialism grew in confidence and definition during the first decades of the twentieth century, strengthened by French anticolonial discourse and hardened by the insensitivities of the French authorities. As elsewhere, educated youths were at the vanguard of nascent revolutionary movements that took the place of older, less radical movements.

New Stirrings of Opposition

From the beginning of French rule, some scholar-officials, mindful of Vietnam's struggles for independence in the past, resisted collaboration and maintained honor even at the price of family ruin and death. But most, even after exposure to modern nationalism, chose to serve the emperor, hoping to preserve their status and scholarship while passively upholding French rule. A few, however, were attracted to ideas subversive both to colonial rule and to the traditional order, which they saw as an obstacle to a better society and to political independence. France was one source of such ideas, but other examples were closer at hand. By the turn of the century, Vietnamese scholars were reading texts by such Chinese reformers as Kang Yuwei and Liang Qichao, as well as Yan Fu's translations of works of Spencer and Mill. A movement sprang up to reform Vietnam through the "new learning." Phan Boi Chau (1867–1940) and Phan Chu Trinh (1872–1926), unrelated though they bore the same surname, represented two facets of "learning from the West." Both men received classical educations and passed the important regional examination in 1900, but both attacked the status quo and were subjected to exile and imprisonment.

When Phan Boi Chau traveled to Japan in 1905, he immediately found himself in the midst of Chinese reformers with whom he shared a profound Confucian background and an intense distress at the state of government back home. In 1905 Liang Qichao himself expressed his sympathy for the plight of the Vietnamese under colonialism by publishing and contributing a preface to Phan's *History of the Loss of Vietnam.* This book advocated the "new learning" and conveyed an intense nationalism, containing veiled incitements to armed uprising against the French.

Phan Boi Chau's "Travel East" Movement, though short-lived, had a lasting influence. At its height in 1907, it brought approximately 200 young Vietnamese to study in Japan. He did not formulate a coherent ideology or program, but focused on expelling the French, and increasingly advocated doing so through violent revolution. However, in 1908, an agreement between Japan and France led to Phan's expulsion from Japan and the end of his movement. After the French succeeded in having him deported, and he continued his advocacy from China, where he sought the support of successful Chinese revolutionaries after 1911. In 1913, he masterminded terrorist incidents in Vietnam that killed two French army officers and a high-placed collaborator. Sentenced to death in absentia, he remained abroad until, in 1925, French authorities finally brought him back under arrest to face a new trial that produced a new death sentence.

One of those who heeded the call to "travel east" was Phan Chu Trinh, who was politically more moderate, but culturally more radical than Phan Boi Chau. His hero was Fukuzawa Yukichi, Japan's foremost proponent of Western-style "enlightenment." In 1907, Phan Chu Trinh helped found a school in Hanoi modeled after the one established by Fukuzawa that eventually became Keiō University. Phan Chu Trinh, more than Phan Boi Chau, was a master of reasoned debate and the use of symbolic gestures to defy colonial rule. He took care to dress fashionably in Western clothes made from local Vietnamese materials. In one lecture at the school, he skillfully chided the Vietnamese for their subservience to both Chinese and Western domination when he urged Vietnamese men to cut their traditional Chinese-style chignons in favor of short haircuts:

> It was not until the Ming invaders came in and . . . compelled us to imitate them that our men began to let their hair grow and wore it in a bun. . . . But today . . . Heaven has opened our minds. We have awakened and the whole nation is modernizing. So go out and cut your hair! Don't leave any more land for that stupid gang of parasites to colonize on top of your heads, from which they can suck your blood![7]

In the wake of such arguments, short haircuts for men became subtly defiant of French rule, and the French were helpless to protest.

The Hanoi school and similar endeavors did not survive government repression, but the work of both Phans showed young Vietnamese in pursuit of a new identity how they could selectively borrow from the West along the lines of their Chinese and Japanese predecessors. Meanwhile, Trinh, the nonviolent reformer, was arrested in the wake of anti-tax rioting in Annam in 1908, and sent to the penal island of Con Son, notorious for its "tiger cages." His sentence was commuted to house arrest in 1911, but then he was allowed to leave for Paris, where he wrote articles attacking French rule and welcomed anti-French Vietnamese to his home. After his death and funeral in 1926, the incoming French governor-general commuted Chau's death sentence to house arrest in response to widespread demonstrations and strikes led by thousands of enraged students and others mourning the fate of the two leaders. By this time, the two Phans, despite their differences, "had become linked in the popular mind as the towering symbols of scholarly patriotism, revered symbols of fortitude and continuity with the past."[8]

Ferment Intensified: The Twenties and Thirties

In Vietnam, as in China, the 1920s were years of ferment, particularly among young people struggling to redefine what it meant to be Vietnamese even as they rejected much of the old culture while living under a colonial regime that proclaimed the virtues of the French Revolution but did not grant its Vietnamese subjects equality, liberty, or fraternity. Like the Japanese in their colonies, the French made ample use of their police power while both encouraging and withholding full participation in their polity and world. At the 1926 trial of Nguyen An Ninh (1900–1943), his translation of Jean-Jacques Rousseau's *Contrat Social* was even presented as evidence of sedition. The prosecution in this case may have been unusually obtuse, but the contradiction in French policies had always existed. After his release from prison, Ninh was drawn to, though he did not join, Cao Dai. He remained politically active and was eventually killed in prison by the French, who were apprehensive that the Japanese might use him.

A burgeoning vernacular press reflected and promoted intellectual and cultural change. While some preferred to publish in the less strictly controlled French language newspapers and periodicals, many sought a wider audience by writing in the *quoc ngu* press, which originated in 1865 but was just coming into its own. A new literary style influenced by French literature called for the purging of Chinese expressions and references. Confucianism, religion, and the purpose of art were among topics hotly debated, as was the role of women. New styles of dress and hair took hold, while satirists mocked old customs and realists depicted the lives of rickshaw pullers, servants, and other members of the urban underclass.

Cultural radicalism did not necessarily entail political radicalism. Nguyen Van Vinh (1882–1936), for instance, was a widely read translator, journalist, and essayist who even in his most acerbic writings never turned against the French politically. One of his many publications was a translation of *The Tale of Kieu* (see Chapter 6, p. 119 and Figure 18.4) from *nom* into *quoc ngu*. This set off a storm of controversy over the appropriateness of Kieu as a symbol for Vietnam or a model for Vietnamese womanhood. Among those most ardently championing Kieu was Pham Quynh (1892–1945), a prominent, neotraditional journalist intent on preserving a Vietnamese essence as well as an advocate of educating upper-class women. Loyal to the old court, he became head of the imperial cabinet and minister of education (1932).

Others became increasingly radical, joining such organizations as the Vietnamese Revolutionary Youth League, founded in 1925 by Ho Chi Minh, or the Nationalist Party of Vietnam, started in 1927 and deeply influenced by Sun Yat-sen. After a major revolt in Tonkin in 1917 led by prisoners in a penitentiary and mutinous Vietnamese troops, violence returned to a small scale until 1930, when Vietnamese troops mutinied at Yen Bay near Hanoi. After the mutiny was suppressed, thousands were sent to brutal, overcrowded, mismanaged prisons where they became radicalized. As the prison authorities themselves realized, "inmates at Saigon Central Prison are receiving a comprehensive communist education."[9] The same happened at other prisons, and a period in prison was to become almost a requisite for the top Vietnamese Communist leadership. Ho Chi Minh was exceptional only in that he served his prison time outside the country.

The Rise of Ho Chi Minh

The Nationalists suffered a grievous blow when 13 of their leaders were guillotined following the uprising at Yen Bay. One lesson drawn from this fiasco was the need for careful organization, analysis, planning, and guidance like that provided by the Comintern, and for an inspiring leader who could unify the different groups.

That leader was the man born a Nguyen but later known as Ho Chi Minh (1890–1969), who was almost 40 at the time he presided over the founding of the Vietnamese Communist Party in February 1930 (name changed to Indochinese Communist Party in October 1930). Ho (then known by another name) had left Vietnam in 1913 and first gained public attention by his unsuccessful attempt to petition the Versailles Peace Conference (1919) to grant Vietnam self-determination. His bitter disappointment in the treaty resembled that of the Chinese participants in the May Fourth Movement. As it did with some Chinese leaders, this failure induced him to seek more radical solutions and more effective means. In Paris he joined the French Socialist Party, and in 1920 he was a founding member of the French Communist Party. He then spent over a year in Moscow (June 1923 to November 1924), where he studied at the University of the Toilers of the East and participated in the Fifth Comintern Conference. After going to Canton in 1924, he spent the next six years primarily organizing revolutionary activities among Vietnamese expatriates in various parts of Asia. Imprisoned in Hong Kong in June 1931 at the request of the French, he managed to get released in December 1932 and to reach Moscow in the spring of 1934. In the fall of 1938 he was able to return and resume operations, first from China and finally from a base within Vietnam itself—but not before experiencing life in a Chinese prison. The dramatic story of Ho's revolutionary career, his voluminous writings (poetry as well as prose), his powers of persuasion, his devotion to the cause, his personal affability and good humor under trying circumstances, along with his skill at strategy and inclination to move gradually at home and abroad gave him a solid reputation. His stature was to be further enhanced by his conduct during and after World War II, ultimately securing his place in the eyes of many Vietnamese as the wise and benevolent father of the revolution. However, on the eve of the war, much of his work still lay ahead.

II. Korea under Japanese Colonial Rule

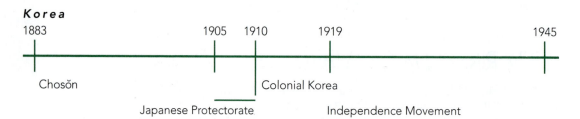

Setting the Stage for Conquest

The Japanese Takeover

Japanese Colonial Rule

The Independence Movement

The Origins of Korean Communism

The Nineteen-Thirties

World War II in Korea

Effects and Legacies of Japanese Rule

Korea's period as a colony, 1910 to 1945, was shorter than that of Vietnam, but is remembered with equal anger and regret. In both cases it began with the collusion of the traditional authorities. In Korea this occurred when Korea's own government signed the peninsula over to the Japanese in return for favored treatment and emoluments. This fact still disturbs Koreans today, just as Japan's treatment of the Korean people during the colonial era continues to cloud relations between the two countries.

Japan's reasons for taking Korea were not limited to national security. The Japanese believed their country was overpopulated, and the mainland of Asia was one obvious place to send people and seek resources for their continuing economic modernization. As they were taking Korea, certain Japanese planners had their eye on Manchuria to the north and even dreamed of moving into China and eventually creating a Japanese-led empire of "Asia for Asians." In this context, the annexation of Korea may be seen as one step in the process that culminated in the Pacific War.

Setting the Stage for Conquest

The Treaty of Shimonoseki that ended the Sino-Japanese War in 1895 defined Korea as a sovereign state and formally ended China's historic role as Korea's suzerain and protector. At the beginning of the war, Japanese stationed in Seoul had lost no time taking control of the Korean government. Working through the enlightenment faction (*kaehwa dang*) of young Koreans who saw Japan as a model for their own country's modernization, they had promulgated changes known as the Kabo Reforms. These had included dissolution of all traditional ties to China, a thorough restructuring of the Korean government as a constitutional monarchy, and a catalog of social reforms that outlawed slavery, ended the civil service examination system, abolished class distinctions, and alienated the ruling *yangban* establishment. Japanese forces virtually occupied the Kyŏngbok Palace throughout the war, warding off objections to the reforms. However, a backlash developed as members of the Queen's political faction persuaded the royal court to try to use Russian influence to check Japan. When this policy became evident following the Shimonoseki Treaty, the Japanese retaliated by sending assassins to murder Queen Min. The murder shattered politics in Seoul and sent King Kojong fleeing from the palace to live for over a year in the Russian legation as the guest of the Russian minister. This was the peak of Russian influence in Korea, from 1896 to 1898.

Though the excessive ambition of Japanese officials in Korea had backfired, Koreans could not agree on a program to bolster defenses and assure Korea's survival as an independent country. As soon as it appeared that Russia was in the ascendancy, other Western powers demanded and received economic concessions from King Kojong to let them profit from mining, electric power, railroad construction, and other modern investments. One response came from a group of Western-educated intellectuals who started an "Independence Club" and published Korea's first modern newspaper, arguing that trying to play foreigners off each other with concessions was a poor way to assure the country's independence. Rather, the leadership should resist foreign encroachment, build up its military defenses, and reform its institutions. The Independence Club advocated modern freedoms and used public rallies to generate support. This brought countermeasures from the Establishment. When squads of hired market "peddlers" used violence to break up one of the rallies, the club went into a steep decline. By the end of 1898 it was out of business.

The Japanese Takeover

When King Kojong left the Russian legation in 1897, he moved to a new palace facility that was located in close proximity to the Western legations. For several years he enlisted the help of the Western diplomatic community to counteract Japanese pressure. In 1897 he declared that Korea was now an "empire" (to be known as Taehan Cheguk, the "Great Han Empire"), and for the first time in Korean history declared himself an "emperor" with the right to offer sacrifices to Heaven, a prerogative theretofore reserved to the Emperor of China (see Figure 12.6). Meanwhile, more Koreans were discovering the outside world, as government emissaries, as students assigned to higher studies, and as laborers such as the ones hired to work in the cane fields of Hawaii.

However, in 1902 England and Japan concluded an alliance that essentially eliminated British objections to Japanese expansion in Korea. In 1904, Japan attacked the Russian naval squadron at Port Arthur on the Liaodong Peninsula, and opened the Russo-Japanese War. This conflict, which brought Russian and Japanese armies to Korea and eventually centered on battlefields in Manchuria, wore down both sides until, in May 1905, the Japanese were able to win a decisive naval engagement in which Russia's main battle fleet was sunk in the Tsushima Strait. Japan's victory in the Battle of Tsushima Strait led to a peace conference at which U.S. President Theodore Roosevelt brokered a treaty at his summer home in Portsmouth, New Hampshire.

The Portsmouth Treaty ended the Russo-Japanese War by dividing the region into spheres of influence. The Russians kept their railroad interests in northern Manchuria, and Japan gained the South Manchurian Railroad running from Harbin to Port Arthur/Dairen (today's Luda) as well as an exclusive sphere in Korea, where its "paramount interests" were recognized both by Russia and, in effect, by the United States, which had mediated the agreement. Russia thus

FIGURE 12.6 Hwanggung-u Pavilion (Temple of Heaven), site of the proclamation raising Korea to the status of empire. (Photograph c. 1925.)
Collection Donald N. Clark.

withdrew from Korea; and with England in a formal alliance with Japan and the United States recognizing the terms of the Portsmouth Treaty, there was no one to oppose Japanese forcible imposition of a protectorate on the Korean government in November 1905. Indeed, the Japanese waited until they had guaranteed American nonintervention through the Taft-Katsura Agreement of 1905, whereby the United States promised not to interfere in Korea in return for Japan's pledge to accept U.S. colonization of the Philippines.

From 1905 until 1910, Japan made Korea a "protectorate." This was a step short of outright colonization, since a protectorate technically retains its sovereignty. Japan took over Korea's foreign relations and disbanded its army, but the Korean government retained administrative charge of domestic matters for a while longer. Japan's annexation of Korea—that is, colonization—did not come until 1910.

The Korean people did not simply accept the events leading up to the Japanese protectorate. Prince Min Yŏnghwan (1861–1905), a member of the late queen's family, committed suicide in protest. Local leaders raised irregular militia units to resist the presence of Japanese in their area, calling themselves *ŭibyŏng* ("righteous troops") after the spontaneous local militia that had fought the Japanese invaders in the 1590s. Their violent resistance was augmented by angry Korean farmers who saw Japanese land developers conduct uninvited surveys with the intention of buying up their land and selling it to Japanese. Koreans founded voluntary associations and started newspapers in attempts to rally the populace for "self-strengthening." Korean educators started modern schools in hopes that studying modern subjects could prepare the younger generation to restore Korea and recover its independence. In 1907, as waves of despair swept Korea, many joined the recently legalized Christian church, associating themselves with Western religion and mission education in the same hope. Indeed, one reason for the growth of Christianity in Korea was its appeal as an alternative to Japanese ideas regarding reform and social transformation.

Korean resistance grew significantly in 1907 when Resident-General Itō Hirobumi ordered the disbanding of the royal Korean army. Many soldiers refused to lay down their arms, and joined the "righteous troops," bringing forth new waves of Japanese repression. King Kojong attempted a last-minute appeal to the world community protesting his country's complete loss of independence, but the appeal, which was aimed at diplomats meeting at The Hague in the Netherlands, was discovered and blocked by the Japanese. Japan then proceeded to extend its control over Korea, forcing the abdication of King Kojong and giving Resident-General Itō Hirobumi authority over Korea's Finance, Justice, and Home ministries. Itō's control of Korea's defenses, finances, courts, police forces, and internal administration now made him Korea's *de facto* ruler. There only needed to be an occasion to take Korea outright. The occasion came with An Chunggŭn's assassination of Itō on the platform of the railroad station in the Manchurian city of Harbin in 1909. The following year, after arranging pensions, payments, and honors for Korea's leading *yangban* noblemen, Japan annexed Korea on August 22, via a treaty that dissolved the Chosŏn monarchy as Korea's government and Korea itself as a nation. Korea acquired a new Japanese name, Chōsen, and the Japanese governor-general of Chōsen was its new ruler.

Japanese Colonial Rule

With their annexation to Japan as a colony, the Koreans lost more than the right to govern themselves: they lost the rights to assemble, to join groups that were interested in politics, to publish, and to speak freely. Many lost their lands through Japan's manipulation of a land survey that vested much good farmland in the hands of the colonial regime and of Japanese land development companies that were designed to transfer it to Japanese investors. They lost their right to participate in local affairs through the reorganization of all government affairs and the appointment of Japanese bureaucrats to administer the provinces, counties, townships, and villages. Their most significant part in the new colonial structure was as hired policemen who assisted in the control of their own people.

At the top of the Japanese colonial structure, the governor-general was a uniformed army general, Terauchi Masatake, appointed by the prime minister of Japan, but in fact a law unto himself in Korea. The governor-general was the colony's chief executive, chief justice, and its only legislator. He had personal command of the Chōsen Army, a military force headquartered in Seoul with units spread across the peninsula. He had personal command of the police, who were actually military police, or gendarmes (infamously known as the *kempeitai*). Under

朝鮮總督府（京城名所）
The Government General of Chosen, Keijo.

FIGURE 12.7 Government-General Building, Seoul, built in 1926 and demolished in 1996. Large enough to house a new bureaucracy, this site held the administrative ministries that Japan imposed on its Korean colony.
COLLECTION DONALD N. CLARK.

his direction, the colony acquired a bureaucracy divided into ministries that mirrored the structure of the home government in Tokyo, though it was a completely separate and autonomous structure (Figure 12.7). The colony financed itself through its own system of revenue collection in a separate currency denominated in yen, like that of Japan proper, but issued through the Bank of Chōsen.

Governor-General Terauchi moved to break all forms of Korean resistance as quickly as possible. After forbidding political activity, he went after groups and individuals who were potential rallying points, imprisoning writers, teachers, and religious leaders as examples, even when the charges against them were flimsy and obviously exaggerated. Then, the government-general promulgated many types of laws and regulations, requiring licenses for many kinds of enterprise. The imposition of standards for licenses to teach, practice medicine, or handle money was a way of standardizing procedure. However, the power to grant or withhold licenses was also a key tool of the colonial bureaucracy as it sought to punish and reward Koreans according to their degree of cooperation. As Mark R. Peattie has written:

> Korea now entered the dark epoch known to its chroniclers as the "period of military rule," a term that in English hardly conveys the crushing impact of the Japanese army and police on every aspect of Korean life.

"Regulations of every kind poured forth wildly and were as harshly enforced," noted a Japanese journalist in Korea at the time, adding that "so completely were the people's liberties restricted that the entire peninsula could be said to have been militarized"[10]

The land survey that was conducted between 1910 and 1918 mapped the peninsula and classified the land according to use and type (forest land, farm land, coastline, and so on) and required owners to produce proof of ownership. This presumably simple requirement trapped many squatters, tenant farmers, and sharecroppers—Korea's poorest peasants—into losing their livelihoods when they could not produce documents or failed to understand Japanese instructions. Better-prepared Koreans who were able to prove their titles, however, kept their land and, along with many newly arrived Japanese buyers, even increased their holdings, thus adding to the pattern of rural land concentration. The gap that had always existed between rural landlords and poor peasants was thus widened by colonial policy, helping set the stage for the violent left-right confrontations that followed the liberation of Korea in 1945.

Japan took charge of Korea's modern facilities as well, controlling transportation, communications, banking, and manufacturing. Japanese firms quickly came to dominate mining, construction, chemicals, and other modern industries. Japanese goods flooded the Korean retail market, driving many Koreans out of business. Only the biggest Korean companies, backed by large Korean fortunes concentrated in family holdings, were capable of surviving Japanese competition. Most needed to align themselves with the government-general and the Japanese market. In effect, they became part of the Japanese power structure in the colony.

In place of traditional Korea's highly informal educational system, which had consisted of tutors and small village academies that fostered literacy in classical Chinese and prepared students for the civil service examinations, the Japanese introduced a plan to deliver mass education at the elementary level. For this they needed teachers, and they encouraged middle schools and private academies to meet government standards for elementary teacher training. The plan was to produce "loyal and obedient" subjects of the Japanese emperor through primary schools (four years) and secondary schools (four years for boys, three for girls). However, the process of building and equipping schools and training teachers for a wholly new Korea-wide educational system took a very long time. By 1919 only 3.7 percent of Korea's school-age children were enrolled in government schools, while three times that number were still studying in village *sŏdang*. In 1929 the regime adopted a plan to establish an elementary school in every Korean *myŏn* (township) and one high school in each of the 13 provinces. By the end of the colonial period, however, only a small percentage of Korean children had ever been to a government school. Rather, the schools served mainly the children of Japanese residents in Korea by a ratio of two to one. Their language of instruction was Japanese, and their curriculum, especially in the 1930s as war approached, aimed at fostering respect for the emperor and Japan's national heroes.

The Independence Movement

The high point of Korean resistance to Japanese colonial rule came in 1919, when a coalition of religious leaders signed a declaration of independence and started a nationwide wave of protests that lasted for more than a year. The Korean independence movement, commonly known as the "Samil Movement" (because of the Korean pronunciation of "Three-One," indicating March First, the day of its outbreak), was influenced in partly by external events—the Russian Revolution, the Versailles Peace Conference, President Woodrow Wilson's Fourteen Points, and the May Fourth Movement in China—and partly by Korean students who had gone to Japan for higher studies and subsequently reflected on the plight of their home country. The independence movement surprised the government-general of Chōsen, which responded with great violence, using the *kempeitai*, the army, the police, and even firemen wielding pikes against the demonstrators. The movement, which was meant to be nonviolent, had its violent moments. Koreans attacked *kempeitai* units and Koreans in the colonial police force. Japanese forces even felt obliged to enter southeastern Manchuria in pursuit of Korean settlers who were attacking Japanese border stations. The Korean independence uprising did not end until late 1920, and only after costing the lives of numerous Japanese and thousands of Koreans.

Korea's independence movement embarrassed many Japanese. Although Koreans who wanted countries like the United States to condemn Japan were disappointed by the lack of interest or response abroad, the Tokyo government was sufficiently chastened to try a new approach in Chōsen. Instead of an army general ruling under "military rule," Korea got an admiral, Saitō Makoto (1919–1927), who ushered in a period of "cultural rule" with the goal of persuading Koreans to support the colonial program and accept Japanese direction. An important part of Admiral Saitō's program was to grant concessions that were highly symbolic but did not seriously undermine Japanese power. He allowed Koreans to start their own Korean-language newspapers and magazines. He granted a demand to establish a government university in Korea so Korean students could have access, at least in principle, to higher studies in their own country. Saitō relaxed many of the more obnoxious regulations and allowed Koreans to associate in a wide variety of civil society organizations. One of the most interesting of these was the Korean Products Promotion Society begun by Cho Mansik (1882–1950), following Gandhi's example in India, to persuade Koreans to buy only products made in Korea by Koreans. Another thread was the study of Korean history and culture, an outgrowth of the efforts at self-strengthening through education that had begun in the protectorate period. Research into the Korean language led to spelling standardization, the production of a national dictionary, and even the writing of modern novels in Korean.

Saitō even allowed the formation of a national organization to discuss politics—albeit under close surveillance. Koreans used this period to discuss how they should continue pushing for independence. Some argued that the Japanese were too strong to be defeated and would have to be accepted while Koreans tried to preserve their culture through studies of history and literature and by educating young Koreans to work toward liberation. Using language approximating ordinary speech, Yi Kwangsu (1892–1950?) published novels such as *Heartless* (1917), conveying national pride, and the poet Yi Sanghwa asked "Does Spring Come to Stolen Fields?" (see Box 12.1). Publication of such literature was itself a political act. A Korean organization called the Sin'ganhoe (New Korea Society, 1927–1931) brought together people from across the political spectrum. At one end were the "cultural nationalists," conservatives who wanted to preserve the culture of Korea without necessarily overthrowing the colonial regime or the social and economic relations permitted by the Japanese. At the other end were left-wing socialists and even a few revolutionaries, who advocated violence not only to overthrow the government-general but also to restructure Korean society and redistribute wealth.

Admiral Saitō's decade of "cultural rule" had moments of disturbance as Koreans showed that they had not accepted the essence of Japanese domination. Korea's last "emperor," the prince who had reigned symbolically from 1907 to 1910, died in 1926, and his funeral was an occasion for muted protest. In 1929 in Kwangju, fighting broke out between Korean and Japanese students over an incident in which a Japanese boy had molested a Korean girl at a train station; when the colonial police tried to break up the fights, the people rose up in rioting.

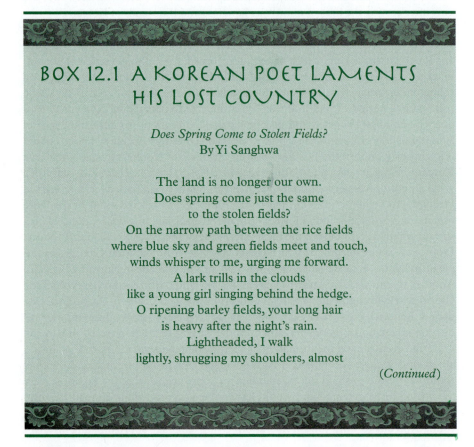

BOX 12.1 A KOREAN POET LAMENTS HIS LOST COUNTRY

Does Spring Come to Stolen Fields?
By Yi Sanghwa

The land is no longer our own.
Does spring come just the same
to the stolen fields?
On the narrow path between the rice fields
where blue sky and green fields meet and touch,
winds whisper to me, urging me forward.
A lark trills in the clouds
like a young girl singing behind the hedge.
O ripening barley fields, your long hair
is heavy after the night's rain.
Lightheaded, I walk
lightly, shrugging my shoulders, almost

(Continued)

BOX 12.1 A KOREAN POET LAMENTS HIS LOST COUNTRY (CONTINUED)

dancing to music the fields are humming—
the field where violets grow, the field
where once I watched a girl planting rice, her hair
blue-black and shining—

I want
a scythe in my hands, I want
to stamp on this soil, soft as a plump breast;
I want to be working the earth and streaming with sweat.

What am I looking for? Soul,
my blind soul, endlessly darting
like children at play by the river,
answer me: where am I going?
Filled with the odor of grass, compounded
of green laughter and green sorrow,
Limping along, I walk all day, as if possessed
by the spring devil:
for these are stolen fields, and our spring is stolen.

Peter H. Lee (ed.), *Modern Korean Literature: An Anthology* (Honolulu: University of Hawaii Press, 1990), p. 80.

The Origins of Korean Communism

The Korean Communist Party (better known as the Korean Labor Party, or Chosŏn Nodongdang) began as several factions in several places, first in 1918 among Koreans in Irkutsk, Siberia. In 1920 in Shanghai, the exile Yi Tonghwi (1872–1935) founded a Korean Communist Party based on an earlier socialist group. The two Korean communist organizations fought each other in a bloody confrontation in the town of Alekseyevsk, Siberia, in 1921; and though many Korean leftists were disgusted at their rivalry, the movement grew as an amalgam of elements committed to revolutionary change in their homeland. Korean students in Japan, such as the ones who had helped inspire the 1919 independence movement, were also attracted to left-wing ideas that pointed to armed struggle.

The idea that violence was necessary to preserve Korean identity offended the cultural nationalists in the Sin'ganhoe. Many of the cultural nationalists were beneficiaries of privileges under the colonial system as it existed: that is, Japanese education and Japanese-sanctioned family wealth. Additionally, while cultural nationalists controlled the Society's national leadership, leftists tended to lead the branch organizations across the country. These groups proposed going much further than liberating Korea from Japanese rule. They advocated a redistribution of wealth and privilege through a social revolution, as well. The two wings of the nationalist movement were therefore at odds, and it was no surprise when their short-lived attempt at cooperation collapsed with the end of the Sin'ganhoe in 1931. The two wings of Korean nationalism never again worked together.[11]

The united front of the Sin'ganhoe had afforded Korea's communists a certain shelter. Their isolation after 1931 forced them into a life-or-death confrontation with the Japanese authorities, who were anti-communist and who had embarked on a program of militarization and expansion on the continent after the Manchurian Incident of 1931. There was no place for toleration of communists in the Japanese plan, and the colonial government in Korea made a concerted effort to annihilate all factions of the Korean Communist Party. In order to survive, the Korean left wing had to go underground or leave the country. Some groups went into exile in China, first in Shanghai, and later when the Chinese Communist Party ended its Long March in Yan'an, with the CCP in Shaanxi Province. Others migrated to the Soviet Far East, seeking safety in the maritime province by living as ethnic Koreans in Russia. Still others attempted to carry on a guerrilla war in the mountains of the Korea-Manchuria border, raiding Japanese outposts and creating mayhem wherever possible. It was with this faction of Korean communists that future North Korean leader Kim Il-sung (1912–1994) made his reputation.

The Nineteen-Thirties

Japan itself abandoned democracy in the 1930s and chose militarism and war in an effort to expel Western imperialism and widen its control over an "Asia for Asians" (see Chapter 13). Korea was transformed into a staging area for this effort as Japanese armed forces invaded Manchuria in 1931 and north China in 1937. Korea's first sense of this situation came with the replacement of Admiral Saitō with a new ruler, army general Ugaki Kazushige (1868–1956), in 1931. Ugaki's economic task was to organize the infrastructure of Korea to supply the Japanese military in Manchuria and China. For example, he started developing the east coast of Korea as an integral part of the metropolitan Japanese economy. Ch'ŏngjin, on the northeast coast of the peninsula, was turned into a major port and railhead for transportation directly from the Sea of Japan (or "Eastern Sea" as it is known in Korea) to Jiandao, the area of southeastern Manchuria whose population is largely Korean, and onward to Mukden (Shenyang) and the Manchurian railroad network. A Japanese oil refinery was built at Wŏnsan, a chemical factory was built at Hamhŭng, and elaborate waterworks were built in the mountains and

FIGURE 12.8 Nandaimon-dōri (today's Namdaemun-no), a main square of colonial-era Seoul with key Japanese institutions (Bank of Chōsen on the left, main post office on the right). COLLECTION DONALD N. CLARK.

along the Yalu River to generate electrical power. Much Korean cropland was turned to cotton and wool production to help equip the military forces—and to reduce the threat of Korean competition for Japanese food growers. The result was a trend away from food production in Korea, which harmed the Koreans, and toward manufacturing, which supported Japanese military expansion.

In political terms, General Ugaki began the complete acculturation of the Korean people as Japanese citizens and subjects of the emperor. To this end, he launched propaganda campaigns, matching those already under way in Japan, telling people to regard Korea and Manchuria as historically one, to think of Japan and Korea as united in a single body, and to think of the self as a part of the great national entity, or *kokutai*. As good imperial subjects, Koreans were exhorted to speak only the "national language" (*kokugo*), which was Japanese. Korean schoolchildren were taken to Shinto shrines that had been built originally for Japanese residents on the peninsula and made to bow to the spirits of the nation's heroes, including Japanese soldiers who had died in the wars to subjugate Korea.

General Ugaki's successor was another army general, Minami Jirō (1874–1956), who carried the program much farther. While continuing Ugaki's economic program, he initiated outright repression of Koreans in a program that approached cultural genocide. It became a crime to speak Korean in school or to refuse to attend "patriotic" ceremonies at Shinto shrines. Studies of the Korean language were deemed subversive, and cultural nationalists who were devising standards for spelling words in *han'gŭl* were rounded up and imprisoned. Civil society groups, both secular and religious, were subjected to police surveillance and their leaders were arrested, interrogated for long hours, and often jailed to guarantee loyalty. Ultimately, all organizations in Korea were required to amalgamate into federations whose primary purpose was avowed to be support for the emperor and the war.

World War II in Korea

Mobilization laws in 1938 began labor drafts that shipped many Koreans to Japan against their will in order to do the dirtiest and most dangerous industrial work, such as coal mining. Even young women were drafted, into the infamous "comfort women" corps, and were transported to forward army units to serve as sex slaves for Japanese soldiers. As part of the mobilization, trusted Korean men were recruited for the first time to serve in the Japanese armed forces, a consequence of the increased manpower requirements of the full-scale invasion of China. As materials and commodities became scarce, Koreans experienced ever-stricter rationing of everything from food, fuel, and medicine to newsprint and building supplies. Destitute Koreans scratched for food on the desiccated mountainsides of "fire-lands" (*hwajŏn*) created by the most primitive slash-and-burn farming methods. The colonial government made the Koreans donate their pots, pans, and wedding rings in metal-collection drives, and their cash in special civilians' collections to pay for warplanes. Leather was so scarce that bankers and professors lined their shoes with fresh newspaper scraps each morning. During the war, speaking Korean was forbidden altogether, and Koreans were required to choose Japanese surnames for themselves, trading their hallowed ancestral Kims and Yuns for Japanese names like Kanemura and Yamaguchi. Under a strict news blackout, little news reached Korea apart from the glowing reports of victories generated by the national Domei News Agency. Near the end of the war, when B-29 contrails appeared in the air as American bombers headed for Manchuria, Koreans concluded that the war was ending in defeat for Japan. After the Cairo conference in December 1943, there were also reports of an Allied agreement to liberate Korea. Nevertheless, the collapse of Japan came as a surprise to most Koreans. It was particularly shocking for Koreans who had cast their lot with the Japanese when they realized that there was likely to be a reckoning between those who had suffered most under Japan and those who had found ways to get along and even to prosper.

Effects and Legacies of Japanese Rule

Economic Misdevelopment. Koreans, like Vietnamese, take offense at assertions by their former colonizers that they should be grateful at least for the physical improvements that were made in their country by the colonial government. When

BOX 12.2 "BECOMING JAPANESE"

Starting in 1937, the colonial administration launched an effort to transform Koreans, Taiwanese, and other colonized peoples into imperial subjects through the ideological policies of assimilation. Laws requiring Koreans and Taiwanese to speak Japanese, to worship at Shinto shrines, and to adopt Japanese names were an important part of this effort. For the colonized, compliance was more a matter of survival than conviction.

Yi Okpun (b. 1914), a housewife from Seoul, later recalled how she was forced to bow at Shinto Shrines:

> Of course we had to go up to the shrine on Namsan (South Mountain). The head of our neighborhood group was Japanese; that's why we had to do everything he said. If we didn't go, we didn't get any food ration.
>
> We didn't go alone. A whole group went—out whole neighborhood cell, about ten households, you know. Even with my babies, I had to take the streetcar, then walk all the way up the hill. It was hard.
>
> We had to go up a lot, sometimes once a week, certainly two or three times a month. The ceremony took about, let's see, thirty minutes. They pour some water, you clap your hands, then you come down and get the food ration stamps.
>
> Later when we changed our name, I just followed whatever my husband said. I didn't care. Just get the food ration card!

Kim Wŏn'gŭk (b. 1918), who grew up in what is today North Korea, recalled how his clan made the decision to adopt Japanese style names:

> My clan had several meetings with lots of debate about whether to go along with the name change. Some were dead set against it, but finally after several meetings, they gave in.
>
> I attended some of the meetings just to listen—I was too young to speak up. Those in favor said that without a Japanese name you could not do business with the Japanese, could not get jobs, could not send your children to school—in fact, could not do much at all. They said it was only a formality, our hearts were still Kim and we would always remain Kim. So we should just go along.

(Continued)

BOX 12.2 "BECOMING JAPANESE" (CONTINUED)

The patriarch of our local clan, an elder who commanded respect, at the third meeting, gave his opinion, which counted heavily. He said we should not draw undue attention to ourselves. Not stir up trouble. So the factions gave in and went along with the patriarch.

At last in our region, those who did not change their name to Japanese were the first targets of the draft to the factories.

Kang, Hildi. *Under the Black Umbrella: Voices from Colonial Korea*. Ithaca: Cornell University Press, 2001), pp. 113, 119.

Japanese cite the hydroelectric dams, ports, railroads, highways, schools, mines, factories, and myriad buildings that were left behind for Koreans to use when Japan was forced to withdraw from the peninsula, Koreans argue that none of these things were constructed for their benefit. No doubt the Koreans did use much that the Japanese left behind after 1945. But the Koreans are correct in noting that Japan rather misdeveloped Korea—for example, creating a chemical industry that was geared to munitions, a banking system that was aimed at providing for Japanese investors, and a land system that favored big landowners and destroyed small farms.

Fear and Coercion.   As in Vietnam, coercion was a basic feature of colonial rule in Korea. The Japanese would have preferred to see Koreans voluntarily accept their control and guidance, but it was enough merely to make them obey. Attempts to convert the Koreans and turn them into loyal subjects of the Japanese emperor were a dismal failure. Admiral Saitō failed to co-opt them with his "cultural policy" in the 1920s, and General Minami was only able to win sullen acquiescence at gunpoint in the late 1930s. Fear was an essential element of Japanese rule in Korea, and Koreans were kept in a constant state of worry that the colonial police would target them or their family members. The arbitrariness of Japanese arrests was proof that the colonial authorities would not hesitate to punish some Koreans to intimidate the rest.

Social and Psychological Disruption.   As was the case in all colonies, Japanese rule was highly disruptive to Koreans, socially and psychologically. As the shapers of modern life for Korea, Japan introduced modern methods of government, education, industry, and mass communication. Koreans thus were given a taste of modern systems and a desire to participate in them. However, while they were exposed to new structures and opportunities, Koreans were by and large confined to lower levels within those structures. The Japanese began a system of mass education, for example, but only at the elementary level. A Korean student had to go to Japan and "become Japanese" if he or she wanted training beyond middle school. The more Korean identity a person retained, the less likely he or she was to advance into positions of responsibility—or more rarely still, of authority. This was logical from a Japanese point of view, but it was deeply troubling to Koreans.

Instilling the Idea of Japanese Superiority. As a rule, no colonial system accepted the colonized people as equals of the colonizers. The Japanese in Korea regarded themselves as innately superior to the Koreans, and they made much of their own efforts to "civilize" and "improve" the Koreans, who it was said, were incapable of governing themselves. One of the tragedies of colonialism is that many of the colonized accept this premise and learn to regard themselves as inferior. Many Koreans became conditioned to admiring the Japanese, their manifest sense of purpose, and their political, military, and economic skills. Koreans learned to do many modern things from their Japanese rulers. The postwar years offer many examples of Koreans continuing to do things the Japanese way, from school uniforms to popular music to police and army methods. South Korea's late twentieth-century economic prosperity was patterned on Japanese models, and the famous Korean conglomerates such as Hyundai and Samsung are called *chaebŏl*, the Korean version of the Japanese term *zaibatsu*.

The Bitter Fruits of Collaboration. These accumulated social, economic, and institutional distortions were part of the legacy of colonial rule that Japan left behind in Korea after being defeated in 1945. Korean politics exploded as Koreans accused one another of collaboration and betrayal, particularly during the war years when the Japanese had pushed hard to get Koreans to support the war effort in public. Koreans who had served in the Japanese colonial bureaucracy and police organizations were condemned as national traitors. Intellectuals who had supported Japan in public statements were condemned, even though some of them, like Ch'oe Namsŏn (1890–1957), the primary author of the 1919 Independence Declaration, and Yi Kwangsu, the country's leading novelist, had towering reputations as cultural nationalists. Wealthy businessmen and landowners stood accused of supporting the Japanese in order to save their fortunes. Christians fought one another over the fact that some had bowed to government pressure and worshipped at Shinto shrines while others had refused and gone to jail. The collaboration issue was also central to the separation of North and South Korea under left and right political factions after the war. In the north, the Soviet-backed leftist regime of Kim Il-sung sought out collaborators of every type and identified them as enemies of the people, in some cases divesting them of the assets that they had managed to maintain through the colonial period. North Korea got considerable propaganda value out of the fact that collaborators were relatively safe in the south, even protected under the U.S. military occupation and later, under the Republic of Korea, as we shall see in Chapter 14.

III. Taiwan

Taiwan

1883   1895   1945

| Under Qing Rule | Colonial Taiwan |

When Japan acquired Taiwan as its first colony in 1895, it did so with many of the same objectives that subsequently prompted it to seize Korea, and the Japanese implemented many of the same policies in both colonies. Consequently, the inhabitants of the island shared many of the experiences of their fellow colonials, but in the final analysis, the differences between Taiwan and Korea, then as now, loom at least as large as the similarities.

One difference was that in 1895 the people on Taiwan were given two years in which to decide between staying on as Japanese colonials or moving to the mainland as subjects of the Qing. The latter choice proved attractive to a good number of the local elite. This included men who had staked their future on the examination system, for by the time of the Japanese takeover, the "gentrification"[12] of what had once been a frontier elite was well advanced. It was to serve their needs that between 1860 and 1893, fourteen academies had been established on the island, which only in 1885 had been elevated to provincial status.

The departure of 6,400 people, about 2.3 percent of the population, no doubt removed some potential leaders of resistance, but as it was, the Japanese occupation began with five months of fighting. The Taiwanese, however, lacked coordination. The "Republic of Taiwan," declared by the last Qing governor, lasted only 12 days. Until 1902 the Japanese faced occasional scattered attacks. Even after Japanese authority had been firmly established over the Han (ethnic Chinese) population (2,890,455 according to the 1905 census), armed clashes continued with Taiwan's original inhabitants (estimated at 122,000 in 1909), who occupied the central highlands and continued to lose ground as they had under the Qing. It was their misfortune that their forest contained camphor trees. Camphor, turned into a government monopoly by Japan, was a prime export, in great demand for use in the manufacture of smokeless gunpowder.

Camphor, as well as hemp, also figured in Taiwanese outrage at Japanese assertion of authority over forests, a policy that provoked armed resistance even before the Ta-pa-ni uprising (1915), which lasted a month and is estimated to have cost 1,000 lives. Less anticolonial resistance occurred in Taiwan than in Korea or Vietnam, but there was resistance nevertheless.

As in Korea, the governor-general of Taiwan was the supreme administrative and judicial authority. Until 1919 he was a military man, but from 1898 to 1906 civil administration was in the hands of Gotō Shimpei (1857–1929), a medical man responsible for much of the basic framework of the Japanese colonial system.

A major objective, accomplished by 1905, was for Taiwan to pay for itself despite continuing heavy government expenditures. To rationalize their administration, the Japanese conducted a land survey and a census. As later in Korea, the colonial authorities relied heavily on the police for a wide range of services, including tax collection, agricultural, hygiene, water supply and sanitation services. However, in Taiwan, unlike Korea, the Japanese controlled these matters by cleverly adapting an old Chinese system of mutual responsibility (*baojia*), under which the population was organized into groups of (theoretically) 100 households, each composed of units of 10. In contrast to the ineffectiveness of this system on the mainland, in Taiwan the *hokō* system (pronouncing the term the Japanese way) became the instrument by which the state reached down into the villages to affect each individual, something beyond the ability of all Chinese mainland governments prior to 1949. However, only the Han population was organized in this manner.

The *hokō*, along with earlier guard units composed of Han settlers and acculturated aborigines, supplied the manpower for a local militia who acted as police auxiliaries. They not only provided security and surveillance, but undertook road repair and even railroad maintenance, as well as contributing to various rural campaigns. They also constituted a heavy burden on the population, who in addition to the regular taxes, were saddled with *hokō* dues and had to supply labor when needed. Though nominally the *hokō* leaders were elected by the households, the system was controlled by the police, which came to include 20 to 30 percent Taiwanese, but remained firmly under Japanese command.

As in Korea, the Japanese developed the Taiwan economy, but did so to meet their own needs and serve their own purposes. A central bank (The Bank of Taiwan, 1899) issued currency and sought to manage the economy. By the time Japan acquired Taiwan, it was an exporter of tea and sugar as well as camphor, but the sugar industry was faltering. The Japanese changed that, turning Taiwan into a major producer of sugar, able to fulfill their domestic needs and thus saving foreign exchange that otherwise would have gone for sugar imports. Along with tea, the Japanese also fostered rice cultivation and initiated irrigation projects. They also developed the network of roads and railways and improved the harbors for ocean shipping. Modern postal and telegraph systems were established. Beginning with Gotō, they were also very active in public health. The death rate was reduced, and by 1945 the population had nearly doubled.

Consumer industries included food processing, logging and textiles—but not until Japan began preparing for total war did heavy industry get started. The completion of the Sun Moon Lake Electrical Generation Plant (1935) was a milestone. Aluminum, textiles, iron, cement, and chemical industries grew in what nevertheless remained an essentially agrarian economy.

As in Korea, there were local people of wealth and education who worked with the Japanese-dominated establishment. There was the ambivalence about education that we have already noted in Indochina and Korea. True, schools were established, but initially there were only lower-level and inferior schools for the Taiwanese, in contrast to the higher levels of education available to Japanese who settled in Taiwan. In 1928, an imperial university was established in Taipei, but it had three times as many Japanese students as it did Taiwanese. In 1945 there was only one Taiwanese professor on its faculty.

As shown by the establishment of the university, in Taiwan as in Korea, there was a relaxation of control in the 1920s followed by the severity of the 1930s. In the 1920s, Japanese liberals talked of eventual assimilation, and there was a temporary and limited loosening of the colonial reins, with greater tolerance for Taiwanese to express their own views at home as well as in Tokyo. In 1921, a Taiwanese intellectual even demanded the abolition of the *hokō* system. Although some changes were made, it was not abolished until two months before Japan surrendered in 1945. To follow Siomi Shunji's analysis, from 1895 to 1920 the police were the prime movers, but during the next quarter of a century they were a background force.[13]

Stimulated by developments in China and Japan, there was a quickening of intellectual life in Taiwan and among Taiwanese in Tokyo, with movements to forge a new and modern culture and to write in the vernacular about current concerns. The main character of the first novel written by Lai Ho (1894–1943), often considered the father of modern Taiwanese literature, was a Taiwanese vegetable seller whose small manual scale for weighing his sales was broken by Japanese policemen. A central issue facing Lai and a new generation of younger writers trying to forge a Taiwanese identity was that of language, as classical Chinese was rapidly becoming obsolete, and the new literary language that gained currency on the mainland after the May Fourth Movement was based on a vernacular incomprehensible to the people of Taiwan. Lai Ho himself was really most at home in classical Chinese, which he had to translate into the local vernacular.

One solution was to write in Japanese. From the start, the Japanese had encouraged people to learn Japanese, and by the 1930s there was a substantial audience for writers such as Wu Cho-liu (1900–1976), whose *An Orphan of Asia* expressed a sense that Taiwan had been abandoned by its Chinese parents and yet had never become a full-fledged member of its new Japanese household. The problem of defining Taiwan's place in the world was to persist long after the Japanese were gone.

As in Korea, during the 1930s, and especially during the war, there were campaigns to have Taiwanese adopt Japanese names and worship at Shinto shrines, but these did not make them into first-class subjects of the emperor. Taiwanese men did fight in the imperial army, and Taiwanese living on the China coast enjoyed status as Japanese subjects, forming an imperial vanguard much as Korean settlers did in Manchuria. However, many Taiwanese suffered under the heavy hand of Japanese rule. Like the people in Japan itself, they were totally surprised by the defeat of Japan. However, they welcomed reversion to Chinese rule, despite not having been consulted.

Notes

1. Ngo Vinh Long, *Before the Revolution: The Vietnamese Peasants Under the French* (New York, NY: Columbia Univ. Press, 1973), p. 14.

2. Andrew Hardy, "The Economics of French Rule in Indochina: A Biography of Paul Bernard (1892–1960)" *Modern Asian Studies,* vol. 32, no. 4 (10, 1998), p. 813.

3. Dao Duy Anh, as quoted in Neil Jamieson, *Understanding Vietnam* (Berkeley, CA: Univ. of California Press, 1993), pp. 91–92.

4. William Duiker, *The Communist Road to Power in Vietnam* (Boulder, CO: Westview, 1996), pp. 11–13.

5. Ngyuen Ngoc Bich, ed. and trans., *A Thousand Years of Vietnamese Poetry* (New York, NY: Alfred A. Knopf, 1975), pp. 82, 84–85.

6. Truong Buu Lam, *Colonialism Experienced: Vietnamese Writings on Colonialism 1900–1931* (Ann Arbor, MI: The Univ. of Michigan Press, 2000), p. 11.

7. Quoted in Jamieson, *Understanding Vietnam,* pp. 59–60.

8. Hue-Tam Ho Tai, *Radicalism and the Origins of the Vietnamese Revolution* (Cambridge, MA: Harvard Univ. Press, 1992), p. 146.

9. Peter Zinoman, *The Colonial Bastille: A History of Imprisonment in Vietnam, 1862–1940* (Berkeley, CA: Univ. of California Press, 2001), p. 218, quoting materials in the Centre des Archives d'Outre-Mer, Aix-en-Province, France.

10. Mark H. Peattie, "The Japanese Colonial Empire, 1895–1945," in Peter Duus, ed., *The Cambridge History of Japan,* vol. 6: *The Twentieth Century* (Cambridge, U.K.: Cambridge Univ. Press, 1988) p. 231.

11. This theme is developed in Pang Kie-chung and Michael Shin, eds., *Landlords, Peasants, and Intellectuals in Modern Korea* (Ithaca, NY: Cornell East Asia Series, 2006).

12. Robert Gardella in Murray A. Rubinstein, ed., *Taiwan: A New History* (Armonk, NY: M. E. Sharpe, 1999), p. 180.

13. Hui-yu Caroline Ts'ai, *One Kind of Control; The Hokō System in Taiwan Under Japanese Rule, 1895–1945* (PhD Dissertation, Columbia Univ., 1990), pp. 494–95, citing Shunji's essay as translated into Chinese by Chou Hsien-wen in *T'ai-wan yin-hang chi-kan,* comp. T'ai-wan Yinhang Ching-chi Yen-chiu-shih, vol. 5, no. 4 (Taipei, Taiwan: Bank of Taiwan, 1953), pp. 267–68.

East Asia: The Thirties and World War II

The fate of Nationalist China and Imperial Japan became fatally intertwined when Japan seized Manchuria in 1931, entering into what in Japan is now called "a dark valley." These were dark years in the rest of the world as well. In the wake of the Great Depression, people in many countries, desperate for vigorous action, accepted dictatorship of one kind or another as the most effective way of pulling through. While the Soviet Union (U.S.S.R.) claimed to be on the road to communist utopia, it was not only in Italy and Germany that there were people who viewed Fascism as the wave of the future. In Japan, militarists seized power from the political parties, and in China, too, the military gained in power and prestige.

During most of the 1930s, the Western Democracies were preoccupied with domestic problems, and the strongest, the United States, was committed to isolationism. International statesmanship was at a low ebb. The failure of the League of Nations to respond to Japanese aggression in Manchuria revealed the inability or unwillingness of any government to do more than pay lip service to the principles of collective security.

The Manchurian Incident and Its Consequences

The Japanese government derived its legitimacy from the emperor, but the ruling political parties confronted charges that they were betraying their sacred trust. In the name of the emperor, the enemies of constitutional government criticized the political manipulations of the Diet leaders, their ties to business, and their policies of accommodating the West and conciliating China, exemplified by the Washington Conference of 1921–1922. Such sentiments animated the members of various patriotic organizations and prevailed in the army, which was chafing from the cuts made in its budgets and restrictions imposed by civilian administrations. Military leaders' dissatisfaction with the political ethos and government policies fused with their sense of being responsible only to the emperor. There were calls for a "Showa Restoration," and discussion about the emperor's divinity as the embodiment of the national polity (*kokutai*), a term that became an "incantatory symbol,"[1] its vagueness making it even more powerful.

Among the most vehement critics of party government were radical egalitarians like Kita Ikki, who favored nationalizing industry, and radical agrarians like Gondō Seikyo (1868–1937), who would have abolished industry altogether and returned Japan to rural simplicity. Although their visions of the future differed, they agreed on two things: that the existing government obtruded on the imperial will and must be swept away, and that Japan had a divine mission overseas. Such ideas formed the agenda for small societies of extremists given to direct action, such as the Cherry Society, which planned an unsuccessful military coup in Tokyo in March 1931. The membership of this society consisted entirely of army officers, none higher in rank than lieutenant colonel.

The assassination of the Manchurian warlord Zhang Zuolin in 1928 was the work of men such as these. They hoped that Zhang's murder would trigger a war in which Japan would conquer this vast, strategic, and potentially wealthy area. This did not happen, but another attempt to start a war appealed to the superpatriots, not only because Japan might gain Manchuria but also because the war would strengthen their support in the army, increase the army's power and popularity at home, and undermine the party government and the "weak" foreign policy they so detested.

Emphasis on Manchuria was also consistent with the thoughts of more analytical army men, like Ishiwara Kanji (Ishihara Kanji, 1886–1949), who developed the plan of attack. He and other students of World War I wanted Japan to control the economic resources of Manchuria as a step toward attaining the economic independence required for waging total war. Many officers, concerned with the possibility of war with the Soviet Union, were also mindful of Manchuria's strategic value.

In the fall of 1931 the time seemed ripe, for China was hampered by floods in the Yangzi Valley and the Western powers were neutralized by the Depression. Ishiwara and other officers serving with the Japanese Army on the Liaodong Peninsula masterminded the seizure of Manchuria. These officers, none higher than colonel, fabricated a Chinese attempt to sabotage the South Manchuria Railway Company as an excuse for hostilities, and then ensured that the fighting continued until the army controlled Manchuria. Although certain high army officials in Tokyo probably knew of the plot, it was performed without the knowledge, let alone the authorization, of the civilian government in Tokyo, which once informed, tried to halt the operations but found itself powerless to do so. An attempted military coup in Tokyo in October did not immediately topple the government, but it did succeed in intimidating civilian political leaders. The Wakatsuki government, divided and helpless, resigned in December. A Seiyūkai government under Inukai Ki (Inukai Tsuyoshi, 1855–1932) followed, and for another half year it tried to maintain a semblance of party control.

Events moved swiftly on the continent and at home. In Manchuria, the army consolidated its hold and established a puppet state, which early in 1932 declared its independence from China. Manchukuo, as it was known, was placed under the titular rule of Puyi who, as an infant, had been the last emperor of China—but it was actually controlled by the army. Meanwhile, the fighting had spread to China proper; for six strenuous weeks, Japanese and Chinese fought around Shanghai until a truce was arranged. However, the Chinese rebuffed Japan's efforts for a settlement recognizing Manchukuo. The League of Nations condemned Japan, and Japan subsequently withdrew from the organization in March 1933. The failure of the League to do anything more than talk was certainly noted by Mussolini and Hitler.

After Japanese troops crossed the Great Wall in the spring of 1933, a truce was concluded in May of that year that left Japanese troops in control of the area north of the Wall and provided for a demilitarized zone whose boundaries were marked by the railway line running between Beijing, Tianjin, and Tanggu. The Japanese were able to establish a puppet regime in that area, and they exerted continuous pressure on North China. In December 1935, Japanese army officers failed in their plans to engineer a North Chinese puppet regime, and full-scale war broke out in the summer of 1937. Meanwhile, in Manchuria, and now also in Korea, the Japanese concentrated on the development of heavy industry, building up an industrial base on the continent under army control.

Japanese Politics and the Road to War

At home, too, 1932 was an eventful year, as members of the patriotic societies continued to further their cause by assassinating prominent men, including the head of the Mitsui *zaibatsu*. On May 15, they raided the Tokyo power station, a bank, Seiyūkai headquarters, and the official residence of the prime minister. They assassinated Inukai in his home.

When the men responsible for the May 15 violence were brought to trial, they were treated with great respect. They were allowed to expound their doctrines for days at a time, and were effectively given a national podium from which to proclaim the selflessness of their patriotic motives. Consequently, they largely succeeded in portraying themselves as martyrs. The light sentences meted out at the conclusion of the lengthy trials further discouraged those who hoped for a return to civilian rule. Instead, power shifted away from the political parties and into the hands of civilian bureaucrats and, especially, the military. In 1936, the leftist Social Mass Party managed to win half a million votes. The following year that party's total climbed to 900,000 votes, and it captured 37 seats in the lower house of the Diet. In that same election the Seiyūkai and Minseitō together polled some 7 million votes, giving them 354 out of a total of 466 seats. But their showing in the polls was to little avail. The parties were too weak to control the military. Those who wished to preserve constitutional government chose to compromise with the military establishment in the hope of averting a complete overthrow of the existing order.

Saionji, the last of the *genrō*, hoped to protect the throne from involvement in politics and therefore attempted to achieve political stabilization through a national unity government, in which every power center was represented. However, this had only partial and temporary success. The next two cabinets, in office from May 1932 to March 1936, did include party men, but were headed by admirals, who were considered more moderate than potential prime ministers from the army.

The divisions within each of the power centers made for continued instability. Within the bureaucracy, there was rivalry between ministries, as well as disagreement between conservative officials and technocrats who envisioned radical restructuring of state and society.

The military, too, was divided. The army and navy frequently clashed, and breakdowns in discipline during the actions in Manchuria reflected disunity in the army itself. The lines of army factionalism were complex: For example, there was a division between Central War College alumni and those who had attended officers' training school. However, two main groups stood out. The more extreme faction, led by Generals Araki Sadao (1877–1966) and Mazaki Jinzaburō (1876–1956), was known as the Kōdōha, or "Imperial Way Faction," because it emphasized the imperial mystique and advocated an ill-defined doctrine of direct imperial rule. Like the radical civilian theorists of the right, it opposed existing political and economic institutions, and sought a moral and spiritual transformation that would assure a glorious future for both army and country. In contrast, the Tōseiha, or "Control Faction," led by General Nagata Tetsuzan (1884–1935), the leading proponent of total war, and including Ishiwara and Tōjō Hideki, gave priority to the buildup of the economy and the transformation of Japan into a modern military state.

For a few years the advantage lay with the Imperial Way Faction, but it suffered a setback in 1935 when General Mazaki was dismissed from his post as director-general of military education. A lieutenant-colonel retaliated by assassinating General Nagata. The Control Faction responded by arresting the officer and planning the transfer of other firebrands to Manchuria. The lieutenant-colonel's trial was still in progress when, on February 26, 1936, a group of junior Kōdōha officers, commanding over 1,000 men, seized the center of the capital and killed a number of prominent leaders, although some of their intended victims, including Prime Minister Admiral Okada Keisuke (1868–1952), managed to elude them. The young officers hoped that their action would topple the old system and that Generals Araki and Mazaki would take the lead in restructuring the state, but these senior generals remained aloof. As in 1928, the emperor intervened, and the navy responded to the crisis with vigor. On the third day of the insurrection, the rebels surrendered. This time the leaders were tried rapidly and in secret. One of those who perished at the hands of a firing squad was Kita Ikki, who had not participated in the mutiny but was too closely associated with the young officers and their movement to escape punishment.

The elimination of the Imperial Way Faction actually increased the army's political power because it could now threaten a second mutiny if it did not get its way. The army still had to consider the wishes of other components of the power elite, but it was able to secure a substantial increase in military spending. Japan now withdrew from the naval limitation agreement, opening the possibility that it might have to confront the combined might of the Western powers and the U.S.S.R. The army's strategic planners thought primarily in terms of a war with the latter, thus providing a strong inducement for Japan to sign an anti-Comintern Pact with Hitler's Germany in December 1936.

Domestically, there ensued an intensification of propaganda and indoctrination, coupled with a continuation of repression directed at the radical left and those whose ardor for emperor and national polity (*kokutai*) was deemed insufficient. The most notorious case occurred in 1935, when Minobe Tatsukichi, the distinguished legal theorist, was charged with demeaning the emperor by considering him merely "the highest organ of the state." Minobe defended himself with spirit, but was forced to resign from the House of Peers. In 1936, while living in seclusion, the old man suffered an attempted assassination that left him wounded. By that time, his books had been banned. Censorship became more severe, and expressions of intense national chauvinism filled the media.

The abandonment of the gold standard and the military buildup stimulated the economy and enabled Japan to recover from the depth of the depression, but agriculture remained depressed, and small firms benefited much less than did the *zaibatsu*.

China: The Nanjing Decade— An Uneasy Peace

From 1927 to 1937, the Nationalist government in Nanjing avoided war with Japan, but these were hardly peaceful years. Even after the completion of the Northern Expedition in 1928, the government actually controlled only the lower Yangzi Valley. Elsewhere it was dependent on the unreliable allegiance of local warlords. In 1930, the government secured its authority in the North after waging a costly campaign with heavy casualties against the combined armies of two warlords. Nanjing was strengthened by this victory, but lacked the power to subdue once and for all the remaining warlords. Some warlords could still claim that they stood for national goals. This reinforced the Nationalists' desire and tendency to give highest priority to building military strength, even before Japan's seizure of Manchuria and the threat of further Japanese aggression made such a policy imperative.

At home, the Nanjing regime had to deal with warlords and the Communists. The government's policy toward the warlords was to temporize, try to prevent the formation of antigovernment warlord coalitions, and to settle for expressions of allegiance until it could establish central control. Its power and prestige were increased when it defeated a rebellion in Fujian in 1933–1934, and especially after it obtained control over Guangdong and the submission of Guangxi in 1936. Its campaigns against the Communists provided occasions for the dispatch of central government troops into warlord provinces, especially after the Communists began their Long March in 1934, and similarly the Japanese threat proved useful in eventually bringing certain warlords into line. Thus the trend favored Nanjing, but the actual balance between central and local power varied widely in different parts of China. The tenacity of the warlord phenomenon in certain regions is illustrated by Sichuan, in parts of which warlords remained powerful even after the Nationalists moved their wartime capital to that province. Similarly, Xinjiang, in the far west, remained virtually autonomous.

The Nanjing Decade—Domestic Policies

The regime's military emphasis was reflected in government spending, with 60 to 80 percent of the annual outlay going to military expenses and debt service. The latter amounted to about a third, reflecting heavy government borrowing, but military considerations were also paramount in such civil projects as road and railway construction. Taking the place of the ousted Russian military advisors were a series of German military men, who tried to introduce German military doctrines (including concepts of military organization not necessarily suitable to the Chinese situation) and helped arrange for the import of German arms and munitions. In 1935, at the height of their influence, there were 70 German advisors in China, but their number decreased after Germany and Japan signed the anti-Comintern pact in December 1936. The last were recalled in 1938. Noteworthy within the army were the graduates of the Whampoa Military Academy, particularly those who completed the course during Chiang Kai-shek's tenure as director, because they enjoyed an especially close relationship with their supreme commander.

It was Whampoa graduates who, during 1931, formed the Blue Shirts, a secret police group pledging complete obedience to Chiang Kai-shek. They and the so-called CC Clique (led by two Chen brothers trusted by Chiang) were influenced in ideology and organization by European fascism. The Blue Shirts were greatly feared because of their spying and terrorist activities, including assassinations.

The CC Clique, too, had considerable power, but failed in its prime aim, which was to revitalize the Guomindang. After the split with the Communists in 1927, the Guomindang purged many of its own most dedicated revolutionaries. One result was that young activists, often from the same modern schools that had earlier supplied recruits for the Guomindang, were drawn to the Communist party. Another result was the creation within the ruling party of an atmosphere attractive to careerists who, concentrating on their own personal advancement, were disinclined to rock the boat. Meanwhile, Chiang ensured that the party remained just one of several centers of power.

The deterioration of the party was a particularly serious matter, because the Nanjing government suffered from factional politics and favoritism as well as from bureaucratic overorganization, which spawned departments with overlapping functions and countless committees grinding out lengthy reports and recommendations, detailing programs that consumed vast quantities of paper but were rarely implemented. Coordination was poor. It sometimes happened, for example, that government censors suppressed news items deliberately issued by the government itself. The conduct of official business lumbered along unless quickened by the personal intervention of Chiang Kai-shek, whose power was steadily increasing. His power was based on the loyalty of the military, the Blue Shirts, and core partisans such as the CC Clique, the financial backing of bankers and businessmen (including the relatives of Chiang's wife), and on Chiang's manipulation of various political cliques and factions. The Soong family deserves special mention, for it included not only Sun Yat-sen's widow, who was politically inactive during the 1930s, but also the decidedly active wife of Chiang Kai-shek, another sister who married the notoriously corrupt H. H. Kung, and T. V. Soong, a brother who was a reformist finance minister. Chiang was indispensable, but lacked the charisma to inspire his officials, who feared rather than loved him. Nor did he have the gift of eloquence with which to rouse the people had he so desired. Negative sanctions, such as the executions sporadically ordered by Chiang when an exceptionally flagrant case of corruption was brought to his attention, were not enough: the regime lacked drive and direction.

The regime was also weak ideologically. Sun Yat-sen became the object of an official cult, but his ideas were not further refined or developed. Nor was political tutelage enacted. Instead, emphasis shifted toward a revival of Confucianism. In contrast to Sun's admiration for the Taipings, Chiang sought to emulate Zeng Guofan, who had crushed the Taipings by revitalizing Confucian values. Chiang's regard for Confucius and Zeng was already apparent during his days at Whampoa, but became even more obvious in 1934 when he launched an extensive program to foster traditional values, known as the New Life Movement. He exhorted the populace to observe four vaguely defined Confucian virtues and spelled out the criteria for proper behavior in detailed instructions. The people were to sit and stand straight, eat quietly, refrain from indiscriminate spitting, and so forth, in the hope that they would thus acquire discipline. It did not work. Officials and commoners continued to act much as before. The government never did devise an ideology able to arouse the enthusiasm of its own personnel, command the respect of the people, or convince intellectuals. Censorship clearly was not the answer, although even foreign correspondents were subjected to it, some complaining that China was worse than Japan.

Local government under the Nationalists was equally ineffective. They restructured county governments and established four bureaus charged with education, construction, public security, and finance. They even attempted to reach beneath that level by assigning officials to the wards into which they divided the counties, but they failed to wrest control over taxes and local security from the entrenched local elite, who in practice, continued to wield power. Like its predecessors, the Nanjing regime failed to mobilize the financial or human resources of the village. With income from land taxes remaining in the provinces, government finances came primarily from the modern sector.

Despite early links with the business community, the Guomindang tended to treat business as an exploitable source for revenue rather than as an asset to be fostered for national strength. During 1928 and 1929, China finally regained the tariff autonomy lost in the Opium War, but this barely helped China's industries because exports were subjected to the same tariffs as imports, and imported raw materials were taxed as heavily as were finished goods. In 1933, heavily in debt to the banks, the government took control of the banking system in a move that benefited the treasury but not the private sector. Overall, the modern sector grew during the first 10 years of Nationalist rule, but only at roughly the same pace as during the years between the fall of the Qing and the establishment of the regime in Nanjing.

During the early 1930s, the traditional agrarian sector of the economy, which accounted for most of China's production and employed the vast majority of its people, was afflicted by severe weather conditions, numerous additional surtaxes (later changed to special assessments), and the decline in commodity prices brought on by the Great Depression. Climate, as well as taxation and exposure to international markets varied widely, making generalization very risky. Even in provinces like Jiangsu and Zhejiang, firmly controlled by the government, taxes paid by one district often far exceeded those paid by another. When the international price of silk collapsed, peasants dependent on sericulture, such as those of Wuxi County in Jiangsu, were badly hurt. Parts of the north were no better off.

Statistics for parts of northern China indicate that by 1934–1935 nearly half of the peasant households were farming less than 10 mu (1 mu = .167 acres), when 15 were needed for subsistence, reflecting a deepening agrarian crisis. Everywhere, since the government did nothing to change the status quo in the villages or on the land, the poorest and the weakest suffered most. Like so much legislation promulgated during those years, a law passed in 1930 limiting rents to 37.5 percent of the harvest was not enforced. Payments of 50 percent were common and 60 percent was not unusual. Programs for developing cooperatives and fostering rural reconstruction were organized, but their benefits rarely filtered down to the rural poor. In 1937 there was a price recovery and harvests were good, but by that time millions had suffered bitter poverty and despair.

Chiang Kai-shek and his supporters wanted to unify the country and stabilize society. They wished to consolidate the revolution that had brought them into power, not expand it. Consequently, they put a premium on suppressing forces pushing for continued revolution, and were intent on destroying the Communists, who maintained that the revolution was unfinished and proclaimed their determination to lead it to completion. To Chiang Kai-shek nothing was more urgent than the elimination, once and for all, of his old enemies. For the CCP, too, these were crucial years.

The Chinese Communists, 1927–1934

The Shanghai massacre and the subsequent suppression of the CCP and its associated labor movement effectively eliminated the party as an urban force, altered its geographical distribution, and profoundly affected its strategy and leadership. For years it remained unclear what direction it would take. Neither the Comintern in Moscow nor its Chinese followers were willing simply to ignore the cities. Urban insurrection was tried but failed. The Canton Commune (December 1927) met with profound popular apathy and lasted only four days. The use of armed force to capture cities such as Changsha in Hunan in 1930 also failed. Although no one was ready to say so, at least in public, Moscow clearly did not have the formula for success. Meanwhile, in China, various groups and factions contended for power and the adoption of their policies.

One of these groups was the CCP military force, reorganized in the mountains on the Hunan-Jiangxi border, where in the spring of 1928, Zhu De (1886–1976) joined Mao Zedong, who had arrived the previous fall. In command of some 2,000 troops, the two men laid the groundwork for the Red Army, with Zhu in military command and Mao in charge of political organization and indoctrination. As Mao was to say in 1938, "Political power grows out of the barrel of a gun. Our principle is that the party commands the gun; the gun shall never be allowed to command the party."[2] Through indoctrination, the recruitment of soldiers into the party, and the formation of soldiers' committees, Mao secured the control of the party over the army. On the military side, Zhu and Mao emphasized guerrilla warfare, which puts a premium on mobility and surprise, rapid retreats to avoid battle with superior enemy forces, lightning strikes to pick off small contingents of the enemy, and constant harassment to keep the enemy off balance. Essential to this type of warfare is popular support to provide intelligence, supplies, and recruits, as well as cover for guerrillas under enemy pursuit. Peasant participation and support were secured by redistributing land and furthering the revolution in the countryside.

This strategy focused on the development and expansion of rural CCP-controlled bases. In the early 1930s there were a number of such areas, with the largest in Jiangxi, where the founding of the Chinese Soviet Republic was proclaimed in December 1931. The basic agrarian policy was "land to the tiller," involving the confiscation of large holdings for reassignment to the poor, with "middle peasants" left largely unaffected. However, there was a good deal of disagreement over definitions, as well as wide variations in the degree of local implementation of the program. In Jiangxi, Mao and Zhu were strong, but they had not won complete acceptance of either their program or their leadership, even after party headquarters were moved from Shanghai to Jiangxi in recognition of the new CCP power center; a defeat for those oriented toward the Comintern in Moscow. Factionalism continued to threaten party unity, but the most severe challenge was external.

Chiang Kai-shek's first three "annihilation campaigns" (1930–1931) helped strengthen rather than weaken the CCP, as the Red Army employed its tactics to good effect, capturing weapons, men, and land. The fourth campaign (1932–1933) again ended in defeat for the Nationalists. In the fifth campaign, begun late in 1933, Chiang, on German advice, changed his strategy. Deploying some 750,000 men supported by 150 airplanes, he surrounded the Jiangxi Soviet and gradually tightened the circle of his blockade. When, in the fall of 1934, their situation became untenable, the Communist forces abandoned their base, broke through a point in the blockade manned by former warlord armies, and began their Long March (Figure 13.1).

The Long March

When the Communists left Jiangxi, their first priority was survival and their destination unclear. That was settled in January 1935 in an important conference held at Zunyi in Guizhou, where it was decided to proceed to Shaanxi, where a small soviet was already in place. In Shaanxi the CCP would be out of easy reach of Guomindang armies. They would be able to act on their declaration of war against Japan, and they might even hope for some aid from the U.S.S.R. At Zunyi, Mao gained a new prominence, although he did not actually control the party until the 1940s.

The march itself was a heroic vindication of Mao's belief in the power of human will and determination. In just over a year, the marchers covered some 6,000 miles, traversing snow-covered mountain passes where they froze in their thin clothes and crossing treacherous bogs and marshes. To the hardships provided by nature was added the hostility of man, for there was rarely a day without

FIGURE 13.1   China, 1930–Spring 1944. The Long March.

some fighting. At one point they had no alternative but to cross a mountain torrent spanned by a 13-chain suspension bridge from which the enemy, armed and waiting on the other side, had removed the planks.

The six- or seven-day crossing of grasslands in the Chinese-Tibetan border region was a terrible ordeal. Here heavy rainfall and poor drainage had created a waterlogged plain on which green grass grew on multiple layers of rotting grass beneath. First a vanguard was sent to chart the way, and in the central grasslands they could find no place dry enough to sleep, so the marchers had to remain standing all night long, leaning against one another. The rest of the army followed through the slippery, treacherous terrain, trudging on despite hunger and fatigue, trying to ward off rain and hail and survive the unbearable cold of the nights. Since the men and women carried only a very small amount of grain, they subsisted mostly on wild grasses and vegetables eaten raw because there was no firewood for cooking. Sometimes the vegetables turned out to be poisonous, and the stagnant water reportedly smelled of horse's urine.

The marchers succeeded in overcoming this and other obstacles. Some of the women even gave birth. But many perished. Of about 100,000 who set out from Jiangxi, less than 10 percent completed the march. Some were left behind to work in various areas, but most perished. The loss was only partially offset by new recruits who joined along the way. After completion of the march, including those already in Shaanxi, the Communists, led from Mao's headquarters in the caves of Yan'an, were about 20,000 strong.

The survivors of the march emerged toughened and filled with a sense of solidarity forged by shared hardships. There was also a heightened self-confidence, a conviction that the movement would surmount all obstacles. Something of this spirit is conveyed in a poem Mao wrote shortly before reaching Shaanxi:

> Lofty the sky
> and pale the clouds—
> We watch the wild geese
> south till they vanish.
>
> We count the thousand
> leagues already travelled.
> If we do not reach
> the Great Wall we are not true men.
>
> High on the crest
> of Liupan Mountain
> Our banners billow
> in the west wind.
>
> Today we hold
> a long rope in our hands.
> When shall we put bonds
> upon the grey dragon?

The saga of the Long March remained a source of heroic inspiration for decades. The last veteran of the march did not leave the stage until the death of Deng Xiaoping in 1997.

United Front and War

Even with the Communists in Shaanxi, Chiang remained determined to crush them rather than turn to combating Japanese aggression. However, the Communist call for a united front against Japan had wide appeal and was especially welcomed by the troops of Marshal Zhang Xueliang, who had been ordered to end resistance against the Japanese in Manchuria in 1931 and move south with his armies to Xian. Zhang's forces were less than enthusiastic in fighting the CCP. To breathe life into the anti-Communist campaign, Chiang Kai-shek flew to Xian in December, 1936. But he had misjudged the situation. Instead of pledging themselves to renewed anti-Communist efforts, Marshal Zhang and some of his men seized Chiang and held him prisoner for two weeks while his fate was negotiated. Exactly what transpired is not clear, but the CCP, agreeing with Stalin's policy of forming a worldwide united front against fascism, intervened with Marshal Zhang. Chiang was finally released after agreeing to terminate his campaign against Yan'an and lead a united front against Japan. He was China's most distinguished military man at the time, the leader of the government recognized as legitimate at home and abroad, and the heir to the mantle of Sun Yat-sen. Even his enemies saw him as the only man possessing the political, military, and ideological authority to lead China in an effort to stop the Japanese.

Following Chiang's 1936 success against Guangdong and Guangxi, the formation of the Chinese united front in 1937 dismayed Japanese army officers intent on dominating China. Ever since 1933, there had been a constant danger that an unplanned military incident might escalate into a major war. This is, in effect, what happened when the Chinese held firm and refused further concessions following a clash between Chinese and Japanese soldiers on the Marco Polo Bridge outside Beijing in July 1937. Thus began the second Sino-Japanese War that in 1941 merged into World War II, although this is not what Japan intended in 1937.

The fighting went badly for the Chinese. By the end of July, the Japanese were in possession of Beijing and Tianjin, and in August Japanese forces attacked Shanghai, the main source of Nationalist revenue. Here Chiang used some of his best German-trained troops in three months of heroic and bloody fighting with very heavy casualties. After Shanghai fell, the Chinese retreated in disarray, failed to take a stand at Wuxi as planned, but poured into Nanjing, which fell in December. The Nanjing Massacre followed. Japanese soldiers, backed by their superiors, went on a rampage, terrorizing people, killing, raping, burning, and looting for seven weeks (see Box 13.1). Sixty years later the number of people who perished remains a matter of bitter contention—as though sheer numbers can measure the horror. The figure inscribed in the memorial erected in Nanjing (1985) is 300,000. How and why it happened, and the lessons to be drawn therefrom, continue to generate intense controversy and stimulate reflection. The Japanese acquired a reputation for terrible cruelty, which stiffened the Chinese determination to resist and continued to cast a pall long after the war.

After Nanjing, the Japanese maintained and continued their offense, taking Canton in October and Wuhan in December, while Chiang, refusing to submit, adopted a strategy of "trading space for time." As the war escalated, so did the Japanese government's aims and rhetoric. What had begun as a pursuit of a pro-Japanese North China turned into a holy crusade against the West and Communism. In 1938, unable to obtain Chinese recognition of Manchukuo, the government of Prime Minister Prince Konoe Fumimaro (1891–1945) declared Chiang's regime illegitimate, and vowed to destroy it. In November, Konoe proclaimed Japan's determination to establish a "New Order in East Asia" to include Japan, Manchukuo, and China in a political, economic, and cultural union: a bastion against (Western) imperialism and against Soviet Communism. Those who did not see the light were to be brought to their senses by force. Originally, in the summer of 1937, Japanese plans had called for a three-month campaign by three divisions, at a cost of 100 million yen, to destroy the main Chinese force and take possession of key areas while waiting for Chiang to ask for peace. But by the following spring they were preparing orders for 20 divisions, and had appropriated over 2.5 billion yen with promise of more to come.

The Nationalist government moved its wartime capital to Chongqing in Sichuan. Many refugees followed the government to the southwest (Figure 13.2).

BOX 13.1 THE NANJING MASSACRE— AN EYEWITNESS ACCOUNT

John Rabe (1882–1950) was a German businessman who had lived in China since 1908 and took a lead in establishing the Nanjing Safety Zone to protect Chinese refugees during the Nanjing Massacre. He was and remained a Nazi, but his ideological commitment is not apparent in his deeds or diary. A statue in his honor now stands in the Nanjing Massacre Memorial Hall in Nanjing.

Rabe's diary was not made public until 1996 and was used by Iris Chang, in her bestselling book, The Rape of Nanking *(1997). That book is open to criticism, but Rabe appears to have been an accurate chronicler. Nevertheless, his diary and the true nature of what happened are still matters of intense debate, especially in Japan. The passage below describes the scene on December 16, 1937, three days after Nanjing had fallen, as Japanese soldiers sought entry into the Safety Zone where thousands of Chinese had taken refuge.*

I've just heard that hundreds more disarmed Chinese soldiers have been led out of our Zone to be shot, including 50 of our police who are to be executed for letting soldiers in.

The road to Hsiakwan is nothing but a field of corpses strewn with the remains of military equipment. The Communications Ministry was torched by the Chinese, the Y Chang Men Gate has been shelled. There are piles of corpses outside the gate. The Japanese aren't lifting a hand to clear them away, and the Red Swastika Society associated with us has been forbidden to do so.

It may be that the disarmed Chinese will be forced to do the job before they're killed. We Europeans are all paralyzed with horror. There are executions everywhere, some are being carried out with machine guns outside the barracks of the War Ministry. . . .

As I write this, the fists of Japanese soldiers are hammering at the back gate to the garden. Since my boys don't open up, heads appear along the top of the wall. When I suddenly show up with my flashlight, they beat a hasty retreat. We open the main gate and walk after them a little distance until they vanish in dark narrow streets, where assorted bodies have been lying in the gutter for three days now. Makes you shudder in revulsion.

(Continued)

BOX 13.1 THE NANJING MASSACRE— AN EYEWITNESS ACCOUNT (CONTINUED)

All the women and children, their eyes big with terror, are sitting on the grass in the garden, pressed closely together, in part to keep warm, in part to give each other courage. Their one hope is that I, the "foreign devil," will drive these evil spirits away.

Rabe, John. *The Good Man of Nanking: The Diaries of John Rabe,* edited by Erwin Wickert and translated from the German by John E. Woods. (New York: Knopf, 1998), pp. 75–77.

FIGURE 13.2 *Refugees Crowding onto Trains Bound for Guilin,* Cai Dizhi. Chinese refugees escaping from Japanese-occupied territory followed the Chinese Nationalist government southwest to its temporary wartime capital in Chongqing. Scenes like this were common from 1937 to 1938. Woodcut.

From *Woodcuts of Wartime China, 1937–1945,* Yonghua Iingxin, ed. (Taiwan: L. Ming Cultural Enterprises, Dist.).

Universities and hundreds of factories were transported piecemeal to help the war effort in Chongqing, where Chiang held on gamely. Before the Japanese attack on Pearl Harbor (December 1941), China obtained financial assistance from the United States and U.S.S.R., and Stalin sent some pilots stationed in Gansu Province. During 1939 to 1941, Chongqing suffered repeated bombings. Not until August 1941 did help come in the form of the Flying Tigers, volunteer American pilots later incorporated into the Fourteenth U.S. Air Force, commanded by General Claire L. Chennault. However, the West's support remained primarily moral, and the U.S.S.R. alone sent some official assistance. Meanwhile, during 1939 to 1941, fighting on the ground was limited to skirmishes, with both sides working to consolidate their positions.

In 1940 the Japanese established a puppet regime in Nanjing headed by Wang Jingwei, the erstwhile follower of Sun Yat-sen and leader of the left wing of the Guomindang. However, like a similar regime established earlier in Beijing, it was clear to the Chinese populace that the Japanese were pulling the strings.

Expansion of the War into a Pacific War

A major Japanese foreign policy concern during the 1930s was relations with the U.S.S.R. During 1938 and 1939, there were several military clashes in the border area along Russia's frontier with Korea and Manchukuo. In these operations, quite large in scale and involving the deployment of armor, Japan was defeated. During 1937 to 1940, there were three military confrontations along the Russian frontier with Korea and, far more seriously, along the Mongolian border with Manchukuo. These operations, which increased in scale, involved the deployment of armor, artillery, and aircraft. The Japanese fought well, but the Soviets proved more than a match. The last and most severe conflict cost Japan 180,000 men and resulted in an armistice.

Japan was caught off guard diplomatically when Germany, without any warning, came to terms with the Soviet Union in August 1939. Japan was therefore neutral when World War II began in Europe shortly thereafter. However, the dramatic success of the German blitzkrieg strengthened the hands of those in Tokyo who favored a pro-German policy, and in September 1940, Konoe signed the Tripartite Pact, forming an alliance with Germany and Italy.

The Germans again surprised the Japanese in June 1941 when Hitler invaded Russia. Some army men wanted Japan to join the attack on the U.S.S.R. As Alvin D. Coox pointed out, they saw this as a way out of the China impasse, "apparently convinced that the best way to climb out of a hole was to widen it."[3] However, the navy wanted to advance into the oil- and mineral-rich south. Officially, Japan claimed its mission to be the creation of a "Greater East Asian Co-Prosperity Sphere," supposedly for the economic benefit of all in the region but actually centered on Japan, for the underlying reality was that the resources of Southeast Asia were essential for Japan's economic security.

Konoe hoped that, armed with the Tripartite Pact, he would be able to reach his aims without going to war with the United States, but the American government was becoming increasingly alarmed over Japanese expansion. When in the summer of 1941 Japan moved troops into southern Vietnam, the United States, Britain, and Holland (then in control of the East Indies, modern Indonesia) retaliated by applying the economic sanctions they had withheld in 1931. An embargo on scrap iron was serious, but the crucial product cut off from Japan was oil. America and Japan were on a collision course. To quote Michael Barnhart, "The Japanese Empire was determined to retain the rights and privileges it considered necessary for its economic and political security. The United States thought these rights and privileges contrary to its own deeply held principles and to the survival of what were now in effect its allies in the struggle against global aggression."[4] The United States was determined that Japan should withdraw from China as well as Indochina. For Japan, this would have meant a reversal of the policy pursued in China since 1931, and the relinquishment of the vision of primacy in East Asia. Dependent on oil and rubber from Southeast Asia, the Japanese were in no position to carry on protracted negotiations. They had to fight or retreat. It is a bitter irony that Japan now prepared to go to war in order to attain the self-sufficiency that its proponents of total war had once considered a precondition for war.

When it became clear to Konoe that the situation had reached an impasse, he resigned, to be followed by General Tōjō Hideki (1884–1948), prime minister from October 1941 to July 1944. When last-minute negotiations proved fruitless, the Japanese decided on war as the least unpalatable alternative. It began on December 7, 1941, with a surprise attack on Pearl Harbor in Hawaii that destroyed seven American battleships and 120 aircraft, and left 2,400 dead. With the United States and Japan at war, Hitler, too, declared war against the United States, but German-Japanese cooperation during the war remained limited.

The Course of the War

At first the war went spectacularly well for Japan. By the middle of 1942 Japan controlled the Philippines, Malaya, Burma, and the East Indies. Japan was also in charge in Indochina (officially under the jurisdiction of Vichy France), and enjoyed the cooperation of a friendly regime in Thailand. However, contrary to hopes in Tokyo, the United States, far from being ready to negotiate a quick peace, mobilized for full-scale war.

In June 1942 Japan suffered a major defeat when it was checked at the battle of Midway, 1,200 miles northwest of Hawaii (Figure 13.3). The Americans, taking advantage of advance knowledge of Japanese movements obtained from breaking the Japanese secret code, destroyed many Japanese planes and sank four Japanese aircraft carriers while losing only one of their own. Three more years of intense warfare, including bloody hand-to-hand combat, lay ahead, but the American use of aircraft carriers and the extensive deployment of submarines, which took a tremendous toll on vital Japanese shipping, were two of the factors contributing to

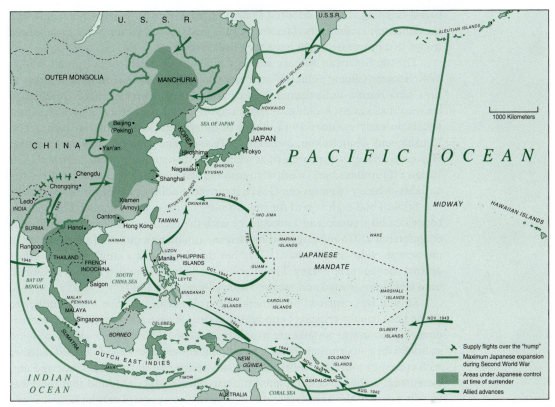

FIGURE 13.3 The Pacific War.

Japan's ultimate defeat. Another was the island-hopping strategy whereby the American forces seized islands selectively for use as bases for further advances, bypassing others with their forces intact but out of action. One consequence of this strategy was that while the Allies wanted Japan to remain bogged down in China, China itself was not a major war theater.

China at War

The conviction that eventually the United States would enter the war sustained Chiang Kai-shek during the long years when China faced Japan virtually alone. When this did happen, it buoyed the spirit of the Chinese, now allied to the one country powerful enough to crush Japan. More material forms of support were soon forthcoming, although there was never enough, because in 1942 Japan cut off Chongqing's last land route to its allies by seizing Burma and closing the Burma Road. Thereafter, supplies had to be flown in from India to Yunnan over the Himalayas (the "hump"). In addition, China ranked low in the American war effort. The Allies decided first to concentrate on the defeat of Germany, and the island-hopping strategy adopted against Japan largely bypassed China, although the Allies appreciated the fact that China tied down vast numbers of Japanese troops that otherwise might have been used elsewhere.

The top American military man in China was General Joseph Stilwell, who in 1942 became Chiang's chief-of-staff as well as commander of American forces in the China-Burma-India theater. Stilwell was a fine soldier. Chennault disregarded his warnings against building airbases unprotected by ground troops, bases from which, in early summer 1944, heavy bombers attacked industrial facilities in Kyushu and Manchukuo, airfields in Taiwan, and oil refineries in Sumatra. However, Stilwell was proven right when later that summer Japan launched their Ichigo ("Number One") campaign into Hunan and Guangxi and captured the airfields. A heavy blow for the GMD, it proved a hollow victory for the Japanese.

Stilwell had high regard for the ordinary Chinese fighting man, but scarcely concealed his irritation and impatience with the inefficiencies and corruption he encountered in Chongqing, and his disgust at Chiang's policy of preparing for a postwar showdown with the CCP rather than joining in a single-minded effort against the Japanese enemy. The relationship between the two men deteriorated until Chiang requested and received Stilwell's recall in 1944.

Stilwell was replaced by General Albert Wedemeyer, who was friendlier to Chiang but equally critical of conditions in the Chinese army, which were horrendous. Induction was tantamount to a death sentence. Those who could afford to do so bribed the conscription officer. The remainder were marched off, bound together with ropes, to join their units, often many miles and days away. Underfed and exhausted, many never completed the trip. Those who did found that food was equally scarce at the front and medical services almost completely lacking.

Misery and corruption were not unique to the military. Even in times of famine (as in Henan, 1942–1943) peasants were sorely oppressed by the demands of the landlord and the tax collector. Meanwhile, the urban middle class suffered from mounting inflation, which had reached an annual rate of 40 to 50 percent between 1937 and 1939, climbed to 160 percent for 1939 through 1942, and mounted to an average of 300 percent for 1942 through 1945. By 1943, the purchasing power of the salaries paid to bureaucrats was only one-tenth what it had been in 1937, while teachers were down to five percent of their former earnings. The result was widespread demoralization of the military and civilian populations under Nationalist control. The secret police were unable to root out corruption. Government exhortations and the publication of Chiang Kai-shek's book *China's Destiny* (1943) failed to reinvigorate ideological commitment to the government and party.

A major reason for the wartime deterioration of the Guomindang was that Japan's seizure of the eastern seaboard and China's major cities deprived the Nationalists of the great business centers of eastern China (especially Shanghai). In Sichuan, they were dependent on the elements in society that were most resistant to change and reform. Moreover, Chiang, hoarding his strength for the coming showdown with the CCP, was unwilling to commit his troops to battle with the Japanese more than was absolutely necessary. Consequently, he missed whatever

opportunity existed for building a modern
Chinese force with American assistance, and for
translating anti-Japanese nationalism into support for his own regime.

The shortcomings of the Chongqing government were highlighted by the accomplishments of the Communists, headquartered in
Yan'an (Figure 13.4). From 1937 to 1945, the
party expanded its membership from roughly
40,000 to over 1 million, and its troop
strength increased tenfold to an estimated
900,000, not counting guerrillas and militia-
men. Furthermore, the Communists enjoyed
widespread peasant support in northern
China, where they established themselves as
the effective government in the countryside
behind the Japanese lines. The Japanese, concentrated in the cities and guarding their lines
of supply, did not have the manpower to patrol
the rural areas constantly and effectively.

FIGURE 13.4   Jiang Qing (left) and Mao Zedong in
Yan'an, 1960. After the Long March and during the war,
the Chinese Communist Party leaders lived and worked
in the Yan'an caves.
REVOLUTIONARY WORKERS ONLINE.

In the areas nominally under Japanese control, the Communists skillfully pursued policies to fuse national resistance and social revolution. The key to their
ultimate success was mass mobilization of the peasantry, but the mix of policies
and the pace of change varied according to local conditions. Carefully avoiding
premature class warfare, they frequently began by organizing the peasants to wage
guerrilla war, enlisting support from the village elites for the war effort, and manipulating them into going along with rent and interest reduction. Building up their
military power, they enlisted elite support even as they undermined elite power.

Crucial was the creation of new mass organizations led by poor peasant
activists, who freed from the exactions of landlords and given a voice in government, became enthusiastic supporters of the party and government. The peasant
associations and local party branches took the lead in effecting changes in taxation
and reducing rent and interest payments, thus destroying the economic foundations of the old system. Similarly, new energies were released by organizing women
and young people in an attack on traditional family authority. Actual or potential
rivals such as secret societies or bandits were attacked and eliminated. The twin
lessons of nationalism and revolution were emphasized for the people through
indoctrination programs and a campaign to combat illiteracy, conveying new ideas
to the peasantry even as they gained access to the written word, shattering the old
monopoly on learning.

The Japanese patronized puppet armies and even tolerated trade with the
Guomindang-controlled areas of China, but the Wang Jingwei regime never gained
credibility, being too obviously controlled by the Japanese. At best, life in occupied China went on as usual, but Japanese arrogance alienated many Chinese.
Humane behavior on the part of some individuals was overshadowed by acts of

cruelty that evoked Chinese hatred and resistance. An example is the notorious "kill all, burn all, destroy all" campaign carried out in 1941 and 1942 in parts of northern China in retaliation for a CCP offensive. Implemented literally, the Japanese hurt the CCP badly, but they also helped turn apolitical peasants into determined fighters.

The policies and record of the CCP also helped attract urban intellectuals. To insure discipline and preserve the cohesion of a movement swollen by new adherents, the party under Mao (now firmly established as leader) organized a rectification campaign to ensure "correct" understanding of party ideology and to bring art and literature into line. Art for its own sake or for self-expression was condemned, and those guilty of being insufficiently mass-oriented were induced to confess their faults. Many were sent to work in villages, factories, or battle zones to "learn from the masses."

From the war, the CCP emerged stronger than it had ever been before. The outcome of the civil war that followed was by no means obvious to observers at the time, but it is one of the ironies of the war that the Japanese, who proclaimed that they were combating communism in China, instead contributed to its ultimate victory.

Japan at War

Well before Pearl Harbor, the effects of the continued war in China were felt by the Japanese people as militarization and authoritarianism increased at home. The National General Mobilization Law of 1938 strengthened the prime minister at the expense of the Diet, and the government began to place the economy on a war basis, with rationing, economic controls, and resource allocations administered by a bureaucratic elite drawn from the most prestigious universities. Getting the various centers of economic and political power to pull together remained a problem, but a precedent was set for government to direct the economy, institutions for this were founded, and Japan gained a cadre of economic and social bureaucrats.

The war entailed a greater role for government in agriculture as well as in industry and commerce. The war years were hard on rural landlords, already hurt by the depression, while ordinary tenant farmers benefited from measures to control inflation, such as rent control (1939), as well as government efforts to increase production by allocating fertilizer. In the last years of the war, the government paid much larger bonuses to farm operators than to noncultivating landlords, who emerged from the war much weakened. As Ann Waswo has shown, "in purely economic terms and in terms of local political influence, ordinary farmers made significant gains."[5] As ever, war proved a potent catalyst for change.

In October 1940, the political parties were merged into the Imperial Rule Assistance Association, which, however, did not become a mass popular party along the lines of European fascism, but served primarily as a vehicle for the dissemination of propaganda throughout Japan. Similarly, labor unions were combined into a single patriotic organization. Great pressures were exerted to bring educational institutions and the public communications media into line so that Japan would speak with one collective voice.

To effect the "spiritual mobilization" of the country, the government tried to purge Western influence from Japanese life. As one writer put it, "While the black ships that represent the material might of the West have left, a hundred years later the Black Ships of thought are still threatening us."[6] Prominent intellectuals insisted on Japanese uniqueness and exceptionalism, and drew on German concepts of irony and angst, nostalgia for the past, and the aesthetics of death, subjectivity, and poetry to attack the "modern" at home and abroad. Foreign radical and liberal ideas banned from theoretical discourse, and popular culture was purged. Permanent waves and jazz, so popular during the 1920s, were now banned. Efforts were made to remove Western loanwords from the language, and the people were bombarded with exhortations to observe traditional values and revere the divine emperor. Heterodox religious sects with no ostensible political agenda were suppressed, and in a "triumph of religious stateism,"[7] all religions were subordinated to the imperial cult. To mobilize the public down to the ward level, the people were formed into small neighborhood organizations.

Colonial East Asia during the War

Japan's attempt to win over the population of the conquered areas by encouraging their native religious traditions, exploiting their resentment against Western imperialism, and teaching them the Japanese language was more than offset by Japan's own imperialistic exploitation, by the harshness of its rule, and by the cruelty of its soldiers. The slogan "Asia for the Asians" did not disguise the realities of what Mark R. Peattie has characterized as a "mutant colonialism." In his words, "the tightening demands on the energies, loyalties, and resources of Japan's colonial peoples by a nation at war with much of Asia and most of the West transmogrified an authoritarian but recognizably 'Western' colonial system into an empire of the lash, a totalitarian imperium, that dragged along its peoples as it staggered toward defeat."[8]

As indicated in Chapter 12, conditions were particularly harsh in Korea, but in Taiwan, too, there was a campaign to assimilate the population and turn them into people who spoke Japanese, had Japanese names, and even worshiped at Shinto shrines. Although Taiwanese were regimented and controlled at home, Taiwanese entrepreneurs took advantage of new opportunities in Manchuria and elsewhere, and young people responded positively to efforts to recruit them into the Japanese military. The largest contingent served on Hainan Island, where many perished. However, overall, people in Taiwan as well as Korea welcomed Japan's defeat. When Nationalists forces arrived in October 1945, they were welcomed as liberators.

Japanese forces dominated Vietnam, although until the fall of Vichy France in March 1945, they left the Vichy French colonial administration in place. The Japanese conducted a cultural campaign claiming that they had come as liberators from all European colonialism and seeking support especially among Buddhists, while the French encouraged and gave new freedoms to Catholics. Resisting both Japanese and French were the Viet Minh (short for Viet Nam Doc Lap Dong Minh or "League for the Independence of Vietnam"), established in the northwest by Ho Chi Minh when he returned to Vietnam in 1941. Viet Minh policy was to postpone the Marxist revolutionary agenda for the sake of forming a broad nationalist coalition and in the hope of gaining assistance from the Allies. The policy resulted in Ho's cooperation with the American Office of Strategic Services in 1944. That the United States would support the reimposition of French colonialism was not apparent by war's end.

Elsewhere in Japan's bloated empire, the colonial authorities were replaced by Japanese-controlled puppet regimes. The history of Southeast Asia is beyond the scope of our text, but we should note that while Japan won no friends, it shattered the myth as well as the actuality of Western hegemony and thus paved the way for the end of colonialism—ultimately throughout the globe.

The End of the War

The closer the American forces came to the Japanese homeland, the easier it was for them to bomb Japan itself. Such raids were aimed at economic targets and population centers as well as military and industrial installations. Incendiary bombs were dropped in order to sap the morale of the people, who by the last years of the war, were suffering from scarcities of all kinds, including food and other daily necessities, many of which were available only on the black market.

In July 1944, after the fall of Saipan, largest of the Mariana Islands, General Tōjō was forced out of office, but there was no change, either in the fortunes of war or in policy, under his successor, General Koiso Kuniaki (1880–1950). Koiso remained in office until April 1945, when he was succeeded by Admiral Suzuki Kantarō (1867–1948). Some civilian leaders sent out peace feelers to the Allies, but their efforts were hampered by the noncooperation of the Soviet Union, anxious to have the war continue long enough to allow it to participate, and by the demand issued at Potsdam in July 1945, insisting on Japan's unconditional surrender. This demand reflected the Allied belief that it had been a mistake to allow World War I to end in an armistice rather than in a full capitulation, permitting Hitler to claim that Germany had been "betrayed" into defeat, not beaten on the field of battle. Determined not to commit a similar mistake, the Allies now demanded an unconditional surrender, which stiffened the resistance of Japanese leaders concerned over the fate of the emperor.

The last year of the war was especially terrible; on one night in March 1945, some 100,000 people died as the result of a firebomb raid on Tokyo, and a similar

FIGURE 13.5 *Hiroshima*. Through the vault over the Memorial Cenotaph for the Atomic
Bomb Victims can be seen the Atomic Bomb Memorial Dome. The steel skeleton of the dome
and the gutted building (formerly the city's Industrial Promotion Hall) have been left standing
unaltered, in witness to the tragedy.
TIME & LIFE PICTURE COLLECTION/GETTY IMAGES.

raid in May devastated another large part of Japan's capital city. Meanwhile,
bombers created an "iron-storm" over Okinawa, sending local people to seek
refuge in caves, where some would perish when Japanese soldiers forced them into
"compulsory group suicide."[9] Short of resources, and with its cities in ruins,
during the last months of the war Japan was reduced to desperate measures, such
as the use of flying bombs directed by suicide pilots, called "kamikaze" after the
"divine wind" that once had saved the land from the Mongols.

Tokyo and other major cities had been practically leveled by conventional
bombing, but on August 6 the United States dropped an atomic bomb on
Hiroshima (Figure 13.5) in southwestern Honshu, razing over 80 percent of the
buildings and leaving some 200,000 people dead or injured and countless others
to continue their lives under the specter of radiation sickness. Two days later, on
August 8, the U.S.S.R. entered the war, and the next day the United States
dropped a second atomic bomb, this time on Nagasaki.

Recent scholarship shows that all along the emperor paid careful attention to
the war without intervening in actual military operations. But now his throne was
at stake. According to Edward J. Drea:

> In the face of total defeat, he valued the imperial institution more than his
> people, his army, and his empire. . . . Perhaps more than fire raids, atomic

bombs, the Soviet entry into the war against Japan, and the specter of invasion, it was the threat to his imperial ancestors, and therefore the survival of the imperial institution itself, that provided the steel otherwise missing from Hirohito's regal backbone.[10]

In any case, twice during these fateful days a government deadlock was broken by the personal intervention of the emperor, each time in favor of peace. Even after the final decision for peace, diehards tried to continue the war by a last resort to violence in the tradition of the terrorists who had first helped steer Japan toward militarism and war. They set fire to the homes of the prime minister and president of the privy council and invaded the imperial palace in search of the recording of the emperor's peace message, but they failed. When all was lost, several leaders, including the war minister, committed ritual suicide.

On August 15, the imperial recording was broadcast over the radio, and throughout Japan the people, for the first time, heard the voice of their emperor. In the formal language appropriate to his elevated status, he informed them that the war was lost. This is how Ōe Kenzaburō, the future winner of the Nobel Prize for literature, 10 years old at the time, recollects the impact of the broadcast:

> The adults sat around their radios and cried. The children gathered outside in the dusty road and whispered their bewilderment. We were most confused and disappointed by the fact that the Emperor had spoken in a human voice, no different from any adult's. None of us understood what he was saying, but we had all heard his voice. One of my friends could even imitate it cleverly. Laughing, we surrounded him—a twelve-year-old in grimy shorts who spoke with the Emperor's voice. A minute later we felt afraid. We looked at one another; no one spoke. How could we believe that an august presence of such awful power had become an ordinary human voice on a designated summer day.[11]

Notes

1. The term "incantatory symbol" comes from Masao Maruyama, in Ivan Morris, ed., *Thought and Behavior in Modern Japanese Politics,* expanded edition (New York, NY: Oxford Univ. Press, 1969), p. 376.

2. Stuart R. Schram, *The Political Thought of Mao Tse-tung* (New York, NY: Frederick A. Praeger, 1963), p. 209.

3. Alvin D. Coox, in Peter Duus, ed., *The Cambridge History of Japan,* vol. 6: *The Twentieth Century.* (Cambridge, U.K.: Cambridge Univ. Press, 1988), p. 324.

4. Michael A. Barnhart, *Japan Prepares for Total War: The Search for Economic Security, 1919–1941* (Ithaca, NY: Cornell Univ. Press, 1987), p. 234.

5. Ann Waswo in *The Cambridge History of Japan,* vol. 6, p. 104.

6. Kamei Katsuichiro quoted in Kevin Michael Doak, *Dreams of Difference: The Japan Romantic School and the Crisis of Modernity* (Berkeley, CA: Univ. of California Press, 1994), p. 101.

7. Sheldon Garon, *Molding Japanese Minds: The State in Everyday Life* (Princeton, NJ: Princeton Univ. Press, 1997), pp. 84–87.

8. Mark R. Peattie in *The Cambridge History,* vol. 6, p. 269. For "mutant colonialism," see p. 234.

9. Norma Field, *In the Realm of a Dying Emperor* (New York, NY: Vintage Books, 1993), p. 61.

10. Edward J. Drea, *In the Service of the Emperor: Essays on the Imperial Japanese Army* (Lincoln, NE: Univ. of Nebraska Press, 1998), p. 215.

11. Ōe Kenzaburō, *A Personal Matter,* trans. by John Nathan (New York, NY: Grove Press, 1968), pp. vii–viii.

Part Four

East Asia in the Second Half of the Twentieth Century

Throughout East Asia, as across the globe, World War II was followed by a period of change unprecedented in its rapidity and scope, affecting the direction of civilizations, economic systems, social structures, and the lives of millions of people.

The war destroyed the Japanese Empire, confirmed the eclipse of the Western European powers begun by World War I, and hastened the end of the old colonialism. In Asia, the British Empire was dismantled as India and Burma attained independence (1947), followed by the Malay Peninsula (1957), leaving only Hong Kong as a Crown Colony—and it was scheduled to revert to Chinese rule in 1997. However, the Dutch in Indonesia and, especially, the French in Indochina resorted to military means in a futile attempt to preserve their colonies.

The war left only two superpowers, the United States and the Soviet Union, with the capacity to exercise major influence over events in East Asia. By 1947 they had developed a bitter rivalry and a "cold" war.

To quote I. M. Roberts:

Even if the Cold War stopped short of actual armed conflict between the two principals, subversion, bribery, murder, espionage, propaganda and diplomatic quarrelling long gave fresh colour to the basic premise, that it was impossible for communist and non-communist societies to cooperate and relate to one another in the way civilized societies had once believed to be normal.*

As announced by President Truman in 1947, the American policy of "containment" was determined to prevent the extension of the U.S.S.R. and of communism everywhere. All too often, this policy was pursued without regard for local conditions, about which the American public and even policy makers were ill informed. American policy became even more important after the end of the Cold War left the United States the only remaining super power.

---

*I. M. Roberts, *Twentieth Century: The History of the World, 1901–2000* (New York: Viking, 1999), p. 462.

14

The Aftermath of World War II

The results of the war were most immediately apparent in Japan, which had to submit to foreign occupation and relinquish not only Manchuria and other areas seized since 1931 but all lands acquired since 1895, most notably Taiwan and Korea. For China and Korea, the war led to further fighting but, as in Japan, the basic parameters of postwar history were in place by the early 1950s. The triumph of the Chinese Communists, the division of Korea, and the remolding of Japan all occurred within those years. Only the future of Vietnam remained in doubt, but because this too had its immediate roots in the war and postwar periods, we have included it in this chapter. In all four countries the imperatives of the Cold War interacted with domestic forces.

I. China: Civil War and Communist Triumph, 1946–1949

Aug. 1945	Dec. 1945	Jan.–April 1946	October 1948	November 1948	October 1949
End of World War II	Marshall Mission	CCP-GMD Truce	CCP gains Manchuria	Battle Huai-Hai	PRC established

When Japan surrendered, Chiang Kai-shek, with American concurrence, directed Japan's generals in China to submit only to Nationalist forces. To enable the Guomindang armies to accept the Japanese surrender, the United States transported them by water and by air to areas of Japanese occupation. However, they were not allowed into Manchuria until January 1946. Manchuria had been occupied by the U.S.S.R. during the last days of the war, and the Soviets, intent on harvesting the Japanese military and industrial assets there, did not completely withdraw their troops until May 1946. By that time they had allowed the CCP to gain substantial control of the Manchurian countryside. Chiang Kai-shek, determined to recover the territory where the Japanese had begun their aggression in 1931, disregarded American warnings against overextending his forces and dispatched almost half a million of his best troops to Manchuria.

During the year immediately after the war, the Nationalists appeared to have superior resources. Recognized as the legitimate government of China by all the Allies, including the Soviet Union, they had three or four times as many men under arms as their Communist rivals and enjoyed a similar advantage in armament. They were, therefore, in no mood to make concessions to the CCP The Communists, on the other hand, had come through the war battle-hardened, with well-established support in the countryside and high morale. Their leaders, too, were convinced that victory would ultimately be theirs in the coming struggle. It was against this background that in December 1945, President Truman sent General George C. Marshall to China to mediate between the two parties. Given their history of conflict, divergence of views, and confidence in their respective causes, the American initiative was probably doomed from the start. Marshall's efforts were also undercut by American support of the Nanjing government, even though President Truman stipulated that large-scale aid to China was contingent on a settlement. As during Mao's visit to Chongqing in August through October (Figure 14.1), there was a show of cordiality, but the Marshall mission produced only a brief breathing spell before fighting erupted in mid-1946.

Initially, until July 1947, the Guomindang armies enjoyed success, even capturing the wartime CCP capital at Yan'an. However, these were hollow victories.

FIGURE 14.1   Mao Zedong (left) and Chiang Kai-shek exchange toasts at Chongqing during a welcoming party for Mao Zedong. August–October 1945.
© BETTMANN/CORBIS (BE046254).

Like the Japanese before them, in northern China and Manchuria the Guomindang controlled only the cities in the midst of a hostile countryside. Moreover, the military efficacy of the armies was undermined by the rivalries between commanders, by Chiang Kai-shek's penchant for micromanagement from afar, and by his concern that a possible rival might amass too much power. Additionally, the harshness and corruption that had sapped the soldiers' morale during the war against Japan were more demoralizing now that they were supposed to fight fellow Chinese.

In other respects, too, far from stimulating reform, the defeat of Japan resulted merely in the transfer to the rest of China of the ills that had been incubating in wartime Chongqing. A nation badly in need of political, economic, and social reconstruction was subjected to a heavy dose of autocracy and to galloping inflation. Liberal reformers, disillusioned by the corruption and alarmed at the prospect of civil war, tried to rally the opposition. One leader of this non-Communist opposition to the Guomindang was Wen Yiduo (1899–1946), a professor at Qinghua University at its wartime campus in Kunming, who encouraged Chinese hoping for a rebirth of democracy and greater freedom to criticize the government. However, the Guomindang responded to these calls for reform by assassinating the critics. In 1946, Guomindang agents assassinated Wen Yiduo just after he gave a fiery eulogy for one of his murdered colleagues. Wen's death shocked China and exposed the ruling group's desperation to retain power.[1]

Intellectuals and students were not the only ones disenchanted with the regime; many suffered from the arrogance of the Nationalist soldiers and the rapacity of those with political connections. The situation was particularly bad in Taiwan, where carpetbaggers from the mainland enriched themselves at the expense of alleged Taiwanese "collaborators"—a convenient charge against any uncooperative

Taiwanese who had done well during the preceding half-century of Japanese rule. When the Taiwanese rioted in protest in 1947, the Nationalist government responded with brutal and bloody repression. The exact number of casualties is not known; however, Taiwanese leaders in exile claimed that over 10,000 were killed.

The government, inefficient as well as autocratic, proved unable to halt rapidly accelerating inflation that threatened all those whose incomes did not keep up with rising costs. Toward the end, people in the cities had to carry enormous bundles of paper money on their daily rounds of shopping for the necessities of life.

In the CCP areas, on the contrary, a disciplined and well-organized political and military leadership offered credible leadership. Unlike the Guomindang, which promised reform only after the fighting was finished, the CCP implemented one change after another. A crucial and impressive demonstration of their expertise in mass mobilization took place in Manchuria, where they took advantage of the opportunity granted them by the Soviet Union before it withdrew. Here, once their military presence was established, they were able in a mere 18 months to transform indifferent, suspicious peasants into ardent participants in and supporters of the party and of the military campaigns directed by the brilliant general Lin Biao (1907–1971). Cooperation was secured by a mixture of hope and fear that varied with groups and individuals. Party cadres led a series of carefully orchestrated campaigns attacking and systematically displacing the old local elite that could no longer summon support from a provincial or regional elite that had been undermined and compromised during the preceding 14 years of Japanese rule. The campaigns culminated in land redistribution (Figure 14.2), which revolutionized the local power structure.

The contrast between CCP dynamism and Guomindang decay helps explain more than the outcome; it also helps explain the unexpected rapidity of the course of events. The military turning point came in July 1947, when Communist armies

FIGURE 14.2 *Seizing the landlord and transporting his movable property. Dongbeizhibao,* October 9, 1947. Energized by the Chinese Communist Party's campaign for land redistribution, local populations reversed the traditional power structures.

FROM ANVIL OF VICTORY: THE COMMUNIST REVOLUTION IN MANCHURIA, 1945–1948, BY STEVEN LEVINE. COURTESY COLUMBIA UNIVERSITY PRESS.

attacked along several fronts in northern China. In Manchuria, Lin Biao commanded a campaign that put the Guomindang forces on the defensive and ended in October 1948 by completely routing them. During that same month and into November, the last great battle of the war was fought at the strategic city of Xuzhou on the Huai River where the Beijing-Nanjing Railway line joins the Longhai line that runs from Shaanxi to the sea. Around half a million men on each side were involved in this battle, generally known as the battle of Huai-Hai after the Huai River and the Longhai Railway. When it was over, the Nationalists, under Chiang Kai-shek's personal command, had lost 200,000 men and no longer had any way to supply their forces to the north. In January 1949, Nationalist generals surrendered Beijing and Tianjin. Throughout the campaigns, the Communist army's victories led to the capture of valuable military equipment and supplies and increased its manpower as Nationalist soldiers defected or surrendered and were incorporated into the People's Liberation Army.

During 1949 the Communists continued their advance. They crossed the Yangzi in April, took Nanjing the same month, and controlled Shanghai by the end of May. On October 1, Mao Zedong, in a great ceremony in Beijing, formally proclaimed the establishment of the People's Republic of China. There was still some fighting in the south, but clearly the CCP had won control of the Chinese mainland. Meanwhile, Chiang Kai-shek and the Nationalists took refuge on Taiwan and vowed continued resistance.

The triumph of the Communists in 1949 began a new chapter in China's long history. It was the result of a long revolutionary process that had started well before the founding of the CCP, but in terms of the party's own programs and goals, the revolution had only just begun.

II. Japan: The Occupation, 1945–1952

1945   1952   1956

End of Occupation

Ends and Means

Social Policies

Economic Policy

The End of the Occupation

The war left Japan in ruins, its cities largely destroyed, the economy wrecked. About 40 percent of Japan's total urban area was wiped out, including 65 percent of residential housing in Tokyo, 57 percent in Osaka, and 89 percent in Nagoya, Japan's third largest city. At the time of the surrender there were 9 million homeless. Hunger, despair, psychic shock, and fear pervaded the country. In preparation for the arrival of the victors, the Japanese evacuated many women to the countryside, and even the government ordered its female employees out of town. It is easy to imagine people's relief when such measures turned out to have been unnecessary.

Ends and Means

The Occupation's mission to demilitarize Japan and turn the country into a peaceful and democratic state was accepted with enthusiasm by a staff composed partly of New Dealers and by General Douglas MacArthur, its head. Despite, or because of, their lack of preparation, the Americans were convinced they had the answers, and their conviction of the righteousness of their values and policies remained firm, even after the onset of the Cold War induced them to change course from "demilitarization and democratization" to building Japan into a reliable ally.

Officially, the Occupation was under the authority of the Far Eastern Commission, which sat in Washington. Its members included representatives of all the countries that had fought Japan, but despite the presence of some British and Commonwealth officials, the Occupation was essentially American. The Japanese government continued to function, but did so according to the directives and "suggestions" of the Occupation authorities under General MacArthur, Supreme Commander for the Allied Powers (SCAP), who regarded the Japanese as an immature people ready for and in need of tutelage. In MacArthur, the Occupation had a leader who won easy credibility: a commanding figure, a "blue-eyed shogun," convinced of his historic mission, a military man who commanded respect, exuded confidence, and had a flair for drama. The process of policy formation was complex, involving Washington, the Occupation bureaucracy, and the Japanese, and reflecting divisions within as well as among these groups; but MacArthur had a strong hand in fashioning and interpreting, as well as administering, policy.

At the outset, the Occupation faced the pressing tasks of disarming the Japanese military and providing enough relief to prevent famine. The widespread destruction of capital goods and industrial plants, a soil starved for lack of fertilizers, the loss of the natural resources from the former empire and of the entire merchant fleet, and the need to feed around 6 million Japanese expatriates and refugees from overseas threatened economic catastrophe. In this situation, suffering was unavoidable. By supplying food and medical supplies, the Occupation authorities helped avert the worst, but the alternative to the black market was starvation. It was not until 1947 that the United States became seriously concerned with rebuilding the Japanese economy. Even in 1948 a magazine editorial complained, "in today's Japan, the only people who are not living illegally are those in jail."[2]

Demilitarization entailed the dismantling of the military establishment and a purge from positions of political and economic leadership of those most closely associated with leading the country to war. Outside of Japan—and excluding the U.S.S.R. and parts of China controlled by the CCP—5,700 individuals were tried by 50 military tribunals with the result that 984 were sentenced to death, among them 173 Taiwanese and 148 Koreans. A total of 28 top leaders charged with responsibility for the war were tried in Tokyo by an international tribunal of 11 judges that sat in Tokyo from May 1946 to April 1948 and included a Chinese, a Filipino, and an Indian jurist, but no Koreans. When the sentences were handed down in November 1948, seven leaders were condemned to die, including Tōjō, the rather colorless general who had headed Japan's wartime government. His role during the war had been more like a chairman of the board than a dictator, but wartime propaganda had cast him as a Japanese Hitler. The lengthy judicial proceedings produced voluminous records, but never attained the legal clarity nor the moral authority achieved by the trial of Nazi leaders at Nuremberg.

In the end, around 200,000 persons were purged, about half of them from the military. However, most of these men were later reinstated, and some became very prominent. The military elite lost the most, but the decision of the Occupation to operate through, rather than replace, the existing government made for a high level of continuity within the bureaucracy. This contributed to the continuing importance of the bureaucracy even after a new constitution placed government on a new footing.

Although he had sanctioned a war fought in his name, the emperor was not charged with war crimes, nor was there a judicial inquiry into the part he had played. Instead, SCAP's policy was to use the emperor's authority while demystifying his person and throne. He was pressured to substitute a more open lifestyle (akin to that of the British monarch) for the secluded and ritualized existence traditionally led by Japanese emperors. An example of the demystification process was the emperor's unprecedented visit to MacArthur at SCAP headquarters. The resulting photograph (Figure 14.3), showing the stiffly formal emperor standing next to the open-shirted general, caused considerable shock and dismay throughout Japan. In his New Year's message of 1946, the emperor publicly denied his divinity, and under the new constitution he became

FIGURE 14.3 General Douglas MacArthur, Supreme Commander for the Allied Powers (SCAP) occupation forces, and Emperor Hirohito of Japan, soon to publicly deny his divinity.

© AP/WIDEWORLD PHOTOS (APA5163982).

a symbol of the nation. For the remainder of his life he never acknowledged any responsibility for the war, setting an example not lost on his subjects.

This constitution, which went into effect in May 1947, was drafted and practically dictated by the Occupation. It stipulated that sovereignty belongs to the people, placed the highest political authority in the hands of the Diet (to which the executive was now made responsible), and established an independent judiciary. Another noteworthy set of political changes were those decreasing the power of the central government, particularly the Home Ministry, and fostering local self-government. Accompanying these structural changes were provisions for universal suffrage and human rights, including the equality of women. A unique feature was the renunciation of war. Article IX stipulates, "The Japanese people forever renounce war as a sovereign right of the nation and the threat or use of force as a means of settling international disputes" and goes on to say, "land, sea, and air forces, as well as other war potential, will never be maintained."[3] In this way, the authors of the constitution sought to incorporate peacefulness into the very framework of the new Japanese state.

Social Policies

The authorities at SCAP headquarters knew that Japan could not be turned into a democracy simply by changing the political system. Consequently, they tried to change Japanese society itself. Since many American officials lacked previous study or experience in Japan, they tended to rely excessively on American prototypes without taking into sufficient account Japan's own experience and situation. Thus they restructured the educational system to conform to the American sequence of elementary school, junior high school, high school, and college, and forced the Japanese to eliminate their old technical schools and special higher schools, which previously covered the eleventh to thirteenth years of education and prepared students for university study. Under the old system, only the student elite had access to a university education, but under the new, all students were to be given equal educational opportunities through high school. In an effort to expand opportunities for higher education, many of the old technical and higher schools were upgraded to become universities. However, these new universities were not of a quality comparable to the old established schools like Tokyo University. Competition for admission to this and other prestigious universities remained brutal. Students found themselves embroiled in a veritable "examination hell."

In order to reform the content of education, the Occupation abolished the old ethics courses and purged textbooks fostering militaristic and authoritarian values. Its attack on these old values was rather successful, especially since they had already been largely discredited by defeat. Similarly, language reform found ready acceptance: the list of standard characters, many of them simplified, issued by the cabinet in 1946 (1,850 *tōyō kanji*) required only minor modifications and additions when revised in 1981 (the current system of 1,945 *joyō kanji*).

The Occupation was rather less successful in its attempts to create a positive sense of individual civic responsibility and citizenship. Social change entails a transformation of values, and thus naturally takes longer than institutional change; but changes in the legal system can encourage social change. Among the Occupation's notable efforts in this direction were measures to enhance the status of women and limit the powers and privileges of the family's male head. The new constitution stated explicitly in Article XXIV, "Marriage shall be based upon the mutual consent of both sexes, and it shall be maintained through mutual cooperation, with equal rights of husband and wife as a basis." The presence of many thousands of Americans in their country also gave the Japanese an unusual opportunity to observe foreign mores. It may have encouraged them to become somewhat more relaxed toward authority, and also stimulated a measure of cosmopolitanism.

Economic Policy

It was generally recognized that the desired political and social changes demanded an economic foundation, and the authorities set about restructuring the Japanese economy. Most successful in this respect was the program of land reform. This prohibited absentee landlordism and restricted the amount of land a resident landowner could hold to a maximum of seven acres to work himself and another two acres to rent out (except in Hokkaido, where the average farm was 12 acres, because the climate precludes intensive rice cultivation). Anything in excess had to be sold to the government, which resold it to former tenants. There was provision for compensation for the landlords, but inflation made this meaningless. The old inequity in the countryside was eliminated. In terms of productivity, too, the land policy was a success, for the agrarian sector was the first to recover.

In the urban industrial sector, the Occupation began by trying to eliminate, or at least reduce, the concentrations of economic power, which Americans viewed as a major component of Japanese authoritarianism. One policy was to foster labor unions. The constitution guaranteed the right of workers to organize and to bargain and act collectively. As intended, a vigorous union movement developed, but contrary to American wishes, the Japanese unions did not, like the American AFL and CIO, limit themselves to economic demands. Much like European unions, they were political in orientation, developing into labor arms of the Socialist and Communist parties. In February 1947, the Occupation banned a planned general strike, and thereafter was less friendly toward the unions. Laws prohibiting public employees from striking followed.

On the management and ownership side, the Occupation did break up the old holding companies and purged the old *zaibatsu* families from positions of economic leadership. Contrary to initial expectations, however, this did not lead to genuine decentralization. Where old systems were broken up, new and equally pervasive patterns of trade and finance developed, bearing a marked resemblance to the old. Furthermore, a plan to break up operating companies petered out: of

1,200 companies initially considered, only 28 were dissolved. Economic power and decision making remained concentrated. The reasons for this are instructive for understanding the accomplishments and failures of the Occupation as a whole, for they include both a Japanese and an American component.

On the Japanese side, strong support for land reform contrasted with a marked lack of enthusiasm for American-style trust busting. Few shared the American faith in the ultimate benefits of maximum competition. Instead, many felt that Japanese companies needed to be large in order to compete in the international market. Radicals and conservatives disagreed about ownership and control, not about the structure of industry and commerce.

Decentralization of the economy also faltered because it was abandoned in the shift of American policy already signaled by the ban on the 1947 general strike. In an atmosphere of mounting Cold War tension, and in line with what is frequently called the "reverse course," economic and strategic considerations came to prevail. Increasingly, the United States saw Japan, called by the Secretary of State "the workshop of Asia," as a potentially valuable and much-needed ally after the victory of the Chinese Communists in 1949. On the advice of Joseph Dodge, a Detroit banker sent out by Washington in 1949, in April of that year the value of the yen was set at 360 to the dollar—low even then—to encourage exports by making Japanese goods inexpensive abroad, and to promote frugality at home. In May, the Ministry of International Trade and Industry (MITI) was formed by merging the Ministry of Commerce and Industry and the Board of Trade, "constituting a greater centralization of economic authority than had been achieved at the peak of Japan's mobilization for war."[4] Meanwhile, the Ministry of Finance exercised paramount sway over budgets and monetary policy. Both would continue playing these roles long after the Occupation came to an end.

More than just labor and economic policies was affected by the policy shift. Communists were purged (1949–1950), and others who had earlier been purged were allowed to reemerge in public life. Since an armed ally, capable at least of self-defense, would be more valuable than one unarmed, the United States had second thoughts about Japan's renunciation of military force as written into the constitution.

Dodge's deflationary policies led to economic decline until the outbreak of the Korean War in June 1950 brought a flood of orders for equipment and supplies, a procurement boom that gave an enormous boost to the faltering economy. Even after the war, orders to supply American troops and bases continued to benefit the Japanese economy. Under American encouragement, Japan also created a paramilitary force of 75,000.

The End of the Occupation

The ending of the Occupation, a subject broached by General MacArthur as early as 1947, was delayed largely because of Soviet opposition. Although the Occupation continued, by the time MacArthur took command in Korea in July

1950, its work was practically complete. Dismissed by President Truman, he departed from East Asia in April 1951. Though in his subsequent testimony to Congress he spoke glowingly of the Japanese, they were distressed to hear him compare them to children.

Under the Occupation, electoral politics was reintroduced, and political parties representing a broad range of ideas and a variety of interests battled for votes. The Diet again became the central arena for national politics. The leading political personality to emerge during the Occupation was Yoshida Shigeru (1878–1967), a former diplomat who had opposed the military leadership in Japan during the 1930s. Yoshida dominated Japanese politics for the better part of a decade, serving as prime minister in 1946 and 1947, and again from 1948 to 1954. A coalition of conservatives and socialists of various shades of radicalism held power briefly in 1947 to 1948, but was unable to create a viable government, partly because of divisions within its own ranks, and partly because of Occupation hostility toward socialism. Upon reassuming the prime ministership, Yoshida called a new election. Held in 1949, it provided his Liberal party with an absolute majority.

It was Yoshida who signed the peace treaty in San Francisco in September 1951, which was ratified the following April and accompanied by a defense treaty that provided for American bases in Japan and continued occupation of Okinawa. At the insistence of the U.S. Senate, Japan signed a parallel treaty with the Chinese Nationalists on Taiwan and agreed to follow the American policy of nonrecognition and containment of the People's Republic of China (P.R.C.). The U.S.S.R. was not a party to the San Francisco treaty. Formal diplomatic relations were established in 1956, but Moscow and Tokyo could not agree on the disposition of four small islands, and entered the twenty-first century without ever signing a peace treaty to conclude World War II with Russia.

Assessments of the Occupation must naturally take into account later history, as so many institutions and practices of contemporary Japan are rooted in this period. What came to be known as the Japanese model of bureaucratic capitalism has been dubbed the "SCAPanese model."[5] There are people who think the reforms went too fast and too far, and others who deplore the "reverse course" taken in response to the Cold War and the persistence of certain traditional institutions and patterns. These include the treatment and retention of the emperor, the role of the bureaucracy, the relationship between government and business, and failure to adhere strictly to Article IX.

Clearly, the Occupation brought about major changes, but it was most successful in areas where there were Japanese precedents and substantial support. This was true of much of the political program, the land reform, and the advocacy of liberal values. Representative institutions, after all, went back to the nineteenth century, and demands for land reform, for equality, and opposition to authoritarianism all predate the rise of militarism. The movement for women's rights had begun in the 1910s. Despite misconceptions and mistakes, and despite the contradiction inherent in a plan to foster democracy by command, many Occupation reforms took hold.

The Occupation also had unplanned side effects, including the influx of foreign culture. Intellectuals who were eager to catch up with the recent Western developments devoured translations of Western books. Many turned to Marxism, but the whole spectrum of ideas found translators and readers. Popular culture was more open than ever to foreign influence. In some respects, the scene resembled that after the First World War. It did not take the Occupation to introduce the Japanese to baseball and jazz. However, this time change went deeper, and there was to be no adverse reaction as in the 1930s. If anything, the doors opened by defeat and occupation are even more widely open today.

III. Korea: Liberation, Division, and War, 1945–1953

| 1945 | 1948 | **Democratic People's Republic of Korea** | 1953 | 1956 |

Republic of Korea

DPRK and ROK
created 1948

Korean War 1950–1953
(armistice)

Liberation and Division

The Birth of Rival Republics

The North-South Civil War

International Intervention in the Korean Civil War

The Korean Armistice

Liberation and Division

Japan's forced withdrawal from Korea did not end foreign rule on the peninsula. Koreans who were expecting to be liberated and then to run their own affairs after Japan's defeat were gravely disappointed. The Soviet Union's entry into the Pacific War on August 8, 1945, led American planners to realize that if all of Korea, like Manchuria, fell under Soviet occupation, communist forces would be positioned dangerously near Japan. To block the Soviet advance, American planners suggested dividing Korea along the 38th parallel, allowing Soviet occupation of the territory north of the line, but holding the south for occupation by the United States Army. The Soviet Army, which was concentrating on occupying Manchuria, agreed.

Though there were Korean exile groups in the Soviet Union, China, and the United States that wanted to return immediately and compete for leadership, neither the Soviets nor the Americans were prepared to let them control the newly liberated peninsula. Assuming that the long-defunct monarchy was in no position to return to power and that the exiled groups lacked legitimacy, the Allies deemed Korea unready for self-government—giving little heed to the last moments of the war when volunteers in the country's valleys, villages, and towns had stepped forward to keep their local markets and farming routines going, and to make administrative decisions for the places where they lived. These committees soon became widely known as "people's committees" (*inmin wiwŏnhoe*). They sprang from many types of organizations that had existed during the colonial era: old-style village elders, young politically active students, and labor organizers who once had tried to set up unions called *chohap*. Whatever their origins, they reflected a spontaneous effort by Koreans to take charge of their own lives. Their politics were leftist; that is, they wanted to reorganize the social and economic system that privileged the wealthy, particularly landlords and big businessmen, many of whom were accused of having profited through collaboration with Korea's Japanese rulers. In Seoul, a coalition of national leaders formed themselves into an umbrella organization called the "People's Republic," seeking to knit the People's Committees together into a national system of self-rule. A separate coalition of conservatives also formed, aimed at maintaining the status quo economic system. Behind this was a largely Japanese-educated elite that included wealthy Koreans from established lineages that had survived the fall of the Korean monarchy and 35 years of Japanese rule, many of whom retained extensive landholdings and owned modern businesses. This property-owning class was disinclined to allow a free discussion of social classes and Japanese collaboration; rather, it wanted a political system that would allow it to maintain its economic position.

The American military men who arrived to occupy South Korea in September 1945 suffered from a nearly total ignorance about Korea and the political cauldron that was boiling there when they arrived. The Americans assumed that the Koreans were a primitive people unfit to govern themselves, disregarding their long tradition of autonomy prior to the Japanese takeover in 1910. During the war, American planners had discussed putting Korea under an international trusteeship after the defeat of Japan, but no proper plans had been developed. When Korea was hurriedly divided along the 38th parallel between U.S. and Soviet forces, it was hoped that the two "trustees" would cooperate to find a way to launch Korea as an independent country. No one knew how this might be done, or which Korean leaders might be best qualified to form a Korean government. When the Americans discovered that most Koreans in the southern zone were bitterly opposed to the idea of foreign "trusteeship," believing that it was just another form of colonial domination, the United States tried to abandon the trusteeship formula. The Soviets, however, maintained that trusteeship was a sound policy, and they accused the Americans of changing the arrangements so they could create an anti-Communist state in South Korea, thereby making the country's division permanent.

The Americans and Soviets argued over these points in Korea as the Cold War was breaking out, and the United States went from thinking of the Soviet Union as a wartime ally to regarding it as a worldwide rival bent on conquest. In 1947, President Truman announced the doctrine of containment. The United States thereby pledged to block the expansion of Communism and vowed to fight Communist attempts to undermine "democratic" governments, that is, governments friendly to the United States. The presence of Soviet forces in North Korea therefore came to appear as a menace to American-occupied Japan, as well as to the non-Communist territory in South Korea. American policy assumed the goal of protecting South Korea from Communist control, thus angering the Soviets and their left-wing Korean Communist allies, and leading to a hardening of the 38th parallel into a permanent boundary between two rival Korean states in the north and south.

The Birth of Rival Republics

The alienation between the Korean political left and right that had developed under Japanese rule was also present in North Korea, where the Soviet occupation forces pushed aside centrist political leaders and installed left-wing Communist Koreans in their stead. The Korean government that took form under Soviet occupation was led by the ethnic Korean Kim Il-sung (Kim Ilsŏng, 1912–1994), who had spent the war years as an officer in a Korean unit of the Soviet Red Army. Among Korean Communists, Kim was known as a long-time guerrilla fighter who had engaged in numerous raids and small battles with the Japanese along Korea's Manchurian border during the 1930s, before finally being driven into Russian territory. With Russian backing, Kim's interim regime launched an attack against those who had collaborated with the Japanese and against all elements of Korean society that had maintained or gained wealth under the Japanese colonial system. These included large landholders, businessmen, former employees of Japanese enterprises, and others seen as socially privileged. Others labeled "class enemies" of the Korean working people included many Christians, intellectuals, and small capitalists whose ideologies conflicted with the vision of a Communist-ruled Korea. After being identified as "enemies of the people," many were stripped of their property and left with little choice but to leave the area ruled by the Communists. With poverty and civil war raging to the north in Manchuria, most chose to go south.

The Americans and anti-Communist Koreans in the south drew attention to northerners who were "voting with their feet" by migrating south to live in "freedom." As the left-wing regime consolidated its control in the north with Soviet backing, and the right-wing consolidated its control in the south under American sponsorship, the two Koreas drew apart. The conflict between their two visions for Korea's future was the basis for the protracted national division that has continued for more than half a century. It also appeared to merge with the worldwide conflict between Capitalism and Communism, making Korea an unfortunate testing ground in the Cold War. When the United States decided to end its military occupation of the south, it turned the problem of creating a "free" Korean government over to the

United Nations. In 1948, the U.N. attempted to organize a national election for a representative assembly to draft a constitution and create a government. In North Korea, however, this was interpreted as a ploy to use the larger population of the south to create a government in which the left would be a disadvantaged minority. The Kim Il-sung regime, with Soviet support, refused to allow U.N. teams into North Korea to set up the election. The election went ahead only in the southern zone. It created a constitution-drafting body that founded a republic whose legislature elected the American-educated Syngman Rhee (Yi Sŭngman, 1875–1965) as the first president of the "Republic of Korea" (R.O.K.). The following month, the Soviet-backed left-wing assembly in North Korea created the "Democratic People's Republic of Korea" (D.P.R.K.) and confirmed Kim Il-sung as its Supreme Leader.

The North-South Civil War

The "Korean War" is usually said to have started with North Korea's invasion of the South on June 25, 1950, and ended with the armistice at P'anmunjŏm on July 27, 1953. However, that three-year period might be better understood as the international phase of a civil war between the Korean left and right that began in 1946 and did not end until the U.S.-backed R.O.K. Army had eliminated the last Communist guerrillas in the South in 1955.

During the initial phase of the war, between 1946 and 1949, the Communists in the northern zone tried to keep left-wing elements alive and active in the south. As the Soviets gradually handed power over to the Korean Workers Party (KWP) under Kim Il-sung, the KWP pursued its belief that the common people of the south were eager for revolution. It was thought that they only needed the right kind of opportunity to rise up against South Korea's conservative elites and their American protectors. However, though there were many strikes and other manifestations of social and economic discontent, the Americans were able to suppress them by using Koreans from the former colonial police force, the former Japanese imperial armed forces, and their own military police. The most serious rebellions were aimed at blocking the 1948 election and the creation of a separate state in South Korea. The worst, on Cheju Island, cost an estimated 30,000 lives.

Koreans in the south were deeply troubled by all these events. The R.O.K. Army and National Police did not get along, and on occasion they even fought each other. In October 1948, leftist elements within the R.O.K. Army mutinied at the southern port of Yŏsu, calling down repression at the hands of army elements loyal to Seoul. By the end of 1949, however, the Seoul government had managed to reduce the left wing in South Korea to a sullen acquiescence. The country's Communist leaders were forced to gather in the north and ponder other ways to reunite the country.

In the early months of 1950, Kim Il-sung settled on a plan to invade the south in hopes of sparking the uprising that he thought would be the key to reunification.

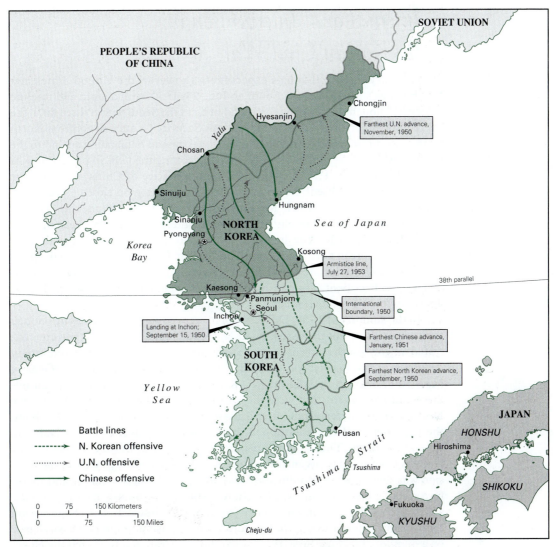

FIGURE 14.4　Korean War.

It is likely that he was encouraged by external developments, particularly the Communist victory in China and signals from the United States that it would not use force to defend the Seoul regime. He consulted with leaders in Beijing and Moscow and received pledges of military aid. He calculated that his own troops, many of whom had acquired battle experience while helping the Chinese Communists fight Japan and the Guomindang, would easily overwhelm the inexperienced R.O.K. Army. He also counted on the advantage of surprise. He thought he could take Seoul within a few days and cause the Syngman Rhee regime to collapse. The rest of the country would then fall quickly under his control.

International Intervention in the Korean Civil War

Contrary to Kim Il-sung's expectations, however, the United States met North Korea's invasion of the South on June 25, 1950, with a rapid and resolute response. Though the invading forces did in fact take Seoul within three days, the United States persuaded the United Nations Security Council to confront North Korea with a resolution branding it as an aggressor and demanding an end to the fighting. At the time, the Soviet Union was boycotting the U.N. in protest over its refusal to admit the P.R.C. as the legal representative of China, and with the Soviet ambassador absent the Security Council resolution on Korea passed without a veto. When the North Koreans ignored the U.N. action, the Security Council passed a second resolution creating a United Nations peacekeeping force to repel the North Korean invasion and restore the 38th parallel as the line between the Korean north and south. The Security Council delegated to the president of the United States the authority to appoint the U.N. Commander-in-Chief, and President Truman named General Douglas MacArthur, then in Tokyo, to lead the counterattack.

In the summer of 1950, D.P.R.K. forces proved to be almost strong enough to overrun all of South Korea. As U.N. troops reached Korea, they concentrated in the southeastern corner of the peninsula, helping the remaining defenders maintain what was called the "Pusan Perimeter." In this area General MacArthur began to rebuild the R.O.K. Army and to introduce the foreign soldiers and equipment that were meant to roll back the invasion. Though the North Koreans defeated the first American units that came to oppose them, the defenders rallied and stopped the Communist advance at the Naktong River, near Taegu. This holding operation bought precious time for the United Nations Command to organize a counterattack. North Korea's view of the invasion was that national reunification was an internal Korean matter and therefore nobody else's business. The United States, on the other hand, saw the attack across the 38th parallel as an international issue, an act of aggression that violated international law. The Americans' decision to intervene was based on a number of factors. First, the Truman Administration interpreted the North Korean invasion as a ploy by the Soviet Union to enhance Communist influence in East Asia. A Communist success in Korea would surely put great pressure on Japan, encouraging left-wing elements there and making it harder to reconstruct Japan as an American ally. Second, the United States saw the invasion as a test of the Containment doctrine, an attack on an American client that could not go unanswered without casting doubt on promises that America had made to defend allies around the world. America's failure to respond would raise doubts about U.S. promises to protect the members of the newly created NATO alliance. Third, the Truman Administration was itself under domestic attack for "allowing" China to "go Communist" the previous year. With congressional elections due in November 1950, the President's supporters knew that they could not let the Republicans add Korea to their list of Democratic foreign policy disasters. Fourth, the D.P.R.K. attack was seen as a blatant violation of the United Nations Charter, which required a resolute response from the United Nations to punish acts of aggression. It was considered important to prove that the United Nations, unlike the League of Nations after World War I, had enforcement power and would not tolerate an open attack by one nation-state upon another. Finally, many American leaders felt that they had a moral obligation to uphold the government that the United States had established in Seoul and to defend the people in the southern zone from forced submission to Kim Il-sung's regime.

Sixteen member nations of the United Nations contributed troops to the United Nations Command in Korea. The biggest contingents, of course, were the R.O.K. Army and forces from the United States. President Truman referred to the U.N. intervention in Korea as a "police action," though to the soldiers on the ground it looked and felt like a full-scale war.

A decisive shift in the war occurred on September 15, 1950, when General MacArthur commanded an amphibious landing at the port of Inch'ŏn, 22 miles west of Seoul, and recaptured the southern capital within two weeks. Korea's geography is such that he effectively blocked the northward escape of the North Korean invaders in the south and captured them by the thousands. It appeared that the U.N. peacekeeping force had succeeded in its mission, to restore the Republic of Korea and reestablish the 38th parallel as its boundary with the D.P.R.K. Buoyed by this success, however, the United Nations decided to expand the mission to invade the north. U.N. forces crossed the 38th parallel in early October, took the D.P.R.K. capital of P'yŏngyang, and advanced as far as the Manchurian border, triggering fears in China that they might continue their advance into China.

In Beijing, Chinese leaders sought assurances that this would not happen, and although President Truman repeatedly said that he did not want the Korean War to turn into World War III, the Chinese were not convinced that MacArthur would not try to roll back the Communist revolution in their country. With American leaders making statements that threatened China and talking loosely about using nuclear weapons to win a decisive victory against Communism in Asia, the P.R.C. prepared to intervene on the Korean peninsula. Adding to their concerns over the fighting in Korea was the fact that the United States had positioned the U.S. Seventh Fleet in the Taiwan Strait to defend the defeated Chinese Nationalists on Taiwan. Indeed, the Korean War brought a renewed American commitment to maintaining Taiwan, using U.S. military forces and aid to interfere in what the Chinese Communists regarded as an internal affair— the secession of a Chinese province under "rebel" Guomindang control. Perceiving a broad threat from the United States under cover of the United Nations, the P.R.C. positioned a force exceeding 250,000 in the mountains of northern Korea and near the end of November 1950 attacked R.O.K., U.S., and other U.N. forces in North Korea. The result was a debacle for many U.N. units, which actually had to fight their way back across the 38th parallel. By January 1951, the combined Chinese and North Korean armies had taken Seoul once more. It was only with difficulty that the United Nations Command was able to push them back, to a battle line that was north of the city not far from the original north-south boundary.

The Korean Armistice

In the spring of 1951, truce negotiations began in a tent on the battlefront and continued for two years during which the warring armies fought bloody engagements along the width of the Korean peninsula. American aircraft pounded targets in North Korea, reducing the major cities to rubble and obliterating North Korean agriculture and industry. Believing that aerial bombing would break North Korea's will at the negotiating table, American commanders destroyed dams and dikes in a way that caused floods and famine. Much of the D.P.R.K. government and surviving small industries were driven into caves and tunnels while ordinary people remained exposed in places that were bombed to break North Korean morale even when they had no military significance.

Meanwhile, streams of refugees collected in South Korea's cities where there was no bombing but also no employment and little food. International relief agencies alleviated the worst suffering, but when the war ended with a hard-fought truce in July 1953, Korea's economy and morale, North and South, had been shattered. The truce was signed at the village of P'anmunjŏm by representatives of North Korea, China, and the United Nations. An American general signed for the United Nations, representing all the armies that had fought on the U.N. side, including the R.O.K. Army. No representative of the Republic of Korea signed the truce document, a fact that the D.P.R.K. has always used as a reason to label the Seoul government as a puppet of the United States. Indeed, under a 1950 agreement, the Commander-in-Chief of the United Nations Command, who was always an American general, retained operational control of R.O.K. forces in wartime and authority over R.O.K. forces that were assigned to defend against North Korean attack for the rest of the twentieth century.

Estimates of Korean War casualties vary widely. More than 2 million Koreans, most of them civilians, lost their lives in the north and south. Among them were an estimated half-million D.P.R.K. and 300,000 R.O.K. soldiers. Chinese battle deaths were at least 320,000, though some estimates range as high as 900,000. The United States suffered 54,246 dead, including 33,629 killed in action. The British Commonwealth and other U.N. contingents lost nearly 5,000 killed in action. Estimates of the wounded and others who died from causes related to the war number in the millions. The United States alone suffered 103,284 wounded.

IV. The Vietnamese Struggle for Independence, 1939–1956

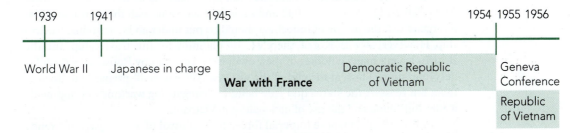

1939	1941		1945		1954	1955	1956

World War II   Japanese in charge   **War with France**   Democratic Republic of Vietnam   Geneva Conference   Republic of Vietnam

Vietnam during World War II

The 1945–1950 Period

The Defeat of France in Indochina

The Geneva Conference on Indochina

The United States and Ngo Dinh Diem

As previously noted (Chapter 12), there are many similarities between the post-colonial situations in Korea and in Vietnam. One of the most obvious is the importance of the American role in a country that was divided between competing left- and right-wing factions. Related to that is the astonishing lack of knowledge on the part of the Americans who made decisions that shaped events in Korea and Vietnam. Indeed, at the height of the Vietnam War, even after decades of American involvement, a senior American official acknowledged that, "There has never been an official of Deputy Assistant Secretary rank or higher (including myself) who could have passed in office a midterm freshman exam in modern Vietnamese history, if such a course existed in this country."[6]

Vietnam during World War II

America committed ground combat forces to Vietnam in 1965, but American involvement in Vietnam can be traced to 1940, when France fell to the Nazis and the French colonial apparatus in Vietnam started collaborating with the Axis, opening North Vietnam to incoming Japanese forces. The United States protested the expansion of Japanese military power into Indochina at that time and began clearing the decks for war in the Pacific, evacuating American civilians and increasing economic sanctions against Japan. In 1941, when Japan moved into southern Vietnam, the United States cut off all economic relations with Japan and, in effect, set the stage for the events at Pearl Harbor and beyond.

During World War II, President Franklin Roosevelt several times asserted his belief that French rule in Indochina had been brutal and should not be reestablished. At the Tehran Conference in 1943 and again in discussions with the British in 1944, he argued that the people of Indochina should be put under an international trusteeship. However, as with Korea, there was no planning for this trusteeship, and the British, having many colonies of their own, were annoyed by Roosevelt's push for decolonization. Thus, at the end of the war, the Allies were ill-prepared to do anything but reassert the status quo ante bellum, disregarding wartime developments within Indochina and the rise of nationalism in Vietnam.

In July 1941, Japanese imperial forces took control of all five *pays* of French Indochina—the three areas of Vietnam (Tonkin, Annam, and Cochin China) plus Laos and Cambodia. Of these, Tonkin and Annam were nominally under the figurehead emperor Bao Dai, scion of the Nguyen dynasty, Cochin China was under direct French rule, and Laos and Cambodia were under "protected rulers" of their own. The Japanese kept Bao Dai in place in Tonkin and Annam, letting him believe that they were positioning him to lead a renewed Vietnamese empire (De Quoc Viet Nam). Bao Dai thus transferred his cooperation to the Japanese, who to his great disappointment, ended up manipulating him as a puppet ruler during the war years. In Cochin China, for most of the war, the Japanese allowed French officials to continue working under their direction.

Meanwhile, Ho Chi Minh made contact with American intelligence officials in China and developed a relationship that he hoped might encourage the Americans to support him after the eventual expulsion of Japanese forces from Indochina. He transferred his base of operations from China to northern Vietnam, returning home for the first time in 30 years. There, in the mountains, he created a nationalist organization that he called the League for the Independence of Vietnam, known as the "Viet Minh."

On March 9, 1945, the Japanese military in Indochina took complete control, removing the French from their positions in Cochin China. No doubt this was a step in contemplation of the imminent Allied victory, but it is important to note that for several months in 1945 there was no French administration at all in Indochina. While the Japanese used Bao Dai in Vietnam, Ho Chi Minh, believing he had American support, tried to influence Allied policy in favor of his own movement. When Japan announced its surrender in August, Ho Chi Minh and his Viet Minh forces marched into Hanoi, took control of government buildings, installed themselves in office, and successfully demanded the abdication of Bao Dai in the old imperial capital of Hue.

In Europe, however, the Allies were making different arrangements for postwar Indochina. With the death of President Franklin Roosevelt, the U.S. Government muted its criticism of colonialism in general, and at the Potsdam

Conference in July, President Harry Truman agreed to a British plan to accept the surrender of Japanese forces in southern Vietnam while the Chinese Nationalists accepted it in the north, above the sixteenth parallel. Like the trusteeship formula for Korea, the plan for Vietnam took no notice of Vietnamese wishes and ignored the emerging nationalist appeal of the Viet Minh. Rather, the British took the lead in reasserting Western control, preparing the way for a return to French colonial rule.[7]

The arrival of British forces in August and September created considerable chaos in southern Vietnam. The city of Saigon was wracked with violence as French legionnaires, liberated by the British from Japanese detention, turned guns on Vietnamese collaborators and confronted agents of the Viet Minh. Angry Vietnamese struck back, no longer respectful of the French after having seen their humiliation during the war. In October, French forces, assisted by the British, landed in the Mekong River Delta and ejected the Viet Minh from Saigon—or so they thought. Viet Minh agents quickly returned. French historian Philippe Devillers later wrote,

> If we departed, believing a region pacified, the Viet Minh would arrive on our heels. . . . There was only one possible defense, to multiply our posts, fortify them, arm and train the villagers, coordinate intelligence and police. What was required was not [our] thirty-five thousand troops but a hundred thousand. . . .[8]

The 1945–1950 Period

In northern Vietnam, after a short-lived intrusion of Chinese forces sent to exercise their part of the bargain at Potsdam, Viet Minh operatives retained control. On September 2 in Hanoi, Ho Chi Minh proclaimed the founding of the Democratic Republic of Vietnam (D.R.V.) under Viet Minh leadership, quoting from the American Declaration of Independence that "all men are created equal" and that the new government stood for "life, liberty, and the pursuit of happiness."

The world, however, did not respond. The United States did not recognize the D.R.V., and by the end of the year it was plain that it had opted to support France. Officials in the European Bureau of the State Department, arguing that France's postwar recovery required the rebuilding of its overseas empire, prevailed over officials in the Far Eastern Bureau who warned that French rule would soon prove untenable in Indochina and that the colony would turn out to be an unbearable burden.

During 1945 and 1946 the French fought their way back into control over the towns and villages of southern Vietnam. Though there were periodic pauses in what amounted to a war between the French and the Viet Minh, Ho Chi Minh appeared certain that his own people would prevail in establishing their independence. The French, on the other hand, trusted in their superior weaponry to reestablish their control. Accordingly, the cease-fires were always short-lived, with France and the D.R.V. repositioning themselves for renewed hostilities. In March of 1946, for example, France and the D.R.V. agreed that the D.R.V. should join the French Union subject to a nationwide vote by the Vietnamese people. The deal called for France to transform Cochin China into a separate state, meaning that the D.R.V. would have to give up claims to uniting the entire country under its sway, and that France would keep forces in southern Vietnam until 1952. When the Viet Minh decided that the price was too high, the agreement broke down. By the end of the year the two sides were at war once again.

By 1947, the cost of the fighting in Indochina had become intolerable for France. In Paris, government officials started searching for an exit strategy. In order to save face and to maintain their economic position in Vietnam, they were determined not to allow Ho Chi Minh a complete victory. They began searching for a non-Communist alternative to Ho who could create a rival government that the people might actually prefer if given a choice. They wanted the former emperor, Bao Dai, who was living in Hong Kong at the time, to return and head their alternative government. Though Bao Dai had abdicated in September 1945, ending the Nguyen dynasty as well as his own reign, the French hoped that his residual cachet would serve to rally Vietnam's non-Communists. When, after considerable turmoil, France created the Associated State of Vietnam in 1949, Bao Dai became its *chef d'état* (chief of state). As a member of the French Union, the Associated State of Vietnam had the right to manage its internal affairs, but French officials retained control of its finances, the economy, and such vital functions as law enforcement. France thus succeeded in transforming at least the southern part of its colony into a puppet state—one that claimed sovereignty over all of Vietnam, including Annam and Tonkin as far north as the Chinese border.

The outside world reacted coolly to the new French client government in Saigon. In Washington, State Department factions resumed arguing about whether French colonialism or Asian nationalism was more deserving of American support. Some wondered if the Bao Dai government was sufficiently autonomous to deserve recognition.

In 1948, U.S. Secretary of State George Marshall had proclaimed that "the objectives of the United States can only be obtained by such French action as will satisfy the aspirations of the people of Indochina."[9] However, not long after the Communist victory in China, both the People's Republic of China and Soviet Union recognized the D.R.V. under Ho Chi Minh. This made Vietnam an urgent foreign policy problem for the Truman Administration by appearing to be another "defeat" in a long series of "losses" to Communism. Dean Acheson, Marshall's successor as secretary of state, declared that Soviet and P.R.C. recognition of the D.R.V., "should remove any illusions as to the 'nationalist' nature of Ho Chi Minh's aims, and reveals Ho in his true colors as the mortal enemy of native independence in Indochina."[10] Putting anti-Communism ahead of all other considerations in Indochina, the United States immediately recognized the Associated State of Vietnam. Acheson explained the step as a way of expressing "displeasure with Communist tactics which are obviously aimed at eventual domination of Asia, working under the guise of indigenous nationalism."[11] In May 1950, the United States went further by granting France US$10 million for military operations against the Viet Minh.

Throughout the late 1940s, fighting continued throughout Indochina. In Laos and Cambodia as well as Vietnam, French forces struggled to reassert their colonial regimes. In areas of northern Vietnam that were fully under their control, the Viet Minh instituted economic reorganization along socialist lines. This involved a certain amount of violence as the D.R.V. dealt with former collaborators, but Ho Chi Minh put the anti-imperialist cause ahead of the antifeudal struggle, and postponed large-scale land reform. Production and efficiency increased in areas that were free of fighting, and though some people dreaded conscription, much of the population supported the Viet Minh both for their resistance against the French and for their domestic policies.

The Defeat of France in Indochina

Viet Minh planners knew that their war would be long and costly. They recognized that the French would have the early advantage but that as the Viet Minh recruited and trained their troops, the advantage, in the north at least, would pass to those who better knew the terrain, language, and aspirations of the people, who on the whole, hated French rule. Early in 1950, the Viet Minh commander Vo Nguyen Giap won an important battle in the Red River Valley. More victories followed throughout the year, with French forces being decimated by effective Viet Minh tactics backed by an increasing supply of weapons from China.

After recognition by the Soviets and Chinese Communists, and under conditions of warfare during which Chinese advisors tried to nudge the D.R.V. farther to the left, life in the Communist-controlled area took on a more political coloration. Stresses increased as the former Indochinese Communist Party regrouped along national lines, creating separate movements in Vietnam, Laos, and Cambodia. In the D.R.V., the government stepped up enforcement of ideological purity and encouraged open class criticism of landowners, intellectuals, and other elite members of society, people who might have supported the independence effort if it had not cost them so much personally.[12]

As the war in Korea heightened American fears about the "march of Communism," the U.S. government stepped up its military aid to the French in Indochina. In 1952, after the battlefront had settled down somewhat in Korea, Americans turned their attention to other parts of Asia. Planners became concerned that if the Communists were successful in Vietnam, neighboring countries would also succumb to Communist conquest or revolution, making for a chain reaction that was likened to a row of falling dominoes. This "domino theory" raised the stakes in Vietnam. The United States disliked supporting colonialism, but it seemed that American-backed military action against the Viet Minh was the only way to keep the first domino from falling. With luck, it might buy time for the Associated State of Vietnam to develop into a viable nation. In the Philippines and Malaya, Western-backed anti-Communist counterinsurgency campaigns appeared to be defeating the local Communists. Perhaps the same result could be achieved in Vietnam.

Until 1953, the French had relied on their better weapons to defeat the Viet Minh and had been unable to field a very large army in Indochina. In that year, however, the new French commander in Vietnam, General Henri Navarre, devised a plan whereby more than 300,000 troops would be recruited from the local population. This "yellowing" of forces, as it was called, would enable the French to blunt the Viet Minh's home-ground advantage while enabling them to confront the Viet Minh in force with troops and weapons paid for by the United States. Enthusiastic about this plan, the Eisenhower Administration pledged $384 million, bringing total U.S. support for France in Vietnam to $500 million per year.

In May 1954 the Navarre Plan met its test in Dienbienphu, a fortified point near the Laotian border in western Tonkin. For many months the Viet Minh had been trying to draw French forces westward, away from their strongholds in the Tonkin Delta. As the Communists pulled westward, the French became concerned about Viet Minh expansion into Laos, and ordered General Navarre to provide protection for the Laotian capital of Luang Prabang. Navarre decided to do more than block Viet Minh expansion: he decided to set the stage for a battle that would turn the tide and deal the D.R.V. a decisive defeat. For many weeks in early 1954, French forces ostentatiously occupied the Dienbienphu valley, setting up artillery at will and reinforcing their main post for the battle. The Viet Minh did not interfere, preferring not to waste their efforts against superior firepower. Instead they bided their time, recognizing that the French were digging into positions that they would be hard pressed to defend or reinforce once the battle began.

General Giap then did something that the French had not thought possible: he gathered a force of 100,000 men and had them haul disassembled heavy artillery and anti-aircraft pieces into the mountains around Dienbienphu. Winter clouds provided cover and much of the work was done at night. On March 12, 1954, Giap opened fire on the French fort and started capturing French outposts throughout the valley. As shells rained down on Dienbienphu, attempts to resupply the French fort by air were met by withering antiaircraft fire from the hills. In Washington, French representatives begged the United States for a quick and massive American intervention, and Eisenhower Administration officials briefly considered using nuclear weapons. The battle went on for six weeks until, on the night of May 6, D.R.V. forces overran the French garrison, forcing surrender. The Dienbienphu debacle was universally seen as the endgame for France in Indochina. The Navarre Plan had failed, and although the fighting continued elsewhere in Vietnam, the election of Socialist Premier Pierre Mendes-France in June tilted the Paris government toward complete withdrawal.

The Geneva Conference on Indochina

The French flag fell at Dienbienphu on the day before the great powers were to convene a conference at Geneva to discuss the future of Indochina. When the conference began on May 8, 1954, the United States was still hoping for a military victory over the Communists in Vietnam. However, the Americans had also

BOX 14.1 DIENBIENPHU—
THE HORRORS OF WAR

The people suffering and dying at Dienbienphu were hardly unique, but for the sake of balance the horrors of war have not previously appeared in our boxes. This account by the French journalist Jules Roy can serve as a reminder of all those who suffered and died (civilians as well as soldiers) in World War II and earlier wars, as well as of the slaughter yet to come in Vietnam.

[Dr.] Grauwin felt like crying. The terrible sight of broken bodies and blown off heads filled him with both horror and rage. To reach the shelter where he snatched a few hours' rest, he had to step over piles of amputated limbs. . . . With his friend Gindrey, he operated, sawed bones, wound yards of intestines, stitched chest wounds and got rid of the hundreds of corpses which had overflowed from the morgue and were covering the helicopter landing ground, the roof to the messes and the dormitories.

Inhumanity and barbarity on the part of the Viet Minh? Who respected the laws of war and who broke them? It was easy to remain unmoved when French fighters machine-gunned the parties of orderlies and porters carrying Viet wounded through the bush on bamboo and nylon stretchers to the hospitals in the rear, but one felt sick with horror when Giap's gunners fired on planes bearing Red Cross markings.

Neither side observed the rules of war. Jules Roy concludes:

I would feel ashamed by the evidence against us only if Dienbienphu had suddenly run short of blameless captains, heroic doctors and poor devils who possessed nothing in the world except human life and honor.

Jules Roy, *The Battle of Dienbienphu*, trans. from the French (New York: Carroll & Graf Publishers, 1984), pp. 190–93.

become disillusioned with French methods and capabilities. They would have been glad to see France ejected from Indochina if it had not meant a certain victory for the Communists. Fearing that the Geneva Conference would conclude by providing for a French exit in exchange for handing too much to the Viet Minh, the Eisenhower Administration refused to participate as a regular member of the conference. Instead the United States sent an "observer" delegation so that it would not be bound to support the conference's decisions. The Associated State of Vietnam likewise attended as an observer. With Washington and Saigon on the sidelines, the participants were the United Kingdom and Soviet Union (as co-chairs), France, China, the D.R.V., and the other two "Associated States of Indochina," which were Cambodia and Laos.

The delegation from the Democratic Republic of Vietnam arrived at Geneva expecting to be recognized as winners of the Vietnamese fight for independence. In this they were supported by the Soviet Union and China. However, the British and French, backed by the Americans, refused to give the D.R.V. more than its forces had won on the battlefield, that is, Tonkin. It was only after many weeks of difficult negotiations that the conferees produced a series of agreements on July 21 that set the stage for the next phase of Vietnamese history. The provisions included:

- An immediate cease-fire between French and D.R.V. forces in Vietnam, Cambodia, and Laos, withdrawal of all combatants to their respective zones, and the return of all refugees.

- The division of Vietnam into northern and southern zones at the 17th parallel, with the D.R.V. in control in the north and the Associated State of Vietnam controlling the south.

- The promise of national elections in both zones within two years, to create a unified government for all of Vietnam by popular consent; a French force to remain in Vietnam to guarantee the election followed by a complete French withdrawal.

- Creation of an International Control Commission made up of Canada, India, and Poland to supervise implementation of the agreements.

- No new foreign bases to be allowed in either zone, and no membership in any externally controlled military alliance.

Although the United States did not sign the Geneva Accords, American observer Walter Bedell Smith gave a statement pledging the United States not to use force to oppose the implementation of the agreements.[13] The Eisenhower Administration was distressed that the D.R.V. had been granted control as far south as the 17th parallel. To make the best of the situation, the United States turned its attention to supporting the Associated State of Vietnam in the south.

The United States and Ngo Dinh Diem

While the conference was taking place in Geneva, change had overtaken the government in Saigon. Chief of State Bao Dai had appointed a new prime minister named Ngo Dinh Diem (1901–1963), commissioning him to create a new post-Geneva government. Diem had once served the French, but had resigned in protest in the 1930s. In 1945 the Japanese had briefly tried to recruit him, as had

Ho Chi Minh. In 1950 he was invited to Michigan State University where he began an ultimately successful public relations campaign to win the notice of American politicians and Catholic leaders. With the backing of such figures as Supreme Court Justice William O. Douglas, Senators Mike Mansfield and John F. Kennedy, and Francis Cardinal Spellman, head of the Catholic church in New York, Diem appeared to Bao Dai to be someone who could win American support in place of the French. Diem's family home was near Hue, in Annam, and his family had had ties to the old imperial court. He was not well known in the south—indeed, he thought southerners as a group lacked the kind of discipline that was needed for victory over the D.R.V.[14]—and he installed many associates in cabinet and other high positions who lacked political followings in the south. He also installed his brother, Ngo Dinh Nhu, as head of the country's internal security forces. In 1955, the Ngo government wrote a constitution, and Ngo Dinh Diem became president of the Republic of Vietnam (R.V.N.).

When Ngo Dinh Diem arrived in Vietnam in 1954 he had to struggle to win public acceptance. He was not well known in the south, and his years abroad further clouded his legitimacy as a national leader. He was single in a country that prized family lineages, a Catholic in a country where most people practiced a mixture of Confucianism, Buddhism, and animism, and he owed his appointment to foreigners, in this case Americans. There were attempts to overthrow him from the beginning, by army elements and political challengers. American officials, though they privately expressed doubts about his capabilities, could not afford to let him fail. They increased aid, both covert and overt, funneling hundreds of millions of dollars into his treasury and introducing weapons and military assistance in violation of the spirit of the Geneva Accords. Seeing time as the enemy—the elections were to be held in two years—they labored to boost Diem's government in public esteem. President Eisenhower pledged full American cooperation in return for "reforms," meaning democratization. But democracy was not notably in Diem's nature. Moreover, the U.S. Central Intelligence Agency helped Washington send mixed signals to Diem, using various illegal and unethical means to help him maintain power without needing to build democratic support. In the 1955 referendum that created the Republic, for example, CIA agents showed Diem's government how to fix the vote by printing the antimonarchy ballots in red, the color of good luck, and the pro-monarchy ballots green, the color of bad luck. In some cases, Diem's police attacked voters with green ballots. The rampant vote tampering means that it is impossible to tell what the voters actually wanted, but the will of Diem and the Americans prevailed.

American efforts to promote the Saigon government and undermine the D.R.V. had started immediately after the Geneva Accords. During the interval in the summer of 1954 when people were allowed freely to migrate from one zone to the other, American propaganda emphasized that Catholics in the D.R.V. zone would be persecuted by the Communists. As a result, Catholics were an important part of the estimated 800,000 refugees who poured from the north into the south, enabling the Americans to point to the huge number of Vietnamese "voting with their feet." CIA operatives used fortune tellers to predict dire things for the D.R.V. zone, and dropped leaflets with propaganda messages intended to frighten northerners into migrating to the south. In other instances, CIA teams ran guns to anti-Communist guerrillas in the north, sabotaged the Hanoi city bus system, instructed Saigon police interrogators in torture methods, and organized English lessons for the mistresses of high Vietnamese officials.[15] However, these things did little to win popularity for the Ngo Dinh Diem regime, which increasingly was seen as corrupt and unworthy of support.

However, in the Democratic Republic of Vietnam, conditions were also depressed. Ho Chi Minh's regime had a hard time delivering the promised benefits of socialism. After the deprivations of World War II and the long war with France, the infrastructure of the northern economy was badly dilapidated. The D.R.V. had to import food and accept foreign aid from other socialist states. In addition, there was real opposition to the D.R.V.'s communist methods for redistributing land and punishing landlords and businessmen who had exploited the working class. To consolidate their control, the Viet Minh rounded up, tried, and executed many "class enemies" who had done nothing worthy of such extreme punishment. This in turn generated great bitterness that undermined the legitimacy of Ho Chi Minh and gave the Republic of Vietnam grounds to accuse the D.R.V. of injustice and tyranny. Ho himself admitted that his government had made many mistakes, and as the time for the 1956 election that had been arranged at Geneva approached, he vowed to do better.

However, the election never took place. President Eisenhower later wrote in his memoirs the he believed that, "had elections been held as of the time of the fighting, possibly 80 percent of the population would have voted for the Communist Ho Chi Minh as their leader rather than the Chief of State Bao Dai."[16] This fact had not changed in 1955, when Ngo Dinh Diem elevated himself to the presidency of the R.V.N., and there was little hope of defeating Ho Chi Minh in 1956. Under the circumstances, when the D.R.V. proposed consultations with Diem regarding the election, Diem refused. The United States briefly fretted that Diem was making the R.V.N. side look bad, but ultimately went along, saying that conditions for the election "were not ripe" yet. American were strongly convinced that the Vietnamese people, given the right conditions, would come to support the democratic-capitalist leanings of the Saigon government over the communist leanings of the Ho Chi Minh regime. The objective would be to "build a nation" in the south that would simultaneously demonstrate the advantages of democracy and the failings of communism. This undertaking would prove to be easier said than done.

Notes

1. For the eulogy, in which Wen Yiduo attacked Chiang Kai-shek personally and predicted that the Guomindang leaders would meet the same fate as Mussolini and Hitler, see Pei-kai Cheng and Michael Lestz with Jonathan D. Spence, *The Search for Modern China: A Documentary Collection* (New York, NY: W. W. Norton, 1999), pp. 337–38.

2. Quoted in John W. Dower, *Embracing Defeat: Japan in the Wake of World War II* (New York, NY: W.W. Norton, 1999), p. 97.

3. Article IX of the Constitution. A convenient source is David John Lu, *Sources of Japanese History,* vol. 2 (New York, NY: McGraw-Hill, 1975), pp. 193–97.

4. Dower, *Embracing Defeat,* p. 544.

5. Ibid., p. 558.

6. Daniel Ellsberg, *Papers on the War* (New York, NY: Simon Schuster, 1972), p. 28, quoted in Stanley Karnow, *Vietnam: A History* (New York, NY: Penguin Books, 1984), pp. 150–51.

7. For Great Britain's role in the return of the French to Vietnam at the end of the war, see David G. Marr, *Vietnam 1945: The Quest for Power* (Berkeley, CA and Los Angeles, CA: Univ. of California Press, 1995), particularly Chapter 5, pp. 297–46.

8. Quoted in Karnow, *Vietnam,* p. 171.

9. Quoted in Chester Cooper, *The Lost Crusade: America in Vietnam* (New York, NY: Fawcett, 1972), p. 85.

10. Quoted in Robert D. Schulzinger, *A Time for War: The United States and Vietnam, 1941–1975* (New York, NY: Oxford University Press, 1997), p. 42.

11. Karnow, *Vietnam,* p. 223.

12. William J. Duiker, *Ho Chi Minh: A Life* (New York, NY: Hyperion, 2000), pp. 434–39.

13. Robert F. Randle, *Geneva 1954: The Settlement of the Indochinese War* (Princeton, NJ: Princeton Univ. Press, 1969), pp. 343–44.

14. Duiker, p. 468.

15. Neil Sheehan, ed., *The Pentagon Papers as Published by the* New York Times (New York: Bantam, 1971), pp. 13–21.

16. Dwight D. Eisenhower, *The White House Years: Mandate for Change* (New York, NY: Signet Books, 1963), p. 449.

China under Mao

When Mao Zedong proclaimed the People's Republic on October 1, 1949, it marked a watershed in the history of modern China. After a century of internal disintegration and foreign aggression, China made a new beginning under leaders deeply committed to the revolutionary transformation of the nation. Mao and his associates were determined to create an egalitarian society and to make China strong and prosperous.

In taking control of the entire country and then restructuring Chinese society, the new leaders faced problems as immense as China itself. They were dedicated Marxists, and in their march to power had brilliantly adapted the foreign ideology to Chinese conditions. The challenge that now awaited them of transforming China in the spirit of that ideology proved a formidable one, and the course they took was anything but smooth.

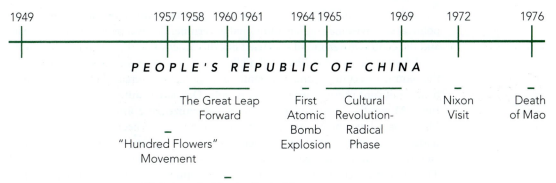

PEOPLE'S REPUBLIC OF CHINA

I. Consolidation and Construction Soviet Style, 1949–1958

Government and Politics

Foreign Relations and the Korean War

Economic Policies

Thought Reform and Intellectuals

The People's Republic of China (P.R.C.) began with an initial period (1949–1952), during which the regime consolidated its rule and forged the basic framework of a new sociopolitical order. This was followed by a period of Socialist Construction (1953–1958), initiated by the first Soviet-style five-year plan— begun in 1953, but not published until 1955.

Government and Politics

Following the example of the Soviet Union (U.S.S.R.), the Chinese formed parallel government and party structures with high party officials appointed to top government posts. Thus, Mao headed the party as Chairman of the CCP Central Committee and, until 1959, was also officially head of state. High party members also held positions of leadership in various quasi-official organizations such as trade unions, and as earlier, party members served as political commissars in the army, which reported to the Military Affairs Commission headed by Mao.

Administratively, China was divided into provinces, which remained the primary political subdivisions after an additional governmental level between the provinces and the central government was tried but discarded. The three most highly populated metropolitan areas, Shanghai, Beijing, and Tianjin, were placed directly under the central government, and "autonomous regions" were created in areas inhabited by a significant number of minority people. One such "autonomous region" was Inner Mongolia. (The new government recognized the independence of Outer Mongolia, where the Mongolian People's Republic had been established in 1924 under Soviet sponsorship.) The other autonomous regions were Guangxi, Ningxia (southeast of Inner Mongolia), and the vast western regions of Xinjiang and Tibet. The latter was incorporated into the People's Republic after Chinese troops entered that mountainous land in October 1950, but Tibet did not receive autonomous region status until 1965. Aside from their strategic importance, the Inner Asian territories were significant because the government had to deal with the interests and sensitivities of their ethnic minorities.

A major step toward realizing the egalitarian aims of the revolution was taken in 1950 with the promulgation of a marriage law that gave women political and economic equality as well as equal rights to divorce. Women were free to participate in the work force and pursue careers, although, in practice, this did not release them from their traditional household responsibilities.

The cohesiveness of the party leadership, forged during years of struggling side by side, was an important success factor in the new system. The only political conflict to erupt openly was an attack on Gao Gang, the CCP leader in Manchuria who was accused of separatist ambitions. Additional factors were Gao's ties with the Soviet Union and the issue of Soviet influence in Manchuria. Gao's suicide was reported in 1955. At this juncture, Rao Shushi, who was based in Shanghai, was also purged. Both leaders, in charge of prime industrial centers, were accused of "operating independent kingdoms" and of forming a political alliance.

To achieve its goals, the leadership launched massive national campaigns in what became a pattern. Thus, during 1951 through 1952 there was a "three antis" campaign against waste, corruption, and bureaucratism, aimed at disciplining the greatly enlarged CCP membership. Additionally, there was a "five antis" campaign against bribery, tax evasion, fraud, the stealing of state property, and the theft of economic secrets. As a result, many wealthy men had to pay heavy fines. In line with Mao's *On the New Democracy* (1940), members of the "national bourgeoisie" were initially tolerated, and only capitalists with Guomindang or foreign ties were labeled enemies of the revolution. Gradually, however, private companies were turned over to the state, although their former owners often remained as managers.

Not all drives were directed against human evildoers; there was also a concerted attack on the Four Pests: a war against rats, sparrows, flies, and mosquitoes. Although the inclusion of sparrows was misconceived, it was partly by such campaigns that the P.R.C. achieved enormous improvements in public health. Furthermore, by involving all the people in these campaigns, the leadership made use of China's greatest asset (manpower) while giving the people a sense of participation and pride in the resulting accomplishments.

Foreign Relations and the Korean War

The Communist victory was hailed with enthusiasm in Moscow and bitterly deplored in Washington. Partly for ideological reasons and partly in response to continued, even if unenthusiastic, American support for the Nationalists, the CCP adopted a policy of "leaning to one side," formally aligning itself with the U.S.S.R. in a treaty in February 1950, a product of Mao's first visit to Moscow (and, in fact, his first trip outside China). However, relations between the two allies were not easy, for Stalin drove a hard bargain and was slow to relinquish special interests in Manchuria and Xinjiang. Still, the relationship with the U.S.S.R. was crucial for China because the Soviet Union provided a model for economic and political development as well as moral, political, and economic support.

On the American side, some observers were disgusted with Chiang Kai-shek, but most continued to view him as China's savior, a view fostered by wartime propaganda and the efforts of ex-missionaries, politicians, and other supporters. Many, in and out of government, failed to appreciate that the CCP were nationalists as well as communists. All this impeded the easing of tensions between Washington and Beijing, but it is clear that "both Chinese and American leaders were interested in and groping uneasily toward accommodation."[1] However, time ran out with the beginning of the Korean War in June 1950 (see Chapter 14).

The Korean War did not alter the international configuration of power in East Asia, but it did embitter Sino-American relations. Each side was now completely convinced of the enmity of the other. In the United States, proponents of a moderate China policy were removed from influence and subjected to slander. The Nationalist regime on Taiwan was given economic and military assistance, and in 1954 the United States signed a mutual defense treaty with the government of Chiang Kai-shek. Meanwhile, American troops remained in Korea and on bases in Japan. The Chinese, alarmed by these developments, felt confirmed in the wisdom of allying themselves with the U.S.S.R. While the Chinese viewed America as an imperialist aggressor, throughout the 1950s many people in the United States, even those in high places, considered the People's Republic to be little more than a Soviet satellite.

If the Korean War merely froze the participants into their Cold War postures, it also enhanced China's international status by demonstrating the ability of its peasant army, a bare year after the triumph of the revolution, to resist the formidable armed might of the United States. Within China, the Korean War helped the government to mobilize the people under the banner of national resistance and created its share of national heroes. Above all, it meant that the revolution had now been tested in foreign as well as domestic war.

Abroad, Beijing's representatives played an important role in the Geneva Conference on Indochina (1954) and at the conference of Asian-African states held at Bandung (Indonesia) in 1955. However, the Nationalists retained the

China seat at the United Nations, and the United States prevailed on most of its allies to join it in withholding recognition of the P.R.C. The buildup of Nationalist strength on Taiwan rankled Beijing, but with the U.S. Seventh Fleet patrolling the Taiwan Strait, actual fighting was limited to sporadic shelling of two Nationalist-held islands off the coast of Fujian Province.

Economic Policies

Economic matters were of central concern to the new government from the start. It had inherited a land ravaged by war and floods, with both agricultural and industrial output severely decreased from prewar levels, and the monetary system wrecked by inflation. In addition, the underlying economy had serious structural weakness. In the agrarian sector, the prevalence of small, uneconomical, scattered landholdings and uneven land ownership helped to perpetuate traditional farming techniques and discouraged investment and capital formation. The industrial sector, on the other hand, consisted primarily of light industry concentrated around Shanghai and heavy industry in Manchuria. The latter had been developed to meet the requirements of foreign capital rather than the needs of China and its people.

Any government would have had to restore and strengthen the economy, but as Marxists, China's new leaders were also committed to the transfer of the means of production from private to public ownership and the creation of an egalitarian system of distribution. Their aim was to create a socialist state with a strong proletarian (working-class) base. The necessary precondition was vigorous industrialization, and because this was also necessary for national strength, economic ideology and patriotism equally demanded such development.

By 1952, despite the strains of the Korean War, the economy had been restored to prewar levels. Factories had returned to operation, railway lines were repaired, and inflation was brought under control. In the cities, the private sector was temporarily retained and even encouraged, but control over materials and marketing, as well as wages, prices, and working conditions, was in the hands of the State. Meanwhile, in the countryside, land redistribution occurred by mobilizing the suppressed fury of the rural poor rather than by governmental decree. Landlords were denounced and humiliated in public trials and at mass "speak bitterness" meetings. The more fortunate ones were allowed to retain enough land to support themselves, but many lost their lives. The campaign became associated with a general suppression of potential counterrevolutionaries during the Korean War. In the end, a more equitable distribution of land was accompanied by a change of village leadership, now drawn from the poor peasantry.

The achievements of the first three years of the People's Republic were viewed as merely a preamble for further socialization and economic development. A planning organization was established, as was a statistical bureau. In 1953 China took its first modern census, which showed a total population of 582.6 million on the mainland. Although its accuracy has been questioned, this figure is accepted as a general indication of China's population at the time.

China's First Five-Year Plan followed the U.S.S.R. model of economic development in stressing heavy industry, with some 85 percent of total investments going into this sector. The Soviet Union supplied technical assistance (plans, blueprints, and so forth), helped train Chinese technicians (28,000 Chinese technicians and skilled workers went to the U.S.S.R. for training during the 1950s), and sent about 11,000 of its own experts to work in China. Development was accelerated by importing entire plants from the Soviet Union. Most of the remaining private sector was eliminated. Control over the plants was given to professional managers and technocrats, whose prime responsibility was to carry out government economic directives. To enable them to do this, they were placed firmly in charge of their factories.

Since loans advanced by the Soviet Union amounted to only three percent of China's total state investments, the financing of this industrialization effort was predominantly Chinese. These funds came out of the government's budget. The government, in turn, derived revenue from taxes and from the income of state enterprises. Ultimately, a considerable portion of investment capital came from agriculture, which remained the heart of the Chinese economy.

To increase output and channel agricultural surplus more effectively into capital formation, the government in 1953 began a more radical transformation of land management. To replace the existing system of small fields, individually owned and worked, the government planned to collectivize agriculture by pooling land, labor, and other resources. This was to be accomplished in stages. First, "mutual-aid" teams, which shared labor, tools, and work animals, were organized. The next stage was to create village producers' cooperatives that also pooled land.

Initially, agricultural collectivization was planned as a gradual program, because the Chinese leadership wanted to avoid the terrible bloodshed and suffering that had accompanied Stalin's rapid collectivization in the U.S.S.R. Mao, however, in a major speech delivered in July 1955, drew on the experience of the Chinese as distinct from that of the Russian Revolution, and reaffirmed his faith in the revolutionary spirit of the Chinese peasantry. Just as the peasantry had been in the vanguard of the revolution that gave birth to the People's Republic, it would now lead the nation to socialism. In Mao's view it was the party, not the people, that was dragging its feet. The immediate effect of Mao's speech was an acceleration in the agricultural collectivization program, leading to its nearly complete accomplishment within a single year (1955–1956); and the timetable for full collectivization was set ahead. This speech marked the emergence of a radical Maoist strategy for economic development. In 1957, the process of collectivization was completed.

At the end of the First Five-Year Plan, the Chinese viewed the results with considerable satisfaction: The government was now firmly in control of the industrial sector; agriculture had been reorganized; iron, coal, and steel production targets had been exceeded; and industrial output doubled from 1953 to 1957. Altogether, remarkable progress had been made on the road to industrialization. Of course, problems existed. One was the widening gap between city and country, a problem that has plagued all industrializing countries but was of special concern in China, where the peasantry remained the majority and where the party leaders identified with it. Another problem was the reemergence of bureaucracy and the transformation of a revolutionary party into the mainstay of the establishment.

Thought Reform and Intellectuals

The leaders of the People's Republic were convinced of the scientific correctness of their doctrine as well as its moral righteousness, and they believed that virtually everyone could be brought to share their vision and act accordingly. They were optimistic not only about the course of history but also about human nature. In keeping with tradition, they had faith that everyone could attain moral perfection, now redefined in terms of an ideal socialist person. It was their belief that given the proper environment and correct guidance, people would become selflessly devoted to revolution and community.

Naturally, the most promising were the young, uncontaminated by the old society, and the government ensured that they were educated in the new values. Special attention was paid to the political awareness of Communist Party members and cadres, who were relied on to set examples of personal conduct and lead the people. To further the thought reform and moral transformation of even the most unpromising individuals, the authorities devised techniques of group discussion, self-criticism, and public confession. By using the individual's own feeling of moral inadequacy and guilt, and by applying external pressures, the authorities induced people to renounce old values and prepared them for conversion to the new faith. The most famous example of such a change of heart, accomplished in the controlled environment of a correctional institute, was provided by Puyi. As an infant he had been the last occupant of the Qing throne, and more recently he had served the Japanese as puppet ruler of Manchukuo. After undergoing thought reform, he reemerged as a citizen in good standing.

Not just prominent personages spent time in small discussion groups; ordinary people also analyzed their lives as well as problems or incidents at their places of work. In this way, the new ideology was transmitted to the people, and they were taught to use it with everyday problems. At the same time, social pressures were applied to make everyone conform with accepted standards of behavior.

The thought reform of intellectuals, already a target of Mao's wartime rectification campaign (see Chapter 13), remained difficult. Highly trained and educated people were a rare and precious resource for a nation bent on industrialization and modernization. Yet few came from peasant or worker backgrounds. More serious than their class background was the persistence of traditional elitist attitudes among intellectuals, as well as their critical habits of mind. They tended to resent taking directions from party cadres less well educated than themselves. The Communist Party needed their special knowledge and skills, but it was unclear if the party could trust them.

With education and the media under tight party control, the arts, too, served the revolution. While Western-style artists were taught "Socialist Realism," a style intended to inspire, not to mirror life (Figures 15.1 and 15.4), artists working in traditional styles (*guohua*) were accepted as furthering national glory, but urged to incorporate modern subjects in their work (Figure 15.2).

The integration of artists and intellectuals into the new society remained problematic. When, in May 1956, Mao invited writers and thinkers to "let a hundred flowers bloom; let a hundred schools contend," there was little response from intellectuals, wary of exposing themselves to attack. However, in February 1957, Mao said in a speech, "On the Correct Handling of Contradictions Among the People," that nonantagonistic contradictions should be resolved by persuasion rather than force. After some further reassurance, the floodgates of criticism were opened.

FIGURE 15.1 *Chairman Mao Standing with People of Asia, Africa, and Latin America,* Wu Biduan (b. 1926) and Jin Shangyi (b.1934). Notice the new artistic style of Socialist Realism. Oil on canvas, 143 × 156 cm. NATIONAL ART GALLERY OF CHINA, BEIJING.

Criticism was directed not only against the behavior of individual party functionaries and at specific party policies but also at the CCP itself for seeking "to bring about the monolithic structure of a one-family empire."[2] Intellectuals and writers asked for independence from the party's ideological control. Academic problems should be left for professors to solve: "Perhaps Mao has not had time to solve these problems for us,"[3] one history professor suggested.

Mao had intended the campaign to rectify the party, but the criticism was more than he had expected. Weeds grew where he had invited flowers. A full-fledged anti-Rightist campaign developed, beginning in June 1957. Prominent intellectual, literary, and artistic figures disappeared into labor camps, along with over 400,000 others, with the government announcing a target of five percent per organization and the campaign quickening to include a massive purge of party members and cadres. Under these pressures, some saved themselves by denouncing their friends. People with negative entries in their files had their lives ruined. Many of the victims were not fully rehabilitated until after Mao's death. By 1958, few dared object when Mao launched his Great Leap Forward.

Balancing the demands for ideological purity and revolutionary fervor with the professional competence required to operate a modern state and build an industrial system became a fundamental issue. Without the former, a new elite of experts, technocrats, and managers would pursue its own aims and the revolution would be jeopardized. Mao believed that progress toward communist egalitarianism and the building of national strength went hand in hand, but put his faith in Redness, often at the expense of expertise.

II. The Revolution Continued, 1958–1976

The Great Leap Forward

The Sino-Soviet Split

"Back from the Brink," 1961–1965

The Great Proletarian Cultural Revolution: The Radical Phase, 1966–1969

The Winding Down, 1969–1976

By the end of the First Five-Year Plan there were indications that following the Soviet model was not producing the desired economic or social results, but there was no agreement on what should be done. While the party establishment saw a need for only minor adjustments, Mao advocated a far more radical approach. In the subsequent, complicated, often turbulent years, he did not always get his way, but he did prevent the revolution from settling down into comfortable routines.

The Great Leap Forward

The Great Leap Forward was initiated in January 1958, but lost momentum the following year. After 1959 it continued, but without vigor until it was terminated in January 1961. On Mao's initiative, the gradualism of Soviet-style central planning was abandoned in favor of reliance on the energies of the masses imbued with revolutionary consciousness. Mao believed that ideology was a force that could motivate people to heroic accomplishments. History was not confined to a series of well-defined objective stages of economic and sociopolitical development, but could be turned into a process of "permanent revolution" driven by the subjective will transforming the objective world. The P.R.C. had made use of massive manpower in labor-intensive projects all along, projects such as the building of waterways, roads, and other giant construction works. Now the glorification of labor became more intense:

> Labor is joy; how joyful is it?
> Bathed in sweat and two hands full of mud,
> Like sweet rain my sweat waters the land
> And the land issues scent, better than milk.

> Labor is joy; how joyful is it?
> Home from a night attack, hoe in hand,
> The hoe's handle is still warm,
> But in bed, the warrior is already snoring.[4]

The author of these lines, written in 1958, was Yuan Kejia (1921–), who had once been an admirer of T. S. Eliot.

All of China's human resources were to be focused in a giant leap. Through Redness and revolutionary fervor, Mao hoped to accelerate China's economic development and speed the advance toward socialism. The spirit of the people was to be the driving force for continued economic growth and social transformation. Through the catharsis of intense participation, the Great Leap Forward mobilized the emotional involvement of many people in the creation of a new order. They were made to feel that building a strong China should not be left to just experts and technocrats; it was to be done by, as well as for, the people.

As the prime vehicle for this effort, rural communes were formed by combining the already existing cooperatives. By the end of 1958, 98 percent of China's rural population lived in some 26,000 communes. Each averaged about 25,000 people. The communes were divided into production brigades, each corresponding roughly to the traditional village, and these in turn, were divided into production teams. The communes were intended to function as China's basic political as well as economic and social units, integrating all aspects of life. As economic units, they supervised agricultural production and distribution, provided banking services, and ran small factories and machine shops, which were operated at the commune or production-brigade level, depending on the size and degree of specialization of the plant. The communes were further responsible for police functions, they ran schools and hospitals, provided day-care facilities and mess halls, took care of the aged, and staged plays and other entertainments. They represented an ambitious attempt to create new, large-scale communities. But they turned out to be too large, and the cadres who ran them were too far removed from the realities of farming. Their size was therefore reduced, so that by the end of the Great Leap Forward the original number of communes had almost tripled to 74,000, with a corresponding decrease in the size of their memberships. Later the communes lost many of their functions to the smaller production brigades, and peasants were given greater discretion.

There was also a movement to establish communes in the cities by combining or transforming earlier street associations that included the inhabitants of one street (or of several small streets, or of a section of a large street) originally organized for security and welfare. They were now given additional responsibilities for economic enterprises, as well as for educational and medical facilities. In general, the formation of urban communes involved the transfer of authority over factories from central and provincial ministries to the local party committee that controlled the communes. Some of the communes consisted of workers in one large factory, others included the residents of one part of a city, still others, located on the outskirts of cities, included some farmland along with an urban sector. Whatever the form of urban organization, an effort was made to release women for work by establishing mess halls, nurseries, homes for the aged, and service facilities such as laundries.

To enlist popular enthusiasm and encourage local initiative, local authorities were granted substantial leeway in deciding how to implement government directives. The central government still set general economic policy and retained control over the largest heavy industrial plants, but 80 percent of all enterprises were decentralized. No longer were there experts in far-off Beijing making all the decisions and operating with a centralized bureaucracy as in the U.S.S.R.

Literature and the visual arts were intended to be by, as well as for, the people. Teams were sent out to collect the people's literature and to encourage peasants to compose poetry and otherwise participate in the creation of art. In Shanghai alone, some 200,000 people participated in producing 5 million poems. Many thousands undoubtedly were exhilarated at achieving recognition in a field previously reserved for an exclusive elite.

High social and economic expectations were raised by the creation of the communes. According to communist theory, the achievement of a truly communist society entails a change from paying people according to their productivity to paying "each according to his needs." In line with this, experiments were conducted in paying people approximately 70 percent of their wages in kind (produce to satisfy their needs) and the rest in cash according to their productivity. Meanwhile, impressive production targets were announced, including the goal of catching up with British industrial production in 15 years. To the Chinese leaders, the social and economic goals seemed entirely compatible.

If the Great Leap Forward achieved some of its political and psychological goals, it ended in economic disaster and famine. This did not become apparent for some time; the initial statistics of production were impressive, but they turned out to have been grossly inflated. An unanticipated consequence of the Great Leap Forward was a breakdown in China's statistical services, and serious mistakes were made because the government accepted the exaggerated figures forwarded by overenthusiastic local authorities. Some projects originally pursued with enthusiasm later had to be abandoned as unworkable. Perhaps the best known of these was the campaign to use local villagers and materials to create backyard furnaces for making iron and steel. Since this fitted in well with the policy of decentralization and relying on the masses, the plan was vigorously implemented. All over China small furnaces were set up and utensils were melted down, but the furnaces proved incapable of turning out iron of acceptable quality, let alone steel.

The most serious failure of the Great Leap Forward was in agriculture. Misconceived irrigation projects leached nutrients from the soil, and mass mobilization for work projects exhausted and demoralized the people. Here, too, the government worked with misleading statistics, as local units vied with each other in reporting productivity gains. The harvest of 1958 was seriously exaggerated. Relying on faulty expectations and inflated reports, the government took so much grain that in many areas practically nothing was left for the peasants. Massive famine resulted. The number who died is difficult to determine, but 16 to 27 million is a conservative estimate, 30 million is plausible. The Great Leap ended in a stupendous crash.

The Sino-Soviet Split

From the beginning of the People's Republic, there was tension and potential conflict between China and the Soviet Union. As we have seen, the CCP rose to power only after following a path independent of Moscow and its recommendations. Furthermore, the Chinese leadership was as determinedly nationalistic as the Soviets, who under Stalin, operated on the principle that what was good for the Soviet Union was good for world communism. This equation had some plausibility as long as there was only one great communist state in the world, but it was a thesis that the Chinese were bound to challenge.

Initially, the forces holding the alliance together were stronger than those pulling it apart. These included ideological ties and shared Cold War enemies. However, around the mid-1950s serious cracks in the alliance began to appear. One cause of friction was territorial. The Chinese reluctantly accepted the independence of Outer Mongolia, whose historical status resembled that of Tibet, but they were very unhappy about their northern and western boundaries with the Soviet Union. These borders had been drawn in the nineteenth century as part of the imperialism that China's new government pledged to undo. As early as 1954, Chinese publications indicated the country's refusal to accept vast regions of Central and Northeast Asia as permanently belonging to the U.S.S.R.

Another source of trouble was the Chinese desire for recognition as leaders of world communism, as suggested in Figure 15.1. After the death of Stalin in 1953, they expected that Mao would be honored as the leading living contributor to Marxist ideology and the architect of strategies to advance the cause in the "Third World." Instead, Khrushchev denounced Stalin in a famous speech in 1956 that implied the illegitimacy of all "personality cults," including that forming around Mao. Figure 15.1 shows Mao as a world figure. Stylistically, it exemplifies a turning away from Soviet models and "the nationalization of oil painting," a term applied to "any means of imbuing oil painting with recognizably Chinese aesthetics." As illustrated here, one such method was to forgo the effects of light and shadow and favoring "flat patches of unmodulated color rather than painterly textures."[5]

Khrushchev's theory of peaceful coexistence and the U.S.S.R.'s new international stance further irritated the Chinese. Even Mao's opponents within the CCP felt insulted that Chinese leaders had not been consulted before these major shifts in Soviet policy were announced. For their part, the Soviet leaders could hardly be expected to welcome Chinese claims, made during the Great Leap Forward, that their communes represented a higher stage on the road to the ideal society than anything achieved in the Soviet Union after 40 years of Communist rule.

Despite efforts toward reconciliation, such as Chinese support for the Soviet suppression of the Hungarian uprising in 1956, Mao's visit to Moscow in 1957, and Khrushchev's to Beijing in 1958 and 1959, the strains in the alliance continued to mount. Contributing to this was the U.S.S.R.'s unwillingness to exploit its temporary supremacy in rocketry to support a possible Chinese attack on Taiwan, an attack that would have had no hope for success unless the United States were neutralized by Soviet threats. Khrushchev's relatively nonbelligerent stance toward the United States seemed to the Chinese like a cowardly betrayal, while Mao's belittling of the dangers of nuclear warfare made him appear to the Soviets as a dangerous adventurer gambling with the lives of millions. From such a viewpoint, it is not surprising that the Soviets were hesitant about sharing nuclear secrets with the Chinese.

The split became unbreachable in the summer of 1960, when the Soviets withdrew their technicians from China. They even took their blueprints with them. After that, despite limited cooperation during the Vietnam War, relations remained bitter, as China and the U.S.S.R. denounced each other's policies and challenged the Marxist legitimacy of each other's revolutions. While the Chinese charged that the Soviets had deviated from the true revolutionary path, Russian and East European ideologists depicted Chinese aberrations as arising from their lack of a firm proletarian base as well as an inadequate understanding of Marxism.

One aspect of this situation was the Soviet Union's support of India in its disputes with China. Relations between China and India became tense in 1959, after the Chinese asserted their rights under international law and imposed their rule on Tibet, using their soldiers to suppress Tibetan resistance. India's welcome of Tibetan refugees, including the Dalai Lama, the spiritual and sometime secular leader of Tibet, was resented in Beijing. China and India, the world's two most populous nations, were natural rivals for Asian leadership. The resulting tensions would not have led to outright hostility, however, had it not been for a border dispute over a remote area through which China had built a road linking Xinjiang with Tibet. The result was a short border war in 1962, in which the Chinese quickly humiliated the Indian troops. The Soviet Union continued its policy of friendship with India, and China cultivated good relations with India's arch rival, Pakistan. Meanwhile, within the communist world, China defended and allied itself with the bitterly anti-Soviet regime of Albania.

Militarily, the Soviet Union remained the much stronger power, but the People's Republic was also developing its armed strength. A milestone was reached in 1964 when it exploded its first atomic bomb. Although, as indicated by its title, the painting reproduced as Figure 15.2 was understood as celebratory, it may have been an ironic response to relentless pressures on Wu Hufan (1894–1970) to produce art that would serve the revolution and the state, for Wu was a highly sophisticated and sensitive traditional-style painter and a careful student of the paintings of the Four Wangs, who had delighted the court of Kangxi (see Chapter 2). To quote Julia Andrews, "As incongruous as it seems, this painting of the mushroom cloud is one of the most beautiful demonstrations of brushwork to be found during the period." She goes on to cite its "casual lively strokes and subtly varied ink tones."[6]

The bomb did not soften relations between the two communist giants. Numerous border clashes endangered the peace between them, and both feared that the situation might escalate into full-fledged war. Beijing built an extensive system of underground shelters in case of an attack by air. The hostility of the Soviet Union was one of the principal factors that led to a gradual rapprochement between China and the United States during the 1970s.

"Back from the Brink,"
1961–1965

We have borrowed the title for this section from a detailed study focused on one village[7] as it recovered from the Great Leap, but it seems apt for the country as a whole. The failure of the Great Leap Forward led to retrenchment in domestic policies, and a willingness to accept, at least for a while, more modest interim social and economic goals. It was a serious setback for Mao, who continued to emphasize class struggle. He remained party chairman, but in December 1958 had to resign as head of the government. That post was filled by Liu Shaoqi (1898–1969), a hard-working organization man long associated with Mao. Liu had supporters in high party and government positions, but the supervision of the State's administrative machinery, including the various ministries, remained under the direction of the head of the State Administrative Council, who had the title of premier. This position had been held since 1949 by another trusted party veteran, Zhou Enlai. Zhou also served as foreign minister until 1959, and continued even after he left that post to act as China's main spokesman in foreign affairs. By all accounts, Zhou was one of the most capable and versatile of the CCP leaders, a superb political and military strategist, as well as a truly gifted administrator and negotiator.

Another important government position was that of minister of defense. In 1959, Peng Dehuai (1898–1974), a veteran general, was ousted from this post for going too far in criticizing Mao and the Great Leap Forward. He was further accused of pro-Soviet tendencies, and held responsible for overemphasizing professionalism and failing to imbue the troops with sufficient ideological spirit. His successor as minister of defense was another distinguished general, Lin Biao (1907–1971) who was favored by Mao.

Under the direction of Liu Shaoqi, the government relaxed the tempo of social change. There was now greater appreciation of expertise and less reliance on the revolutionary enthusiasm of the masses. There was an increased use of economic rather than ideological incentives: in the communes the more productive workers could earn extra work points, and in the factories there were wage increases,

FIGURE 15.2 *Celebrate the Success of Our Atomic Bomb Explosion*, Wu Hufan. Hanging scroll, ink and color on paper, 1965.

bonuses, and promotions to be earned, measures later castigated as "economism." Peasants, while still under the obligation to produce a fixed amount of grain for the State, were allowed small private plots and permitted to sell on the free market whatever they could grow on these.

No longer able to rely on the U.S.S.R. in the international arena, China in 1964 channeled investments into creating a "Third Front," described as "a crash program to build heavy industry in inland provinces away from the militarily vulnerable coastal and northeast areas."[8] Despite political turmoil, this effort continued until 1971, augmenting the damage already inflicted on the environment by misguided dam building and other abuses during the Great Leap Forward. From the beginning, as in the campaign against sparrows, Mao and his followers advocated and pursued the conquest of nature.

After the great exertions and the disappointments of the Great Leap Forward, there was a natural slackening of revolutionary fervor and subsequently the pace of change. This alarmed Mao, who sought to combat this trend by initiating a socialist education movement in 1962 without, however, much effect. Furthermore, thinly veiled attacks on Mao himself now appeared in print. Among them was the historical play, *Hai Rui Dismissed from Office*, written by the deputy mayor of Beijing. In this play the sixteenth-century official (see Chapter 2) was portrayed sympathetically as an honest minister who stood up for the peasants and was dismissed by a foolish and autocratic emperor. What was implied was a critique of Mao's own dismissal, in 1959, of Minister of Defense Peng Dehuai. In November 1965 an article was published in the Shanghai press denouncing this play. Thus began the Cultural Revolution.

The Great Proletarian Cultural Revolution: The Radical Phase, 1966–1969

The Cultural Revolution was profoundly ideological and strongly political. It was cultural in the broadest sense, for it sought to remold the entire society and to change the consciousness of the Chinese people. Utopian in its aims, it was disastrous in its results. Its moving force was Mao himself, determined not to allow the revolution to drift into Soviet-style revisionism, resolved to combat the reemergence of old patterns of bureaucratic arrogance and careerism, convinced that drastic measures were necessary to prevent the entrenchment of new, vested interests in state and party, and hungry to resume personal control. Now an old man, Mao was unwilling to rest on his laurels as the father of the revolution. He actively involved himself in the Cultural Revolution and dramatically displayed his physical vigor by publicly swimming some 10 miles across the Yangzi River five months before he turned 74 in 1966.

The obstacles to the Cultural Revolution were formidable, because it affected the interests of a majority of party functionaries both at the center of the bureaucracy and in the provinces. However, Mao's assets included more than just his unequaled prestige; they included the support of the People's Liberation Army, which under Lin Biao, emphasized guerrilla-style revolutionary spirit and fostered solidarity among officers and men by deemphasizing rank. In the summer of 1965, insignia of rank were abolished and uniforms in no way differentiated officers and men. Mao and other leaders hoped similarly to eliminate the distinctions and privileges of rank in society.

To accomplish this required the destruction of the Establishment. To carry on the battle, the country was inundated with copies of *Quotations from Chairman Mao,* the omnipresent Little Red Book cited on all occasions as the ultimate source of authority. Mao himself was glorified as never before. His sayings and pictures were everywhere; his writings were placed on family altars, his name filled the air; some villages began meetings by people holding hands and dancing to the tune of "Sailing the Seas Depends on the Helmsman, Making Revolution Depends on Mao Zedong's Thought."

The vanguard and shock troops of the Cultural Revolution were the Red Guards, young people mostly born since the founding of the People's Republic. Mao hoped that their youthful spirit would revitalize the revolution and rescue it from sinking into comfortable revisionism. In his view, it was not enough for these young people merely to read theoretical and historical works and to sing revolutionary songs. They must actually live and make revolution, so that they would be molded by direct personal revolutionary experience. As Mao had said, "a revolution is not a dinner party" (see p. 236). Going on their own "long marches" was not enough. The Red Guards were responsible for many excesses as they organized public humiliations of prominent people, administered beatings, took captives, ransacked houses and destroyed books, art, and anything old or foreign. Many people were beaten to death or committed suicide, while countless others were humiliated, imprisoned, and/or sent to labor on the land (Box 15.1). Among the most enthusiastic participants were urban youths of questionable class background proving to others and themselves their revolutionary purity.

Opposition to the Red Guard and the Cultural Revolution was considerable. In many places the local authorities were able to draw on popular support. There was rioting, and pitched battles were fought between rival groups, each claiming to represent the thought of Mao. Much of the information on these struggles comes from numerous posters written in large characters. Mao himself, in August 1966, wrote such a poster, "Let Us Bombard the Headquarters."

Many party headquarters were attacked, and the party was crippled. Leaders of the government, from Liu Shaoqi down, were made to confess their sins in public and then removed from public view. Universities were closed, scientific and scholarly journals ceased publication (although nuclear development went on apace), intellectual and cultural life was disrupted, and there was turmoil in the cities. However, Zhou Enlai managed to keep the basic machinery of government working, and was able to protect some from attack. Meanwhile, Mao's wife, Jiang Qing (c. 1914–1991), and Mao's secretary, Chen Boda (1904–1989), emerged as leaders of the Cultural Revolution group.

Writers and artists were prominent among the victims of the Cultural Revolution, and a narrow orthodoxy was also enforced in the other arts. Jiang

BOX 15.1 THE TIGRESS FALLS

The turmoil created by the red guards led to great suffering and released deep animosities. The following took place in a village in Hebei. The woman in question had no doubt earned her nickname, but ironically, she is made to suffer for excessive devotion to the nation and blamed for the policy of her husband whose powerful connections protect him from attack.

In mid January [1967] Beijing red guards dragged bound-foot Xu to a rally at the clubhouse. Villagers denounced grain-requisition policies. Geng was responsible, but villagers cursed his wife. One grabbed the Tigress by the collar and exploded into her face, "You old hag, you sifted and selected, selected and sifted, until there wasn't a single grain of sand in the grain. You delivered this good grain to the state. You didn't want to leave anything for us, did you?" Another shouted. "You delivered the best grain to the state. We harvested it and dried it. But you delivered it. We didn't have enough to eat!". . . .

The meeting roared approved for ousting Xu. A white dunce cap, symbolizing a descent into hell, was placed on her head. The rebels dragged her forward on tiny feet and paraded her. Stumbling, confused, 56 years old, worn out, wounded, she still shouted, "Long live Chairman Mao!" People screamed back insults, demanding she be silenced. How dare a counterrevolutionary invoke Mao's name! They pushed her head down and shut her up. Xu tried to shout again, "Long live Chairman Mao!" Someone hit her. She hobbled ahead and tried to raise her slogan again. Enraged, local people pressed forward and beat her.

Edward Friedman, Paul G. Pickowitz, and Mark Selden, *Revolution, Resistance, and Reform in Village China* (New Haven: Yale University Press, 2005), p. 97.

Qing, herself once an actress, championed revolutionary operas. In place of traditional Chinese opera, audiences were now treated to dances on the theme "We Are So Happy Because We Are Delivering Grain to the State" or expressing joy at the completion of an electric power plant.

The Cultural Revolution reached its most radical phase in early 1967. At the beginning of that year, a dramatic series of events in Shanghai led to the triumph of a workers' movement that was able to overthrow the local party apparatus by overcoming factional divisions. In February, the workers formed a People's Commune, which lasted only 19 days because Mao, thinking it too radical, did not endorse it. He preferred the formation of "revolutionary committees" in which the army played a leading role. With the party out of commission and the country badly divided, the army grew in importance as the single organized and disciplined institution capable of forceful action on a national scale. However, the revolution developed a new "ultraleft" intensity before the army was called to calm the situation. In the summer of 1967, hundreds of thousands demonstrated in Beijing against Liu Shaoqi and Zhou Enlai. Radicals even occupied the foreign ministry for two weeks. Outside of the capital, the army killed countless numbers in clashes with opponents. The most dramatic events took place in July, when the army intervened to suppress insurgents in Wuhan. Further violence ensued elsewhere. Finally, in September, Mao and the leadership turned toward the army to restore order. The Red Guards were disbanded in July 1968.

Military men were prominent on the various revolutionary committees set up to administer provinces, factories, and communes as the Cultural Revolution continued, increasingly under army auspices. The revolution came to an end in 1969. In April of that year, a party congress officially confirmed the new prominence of the army by adopting a new constitution designating Lin Biao as Mao's successor.

An important official criterion for party membership was class background. "Bad elements," such as the descendants of landlords, rich peasants, capitalists, and "rightists" continued to face obstacles in career advancement.

Earlier, party cadres and intellectuals had been "sent down" to work the land among the peasants, and now thousands of Red Guards were similarly removed from the cities for a stint of labor in the fields. This was a practical measure for restoring order, however, it also had a theoretical basis in the "mass line," which embodied Mao's conviction that the people were the source of valuable ideas and that the function of leaders was to obtain these ideas from the masses, to concentrate and systematize them, and then take them back to the masses. In other words, the function of leaders was to learn humbly from the masses and then to teach them. The idea was that leaders would identify with the common people, but the actuality was that for 10 years most of China's best and brightest had to suffer physical hardship and mental anguish and despair. Some were never to make it back to the cities, and numerous others would never be able to make up for years lost in education and training. China was to pay a heavy price for the loss of 10 years of educational, intellectual, and technological advance.

The Cultural Revolution saw the resumption of Great Leap Forward trends that had been discarded during the early 1960s. A policy of economic decentralization and provincial self-sufficiency was emphasized as consistent with the Third Front program as well as with Maoist ideology. Again, Redness was emphasized over expertise and private economic incentives. Again, the focus was on the rural sector, which benefited from programs that extended medical care and education. Plants were built in rural areas to manufacture and repair farm machinery, produce fertilizer, and process local products, thereby diminishing the distinction between city and country. There were experiments in calculating work points for farm work on the basis of political criteria rather than in terms of an individual's productivity. Similarly, in urban factories there were provisions for greater worker participation in factory management and programs to lessen the distinction between workers and managers as well as between mental and manual labor.

The Winding Down, 1969–1976

Although the Cultural Revolution was officially ended in 1969, Jiang Qing and her associates retained control over the media and cultural affairs. During the next seven years radical Maoists remained influential in national politics and had some victories. Nevertheless, there was a gradual turn to moderation. The party was rebuilt, and moderate leaders reappeared. Mao himself wanted to curb the power of the military and turned against Lin Biao, whose downfall came in the autumn of 1971. Allegedly, Lin tried to save himself by staging a coup, and when that failed, he attempted to flee in an airplane that crashed in Mongolia.

The fate of Liu Shaoqi and Lin Biao demonstrated the hazardous position of those marked for the succession, but Zhou Enlai, as usual, was on the winning side. Zhou continued as premier, and with Mao aging, he was more influential than ever. Army influence decreased and more moderate economic policies were adopted. There was a general relaxation of emphasis on revolutionary fervor. For example, when universities were first reopened in 1970, after a four-year hiatus, admission was based on recommendations from comrades in the candidate's work unit and the approval of the appropriate revolutionary committee, but in 1972 academic criteria for admission were reintroduced. Additionally that year, the first scientific periodicals reappeared but with an emphasis on applied science. Public exaltation of Mao was toned down. There were even attacks on the Little Red Book; CCP members were now urged to pursue a thorough study of Marxist writings.

During 1973 to 1974, Lin Biao, though dead, was further denounced in a campaign linking him with Confucius. Both men were portrayed as "political swindlers" and sinister reactionaries. Confucius was depicted as representing a declining slave-owner class, while Lin Biao was charged with wanting to restore capitalism, each man exerting himself to reinstate an outdated system. The campaign against Confucius and Lin Biao was a sign of the continuing influence of the Cultural Revolution leaders' attack on the past, but the ancient philosopher and modern general made a strange pair, and very likely Confucius was actually a surrogate for Zhou Enlai.

The politics and ethos of the time are illustrated in Figure 15.3. The slogan spanning and dominating the entrance reads "Workers, Peasants, and Soldiers Are the Main Force Criticizing Lin and Criticizing Confucius." Parking their bicycles and small tractors outside the gate, people have entered the compound to peruse wall posters elaborating the case against the two villains while loudspeakers, high on

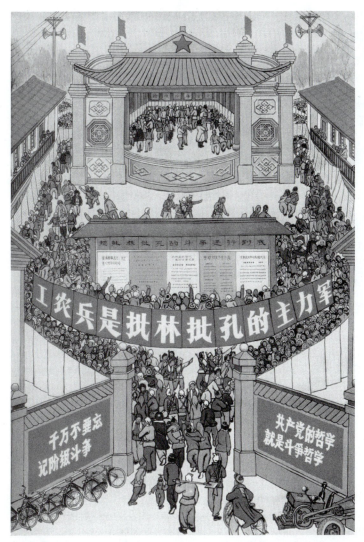

FIGURE 15.3 *Repudiating Lin Biao and Confucius,* Yang Zhixian. Like many peasant paintings, this one employs bright colors. Here vivid red predominates. Peasant painting exhibited in Beijing in 1973.

FROM *PEASANT PAINTINGS FROM HUHSIEN COUNTY.* COMPILED BY THE FINE ARTS COLLECTION SECTION OF THE CULTURAL GROUPS UNDER THE STATE COUNCIL OF THE PEOPLE'S REPUBLIC OF CHINA (PEKING, 1974).

their poles like their counterparts everywhere, blare out announcements, slogans, and revolutionary music.

Most peasant paintings do not serve overt political campaigns but celebrate rural life and work. Their urban counterparts were paintings showing people working in factories. Many show women at work, for China was determined that women were to become fully equal with men (Figure 15.4). In China, as in the Soviet

FIGURE 15.4 *Wo shi haiyan (I Am a Seagull)*, Pan Jianjun (designer/artist), c. 1973. Chinese poster showing a strong, exuberant woman defying the elements to bring modernity to the countryside.

Union, the challenges and triumphs of a socialist society were the main topics of art and literature, depicted in "socialist realism" style.

Peasant and "social realist" painting represent a break with old styles of painting, but others artists painted new subjects in a traditional way (Figure 15.1) or placed modern subjects in an essentially traditional setting rendered in a traditional manner, as in Qian Songyan's *Ode to Ya'an*, paying homage to the location of the Chinese Communist Party victory where the revolutionary Yan'an spirit supposedly held sway (Figure 15.5).

During the 1960s and 1970s, workers and peasants were still encouraged to participate in the creation of art. There were efforts at collective writing and painting. Another arrangement allowed part-time authors to get a day off from their factory jobs in order to write. Professional writers were periodically "sent down" to factory or commune so that they would not lose touch with the people. As a matter of routine, they invited popular criticism of their work and responded to suggestions for changes. For example, before *The Golden Road* (1972) was published, 200 copies were sent to communes and factories for criticism. This novel by Hao Ran (Liang Jinguang, 1932–), which went on to sell 4 million copies, dealt with the change from individual farming to the formation of mutual aid teams. In all arts, the same themes occur repeatedly: the ideals and struggles of the revolution, the wisdom of Mao, the heroism of soldiers, the triumph of socialist virtue over selfishness, and the glory of work.

During and after the Cultural Revolution, Chinese relations with the Soviet Union remained tense, even though both powers supported North Vietnam in its war against the Saigon regime and the United States. Concern over Soviet intentions heightened to alarm when the U.S.S.R. invaded Czechoslovakia in 1968 and Party Secretary Leonid Brezhnev announced that the U.S.S.R. had the right to intervene in socialist countries, which he accorded only "limited sovereignty." Fears of a Soviet nuclear strike, actual troop deployments along the lengthy Sino-Soviet frontier, and armed clashes in Manchuria induced China to seek broader diplomatic contacts with the United States. Although Chinese personnel did assist the North Vietnamese, there was no repetition of Korea. Chinese terrain was not threatened and no massive intervention by Chinese troops took place. Meanwhile, a channel of communication was maintained with the United States through periodic meetings of the ambassadors of the two countries, held first in Geneva and later in Warsaw. The fall of Lin Biao and the emergence of Zhou Enlai increased the prospect for improved Sino-American relations.

A contributing factor on the American side was the intention of President Nixon, elected in 1968, to withdraw the United States from the war in Vietnam. As long as China and the United States were committed to the opposing sides of a war that was raging at full force and threatening to escalate still further, substantial improvement in Sino-American relations remained highly unlikely. Nevertheless, a high-level Sino-American dialogue did not have to wait for the actual end of the war—a shift in direction toward peace was enough. By 1971 both sides were ready to talk. A new approach to China (known as "Triangular Diplomacy" because of the American strategy to play its two rivals—China and the U.S.S.R.—off each other) was deemed a logical corollary of the Kissinger-Nixon concept of international balance-of-power politics. The Chinese were receptive. The Sino-American rapprochement began informally with a Chinese invitation of an American ping-pong team, whose members were personally greeted by Zhou Enlai. Next, President Nixon's visited Beijing in February 1972, resulting in the Shanghai Communiqué, which provided for partial normalization and paved the way for the resumption of full formal diplomatic relations in 1979. In 1971, even before the Nixon visit, the United Nations had voted to admit the People's Republic in place of the Nationalists, and the new American stance now removed the last obstacle to recognition by most countries.

FIGURE 15.5 *Ode to Yan'an,* Qian Songyan (1898–1985). A pagoda and a transmission station face each other across a space defined, as in traditional landscapes, by mist and clouds rendering just barely visible the entrances to Yan'an's famous caves. Print.
COLLECTION CONRAD SCHIROKAUER. PHOTOGRAPH © LORE SCHIROKAUER.

Two deaths dominated the news in 1976. When Zhou died in January of that year, his enemies banned public mourning, but were unable to prevent a massive gathering at the Martyrs' Memorial in Beijing's great Tiananmen Square on China's Day of Mourning in April. This expression of reverence for the late premier was tantamount to a rejection of the Cultural Revolution. Mao, aged and ailing, still had sufficient authority to designate Hua Guofeng (1921–) as Zhou's successor.

Hua was soon called upon to demonstrate his administrative talents, for in July China's worst earthquake in four centuries devastated Tangshan, an industrial and mining city 100 miles from Beijing. Close to a quarter of a million people lost their lives. Historically, people would have interpreted this as a signal of further shocks to come—and they would have been right, for on September 9 Mao died. Architect of the triumph of the CCP, Mao presided over the successes of the revolution, but was also responsible for its failures and for needless suffering, hardship and dying. His passing marked the end of an era.

Notes

1. Warren I. Cohen, ed., *New Frontiers in American-East Asian Relations* (New York, NY: Columbia Univ. Press, 1983), p. 144.

2. Quoted in Merle Goldman, *Literary Dissent in Communist China* (Cambridge, MA: Harvard Univ. Press, 1967), p. 192.

3. Quoted in Goldman, p. 193.

4. Hsu Kai-yu, *The Chinese Literary Scene—A Writer's Visit to the People's Republic* (New York, NY: Vintage Books, Random House, 1975), p. 227.

5. Julia F. Andrews, "The Victory of Socialist Realism: Oil Painting and the New Guohua," in Julia F. Andrews and Kuyi Shen, *A Century in Crisis: Modernity and Tradition in the Art of Twentieth-Century China* (New York, NY: Guggenheim Museum, 1998), p. 230.

6. Julia F. Andrews, *Painters and Politics in the People's Republic of China, 1949–1979* (Berkeley, CA: Univ. of California Press, 1994), p. 303.

7. Edward Friedman, Paul G. Pickowicz, Mark Selden, *Revolution, Resistance, and Reform* (New Haven, CT: Yale Univ. Press, 2005), title of Chapter 2.

8. William A. Joseph, Christine P. W. Wong, and David Zweig, *New Perspectives on the Cultural Revolution* (Cambridge, MA: The Council on East Asian Studies/Harvard University, 1991), Introduction, p. 2.

16

The Chinese World since Mao

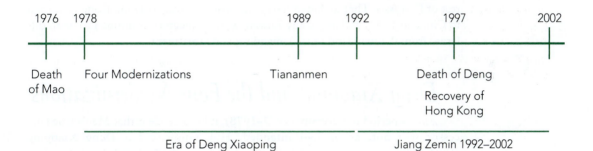

After the death of Mao Zedong, China embarked on a profound change of course. Many policies from the previous quarter of a century were reversed, and new measures were adopted that bore scant resemblance to those either of Mao or of his more conventional opponents. The economy changed dramatically, and by 2000 China was growing at the fastest rate in the world, creating both new problems and opportunities. All spheres of life were affected, but in different ways and at different speeds. Artistic and intellectual change were most intense; politics and its institutions lagged.

China's relationships to the external world, both in East Asia and beyond, also changed. One factor initially spurring China's leaders to adopt new policies was the recognition that it had fallen behind the impressive achievements of the rest of East Asia. That included Japan and Korea as well as Hong Kong (returned to China in 1997) and especially Taiwan, whose trajectory continued to be so different from the mainland as to demand separate treatment.

Deng Xiaoping and the Four Modernizations

After a period of adversity (1977–1978), it became clear that Mao's true successor was not, as he had intended, Hua Guofeng but Deng Xiaoping (1904–1997). Deng was a party veteran who, during the Cultural Revolution, had been removed from office and denounced as second only to Liu Shaoqi in "taking the capitalist road," but more recently Deng had enjoyed the backing of Zhou Enlai. In July 1977, Deng became first deputy premier, and by 1978 he was clearly China's most powerful political figure. Blamed for all the ills of the Cultural Revolution were the "Gang of Four," led by Jiang Qing, Mao's widow, who insisted, in vain, that she had simply been carrying out Mao's directives. By November 1980 the new leadership under Deng felt sufficiently secure to put the Gang of Four on trial and have it televised. In January 1981, Jiang Qing and another leader were given suspended death sentences, later commuted to life imprisonment. Hua Guofeng was soon shunted into political obscurity.

Deng's program was epitomized by the slogan "The Four Modernizations," first introduced by Zhou Enlai in 1975. Directed at agriculture, industry, science, and defense, the aim was to turn China into a modern industrial state. The years since 1952 had seen considerable economic progress, but China remained an underdeveloped country. Furthermore, the Cultural Revolution had taken a heavy toll in lost educational and technological progress. Now, under Deng, merit, not revolutionary virtue, was rewarded. Professionalism and individual initiative were encouraged, and market forces were allowed greater scope.

There were drastic changes in the countryside as agriculture was decollectivized. In 1982, communes lost their social and political authority, and their economic power was also curtailed. Under the "responsibility system," peasants were assigned land on contracts to produce a certain amount of grain, and increasingly won the right to decide on just how to do this and the right to dispose of any surplus produce on the open market. The amount of land assigned depended on the number of people in each family, an arrangement that seemed new but actually resembles both the 1951 Land Reform and the "equal-field system" enacted in 486 C.E. and discarded in the eighth century. Gradually, restrictions on commercial activities were eased, and enterprising peasants did notably well.

Similar changes took place in light industry and commerce, but at a slower pace. Official enterprises were expected to justify their existence by making a profit, government regulation was decreased, and individuals were allowed to open restaurants and workshops. Under a new open door policy welcoming foreign companies, special economic zones encouraging foreign investment were established. The most extraordinary of these, Shenzhen, not far from Hong Kong, mushroomed into an "overnight" boomtown. At the same time, the skylines of first Beijing, then Shanghai, and more recently even cities in the interior, were being transformed by high-rise buildings, among them international luxury hotels where the affluent traveler could savor China in luxury and at an antiseptic distance.

Mao Zedong had once seen China's large population as an asset, but even before his death it became clear that China's future would be dim if the population continued to grow without restraint. In the early 1970s, China adopted a vigorous birth-control program (see Box 16.1). Even so, the population continued to increase, topping 1 billion in 1982. In the cities, the birth rate had fallen even before severe pressures insured virtually full compliance with the one-child-per-couple law. However, this was not the case in the countryside, where children continued, with good reason, to be regarded as an asset to a family.

Industrialization and population growth put additional strains on China's already hard-pressed environment. We will return to them in our discussion of the 1990s, but it is worth noting here that air and water pollution were on the rise, and that land erosion had already turned the Yangzi River into a second Yellow River. In the mid-1980s, topsoil loss of more than 5 billion tons annually deprived China of more soil nutrition than that produced by its entire synthetic fertilizer industry. Major programs of reforestation were one positive response, but in general the environmental degradation accelerated. The State's obligation to protect the environment was included in the 1982 constitution, and a body of law ensued, but the Four Modernizations were not concerned with environmentalism.

Some, mostly elderly, party leaders objected to the pace of change, but there were also voices at the opposite end of the political spectrum calling for more rapid liberalization. They found expression in postings on Beijing's "Democracy Wall," where, for a time, people could freely state their views. Especially notable was a poster put up in December 1978 by Wei Jingsheng (1949–), a young man who worked as an electrician and had served in the army for four years. In his poster, Wei called for democracy as a Fifth Modernization necessary for the attainment of the other four.

This was too much for Deng and the political leadership. The wall was abolished. In May 1979 Wei was arrested. Subsequently, he received a 15-year sentence. Instead of a Fifth Modernization, Deng, in March 1979, proclaimed "four cardinal principles" as guides for the future.

BOX 16.1 CHINA'S ONE-CHILD POLICY

The following are regulations from a family planning policy enacted in Sichuan province in 1987. Although the one-child family was the norm, couples that met certain requirements were permitted to have a second child. For instance, if the first child had a nonhereditary disease and could not perform physical labor, if the husband or wife was the only son or daughter for two generations, if a parent was a disabled veteran of a certain rank and standing, or if the couple were overseas Chinese who returned to Sichuan, a second child was permitted. Infringements were punished through fines and other disciplinary action.

Article 1. To practice birth planning, exercise control over the population, and improve the quality of the population, and improve the quality of the population so that population growth would be suited to economic and social development plans, these regulations are enacted in accordance with the People's Republic of China (PRC) Constitution, PRC Marriage Law, and relevant regulations of the state, and in connection with Sichuan's actual realities.

Article 6. Late marriage and late births are encouraged. Late marriage means that both men and women are married three years later than the lawful age [of 20 for women and 22 for men]. Late births mean births by women aged 24 and above.

Article 27. Regarding those who insult, threaten, and beat doctors, nurses, and working personnel in charge of birth planning work or use other methods to obstruct birth planning, the public security organs will handle the cases in light of the "PRC Regulations Concerning Public Security Management and Punishment." If the practices constitute an offense, the judicial organs will investigate and affix the responsibility for the offense according to the law.

Article 29. Drowning, abandoning, selling, and maltreatment of girl babies and their mothers are prohibited. Regarding those involved in any of these practices, the units where they work or the leading organs concerned should educate them through criticisms and disciplinary sanction in light of the seriousness of the case . . .

Patricia Buckley Ebrey, ed., *Chinese Civilization: A Sourcebook.* Second edition (New York: The Free Press, 1993), pp. 478–480.

The Four Cardinal Principles

The four principles aimed to consolidate Deng's policy of economic but not political liberalization. They consisted of "the socialist road," "the dictatorship of the proletariat," "the leadership of the CCP," and "Marxism-Leninism and Mao Zedong Thought." In practice, as in theory, all four were vague at best. In 1981, "socialism with Chinese characteristics" was adopted as the official policy, postponing the attainment of utopian egalitarianism into the distant future. The "socialist road" was intended to be long, with China deemed to be only in the "initial stage of socialism," as Premier Zhao Ziyang (1919–2005) put it at the Eleventh Party Congress in 1987. That same year, the mayor of Shenyang was quoted as saying, "When used to promote the development of China's socialist economy, bankruptcy, leasing, shareholding and these sorts of things are no longer capitalist."[1]

Of the other cardinal principles, the leaders took "the leadership of the CCP" most seriously, and brooked no challenge to the political dominance of their party, which they equated with "the dictatorship of the proletariat," the orthodox Marxist label for the stage between revolution and the withering away of the State that would usher in true communism.

The status of "Marxism-Leninism and Mao Zedong Thought" was more problematic. Nineteenth-century self-strengtheners had once firmly believed in the Confucian ends they meant to serve with novel and foreign means, but China's new leaders conveyed no similar depth of conviction. To many it seemed that the official ideology commanded little more than lip service, while acquiring and enjoying personal wealth became common goals. China took on a new look as revolutionary posters and slogans gave way to commercial advertisements on billboards and in the media, clumsy at first but then "gradually transmogrified into slavish imitations of Hong Kong, Taiwanese and Japanese models." Geremie R. Barmé goes on to point out, "The world presented in such advertising was one nearly entirely divided from the ideological landscape constructed by the party." Referring to the vision projected by international consumerism and playing off Marx's denunciation of religion, he concludes, "During the early 1990s, this vision of the consumer's paradise, rather than the state religion of Marxism-Leninism and Mao Thought, became the true opiate of the masses."[2]

Intellectual Life and the Arts in the Eighties

It was a heady time, stimulated by a deluge of new ideas, forms, and styles. The period began with the "literature and art of the wounded," as artists and writers gave expression to their suffering during the Cultural Revolution. This was followed by a "search for roots," expressed not only in literature but in films, such as "Yellow Earth," directed by Chen Kaige (1952–), who along with his fellow "fifth generation" director, Zhang Yimou (1952–), won international acclaim for Chinese film. One of the many writers expressing similar sentiments was Mo Yan (Guan Moye, 1956–) whose *Garlic Ballads* depicts, with great human sympathy, the bitter life of peasants suffering at the hands of arrogant party cadres. He also wrote *Red Sorghum,* in which the villains are the Japanese military in China during World War II. Made into a movie directed by Zhang Yimou, it shocked the Chinese audience, but won the best picture award at the Berlin Festival in 1988.

Some writers turned more to psychological themes or to the interplay of human feelings, and engaged in stylistic experiments such as the flow of consciousness technique used by Wang Meng (1934–), Minister of Culture from 1987 to 1989. Others favored the magic realism of Gabriel García Márquez. Meanwhile, Chinese intellectuals in all fields rejoined the international intellectual community and undertook a reexamination and reevaluation of their own past. Foreign scholars were welcomed, notably at conferences on Confucius and Zhu Xi (1987) held in the philosophers' home provinces (Shandong and Fujian, respectively). Temples and monuments were restored, as were mosques and churches. Jiang Qing's revolutionary operas disappeared from the stage, and Arthur Miller was invited to help prepare a Chinese performance of *Death of a Salesman* (1985).

Now, too, the Chinese public had its first look at modern artists ranging from Picasso to Jackson Pollock. While members of the Obscure School of Poetry expressed their alienation in verse, avant-garde painters depicted faceless figures set in endless, barren space. Some determined nonconformists, such as the Dada group of Xiamen, Fujian's largest city, sought to smash all frames. Like the original proponents of Dada in post–World War I Europe, they mocked all art. Proclaiming the end of art, they ended their 1986 exhibit by burning all the works on display. In 1985 in Beijing, the brothers Gao Zhen and Gao Qiang inflated hundreds of balloons and condoms and called it a "midnight mass." A kindred spirit was Xu Bing (1955–), who devoted three years of hard work to compose his *Book from the Sky* that no one can read, thus challenging the viewer to reflect on the nature of writing, language, art, and life in a postmodern world (Figure 16.1).

The spirit of iconoclasm and revolt was not limited to the highbrow. Many aspects of western popular culture found a following in China, where Japanese and Taiwanese pop tunes were widely enjoyed and rock and roll gained an ardent audience. In the mid-1980s, Beijing's own Cui Jian (1961–), "the John Lennon of China,"[3] formed a rock group whose records were best-sellers, much to the puzzled dismay of the Establishment.

While raucous music and critical writings continued to find an audience among students and intellectuals, the regime, guided by Deng, was concerned not to let matters get out of hand. However, for approximately 10 years the leadership refrained from strong-arm measures that could alienate the intellectuals whose cooperation was needed for modernization. Thus, campaigns against "cultural pollution" (1983) and "bourgeois liberalism" (1987) were relatively mild.

Still, pressure for change mounted. An outspoken advocate of openness in government, free speech, and political pluralism was the astrophysicist, party member, and university vice president Fang Lizhi (1936–1986), who encouraged his students to campaign for genuine local elections in Anhui, where his university

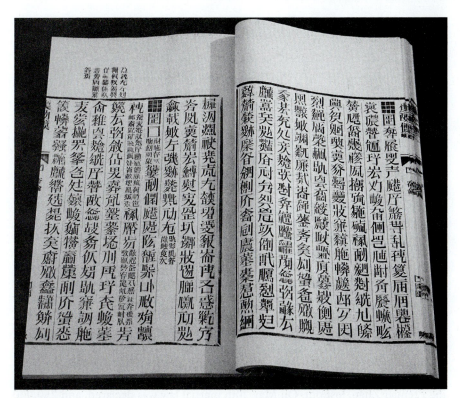

FIGURE 16.1 Detail view of the nonsense characters on the printed pages of the books from *Book from the Sky* (1987–1991) by Xu Bing. At first glance the writing looks like Chinese, for the characters are composed of elements found in traditional writing. They are, however, nonsense characters invented by the artist. Mixed media installation: hand-printed books, ceiling and wall scrolls from intentionally false letter blocks.

was located. The movement spread from Anhui. In December, some 30,000 students demonstrated in Shanghai, and there were further demonstrations in Tianjin, Nanjing, and Beijing. In response, the government removed Fang from his job and expelled him from the CCP Over a million students were sent to spend the following summer recess in the countryside.

For roughly 10 years Deng successfully orchestrated Chinese transformation, and in 1987 he had the satisfaction of seeing the Thirteenth Party Congress affirm the general directions of his policies, including the primacy of economic development. This session also marked the retirement of a substantial number of the old guard, who were generally replaced by men more inclined to "seek truth from facts," an expression found in the *History of the Han* (*Han Shu*, first century C.E.), taken up by Mao, and used as a slogan by Deng. Deng now felt sufficiently confident to resign as deputy premier although, significantly, he retained his chairmanship of the Military Commission for two more years.

Tiananmen (The June 4th Movement)

The policy of mild repression of demands for democracy and human rights failed to deter student activism or dampen student demands for greater freedom of speech and of the press, an end to favoritism and government corruption, the right to form their own organizations, and for the people to have a greater say in government. In the spring of 1989 the government was caught off guard when students demonstrated, boycotted classes, held sit-ins, and occupied Beijing's huge Tiananmen square in their determination to be heard.

With the approach of the seventieth anniversary of the May Fourth Movement, students and officials alike were aware of the occasion's historical significance, as was the press, now including international television as well as print media. Marches and demonstrations on May 4 quickened the movement, but did not settle anything. On May 13, two days before the state visit of Premier Mikhail Gorbachev, over 200 students began a hunger strike supported by thousands of Beijing residents. When Gorbachev arrived, the government had to change the program and avoid Tiananmen. By May 16, the number of hunger strikers had increased to over 3000. Meanwhile, as the movement gathered steam, students in many other cities demonstrated in support. Most alarming to the government, ordinary people, including factory workers, increasingly became involved.

Opposition within the government prevented even a mild compromise with the students, who were not well organized and did not speak with a single voice. When Deng Xiaoping asserted his leadership, the government moderates, including Premier Zhao, lost out. On May 20th martial law was declared, and 250,000 soldiers were brought into Beijing, where they were greeted by roadblocks and demonstrations. On May 29th, in a show of determination, radical students erected a large statue of the Goddess of Democracy holding high the torch of freedom (Figure 16.2). A young girl read their statement:

> Today, here in People's Square, the people's goddess stands tall and announces to the whole world: a consciousness of democracy has awakened among the Chinese people! The new era has begun! From this piece of ancient earth grows the tree of democracy and freedom, putting forth gorgeous flowers and a bountiful harvest of fruit.[4]

The goddess became the symbol of their movement, and Cui Jian's "Long March Rock" was their anthem.

Echoing the May Fourth Movement of 1919, the events centering on Tiananmen are known as the June 4th Movement because the end came early on June 4 when, shortly after midnight, columns of tanks and armored cars charged into the city and on to Tiananmen, crushing barriers and shooting anyone in the way. After the soldiers destroyed the student encampments and the statue on the square, the violence escalated. Many student and civilians were shot down, and some soldiers died too. The carnage overwhelmed Beijing's hospitals, many of which were forbidden to treat civilian casualties. Nor could they or anyone else compile statistics of the dead and wounded.

FIGURE 16.2 *Goddess of Democracy,* Tiananmen Square, Beijing, May 30, 1989. Radical students erected the statue to democracy, and tanks and soldiers destroyed it six days later in their violent assault on Tiananmen Square.
© Peter Turnley/Corbis (TL009252).

Military suppression was followed by the arrest, and in some cases execution, of student leaders in the capital and elsewhere. Others found their way into exile in the West, where some continued as leaders of a nonunified and contentious political/intellectual community. Fang Lizhi, too, found freedom abroad. In 1997, after a second imprisonment, Wei Jingshen also found sanctuary abroad. After 1989, Chinese voices in many parts of the world presented alternatives to the ideology and policies proclaimed by Beijing. In the 1980s the telephone, photocopier, and fax helped undermine the government monopoly on information, which proved even more difficult to sustain with the spread of email, the cell phone, and the internet toward the end of the century. The leadership's credibility now depended not on the old ideology but on its performance, especially its economic performance.

State, Economy, and Society in the Nineties and Beyond

An immediate result of Tiananmen was that Deng's protégé, Premier Zhao Ziyang, was forced out of office and placed under house arrest. His place was taken by Jiang Zemin (1926–). In 1992, the octogenarian Deng made a dramatic tour of the south, proclaiming his determination to continue the pragmatic economic policy. After this trip, though still considered China's paramount leader, Deng faded into the background, allowing Jiang to establish himself and ensure a smooth transition when Deng died in 1997. Essentially, Jiang continued Deng's policies of economic liberalization without relaxing CCP control over politics and public discourse. Indeed, economic liberalism while maintaining political control became the hallmark of Jiang's leadership and legacy. Indicative of this dual policy was his speech of July 1, 2001, declaring that capitalists should be welcomed into the Communist Party and the subsequent closing of a publication named *The Pursuit of Truth* for criticizing this extraordinary departure from Marxist practice. Jiang redefined the role of the party as representing, "advanced productive forces, advanced Chinese culture, and the fundamental interests of the majority."[5] These "Three Representations" were billed as major theoretical contributions, and seen as a bid by Jiang to gain status as a thinker before relinquishing his post as General Secretary of the Chinese Communist Party in November 2002.

Two years later, Jiang also gave up his position as chairman of the Military Commission, thus consolidating the power of the new general secretary, Hu Jintao (1942–), who continued to combine policies of economic liberalization with strict one-party rule and the monitoring of channels of communication including the internet. In place of Jiang's "Three Representations," Hu stressed "advancedness" (or advanced nature, *xiangjinxing*). For example, when marking the 85th anniversary of the founding of the Communist Party, Hu said, "history proves that only when the party maintains its advanced nature can it push forward both the party's and the people's mutual interests, develop advanced production and advanced culture, and realize the interest of the vast majority of the people."[6] In the same speech he called for a crackdown on corruption but otherwise left himself room to define "advanced."

The CCP still controlled the State, but with the State no longer "commanding" the economy, the relationship between State, economy, and society changed. The direction of economic change remained largely the same, though there were times of pause and hesitation. Under the direction of Zhu Rongji (1928–), like Jiang an engineer by background, and a former mayor of Shanghai, the economy weathered bouts of inflation peaking in 1988 and 1995, and the government continued to encourage foreign investment and trade, negotiating its way into the World Trade Organization in 2000. Whereas previously people had depended on their work unit to supply everything from housing to entertainment, these functions were now privatized, with the result that in Shanghai and other eastern cities a hundred stores blossomed, a thousand restaurants contended, and advertisements urged, "buy a house and become a boss."[7] The private sector prospered, but not everyone could become a boss.

The government reduced the scope of the state-run sector and announced its determination to continue doing so, because these enterprises were inefficient, frequently lost money, drained funds, and weakened the state banks on which they depended. However, the government had to proceed gradually because of the threat of social unrest posed by workers deprived of the security of their "iron rice-bowls." The labor market was already swollen by about 60 million peasants who were annually leaving their villages in search of better pay. The urban and rural unemployed formed a "floating population" that appeared in China's major cities looking for a day's work.

In the countryside, peasants received longer leases on their land, but continued to be required to sell a quota of grain to the State, which was anxious to maintain grain self-sufficiency. At the same time, many peasants now engaged in rural industries, which came to account for 60 percent of China's industrial output but did not solve the problem of rural poverty. Like other governments at the time, the P.R.C. authorities accepted a widening income gap as the price of economic growth.

Although a rail line linking Tibet to the rest of China was completed in 2006, emphasis was on constructing super highways to provide escape from the traffic jams that clogged city streets and to encourage China's newly affluent to pursue their love affair with the automobile. While China's automobile industry was gearing up for entry into world markets, there was little public concern over whether China was "advancing" in the right direction. However, as the economy boomed in the first decade of the twenty-first century, China's internal transformation accelerated and China became a major factor in international commerce. The sense that China was indeed advancing in the world was given a boost by the award of the summer 2008 Olympics to Beijing.

Similarly in line with global trends, China moved in the directions of market economics, but the government often gave mixed political and economic signals. Heavy taxes, land requisitions, autocratic and corrupt officials, and/or severe water pollution elicited peasant petitions (70,000 in 1995) and demonstrations, some large and violent. One response was the provision for village elections, "as a safety valve to let the peasantry vent their dissatisfaction." Jean C. Oi goes on to point out that different constituencies and different agendas left China "a country riddled with policy contradictions."[8]

The new relationship between State and society is unstable and difficult to define, as is reflected in the proliferation of labels proffered by Western academics, including, but by no means limited to, "capitalism with Chinese characteristics," "capital socialism," "state-socialist corporatism," "symbiotic clientism," "Confucian Leninism," and "bureaupreneurialism." The proliferation of terms reflects the inadequacy of traditional categories as well as the blurring of the line between State and society. It also reflects the variety of relationships in China between State and society. The initiative for action has largely passed to local, especially county, levels, which helps explain this variety. Following the penchant for fours favored in the post-Mao years, Richard Baum and Alexei Shevchenko have characterized local governments as "Entrepreneurs, Patrons, Predators, and Developers." One of their major conclusions is that the situation "augurs neither the continued potency of the central party state nor the emergence of a pluralistic civil society but the proliferation of quasi-autonomous (and potentially corrupt) local economic empires."[9]

The potential for corruption was fully realized in what Lionel Jensen has aptly termed a "hybrid political economy" and in "the moral confusion wrought by a contradictory ideology."[10] Corruption riddled the country, and crime was increasing. Nor was malfeasance by any means purely local. In August 1999, China's auditor-general reported that one fifth of China's annual revenue had been "misappropriated," that all 18 provincial governments were guilty, and that the Ministry of Water Resources was building luxury office buildings rather than much-needed dams and dikes. Meanwhile, government censorship was ineffective in its attempt to suppress accounts of suffering and corruption in the countryside such as *Will the Boat Sink the Water* by Chen Guidi and Wu Chuntao (2003), said to have sold 7 million pirated copies.

The Environment

Industrialization and the efforts to meet the needs and aspirations of a population estimated at 1.374 billion in 2006 placed great strains on the environment. Air and water quality both posed health threats. China's major cities were shrouded in permanent haze, and people breathed polluted air not only outside but even indoors, where it especially threatened women cooking over stoves burning raw coal. Most coal remained untreated, and most women, though theoretically the equals of men, remained unliberated from the stove. China was on pace to replace the United States as the planet's foremost producer of greenhouse gases. Meanwhile, China's polluted air reached the west coast of the United States. Roughly one third of this was dust with sulfur, soot, and trace metals from burning coal, while other fossil fuels accounted for the rest. In 2006, the U.S. Environmental Protection Agency estimated that there were days when nearly 25 percent of the particulate matter in the skies above Los Angeles could be traced to China.

Water, too, can be lethal in China. As Elizabeth Economy reported, "The river runs black."[11] Irrigation water is often contaminated by discharge. In the case of a village in Gansu inhabited by descendants of Confucius, the village leaders were able to obtain some redress only after challenging managers of a fertilizer plant to drink some water from a stream they had poisoned. The whole world took note when in November 2005 a chemical explosion polluted the Songhua River producing a 50-mile-long slick that forced Harbin, a city of 3.8 million people, to lose its water supply for five days.

Pollution is not the only water problem. In the north, water tables have sunk alarmingly and water shortages are severe. The diversion of Yellow River water for irrigation has reduced the transport of silt to the sea. Instead, it is deposited on the riverbed, raising it above the surrounding countryside and posing again the old threat of devastating floods. Meanwhile, recurrent floods inundated southern regions. Not until 1999 did the government officially acknowledge that chopping down trees in the headlands of the Yangzi helped cause this. There have been people in and out of government who were aware of the problem, but environmental policies formulated in Beijing were often ignored locally, especially when the problem mostly affected people downriver or far away.

However, the government, too, contributed to the destruction of the environment. In 1992, it approved a major project to dam the Three Gorges of the Yangzi River in order to address China's need for clean energy and flood control, and to open Sichuan, China's most populous province, to oceangoing vessels. The waters of the river were diverted in 1997, and the dam is scheduled for completion in 2009. It will be 170 meters high and will run for two kilometers, comparable to a four-story building a mile wide, and will cost much more than the optimistic official estimate of $25 billion. It will displace well over a million people and inundate priceless cultural sites. The government discounted warnings about the potential disasters posed by the buildup of silt behind the dam, unpredictable geologic effects, the dangers of forming a lake even more polluted than the present river, and possible adverse effects downstream. Nor was it impressed by the turning of world opinion against megadams. While energy generation and water control could be achieved more cheaply and less dangerously by a series of small dams, these would not provide maritime access to Sichuan, where Chongqing is growing into a huge metropolis.

Whether and to what degree the laws on the books and increased awareness can avert the worst environmental destruction remains to be seen. The example of what the wealthy nations do will be a factor. Meanwhile, in some places local gods have sometimes been enlisted to defend the local environment.

The Revival of Religion

One response to the loosening of central government reins was the reemergence of religion, condemned long before the Cultural Revolution by Karl Marx himself as the "opiate of the people." Village temples to local and lineage deities were rebuilt, traditional burial practices resumed, and traditional beliefs and practices such as geomancy (*fengshui;* see Chapter 1) resurfaced. These cults and practices were still denounced as "superstition" by the political and intellectual establishment, which distinguished them from "legitimate" religions such as Buddhism, Daoism, Islam, and Christianity. As Stephen Feuchtwang attests, partly on the basis of personal observation, "In some places new religious buildings were tolerated, in others the Public Security forces periodically destroy them."[12] Much depended on local authorities and circumstances. For example, at Black Dragon Pool in northern Shaanxi, the head of the officially sanctioned Cultural Management Institute also heads the temple association, and the Institute is responsible for the upkeep of the Black Dragon god's temple and the conduct of its main annual festival, featuring a tour by the god around the dry land to bring rain.

During the Cultural Revolution there was a tendency to elevate Mao to a superhuman status, and now tens of thousands of pilgrims have visited a monastery in Hunan, Mao's native province, where:

> some pray for the safety and harmony of family members while others ask Mao to cure chronic diseases. [Members of] the latter group are given a glass of "holy water" after their prayers. Those who feel Mao has listened to their prayers thank him for the kindness received.[13]

Some mosques and churches, converted to factories during the Cultural Revolution, were returned to their congregations and became once again places of worship sanctioned and supervised by the State. Chinese Catholics remained separated from Rome, as the government refused to let them obey the pope, and neither Catholic nor Protestant missionaries were permitted into the country. Unsupervised worship in private houses was also prohibited. However, the loss of credibility of official materialism provided fertile ground for those seeking something beyond the quest for wealth and the passing satisfactions of consumerism.

The State remained suspicious of religion as an alternate source of authority and potential nucleus of resistance. Officials were particularly wary of Vajrayana Buddhism in Tibet and Islam in Xinjiang and Qinghai. However, the government's concerns were not limited to peripheral minorities such as these. It was taken aback, and the security apparatus was caught by surprise, when 10,000 followers of *Falungong* quietly assembled in Beijing to protest the outlawing of their sect. Led from New York by its exiled founder, the sect, estimated by the government to have 70 million adherents, offered spiritual and physical health through dance like *qigong* exercises and mental concentration. Its leader insisted from the start that it was nonpolitical, but the authorities were alarmed at its ability to mobilize thousands, and troubled that its membership was largely middle-aged and well-integrated members of the community, some even belonging to the CCP. It was outlawed, and periodic arrests and trials followed.

The suppression of religious expression and the arrest of political dissidents continued in the face of international concern over human rights. While avoiding a second international outrage like Tiananmen, the regime continued attempts to stamp out any sparks of separatism it feared might catch fire in Tibet or elsewhere. In international relations, particularly with the United States, the human rights issue continued to smolder, only to be doused by geopolitical and geoeconomic considerations. This was especially the case when, after September 2001, China gave its support to the American war on terror.

Foreign Relations and Hong Kong

Foreign relations during the late 1970s and 1980s remained within the pattern set earlier, and China remained at peace except that conflicting ambitions in Cambodia prompted an unsuccessful invasion of Vietnam in 1979. Sino-Vietnamese relations remained tense for some time. There were border clashes in 1985, but relations improved in the late 1990s. China did not engage in any further military combat, but still concentrated on modernizing its military.

China's relations with the Soviet Union became more cordial, especially after the U.S.S.R. withdrew from Afghanistan in 1988, while the fall of Communism in Eastern Europe and the disintegration of the Soviet Union were taken by China's rulers as warnings of what could befall them and their country.

Full diplomatic relations with the United States were established on January 1, 1979. Although Chinese wariness of the only remaining superpower was balanced by American unease over an emergent giant, relations remained generally cordial while trade grew and Americans entered into joint ventures with Chinese partners. With its business community enthralled by the old Western dream of an unlimited Chinese market, the United States tolerated widening trade deficits, and in the first year of the new century agreed to forgo annual reviews of China's generally unsatisfactory human rights situation. As already noted, that same year China was admitted to the World Trade Organization.

A notable diplomatic success was the agreement signed in 1984 with Great Britain to return Hong Kong to Chinese sovereignty in 1997. China in turn guaranteed that for the next 50 years Hong Kong would retain its own laws and institutions. The People's Republic thus acknowledged the economic importance of Hong Kong, which by the mid-1980s, had developed into a major world financial and trade center with a thriving manufacturing sector. Symbolizing the future, China's Central Bank erected the city's tallest skyscrapers (1982–1990), designed by I. M. Pei (Ieho Ming Pei, 1917–), the Chinese-born American architect who in 1983 had received architecture's highest award, the Pritzker Prize. I.M. Pei's Bank of China building remained the signature building of the new Hong Kong, rivaling the new Hong Kong and Shanghai Bank headquarters designed by the British architect Norman Foster. Numerous other towers subsequently sprang up to enhance the city's skyline.

Much younger than I. M. Pei, and not nearly as famous, was Yuen Kwok-chung (1963–), whose *Triptych* (Figure 16.3), exhibited at the 1994 Hong Kong Contemporary Art Biennial Exhibition, invites the viewer to see the barcode as the true flag of Hong Kong and infer that commercial consumerism (often mediated through Hong Kong) is what links the United States. and the P.R.C. The Chinese title, "study hard and make progress every day," would make a splendid slogan for a textbook, but here heightens the sardonic effect. Fortuitously, in the exhibition catalog *Triptych* is preceded by a painting titled *Perplexity* and followed by *Coiling Incense Smoke.*

Though *Triptych* represents the money-making spirit of Hong Kong and of would-be Hong Kongs further up the Chinese coast, the city also provided a haven for those like the noted philosopher of "New Confucianism," Mou Zongsan (1909–1995), and highly original painters like Irene Chou from Shanghai (see Afterward Figure A.1) and Liu Guosong from Taiwan (Figure 16.5).

With the erosion of its old ideological base, the government of the P.R.C. had the option of seeking legitimacy from its economic performance—the success of

FIGURE 16.3   *Triptych 1994,* Yuen Kwok-chung (1963–). Most people in the People's Republic at this time would probably recognize the American flag as well as their own but had never seen a barcode. That, however, was a familiar symbol in Hong Kong. Acrylic on canvas, 184 × 290 cm.
© YUEN KWOK-CHUNG. USED BY PERMISSION OF THE ARTIST.

"managed consumerism," as Richard Kraus has termed it. Alternatively, it could emphasize "orchestrated nationalism"[14]—orchestrated lest it get out of hand in demonstrations that could interfere with the conduct of foreign policy and might even threaten the established order. During the 1990s it pursued both consumerist and nationalist aims. With Hong Kong safely in the fold, the de facto independence of Taiwan remained a major irritant.

While chafing over foreign criticism of its suppression of human rights in Tibet and elsewhere, it was particularly troubled by Taiwan's failure to be persuaded of the benefits of its "one country–two system policy." On the eve of Taiwan's presidential elections in 1996, the P.R.C. fired missiles and conducted naval maneuvers in a show of force, and as the new century began, the future of P.R.C.-Taiwan relations remained very much in doubt.

Intellectuals and Artists in the Nineties and Beyond

In the P.R.C., the authorities continued to jail dissidents and refused to tolerate political opposition. They allowed people to choose their own jobs but no longer guaranteed them a job. Overall, the government gave people more latitude

FIGURE 16.4 Shanghai Museum (1996), architect Xing Tonghe. The circular building placed on top of a square recalls the tradition that heaven is round and earth is square, while the arches on the roof resemble the handles on ancient bronzes.
PHOTOGRAPH © LORE SCHIROKAUER.

in the conduct of their lives, letting them enjoy their electric appliances and other new possessions. People were allowed freedom of movement. The arts continued much in the spirit of the 1980s, producing a profusion of styles and agendas, frames and shattering of frames, as well as a renewed appreciation of tradition, including Confucianism. An unusually satisfactory marriage of new and old was the Shanghai Museum (Figure 16.4), by the Shanghai architect Xing Tonghe, completed in 1996 to house the city's treasures, including China's foremost collection of bronze vessels from the first dynasties.

Many prominent artists from the 1980s remained productive. Wang Meng fought off his critics and advocated cultural pluralism with the market as judge. In 1992 he founded *Green Leaves,* a journal on the environment. Mo Yan published *Wine Republic.* Characterized by David Der-wei Wang as a "Swiftian satire and Kafkaesque fable," it follows a detective sent to a country where people eat children. Wang comments:

> In a world where the high and the low, the fragrant and the putrid, mingle, nobody has clean hands; the protagonist is fittingly murdered by being

drowned in a manure pit at the end of the novel. Eschatology and scatology turn out to be two readings of the same reality.[15]

In 1995 Chen Kaige directed *Farewell My Concubine,* which found a warm reception overseas. The work of some of the most experimental artists was confined to their apartments, while the audience of others, like the computer artist Feng Mengbo, was primarily overseas. Feng, a resident of Beijing, explained the thought behind his series of paintings "Taxi! Taxi!—Mao Zedong I–III" as follows:

> In 1990, when I was still at the academy, I suddenly realized that the way Mao Zedong waved his hand at the army [of Red Guards] gathered in Tiananmen Square during the Cultural Revolution was very similar to the way people wave to hail a taxi. So I copied the image of Mao waving and put a common yellow taxicab in front of him—the kind you see everywhere in Beijing today.[16]

Mao had been taken off his pedestal and made to hail a cab. Once inside he was likely to encounter a Mao traffic safety charm. To recover from the shock would he have taken a swig of "The East is Red" health drink, thirsting for the days when this had been the anthem of the revolution?

Cui Jian, the rock star, had his ups and downs, but mostly was tolerated by the authorities and allowed to perform at home and abroad. David Fricke, critic for *Rolling Stone,* heard him in concert in 1995 and wrote:

> But just as he challenges the arthritic authority of his country's leaders, Cui tolerates no laws or limits to his music. The rumble of Chinese barrel drum fattened the surge of angular guitar grooves. Beastie-style beats, fierily Jamaican ska and the roadhouse rattle of early Springsteen collided in such anthemic fireballs as "The Other Shore," "Together we confront the same reality—Together we sing a song loudly."[17]

Listeners will need to judge the results for themselves as postmodern Chinese intellectuals engage "in a new search for a real 'hybridization' or 'hybridity' based on a dialectical synthesis beyond the old dichotomies between the traditional and the modern, the particular and the universal."[18]

One dichotomy that was breaking down was that between the thought and symbolic world of artists and writers living in the People's Republic and those living elsewhere in a Chinese or semi-Chinese world. While critics worried about the hybrid culture, the mixing of elements from different traditions continued such that when a joint exhibit was held in New York in 1999, it was often difficult to distinguish the works of those in the P.R.C. from the works of those outside (see Box 16.2). Mainland exiles in America, Europe, Australia and New Zealand, as well as artists and writers from Taiwan, contributed to "a China defined not by geopolitical boundaries and ideological closures but by overlapping cultural and shared imaginative resources."[19] Others embraced a global perspective.

BOX 16.2 CHINESE ARTISTS ABROAD IN PERSON AND ON THE INTERNET

The Gao brothers are among the Chinese artists who addressed all people every-where. It is therefore appropriate that the source of this box is from cyberspace, which knows no boundaries. Perhaps some of our readers will want to give the Gao brothers a hug.

THE UTOPIA OF HUGGING

A performance by the Gao Brothers from Beijing at Arboretum Park, Nottingham/UK, SUNDAY APRIL 30, 2006 FROM 11:30 AM. A video of the Nottingham Hug will be online 3 hours later [14:30 GMT] at http://world-hug day.net/Nottingham

As part of their global World Hug Day performances, internationally renowned Chinese artist brothers Gao Zhen and Gao Qiang invite you to participate in the most ambitious event of the series to date; a group embrace of epic proportions orchestrated at the Networking Artists Network [NAN] conference and representing the first ever mass hugging to be staged in the British Isles.

Volunteers wishing to take part in the performance are invited to come to Arboretum Park where they will be directed with hundreds of others by the Gao Brothers to embark on a hearty fifteen-minute hug with a stranger, followed by one gigantic hugging cluster formed by the entire group, all accompanied by the music of J.S. Bach. Speaking about their first performance of a group hug THE UTOPIA OF HUGGING [Shangdong Province, China, September 2000] the Gao Brothers explain:

"We invited some 150 volunteers, who were previously strangers to each other, to participate. We asked the participants to choose a person at random for a hug, which they would then do simultaneously with hundreds of other couples. We then asked everyone present to cluster into one big group hug. Since then, we personally have hugged hundreds of strangers, and organised group hugs amongst strangers in different public locations and in different ways all across China."

(continued)

BOX 16.2 CHINESE ARTISTS ABROAD IN PERSON AND ON THE INTERNET (CONTINUED)

World Hug Day series will continue in Marseille on the 9th of June, running concurrent with an international traveling photo exhibition documenting all performances so far. The event will be followed by a press-conference/presentation with the Gao Brothers and their co-organising partners from artists' group Digital Art Projects at the nearby Waverley lecture theatre of Nottingham Trent University from 12:30 onwards.

http://www.turbulence.org/blog/archives/002330.html

Taiwan

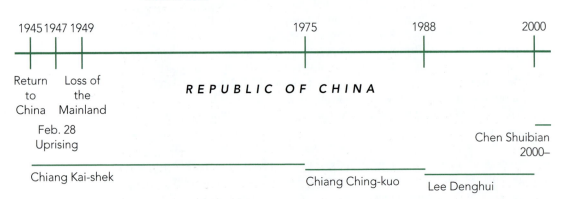

As noted in Chapter 14, Taiwan's first two years under the Guomindang controlled Republic of China were so oppressive that they provoked the violence of 1947. The Guomindang actions resulted in the decimation of the Taiwanese elite. Ironically, this removed not only resistance to the political dominance of the Nationalists but also a potential source of opposition to land redistribution and other economic reforms undertaken during the 1950s with American backing, pressure, and advice. As in postwar Japan, the end of landlordism had profound economic and social effects.

During the Japanese years, Taiwan had acquired much of the necessary infrastructure for industrialization, and many of the approximately 2 million civilian refugees who fled from the mainland also brought training and skills that contributed to the development of light industry and commerce. The large sums of money that the Nationalists brought over with them provided capital. Until terminated in 1966, American economic aid also helped, and once the Japanese economy had recovered, Japanese companies invested heavily. The government generally supervised and advanced development, first building up infrastructure and then fostering exports. In 1965, it created special Export Processing Zones where companies enjoyed tax incentives and were free of import taxes as long as they exported whatever they made or assembled.

Culturally, the government saw its mission as preserving old Chinese traditions. Taiwan became the home for institutes of higher learning. The use of the local Taiwanese language was suppressed and, as in the P.R.C., instruction was in Mandarin. A museum was built to house the priceless Palace Collection the Nationalists brought with them from the mainland.

While mainland artists were caught in political storms, artists in Taiwan and elsewhere were free to explore new ways to draw on their tradition in creating forms of expression suitable for the twentieth century. One of the most gifted artists was Liu Guosong (Liu Kuo-sung, 1932–), who was born in Shandong, educated in Taiwan, established as a painter there, taught many years in Hong Kong, and returned to Taiwan before retiring to California. As Liu explained, "We are no longer ancient Chinese nor modern Westerners . . . If it is false for us to copy old Chinese paintings, isn't it the same to copy modern Western painting?"[20] Liu is deeply conversant with both traditions. He painted a distinctive series on the sun and moon, continued to experiment with textures and techniques, and later painted abstractions that suggested the metaphysics of mountains.

Under the Guomindang, the Republic of China remained ideologically committed to the reunification of China and to Sun Yat-sen's Three Principles of the People. Until ousted from the United Nations in 1971, its claim to speak for China was widely accepted abroad. At home, although the Guomindang was reformed, it remained dictatorial, refusing to share substantive power with the Taiwanese, that is, people of Chinese stock who had settled on the island before 1945. Though the native Taiwanese did win elections to local governments, real control remained in the hands of the central government. Prosperity and repression kept dissent to a minimum. Among those imprisoned on Green Island was Bo Yang (1920–), given 10 years for translating an English-language comic deemed insulting to Chiang Kai-shek. His acerbic critique of Chinese ways won him a wide readership on the mainland.

When Chiang Kai-shek died in 1975, there was an easy and smooth passing of power to his son Chiang Ching-kuo (in *pinyin*, Jiang Jingguo, 1910–1988). Progress was sufficient for the economy to emerge from both the oil crisis and the diplomatic defeats of the 1970s in good shape. As in Japan, there was a turn to more advanced technology such as computers. In 1980, the state established a science-oriented industrial park and an electronics industry.

FIGURE 16.5 *The Metaphysics of Rocks,* Liu Guosong. The artist uses calligraphy, brushwork, and collage. Ink and acrylic with collage on paper, 1968, 68.6 × 67.3 cm.

© Liu Kuo-Sung. Used by Permission of the Artist.

By that time, Taiwan had attained a level of per capita income second in Asia only to Japan. In many ways, it became a modern country. By 1979, over half the people owned a color television and 90 percent had refrigerators. During the 1980s, air-conditioners became common while cars largely captured the road dominated previously by motorbikes.

The normalization of U.S. relations with the P.R.C. meant that relations with Taiwan were formally downgraded. Semi-formal relations were maintained, but the Guomindang's claim to the rulership of all China was weakened, and those born in Taiwan who coupled demands for democratization with calls for a Republic of Taiwan found their case strengthened. Chiang Kai-shek's response had been repression, but his son alternated between jailing leaders of the opposition and instigating reform. The latter was predominant during his last two years, when martial law was revoked, press restrictions were eased, and the prohibition against opposition parties relaxed.

These reforms allowed the Democratic Progressive Party (D.P.P.) to field candidates in the election of December 1986. Inhabitants of Taiwan were, for the first time in 38 years, allowed to visit relatives on the mainland. The government was confident that they would return with an appreciation for the higher standard of living they enjoyed on Taiwan. In practice, even the post-1945 newcomers came to see themselves as different from mainlanders and as having much in common with their fellow Taiwanese.

When Chiang Ching-kuo died in January 1988, he was succeeded by Lee Teng-hui (Li Denghui, 1923–), a Taiwanese with a Ph.D. in agricultural econom- ics from Cornell, who brought more Taiwanese into the top party and government posts and included 14 holders of American doctorates in his cabinet. The emer- gence of a strong middle class, strong advances in education, and continuing afflu- ence provided fertile ground for continued movement in the direction of greater democracy, while the ultimate nature of a Taiwanese identity remained in dispute. The GMD won the election of 1989, but the D.P.P. gained ground. Despite the P.R.C. show of force, Lee was victorious in Taiwan's first direct popular presiden- tial election in 1996. However, he had to face both D.P.P. opposition and divisive- ness within his own party that led to a major defection in 2000.

In the election of 2000, Chen Shui-bian (1951–) of the D.P.P., with 39.3 per- cent of the vote, defeated two rival candidates to become the Republic of China's youngest and first non-GMD president. His vice president, the women's rights advocate Lu Hsiu-lien (Xiulian, Annette Lu, 1944–) was the first woman elected to that high office. Elected on a promise to put an end to widespread corruption, Chen, on assuming office, played down his Taiwanese nationalism and indicated he would give priority to domestic house-cleaning but by June 2006 was so embroiled in corruption charges that 119 of the 221 members of the legislature voted to remove him. This was more than half, but since it fell short of the two- thirds vote needed for recall, he remained in office.

Beijing made it clear that it would not rule out the use of force if Taiwan declared independence. The example of a party losing an election to an opposition running on an anticorruption platform must have been distasteful and unnerving to those deeply implicated in the mainland status quo. However, business rela- tions continued to flourish and Taiwanese investments in the mainland increased steadily despite efforts by the Taiwanese government to persuade companies to diversify by investing in other countries such as Thailand, Vietnam, and India.

Notes

1. Christopher R. Wren, "Comparing Two Communist Paths to 'Reform,'" *The New York Times,* Sept. 6, 1987, Section 4, p. 2.

2. Geremie R. Barmé, *In The Red: On Contemporary Chinese Culture* (New York, NY: Columbia Univ. Press, 1999), p. 123.

3. Shen Tong, *Almost a Revolution* (Boston, MA: Houghlin Mifflin, 1990), p. 310, as quoted in

Andrew E. Jones, *Like a Knife: Ideology in Contemporary Chinese Popular Music* (Ithaca, NY: East Asia Program, Cornell Univ., 1992), p. 95.

4. Quoted by Wu Hung, *Remaking Beijing: Tiananmen Square and the Creation of a Political Space* (Chicago, IL: Univ. of Chicago Press, 2005), p. 46, which cites Hsing-yuan Tsao, "Birth of the Goddess of Democracy" in Jeffrey N.

Wasserstrom and Elizabeth Perry, eds., *Popular Protest and Political Culture in Modern China,* 2nd edition (Boulder, CO: Westview Press, 1994), p. 145.

5. *The New York Times,* August 16, 2001, p. A13.

6. *The New York Times,* July 1, 2006, p. A4

7. *Xinmin wanbao (New People's Evening News),* Shanghai, May 11, 1994, as quoted by Deborah S. Davis in her introduction to *The Consumer Revolution in Urban China,* ed., Deborah S. Davis (Berkeley, CA: Univ. of California Press, 2000), p. 9.

8. Jean C. Oi, "Two Decades of Rural Reform in China: An Overview and Assessment," *The China Quarterly* no. 159 (Sept. 1999), p. 627.

9. Richard Baum and Alexei Shevchenko, "The State of the State," in Merle Goldman and Roderick MacFarquhar, eds., *The Paradox of China's Post-Mao Reforms* (Cambridge, MA: Harvard Univ. Press, 1999), pp. 345 and 349. The list of labels at the beginning of this paragraph is taken from the same source, where each label is documented.

10. Lionel M. Jensen, "Everyone's a Player, but the Nation's a Loser: Corruption in Contemporary China," in Timothy B. Weston and Lionel M. Jensen, *China Beyond the Headlines* (Lanham, MD: Rowman & Littlefield, 2000), p. 42.

11. Elizabeth C. Economy, *The River Runs Black* (Ithaca, NY: Cornell Univ. Press, 2004).

12. Stephen Feuchtwang, "Religious Resistance," in Elizabeth J. Perry and Mark Selden, eds., *Chinese Society: Change, Conflict and Resistance* (London,

U.K. and New York, NY: Routledge, 2000), p. 171.

13. *Eastern Express,* October 5, 1955, p. 39, as quoted in Elizabeth J. Perry, "Crime, Corruption, and Contention" in Goldman and MacFarquhar, *The Paradox,* p. 323.

14. Richard Kraus, "Public Monuments and Private Pleasures in the Parks of Nanjing: A Tango in the Ruins of the Ming Emperor's Palace," in Deborah S. Davis, ed., *The Consumer Revolution in Urban China,* p. 306.

15. David Der-wei Wang, *Fin-de-siecle Splendor: Repressed Modernities of Late Qing Fiction, 1849–1911* (Stanford, CA: Stanford Univ. Press, 1997), p. 332.

16. Quoted in Geremie R. Barmé, *In the Red: On Contemporary Chinese Culture,* p. 231.

17. David Fricke, "Cui Jian: New York, The Bottom Line, Aug. 31, 1995," *The Rolling Stone,* November 2, 1995.

18. Min Lin with Maria Galikowski, *The Search for Modernity: Chinese Intellectual and Cultural Discourse in the Post-Mao Era* (New York, NY: St. Martin's Press, 1999), p. 197.

19. David Der-wei Wang, "Chinese Fiction for the Nineties," in David Der-wei Wang and Jeanne Tai, eds., *Running Wild: New Chinese Writers* (New York, NY: Columbia Univ. Press, 1994), p. 238.

20. Quoted in Chu-tsing Li, *Liu Kuo-sung—The Growth of a Modern Chinese Artist* (Taipei, Taiwan: The National Gallery of Art and Museum of History, 1969), p. 32.

17

The New Japan

Key Dates

1952	Termination of the Occupation
1954	Resignation of Prime Minister Yoshida
1955	Formation of the Liberal Democratic Party (L.D.P.)
1956	Admission of Japan to the United Nations
1960	Demonstrations against Continuation of U.S.–Japan Mutual Security Treaty
1968	Kawabata Awarded Nobel Prize
1971	Floating of the Dollar
1972	Visit of Prime Minister Tanaka to Beijing
1976	Lockheed Scandal
1980	Automobile Production Exceeds That of U.S.
1989	Death of Shōwa Emperor; Recruit Scandal
1990	Stock Market Plunge
1991	Begin Decade of Weak Economy
1993	L.D.P. Crisis
1994	Ōe Awarded Nobel Prize
2001–2006	Koizumi Prime Minister

After regaining independence in 1952, Japan achieved such phenomenal economic growth that by the 1970s it had become one of the world's industrial giants. By the 1980s, people in the United States and Britain were turning to Japan for lessons in industrial management. Despite a setback in the last decade of the century, Japan remained an economic power second only to the United States.

Japan's economic growth was part of a broader transformation that affected every aspect of life. The pace of change was steadier than in China, but that did not make it less extensive or profound. The absence of the drastic shifts in direction, such as those that punctuated Chinese history, enables us to discuss the new Japan in a single chapter—but makes it harder to periodize.

We have chosen to break our story at 1989, when a new emperor ascended the throne, primarily because the end of the Cold War coincided with the end of the economic exuberance of the 1980s.

I. The New Japan, 1952–1989

The Economy

Government and Politics

The Seventies and Eighties

The Economy

As we have seen, the Korean War greatly stimulated the Japanese economy. Thereafter, Japan continued to profit from access to foreign raw materials, technology, and markets, including those of the United States. Due to popular sentiment, constitutional constraints, and the country's reliance on the American "nuclear umbrella," Japan was freed from the burden of supporting a large and costly military establishment, releasing funds and energies for economic development. At the same time, business benefited from a pro-business political system.

Politically, the period began with Yoshida in power and his Liberal Party in control of the Diet. He remained in office until 1954, when he was forced to resign in the wake of a scandal involving the shipping industry. In the elections of 1955, the Democratic Party, a rival conservative party, won a plurality but not the majority required to govern. It therefore entered into negotiations with the Liberal Party that led to the formation of the Liberal Democratic Party (L.D.P.), which dominated Japanese politics until 1993.

By 1953, economic production had practically returned to pre-war levels, although the volume of trade was still only half of its previous total. After 1954, the economic surge continued, transforming recovery into growth at an average of 10 percent a year from 1955 to 1974 (including over 11 percent during the 1960s). During the 1950s, with government support, great strides were made in heavy industry—despite the fact that Japan lacks raw materials and is poor in energy resources. By building manufacturing plants in port cities, which provided the advantage of low-cost ocean transport, and through the sophisticated application of modern technologies, Japan was able to become the world's leading shipbuilder and the third largest producer of iron and steel (after the United States and the Soviet Union). By 1974, its steel production reached 89 percent of that of the United States. There were investments in chemicals, textiles, and consumer products. The washing machine, vacuum cleaner, and refrigerator of the 1950s were soon joined by the television set and the air conditioner, with the video recorder, microwave, and computer following in the 1980s. Car production reached 10 million in 1966, dubbed "year one of the My-Car Era" by the media. Cameras, watches, and pianos were just a few of the consumer technologies that Japan excelled at—indeed, it is difficult to find an example of Japanese failure in that sector.

Some of these products were built by new companies, such as Sony or Honda, founded by entrepreneurs who took advantage of the opportunities offered by postwar economic dislocation to establish new enterprises. Other ambitious men (in what remained a man's world) reorganized or rejuvenated older companies, often importing technology by buying rights to foreign patents. In the dominant position in the economy, however, familiar old names reappeared, including Mitsui, the world's oldest major firm, as well as Mitsubishi, Sumitomo, and others.

The names were old, but they now designated a new kind of enterprise grouping consisting of affiliated companies (*keiretsu*) rather than the family-centered *zaibatsu* of the prewar period. Each group included a bank, very likely an insurance company, a real estate firm, and a cluster of companies engaged in every conceivable line of business, where its main competitor was most frequently a member of a rival group. The activities of the various member firms of each group were coordinated in periodic meetings of their presidents in presidents' clubs. Interlocking directorships, mutual stock holdings, and internal financing further held the organizations together, although more loosely than in the old *zaibatsu*.

The *keiretsu* grew in size and strength until in the mid-1970s a study by Japan's Fair Trade Commission found that the six major groupings, composed of 175 core companies, held 21.9 percent of all the capital in Japan and had a controlling interest in another 3,095 corporations that held 26.1 percent of the nation's capital. Additionally, these numbers fail to include their substantial investments in other companies that they influenced without controlling.

Among the member firms of these enterprise groupings, the most spectacular were trading companies (*shōsha*) that conducted their business all over the world: exporting and importing, transporting and storing, financing and organizing a host of multifarious projects—an airport in Kenya, a large commercial farm on Sumatra, a petrochemical industry for Iran, or copper mining in Zaire—all linked by communications networks that were unparalleled. Furthermore, Mitsui, Mitsubishi, and the others built their own research organizations, analyzing information, charting future trends, and drawing up plans to provide for future project recommendations. Their experts engaged in city planning, energy research, and ocean research. Japanese companies provided varied services and facilities for their employees, including company dormitories for the unmarried. There were company athletic teams and a host of recreational activities, such as organized outings to mountain retreats. These were intended to foster the health and well-being of the employees, and moreover, to strengthen feelings of group solidarity and identification with the sponsoring firm, which used them to convey an image of paternalistic solicitude. At Toyota, Japan's leading automobile manufacturer, white-collar men received an entire year of training, including a month in a company camp. Recruitment patterns that centered on certain universities, encouraging ties between men entering a company in the same year, an emphasis on longevity in promotions, the practice of extensive consultation, and a strong preference for decision by consensus all helped foster management solidarity.

Japanese companies, especially the large modern ones, retained the loyalty of most employees, who were made to feel that what was best for the company was also best for Japan. This business ideology gained credence from the management's practice of plowing earnings back into the firm so that it could continue to grow and hopefully surpass its rivals. At the same time, the efficacy of persuasion should not be exaggerated, for company extras increasingly became contractual rights subject to collective bargaining, like fringe benefits in other countries, rather than efforts at paternalism. However, management got workers' agreement to moderate wage increases and fringe benefits. The threat of foreign competition was also used effectively, and for many years Japanese companies enjoyed a lower labor bill and more labor peace than many of their competitors in Europe and America. The quest for economic growth gave Japan a sense of national purpose even as it promised an improved standard of living for the people.

Japan's concentration on economic development was epitomized in the income-doubling policy of Ikeda Hayato (1899–1965, prime minister 1960–1964), which provided for the doubling of per capita production in 10 years. The government fostered growth by establishing a political climate favorable to economic expansion, by investing in infrastructure, by adopting appropriate fiscal and monetary policies, and by setting production targets, assigning priorities, and generally orchestrating the economy. It sponsored the bullet train, which in 1964 reduced a long overnight journey between Kyoto and Tokyo to a trip of 3 hours and 10 minutes. The government built roads and dams, and financed the reclamation of coastal lands.

While the Construction Ministry controlled the bulk of infrastructure spending, the Finance Ministry and the Ministry of International Trade and Industry (MITI) coordinated economic growth. The importance of the MITI reflected the crucial role of foreign trade in Japan's economy and the determination of the government to oversee the country's economic, as well as political, relations with other countries. By deploying foreign exchange allocations, manipulating quotas, and establishing barriers protecting native capital from foreign competition, the government channeled the flow of investment funds. It could also extend or deny tax privileges. It thus had a variety of weapons to bring recalcitrant firms into line if persuasion and/or pressures failed. Generally, it preferred to rely on discussion and to act on the basis of a consensus between government and business. Businesses competed with one another within a more tightly defined arena than in most other capitalist nations.

Consensus was possible not only because of the shared aims and interests of government and business but also because of ties between government and the business community. Often these ties were personal, for the men at the top in the private sector and those heading the influential and prestigious government ministries tended to share similar backgrounds (both included a high proportion of Tokyo University graduates). Some of the ties were ideological, since Japan was ruled during these years by conservatives. Other ties were financial, for elections were costly and business constituted a major source of funds for conservative politicians.

Government and Politics

After 1955, the L.D.P. was opposed by the two Socialist parties (the Japan Socialist Party and the Democratic Socialist Party), by the Clean Government Party (formed in 1964, it first ran candidates for the lower house in 1967), by the Communist Party, and by independent politicians. This opposition was too divided to constitute a serious alternative to conservative rule, but it was sufficient to prevent the L.D.P. from gaining the two-thirds majority in the Diet needed for revising the constitution. Some conservatives, concerned about Japan's security, favored the revocation of Article IX so that Japan could acquire its own military power. In view of a dangerous world and in response to American urgings, the Self-Defense Forces were expanded to include well-equipped naval and air arms, and the defense budget continued to increase. However, Japan continued to forgo offensive weapons or capabilities, and total defense expenditures remained limited to one percent of gross national product until 1987.

About one quarter of L.D.P. Diet members were former bureaucrats, as were Prime Minister Ikeda, his immediate predecessor, Kishi Nobosuke (1957–1960), and his successor, Satō Eisaku (1964–1972). Subsequently, only Nakasone Yasuhiro (1982–1987) occupied that position for more than two years. Throughout the period, the well-educated, capable, and prestigious higher bureaucracy wielded great influence on the making and execution of policy.

Dominating the internal dynamics of the L.D.P., and thus determining the composition of Japan's government, was the interplay of political factions. After 1972, all prime ministers came from one of five factions—formal, recognized political groupings built around a leader, usually a potential prime minister. From his faction, a member derived political and financial support in his election campaigns and backing in his attempts to gain high government or party office. In return, he owed his faction leader political support, especially during the complex maneuvering that determined the party presidency and the prime ministership. What counted was skill in assembling political combinations and seniority, not popular appeal.

The L.D.P.'s origin as an association of independently based politicians helps account for the strength of the factions. Another factor was a system of multimember election districts in which there were frequently more conservative candidates than could reasonably expect to win election. Thus, in a five-member district, there might be four L.D.P. candidates with only three likely to win. In such cases, each candidate would build his own local support group aligned with a national L.D.P. faction.

The need to negotiate with the factions set limits on the prime minister's authority. Meanwhile, the national party was constrained at the grass-roots level, where each politician depended on his (or in rare cases her) own local support organization composed of various groups within his constituency. The politician maintained his following by supporting various community activities and offering personal assistance to constituents. He kept his political machine oiled by maintaining a "pipeline to the center," so that he could take credit for obtaining public works and other special-interest legislation. In seeking to fulfill these expectations, politicians depended on the political clout of their faction and a purse kept full by friendly interests. Although the most successful politicians were solidly entrenched, there were enough shifts in political fortunes on both the local and the national levels to provide for political interest. More importantly, the system retained the flexibility to adjust policies to changing circumstances.

For the opposition parties on the left, these were years of frustration. The two Socialist parties were closely associated with labor, each linked to one of the labor confederations. They depended on organized labor for votes, and labor leaders figured prominently in their leadership. Many of their Diet members also came from a labor background. Ideologically, the Socialists ran the gamut from Maoist radicals calling for revolution to moderate reformists. During the 1950s, the Communist party was very weak, but it picked up strength in the late 1960s after adopting pragmatic policies. However, even had they been able to unite, the three leftist parties lacked the strength to topple the L.D.P. regime.

Domestically, the opposition parties viewed with special alarm L.D.P. measures that looked suspiciously like a retreat from Occupation reforms and a return to the past—for example, measures to recentralize the police and education functions and to give Tokyo greater control over local government. Socialist fears were fortified by the prominence in the conservative leadership of men who had held cabinet offices in the 1930s and had been purged from politics by the Occupation authorities. The left was adamantly opposed to government moves to re-create a military establishment, and did what it could to block or at least delay the expansion of the Self-Defense Forces.

The left also objected to the government's pro-American foreign policy, protested against the continued presence of American bases, and against American nuclear weapons and tests. Unrestrained by expectations of forming a government themselves, they engaged in bitter struggles, including boycotts of the Diet and physical disruption, prompting police intervention. The L.D.P. did not refrain from using its majority to ram legislation through the Diet with little regard for the niceties of parliamentary procedure. This is what Minister Kishi did in 1960 to gain renewal of the Security Treaty with the United States, first signed in 1952 along with the peace treaty. The renewal of this treaty prompted demonstrations sufficiently strong to prompt the cancellation of President Dwight Eisenhower's planned visit to Japan.

Political animosity now reached its greatest intensity. Opponents felt that instead of providing for Japanese security, the treaty endangered Japan, threatening to involve it in American wars. The specter of nuclear war was particularly terrifying to a people who had experienced Hiroshima and Nagasaki. The socialists mustered impressive support for their opposition to the renegotiated treaty. Union workers, housewives, students, professors, and members of diverse organizations took to the streets in mass demonstrations in which millions of people participated. There was also a one-day general strike. All this did not block ratification or enactment of the treaty, but Kishi did resign.

After the 1960 confrontation, politics simmered down to less violent exchanges as the success of Japan's economic development became apparent. Ikeda's 10-year plan to double per capital GNP was achieved in only seven years. Although there were student protests against the Vietnam War, the Security Treaty was renewed in 1970 with little trouble.

In 1964, the political scene was complicated by the appearance of the Clean Government Party, formed by the Sōka Gakkai (Value Creation Society), a religious sect. As implied by its name, the party program opposed corruption, but it was vague on other issues. After obtaining 10.9 percent of the vote in the 1969 election, it declined to 8.5 percent in 1972, but remained a presence for the rest of the century. The L.D.P. aroused little enthusiasm. Its patronage networks remained effective in the over-represented countryside, but the party was weak in the cities. Before 1967, its candidates had received over half of the vote, but in the election of that year it declined to 48.8 percent, and continued slowly downward until it bottomed in 1976 at 41.8 percent. Even then, it remained by far the largest vote getter, benefiting from an electoral system that favored rural areas.

The Seventies and Eighties

Unlike China and the rest of East Asia, change in Japan remained gradual. There were neither abrupt reversals nor bold initiatives. We cannot identify any single truly major turning point. However, by 1970 a quarter of a century had transpired since the end of the war, and there were new challenges as well as new opportunities and achievements.

In the 1970s, Japanese resilience was tested by a series of short-term economic and political shocks. The first came in 1971, when the Bretton Woods System of fixed rates of exchange, adopted in 1944, was abandoned in favor of letting national currencies "float" more freely. That year the United States, Japan's largest trading partner, placed a 10 percent surcharge on imports, and it was left to the international monetary market to determine the value of the yen, with the result that it rose, making Japanese goods more expensive overseas but also making imports cheaper. Both these American actions were aimed at reducing, if not eliminating, a mounting U.S. trade-and-payments deficit with Japan, but they proved ineffective, and the problem persisted.

A political blow followed these economic acts when, still in the same year, Washington announced the impending visit of President Nixon to China, an act on which Japan was not consulted and which undercut Prime Minister Satō, who, primarily to please Washington, had been following the unpopular policy of maintaining the fiction that the Nationalist regime on Taiwan was the government of China. In 1972, after Tanaka Kakuei (prime minister, 1972–1974), became the first Japanese prime minister to visit Beijing, Japan recognized the P.R.C.

The next shock came in 1973 when the Arab oil boycott reminded Japan of its dependence on imported energy, and was followed by a quadrupling of the price of this vital import. As a result, during 1974 through 1976 Japan suffered a severe recession. However, the system demonstrated remarkable resilience. An outstanding example was the rescue of the Japanese automaker Mazda, saved from collapse through the cooperation of government-backed financial interests, management, workers, dealers, suppliers, and the local community. This "lesson in managing interdependence" led two American experts to conclude, "Relatively low interest rates, MITI bureaucrats, trade barriers, and the like are, no doubt, important factors in a comparative history of economic growth, but only managers and workers build cars and other products. And their capacity to pull together in a crisis is a crucial measure of a society's strength."[1]

In the late-1970s and 1980s, Japan's emphasis on high technology led to a decrease in dependence on imported raw materials. By 1984, Japan had reduced its use of imported raw material per unit of manufacture to 60 percent less than it had been 20 years earlier. This change also positioned Japan to compete with the emerging economies of such neighbors as Korea and Taiwan. Encouragement was given to electronics, telecommunications, biochemicals, and machine tools. In this way, the economy continued to sustain a population that by 1985 had reached 121 million, up from 65 million in 1930 and about four times the number of inhabitants of Japan at the time of the Meiji Restoration.

As elsewhere, the move away from "smoke-stack industries" hurt the labor movement by reducing the number of its members. Furthermore, the great majority of people considered themselves middle class. Growth of GNP declined to the level of other fully developed countries, but Japan's trade imbalance, especially with the United States, posed a continuing problem. Contrary to expectations, it was not solved by the rising value of the yen, which did, however, facilitate Japanese investment in the United States.

One business response to new conditions was the transformation of Japanese companies into multinationals, a trend that was to continue through the century and into the next as Japanese companies, in addition to trading in world markets, became involved in manufacturing overseas. These operations were generally successful on the factory floor, but it proved more difficult to internationalize management or "localize" the "transplants." In many cases, Japanese companies were resented for reserving the best jobs for those at home, for building factories far from the troubled, job-hungry cities, for favoring their *keiretsu* partners, and generally taking advantage of opportunities abroad denied to foreign companies at home.

In politics as in economics, the system proved vulnerable but resilient. Early in 1976, the Lockheed scandal ("Japan's Watergate") shook the political world, as it was revealed that millions of dollars of the American company's funds had been used to corrupt the highest Japanese government officials. Although prosecutors lacked the independence and tools to be truly effective, they were able to indict the former prime minister Tanaka Kakuei, who was found guilty in a 1983 decision upheld in 1987.

Predictions that the L.D.P. would decline to the point of losing its ability to form a government proved false. It reached a low of 41.8 percent of the popular vote in 1976, but made a strong comeback in 1980. In 1986 it won 49.6 percent of the vote, entitling it to 300 seats, the highest number of the party's history. The party and its internal factional structure remained essentially the same. Despite the Lockheed scandal, Tanaka continued to control his faction until he suffered a stroke in 1985.

The leading political figure in the 1980s was Nakasone Yasuhiro (1918–), who as prime minister from 1982 to 1987, brought an unusually vigorous style of leadership and national assertiveness into the office. Prosperity, self-confidence, and American pressure combined to induce the government in 1986 to exceed the previous one percent of GNP cap in the military budget for the next year. Though the increase was modest, it had symbolic significance. Nakasone was also the first prime minister to visit the Yasukuni Shrine to pay his respects to the Japanese war dead, including 14 men condemned as Class A war criminals. At the same time, the Socialist Party dropped its long-standing opposition to the Self-Defense Forces based on Article IX of the constitution. It now held that the Self-Defense Forces were "unconstitutional but legal." Ten years earlier the Supreme Court had ruled that the constitutionality of the forces was a decision for the legislature to make and had also left it up to the legislature to rectify an electoral system that was unconstitutional in discriminating against urban voters.

Nakasone cooperated with the United States to reduce the trade surplus by emphasizing domestic spending, cooperating on monetary policy, and trying to open Japanese markets to more imported goods. The last of these, however, was difficult in face of powerful, deeply entrenched domestic interests and business patterns. Farmers and construction companies were just two examples of major domestic constituencies on which many L.D.P. leaders had long depended. For the rest of the 1980s, the trade imbalance was more acute than ever. Japan developed expertise in industrial ceramics, robotics, and biotechnology.

The yen remained strong, propelled by a hot economy that sent the stock market soaring and raised land prices to astronomical levels. Japan became a major exporter of capital—building factories and buying foreign debt, prestigious hotels, and trophy real estate such as New York's Rockefeller Center, acquired by a Mitsui affiliate in 1989. Nevertheless, the balance of payments remained in Japan's favor.

In keeping with a general trend in the capitalist world, Japan divested itself of the government railway in 1987 and sold its shares in the National Telegraph and Telephone Company and in Japan Air Lines. By that time, Nakasone had been succeeded by Takeshita Noboru (1924–2000), who headed the Tanaka faction after 1985 but lasted less than two full years (Nov. 1987–June 1989). He was forced to resign under a cloud arising out of revelations that the head of the Recruit group of companies had attempted to buy influence by giving large amounts in shares and money to leading politicians and bureaucrats. The next prime minister, who lied about giving hush money to a mistress, lasted two months. His successor, too, was a weak leader. The L.D.P.-dominated system was coming unglued, and now the financial bubble burst. Between January and October 1990 the stock market plunged 48 percent, and in 1991 recession set in.

II. Society, Thought, and the Arts

Social Change and Quality of Life

Film

Intellectual Life and Literature

The Visual Arts

Social Change and Quality of Life

Economic growth brought unprecedented affluence. The very physiognomy of the Japanese people changed as an improved diet produced a new generation taller and healthier than its parents. By 1990, the Japanese people had the world's highest rate of life expectancy, and this was still the case in 2000 when it reached 74.5 years. Increased longevity strained family values when the golden years turned out disastrously (see Box 17.1).

People now ate more fish and meat. Dairy products became daily staples, and wheat consumption rose steadily. Japan became a nation of coffee as well as tea

BOX 17.1 "THE HATEFUL AGE"

In this 1947 short story, Niwa Fumio (1904–2005) tells the story of a young couple taking care of a pestilent and senile grandmother who steals, urinates on the floor, and keeps odd hours. Her decrepit body was as light as a "sack of charcoal." According to the wife, "granny was like some sort of disease visited permanently upon their family, and now afflicting the third generation." They had to get rid of her. Their solution was to unload her on an older sister living in the countryside. Younger sister Ruriko was charged with carting granny there, and the following passage describes their journey on the train.

The compartment was crowded, but one of the passengers, seeing Ruriko enter with her peculiar burden, offered his seat. Directly opposite her was a woman in her thirties, also accompanied by an old lady. Soon after the train started she addressed Ruriko:

"Excuse me, but where are you taking yours?"

"I'm leaving her at my sister's place in the country."

"Well, we seem to be in the same boat," said the woman, with a sigh. She and Ruriko exchanged the bitter smiles of people who share some painful illness. "How old is she?" the other woman asked.

"Eighty-six."

"Mine's eighty." She glanced about the carriage and went on in a lower voice. "Why on earth do they live on to be eighty? I just can't make it out. They live on and on and on, until they're of no use to anyone—until even they themselves are fed up with living. All that mine cares about nowadays is food, and she can't get it into her head that rice is rationed. She's always accusing us of being mean to her, even though she gets her full ration."

"Mine's the same," said Ruriko. "She's got the appetite of two normal people. I really don't know how she can eat so much, just sitting still all day."

"They're rice-eating spooks!" said the woman, with venom. "Just rice-eating spooks!"

Meanwhile the two "spooks" sat gazing vacantly out of the window at the changing scenery, evidently unaware that they were being discussed. The other passengers had overheard the conversation and were staring with undissembled curiosity at the two old women.

(continued)

BOX 17.1 "THE HATEFUL AGE" (CONTINUED)

From their expressions it was clear that they did not feel they were looking at human beings at all but rather at some strange species of superannuated plant or animal.

Ironically, Niwa himself lived to the ripe old age of 100 and was beset by Alzheimers when he died.

Niwa Fumio, "The Hateful Age" translated by Ivan Morris in Ivan Morris, ed. *Modern Japanese Stories: An Anthology* (Rutland, VT: Charles Tuttle, 1962), pp. 320–348. The quoted passages are on pp. 324, 326–327.

drinkers. During the 1970s, the arch of McDonald's spread from Tokyo's Ginza to the provinces, where it was soon joined by the figure of Colonel Sanders inviting passers-by to partake of Kentucky Fried Chicken, while Mr. Donut and Dairy Queen did their part to propagate fast-food culture American-style.

Changes in dress were equally dramatic. In the 1980s, blue jeans became the universal dress of the young, and pants were worn in public by women of all ages as a matter of course. Conversely, the kimono was reserved for special occasions, but wealthy sophisticates now could prance about in the latest fashions by Japan's world-renowned designers.

Consumerism reigned as old crafts declined, and traditional elegance gave way to modern practicality—except that the modern was not always practical, for during the 1980s so many realized their dream of owning an automobile that the roads were choked and the savvy driver had to learn how to "diagnose traffic paralysis."[2] Fortunately, public transportation within and between cities was excellent, although in Tokyo's rush hour ("crush hour" would be more appropriate) "pushers" had to cram the people quickly into the overflowing subways.

There was a shift of population from the country into cities. Nevertheless, since mechanization reduced the need for farm labor, agricultural production increased. Thanks to the L.D.P., the government purchased rice at several times the international price. The prewar gulf between urban wealth and rural poverty disappeared, and the spread of television accelerated the process, begun by radio, of diminishing the cultural gap. However, despite the omnipresence of the television set, the Japanese remained the world's most avid consumers of newspapers, magazines, and comic books.

Public transportation, communication, and security were excellent, but the environment suffered. Japan's industrial zone, running along the Pacific coast from Tokyo to northern Kyushu, developed into a "polluters' paradise":

> Polluted air choked urban residents with respiratory difficulties, which were fatal in some areas. Water pollution wiped out coastal fishing along the industrial belt. In the cities exhaust from automobiles mixed with pollutants from smokestacks and produced toxic photochemical smog during the day.[3]

Only after Tokyo became enshrouded in a semi-perpetual screen of smog did the government take action. In Mie prefecture asthma was linked to pollution, and in Toyama a river caused cadmium poisoning. Most notorious was the "Minamata Disease" (1953) caused by people eating fish contaminated by methyl mercury discharged by a fertilizer plant in Kyushu. Thanks to obstruction by the company and government connivance, the victims had to wait until 1968 for official acknowledgment that mercury was the cause. In 1973, a group of Minamata plaintiffs prevailed in court and won the largest tort award in Japanese history. In 1978 a National Institute for Minamata Disease was established. The name "Minamata" still conjures up both the deadly threat of environmental pollution and people's determination to fight back.

Government measures taken in the 1970s did ameliorate the problem, but the quality of air and water remained a matter of concern, and excessive dam construction boded ill for the future of Japan's rivers. Visual pollution was all too apparent as Japan's industrial area became one of the ugliest to be found anywhere. While the Japanese people continued to cherish nature in miniature, lovingly tending tiny gardens on the most unlikely bits of land, Japan's business and political leaders, in their rush to modernize, sacrificed much of the natural beauty that had once been Japan's cherished heritage.

In the 1980s, preserving the environment was widely accepted as a public good, leading to the Ministry of Construction-sponsored International Flower and Greenery Exposition in 1990, even as it was planning an airport that would kill the last healthy coral reef in Okinawa. By the end of the 1980s, environmentalists were expressing concern over the situation at home, as well as calling attention to the destruction Japanese companies were inflicting on the tropical forests of Borneo and other lands. If the aims of Japanese environmentalists were similar to those elsewhere, the same was even more true of the forces arrayed against them.

Even before the land boom of the 1980s, the escalating price of land and housing in Japan's large cities forced young married couples to live with their in-laws because they could not afford separate establishments, or to crowd into tiny apartments in drab and monotonous buildings made of reinforced concrete. Raising a family in such confined quarters was no easy task. Although the small apartments reduced women's household chores, releasing time for other activities, the residents of such buildings were slow to develop a sense of community, since they regarded these quarters as temporary, marking a stage of their lives and careers soon to be surmounted.

The absence of grandparents in the new housing was but one of the factors making for discontinuity between the generations. Such discontinuity was not unique to Japan; in other countries, too, rapid changes during the postwar years created a "generation gap." However, in Japan the gap was particularly severe. The younger people grew up in a society that had suddenly become very different from that of their parents, and furthermore, a whole generation of wartime leaders had been thoroughly discredited and the old values blamed for leading the nation to catastrophe. Included were many of the values that had strengthened the cohesiveness of Japanese society.

New lifestyles and values appeared in the factories, as young workers preferred to spend their leisure time manipulating *pachinko* (vertical pinball) machines, playing video games, or listening to rock music rather than going on company outings. They valued skill more than length of service, and tended to regard the factory not as a second home but merely as a place to work. The number of hours they would have to spend there was also decreasing, and a survey conducted in 1990 revealed that workers were more interested in obtaining more leisure than higher pay.

Those fortunate enough to survive a brutal entrance examination system gained admission to universities oriented largely to research and graduate work. Ostensibly paternalistic, the universities demonstrated their supposed concern for the youngest members of the academic community by virtually guaranteeing graduation to all matriculants. Neglected after having worked so hard for university entrance, the students expressed their discontent in radical political activities. Their dissatisfaction helped fuel widespread demonstrations and disruptions in the late-1960s, directed against both national and university policies. Activities of Japanese youth reflected those of youth elsewhere in the world, and similarly, the pendulum swung back to greater conservatism in the 1970s and 1980s.

The loosening of traditional patterns and values presented contemporary Japanese with a wide range of choices but within what remained, by and large, a closely knit society. For example, young people increasingly insisted on making their own selection of a spouse, and they were now always consulted before a marriage was arranged by their parents. Nevertheless, even in love marriages, most young people still asked their employer or teacher to serve as official matchmaker. A surprisingly large number continued to leave the initiative to their parents. Under the postwar legal system, wives as well as husbands could now initiate divorce proceedings; the divorce rate grew but remained low.

Women now had more options. Many remained content with their traditional roles, which gave them a predominant influence over their children and firmly established the home as their field of authority. Although submissive to their husbands in public, most wives controlled the family budget, ran the household, and often treated their husbands as they would an older, somewhat difficult, and rather special child. They accepted their exclusion from much of their husbands' social lives, which the husbands spent largely in the company of fellow workers. Such couples, like their Tokugawa predecessors, led separate social lives. These wives also did not share in their husband's nightlife.

However, as time went on, an increasing number of women chose a career and either a companionate marriage or a single life. They made progress in the

professions and, more slowly, in business, where they often had to choose between temporary employment followed by marriage or the more regular male-oriented career path. The passage of the Equal Opportunity Act in 1985, making sex discrimination illegal, reflected a new consciousness, but the law lacked teeth.

As in all periods of social change, there were some who suffered because change was too rapid and others for whom it was too slow. Among the former were old people, bewildered and distressed by the whirl about them. One of the strengths of the old society had been the dignity and security afforded to the aged, but now cramped quarters and new ideas ate away at old values and threatened traditional comforts. These were people who found that the social rules had changed just when their turn came to reap the rewards the system offered those who played by the rules. While the erosion of respect for the aged diminished the traditional attractions of longevity, forced retirement at an early age (usually 55) and the devaluation of savings because of continual inflation deprived the old of a sense of economic security. Most families did manage to take care of the elderly, and most old people were not shunted off into nursing homes or set up in special retirement communities, but the social arrangements made for the elderly by their children were often grudging and poisoned by resentment.

At the other end of the spectrum were those who felt that change was too slow. They felt stifled rather than supported by a social system that still expected the individual to be subordinate to the group, whether it be family or company. They also balked at conforming to a social hierarchy that had lost much of its theoretical support. The discontented were a disparate group. They included career women frustrated by roadblocks and ceilings, those constrained to maintain and live with parents, and people seeking to fill the vacuum left by the abandoning of the old values with something more solid than consumerism and the race to elevate the economic standing of their country. Their discontent was frequently shared by students and by radicals impatient for a more egalitarian society. Some of the young men without prospects for university study joined motorcycle gangs. However, most worked out a modus vivendi for themselves, and many of the young gradually came to terms with society.

The great majority of the population, however, neither mourned the passing of the old nor were impatient for the arrival of the new. Appreciative of the increase in material wealth, they were nevertheless unsure of the future. Many turned to religion, maintaining home altars, visiting temples and shrine, and going on pilgrimages. Shrines and temples had always offered prayers and amulets protecting against disease, assurance of safe childbirth, and the like. Adjusting to new conditions, many now offered traffic-safety charms while a temple in Tokyo added air safety. Shrines and temples offering examination success were popular with young people. The elderly were serviced by temples offering prayers and amulets to quiet their fears of senility. This had excellent prospects of becoming a growth industry because, as a by-product of longevity, Japan had half a million senile people by 1994, and the average age of the population was rising.

New religious sects arose seeking to satisfy the spiritual hunger and alleviate the mental malaise brought on by the loss of community. As they moved from traditional village to modern city, people sought "a religious frame of meaning relevant to contemporary life."[4] Attracting the largest membership was Sōka Gakkai, the sponsor of the Clean Government Party. Doctrinally based on Nichiren Buddhism, it denounced all other faiths, and insisted that its members proselytize relentlessly and go on a pilgrimage to the head temple at the foot of Mt. Fuji, where an average of 10,000 people a day came to pay their homage. By passing a series of examinations, the faithful could rise in an academic-style hierarchy of ranks. For the devoted members, the sect provided a spiritual community and a sense of personal worth and of belonging to a large, integrated, purposeful group. Others found it more difficult to find new certainties, however, for the world offered a bewildering range of choices.

Not all choices were solemn. Just like today, everyone, not only the devout, flocked to the temples and shrines on festival days when the lanes leading to their gates were lined with stands offering various trinkets, souvenirs, and good things to eat—everything from octopus snacks to chocolate-covered bananas. This combination of piety and fun also accounts for the continued popularity of roly-poly *darumas,* popular doll-like figures named after Bodhidharma, the monk who was thought to have brought Zen to China and later lost his legs after nine years in uninterrupted contemplation. Even the skeptical made sure to paint in an eye and made a silent wish, hoping they would be able to paint in the other eye once their wish was granted. Although ubiquitous, *daruma* also had his special temple (Figure 17.1).

FIGURE 17.1 *Darumas* greet the visitor everywhere in the Hōrinji Temple, Kyoto, founded in 1718 but frequently rebuilt. Commonly known as the *Daruma* Temple, it houses around 8000 *daruma* figurines.

Film

If, as is often said, film was the characteristic art form of the twentieth century, then the worldwide acclaim accorded Japanese films is but one more indication of Japan's full participation in that century's culture. By no means were all Japanese films masterpieces: Japanese companies were second to none in turning out ephemeral entertainments—samurai movies that were the artistic equivalents of American westerns, unbearably sentimental tear-jerkers, horror and monster films, and in the 1970s and 1980s, a wave of erotica with little artistic or social value but plenty of sexual action. Such films, reflecting social stereotypes and people's daydreams, are of considerable interest to psychologists and social scientists, but it is important to remember that the stereotypes they contain—the self-sacrificing but self-centered mother, the wife finding herself, daughters in various degrees of revolt—are never simple mirror images of society. The more ambitious and truly superior films reflected the times and the society, but rose above them. The major films were the creations of quality actors, sensitive cameramen, and above all, great directors who were able to use the medium to create their own personal styles, conveying their own personal visions. If they had anything in common, it was a superb visual sense employed to create an atmosphere. Some may be said to have used the camera to paint their vision on the screen.

Exercising classic restraint in his insistence on a strict economy of means (empty spaces, simple objects, minimal plot) and avoiding anything superficial or artificially clever was Ozu Yasujiō (1903–1963), whose traditionalism also extended to his subject matter, for he was the filmmaker par excellence of the Japanese family. Other directors, like their Chinese counterparts, were highly critical of their country's traditions and values. For example, in *Harakiri* (*Seppuku*, 1962), directed by Kobayashi Masaki, the hero sets out to avenge his son, who had been forced to commit an unimaginably painful *seppuku* (ritual suicide) using a sword with a bamboo blade, but in the end the whole system is revealed to be founded on hypocrisy. Or there is *Night Drum* (*Yoru no Tsuzumi*, also known as *The Adulteress,* 1958), directed by Imai Tadashi, in which a samurai kills the wife he loves. By doing what society demands, he deprives his own life of meaning. Such vivid and moving historical films were among the triumphs of the postwar cinema, part of a continuing and sometimes bitter dialogue with a still-living past.

An outstanding director was Kurosawa Akira (1910–1998). His world-famous *Rashomon* (1950) suggests the relativity of all truth through a demonstration of the power of human subjectivity and self-interest. *Ikiru* (1952) takes the viewer through a Faust-like quest for meaning in life. The main character, a petty bureaucrat dying of cancer, in the end finds fulfillment in one meaningful social act: surmounting endless red tape and bureaucratic obstructionism, he gets a small park built. Kurosawa's mastery of large scenes with vast casts as well as his versatility and creative vigor was apparent in *Ran* (1985), an imaginative metamorphosis of King Lear into sixteenth-century Japan. Like his earlier *Seven Samurai* (1954), it is one of those rare films in which powerful and sensitive acting, beautiful visual composition and realistic detail, story line and structure, friction and harmony, violence and stillness blend into a major artistic statement.

In the 1980s, Japanese studios increasingly churned out films of violence and pornography. Refreshing exceptions were films of Itami Juzo (Ikeuchi Yoshihiro, 1933–1997), who poked fun at the Japanese way of burial in *The Funeral* (1984), noodlemania in *Tampopo* (1986), and tax collection methods in *A Taxing Woman I* and *II* (1987, 1988). His satire on the Japanese mob, *Minbo no Onna—The Gentle Art of Extortion* (1994), provoked the Yakuza (organized crime) to a physical attack on his person. Itami survived this, but later committed suicide, leaving a note explaining this act as proving the untruth of rumors that he was having an affair with a much younger woman.

Intellectual Life and Literature

After the war, Japan rejoined the international intellectual community, participated in scientific and scholarly meetings at home and abroad, and increasingly contributed to specialized disciplines in important ways. Many scholars became conversant in a foreign language, usually English, and all had access to a broad and steady stream of translations.

Writings addressing broader human or philosophical issues, published in journals of opinion and in books, have attracted less attention abroad than have the works of filmmakers and novelists. One reason, no doubt, is the language barrier. Another may be that much was derivative. Additionally, many Japanese intellectuals, like their American counterparts, applied their energies to studying their own society and to addressing their own countrymen. Notably fascinating but problematical has been the literature of exceptionalism (*Nihonjinron*) that burgeoned in the 1970s and continued thereafter to fuel a sense of self-confidence and assertiveness. This literature, which focused on Japanese uniqueness, included the highly respected and stimulating work of such scholars as the psychiatrist Doi Takeo and the sociologist Nakane Chie. Lesser scholars, however, expounded on and frequently took pride in the uniqueness of just about every aspect of Japanese behavior, institutions, and climatic and racial characteristics. Increasing cosmopolitanism did not prevent the persistence of insularity.

What it meant to be Japanese was also one of the themes explored in postwar fiction. After the war, older novelists published manuscripts they could not release during the war, while new writers sounded new themes. An outstanding example of the former is the long novel by Tanizaki translated as *The Makioka Sisters*.

In 1947 Kawabata published the last installment of *Snow Country*. Previous segments of the novel had been published in various journals over the course of the preceding 12 years, as though each part were a stanza in a *renga* (linked verse) rather than a building block for a novel. Kawabata's work resonates with tradition, but he also has his personal obsessions. Roy Starrs has pointed to "the ceaseless attempt of his male heroes to free themselves from their alienation and egotism to achieve a kind of monastic state of grace by a purifying contact with a pure, virginal girl."[5]

Kawabata's novels sacrifice structure and plot for the sake of naturalness and poetry. *A Thousand Cranes* (1948) and *The Sound of the Mountain* (1951) followed, each imbued with the author's visual sensibility and with his concern for beauty and sadness, inseparable as ever in Japanese literature, and evoking what one critic termed a "vibrant silence." Kawabata's method and vision was clearly demonstrated in his Nobel Prize acceptance speech (1968). Translated as *Japan, the Beautiful, and Myself,* it is an evocation of the Japanese tradition, a string of poems and images held together by a perception of beauty and truth.

Japan's literary classics were written by women during the Heian period (794–1185). Subsequently that changed and most of the writers recognized as eminent during the Tokugawa period and in the first years of Meiji were men. Women writers reappeared toward the turn of the century but really came into their own after the war. As Donald Keene pointed out, "At no time since the Heian period had women figured so prominently in the literary world." Appropriately, one of the most distinguished among them, Enchi Fumiko (1905–1986), translated *The Tale of Genji* into modern Japanese (1972–1973). She also wrote realistic novels such as *Waiting Years* (1957) and the subtle and imaginative *Masks* (1958).

A brilliant and versatile but uneven writer was Mishima Yukio (1925–1970), who in a series of well-constructed novels, developed his ideas on such themes as the nature of beauty and the relationships between art and life, warrior and poet. One of his most compelling novels is *The Temple of the Golden Pavilion* (1956). Based on an actual act of arson in postwar Kyoto, it includes powerful psychological and philosophical explorations. A dramatist and critic as well as novelist, Mishima was prolific, self-contradictory, and even self-parodying. He tried to mold his life and his body as he did his art. Wishing to be both athlete and artist, he took up body building and developed a strong torso, but on spindly legs. Seeking to achieve a unity of knowledge and action, as in the philosophy of Wang Yangming, whom he admired, Mishima's culminating act was a dramatic public *seppuku* committed in 1970 after the completion of his final work, a tetrology entitled *The Sea of Fertility.* He was joined in death by a member of his small, private right-wing army. Mishima exhorted the Self-Defense Force to rise up before performing his ritual suicide at its headquarters. Regarded by the public as irrelevant and bizarre, Mishima intended this act to be a fulfillment of his life's work.

A productive writer who was well known abroad was Endō Shūsaku (1923–1996), who in a series of brilliant novels, grappled with the tensions between his Catholic faith and his Japanese heritage. Just as Endō contributed to modern Christian as well as Japanese literature, Abe Kobō (1924–1993) earned an international reputation as an existentialist. He is perhaps best known for his novel *Woman in the Dunes* (1962), subsequently made into a film. In this work as well as later novels such as *Face of Another* (1964), *The Boxman* (1973), and *The Ark Sakura* (1984), and in such plays as *Friends* (1967), Abe explored themes and predicaments besetting the contemporary human condition, including the search for identity.

The search for identity was particularly acute in an age when people had a greater freedom to choose how to live their lives and in that sense was hardly confined to a single country or region. Nonetheless, in Japan as elsewhere, the search for one's personal roots in the past often accompanied the search for identity. Such a search for identity and roots infuses the work of Ōe Kenzaburō (1935–), two of whose novels, *A Personal Matter* (1964) and *The Silent Cry* (1967), were widely read in Japanese and in translation. Insight into psychological complexities of modern people—including the sources of violence, a concern for social morality, and a strong personal symbolism—and his grappling with basic problems of existence in the second half of the twentieth century mark him as a major writer who speaks to the central problems of his age.

The Visual Arts

Like filmmakers and novelists, Japanese painters, potters, and architects won international recognition. As earlier, some artists found their inspiration in, and took their cues from, the latest trends. Japan had its practitioners of abstract expressionism, action painting, pop art, and the various other international art movements, which represented the search for a style appropriate to a bewildering age and often degenerated into fads.

More traditional was the work of artists who strove to create beauty without attempting to convey a symbolic message. Japanese potters, innovators as well as traditionalists, continued to blend shapes, textures, and colors to create works worthy of the tradition.

An old genre in new form was the woodcut. Unlike the earlier *ukiyo-e* artists, their twentieth-century successors took responsibility for the entire process of print making. They did their own cutting and printing, although they might have students assist them in the more routine aspects of the process. Among the finest was Munakata Shikō (1903–1975), also a gifted painter, whose style was influenced by traditional Japanese folk art, but who also developed new techniques. One was to apply color on the back of the print and let it seep through the paper to create gentle, diffused coloring. This helped Munakata create a general decorative effect, as in his rendition of the clothing in *Lady in Chinese Costume* (Figure 17.2). In subject matter his works range from the religious, such as the series of the Buddha's disciples that won him a prize in Venice in 1956, to the sensuous and the whimsical as exemplified by a nude with the artist's eyeglasses resting on her belly. While the disciples are in black and white, many other woodcuts reveal Munakata's love of playing with color. In tone his art is positive—there is no echo here of the agony of the century.

Perhaps the most revealing art of society is architecture. Although many opportunities were missed in the rush of postwar reconstruction, and Japan's industrial centers are among the ugliest cities in the world, there were also buildings of great distinction. The achievements of Tange Kenzo (1913–2005), designer of the Hall Dedicated to Peace at Hiroshima, were recognized internationally when he received the Pritzker Prize in 1987. The swimming pool and sports center he designed for the 1964 Tokyo Olympics won wide acclaim. Thirty years later he designed the Tokyo City Hall Complex (1995). His buildings can also be seen in Singapore, Europe, North Africa, the Middle East, and Minnesota (The Arts Complex in Minneapolis, 1970–1974). In addition to designing superb buildings, Tange involved himself deeply in urban planning.

One of Tange's most creative students was Isozaki Arata (1931–). Postmodernist in rejecting the functionalism of the modernist international style and seeking a "shifting, revolving, flickering style" rather than a "lucid, coherent, institutional style," Isozaki is also an internationalist who could write, "the Katsura Palace, the Parthenon, the Capitoline piazza, and so on all live in a time and place equidistant from us. Anything occurring in the history of architecture even the history of the world— is open to quotation."[6] Such quotation yields new and complex meaning and explains the rationale for Isozaki's Tsukuba Science Center. However, often Isozaki does not quote, and some of his most successful buildings employ solid geometric forms, as in his Museum of Contemporary Art in Los Angeles. Illustrated here (Figure 17.3) is the tower for his arts center in Mito, which although located in a place once famous for historiography, does not refer to anything except itself.

FIGURE 17.2 *Lady in Chinese Costume,* Munakata Shikō, (1946). There are strong hints of Persia and India in Munakata's work. But in the vigor of his lines, his gentle eroticism, and the decorative qualities of his art, he resembles Matisse, and his coloring is reminiscent of Chagall. Woodcut, 21 × 15 inches.

PHOTOGRAPH © "TORNADO" FROM THE SERIES "IN PRAISE OF SHOKIE" BY MUNAKATA SHIKŌ, MUNAKATA MUSEUM IN KAMAKURA.

The diversity of modern Japanese architecture is far too great for any single building possibly to be representative, but architecture can, among other things, be fun. The example of Japanese "pop architecture" in Figure 17.4 was built to house an exhibit on coffee for an exposition celebrating the completion of an artificial island in Kobe. Later, it was turned into a permanent coffee museum and given a more dignified but conventional exterior. Perhaps the cup ranneth over and the joke wore off—humor may be as ephemeral as beauty. Still, it is a splendid museum, housing exhibits on the history, the preparation, and the consumption of coffee and also providing facilities for study and a "training room" for coffee makers. It is a striking reminder that Japan, which had perfected the tea ceremony, now became a world leader in coffee appreciation, famed for its many and varied coffee houses serving the choicest South American beans. A serious beverage befitting hard workers and diligent students, coffee had found a home in Japan.

III. The Nineties and Beyond, 1989–2006

FIGURE 17.3   Art Tower Mito in Mito Ibaragi. 1986–1990. A postmodernist, architect Isozaki Arata often includes historical references in his buildings, but he also delights in the play of space and forms. 328 feet high.

PHOTOGRAPH COURTESY YASUHIROS ISHIMOTO AND ARATA ISOZAKI & ASSOCIATES.

The death of the emperor in January 1989 had little immediate political effect. Most Japanese were happy with the personality of the new, more accessible emperor, the first to have married a commoner. However, the performance of Shinto funeral and enthronement rites as official ceremonies troubled those committed to a secular state. Additionally, the focus on the monarchy drew renewed attention to the past role of the throne in leading Japan into the dark valley of authoritarianism and war. The tendency of high government officials to minimize wartime atrocities, government reluctance to compensate Korean "comfort women" forced into sexual slavery during the war, claims that the Pacific War had been righteous, and the widespread view of the Japanese as history's innocent victims combined to disturb people, at home and abroad, who knew otherwise.

For progressives, Japan had paid far too high a price for development. They saw the system as "a kind of state capitalism brokered by the elites that held the masses in thrall and precluded the emergence of a genuine democratic polity . . . a capitalism brokered by conservative elites in order to achieve nationalist goals."[7] A strong voice for a more positive appraisal was that of Murakami Yasusuke (1931–1993), professor of economics at Tokyo University and author of *An Anticlassical Political-Economic Analysis* (1992). Murakami blamed Japanese imperialism on the West and historical circumstances, and emphasized the positive achievements of Japanese-style developmentalism. A nuanced thinker capable of criticism, he sharply warned against Japanese particularism, but was convinced that there was more than one road to success. He maintained that Japan, with its "capacity to nurture a community of cultural systems,"[8] had achieved a viable way that could serve as a model for late developing nations and enable Japan to be a leader in the post–Cold War world.

The message that there is more than one road to development was a timely one for a world in which only one super-power remained and triumphalism was in the air, but during the 1990s it seemed increasingly less likely that Japan would serve as an economic, let alone political, exemplar. Essentially, the country managed to muddle through the decade, but did not shine.

FIGURE 17.4   Coffee Pavilion, Port-pia Exposition, Kobe, 1981. Takenaka Construction Firm.
Although the era of pop architecture has passed and the coffee museum has changed the face
it shows the world, coffee has found a permanent home in Japan. 82 feet high, c. 72 feet in
diameter.
PHOTOGRAPH © LORE SCHIROKAUER.

As already noted, 1991 marked the real start of the recession. That same year,
Japan contributed $13 billion to the war effort in the Persian Gulf, but did not
send troops. Two years later, however, despite Article IX of the Constitution, it
sent a token non-combatant force to support U.N. peacekeeping in Cambodia. Yet
talk of Japanese membership in an expanded Security Council remained talk, and
a new, more prominent international role eluded the nation with the world's
second-largest economy. If the Persian Gulf War again highlighted Japan's dependence on foreign oil, the conference on global warming held in Kyoto in 1997 was a
reminder that we all live on the same planet.

During the 1990s the economy sputtered along, each small spurt followed by
a stall, so that it neither advanced into sustained recovery nor sank into the depths
of depression. The excesses of spending abroad were liquidated—Rockefeller
Center went bankrupt in 1995. Japan was not as badly hit by the "Asian Crisis" of
1998 as Korea, but nevertheless suffered serious losses. At the end of the decade
there was an uptick, but all too soon it was clear that the banking system remained

unsound and that Japan had not yet found a way back to economic health. The stock market in the summer of 2001 declined to a 17-year low.

Where earlier the Japanese economic system had been widely admired, the pressures now were toward opening its markets to American-style entrepreneurs and foreign companies and goods. By the end of the decade, the *keiretsu* were dissolving as banks sold stocks and companies became more dependent on equity financing. American financial institutions became a major presence.

A number of factors kept the economy afloat. A vital one was Japan's sheer wealth. This enabled the government to finance very substantial deficit spending on public works, to underwrite housing projects and small business loans, and generally to prime the economy. In 1994 it completed the scintillating Kansai Airport. Designed by the Italian architect Renzo Piano (Pritzker Prize winner, 1999), it was built offshore in 18 meters of water on soft foundations that kept subsiding, running the cost up to the enormous figure of roughly $15 billion. In addition to stimulating the economy with construction money, this project gave easy international access to the Osaka area.

There were numerous smaller projects nourishing the politically and economically important construction industry. In 1995 these included 400 dams either under construction or planned. By that time, postwar Japan had already built 1,000 dams, many of which were already clogged by over 1 billion tons of silt. Writing in 1996, Gavan MacCormack described the situation as "an ecological nightmare to which Japan is only beginning to wake."[9] Economic recovery remained Japan's top priority.

The government also sought to stimulate the economy by lowering interest rates, which at one point reached zero. Even so, the yen did not sink precipitously. The balance of payments with the United States remained in Japan's favor, although by 2000 China had replaced Japan as the country with the largest U.S. trade deficit.

An element of strength was Japan's continued technological excellence. People everywhere eagerly bought Japanese cars, laptop computers, and electronics. Robotics led to triumphs in manufacturing and gave birth to toys that delighted children throughout the world. Perhaps robotic cats and dogs will also eventually catch on. Somewhere between a tool and a toy were the cellular e-mail telephones ubiquitous among Japanese teenagers who found a space of their own in cyberspace.

Companies cut back but tried to limit layoffs. People did not prosper, but most continued to work. The authorities worried less about present or future unemployment than about the aging of the population and a declining birthrate that reached 1.29 children per woman in 2003. Women sought and increasingly found more fulfilling roles than that of the traditional mother. A projected decline from some 127 million people in 2006 to 90 million by 2100 raised concern over the adverse effects this could have on Japan's economic growth and international political standing, but so far has stimulated only ineffective government responses.

People had little faith in government, but there was not a sense of urgency sufficiently strong to stir up an effective public demand for radical change in political direction or leadership. The government's failure to prepare for or deal adequately with the earthquake that shook the Kobe area in 1995, officially designated not earthquake-prone, revealed the government's shortcomings. Over 6,000 people died, and the heart of one of Japan's most modern and international cities was destroyed along with a brand new highway, revealing shoddy construction made possible by corruption. Government failure to assure adequate standards was matched by the slowness and inadequacy of its response. In contrast, organized crime stepped in to provide help and relief. The government was effective in suppressing the apocalyptic Aun Shinrikyō sect after it used sarin in a 1995 Tokyo subway attack, but faced with a nuclear mishap in 1999, the government's response was again slow and inept.

On the political stage, the L.D.P. finally disintegrated in 1993 with a major factional exodus, but the first non-L.D.P. prime minister, Hosokawa Morihito, lasted less than a year (August 1993–April 1994) before he too was undone by involvement in yet another scandal. In 1989, under the leadership of Doi Takako (1928–), the first woman to become a major force in Japanese politics, it looked as if the Socialists might grow into a viable second party, but this did not happen. Instead, badly divided and compromised by ill-advised political alliances, they declined. Though the women's vote was important, and two women served in the cabinet for a short time, at century's end over 95 percent of the Diet members were men. With men also in control of the bureaucracy, government and politics remained male domains.

Coalition governments between 1993 and 1996 were hampered by internal rivalry and conflict. One accomplishment in 1994 was a major change in the electoral system, abolishing multi-member districts and providing for a total of 500 seats, 300 from small single-member districts and 200 filled by proportional representation. In 1996, the first election under the new law was held, with the result that a weakened and divided L.D.P. regained power.

Prime Minister Hashimoto Ryutarō (1938–2006, in office 1996–1998) was succeeded by Obuchi Keizo (1937–2000), who died very suddenly and unexpectedly in May, 2000. His successor, Mori Yoshirō (1937–), lost no time causing widespread consternation by calling Japan "a divine nation with the emperor at its core," stating publicly what more circumspect rightist politicians kept to themselves. New elections were held in June with the result that the opposition gained strength, but Mori managed to remain in office until April 2001, when he was succeeded by Koizumi Junichirō (1942–) who owed his position to a landslide victory in provincial party elections rather than through the usual political horse trading by faction leaders.

Koizumi, an unconventional politician noted for an outspoken and frank manner, with an easy sense of humor and something of a bad-boy image, entered office with a broad but vague program of financial reforms, which he warned would cause short-term economic pain for the sake of long-term recovery. Thanks to restructuring the banking system, fiscal policies, and global developments, Japan's economy did finally recover. In 2004 it showed strong growth with China now its main export market. Meanwhile, the globalization of the economy continued to the point that in 2006 Japanese companies built more cars outside Japan than in their own country.

Embedded in the global economy and generally following Washington's lead in foreign policy, Koizumi pleased Japanese nationalists by calling for constitutional change to legalize the military and by visiting the Yasukuni Shrine to pay homage to Japan's fallen soldiers, including those condemned as war criminals. Koizumi took a bold step in appointing an outspoken woman as Japan's first female foreign minister. She was Tanaka Makiko (1944–), the eldest daughter of former prime minister Tanaka Kakuei. In July, Koizumi, Japan's most popular prime minister since World War II, was able to lead the L.D.P. to an electoral victory. This was a personal triumph, but many were disillusioned after he gave in to Foreign Ministry pressure and forced Tanaka out of the cabinet at the end of January 2002. Despite two visits to North Korea, relations with Pyongyang remained tense and Koizumi did not help relations with Korea, China, and other countries by continuing to visit the Yasukuni Shrine. Meanwhile, his administration continued on a course of gradual reform rather than the kind of bold innovation once associated with Koizumi's name. After Koizumi completed his term in September 2006, his successor, Abe Shinzo (1954–), a telegenic and outspoken politician, appeared ready to continue Koizumi's domestic politics while adopting a more hawkish stance in foreign affairs. It was too early to judge the effectiveness of moves to emphasize nationalism in education and to amend the constitution including revocation of Article IX.

An ardent critic of Establishment thinking was Ōe Kenzaburō, who in 1994 became only the second Japanese, or for that matter East Asian, to receive the Nobel Prize for literature. In conscious contrast to Kawabata, he entitled his acceptance speech "Japan, the Ambiguous and Myself," and not long after shocked the public by refusing the Imperial Order of Culture. In 1995, he completed his trilogy *The Burning Green Tree* (*Moegaru midori no ki*, 1992–1995). Like Mishima's tetrology, it ends with a death, but, to quote Susan Napier:

> Unlike Mishima whose dead protagonists leave the living with only a feeling of betrayal and emptiness, or Abe whose characters survive in misery, and above all unlike Murakami whose protagonists commit a sort of suicide to the outside world, Ōe gives us a vision of the outside world revitalized by the sacrifice of a body.[10]

Here Napier points to a positive element present in much of Ōe's writing even as he faces human tragedy. In doing so, he differs not only from Mishima and Abe, who belonged to the recent past, but from Murakami Haruki (1949–), a prominent writer of the 1980s and 1990s who represented a generational shift that Ōe deplored. He said of it:

> In contrast to much postwar writing which fictionalized the actual experience of writers and readers, who, as twenty- and thirty-year-olds, had known war, Murakami and Yoshimoto convey the experience of a youth politically uninvolved or disaffected content to exist within a late adolescent or postadolescent subculture.[11]

Yoshimoto is Yoshimoto Banana (Yoshimoto Mahoko, 1964–) who had adopted "banana" as her pen-name. Both writers are easy to read and prolific. Both were attuned to the market, enjoyed sensational sales, and were found lacking in gravitas by their elders. Both were steeped in popular culture, probably read too many comic books, and have been taken to represent a postmodern commodification of literature. Especially Yoshimoto Banana, beginning with *Kitchen* (1987), is treated as much as a cultural as a literary phenomenon (see Box 17.2). Her novels often depict alternate lifestyles in deadpan, commonplace language. They signal the disintegration of the traditional family, but are bright and cheerful.

BOX 17.2 KITCHEN

Mikage Sakurai, the narrator of Kitchen, *is a young woman in her twenties who has just lost her only relative, her grandmother. She moves in with her grandmother's young acquaintance, Yuichi Tanabe, and his "mother" Eriko, a transsexual who used to be Yuichi's father before his real mother passed away. For a short while, the three of them form a new "family" of sorts. This arrangement falls apart when Eriko is brutally murdered by a male admirer upset to discover that "she" is in fact a "he," and Mikage once again finds herself alone in the world. Her one source of comfort is the gleaming white kitchen of the Tanabe residence, a space in which to cook up new, masterful creations with fresh and tasty ingredients. The following passage touches on death, alienation, urban life, family, and the passage to adulthood in contemporary Japanese society.*

I flopped down on my back and looked up at the dear, familiar ceiling. Right after my grandmother died, I had stared at this same ceiling many an afternoon while Yuichi and Eriko were out. I remember thinking to myself, my grandmother is dead, I've lost my last blood relation, and things can't get any worse. But now they had. Eriko had been enormously important to me. In the six months we spent together she had always been there for me; she spoiled me.

To the extent that I had come to understand that despair does not necessarily result in annihilation, that one can go on as usual in spite of it, I had become hardened. Was that what it means to be an adult, to live with ugly ambiguities? I didn't like it, but it made it easier to go on . . .

After a long absence I was once again in the Tanabe kitchen. For an instant I had a vision of Eriko's smiling face, and my heart turned over. I felt an urge to get moving. It looked to me like the kitchen had not been used in quite a while. It was somewhat dirty and dark. I began to clean. I scrubbed the sink with scouring powder, wiped off the burners, washed the dishes, sharpened the knives. I washed and bleached all the dish towels, and while watching them go round and round in the dryer I realized that I had become calmer. Why do I love everything that has to do with kitchens so much? It's strange. Perhaps because to me a kitchen represents some distant longing engraved on my soul. As I stood there, I seemed to be making a new start; something was coming back.

Yoshimoto Banana. *Kitchen,* translated by Megan Backus (New York: Washington Square Press, 1994), pp. 55–56.

Murakami, who once ran a jazz bar, wrote long novels filled with the music of his youth, interesting situations, and characters not given to reflection. Pico Iyer had this to say about *The Wind-up Bird* (*Nejimaki-dori kuronikuru,* 1994–1995):

> It does not require much reflection that almost every image in the book's 600 pages—a dry well, a haunted house, a faceless man, a dead-end street—stands in some way for a hollowed out Japan, whose motto might be, "I don't think, therefore I am." Again and again, characters say, "I was like a walking corpse" or "I was now in a vacant house" or "I felt as if I had turned into a bowl of cold porridge." Murakami's storytelling ease and the pellucid, uncluttered backdrop he lays down allow moments to flare up memorably. Yet the overall effect of his grand but somewhat abstract novel is to give us X ray after X ray into the benumbed soul of a wannabe Prozac Nation.[12]

In the 1990s, the director Kurosawa, then in his 80s, drew on his earlier films to produce works new in content and technique. An example of the latter, discussed by Stephen Prince, is his use of axial cutting, while the dreams in *Dreams* (1990) represent an old theme given new meaning. Once he had seen dreams as being in tension with social commitment, but now Kurosawa cherished them as "the fruit of pure and human desire," and went on to say, "A human is a genius while dreaming."[13] Be that as it may, it takes a great artist to convey a dream to others. One who was able to do so was Miyazaki Hayao (1941–), who in a series of works, raised film animation to new heights. His *Princess Mononoke* (1997) won widespread popular and critical acclaim. Similarly, *Spirited Away* (2001) broke all box-office records in Japan.

Japanese architects too continued to dream. One who did so with great imagination was Ando Tadao (1941– , Pritzker Prize winner, 1995), a self-taught master who, early in his career, built a lovely, small Christian church in Osaka. Among his most notable subsequent works were an underground temple entered though stairs in a lotus pond (1991) and, on Naoshima, an island in the Inland Sea, a museum/hotel for contemporary art (1995). The art, mostly non-Japanese, is not confined to the inside, but continues outdoors, and includes an enormous pumpkin and a Chinese stone garden. In 1997, I. M. Pei completed his masterpiece, the Miho Museum at Shigaraki. Like Ando's temple and museum/hotel, it is mostly underground, and it too blends in with and makes the most of the natural beauty of the landscape.

As earlier, Japanese artists participated in all the international styles and movements of the day. Some of them spent considerable time overseas. Performance and installations remained popular, conveying the sense that art, like all things, was not forever. A sculptor obsessed with time was Miyajima Tatsuo (1957–), whose *Running Time* (1994) consisted of battery-powered "U-cars," each with a colored, single-number LED (light emitting diode) counter on its roof and with sensors front and back so that the cars changed direction as they randomly bumped each other. The effect has been likened to "glowing numerical fireflies," while the artist himself explained that the "u" refers to the "uncertainty principle," as in the physics of Heisenberg.[14]

Running Time, like the writings of Banana Yoshimoto and Murakami Haruki, is a work in a modern idiom with it own aesthetic appeal. It says something in a new way without reference to what others in the long tradition have said on the subject. Like traditional works of art, it leaves interpretation to the viewer, but unlike them, it does not demand the cultivation of connoisseurship to unlock the message.

Notes

1. Richard Pascale and Thomas P. Roblen, "The Mazda Turnaround," *The Journal of Japanese Studies 9,* no. 2 (Dec. 1983), p. 263.

2. David Plath, "My-Car-isma: Motorizing the Showa Self," in Carol Gluck and Stephen R. Graubard, eds., *Showa: The Japan of Hirohito* (New York, NY: W.W. Norton, 1992), p. 239.

3. Koji Taira, "Dialectics of Economic Growth, National Power, and Distributive Struggles," in Andrew Gordon, ed., *Postwar Japan as History* (Berkeley, CA: Univ. of California Press), p. 171.

4. Ian Reader, *Religion in Contemporary Japan* (Honolulu, HI: Univ. of Hawaii Press, 1991), p. 233, apropos Agonshu.

5. Roy Starrs, *Soundings in Time: The Fictive Art of Kawabata Yasunari* (London, U.K.: Curzon Press, 1998), p. 218.

6. Isozaki Arata in Masao Miyoshi and H. D. Harootunian, eds., *Postmodernism and Japan* (Durham, NC: Duke Univ. Press, 1989), pp. 57 and 59.

7. Kenneth B. Pyle, "The World Historical Significance of Japan" in Kozo Yamamura, ed., *A Vision of a New Liberalism? Critical Essays on Murakami's Anticlassical Analysis* (Stanford, CA: Stanford Univ. Press, 1997), pp. 233 and 237.

8. Ibid., p. 127.

9. Gavan McCormack, *The Emptiness of Japanese Affluence* (Armonk, NY: M.E. Sharpe, 1996), p. 46.

10. Susan J. Napier, "Ōe Kenzaburō and the Search for the Sublime at the End of the Twentieth Century," in Stephen Snyder and Philip Gabriel, eds., *Ōe and Beyond: Fiction in Contemporary Japan* (Honolulu, HI: Univ. of Hawaii Press, 1999), pp. 32–33.

11. Quoted by Snyder and Gabriel on page 2 of their introduction.

12. Pico Iyer in *Time,* vol. 150, no. 8 (Nov. 3, 1997) available at www.time/magazine/1997/dom/ 971103/abook.tales_of_the_html.

13. Kurosawa as quoted in Stephen Prince, *The Warrior's Camera: The Cinema of Akira Kurosawa,* revised and enlarged edition (Princeton, NJ: Princeton Univ. Press, 1999), p. 303.

14. Exhibition catalog. *Tatsuo Miyajima (1957) BIG TIME,* organized by Michael Auping, Fort Worth: Modern Art Museum of Fort Worth and Hayward Gallery London (June 19–August 17, 1997), pp. 25–26.

18

The Two Koreas and Vietnam

When we last discussed Korea and Vietnam, both were divided between northern and southern systems. During the next half-century, the two Korean regimes failed to make peace, but the cease-fire that had ended the fighting in 1953 held, and the people were spared further warfare. In contrast, Vietnam achieved unification in 1975, but only after bitter and prolonged fighting and untold suffering. In both cases, military concerns and military men played a major role in shaping new, postcolonial policies and societies.

I. Korea

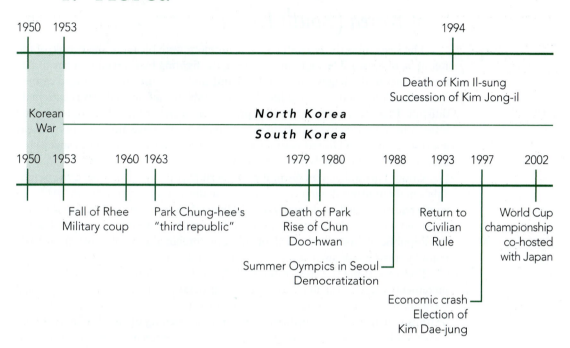

Aftermath of the Korean War in the Republic of Korea (South Korea)

Military Rule and Economic Development in the Republic of Korea

The Republic of Korea since 1988

The Democratic People's Republic of Korea (North Korea) under Kim Il-sung

The Problem of North-South Relations

Aftermath of the Korean War in the Republic of Korea (South Korea)

The years after the cease-fire at P'anmunjŏm were bleak for the people of the Republic of Korea. Throughout the south, the fighting had forced families to flee their homes and villages and seek food and shelter in miserable refugee camps. Returning home and restoring life to some semblance of normalcy was extremely difficult. There was little food to buy, prices were high, and the shattered economy offered little employment to help people recover. Massive amounts of overseas assistance from the United Nations and South Korea's wartime allies succeeded only in keeping the population from starving.

Under Japanese colonialism, the southern part of Korea had been the peninsula's main food-producing region. After the division of the country in 1945, the south had struggled to diversify and industrialize in order to develop a better-balanced regional economy. The Korean War ended that effort, however, leaving the Republic of Korea abjectly dependent on foreign aid for all items, from basic manufactured goods such as clothing to food and other raw materials.

Progress along the long road back from devastation was marked in small increments: an increase in electrical power generation, the building of a chemical fertilizer plant, the opening of a textile factory, more coal for cooking and home heating, construction of a cement plant, and the opening of an oil refinery. In the countryside, a network of government-organized extension agencies provided training and credit to farmers. These efforts were the building blocks for the new national economy, but they were overshadowed always by the overwhelming problem of Korea's national division, the need to maintain a large standing army, and the question of whether war would break out again and destroy everything. It was a bitter time for the Korean people, and it took enormous courage and determination for the country to survive.

The Korean War era greatly affected Korea's artists and writers. Liberation itself, so full of hope in the beginning, led immediately to a struggle to redefine Korean identity in terms of north and south, suddenly repoliticizing the arts in terms of the Cold War. On top of recriminations about collaboration with the Japanese—in a famous case, the novelist Yi Kwangsu was accused of collaboration—Korean intellectuals also had to deal with the nation's own alienation, producing, in the words of Marshall Pihl, "a literature [that] was little better than a deformity incapable of expressing the wholeness of the Korean experience."[1] The Korean War era itself was full of human drama, and did eventually lead to a rich output of novels and stories by writers such as Hwang Sunwŏn, Kim Tongni, and Cho Chongnae among others.[2]

President Syngman Rhee, who remained in office as President of the Republic of Korea until 1960, retained much personal prestige. His administration's record, however, was disappointing, and his ruling Liberal Party was notoriously corrupt. Rhee exploited popular emotions to rally support, inveighing against an array of demons that included North Korean Communists and the Japanese. He told his people that the Communists were poised to invade at any moment, and that the people must support his regime as the best hope of deterring a new war. He told them that the Japanese wanted to colonize Korea again, and that Koreans should not accept Japanese aid or allow Japanese investment to help them rebuild. On occasion he also criticized the United States for interfering in Korea's internal affairs and trying to take advantage of the Korean people, though his government was a major beneficiary of all types of American aid—political, economic, and military. As a result, the Republic of Korea was an isolated nation. Its main relationships were with the United States and its anti-Communist clients, notably the Republic of China on Taiwan and the Republic of Vietnam based in Saigon.

Rhee was president for 12 years, being reelected in 1952 and 1956. These two elections were irregular, but his third attempt at reelection in 1960 was so blatantly corrupt that the people rose up in protest. After demonstrations swept South Korea in March and April 1960, Rhee was forced to resign, and he retired to Hawaii, where he lived in exile.

Between the summer of 1960 and May of 1961, the Republic of Korea was governed by a democratically elected government under a new, parliamentary-type constitution. Prime Minister Chang Myŏn (John M. Chang) wrestled with the country's ongoing economic and political problems while trying to maintain democratic freedoms of assembly, expression, and association. His time in power was short—less than a year, during which he was unable to get the economy under control, and many of his countrymen feared that the country was in danger of being torn apart by dissident factions. It was for these reasons, and ostensibly to restore a sense of social discipline and national direction, that elements of the R.O.K. Army struck in a coup d'état on May 16, 1961, overthrew the Chang government and constitution, and began ruling under martial law.

Military Rule and Economic Development in the Republic of Korea

In a way, it was predictable that the South Korean military would rise to power in a coup. The army was the best-organized and disciplined element in the country, and it was heavily armed. In 1961, the R.O.K. Army was one of the largest in the world. When the coup came, in May 1961, the United States, having created, trained, and equipped the South Koreans to hold the line on the "frontier of freedom," found itself in no position to oppose it and thus allow the messy democratic experiment of Prime Minister Chang Myŏn to continue. Instead, the U.S. reluctantly accepted the idea that conditions required the establishment of a firm central authority in Seoul, even if it meant a military dictatorship. In turn, the Korean Army promised to organize a bootstrap effort to achieve modernization and an eventual return to elections and constitutional rule.

Korea remained under direct military control for two years. The coup leader, Major General Park Chung-hee (Pak Chŏnghŭi, 1917–1979), presided over a tight circle of military men whose power derived from their personal networks. They began as a group of alumni from the same class of the Korean Military Academy. As they created their new state structure, they invented new institutions and assumed new, civilian-style positions. One of the coup planners, Lieutenant Colonel Kim Chŏngp'il (Kim Jongpil, 1926–), became head of the Korean Central Intelligence Agency (KCIA), a type of secret police that monitored not only national security but also the economy, political activities of individuals, the press, the universities, and religious and labor leaders. Kim Chŏngp'il also founded a new political party through which the army leaders, after "retirement," ran for civilian office in 1963, winning elections that gave them a majority in the National Assembly and installed General Park as President of the Republic of Korea.

With his men ensconced in control of the army, administration, economy, and National Assembly, General Park single-mindedly pursued the goal of economic betterment for the people of Korea. His methods remain a topic of controversy in South Korea. Though his leadership was strict, he was seen as personally honest. He took the country and its low-wage workers on a forced march. Progress was made, but the price was high. Yet there is a rough consensus that conditions in 1961 required assertive leadership and that the Army was in a logical position to "save the nation."

As president, General Park supervised a central Economic Planning Board that laid out a series of five-year plans providing for the consolidation of Korea's economic infrastructure, and setting ambitious production targets. The results were remarkable. From the beginning, the five-year production targets were met ahead of schedule and were followed by ever more ambitious goals. By the end of the 1960s, there were noticeable improvements in the supplies of food and energy, as well as in areas such as public health and education.

Using his political clout to "normalize" relations with Japan, Park obtained a package of loans and aid that helped jump-start the industrialization process. He contributed two Army divisions to the U.S.-led effort to defend the Republic of Vietnam, with Washington paying Seoul in dollars for all the costs of the deployment, thus providing the R.O.K. with a valuable flow of foreign exchange. The United States also granted preferential status to Korean companies that bid on construction projects such as runways and port facilities in the Republic of Vietnam. Their participation in Vietnam enabled South Koreans to feel that they had "repaid" the United States for saving them from their own near-takeover by the North Korean Communists in the early 1950s. It also made them feel that they were on the verge of becoming a true industrial trading nation.

One of President Park's signature programs was the Saemaŭl ("New Community") Movement that was aimed at boosting productivity and raising living standards in the countryside. The Saemaŭl Movement helped farmers get credit, fertilizer, and pesticides, and brought electricity, safe water, better roads and communications, more schools, better health, and birth control to South Korea's villages. Korea's rural areas underwent significant changes as living standards rose—and as many of the rural youth were lured to the cities, where life seemed to be improving even more rapidly. In a single generation, the population of South

Korea went from 80 percent rural to 80 percent urban, and the nation was unified as never before by the power of common experience and mass communication.

Despite dramatic progress, there continued to be disparities in the distribution of burdens and benefits. Farm people continued to do backbreaking work that was only partly alleviated by mechanization. Factory workers powered production in the R.O.K., but they labored in wretched conditions with few safeguards from injury or illness. The Park government kept tight control over labor and forbade strikes. Labor organizers, who tried to teach workers how to band together for better working conditions, often ended up in jail. Low wages and scant workers' benefits were keys to the country's economic growth, achieved on the backs of its workers. It is not an exaggeration to say that an entire generation of South Koreans sacrificed themselves to create the relative prosperity that their children now enjoy.

Big business, on the other hand, received considerable support from the Park government as it tried to emulate imperial Japan in the creation of favored conglomerates called *chaebŏl* (the Korean equivalent of the Japanese term *zaibatsu*). The government intervened to guarantee financing for these clusters of companies, some of whose names are now famous around the world. The Samsung *chaebŏl*, for example, started as a textile manufacturer and branched out into light electronics, household appliances, cameras, and computers. Components of the Hyundai *chaebŏl* included construction, shipbuilding, automobiles, department stores, and tourism. Government favoritism nurtured the *chaebŏl*, which in turn, created jobs, exported Korean goods to earn hard currency, and occasionally returned the favor by supporting government candidates financially. As products from South Korea won market share overseas, the *chaebŏl* came to control a large part of the national economy.

Development of the *chaebŏl* conglomerates concentrated enormous wealth in the hands of relatively few large capitalists, and by the 1970s there were irresistible demands from workers for a better share of the nation's new prosperity. In 1979, amid a wave of labor unrest, President Park Chung-hee was assassinated by one of his own deputies. Within months a new military strongman emerged. He was General Chun Doo-hwan (Chŏn Tuhwan, 1931–), who used his partisans in the army to seize control, first of the military, and then of the nation itself. In the process, he crushed a popular uprising against him in the southwestern city of Kwangju in May 1980, a disastrous move that cost the lives of hundreds of civilians. Though Chun manipulated the factions of his followers and the nation's laws to seize the presidency, and was able to rule from 1980 until 1988, the Kwangju massacre made him one of the most hated figures in the history of the Republic. He was regarded as an illegitimate president because of this rise to power and he remained in power through threats and use of police power.

The city of Seoul won the bid for the 1988 Summer Olympics, and despite Chun Doo-hwan's dubious presidency, South Koreans worked hard to set the stage for a grand international show. Korea enjoyed a surge in construction; the *chaebŏl* boomed; and despite concerns over possible interference by the North, the 1988 summer games were a great success.

The Republic of Korea since 1987

South Koreans saw the 1988 Summer Olympics as their international debut, the celebration of their emergence from poverty to prosperity and from dictatorship to democracy. Indeed, the approaching Olympics, with all the international attention that came with preparation for the games in Seoul, helped deter the Chun government from crushing the emerging Korean democracy movement in the mid-1980s. As his presidential term was ending in 1987 on the eve of the Olympics, he sought to prolong military rule by picking Roh Tae-woo, an army general and main supporter, as his successor. Hundreds of thousands of South Koreans, including middle-class housewives and office workers, poured into the streets to demand an open election to pick the next president. The massive demonstrations, with the Olympics just around the corner and the world community worrying that Korea was not a safe place for the games, forced candidate Roh Tae-woo to repudiate his mentor's high-handed tactics. Roh agreed to a quick change in the procedure that would allow popular voting for president. Ironically, the opposition split between two candidates and handed him the election anyway, by plurality. Nonetheless, the corner had been turned. By ending the military's lock on leadership, the stage was set for South Korea to emerge as a full democracy. Roh's five years as president were marked by increasing liberalization, a freer press, and expanded freedom to think, associate, travel, and worship. Additionally, the R.O.K. made startling new overtures toward China and the Soviet Union. Opening relations with the communist countries helped promote South Korea as a worldwide economic power. There was change at home and abroad. Belief in their own achievements and increased national confidence convinced Koreans that they did not need to organize everything around the fearful memory of the Korean War. The growth of civil society, the high level of education, the success in the world markets, and recognition and respect from other countries created the atmosphere for a new era in national life.

If the transition from military dictatorship to democracy was at the heart of this national mood, the individual who symbolized it was Kim Dae-jung (Kim Taejung, 1925–), a longtime opposition leader from southwestern Korea. Kim Dae-jung had made a career of challenging dictatorship, even daring to challenge President Park Chung-hee as he ran for reelection in 1971. When Kim nearly won that election, Park launched a campaign of persecution against him, variously imprisoning him, putting him under house arrest, kidnapping him, and more than once trying to kill him. When Kim publicly opposed the emerging strongman Chun Doo-hwan in 1980, Chun had him sentenced to death. It took an international outcry to get the sentence lifted. Kim went into exile in the United States, returned home in 1985, and was one of the challengers in the presidential election of 1987.

By the early 1990s, the 44 million citizens of the Republic of Korea were enjoying a standard of living unimagined in the 1970s. Full employment and universal literacy, together with strong community values, pride, and purpose seemed to be working. Amid continual fear of renewed war with the North, traffic jams, industrial pollution, and labor unrest, the people nevertheless found that they had time for vacations, reading, and television watching, and money for luxury goods. Many ordinary Koreans became wealthy overnight by selling suburban farmland that was in sudden demand for housing in the country's booming urban areas. These profits fueled investments and consumption, paid for college educations, private cars, and even relocation to such places as Los Angeles and New York. People sported fine clothes, cell phones, and jewelry. Seoul came to offer fine dining, several prime arts centers, a world-class film industry, and stores selling everything from books and CDs to imported foods and heavy appliances. Between 1993 and 1997, under Kim Young-sam (Kim Yŏngsam, 1927–), the first civilian president since 1963, the dream of modernization seemed at last to have come true.

However, beneath the surface there was much instability. In the name of "globalization," the R.O.K. government had permitted money to flow too freely between Korea and foreign financial institutions. The Korean conglomerates in particular had taken on too much debt to finance expansion into areas that proved too risky, and the debts suddenly turned bad in 1997. Unable to repay short-term loans, several of South Korea's biggest *chaebŏl* suddenly found themselves facing bankruptcy. When the Korean government was unable to save them, the country's banking system proved short of funds to pay its international obligations. Only days before the presidential election of 1997, citizens of the R.O.K. were obliged to watch in humiliation as the outgoing Kim Young-sam administration was reduced to begging for billions of dollars in emergency loans from the International Monetary Fund (IMF). A hurried IMF bailout amounting to $57 billion—the largest ever arranged by the Fund—temporarily enabled the R.O.K. to survive the crisis. In return for the bailout, the IMF demanded control of South Korea's financial system and the institution of strict austerity measures. Massive layoffs created disturbances across the economic spectrum, and ordinary Koreans paid a high psychological and social price for their government's mismanagement.

The leader who inherited this situation was Kim Dae-jung, who was finally elected president in December 1997. When he took office in February 1998, he asked the people to accept unemployment, the closure of badly run banks and businesses, and a sell-off of distressed components of the big Korean conglomerates. The strong medicine took effect within a year of the crash, and by the year 2001 the R.O.K. economy was recovering well. Though there were many signs of lingering trouble, most Koreans had jobs again and much of the underlying instability had been eliminated. President Kim Dae-jung deserved some credit, but again it was the Korean people who were disciplined in meeting a crisis with hard work and determination. The "IMF Crisis" remains a bitter memory in South Korea, not merely because of the humiliation that came with the imposition of IMF rules on the economy but also because it revealed that instability and corruption were ongoing problems seemingly embedded in their system. Some referred to this problem as "the Korean disease," and fretted that it would remain indefinitely as a curse into the future.

South Korea's greatest triumph, when it came, was a different sporting extravaganza: the co-hosting (with Japan) of the 2002 FIFA World Cup. As soccer teams from around the world converged on the two nations, Korea and Japan as hosts were given honorary slots in the first round. To everyone's astonishment, the Korean team advanced into the quarter finals, touching off wild enthusiasm in the streets as "Red Devils" (Korean soccer fans in red t-shirts), swarmed before giant TV screens to watch their team proudly. Unlike the 1988 Olympics, whose success had been marred by low attendance and a series of controversies, the 2002 World Cup in Korea was an unalloyed national joy with a proud afterglow that lingered for years. This sense of having "arrived" was fortified by the spreading of the "Korean Wave" (*hallyu*) across Asia, as Korean films, popular music, television dramas, and fashions became popular in neighboring countries. Japanese Prime Minister Koizumi Junichiro was known to have followed the Korean soap opera "Winter Sonata" along with millions of Japanese housewives, many of whom jetted over to Seoul just to visit places where "Winter Sonata" had been filmed. This was heady stuff to the South Koreans, and the attention helped them heal the wounds of the earlier IMF Crisis.

The Democratic People's Republic of Korea (North Korea) under Kim Il-sung

Kim Il-sung's decision to reunite the country by military force in 1950 turned out to have been a massive mistake. The southern population did not rise up as expected to welcome his army, and he miscalculated the intentions of the United States and United Nations. When the tide of battle turned after the Inch'ŏn Landing and the D.P.R.K. itself was in danger of being overrun by United Nations forces, Kim Il-sung had to accept intervention by the People's Republic of China. The second and third years of the war brought a rain of bombs from the U.S. Air Force as it tried to force the communist side to surrender or agree to a cease-fire. Though the bombing was of questionable political value, it did succeed in pulverizing most of the D.P.R.K.'s industrial plants and reducing the quality of life in the north to mere subsistence. By the end of the war, the citizens of the D.P.R.K., though still tough and determined, were unable to provide for themselves.

North Korea's physical recovery was enhanced by postwar aid from China, the Soviet Union, and the socialist countries in Europe. In P'yŏngyang there were recriminations. When challenged or criticized, Kim Il-sung responded by purging rivals and instigating a reign of terror. He blamed the wartime disaster on bad advice, noting that Pak Hŏnyŏng, the leading southern communist, had assured him that the people of the south were poised for revolt and waiting for their chance to rise up and welcome the North Korean army. When this proved wrong, Kim accused Pak of secretly working for the Americans, and had him executed as a spy. In this atmosphere, which came to resemble that of the Soviet Union under Stalin, personal loyalty to the "Great Leader" became the foremost criterion for success and survival in the D.P.R.K. Thus, Kim Il-sung was able to escape judgment for the disasters that he had brought upon his people.

One feature of Kim Il-sung's rule was the invention of the North Korean political philosophy known as *juch'e,* which means "self-reliance." One purpose of the
"*juch'e* idea" was to inspire the people to work hard to achieve true national independence from foreign aid and control. Another was to establish North Korea as
neutral in the ideological disputes that were developing among the socialist countries. However, true self-reliance was beyond North Korea's capabilities. When the
communist superpowers phased out foreign aid, North Korea continued to
depend on a system of barter trading, whereby it traded raw materials such as
lumber and minerals to the Soviet Union for goods such as oil. North Korea also
exchanged labor for imports, by sending workers to help clear timberland in
Siberia. In the 1960s and 1970s, this combination of reconstruction at home, aid
from abroad, and barter trading enabled North Korea to outdistance the south in
restoring the economy. Though North Korean workers enjoyed little freedom of
expression or movement, having to work wherever they were assigned for pay that
was extremely low by world standards, the State provided their housing, education, health care, and other necessities of life.

North Korea recovered faster than the south due mostly to massive socialist-
bloc aid and a centrally controlled economy; however, its growth slowed and
performance began to lag behind that of the south. It developed economic imbalances and commodity shortages owing to poor management and to its imposed
isolation by the international community, led by the United States. For decade
after decade, American diplomatic pressure effectively prevented North Korea
from taking advantage of the planning and funding resources that were available
to the Republic of Korea as well as other developing economies around the world.
As a result, the D.P.R.K. was almost entirely reliant on the socialist community
for vital assistance with energy, manufacturing goods, and basic technical training.
The D.P.R.K. developed along lines favored by the Soviet Union, with emphasis
on central direction and heavy industry such as railroads, steel, and chemicals at
the expense of consumer goods manufacturing. The D.P.R.K.'s enormous military
establishment also drained resources from the budget. This meant that daily living
standards for ordinary people did not rise as they did in the south, where consumer goods were a much higher priority. By the 1980s, when South Korea
became one of the trading powers of the Pacific Rim, making money by exporting
textiles, electronics, automobiles, and other consumer items, North Korea
remained preoccupied with food sufficiency and the export of raw materials to
pay for whatever consumer goods it could afford to buy.

North Korea's foreign relations were similarly lopsided, as the D.P.R.K.
remained isolated from the mainstream of world organizations and excessively
reliant on support from the socialist community. As a state with an avowedly
Marxist-Leninist political philosophy, the D.P.R.K. claimed to be committed to
world revolution. It was fundamentally hostile to Western-style democracy and
capitalism, and its steady output of invective against the United States, Japan, the
R.O.K., and the West in general, while not damaging, won few new friends.

Occasionally, the D.P.R.K. took action in ways that aggravated its isolation.
For example, in 1968 a team of D.P.R.K. agents almost succeeded in assassinating

President Park Chung-hee in Seoul. The D.P.R.K. captured a U.S. Navy intelligence ship that was accused of violating North Korea's territorial waters, letting nearly a year pass before releasing the crew. In 1969, the D.P.R.K. shot down an American intelligence plane. In 1983, D.P.R.K. agents planted a bomb that killed many members of the South Korean cabinet during a visit to Rangoon, Burma (Myanmar) and just missed killing President Chun Doo-hwan. In 1987, they planted a bomb on a South Korean airliner that blew up over the Andaman Sea, killing more than 200 passengers and crew. These and other "revolutionary" actions succeeded in getting the D.P.R.K. labeled a "terrorist state," and eroded the willingness of governments around the world to do legitimate business with it. North Korea also engaged in a lively arms export trade, selling guns and missiles to countries such as Iran and Libya. The D.P.R.K., after decades of economic pressure and sanctions from the West, had little besides weapons worth exporting. Of course, such weapons sales to adversaries of the Western democracies merely aggravated the situation and did little to encourage the lifting of sanctions or to repair the Kim regime's reputation for state-sponsored terrorism.

When the socialist community collapsed in Eastern Europe and the Soviet Union fell, North Korea was forced to pay for many goods for which it had formerly traded. When the Russian Federation started demanding cash for the oil it had been bartering to North Korea, and China followed suit, North Korea suffered an immediate energy shortage that brought its national economy to a standstill. The lack of fuel for transportation affected production at all levels and led to many system breakdowns. With North Korea's history of state terrorism, the world was not sympathetic to its plight. There was a dramatic contraction of the national economy and severe hardships for the people of North Korea in the mid-1990s. This was further aggravated by weather disasters that ruined crops and caused famines in certain parts of the country, and hundreds of thousands of vulnerable people, mainly older citizens and children, perished.

Kim Il-sung, commonly referred to by northerners as their "Great Leader," was President of the Democratic People's Republic of Korea, the head of its ruling Korean Workers Party, and commander-in-chief of its armed forces from 1948 until his death in July 1994. The people of North Korea, by all accounts, are a patriotic population who believe that they owe everything to their late leader. They revere his memory and they respect his son and successor, Kim Jong-il (1942–). However, Kim Il-sung used the people's respect to construct a remarkable personality cult. Statues of Kim Il-sung, some 50 or 60 feet high, were erected all over the country during his lifetime. The people were told to wear Kim Il-sung buttons on their clothes to indicate their loyalty and to welcome him warmly when he came to visit factories and farms to give them "on-the-spot guidance." The country's top university bears his name, as do many other institutions. North Korean history books assign him a major role in defeating Japan in World War II. Various Kim family members and in-laws have occupied many key positions in the regime. Early in his career, his son Kim Jong-il became known as the ruling party's "party center" and the country's "Dear Leader," titles that identified him as the likeliest candidate to succeed the "Great Leader" himself.

Outsiders sometimes have trouble fathoming North Korean political culture, rejecting the legitimacy of the Kim personality cult and dismissing North Korea as a country ruled by irrational people who cannot comprehend modern civilization or even what is in their own best interests. The U.S. government has variously labeled North Korea a "terrorist state," a "rogue state," and a "state of concern." For many years, Westerners have been assessing North Korea and predicting a collapse that has never come. The mysterious survival and resilience of North Korea baffles those who think in Western terms and judge by Western standards. However, history as the North Koreans have experienced it can offer us some clues about their motivations and political culture.

The Democratic People's Republic of Korea has been isolated from the non-Communist world virtually from its birth in 1948. Very few North Koreans have been outside their country. Few have studied foreign languages or met foreigners other than Chinese and Russians. The entire system has been locked down under tight information control. North Koreans read few foreign books and see virtually no foreign films or newspapers. They have not enjoyed the music that has helped shape the modern age. Instead, the popular culture of the D.P.R.K. has been inward-looking, drawing lessons from North Korea's own experience. One lesson is xenophobic: foreigners are a threat. Another is pride in surviving the Korean War and a determination to avenge the national damage caused by perceived Western (that is, American) imperialism. Another is a hatred of Japan arising from the colonial past.

When it comes to formative influences from Korea's history, the D.P.R.K. remembers the hereditary monarchy of the Chosŏn dynasty, the system that preceded Japanese colonialism, and the elite Confucian bureaucracy that supported it. Despite resentment of Japanese colonialism, the North Korean system also draws lessons from imperial Japan. For example, in World War II, Japan used the term *kokutai* ("national body," or "national polity") to speak of Japan and its people as an organic whole headed by the emperor. The second syllable of the Korean word *juch'e* is the same as the "tai" of the Japanese word *kokutai*, carrying some of the same emotional meaning that attaches to unquestioning loyalty and belonging.

These particular "lessons of history" have created a unique worldview in the D.P.R.K., one that can only be understood by making the effort to imagine what the people there see as their own national interests. They help explain features of the North Korean system: its extreme emphasis on group loyalty, its ultranationalism and fierce determination to claim independence, its resentment of the West, and even its acceptance of a dynastic succession in the passage of power.

When Kim Il-sung died, his country was already in deep trouble. Since the fall of communism in Europe and the end of the Soviet Union, much of the D.P.R.K.'s support system had vanished. The D.P.R.K.'s barter system had ended, and the Kim regime was having to pay for imports of vital commodities such as fuel oil. A rudimentary nuclear power industry had become an international threat, and the D.P.R.K. was under intense pressure to shut it down. The economy that once had outrun its southern rival had started to contract, and famine seemed to stalk the land.

Kim Jong-il succeeded his father during this perilous time. In 1994 he was little known in the outside world. Those who claimed to know him said that he was a spoiled playboy with few skills of his own, and many outsiders predicted that he would be unable to survive whatever power struggles were bound to ensue. In the south, there was talk about going north to take over the wreckage of the communist regime. Some former refugees talked of going back to reclaim their lost property. Yet, despite the severe economic crisis and a desperate shortage of basic needs, Kim Jong-il's regime took hold and managed to survive. In 1998, after showing due reluctance in good Confucian style, the younger Kim accepted his father's title of "Great Leader," and became general secretary of the ruling political party. He left the post of president vacant in memory of his father, however, as if to suggest that the late President Kim Il-sung will always occupy the position in spirit.

The decade following the elder Kim's death was a time of severe trial for the D.P.R.K. In 1997, the combination of flood, drought, and poor policy resulted in a terrible famine that took the lives of between 1 and 2 million people. North Korea's political system classifies citizens according to their support for, and participation in, rule by the Korean Workers Party. As at times in Communist China under Chairman Mao, the descendants of people with the wrong kind of class background are lumped together with suspected opponents of the regime and left out of the rationing system for food and other benefits. An unknown number inhabit a frightful gulag of prisons and concentration camps. While party members and supporters of the system survived the deprivations of the famine and other setbacks between 1995 and 2005, those in marginal categories suffered most. Many fled across the border into China, seeking enough food to survive. Of these, many were helped by South Korean charities, and a small number were assisted to travel through China into South Korea itself, where the government helped them learn how to exist in southern society. They told hair-raising stories of life in the north under Kim Jong-il and thus contributed to international pressure for "regime change" in the D.P.R.K.

North Korea also provoked international concern by insisting on its sovereign right to have a nuclear program, notwithstanding its agreement with the United States in 1994 to freeze its plutonium reprocessing program and to concentrate on making electricity only in relatively safe "light water reactors" supplied with South Korean, Japanese, and American assistance. In October 2002, North Korean officials admitted to an ongoing program to enrich uranium, technically not an issue covered by the 1994 agreement, but definitely a violation of the spirit of the agreement as well as earlier commitments to "denuclearize" the Korean peninsula. The U.S. administration of George W. Bush took this as an opportunity to scuttle the 1994 arrangements and to denounce North Korea once again as a rogue state. Relations with the United States, never good, went from bad to worse. In 2003, at the insistence of the Bush Administration, Russia, China, Japan, and South Korea joined the DPRK and the United States at a table in Beijing to being what has come to be known as the "Six Party Talks." The North Koreans demanded that the United States offer a nonaggression promise, a peace treaty, and bilateral relations before they would discuss the future of their nuclear program. The United States offered limited security assurances but made a point of refusing bilateral talks, insisting that negotiations proceed exclusively in the "Six Party" forum. This, in effect, created a stalemate during which the North Koreans proceeded to develop their nuclear facilities and a parallel program of missile development, without effective restraint. To make their point, the North Koreans tested a variety of potentially dangerous missiles in July 2006, reminding the world of the need to find a better way to deal with the situation.

The impasse between the United States and North Korea continued through the end of 2006, with each side accusing the other of bad faith and aggressive intentions. While the Bush Administration refused to engage the North Koreans directly, P'yŏngyang went ahead with its nuclear program, refining plutonium from waste from its power reactor at Yongbyon. In early October 2006 it detonated its first nuclear device in an underground test. The U.N. Security Council promptly responded with a resolution condemning the test and calling for tighter sanctions, though probably to little effect. The United States continued to hope that China somehow would pressure the D.P.R.K. into restraining itself, and the D.P.R.K. kept asserting its right to a nuclear deterrent in the face of what it saw as an American goal of "regime change" in P'yŏngyang.

The Problem of North-South Relations

The problem of national reunification had been at the top of the agenda for both Koreas since the armistice in 1953. Since the two systems are incompatible, it is hard to see how they might be reunited without the extinction of one or the other. With huge armies on either side of the border mutually ruling out a military solution, it has been necessary to seek common ground in pursuit of national reunification. To be sure, powerful interests on both sides are heavily invested in the status quo, chief among them the military establishments whose very existence is premised on a continuing military stalemate. However, in the 1990s there were small steps toward relations between the two regimes that raised hopes for some degree of contact and reconciliation.

The two Koreas have floated many reunification proposals over the years. Most of these have seemed to be propaganda initiatives, advanced in terms that were designed to be rejected by the other side. Each claims to be the "legitimate" or "legal" government of the Korean people. The D.P.R.K. points out that the United States (more properly the United Nations Command) signed the armistice document for the U.N. side, and that it is the United States, and not its puppet the R.O.K., that should handle the business of changes in the armistice leading to reunification. The United States insists that the two Koreas talk to each other, that is, that the R.O.K. and D.P.R.K. should deal with each other as equals. Thus, even the beginning of a conversation between the two has meant a concession by the northern side.

The multiple disasters in the D.P.R.K. during the 1990s have softened the northern position somewhat. Another change has been the R.O.K.'s active pursuit of better relations with communist countries since 1988, including the former socialist countries of Eastern Europe and the Soviet Union, and today the People's Republic of China and Socialist Republic of Vietnam. From 1993 through 1997, the Kim Young-sam Administration in South Korea pursued a hard line against the north, for example, greatly offending the D.P.R.K. by its ostentatious lack of mourning for the death of the "Great Leader" in 1994. The Kim Dae-jung administration, however, has pursued a much softer "Sunshine Policy" toward North Korea, tolerating insults and steadily promoting trade and "confidence-building" measures. As a result, southern companies have built factories in the D.P.R.K. and created a steady flow of goods between the two sides, creating stakes in peaceful interaction. Many southerners have visited the north, and numerous are working on projects there. Indeed, the most astonishing product of the Sunshine Policy was the visit, in June 2000, of President Kim Dae-jung to P'yŏngyang to shake hands and talk with Chairman Kim Jong-il (Figure 18.1). The event was heavy with symbolism and promises of change. It capped a process of conciliation for which Kim Dae-jung was awarded the Nobel Peace Prize later in the year. Although the unification process reverted to its normal glacial pace, the people of South Korea, and presumably some citizens of the D.P.R.K., had a welcome chance to see one another as countrymen.

As South Korean President Kim Dae-jung's term was ending, a little-known labor lawyer named Roh Moo-hyun surprisingly succeeded him in office, in 2003.

FIGURE 18.1 The "Sunshine Policy:" South Korean President Kim Dae-Jung Greeting North Korean Leader Kim Il-Jong in P'yŏngyang, June 2000.
AP/WIDE WORLD PHOTOS.

Roh defeated much better established candidates partly because of an unprecedented internet campaign that recruited masses of younger voters and demonstrated the effect of Korea's emergence as one of the world's most wired societies. A second factor was a wave of anger against the United States over a number of issues ranging from friction over the U.S. military presence in Korea to President Bush's placing North Korea in the "axis of evil," which offended South Koreans as well. Roh's performance in office was somewhat erratic: at one point he publicly considered resigning, and at another he was impeached by the National Assembly and returned only by verdict of Korea's Constitutional (Supreme) Court. One constant was Roh's continued commitment to Kim Dae-jung's "Sunshine Policy" toward the North, a stance that angered many conservative southerners but succeeded in opening many new avenues of communication with the Kim Jong-il regime. Of these, perhaps the most substantial was the opening of a special economic zone in the area between the DMZ and the northern city of Kaesŏng, using South Korean capital and North Korean labor to produce consumer goods. The arrangements for the Kaesŏng economic zone were widely recognized as a dress rehearsal for what could happen if and when North Korea opens up for outside investment and participation in the world economy. Kaesŏng encourages observers that North Koreans can prosper by exporting shoes, soccer balls, and electronics instead of missiles.

II. Vietnam

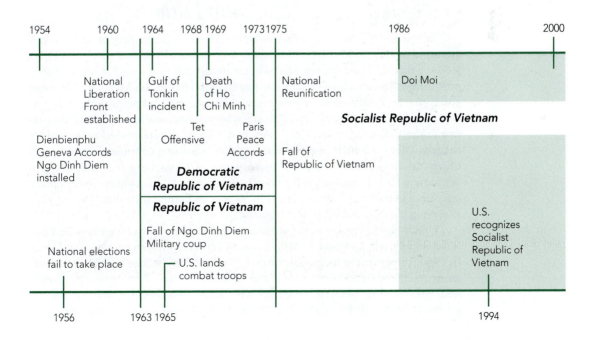

The Regime of Ngo Dinh Diem

The Fall of Diem and American Escalation, 1963–1968

Maintaining a Society at War: South Vietnam

Maintaining a Society at War: The D.R.V.

The Vietnam War: The Final Phase

The Socialist Republic of Vietnam: The First Decade, 1976–1986

Doi Moi, 1986–Present

The failure to hold elections in 1956 left Vietnam divided, with governments in the north and south fighting each other, striving to establish their legitimacy, achieve economic and military strength, and to form their people into a strong state capable of dominating the entire country. Prolonging and deepening the conflict between them was the intrusion of foreign powers, particularly the United States.

The Regime of Ngo Dinh Diem

In the 1950s, the government of Ngo Dinh Diem in Saigon made many attempts to win support from the people of southern Vietnam. However, Diem lacked a natural constituency. His political base, such as it was, consisted of support from refugee Catholics from the north, landlords of the Mekong Delta, and government officials whose salaries he paid. His second, and perhaps more important prop, came from American officials who saw him as Vietnam's best alternative to the Communist Ho Chi Minh, and who were determined to ensure his success. Diem was little known in his country's farming communities and small towns. In those areas, popular discontent was fanned by the arrival of his appointees to rule and tax the peasants—police and civil administrators more interested in pleasing their superiors in Saigon and lining their own pockets than in serving the interests of the local people.

Under Ngo Dinh Diem, the government of the Republic of Vietnam (R.V.N.) faced many urgent problems. Millions of peasants did not own their own farms. In 1960, 15 percent of the people owned 75 percent of the land, but Diem consistently postponed a long-promised land reform program. Consequently, discontent rose among landless peasants who were disappointed by the central government, which felt entitled to tax them, draft their sons into the army, and harass suspected political opponents, but felt no obligation to improve their living conditions and public services.

Revolutionary elements took full advantage of unhappiness in the South Vietnamese countryside. As Diem grew more suspicious of his own people and employed ever more repressive police measures, some of his opponents used terrorism to spread their own influence among the peasants. One tactic was to kill some of the most unpopular Saigon appointees—proving that no one was safe from revolutionary reprisals and winning favor among the most disaffected. Vietnamese communists justified their use of violence as their only choice now that the Republic of Vietnam was excluding them from the legitimate political process.

Antigovernment strikes grew numerous in the late 1950s, when an atmosphere of national emergency settled over the Saigon government. Though the Republic of Vietnam had an elected legislature, Diem dominated it like a king rather than an elected chief executive. Using the "emergency" as an excuse, he devoted much of the American aid meant for development to security purposes. The emergency was also the reason for arresting his critics, often holding them without warrant or trial. Seeking to surround himself with people of unquestionable loyalty, he turned to family members—brothers and their in-laws—to serve in the most sensitive positions. His brother Ngo Dinh Nhu was put in charge of the security forces and given effective police power over the entire population. His brother Ngo Dinh Can was in charge of all government appointments and contracts. Both men quickly acquired reputations for extreme corruption. A fourth brother, Ngo Dinh Thuc, was the Catholic archbishop of Hue and leader of the church in Vietnam.

At the Third National Congress of the Vietnam Workers Party in Hanoi, in September 1960, the members set an agenda that placed national unification on a par with socialist development in the north. The "masses" were identified as the best means to this end, and party leaders said they hoped to bring about the collapse of the Diem regime without provoking large-scale intervention by the United States. To mobilize the masses in the south, the party conceived a "National Front for the Liberation of South Vietnam" (known as the National Liberation Front, or "N.L.F."), designed to rally all of the political factions that opposed the Diem government. The N.L.F. was born on December 20, 1960, on a rubber plantation in the south near the Cambodian border, and it came to represent a coalition of leftist political factions in the south as well as the guerrilla fighters who sapped the strength of the Saigon regime through organized acts of military resistance.[3]

In the early 1960s, the government of the Republic of Vietnam was thrown on the defensive, even in the capital, by opposition from Buddhist groups angry about religious discrimination. The government hired Catholic officials while the army's officer corps was almost entirely comprised of Catholics, with Buddhists relegated to the ranks. Ngo Dinh Nhu, meanwhile, had begun a program of counter-terror against the National Liberation Front, arresting and torturing suspected communists to extract information, and intimidating villagers in a campaign to end their cooperation with N.L.F. agents. He employed special forces, who were effectively his own private army, to attack both N.L.F. members and other political opponents, including Buddhists. When Buddhists staged a protest demonstration in Saigon in May 1963, the Army of the Republic of Vietnam (A.R.V.N.) opened fire on them, killing nine and wounding 14. The public erupted in a furor, which was aggravated by the deaths of several monks who set themselves on fire in public suicides. Ngo Dinh Nhu's wife was once heard referring to these as "Buddhist barbecues."

The Fall of Diem and American Escalation, 1963–1968

The United States, meanwhile, increasingly came to see South Vietnam as a test case in the Cold War: a small country under assault by communist forces backed by foreign powers seeking to extend communist control over all of Southeast Asia. The "domino theory" held that if the Republic of Vietnam fell to communism, Cambodia, Laos, and the rest of Southeast Asia would be ripe for conquest, and therefore the line would have to be drawn somewhere, sometime, before the entire Pacific Rim came under the sway of Moscow and Beijing. American leaders reasoned that it would be better to take a stand in southern Vietnam while "counterinsurgency" could still be effective, than to fight a larger and more difficult war somewhere else. There had been successful "counterinsurgency" campaigns against leftist rebels in the Philippines and Malaya, and the Kennedy Administration was confident that with the right advice, training, and development the Saigon government could overcome the communist effort to disrupt the South Vietnamese countryside. Accordingly, in 1962 the Kennedy Administration dispatched more than 11,000 military advisors and combat support personnel to guide the R.V.N.'s counterinsurgency campaign. However, even this level of American support was unlikely to be helpful if the Saigon government remained corrupt, ineffective, and unpopular.

In the summer of 1963, the United States began getting signals from A.R.V.N. sources that planning was under way for a military coup against Ngo Dinh Diem. The Kennedy Administration, while nominally committed to supporting constitutional governments in allied countries, was sufficiently frustrated with Diem to listen to the coup plotters and to give what amounted to a green light for action. In November, the Americans stood aside while Army generals deposed the Ngo brothers and overthrew their government, killing President Ngo Dinh Diem and his brother Ngo Dinh Nhu in the process. Though shocked at the murders, the American administration quickly gave its support to the generals who headed the new regime.

President John F. Kennedy himself was assassinated in Dallas later in the same month, November 1963. At the time of his death, his top foreign policy officials were engaged in a top-to-bottom review of American policy in Southeast Asia, and contemplating changes that ranged from abandonment of the Saigon government to the introduction of U.S. ground forces in an all-out military campaign.

Kennedy's death interrupted the review, and for the ensuing year the American advisors remained in Vietnam trying to organize the A.R.V.N.'s counterinsurgency campaign. Meanwhile, Kennedy's successor, Lyndon B. Johnson, ran for election in 1964 on an implied promise to keep the United States out of war.

In August 1964, a U.S. naval destroyer, engaged in intelligence and sabotage operations in the Gulf of Tonkin off the coast of the Democratic Republic of Vietnam, was attacked by D.R.V. torpedo boats. A second attack, later proven not to have happened, was reported the following night. Concerned about protection of U.S. forces in the area, President Johnson had Congress pass a resolution, known as the Gulf of Tonkin Resolution, that gave him the authority for whatever was necessary, including military action, to protect American personnel in the region and to shield the nations in the region from communist attack. Most of the congressmen and senators who voted for the Gulf of Tonkin Resolution did not realize that it was, in effect, a declaration of war, and that Johnson eventually would use it as the legal basis for sending more than half a million soldiers to Southeast Asia. Johnson and his successor, Richard Nixon, eventually carried the war to Laos and Cambodia, bombing all three countries and vastly expanding the war, so that it engulfed the societies of the entire region.

An essential element of the war was the D.R.V.'s slow but steady supply of men and materiel to support and reinforce the N.L.F. against the Saigon government and the Americans.[4] After 1964, units of the People's Army of Vietnam (P.A.V.N.) from the north also traveled to the south to fight the A.R.V.N. and Americans. The N.L.F. appealed for support in the provinces of South Vietnam by promising land reform. It also continued to threaten supporters of the R.V.N. and families of A.R.V.N. soldiers, drawing support away from the R.V.N. government. The N.L.F. demanded a role in South Vietnamese politics and a withdrawal of foreign (meaning U.S.) forces. Their northern support came via the "Ho Chi Minh Trail," a system of roads and trails leading southward through the jungles and inland mountains. Much of the Ho Chi Minh Trail passed through the nominally neutral territory of Laos and Cambodia. Much of it was obscured by foliage and invisible from the air. Much of the movement took place at night for protection from American bombing. Branches of the trail led to the Mekong River Delta, just a few miles west of Saigon, where they deposited significant military power virtually on the doorstep of the R.V.N. government. The military objective then was to hurt the Saigon government and American forces so badly that the United States would eventually withdraw, leaving the R.V.N. to face the communist insurgency without outside help.

The effectiveness of the Ho Chi Minh Trail prompted America's campaign to defoliate the jungle and, eventually, President Nixon's decision to send bombers and ground forces into Laos and Cambodia to interfere with the supply lines through neutral territory. These decisions were fateful, for American intervention was the catalyst that led to revolutionary change in Cambodia and eventually the rise of the murderous Khmer Rouge. In Laos, so many American bombs fell on the countryside that the beleaguered Laotians coined the term "ironing" to describe the planting of metal in their fields. The death toll among noncombatants in both countries, collateral victims of the Vietnam War, ran to hundreds of thousands of innocent people. Deaths in Cambodia resulting from the political upheavals related to the war ran to the millions.

In Vietnam, the United States struggled to stabilize the Saigon government. The 1963 coup against Diem was only the first in a series of military uprisings. It took two years to find a combination of generals who could create a semblance of stability. Though the successive military leaders who presided over the R.V.N. between 1965 and 1975 sometimes surprised observers with flashes of competence, the N.L.F. succeeded in convincing many Vietnamese that they were merely agents of the United States.

From 1965 until 1968, the U.S. Military Assistance Command in Vietnam (M.A.C.V.) claimed that combined U.S. and R.V.N. forces, temporarily augmented by units from other "allied" countries such as Australia and the Republic of Korea, were making steady progress against the "Viet Cong," as American and Saigon officials typically referred to the N.L.F. and their allies in the field. Indeed, considering the imbalance in firepower, the N.L.F. and P.A.V.N. seemed badly overmatched. The United States flew fighter-bombers from carrier decks in the Tonkin Gulf wherever it wished, hitting targets in either part of Vietnam at will (Figure 18.2). B-52s from U.S. Air Force bases on Guam and in Thailand dropped more bombs on Indochina than were used in all of Europe and the Pacific during World War II. American, R.V.N., and allied ground forces, equipped and financed by U.S. taxpayers, were well supplied with weapons, ammunition, vehicles, air support, food, and medicine. Americans built ports and landing fields to handle the equipment, and American bases grew into small cities. Americans even tried to alter the environment in Vietnam by sending special planes to spray defoliants on the jungles. The poison, known as "Agent Orange," was meant to remove the natural protection over the Ho Chi Minh Trail and expose the men and trucks beneath to American bombing, but it also caused much additional damage, including genetic defects among Vietnamese and Americans who came in contact with it.

Americans who remembered American victories in World War II had difficulty

FIGURE 18.2 The Pont Doumer, renamed Long Bien Bridge, after U.S. bombing. See Figure 12.1 for an artist's view of the bridge during French colonization.

FROM HANOI, *BIOGRAPHY OF A CITY*, BY WILLIAM S. LOGAN. COURTESY UNIVERSITY OF NEW SOUTHWALES PRESS, SYDNEY. QUOTED FROM *JOURNAL D'UN DIPLOMATE FRANÇAIS*, 1966–1969, BY FRANÇOIS DE QUIRRELLE (PARIS: TALLENDIER, 1992), P. 132.

grasping the reality in Southeast Asia: that lightly armed Vietnamese peasants could get the better of the gigantic military force that Washington sent to Vietnam. Yet the war was not decided by money or numbers. Early in the war at Ap Bac, for example, 2,500 A.R.V.N. soldiers, with their American advisors, helicopters, weapons, and vehicles, were defeated by 200 N.L.F resisters who inflicted heavy casualties on them and destroyed five of their aircraft.[5] Ho Chi Minh (Figure 18.3) explained such events by claiming that the Vietnamese were fighting a patriotic war on their own soil against a foreign—that is, colonial— power, and he argued that the United States had merely replaced France in what was a protracted war of national liberation. Where Americans tended to see the war in terms of days and months, Ho saw it in terms of years and decades. From his perspective, the defeat of the United States—like the defeat of the colo- nial idea everywhere—was certain in the long run. He never wavered in his belief that the Vietnamese cause was just, that foreign intervention in his country was wrong, and that eventually a combination of Vietnamese nationalism and American fatigue would lead to an

FIGURE 18.3 Portrait of Ho Chi Minh. BETTMANN/CORBIS.

American withdrawal and the reunification of Vietnam by his own forces. In this, of course, he was eventually proven correct.

In January 1968, during the lunar new year holiday called "Tet," a combina- tion of N.L.F. and P.A.V.N. units attacked all across the south in an all-out effort to overrun U.S. and A.R.V.N. military positions. The Ho Chi Minh Trail and other N.L.F. supply routes had made it possible to position the attackers at key points throughout the country, and on January 31 they struck seemingly everywhere at once. The streets of Saigon rang with gunfire and the rumble of heavy vehicles as N.L.F. guerrillas actually entered the American Embassy compound and briefly occupied the very heart of the U.S. presence in their country. U.S. and A.R.V.N. defenders struck back, and within a week negated most of the N.L.F's success. In military terms, the defense of South Vietnam during the "Tet Offensive" was a success. However, in psychological terms, Tet was a defeat for the United States. M.A.C.V. officials had been telling the American public that the "Viet Cong" were nearly vanquished and that they could "see the light at the end of the tunnel." The fact that they were caught by surprise humiliated them, and in the United States there were severe repercussions. President Johnson devoted himself to finding a way to negotiate an end to the war, and finally bowed out of the 1968 election, in part because he dreaded being humiliated by the voters at the polls. After the public relations fiasco of Tet, the American people turned against the military effort in Vietnam, and there was a dramatic rise in public protests and antiwar activity, including resistance to the draft. There was a review of America's Vietnam policy, and later in 1968, when M.A.C.V. asked for enough additional soldiers to bring the total to three quarters of a million, Washington refused. By this time, there were 543,000 American soldiers in Indochina, battles were raging and bombs were dropping all over Vietnam, half a million Vietnamese people were becoming homeless every year, and 130,000 Vietnamese civilians were killed or wounded every month.[6] Frustration with the war and incredulity at the U.S. government's inability to get the better of the N.L.F. and Ho Chi Minh were major factors in the election of the Republican Richard Nixon as president in 1968.

Maintaining a Society at War: South Vietnam

Traditional Vietnamese society was based on family and harmony in the community. At the local level, villagers were largely autonomous. Village leaders, though not elected in the modern sense, emerged and asserted themselves by virtue of age, accomplishments, and public respect. In part at least, local communities were governed by consent.

Colonialism weakened this consent through taxation, realignment of property, patterns of labor recruitment, conscription, and institutional intrusions such as the colonial police. Resentment over colonial rule generated modern nationalism in Vietnam. However, it was not until the Diem regime in the 1950s that the countryside experienced revolutionary societal disruption. Some of the disruption was the by-product of establishing representative democracy in Vietnam. Indeed, Diem convened several sessions of his national parliament while he was president, and recruited a high level of voter participation in every election. However, the purpose was not to increase local influence in national affairs. Rather, it was the opposite, to impose Saigon's power on districts in the countryside, to install strangers from the government bureaucracy (invested with armed authority) in their midst, and to take away the power of people to decide local matters for themselves.[7]

Vietnamese society, however, has never been easy to organize by any central authority. The French were never able to control the secret societies such as the Binh Xuyen crime syndicate that developed partly as a response to colonialism. Other groups that opposed French rule were criminalized because of their ideas. Anti-French religious organizations, such as the Cao Dai and Hoa Hao, developed and had to survive in the twilight of the underworld. After the demise of French rule, the R.V.N. government and U.S. military authorities likewise found them troublesome. Indeed, some of America's earliest fiascoes in Vietnam were attempts to buy the backing of the Cao Dai and Hoa Hao sects and the Binh Xuyen syndicate for the Diem regime in the mid-1950s.[8]

The National Liberation Front co-opted many from these strata of southern Vietnamese society as it organized itself, in effect, as a secret society. The people of Vietnam were familiar with this shadowy form of organization. Even their use of terror tactics was familiar, and when N.L.F. guerrillas appeared at night and

took control of a village, the peasants knew better than to report them to the
A.R.V.N. the next day. Having to live under N.L.F. control by night and Saigon's
control by day certainly made the countryside unsafe. One answer was to remove
villagers into "strategic hamlets"—concentration camps where they slept at night
surrounded by fences and South Vietnamese troops. But the villagers hated leaving their houses exposed overnight, and the program was very unpopular. Instead
of winning the "hearts and minds" of the people, the R.V.N. only succeeded in
alienating them further.

The N.L.F. strength came partly from secrecy and terror, yet it also derived
from positive messages of patriotism and independence. Young people across the
country were susceptible to the nationalist appeal, aimed at ridding the country of
what looked like foreign occupation. American forces were known for their disre-
spectful behavior in Vietnam, and often acted like conquerors rather than allies. The
rhetoric of democracy was not as effective as the anger generated by the numerous
racist epithets that were used to refer to the Vietnamese people. Educated Vietnamese
resented the lordly demeanor of American enlisted men spending money on cheap
entertainment in the camp towns that sprang up around U.S. bases.

In the 1960s, life in the Republic of Vietnam was completely militarized.
Military priorities dominated everything. The foreign presence pumped money
into the economy and created many thousands of jobs, but even Vietnamese profiting from the war could see that the American presence made the violence incalculably worse. The war disrupted education and the lives of young men drafted
for army service. The farming economy was disrupted by the fighting and damage
to the supply system. Human rights were ignored as the government spied on citizens and rounded up suspected N.L.F. agents, holding them without trial, sometimes in the infamous "tiger cages."

It is therefore remarkable that after the fall of Ngo Dinh Diem in 1963 and
the escalation of the war by the United States, intellectuals in the R.V.N. actually
acquired more freedom to write and express themselves via literature and journalism. Some of the writing supported the N.L.F. and appealed for freedom from
American domination. Novels, stories, and poems became an important outlet for
the anger that rose from racial and sexual friction with the Americans and the vast
disparities in power that came with the war. Writers looked for ways to express
feelings about the moral ruin of Vietnam, of the damage to families and the nation.
One group expressed itself through romanticism; another through existentialism.[9]
On the N.L.F. side, the writing was more overtly political, following socialist realism to inspire and rally people in the patriotic cause of independence, even when
the words were romantic. In the poem "You Have Got Into University," by Giang
Nam, a resistance fighter imagines a reunion with his sister, who is a student:

> Tomorrow, when the motherland is unified,
> Tomorrow, you will come back and give me lessons,
> And we shall not have to write on the wall with coal any more
> Or dread the horror of the police searches.
> You will say to me "Come on, big brother, courage!"
> And I shall smile, remembering the moonlight,

And our motherland, that gave you wings
And the honor of marching with those up at the front.
I shall need to keep a long sleepless night
To tell you about the South, and its struggle and agony:
"In those days, little sister, I had
But one school on earth—the Revolution!"[10]

Maintaining a Society at War: The D.R.V.

After the French left Indochina in 1954, the Hanoi-based regime of the Democratic Republic of Vietnam under Ho Chi Minh embarked on a revolutionary program designed to make North Vietnam a socialist state. In advance of this transformation, as many as 800,000 northerners fled to the south, migrating with whatever they could carry, in order to escape a violent purge of class enemies. In keeping with Marxist theory, the government carried out a thorough land reform that wrested property from big owners and redistributed it to the landless. The Vietnamese land reform resembled the reorganization of the rural economy in Communist China, involving the identification, trial, and sometimes execution of newly defined criminals. Though the government later expressed regret for the excesses of its overzealous agents, it cost an estimated 50,000 lives.[11]

The government spared the lives of many educated and propertied people because it needed their skills. These were a middle echelon of specialists who staffed the medical care system, mass education system, and mass organizations such as neighborhood committees. Though deprived of their wealth, these useful citizens duly submitted to rule by the Workers' Party (the Lao Dong Party, previously the Indochinese Communist Party). The communist cadres who bossed them were headed by veterans of the longstanding resistance against France, including legendary independence fighters such as Vo Nguyen Giap, Pham Van Dong, and Ho Chi Minh himself, who presided over state and party. Ho became the center of a personality cult, but did not exercise the control wielded by Kim Il-sung in Korea. After some vacillation, the party decided not to follow the Chinese lead but adopted Stalinist policies like those of North Korea, and increasingly sided with the Soviet Union in its dispute with China. The lead in this was taken by Le Duan (1908–1986), a member of the party since its foundation who, when the country was divided in 1954, was put in charge of organizing the communist underground in the south. Le Duan was First Secretary at the time of Ho's death in 1969, and remained in power for the rest of his life.

The population in general appears to have accepted the regime, although it does not appear to have embraced socialism with enthusiasm. As workers, they had little time for politics; when the war in the South started affecting their lives in the late 1950s, they did their duty and continued working in small jobs as farmers, laborers, miners, and tradespeople. Above all, North Vietnam was a very poor country with a primitive agricultural economy faced with the urgent task of social and economic modernization.

Ho Chi Minh and the Lao Dong Party determined first to fight for reunification with the south and expulsion of the foreign forces that were beginning to control the Saigon government. Thus, they opted to continue what they called their "war of national liberation" before trying to modernize their state. For them, the decade from 1965 to 1975 became a time of total mobilization in the struggle to support the N.L.F. in the south and, increasingly, to survive continual bombing by American warplanes.

American leaders imagined that their bombing might cripple the D.R.V. economy and compel the Hanoi government to capitulate or at least abandon the effort in the south. They assumed that the D.R.V. had enough of an industrial economy to be reduced by blowing up ports, railroads, and factories. It was hard for them to grasp the fact that the poverty and simplicity of North Vietnam's mostly agricultural economy created a kind of resilience that helped it withstand attacks from high altitude B-52s and carrier-launched fighter-bombers. The Soviet Union aided Hanoi with anti-aircraft guns and surface-to-air missiles (SAMs) that took a heavy toll on American planes and pilots. After the United States started bombing North Vietnam in 1965, the D.R.V. began collecting downed pilots as prisoners of war. The numbers of killed and missing, as well as the POWs who eventually were returned, became a major issue in U.S.-Vietnamese relations for a generation after the end of the war. It is ironic to note that the supply situation in North Vietnam actually improved during the American bombing because of increased foreign aid from the socialist countries. Trucks that were destroyed on the Ho Chi Minh Trail, for example, were readily replaced with newer trucks from abroad.

The Hanoi government claimed that popular morale in North Vietnam remained high throughout the war, but this is belied by postwar accounts of a general war-weariness that descended after several years of bombing, creating pressure for progress or at least a settlement. This pressure was not the kind envisioned by the Americans, however. It did not propose accepting the legitimacy of the foreign presence in Vietnam or a continued role for the United States, and it did not envision Vietnam as anything other than a socialist state ruled by the Workers Party. It was rather a profound impatience with the length of the struggle and a lack of triumph or satisfaction when things went well in the south. Thus the Tet offensive, which was a political, if not military, victory for the N.L.F. and Hanoi, was recognized as having been extremely costly and by no means an occasion for celebration in the north. The damage wore at North Vietnam's infrastructure, degrading transportation and energy facilities and preventing the kind of economic and social development that might otherwise have been achieved.

Hanoi accepted aid from communist allies, but the Soviets and Chinese Communists were bitter rivals at the time, and the Chinese sometimes blocked the shipment of Soviet aid by rail through their territory. Most Soviet aid came by ship and was delivered in the port of Haiphong, creating a tempting bombing target for the Americans, who, nonetheless, could not afford to bomb Soviet ships. Trade with North Vietnam also came from other Western countries, such as France and Britain, who greatly annoyed the United States by failing to honor America's requests for a boycott of the Vietnamese market.

The Vietnam War: The Final Phase

When Richard Nixon became President of the United States in 1969, he implemented a policy of "Vietnamization," by which U.S. troops were to be withdrawn from Vietnam by stages and R.V.N. Vietnamese forces were to take over more of the fighting, supported by American money and material. Nixon thus hoped to reduce the number of American battle casualties and calm the outrage at home over what was, by then, seen as a failed military adventure. Nixon, however, was determined not to lose the war, and demanded "peace with honor." To effect this, he pursued negotiations with the D.R.V. at a long-running conference in Paris. The negotiations faltered over many points: the participation of the N.L.F., the legitimacy of the R.V.N. government, whether negotiations could proceed while the United States was bombing the D.R.V., and when to release U.S. prisoners from D.R.V. detention. Even the shape of the conference table had to be negotiated (it was round).

The key element of Nixon's pursuit of "peace with honor" was that the United States must not appear to have been defeated in Vietnam. Initially, it seemed that the Nixon Administration was also determined to guarantee the survival of the Republic of Vietnam as well. To force his point on the opposing side, he ordered dramatically increased bombing in neighboring Laos and Cambodia, aimed at increasing the costs of using the Ho Chi Minh Trail. In May of 1970, he sent American forces on an invasion into Cambodia to attack N.L.F. sanctuaries that were dangerously close to Saigon. This attack had a military purpose, but it was a political disaster. In the United States, university campuses erupted with protests against the widening of the war, and at Kent State University in Ohio, the National Guard fired on the protesters, killing four and injuring several others. The sight of uniformed guardsmen firing on American students galvanized opposition to the war and made it necessary, first and foremost, to find a way out.

The Paris negotiations continued in earnest through the middle of 1972. Meanwhile, the Nixon Administration was torn between "hawks," who thought that Hanoi might still be forced to pull out of the south, and "doves," who thought the United States should immediately settle for the best deal it could get and then pull out of Vietnam. The effect of American actions in Southeast Asia are still debated, for it was only after an intensive campaign of carpet bombing by B-52s that Hanoi finally agreed, in January 1973, to a settlement with the United States whereby American prisoners would be returned and U.S. troops would be withdrawn from the south. The belief lingers that Hanoi was "forced" to settle. However, it settled largely on its own terms. The American negotiator, Henry Kissinger, later said that he had wanted a "decent interval" between the American pullout and what was seen as an inevitable final attack by Hanoi to overrun the south. Kissinger and Nixon did not want it to appear that the American pullout had triggered the collapse of the Saigon government and the "bloodbath" that was expected to follow when the communists punished the losers.

The deal held for two years. In March 1975, after Kissinger's "decent interval," North Vietnam renewed the attack on the south with a major campaign that lasted only a few weeks. Saigon fell on April 30, with the last American personnel and helicopters departing in a disorderly crush along with crowds of refugees who feared communist reprisals. The Americans evacuated many Vietnamese who were tainted by collaboration, but left many more behind.

The Socialist Republic of Vietnam: The First Decade, 1976–1986

Victorious at last, the leaders of the Vietnamese Communist Party (previously the Workers' Party) and the new Socialist Republic of Vietnam faced a major task of reconstruction. In the north, industrial and transportation facilities had been much damaged by repeated bombing. In the south, the war left innumerable villages in ruins, vast areas stripped of foliage by napalm and chemicals, millions of homeless people, and an estimated 3.5 million landmines, which for the next quarter of a century caused 2,000 casualties per year.

Moreover, the government faced the challenge of forging the 24 million people of the north and the 22 million of the south into a single socialist nation-state. This most urgently entailed extending socialism to the south. Many southern soldiers, officials, religious practitioners, and intellectuals were sent to "reeducation camps," and trusted party members, often northerners, were placed in positions of authority. In December 1976, the Fourth Party Congress convened under the leadership of Le Duan and declared that socialism could be substantially achieved in 10 years. The unified national government, now calling itself the Socialist Republic of Vietnam, took action accordingly. In 1978, it announced the nationalization of industry and commerce, launching "the second battle of Saigon," aimed at the destruction of the city's traders and shopkeepers. These were mostly ethnic Chinese who operated small enterprises in Cholon, the bustling Chinese quarter of Saigon, which by then had been renamed Ho Chi Minh City. Many of these people were forced into other occupations and/or relocated to "New Economic Zones" in the underdeveloped parts of the country. Thousands of others fled the country, risking their lives in small boats moving through treacherous, pirate-infested waters to find refuge in Hong Kong or Thailand.

Meanwhile, collectivization of agriculture was also extended to the south, at least on paper. However, it ran into resistance, and proceeded unevenly and with very mixed results. Rising prices and bad weather disrupted farm life for several years and frustrated efforts at reorganization. By 1979, it was clear that the economic program was not working. In that year Vietnam, following the Chinese example, partially relaxed economic controls by allowing for a contract system under which farmers could sell their rice on the open market once they had fulfilled their State quota. Collectivization never prevailed in the south: by 1985 official sources reported that no more than 25 percent of farming households had joined any kind of collective organization.

Victory brought neither reduction in military expenses nor peace. As it consolidated its control in the south, the government of the Socialist Republic of Vietnam became concerned about Chinese ambitions in Cambodia and the influence of the

People's Republic of China over the new Khmer Rouge government there. After a series of border clashes with Chinese-backed forces of Pol Pot's Khmer Rouge regime, Vietnamese troops seized the initiative and invaded Cambodia, attempting to set up a satellite regime. The P.R.C. responded in February 1979 by sending an army across the border into northern Vietnam. This military excursion lasted only 17 days, but the threat of renewed invasion forced the Vietnamese military to maintain two large armies at opposite ends of their country. This was in addition to a force of 40,000 that was kept in Laos.

The need to spend up to 40 percent of its national budget on military matters severely restricted the Vietnamese government's ability to advance a reform agenda. Thus, during the first decade of unified Vietnam, the party and government remained under the stern control of Le Duan in a state of neither war nor peace. However, Le Duan's death in 1986 opened up possibilities for change.

Doi Moi, 1986–Present

At its Sixth National Congress in December 1986, the Vietnamese Communist Party adopted a policy of economic liberalization under the slogan "Doi Moi" (literally meaning "renovation"), a term that was sufficiently elastic to cover a wide range of policies. Generally, it meant a reduction of the State's role in the economy in favor of the free market; less government control over agriculture, commerce, and industry; and greater openness to foreign trade and investment.

Concurrently, there was a shift in foreign policy. In 1989, Vietnamese forces were withdrawn from Cambodia and Laos, paving the way for better relations with China. In 1991, after a conference between the two countries' foreign ministers, tensions eased with the P.R.C., but Vietnam remained apprehensive about Chinese expansionism. Robert Templer aptly characterizes the relationship with China as a "guarded friendship" once again.[12] Two tiny groups of islands, known as the Paracels and Spratleys (located in what the Chinese call the "South China Sea" but the Vietnamese insist is the "East Sea"), remained a cause of dispute. Only 33 of these islands lie permanently above water, but it is the possibility of oil beneath them that prompted China and Vietnam, as well as Taiwan, Malaysia, the Philippines, and Brunei to advance claims of sovereignty.

In 1994, the United States lifted its trade embargo and in the following year extended diplomatic recognition. Additionally in 1995, Vietnam gained security and diplomatic leverage by joining the Association of Southeast Asian Nations (ASEAN). There was also an economic side to this, as Vietnam joined the ASEAN Free Trade Area, formed economic ties with ASEAN countries, and received investments from Singapore, Malaysia and other ASEAN members.

Vietnam's economic policy under Doi Moi resembled that of China, except that the State sector remained more important and State regulation continued to be pervasive. As in China, the government sought political stability as well as economic growth, and countenanced no political opposition. Especially after the 1989 Tiananmen uprising in Beijing, the Vietnamese government closely watched the press. However, the discrediting of Marxism-Leninism in Europe and the collapse of the Soviet Union, along with the obvious success of business ventures in China, eroded the credibility of communism in Vietnam and increased the importance of the government's economic and political performance as the basis for its legitimacy.

With this erosion of ideology on top of the social damage resulting from the war, corruption spread on all levels. Corruption aggravated inefficiency and no doubt retarded economic growth. Nevertheless, the economy in Vietnam grew impressively. The country survived the end of foreign aid that came with the dissolution of the Soviet Union, and was able to reorient its trade away from dependence on the former socialist bloc. The most dramatic and highly symbolic achievement was that Vietnam no longer had to import rice, but instead began exporting it. The gross domestic product increased steadily during the 1990s. During the five years prior to the Asian fiscal crisis of 1997–1998, it grew over eight percent a year.

However, the economy had begun to slow down even before the Asian Economic Crisis, in what has been called the first of four "typhoons" of 1997–1998. The second "typhoon" was rural unrest in Thai Binh province in the north, where high taxes and transportation costs had left many peasants impoverished. The third "typhoon" was literally a typhoon, the worst in half a century. Finally, Vietnam was hit by the Asian financial crisis. With its national economy less integrated into the global system than states such as Thailand and the Republic of Korea, Vietnam suffered comparatively less. Nevertheless, it experienced a major decline in foreign investment and trade with its Southeast Asian neighbors, who accounted for 60 percent of its foreign trade and provided 70 percent of its foreign investment.

Government during these years was not dominated by any single individual. Policy decisions were reached by forging agreement among the party's factions, with leaders disinclined to rock the boat. They preferred to maintain social and political stability rather than risk the consequences of taking drastic action to reform, the corruption that was draining state enterprises and undermining the financial and banking system The government continued to promote state enterprises, even as the private sector grew at a much faster rate. During the first five years of the twenty-first century, Vietnam's annual rate of economic growth reached more than seven percent. In June 2006, there was a smooth political transition as the former Deputy Prime Minister Nguyen Tan Dung (1949–) assumed the prime ministership. Dung had extensive experience in economic affairs and is expected to continue emphasizing his country's economic development.

As in many developing countries, modernization is not without consequences for other aspects of life, such as the environment. Plans to build a highway along the path of the Ho Chi Minh Trail represent the government's commitment to large-scale development without much attention to the environmental impact, reminiscent of Japanese dam building and the Three Gorges Dam project in China. In 2006, the government acknowledged the need for action by preparing to establish a special environmental police force.

Doi Moi in Vietnam has been compared to *Perestroika* ("restructuring") in the former Soviet Union, the movement launched by Mikhail Gorbachev the same year that led to *glasnost*, or "openness." In Vietnam there was a similar, though less extensive and certainly less consequential, relaxation of control over artistic and intellectual life. A varied and vigorous literature replaced Soviet- and Chinese-style "social realism," as writers took the pulse of the times. Ho Anh Thai (1960–), who in 1988 published a story about a hypocritical official who watches so much pornography that he gradually turns into a goat, went on to be accepted as a member of the Hanoi Writers' Association. However, the portrayal of party hypocrisy and ruthless careerism presented by Duong Thu Hung (1947–) in *Paradise of the Blind,* also published in 1988, was more than the political establishment could tolerate. Though Duong Thu Hung was part of a troupe that once traveled in the war zones to "sing louder than the bombs," her works were banned, and she was made to serve seven months in prison. Since her 1991 imprisonment she has lived in Hanoi, but can only publish her work overseas. Her *Memories of a Pure Spring* presents a devastating contrast between wartime idealism and postwar cynicism. One of its themes is a harrowing glimpse of Vietnamese prison life.

Bao Ninh (1952–) expresses his own gritty comprehension of Vietnam's recent history in *The Sorrow of War* (1990). War, with all its brutal violence and futility, is just something that happens and that one endures in order to survive in his view. The main character does not lose his humanity, but neither does he return to a fulfilling life. There is little to choose here between victory and defeat. Though the work lacks the hopeful vision sought by the party, Bao Ninh has nonetheless won several prestigious literary awards within Vietnam.

Under circumstances that discourage direct political commentary, writers sometimes resort to historical allegories to make their points. Such is the work of the writer most adored for his command of the language, Nguyen Huy Thiep (1950–), who has used historical settings with contemporary meaning that include controversial treatments of Gia Long, founder of the Nguyen Dynasty, and of Nguyen Du, author of *The Tale of Kieu.* Thiep's impoverished, ineffectual Nguyen Du suggests the general marginalization of artists and intellectuals by the modern political process, as well as the Vietnamese hate-love relationship with China. In his portrait of Gia Long, politicians appear cruel, duplicitous, anti-intellectual, hypocritical, self-absorbed, and egomaniacal. Their pathological fear of social change prevents them from undertaking the reforms necessary to improve society.

FIGURE 18.4 *Story of Kieu* (1972), Nguyen Tu Nghiem. Gouache on paper, 11.5 × 8 inches.

FIGURE 18.5 *Metamorphosis 2000,* Pham Cam Thuong. Caterpillars turning into butterflies are classic exemplars of biological metamorphosis, but this one has a human face. Is he dreaming of the female (butterfly) above him? And do they both occupy the monk's dream—a dream within a dream? Meanwhile, the little fish at the bottom is a reminder of the kinship of all sentient life and the ability of all to metamorphose and dream. Woodblock print, 21 × 27.5 cm.
© PHAM CAM THUONG. USED BY PERMISSION OF JUDITH HUGHES DAY, FINE CONTEMPORARY VIETNAMESE ART.

There has also been a flowering of art in such a variety of styles that it is impossible to single out one artist or work as representative. Nguyen Tu Nghiem (1922–) was trained in Western techniques but developed a style very much his own. While his *A Buffalo Calf Given in Land Reform,* painted in 1968, reflects what was politically correct at the time, he preferred to draw on Vietnamese myths and tradition. It is therefore fitting that he is represented here by his charming and delicate rendering of Vietnam's most beloved classic (Figure 18.4). Pham Cam Thuong (1957–) belongs to different generation, but he too is grounded in the tradition that has provided him subject matter for four books as well as for his art (Figure 18.5). *Metamorphosis* is Buddhist and Vietnamese, but may also suggest a metaphor for the human condition at the turn of the century.

Vietnam never had a Cultural Revolution, but its party and government shared the Marxist aversion to religion, suppressed sects they felt to be subversive, and severely limited those too large to be crushed. The government also discouraged household altars and other aspects of Vietnamese popular religion with mixed results. For instance, ancestors still had to be propitiated so that they would sanction weddings, but now arranged marriages were the exception rather than the rule. The communal house (*dinh*) retained its central place in the religious life of

BOX 18.1 THE LONELY BUDDHA

The Lonely Buddha is a large statue famous for healing people and granting requests. Though placed in the jungle, it does not lack human company. When Philip Taylor visited (most likely in 1998), a monk explained that the Buddha was placed in the jungle in 1953 because it was too large for its intended site in Saigon. However, in a separate conversation, a nun gave a different account:

> The Lonely Buddha was discovered by an elderly farmer in the middle of an area of jungle about ten years ago. The farmer lived and worked nearby. One night as he lay dreaming, the Buddha appeared and gave him instructions how to find the place where he lay abandoned with nothing but wild animals as friends. The next day he followed the directions and found an enormous seated Buddha, with palms facing upward on his lap, collecting pure rainwater. Only after that did the place become widely known and the present complex built.

The nun continued:

> More than thirty years ago, a Buddha image was commissioned from India. The airplane transporting the Buddha to Saigon suddenly lost power when it flew over the Buddha's present location. It was forced to land about thirty kilometers short of its destination . . . Surely there must have been something miraculous concerning the site, for it was strange that a plane could fly all the way from India and yet not make it the final short distance to Saigon. This happened during the American times. Meanwhile, the jungle grew up, government changed and the statue was forgotten and lost to all.

Philip Taylor, *Goddess on the Rise: Pilgrimage and Popular Religion in Vietnam* (Honolulu, University of Hawai'i Press, 2004), p. 247.

the village. The addition of Ho Chi Minh hardly signified a transformation, but the admission of women signaled both major social change and the ability of traditional institutions and practices to accommodate such change.

With the relaxation of controls and a decline in the official Marxist faith, traditional religion has revived and boomed (Box 18.1). Traditional tombs have reappeared in the Mekong Delta and elsewhere, while the hills on the way to the Catholic cathedral at Pham Diem, south of Hanoi, are dotted with crosses. Although it suffers from government hostility, Cao Dai still exists. Throughout Vietnam, the myriad deities in the temples do not lack offerings of incense and fruit.

At the turn of the twenty-first century, Vietnam remains an ostensibly Marxist state that continues to resemble the Chinese state more than it does its Southeast Asian neighbors. This looks very much like the traditional relationship in modern form. Similarly, its apprehensions concerning China have not disappeared, but appear muted into a "background hum."[13]

Finally, after years of war and more years of regrets and hostile memories, relations with the United States have continued to improve. President Bill Clinton was warmly welcomed when he visited in 2000, although his hosts were unreceptive to his concerns for human rights. This may suggest the formation of yet another "guarded friendship," but in 2001 the U.S. Congress passed and President George W. Bush signed an agreement negotiated by the Clinton Administration to normalize trade relations between the two countries. Bush, attending a regional economic meeting in Vietnam, expressed satisfaction at Vietnam's economic progress and openness to the world. Bilateral negotiations with the United States and other countries regarding entrance into the World Trade Organization completed in the spring of 2006 led to Vietnam's admission to membership in January 2007. Vietnam thus joined the dominant system of global trade with all its opportunities and challenges.

Notes

1. Marshall R. Pihl, "Contemporary Literature in a Divided Land," in Donald N. Clark, ed., *Korea Briefing 1993* (Boulder, CO: Westview Press, 1993), p. 83.

2. For an introduction to literature of this period, see Marshall R. Pihl and Bruce and Ju-Chan Fulton, eds., *Land of Exile: Contemporary Korean Fiction* (Armonk, NY: M. E. Sharpe, 1993).

3. William J. Duiker, *Ho Chi Minh: A Life* (New York, NY: Hyperion Books, 2000), pp. 524–25.

4. The American argument that the South Vietnamese insurgency was actually camouflage for a North Vietnamese invasion was presented in a "white paper": U.S. Department of State, *Aggression from the North: The Record of North Vietnam's Campaign to Conquer South Vietnam*, Far Eastern Series 130, publication 7839 (Washington, DC: U.S. Government Printing Office, 1965).

5. This episode is recounted by Neil Sheehan in *A Bright Shining Lie: John Paul Van and America in Vietnam* (Vintage Books, 1988), pp. 212–265.

6. Thomas D. Boettcher, *Vietnam: The Valor and the Sorrow* (Boston, MA: Little, Brown & Co., 1985), p. 341.

7. Allan E. Goodman, *Politics in War: The Bases of Political Community in South Vietnam* (Cambridge, MA: Harvard Univ. Press, 1973), pp. 1–30.

8. George C. Herring, *America's Longest War: The United States and Vietnam, 1950–1975* (New York, NY: John Wiley & Sons, 1979), pp. 51–54.

9. Maurice M. Durand and Nguyen Tran Huan, *An Introduction to Vietnamese Literature*, trans. by D. M. Hawke (New York, NY: Columbia Univ. Press, 1985), pp. 137–143.

10. Ibid., p. 173.

11. U.S. Library of Congress, *Vietnam: A Country Study*, ed. Ronald J. Cima (Washington, DC: U.S. Government Printing Office, 1989), p. 105.

12. Robert Templer, *Shadows and Wind: A View of Modern Vietnam* (New York, NY: Penguin Books, 1998), p. 298.

13. Ibid., p. 301, referring to tensions over the Paracels and Spratleys.

Afterword

All around the globe, the modern era saw the growth in power of the nation-state to a degree unprecedented by any institution in human history even as economic links were formed that became the precursor of contemporary globalization. At the start of the twenty-first century, in East Asia as elsewhere, the State's role in managing national economies was diminishing in the face of a global economic and financial system grown beyond the power of even the strongest state to control. Nevertheless, the nation-state remained the dominant military and political institution, and nationalism remained prevalent. Both globalization and nationalism held promise of a brighter future, but both also entailed dangers. It remains to be seen whether sovereign states can solve global problems when focused on local issues, while national rivalries continue to generate international dangers helping foster the globalization of terrorism.

Nationalist Tensions

Though the two Koreas are often referred to as rivals, their positions on the peninsula are not equal. South Korea has many advantages: twice the population, 30 times the national productivity, incalculably more personal income, and ties throughout the world. North Korea is a small state that relies on its own will and discipline and considerable luck in recent years in turning misfortune to its advantage. Both sides are intensely nationalistic and they accuse each other of subservience to foreign powers. They remember the ordeal of the Korean War and each blames the other for it. They despise each other's rulers and mistrust each other's institutions. It is highly unlikely that they will suddenly drop their differences and embrace each other as members of the same family. Yet underneath all the rhetoric of division, there remains a common language and a deep-seated bond that is demonstrated whenever Korean delegations meet to talk about their hesitant next steps toward reconciliation. The election of South Korean president Kim Dae-jung in 1997 created an opportunity to shift the goal from reunification (which is unlikely) to reintegration, under which each side can keep its national myths and structures, but in which communication is freer and common stakes are developing. President Kim's successor, Roh Moo Hyun, continued to pursue the "Sunshine Policy," but as his sometimes troubled term drew to a close there was considerable disillusionment in South Korea about the policy's meager results. A national reassessment was under way well ahead of the elections scheduled for late 2007. Nevertheless, it is reasonable to hope that communications between the north and south will continue to expand, and that they can become the basis for healing the conflicts that divide the 70 million Korean people.

Despite differences in scale and relative size, the commonalities and disparities between Taiwan and the People's Republic are similar in that the each side rejects the other's political and economic systems and tell different versions of China's modern story. One side—Taiwan—has achieved much greater wealth than the other. There is every sign that the flow of knowledge, goods, and people between Taiwan and the mainland will continue to accelerate, creating common ground and stakes in a peaceful reintegration of the Chinese nation. Though economic reintegration of China is taking place, political reintegration remains a very difficult problem. The P.R.C. insists that it wants peaceful reunification with Taiwan—but on its own terms. Meanwhile, it is willing to wait for changes to occur that will permit political reintegration, whatever those changes might be. However, it will not permit overt secession and the establishment of an independent republic on Taiwan that rejects the principle of Taiwan belonging to "one China." The P.R.C. has made it clear that in such a circumstance, it would intervene militarily to enforce Taiwan's "belonging" to China.

Under this threat from the mainland, the Republic of China on Taiwan continues to proceed cautiously in asserting its intention to move toward independence, even though its president, Chen Shui-Bian, was elected on an independence platform. Other countries, meanwhile, remain nervous about the potential for conflict between the two governments. The United States, which has committed itself to defend Taiwan from encroachment or invasion from the mainland, sometimes aggravates tensions in the Taiwan Straits by selling weapons to Taiwan and making careless references to Taiwan as a "country." Both actions raise hackles in Beijing and remind the P.R.C. that the United States is a main reason why what the P.R.C. sees as a purely domestic issue remains unsolved after more than 50 years.

China and the United States are only two of the "three ever shifting legs on a triangle,"[1] with Japan forming the third. With China now Japan's largest market as well as rival, relations between any two of the three also affects the third, and ultimately the rest of the globe. These legs keep shifting because "patterns of cooperation and rivalry" are unstable, pulled in various directions by economic and political forces.

Economic Globalization

Global economic integration, a continuous, long-term trend in modern history, continues apace along with an almost universal pursuit of economic growth, even at the expense of other values. Thus, economic globalization progresses far more rapidly than global efforts at protecting the environment, for example.

That is certainly the case in East Asia which now includes two of the four strongest, and most global economies on the globe. Japan has been an important factor in the global economy for many years, but more recently Chinese growth has provided a crucial stimulus to world commodity prices, and China, both as exporter of a wide range of goods and as a heavy purchaser of American public debt, has been crucial to the performance of the American economy. Beyond the developed world, China's, as well as Japan's, search for energy (primarily oil) extends to Africa and South America. Meanwhile, the Korean economy and fiscal policies have grown to the point where they have an impact on far-away lands. In all these cases, the values of the market prevail as deals are made with local power holders and environmental degradation continues to spread at dangerous speed.

Given the prominence of Japan and the Japanese model of economic development, adopted by the Park Chung-hee government in South Korea in the 1960s and influential throughout the region, East Asia serves as something of a laboratory for the policy of promoting globalization by encouraging the freest possible flow of capital and goods across international boundaries. Consequently, East Asia has also displayed some of globalization's greatest contradictions. As a theory, globalization rests on the proposition that free trade enriches everyone and creates stakes for the peaceful resolution of conflicts, and is therefore a good antidote to war. Globalization is the realization of what was envisioned at the end of World War II in the "Bretton Woods System" that created the World Bank, the International Monetary Fund (IMF), and the system of free trade promotion that evolved into the World Trade Organization (WTO) of the 1990s.

In theory, globalization is supposed to promote the flow of investment capital from rich countries to poor ones, creating employment and prosperity among less-advantaged peoples as they work to supply the part of the world that consumes most of the products they make. In this way, poor people work to raise their living standards, profits flow to the people who supply the capital, living standards converge, and everyone gets what they need. Unexpected events and distortions in this picture are to be dealt with by infusions of emergency capital (debt) from the IMF.

This theory has worked fairly well in East Asia. Certainly Taiwan and South Korea are shining examples of the rational application of capital and know-how to the problem of developing economies that are very short of resources other than their people. Vietnam after 1986 and the P.R.C. after 1980 are also examples of how parts of this theory—the trade elements of it at least—can be applied to boost national income and living standards. However, the theory has not proved stable or consistent. The economic crisis in South Korea in 1997–1998 was the result of too much foreign capital flowing into Korea in the form of foreign bank loans, without sufficient precautions or regulation. The "globalization explanation" was that corruption and "crony capitalism" had diverted much of the money, creating speculation, excessive levels of debt, and corruption of the system. The IMF bailed Korea out—with emergency loans that had to be paid back. Korea, fortunately, was able to do so, and had righted itself by 2001. The blame went to Korean banks and industries and the Korean government itself, for interrupting the "pure" forces of the market.

The Korean case, however, raised questions about whether the IMF had not actually functioned primarily to guarantee the bad loans, forcing the Koreans to pay them back—in effect punishing the borrowers for reckless borrowing—while protecting the lenders from the consequences of their reckless lending. In the end, ordinary citizens in Korea lost their jobs, Korean companies of all sizes and types were forced to close, and Koreans lost a proportion of their savings through the devaluation of their currency. For them, globalization was definitely a mixed blessing, and it is little wonder that Koreans refer to their economic collapse as the "IMF crisis." The worldwide critique of globalization uses such cases as examples of who actually wins and who actually loses in a system that is advertised as being good for everyone. Reformers point to unmanageable debt, stagnant real wages, massive unemployment, and the misallocation of resources as primary consequences of globalization. These in turn fuel the illiteracy, starvation, uncontrolled migration, trafficking in humans, and even slavery, crime, epidemics, and terrorism that afflict much of the world. These facts of life should not be regarded as solely the circumstances of the "less fortunate," but rather must be seen as coming back to haunt the richer countries of Europe, North America, and East Asia if they remain indifferent to them. The appalling events of September 11, 2001, in New York and Washington should have made that plain.

The experiences of the various nations of East Asia raise interesting questions about whether the neo-liberal theories of globalization are viable in the world as it is, or whether they were created for an imaginary world that does not, and will not ever, exist. Many believe that universal theories such as globalization as advanced by the United States and the West in general lack categories that can account for the variations that exist in the world.

Japan is a case in point. After the collapse of the Japanese stock market and the bursting of the country's much-touted economic "bubble," Japan languished in a recession for almost a decade before beginning a laborious recovery. In the 1980s, Japan had seemed like an unstoppable economic force in the world, its people saving steadily and its investors busily buying property and companies all around the globe. The collapse, however, diminished Japan's presence. It no longer seemed to be such a worthy model, but came instead to be seen more accurately as a unique social and political entity seeking, among other things, to provide lifetime employment to a significant portion of its workers as well as managers, support for small shopkeepers and family farms, and the preservation of big businesses and banks even if they deserve to sink into bankruptcy. Providing full employment, fostering families, protecting the environment, and preserving communities are values of the Japanese society and culture, but not of the market. The same holds for the "crony capitalism" that connects Japan's bureaucracy, big businesses, financial institutions, and political parties. Japan's economic difficulties were attributable to its refusal to sacrifice these values to meet the requirements of the global market.

It seems reasonable to think that all countries retain their own values in similar ways and cannot be expected to be responsive only to global market forces. Similarly, the aging of Japan's population leaves the expenses of retirement, which are particularly onerous because Japanese workers often retire in their fifties, to be borne by steadily fewer younger workers who are marrying later and having fewer children. Japan faces a serious labor shortage in the near future, both because of the falling birth rate and because it lacks established means of absorbing foreign workers into the society. Thus, Japan's non-globalized values and practices stand in the way of adopting one of the most obvious remedies for its imminent labor shortage.

Globalization also has a political aspect, such as in the push from Japan's political right-wing to rearm and assert the military and diplomatic influence, notwithstanding the clear language of Article IX in Japan's "peace constitution." The perceived threat from North Korea drives this, as does a nationalist hunger for recognition in world bodies where the Japanese, for example, want a permanent seat on the United Nations Security Council. Many Japanese lament that their country is an economic giant and a diplomatic pygmy, and leaders of the ruling Liberal Democratic Party seem to be laying the groundwork for a constitutional amendment that will doubtless trigger a furious national debate over Japan's place in the world.

At the other end of the spectrum, Vietnam is going through a much different process, trying to integrate into the world economy in more basic ways. Since 1986, Vietnam has been opening its market and creating entrepreneurial opportunities for its citizens. Burdened by the legacy of post-colonial wars, corruption, and the failures of socialist economics, Vietnam also has to contend with a very young population for which education resources are stretched to their limits. Vietnam has created a stock market, opened its doors to foreign business investment, constructed industrial parks and special economic zones where foreign businesses can take advantage of low-paid Vietnamese labor, and ventured into the world of international finance by borrowing.

The results are dramatic and highly visible in the small vehicle traffic, hustle of shopkeepers and peddlers, as well as the small businesses, repair shops, and restaurants that flourish everywhere. Joining the global economic system has meant greater prosperity, but has also brought increased dependence on forces beyond Vietnam's borders, risking vulnerability to external fluctuations in demand for Vietnam's new products. For example, in the year 2000, Vietnam signed a new trade agreement with the United States. Certain Vietnamese companies sought foreign loans to build catfish farms on the expectation that refrigerated freight airplanes could whisk frozen Vietnamese catfish to stores in the United States. However, American catfish growers, fearing competition from Vietnam, succeeded in getting the U.S. government to increase tariffs on imported catfish. Suddenly, the Vietnamese faced a danger that the globalized catfish market was about to dry up, leaving behind only the globalized debt.

Cultural Globalization

Parallel to economic globalization, one can speak of cultural globalization, both in terms of a youth culture with shared taste in music and dress, and of a global "trans-cultural" avant-garde of literary and visual artists, in which East Asia is well represented. If these people have found inadequate representation in our text, we make amends herewith by including an illustration from one of the earliest of their number, Irene Chou (Zhou Luyun, 1924–), who left Shanghai for Hong Kong in 1949, but now resides in Australia. In an eloquent style very much her own, she addresses issues that transcend our globe and time (Figure A.1). Among the younger generation, we could cite Ha Jin (1956–), winner of the 1999 National Book Award, who once served in the People's Liberation Army, but owes his reputation to novels written in English, and Gao Xingjian (1940–), China's first Nobel Prize winner (2000), who moved to Paris in 1989, where Myung-whun Chung (b. Seoul 1953) was in his first year as conductor of the Paris Opera. Chung was just one of the outstanding East Asians to contribute to musical life far from home. His older sister, Kyung-wha Chung, is an internationally renowned violinist. Similarly, Nam June Paik (1932–2006),

FIGURE A.1 *Coda,* Irene Chou. Working in an individual yet global sensibility that speaks to many cultures, Chou may yet be surprised to find her painting as coda to our book.

© Irene Chou. Used by Permission of Artist and Mandy Lee, Ipreciation Gallery. (http://www.ipreciation.com)

an American born in Korea, won fame with his neon constructions, including a show rendering "postmodern life in cyberspace."[2] In that sense, his reach, like that of Irene Chou, may even be said to extend beyond our globe. The globalization of thought and art often encounters resistance. Neither Ha Jin nor Gao Xingjian can be published in China. The Gao brothers' notwithstanding (see Box 2, Chapter 16), the world's people are not ready to hug each other, and East Asian countries are hardly alone in their suspicion of the outside world.

Everywhere today, change is valued as capable of producing a better society and a better life, but agreement of what would be better for one's people remains elusive. For example, in China and Vietnam people can now change jobs and are free to travel, but tolerance for dissent remains limited. However, the internet and the rise of cheap and easy global communications have implications for political change that worry many of the conservative regimes in East Asia.

The P.R.C. learned this in 1989, when fax machines and satellite television completely undermined its ability to control the flow of news about the Democracy Movement. Now it is bent on censorship and control of cyberspace in a cat and mouse game.

Today, internet access is unknown to ordinary people in North Korea, where the regime depends for its survival on complete control of information. In Vietnam, however, internet cafés abound. Though the government tries to filter what comes in via the World Wide Web, email can put any Vietnamese in instant touch with relatives overseas and other sources of information. This facilitates the free flow of ideas, information about business opportunities, and no doubt, critical thoughts about the shortcomings of the Vietnamese system as it exists. In Vietnam, as elsewhere, the libertarian environment of the internet may serve to be the most authentic and revolutionary globalizing force of all.

Cinema, one of the earliest genres of global influence, remained a major avenue of influence across national boundaries. Film not only told stories but represented whole peoples and ways of life. Hollywood images of American life are notorious for their portrayal of the United States as a sun-drenched suburb and, concurrently, as a nation of violent cities. The coexistence of these two images in the minds of people all over the world are proof of the vast abilities of cinema to further, or distort, understanding. The television age has simply extended this power into the homes of even the most remote communities around the globe.

The influence of cinema, however, was by no means all one way. Kurosawa Akira, Chen Kaige, and Zhang Yimou have already been cited in earlier chapters of our text. To them we should add South Korea's Im Kwŏn-taek (b. 1936), active since the early 1960s in Korea and then in Asian film festivals, who went on to win Best Director at the 2002 Cannes Film Festival for *Chihwaseon* ("Painted Fire"). Park Chan-wook has also won acclaim for his uncompromising treatment of violence in the human soul—notably his "vengeance trilogy," as well as for his treatment of Korean reunification in the film *JSA*. Indeed, Koreans proudly celebrate the spreading popularity of their popular music and television dramas in other regions of Asia—a phenomenon they call the "Korean Wave" (*hallyu*).

Other examples of transnational influence within East Asia, and between the region and the rest of the world, are legion. East Asians have become passionately involved in international sports, whether it be in hosting the Olympics or the competition for the World Cup in football (soccer). In the other direction, East Asian martial arts have won a devoted following in the West.

Religion is another vast field of intense and varied interaction, as seen in the appeal of messages directed at all people by such global religions as Buddhism, Christianity, and Islam, and also in the return of many people to their local, traditional beliefs and gods. This return to local creeds and loyalties is itself a global phenomenon. As in other areas of endeavor, attempts to work out a viable balance between the local and the global remain crucial as the twenty-first century gets under way.

Notes

1. Ellis S. Kraus and T.J. Pempel, *Beyond Bilateralism: U.S.–Japan Relations in the New Asia Pacific* (Stanford, CA: Stanford University Press, 2004), p. 306.

2. Ann Elliott Sherman at http://www.metroactive.com/papers/metro/02.29.96/paik9609.html.

Suggestions for Further Study

The website of the Association for Asian Studies (www.aasianst.org) maintains a list of the numerous websites dealing with East Asia. It also publishes the *Annual Bibliography of Asian Studies* online in many libraries. We have also posted our suggestions on individual topics and periods on the book's companion website (college.hmco.com/info/schirokauer), and we limit our suggestions here to broad surveys that can help readers begin further research. We also suggest that the works we have quoted in our text merit reading in toto.

General

To place East Asian history in a global perspective, see the succinct history of the modern world by China specialist Robert B. Marks, *The Origins of the Modern World: A Global and Ecological Narrative* (Lanham, MD: Rowman & Littlefield, 2002). Michael Sullivan, *The Meeting of Eastern and Western Art: From the Sixteenth Century to the Present Day* (London: Thames and Hudson, 1973, 1989) is informative and perceptive on Chinese and Japanese art. *Asian Religions in Practice: An Introduction,* edited by Donald S. Lopez Jr. (Princeton, NJ: Princeton University Press, 1999) does not discuss Korea or Vietnam, but does deal extensively with East Asian Buddhism. Wm. Theodore de Bary, *East Asian Civilizations: A Dialogue in Five Stages* (Cambridge: Harvard University Press, 1988) is a broad and brief interpretative survey. A different perspective is provided by Gilbert Rozman, *The East Asian Region: Confucian Heritage and Its Modern Adaptation* (Princeton, NJ: Princeton University Press, 1991).

China

Keith Schoppa, *The Columbia Guide of Modern Chinese History* (New York, NY: Columbia University Press, 2000) is the best place to begin further study of topics in Modern Chinese History. The various volumes of the *Cambridge History of China,* edited or coedited by John K. Fairbank, are a major resource. Joseph S. M. Lao and Howard Goldblatt, *The Columbia Anthology of Modern Chinese Literature* (New York, NY: Columbia University Press, 1995) includes fiction, poetry and essays.

Murray A. Rubinstein, *Taiwan: A New History Expanded Edition* (Armonk, NY.: M. E. Sharpe, 2006) covers the entire history of the island.

Korea

Korea: a Historical and Cultural Dictionary, by Keith Pratt and Richard Rutt (Richmond, Surrey: Curzon, 1999) is a good reference tool for anyone embarking on the study of Korea. Many histories of Korea emphasize the modern period, and of these the most commonly used in classrooms is Bruce Cumings's *Korea's Place in the Sun,* 2d ed. (New York, NY: W.W. Norton, 2005). Two other histories survey the whole sweep of Korean history but in different styles: the brief and accessible Keith Pratt's *Everlasting Flower: A History of Korea* (London: Reaktion Books, 2006), and the scholarly and detailed *Korea Old and New: A History* (Seoul: Ilchokak Publishers for the Korea Institute, Harvard University, 1990), by Carter J. Eckert et al. A useful supplement to any of these is the collection of documents and commentaries in Peter H. Lee, Yongho Ch'oe, and Wm. Theodore de Bary, entitled *Sources of Korean Tradition,* 2 vols. (New York, NY: Columbia University Press, 1996–2000).

For the history of North Korea, nothing surpasses Dae-sook Suh, *Kim Il-sung: The North Korean Leader* (New York, NY: Columbia University Press, 1989), though it is necessary to supplement it with more recent information. One of the best recent books is Bradley Martin's *Under the Loving Care of the Fatherly Leader: North Korea and the Kim Dynasty*, by Bradley K. Martin (New York, NY: St. Martin's, 2004). For North and South Korea together, two works stand out: Don Oberdorfer's *The Two Koreas*, rev. ed. (New York, NY: Basic Books, 2002) and John Feffer's *North Korea/South Korea* (New York, NY: Seven Stories Press, 2003). Two outstanding books on the ongoing "nuclear crisis" involving North Korea, now in its second decade, are Leon V. Sigal's *Disarming Strangers* (Princeton, NJ: Princeton University Press, 1999), and Marion Creekmore's *A Moment of Crisis* (New York, NY: Public Affairs Books, 2006), both dealing with negotiations leading to the "Agreed Framework" that froze North Korea's plutonium re-processing program in 1994 (later unfrozen in the standoff between Washington and P'yongyang in 2002–03).

Japan

Gary D. Allinson, *The Columbia Guide to Modern Japanese History* (New York, NY: Columbia University Press, 1999) includes a resource guide. Helen Hardacre, *The Postwar Development of Japanese Studies in the United States* (Leiden: Brill, 1998) provides assessments, complete with bibliography, of the current state of American–Japanese studies on history, foreign relations, art, religion, literature, anthropology, political analysis and law that prove excellent points of departure for further study. *The Cambridge History of Japan* is a major resource. Hitomi Tonomura et al., *Women and Class in Japanese History* (Ann Arbor, MI: Center for Japanese Studies, University of Michigan, 1999) includes essays covering all periods of Japanese history.

Vietnam

Vietnam is included in the *Cambridge History of Southeast Asia* (New York, NY: Cambridge University Press, 1992). Reliable reference works include Bruce M. Lockhart and William J. Duiker, *Historical Dictionary of Vietnam*, 3rd ed. (Lanham, MD: Scarecrow Press, 2006) which is much more extensive than the earlier editions, and Mark W. McLeod and Nguyen Thi Dieu, *Culture and Customs of Vietnam* (Westport, CT: Greenwood Press, 2001). For additional bibliography, see David G. Marr, *World Bibliographical Series*, vol. 147, *Vietnam* (Oxford, U.K: Clio Press, 1993). William J. Duiker, *Ho Chi Minh* (New York, NY: Hyperion, 2000) is now the standard work on the life of the Vietnamese independence leader as well as a useful survey of modern Vietnamese history. The Vietnam War is much documented in the United States, mostly from an American point of view. A standard survey is Stanley Karnow, *Vietnam: A History*, 2nd revised and updated ed. (New York, NY: Penguin Putnam, 1997), whose original edition (1984) served as a companion volume to the 13-part Public Broadcasting Service documentary entitled "Vietnam: A Television History."

Index